THE EREZ SERIES

RABBI ADIN
EVEN-ISRAEL
STEINSALTZ

A CONCISE GUIDE TO
THE SAGES

AN OVERVIEW OF JEWISH WISDOM

A Concise Guide to the Sages
First edition, 2020

Koren Publishers Jerusalem Ltd.
POB 8531, New Milford, CT 06776-8531, USA
& POB 4044, Jerusalem 91040, Israel

www.korenpub.com

This book was published in cooperation with
the Israeli Institute for Talmudic Publication.

Steinsaltz Center is the parent organization of institutions
established by Rabbi Adin Even-Israel Steinsaltz
POB 45187, Jerusalem 91450 ISRAEL
Telephone: +972 2 646 0900, Fax +972 2 624 9454
www.steinsaltz-center.org

ISBN 978-1-59264-564-0, *hardcover*
Printed and bound in the United States

Contents

Torah – Numbers

Torah – Deuteronomy

Sages on the Festivals

Stories from the Sages

Sages on Life

Passages from the Talmud

Foreword

This book contains a compilation of the statements of the Sages from the start of the Second Temple era (approximately 300 BCE) through 700–800 CE. The material includes statements of the Sages of the Mishna, i.e., from the days of the Second Temple until the third century CE. The Sages of the Mishna are typically called *tanna'im*, literally, teachers. Most of their work was in the Hebrew language and can be found in the Mishna and other texts. Those who came later and clarified the statements of the *tanna'im* are the *amora'im*, literally, speakers, who lived from approximately the third century until the sixth century CE. Some of them lived and studied in the Land of Israel and some of them in Babylonia. Amoraic literature contains two elements: the halakhic section, which is found primarily in the Babylonian Talmud and the Jerusalem Talmud, and the aggadic section, which is found in the two Talmuds and the aggadic Midrash. In addition, there is material that appears in the minor tractates of the Talmud, which were edited at a later stage. The core of those tractates originated during the mishnaic period, and they are printed as appendixes to the Babylonian Talmud. Most of the talmudic material is written in a combination of Hebrew and Aramaic. The entire corpus of amoraic literature is considered fundamental and was accepted by all Jews.

Rabbinic literature is called the "Oral Law," because it is not found in the text of the Bible. It was preserved as oral statements that originated with the giving of the Torah and became the focus of study and deliberation throughout the generations. The Oral Law comprises explanations of biblical verses, ancient halakhic traditions not rooted in the text of the Bible, and rabbinic ordinances enacted throughout the generations.

Since the scope of rabbinic literature is enormous, this work is limited to citing the Mishna, the Babylonian Talmud and the Jerusalem Talmud, the minor tractates, and the aggadic Midrash – primarily *Midrash Rabba* and *Midrash Tanḥuma*. The basis of this anthology is largely the aggadic material in the Talmud and in the various works of aggadic Midrash. The matters included here serve as commentary on the written Torah. In addition, there is a treatment of many topics, each with a section devoted to it, addressing Jewish life, the cycle of life, and societal and personal issues. Likewise, there are a large number of anecdotes that relate both to the biblical narrative and to accounts of the lives of the Sages. For clarity, brief introductory statements have been added to each of the segments.

Rabbi Adin Even-Israel Steinsaltz

A Jewish home, at any time or place, cannot be maintained based on the mere identity of its residents as Jews. Whether they conceive of themselves as religious, traditional, or secular, people need to have access to written expression of their tradition through which they can come to know, understand, and "enter" their tradition.

"To enter the tradition" can mean something different for each person. Some are simply curious, others have a particular interest, and there are undoubtedly many Jews who just do not want the worlds of the Jewish spirit to be closed to them. People therefore require bridges and gates to gain access. There is no obligation to use these, but their existence makes it possible for anyone – when that person so desires, to enter, or even to glance within – the way is clear and he or she can do so.

We have thus produced the Erez series, which provides different gates by which one can enter the Jewish tradition. Just as it is told about Abraham's tent that it was open from all four directions in order to welcome guests from everywhere, these books allow anyone, whenever he or she feels like it or finds something interesting, to enter into the tradition.

There are thousands of books that cover, in various ways and at different levels, the materials presented here. However, most of them require prior knowledge and no small amount of effort to be understood. In these volumes, we have striven to give anyone who seeks it a paved road into the riches of the Jewish world. More than merely a gate, we hope that these books can be said to offer their readers a "ride" into the tradition. Each person can get off whenever he or she desires and continue traveling when their interest is reawakened.

These volumes contain some of the fundamentals of Judaism. In each of them there are elements that can be considered hors d'oeuvres that can be snacked upon and others that are more comparable to entrees that require more time for digestion. In either case, the invitation offered by *A Concise Guide to the Sages* in Proverbs (9:5) is relevant: "Come, partake of my bread, and drink of the wine that I have mixed." The books were deliberately designed to be accessible to everyone, whether he or she is highly educated or someone whose source of intellectual stimulation consists of occasionally reading the newspaper. Anyone can enjoy something, whether by means of an occasional taste, or by sitting down to a hearty meal. The way is open and anyone can find the gate appropriate for him or her, without effort.

We have aimed to keep the translation as true to the original Hebrew and Aramaic as possible. As some of these texts are not easy to understand, we have added clarifying comments in square brackets where appropriate. Further explication is appended in notes at the end of certain passages. When we have felt it appropriate to use a transliteration, the transliterated term is first explained and then followed by the transliteration in square brackets. At the end of each book we have provided a glossary of Hebrew terms mentioned in the series. Some of the terms found there may not be found in this book, as we have used the same glossary for all the volumes of the Erez series. *The Reference Guide to the Talmud* has a far more extensive glossary, as is necessary for that work.

Given the antiquity of the texts collected here, there are many occasions where it was impossible to avoid gendered usage, and we have followed the texts themselves in using the male gender as the default.

Each of the volumes in this series stands alone, with only occasional citations connecting them. The first volume, *A Concise Guide to the Torah*, contains the translation of the Torah taken from the *Steinsaltz Humash*; we have abridged the commentary that can be found there. One can take this volume to the synagogue but also peruse it in the comforts of one's home.

The second volume, *A Concise Guide to the Sages*, is an anthology of rabbinic literature, organized by topics. One part includes rabbinic thinking associated with the Torah, while other topics are also addressed: the cycle of the Jewish year, the cycle of life in rabbinic eyes, as well as other topics where a person can find something that fits his or her needs.

The third volume, *A Concise Guide to Mahshava*, addresses spiritual matters. It contains an anthology of non-halakhic literature from the Jewish spiritual tradition: kabbala, Jewish philosophy, the Musar tradition, and hasidic writings. Here too, the texts are presented in a manner that is accessible to all, in clear English. This volume addresses a broad array of topics: Besides comments and explanations on the Torah, there are sections devoted to the cycle of the Jewish year, the life cycle, and fundamental questions of human life such as parenthood, marriage, and death. There are many other topics addressed in this volume and one can open it at random and find wisdom that touches the soul.

The fourth volume, *A Concise Guide to Halakha*, is a survey of practical *halakha*. It does not delve into the sources of *halakha* and provide an opportunity for intensive study but serves rather as a guidebook to what the *halakha* instructs one to do in various situations. In this way the book offers

a summary of the *halakhot* of Shabbat and the holidays, of life cycle events, and of those mitzvot that any Jew is likely to encounter. If one wishes to act in accordance with the *halakha*, he or she will know what to do with the help of this volume. It is written in clear English with a minimum of technical language so that it is accessible to anyone, man, woman, or child. And if he or she decides to act accordingly, may he or she be blessed.

The fifth volume, *The Reference Guide to the Talmud*, is a reprint of the work that was issued as a companion to the *Koren Talmud Bavli*. It is an indispensable resource for students of all levels. This fully revised, English-language edition of the *Reference Guide* clearly and concisely explains the Talmud's fundamental structure, concepts, terminology, assumptions, and inner logic; it provides essential historical and biographical information; it includes appendixes, a key to abbreviations, and a comprehensive index.

For improved usability, this completely updated volume has a number of new features: topical organization instead of by Hebrew alphabet, re-edited and revised text to coordinate with the language used in the *Koren Talmud Bavli*, and an index of Hebrew terms to enable one seeking a Hebrew term to locate the relevant entry.

These books are certainly not the entire Torah, but they are beneficial for any Jew to have in his or her home. If one finds something interesting, or is curious about something, these books offer a resource to investigate that topic. Even if one opens one of these volumes by chance, he or she will gain from reading it, both intellectually and spiritually. In short, these are books that it is convenient to have in one's home.

Our thanks are extended to all the people who participated in the project of writing these books, editing them, and finding the sources therein. We likewise would like to thank the publisher, and those first readers who offered helpful criticism and advice, and finally those generous people whose donations made it possible to create these books.

The Editors

Torah – Genesis

Bereshit

The portion of *Bereshit*, the first portion in the Torah, presents the story of Creation and the central events during the dawn of humanity, but it does so with great concision. The rabbinic literature provides the background and details of those events, along with explanations of their significance.

The following text discusses the letters, and the names of the Creator, with which the world was created; the creation of Man – his uniqueness; why he was created as an individual, not as a species; the considerations that were raised before he was created; the seduction by the serpent; and the motives of Cain in his killing of Abel.

The First Letter in the Torah

The Torah begins with the word *bereshit*, which itself begins with the letter *bet*. The Sages explain why the Torah does not begin with the letter *alef* – the first letter of the Hebrew alphabet.

And why with a *bet*? Because it is an expression of blessing;[1] and not with an *alef*, which is an expression of curse,[2] so that those who live in the world will not say: How can the world, created with an expression of curse, endure? Instead, I am creating it with a *bet*, with an expression of blessing, and perhaps it will endure.

(Jerusalem Talmud, *Ḥagiga* 2:1)

The World Attests to Its Creator

What did Rabbi Akiva respond to a person who sought unequivocal proof of the existence of a Creator?

It happened that a heretic came and said to Rabbi Akiva: This world – who created it? Rabbi Akiva said to him: The Holy One, blessed be He. The heretic said to him: Show me some clear proof! Rabbi Akiva said to him: Come to me tomorrow. The heretic came to him the next day. Rabbi Akiva said to him: What are you wearing? He said to him: A garment. Rabbi Akiva said to

---

1. The Hebrew word for blessing, *berakha*, also begins with the letter *bet*.
2. The Hebrew word for curse, *arira*, begins with the letter *alef*.

him: Who made it? The heretic said to him: The weaver. Rabbi Akiva said to him: I don't believe you; show me some clear proof. The heretic said to him: And what should I show you? Don't you know that the weaver made it? Rabbi Akiva said to him: And you, don't you know that the Holy One, blessed be He, created His world?

That heretic took his leave. Rabbi Akiva's students said to him: What is the clear matter? Rabbi Akiva said to them: My children, just as the house attests to its builder, and the garment attests to its weaver, and the door attests to its carpenter, so the world attests to the Holy One, blessed be He, that He created it.

(*Otzar HaMidrashim* [Eisenstein], *Temura*, p. 583)

📖 Further reading: For more about the existence of the world as proof of the existence of the Creator, see *A Concise Guide to Mahshava*, p. 130.

The Attribute of Justice and the Attribute of Mercy

God has many names, and each name expresses a certain aspect of revelation. The Tetragrammaton, spelled *yod, heh, vav, heh*, known as *Hashem*, the name, expresses the attributes of kindness and mercy, while the name *Elohim* expresses the attribute of justice. The Sages explain why both names are employed in describing the creation of the world.

"This is the legacy of the heavens and of the earth when they were created, on the day that the Lord [*Hashem*] God [*Elohim*] made the earth and the heavens" (Genesis 2:4).

This verse concludes the act of Creation, and in it two names of the Creator are mentioned – Hashem and *Elohim*.

Hashem Elohim – This can be compared to a king who had empty cups. The king said: If I place hot water into them, they will break; cold water, they will shrink. What did the king do? He mixed hot and cold water, and he placed it into the cups and they remained intact. So too, the Holy One, blessed be He, said: If I create the world with the attribute of mercy alone – the sinners will be many;[3] with the attribute of justice alone – how will the world be able to endure?[4] Instead, I will create it with both the attribute of justice and the attribute of mercy, and perhaps it will endure.

---

3. As people will have no fear of God.
4. As people will be dealt with strictly for even the slightest infraction.

The Deliberation with Regard to the Creation of Man

The depiction of the creation of the first human being in the Torah differs from the depiction of the creation of the rest of the creatures. God speaks of this creation in the plural ("Let us fashion"), and the Sages interpret that expression as a deliberation that was conducted either between God and Himself or between God and the ministering angels. This deliberation concerned the question of whether it is indeed appropriate to create humans.

Rabbi Shimon said: At the time that the Holy One, blessed be He, came to create the first person, the ministering angels divided into factions and groups. Some of them said: He should be created! Some of them said: He should not be created! That is the meaning of that which is written: "Kindness and truth have met; justice and peace have touched" (Psalms 85:11).[5] Kindness says: He should be created, as he performs acts of kindness. Truth says: He should not be created, as he is falsehood in his entirety. Righteousness says: He should be created, as he performs acts of righteousness. Peace says: He should not be created, as he epitomizes strife.

What did the Holy One, blessed be He, do? He took Truth and cast it to the earth.[6] The ministering angels said before the Holy One, blessed be He: Master of the Universe, why are You demeaning Your seal? Let truth rise from the earth, as it is written: "Truth will spring from the earth" (Psalms 85:12).

When the Holy One, blessed be He, sought to create the first person, He consulted the ministering angels. He said to them: Shall we make Man? They said before Him: Master of the Universe! "What is a mortal that You remember him, a person that You take him into account?" (Psalms 8:5). He said to them: This person that I seek to create in My world has greater wisdom than you.

What did He do? He assembled all the animals, beasts, and birds and He passed them before the ministering angels. He said to them: What are the names of these creatures? And they did not know. Once He created the first person, He assembled all the animals, beasts, and birds and He passed them before him. He said to Adam: What are the names of these? Adam said: This should be called an ox, and this should be called a horse, and this should be called a camel, and this should be called a vulture, and this should be called a lion. That is what is written: "The man called names for every

---

5. The verse in Psalms describes an encounter between the attributes of kindness, truth, justice, and peace.
6. Leaving a majority of groups supporting the creation of people.

animal and for the birds of the sky and for every beast of the field" (Genesis 2:20).

God said to him: And what is your name? He said: Adam. God said to him: Why? He said to Him: Because I was created from the earth [*adama*]. He said to him: And Me, what is My name? Adam answered: *Adonai*. He said to Adam: Why? Adam answered: Because You are the Master [*Adon*] over all Your creations.

(Bereshit Rabba [Theodor-Albeck] 8; *Pesikta Rabbati* [Ish Shalom] 14: *Para)*

Creation of Man in the Plural

The Sages address the question of why the creation of the first person was formulated in the plural, "Let us fashion man," despite the erroneous conclusion one may make from such wording.

When Moses was writing the Torah, he would write what was formed on each and every day. When he reached this verse, which states: "Let us fashion man in our image, in our likeness" (Genesis 1:26), he said before Him: Master of the Universe, I wonder: Why do You provide grounds for the heretics?[7] He said to Moses: Write, and let one who seeks to err, err.[8] The Holy One, blessed be He, said to him: Moses, this person that I created, won't I establish both greater people and lesser people from him? If the greater people will come to consult with the lesser people, and will say: Why do I need to ask permission with one lesser than I? The lesser people can say to him: Learn from your Creator, who created the heavenly and the earthly. When He came to create Man, He consulted with the ministering angels.

(Bereshit Rabba 8)

📖 **Further reading:** For more about the meaning of the creation of man in the image of God, see *A Concise Guide to Mahshava*, pp. 131, 139.

Man Was Created Alone

There are several explanations provided by the Sages with regard to why one person was created alone, and from him all of humanity developed.

The reason why Adam was created alone is to teach you that with regard to anyone who destroys even one soul from the Jewish people, the verse

---

7. Who may claim that there were multiple gods that created Adam.
8. People can choose to mislead themselves if they wish.

ascribes blame to him as though he destroyed an entire world.[9] And with regard to anyone who sustains even one soul from the Jewish people, the verse ascribes credit to him as though he sustained an entire world. Another reason is due to maintaining peace among people, so that one person will not say to another: My ancestor is greater than your ancestor. Another reason is so that the heretics will not say: There are many authorities in Heaven.[10] Another reason is to tell of the greatness of the Holy One, blessed be He, as when a person stamps several coins with one seal, they are all similar to each other. But the supreme King of kings, the Holy One, blessed be He, stamped all people with the seal of Adam the first man, and not one of them is similar to another. Therefore,[11] each and every person must say: The world was created for me.

(Mishna *Sanhedrin* 4:5)

Creation of Man and Woman

The Sages discuss the creation of the first woman from a perspective that views man and woman as two halves of a single entity.

Rabbi Yirmeya ben Elazar said: When the Holy One, blessed be He, created Adam the first person, He created him androgynous.[12] That is what is written: "Male and female He created them" (Genesis 5:2). Rabbi Shmuel bar Nahman said: When the Holy One, blessed be He, created Adam the first person, He created him with two fronts,[13] and He then split him and made for him two backs – one here and one there.[14]

Rabbi Yohanan said: Adam and Eve were created at the developmental age of approximately twenty years old.

(*Bereshit Rabba* 8, 14)

Further reading: For more about Man and Woman as two halves of a single entity, see *A Concise Guide to Mahshava*, p. 16.

---

9. Because all of humanity emerged from one person.
10. Each of whom created another person.
11. Since the first person was created alone.
12. One with both male and female sexual organs.
13. One male and one female.
14. God separated him in the middle, and two backs were provided for those two fronts, i.e., they were divided into two separate entities.

Preservation of the World

Although God created the world for the benefit of humanity, people bear great responsibility for the preservation of the world.

When the Holy One, blessed be He, created Adam the first person, He took him and showed him all the trees of the Garden of Eden, and said to him: See how beautiful and excellent My creations are, and everything that I created, I created for you. Ensure that you do not ruin and destroy My world, because if you ruin it, there is no one else to restore it.

(Kohelet Rabba 7)

Eve and the Serpent

The Sages discuss the sin of the Tree of Knowledge, explaining the serpent's contentions as well as what caused Eve to convince Adam to eat the fruit.

The serpent went and said to the woman: Is it true that also you[15] are commanded with regard to the fruits of this tree? She said to him: Yes, as it is stated: "But from the fruit of the tree that is in the midst of the garden, God said: You shall not eat of it, nor shall you touch it, lest you die" (Genesis 3:3). From her words,[16] the serpent found an opening through which it could enter [and undermine the prohibition]. The serpent said to her: This command is nothing more than stinginess,[17] as at the moment that you eat from it you will be like God. What does He do? He creates worlds and destroys worlds – likewise, you will be able to create worlds and destroy worlds. Just as He brings death and gives life, you too will be able to bring death and give life.

The serpent went and touched the tree. The tree screamed and said: Wicked one, don't touch me! The serpent went and said to the woman: I touched the tree and I did not die, you too touch it and you will not die. The woman went and touched the tree and saw the angel of death approaching her. She said: Perhaps now I will die, and the Holy One, blessed be He, will form another woman for Adam. I will cause him to eat with me. If we die, both of us will die, and if we live, both of us will live. She went and took and ate of the fruits of the tree, and gave of its fruits to her husband too, so that he would eat with her.

(Pirkei deRabbi Eliezer 13)

---

15. In other words, are the fruits prohibited not only to me but to you as well?
16. Her adding a prohibition against touching the tree, which had not been commanded by God.
17. To prevent you from becoming like God.

📖 **Further reading:** The narrative of the Tree of Knowledge is found in *A Concise Guide to the Torah*, p. 8.

The Killing of Abel

The Sages elaborate on the first murder. Why did Cain kill Abel? What was Cain's reaction after the murder, and what was his punishment?

"Cain said to Abel his brother" (Genesis 4:8). What did Cain say to him?[18] Cain said to Abel: Shall we divide the world between us? Abel said to him: Yes. Abel took his flocks to graze and Cain took the land to cultivate, and they agreed that neither of them would have any claim against the other. When Abel took his flocks, he began to shepherd the flocks, but Cain would pursue him from mountain to valley and from valley to mountain.[19] This went on until they encountered each other and fought. Abel triumphed over Cain and Cain fell beneath him. When Cain saw that Abel had prevailed he began to scream: Abel my brother, do not do me harm. Abel pitied him and released him, and Cain rose and killed him.

Once Cain killed him, he said: I will flee from my father and my mother, who will ask me about him, as there is no one in the world other than me and him. Immediately, the Holy One, blessed be He, appeared to Cain and said to him: You can flee from your parents, but you cannot flee from Me… "Where is Abel your brother?" (4:9). God said to him: Woe unto Abel, as he pitied you and didn't kill you when you fell beneath him, and you rose and killed him.

How did Cain kill him? He made several wounds and several injuries with a stone, in Abel's arms and legs, as Cain did not know from where his life departs. Cain continued striking Abel until he reached his neck…Cain said to God: Master of the Universe, I did not know and I had never seen anyone killed in my life. How could I know that if I smite him with a stone he would die? Immediately, He responded to Cain: "And now, cursed are you from the ground that opened its mouth to take your brother's blood from your hand. When you cultivate the ground, it shall not continue giving its strength to you" (4:11–12).

Cain said before Him: Master of the Universe, do You have informants who inform on people before You? My father and my mother are on earth and do not know that I killed Abel, and You are in the heavens; from where

---

18. The verse does not tell us what Cain said.
19. Wherever Abel would shepherd his flocks, Cain would claim that the land on which they were grazing was his.

do You know? God said to him: Fool! I bear the entire world…Cain said to Him: You bear the entire world and You are unable to bear my iniquity? Is my sin too great to bear? (4:13). God said to him: Since you have repented, depart and be exiled from this place…When Cain departed, every place that he would go, the land would quake beneath him and the beasts and the animals would quake and say: What is this? They would say to each other: Cain killed his brother Abel, and the Holy One, blessed be He, decreed in his regard: "Restless and itinerant you shall be" (4:12).

(*Tanḥuma, Bereshit*)

Noah

The first part of *Parashat Noah* discusses the flood. The Torah recounts the decision of the Creator to destroy all life other than the members of the family of Noah the Righteous, and with him representatives of each species of animal that remained in the ark during the entire duration of the flood. In the second part of the Torah portion the rebirth of humanity is depicted. This beginning is optimistic and heartening, but it is also fraught with the failures of Noah himself and afterward the construction of the Tower of Babel and the punishment of that generation. The portion also contains detailed lists of the nations of the world and their descendants, along with the continued chronicling of Noah's family – which reaches its climax with the appearance of Abram.

Presented here are discussions of the uniqueness of Noah and his relationship with the members of his generation; the sin of the members of the generation of the flood; the construction of the ark; the drunkenness of Noah; and the nature and sin of the members of the generation of the Dispersion, who were the builders of the Tower of Babel.

Noah and His Generation

The Torah relates that Noah was: "A righteous man; he was faultless in his generations" (Genesis 6:9). What is the verse emphasizing? The Talmud cites a dispute with regard to this question.

"This is the legacy of Noah. Noah was a righteous man; he was faultless in his generations" (6:9). Rabbi Yoḥanan says: He was righteous relative to his generation, but not relative to other generations. And Reish Lakish says: He was righteous relative to his generation; all the more so relative to other generations.[20]

Rabbi Ḥanina says: A parable for the explanation of Rabbi Yoḥanan; to what is this matter comparable? To a barrel of wine that was placed in a cellar of vinegar; in its place, near vinegar, its fragrance diffuses,[21] not in its place, not near vinegar, its fragrance does not diffuse.[22] Rabbi Oshaya says:

---

20. If Noah was righteous in such a sinful generation, all the more so would he have been righteous in other generations.
21. It is very conspicuous, and is even more palpable due to the contrast with the nearby vinegar.
22. As the fragrance of the wine is not as powerful and conspicuous in and of itself.

A parable for the explanation of Reish Lakish; to what is this matter comparable? To a flask of perfume that was placed in a location of filth. In its place its fragrance diffuses despite the surrounding filth, and all the more so in a location of perfume.

(*Sanhedrin* 108a)

The Severity of Robbery

What was so severe about the sin of the members of the generation of the flood? According to the talmudic Sages, the generation of the flood was guilty of many and various sins, but the sin that sealed their fate was robbery.

Come and see how powerful robbery is, as the generation of the flood violated every prohibition, but their sentence was not sealed until they extended their hands into robbery, as it is stated: "As the earth is filled with villainy because of them; and behold, I will destroy them with the earth" (Genesis 6:13).

(*Sanhedrin* 108a)

Man and Animal

The Torah relates that during the flood, the Creator destroyed all living creatures – both man and animal – except for those in the ark. In the statements of the Sages, there are several explanations why the animals too were destroyed.

Rabbi Azarya says in the name of Rabbi Yehuda bar Shimon: Every creature in the generation of the flood corrupted its actions: The dog would go to mate with the wolf and the rooster would go to mate with the peacock. That is what is written: "As all flesh corrupted" (Genesis 6:12). It is not written: As all men corrupted; rather: "As all flesh corrupted." Rabbi Lulyani ben Tavrin says in the name of Rabbi Yitzhak: Even the land strayed:[23] People would sow wheat and it would produce rye-grass.

"He obliterated all existence that was on the face of the earth, from man to animal" (7:23). If people sinned, in what way did the animals sin? It was taught in the name of Rabbi Yehoshua ben Korha: This can be explained by means of a parable of a man who built a wedding canopy for his son and prepared all sorts of delicacies for the feast. Sometime later his son died. He arose and dismantled his wedding canopy. He said: Didn't I prepare the entire feast only for my son? Now that he has died, why do I need a wedding

---

23. It produced plants that had not been sown.

canopy? So too, the Holy One, blessed be He, said: Didn't I create animals and beasts only for people? Now that people sin, why do I need animals and beasts?

(*Bereshit Rabba* 28; *Sanhedrin* 108a)

Noah and the Members of His Generation

The Torah relates that Noah alone was righteous in his generation; therefore, only he and his family were rescued. The interactions between Noah and the members of his generation are left undescribed. Did he attempt to convince them to change their ways? Did they respect him, or did they despise and oppose him? The Sages present a more detailed picture of this matter.

Rav Huna says in the name of Rabbi Yosei: The Holy One, blessed be He, warned the generation of the flood for 120 years, so that perhaps they would repent. As they did not repent, He said to Noah: "Make for yourself an ark of gopher[24] wood" (Genesis 6:14). Noah arose and repented and planted cedars. The people of his generation would say to him: Why are you planting these cedars? Noah said to them: The Holy One, blessed be He, seeks to bring a flood to the world, and He told me to build an ark so that my family and I will escape in it. They would laugh at him and ridicule his words. He would water those cedars and they grew. The people of his generation said to him: What are you doing? He responded to them in that same manner, and they would ridicule him. Eventually, he chopped down the cedar trees and was sawing them. The people of his generation said to him: What are you doing? He told them as he had told them previously, and he warned them. Since they did not repent, God immediately brought the flood upon them.

"On that very day, Noah…entered the ark" (7:13). Rabbi Yohanan says: The Holy One, blessed be He, said: If Noah enters the ark at night, all the people of his generation would then say this: We did not know of him. Had we known of him that he was entering the ark we would not have enabled him to enter. Rather: "On that very day, Noah…entered the ark." Let anyone who is in pain speak.[25]

"And the Lord shut it for him" (7:16). Rabbi Levi says: This can be compared to an official who instituted an edict of death in the country, and he took his beloved and incarcerated him in prison and placed his seal upon it. So too: "And the Lord shut it for him." The people of Noah's generation

---

24. A tree from the cedar family.
25. An Aramaic saying, meaning that if an event bothers someone, he may protest against it.

sought to upend the ark, and He surrounded it with lions so they would not touch it.

(*Tanḥuma, Noah; Bereshit Rabba* 32)

Falsehood and Oblivion Seek Refuge in the Ark

The Torah relates that Noah took male and female from every species of living beings so that every species would exist after the flood. The Sages elaborate on that idea and describe how it was not only living beings, but also abstract ideas such as falsehood and oblivion that sought refuge in Noah's Ark.

"Two at a time they came to Noah" (Genesis 7:9). Falsehood came and sought to enter the ark. Noah said to him: You may enter only if you find a spouse to marry. Falsehood encountered Oblivion. Oblivion said to him: Where are you coming from? Falsehood said to her: From Noah, as I went to him and sought to enter the ark but he did not let me. Rather, he told me: If you have a spouse you may enter. If you wish, you will be my spouse. Oblivion said to him: And what will you give me? Falsehood answered: I will agree with you that everything I earn, you take. They agreed that everywhere that Falsehood would earn, Oblivion would take.

Both of them entered the ark. Once they emerged after the flood, Falsehood would go and earn, and Oblivion would immediately take everything. Falsehood came and said to her: Where is everything that I collected? Oblivion said to him: Didn't you agree with me that everything that you earn I take? Falsehood had no response.

(Midrash on Psalms, 7)

Care for God's Creatures

Noah and his family spent a year in the ark with many and various living beings. The Sages describe their daily care for the creatures.

What would Noah feed them? Rabbi Akiva says: He would feed them all, whether domesticated animal, people, undomesticated animal, or fowl, a cake of dried figs, like that which is stated: "And it shall be for you and for them for food" (Genesis 6:21).[26] What is the item that people, as well as domesticated animal, undomesticated animal, and fowl, eat from it? This is a cake of dried figs. But the Rabbis say: No. Rather, each and every species

---

26. Indicating that they all ate of the same food.

would eat the food to which it was accustomed: The camel ate straw, the donkey ate barley, the elephant ate vines, and the ostrich ate glass.[27]

Alternatively…there is an animal that would eat at the first hour of the day, and there is an animal that would eat at the second hour of the day, and there is an animal that would eat at the third of the day, and there is an animal that would eat at the call of the rooster. The Sages say: During the twelve months that Noah stayed in the ark he did not have even a bit of sleep, neither during the day nor during the night, as he was busy feeding the creatures that were with him…. One time, Noah was late in feeding the lion, and the lion bit him and Noah emerged from the encounter limping.

(*Tanḥuma* [Buber], *Noah*; *Tanḥuma, Noah*)

The Olive Leaf

Noah dispatched the dove to ascertain whether the water had receded and it returned carrying an olive leaf in its mouth, indicating that the land and the vegetation had started to be exposed. The Sages explain the symbolism of the dove selecting the olive leaf.

"And behold, it had plucked an olive leaf in its mouth" (Genesis 8:11). Rabbi Elazar says: The dove said before the Holy One, blessed be He: Master of the Universe! Let my food be bitter like the olive and given from Your hand, and let it not be sweet as honey and given from the hand of flesh and blood.

(*Sanhedrin* 108b)

Noah's Intoxication

After emerging from the ark, Noah planted a vineyard and produced wine. He became absolutely drunk from his wine and found himself disgraced in the presence of his family. The Sages say that it is possible to illustrate the progression of the destructive effect of wine on a person by means of a comparison to the conduct of four different animals – an illustration that Satan himself presented before Noah.

When Noah came to plant a vineyard, Satan came and stood before him. [Satan] said to him: What are you planting? Noah said to him: A vineyard. Satan said to him: What is its nature? Noah responded: Its fruits are sweet both when they are moist, as grapes, and when they are dry, as raisins, and one produces wine from it, which gladdens the heart.

---

27. While ostriches do not technically eat glass, they are often observed swallowing bits of glass and small stones which they store in their gullets and use to grind up their food.

Satan said to him: Let the two of us enter into a partnership concerning this vineyard. Noah said: Very well! What did Satan do? He brought a sheep and killed it beneath the vine, thereafter he brought a lion and killed it there, and thereafter he brought a pig and killed it there, and thereafter he brought a monkey and killed it beneath the vine. The blood of the killed animals dripped in that vineyard and Satan irrigated it with their blood. Satan alluded to Noah that before a person drinks wine, he is as innocent as a lamb, which does not know anything, and like a sheep, silent before its shearers. After drinking in moderation he is as powerful as a lion, saying that there is no one like him in the world. Once he drinks excessively, he becomes like a pig, sullied with urine and with something else.[28] Once he becomes intoxicated, he becomes like a monkey: He stands, dances, plays, and utters obscenities before everyone, and does not know what he is doing.

All this befell Noah the righteous. And if it was so for Noah the righteous, with regard to whom the Holy One, blessed be He, was explicit in His praise,[29] all the more so for all other people.

(*Tanḥuma, Noah*)

The Tower of Babel

The actions of the members of the generation of the Dispersion, who were the builders of the Tower of Babel, are cited in the Torah in brief and not fully explained. The Sages elaborated on the motives of the builders of the tower, its nature, the manner of its construction, and the punishment for its builders.

Nimrod said to his people: Come, let us build a great city for ourselves, and settle within it, lest we be dispersed upon the face of the entire land like our predecessors.[30] And we will build a great tower within it,[31] one that will rise to the heavens, as the power of the Holy One, blessed be He, to destroy is only with water, and we will become famous in the world ....

Rabbi Pinhas says: There were no stones there to construct the city and the tower. What did they do? They made bricks and burned them, like a potter does, until they built the tower to a height of seven *mil*[32] ... If during the construction a person fell and died they would pay no attention, but if a brick fell and broke they would sit and cry, and say: How will we replace it?

---

28. A euphemism for excrement.
29. See Genesis 6:9.
30. The generation of the flood, whose corpses were dispersed on the face of the entire earth.
31. That will not be destroyed in a flood.
32. A *mil* is approximately 1 km.

Abraham ben Terah, our patriarch, passed and saw them building the city and the tower, and he cursed them with the name of God, and they despised and dismissed his words like a stone cast to the ground….

Rabbi Shimon says: The Holy One, blessed be He, summoned the seventy angels that surround His royal Throne, and the Holy One, blessed be He, said to them: Let us descend and muddle them into seventy nations and seventy languages. From where is it derived that He said it to them? As it is stated: "Let us descend" (Genesis 6:9). Let Me descend is not written; rather, "Let us descend [and we will muddle their language there," with the pronouns in the plural]. The Holy One, blessed be He, and the seventy angels that surround His Throne of Glory descended and muddled their language, dividing them into seventy nations and seventy languages…they would try to speak with each other but did not know each other's languages. What did they do? Each person took his sword, and these battled with those, and half the world fell by the sword. From there the Lord dispersed them throughout the entire land, as it is stated: "And from there the Lord dispersed them on the face of the entire land" (11:9).

(*Pirkei deRabbi Eliezer* [Higer] 24)

The Generation of the Dispersion and Unity

The generation of the Dispersion sought to wage war against God and to replace Him. Why, then, was the punishment of the generation of the Dispersion less severe than the punishment of the generation of the flood, which was totally destroyed?

No survivors remained of the generation of the flood [other than Noah and his family], while survivors remained of the generation of the Dispersion although their sin was more severe. Because the generation of the flood was steeped in robbery, no survivors remained of them; but with regard to the generation of the Dispersion, because they loved each other, survivors remained of them.

(*Bereshit Rabba* 38)

Further reading: For more about the virtue of peace and unity, see pp. 179, 226, 374.

Lekh Lekha

This entire Torah portion revolves around the figure of Abraham our patriarch. It opens with God's command to Abraham to travel to the land of Canaan and goes on to describe his descent to Egypt and Sarah's abduction by Pharaoh, his parting from Lot and the war that Abraham wages to rescue him, and his going to Gerar. In the latter part of the portion, the Torah relates the marriage of Abraham to Hagar in an attempt to have children, the flight and return of Hagar, and the birth of Ishmael. The portion also presents the covenants established between God and Abraham: the Covenant between the Parts and the covenant associated with the mitzva of circumcision.

The chapter that follows presents statements of the Sages relating to the uniqueness of Abraham and his faith, the manner in which Abraham and Sarah interacted with people, the command to go to the land of Canaan, the covenants that the Creator established with Abraham, and the events tied to the lives of Abraham and his family.

Abraham and the Idols

When God told Abraham to depart from Haran and go to the land of Canaan, Abraham was already seventy-five years old. The Torah relates almost nothing about his earlier life; the Sages elaborate on it, and the following passage tells of Abraham's attitude vis-à-vis the idolaters that were in his family and in his surroundings, and about the challenging test of faith that he withstood when he was cast into the fiery furnace.

Rabbi Hiyya, grandson of Rav Adda of Yafo, said: Terah was an idol worshipper. One day, he went somewhere and designated Abraham his son as storekeeper in his stead. A person would come wanting to make a purchase. Abraham would say to him: How old are you? The customer would reply: Fifty or sixty years old. Abraham would say to him: Woe unto that person who is sixty years old and wants to worship an idol that is one day old. The customer would be ashamed and leave.

Once, a woman came bearing a bowl of finely sifted flour in her hand. She said to Abraham: Here it is for you; offer it before the idols. He stood and took a stick in his hand, broke all the idols, and placed the stick in the hand of the largest idol among them. When his father returned, he said to Abraham: Who did this to them? Abraham responded: Why would I con-

ceal it from you? A woman came carrying a bowl of finely sifted flour in her hand, and said to me: Here it is for you; offer it before the idols. I offered it before them; this one said: I will eat first, and this one said: I will eat first. The largest idol among them took a stick and broke the rest of them. Terah said to him: Why are you mocking me; do the idols know anything? Abraham responded: Do your ears not hear what your mouth is saying?[33]

Terah took him and delivered him to Nimrod [the local ruler]. Nimrod said to him: Let us worship the fire. Abraham said to him: Let us worship the water, which extinguishes the fire. Nimrod said to him: Let us worship the water. Abraham said to him: Let us worship the cloud, which bears the water. Nimrod said to him: Let us worship the cloud. Abraham said to him: If so, let us worship the wind, which disperses the cloud. Nimrod said to him: Let us worship the wind. Abraham said to him: Let us worship Man, who withstands the wind. Nimrod said to him: You speak mere words, [and are not trying to arrive at the truth]; I prostrate myself only to the fire. I am casting you into it; let the God to whom you prostrate yourself come and rescue you from it.

Haran, Abraham's brother, was there, and he stood conflicted about whom to support. He said: Either way; if Abraham prevails, I will say that I am with Abraham, and if Nimrod prevails, I will say that I am with Nimrod. Once Abraham descended into the fiery furnace and was rescued, the people there said to Haran: Whose side are you on? Haran said to them: I am with Abraham. They took him and cast him into the fire and his innards were burned; and he emerged dead during the lifetime of Terah his father. That is what is written: "Haran died during the lifetime of Terah his father" (Genesis 11:28).

(Bereshit Rabba 38)

Abraham's Departure from Haran

The Sages provide a rationale for God's commandment to Abraham to depart from Haran and to go to "the land that I will show you." They also explain the particular difficulty that fulfilling this commandment entailed.

Rabbi Berekhya said: To what was Abraham our patriarch comparable? To a bottle of perfume that was sealed with a tight-fitting lid and placed in a corner. As long as it sat there its fragrance did not diffuse. Once it was moved, its fragrance diffused. So the Holy One, blessed be He, said to Abraham our

---

33. Aren't you yourself admitting that there is no point in worshipping them?

patriarch: Move yourself from place to place, and your name will be exalted in the world.[34] "To the land that I will show you" (Genesis 12:1). God did not say to him: To such and such place, telling him where to go. This wording of the command is an ordeal within an ordeal;[35] is there a person who goes and does not know to which place he is going? What did Abraham do? He took his belongings and his wife.

(*Bereshit Rabba* 38)

The Quality of the Land of Canaan

The Sages explain in what way the land of Canaan was different from other lands.

Rabbi Levi said: At the time that Abraham was traveling through Aram Naharayim and Aram Nahor,[36] he saw the local people eating, drinking, and acting without restraint. He said: I hope my lot will not be in this land. Once he reached the Promontory of Tyre,[37] he saw that the local people were engaged in weeding at the time for weeding, in hoeing at the time for hoeing. He said: I hope my lot will be in this land.

(*Bereshit Rabba* 39)

Abraham and Sarah Draw People Near

The Torah relates that Abraham and Sarah took with them to the land of Canaan "the people whom they had made in Haran." The Sages explain the meaning of this expression.

"The people whom they had made in Haran" (Genesis 12:5). Rabbi Hunya said: Abraham would convert the men and Sarah would convert the women. And what is the meaning of that which the verse states: "Whom they had made in Haran"? It teaches that Abraham and Sarah would bring people into their home, feed them, give them drink, show them love, draw them near, and bring them under the wings of the Divine Presence. You learn that any-

---

34. As the verse states in this context: "I will make your name great" (Genesis 12:2).
35. The hardship of going to an unknown destination within the general hardship of leaving his homeland.
36. Regions in the ancient territory of Aram through which Abraham passed en route to the land of Canaan.
37. The mountains that soar above the coast of Tyre adjacent to the northern border of the land of Canaan.

one who brings one person into the wings of the Divine Presence is ascribed credit as though he created him, formed him, and shaped him.

(*Shir HaShirim Rabba* 1)

Charity and Justice

Through their hospitality, Abraham and Sarah taught their guests to thank the Creator of the world for their food.

Abraham would receive the passersby. After they would eat and drink, he would tell them: Recite a blessing. They would say to him: What should we say? Abraham would tell them to say: Blessed is the eternal God, whose food we have eaten. If the guest would accept it upon himself and recite the blessing, he would eat, drink, and go. If he would not accept it upon himself, Abraham would say to him: Give me what you have [in exchange for what you consumed]. The guest would say: What claim do you have on me? Abraham would say to him: I supplied you with one jug of wine for ten *polar*,[38] one *litra* of meat for ten *polar*, and one loaf of bread for ten *polar*. Who would give you wine in the wilderness? Who would give you meat in the wilderness? Who would give you a loaf in the wilderness? Once the guest would see all this trouble that [Abraham] was causing him, he would say: Blessed is the eternal God whose food we have eaten. And that is what is written with regard to Abraham: "To perform charity and justice" (Genesis 18:19). Initially, charity, and ultimately, justice.[39]

Initially, charity…justice: Initially, he followed the path of charity and kindness; but ultimately, he resorted to a resolute demand, employing the quality of justice.

(*Bereshit Rabba* 49)

Abraham and Sarah's Descent to Egypt

Abraham asks Sarah to declare that she is his sister, lest the Egyptians kill him if it becomes known that he is her husband. The Sages discuss Abraham and Sarah's descent to Egypt and the exchange between Abraham and the Egyptians.

---

38. This is an ancient coin. Ten *polar* is an excessive amount for the food in question.
39. Initially, Abraham followed the path of charity and kindness. Ultimately, he presented a resolute demand, employing the quality of justice.

"It was upon Abram's arrival in Egypt, the Egyptians saw [the woman, that she was very fair.]" (Genesis 12:14). Where was Sarah?[40] Abraham placed her in a chest to hide her, and locked her in it. Once they reached customs, the customs workers said to him: Pay the tariff. Abraham said: I will pay the tariff. [In order to encourage him to open his chest] they said to him: You are bearing vessels, [which carry a high tariff]. Abraham said: I will pay that of vessels. They said to him: You are bearing gold, [which carries an even higher tariff]. Abraham said: I will pay that of gold. They said to him: You are bearing silk, [which carries an even higher tariff]. Abraham said: I will pay that of silk. They said to him: You are bearing jewels, [which carry an even higher tariff]. Abraham said: I will pay that of jewels. They said to him: There is no way out of your opening the chest and showing what is in it. Once he opened it, the entire land of Egypt shone from Sarah's radiance.

(*Bereshit Rabba* 40)

The Promise of Progeny

God promises Abraham that despite his advanced age, he will have innumerable descendants. God shows him the stars, and tells him: "So shall be your descendants." The Sages explain the precise meaning of this expression.

What is the meaning of the verse: "So shall be your descendants" (Genesis 15:5)? Rabbi Levi said in the name of Rabbi Yohanan: To what is the matter comparable? It is comparable to one who set out on the way and he went one, two, three, up to ten days, and he did not find a city, an inn, a tree, water, or a person. After walking for ten days, he saw one tree from a distance. He said: Perhaps there is water beneath it. Once he approached the tree, he found it standing beside a spring. Once he saw that the tree was beautiful, its fruits were tasty, and its branches were beautiful, he sat and cooled himself in its shade. He ate some of its fruits, drank water from the spring; and it was pleasant for him and his soul was restored. When he stood to go, he said to the tree: How can I bless you? What can I say to you? Shall I say that your wood should be beautiful? It is already beautiful. Shall I say that your shade shall be pleasant? It is already pleasant. Shall I say that your branches should be pleasing? They are already pleasing. Shall I say that your fruits shall be sweet? They are already sweet. Shall I say that a spring shall emerge from beneath your roots? A spring already emerges from beneath your roots. Shall I say that you shall stand in a charming place? You already stand in a charming

---

40. First the verse mentions only that Abraham arrived in Egypt.

place. How can I bless you? I bless you that all the saplings that come from you shall be like you.

So too, when the Holy One, blessed be He, created the world, twenty generations stood and they served no purpose, and no righteous person stood among them until after twenty generations, [when Abraham was born]. The Holy One, blessed be He, said to him: Abraham! What can I say to you and how can I bless you? Shall I say that you shall be completely righteous before Me, or that your wife Sarah shall be righteous before Me? You are righteous and your wife Sarah is righteous before Me. Or shall I say that all the members of your household shall be righteous? They are all righteous before Me. How can I bless you? I bless you that all the children that are destined to come from you shall be like you. From where is that derived? As it is stated: "He said to him: So, [i.e., like you] shall be your descendants" (15:5).

(Bemidbar Rabba 2)

Circumcision – Completeness

Abraham is commanded with regard to circumcision, and circumcises himself, Ishmael, and the male members of his household. The Sages describe the unique value of this mitzva.

Rabbi says: Great is the mitzva of circumcision. As despite all the mitzvot that Abraham fulfilled, he was not called complete until he was circumcised, as it is stated: "Walk before Me, and be complete" (Genesis 17:1).[41]

(Tosefta [Lieberman], Nedarim 2:5)

📖 Further reading: For more about circumcision and its profound meaning, see *A Concise Guide to Mahshava*, p. 9. About the circumcision ritual and the manner of its fulfillment, see *A Concise Guide to Halakha*, p. 5.

The Ordeals of Abraham

The Sages have a tradition that Abraham was tested with ten ordeals, or trials of faith. Below is one tradition with regard to what, specifically, these ordeals were.

Abraham was tested with ten ordeals and he withstood them all.

The first ordeal: When Abraham was born, all the prominent members of the kingdom and the priests sought to kill him, and he hid in the house of Haran his brother for thirteen years.

---

41. This verse immediately precedes the mitzva of circumcision.

The second ordeal: He was incarcerated in prison for ten years … and after ten years they sent and brought Abraham to Nimrod, the ruler, and they cast him into the fiery furnace, and the King of glory extended His right hand and rescued him from the fiery furnace, as it is stated: "I am the Lord who took you out of Ur[42] of the Chaldeans" (Genesis 15:7).

The third ordeal: His displacement from his father's house and his homeland. God brought him to Haran, and his father Terah and his mother Atdai died there. Displacement is more difficult for a person than anything.

The fourth ordeal: From the day that the heavens and the earth were created, the Holy One, blessed be He, did not bring famine in the world until the days of Abraham. And this famine was not in all the lands, but only in the land of Canaan, in order to test, by causing him to be dislocated to Egypt, [whether he would keep his faith].

The fifth ordeal: Pharaoh took Abraham's wife Sarah as his wife. Is there a man who sees his wife taken to another man and does not rend his garments in mourning?

The sixth ordeal: All the kings[43] attacked him to kill him. They said: We will initiate the battle with his nephew and then we will initiate the battle with him.

The seventh ordeal: "After these matters, the word of the Lord came to Abram in a vision, saying" (14:12).[44]

The eighth ordeal: "Abram was ninety years and nine years old, and the Lord appeared to Abram; He said to him: I am God Almighty; walk before Me, and be complete" (17:1). The Holy One, blessed be He, said to him: Until now, you have not been complete; circumcise your foreskin and walk before Me, and you will be complete.[45]

The ninth ordeal: Ishmael saw Isaac sitting alone and he shot an arrow, attempting to kill him. Sarah saw and told Abraham. She said to him: Ishmael did such and such to Isaac. Stand and write a document giving to Isaac everything that the Holy One, blessed be He, took an oath to give to you and your descendants. Ishmael the son of the maidservant Hagar will not inherit with my son, with Isaac.[46]

---

42. *Ur* is a Hebrew term for fire.
43. The four kings of Canaan, who took his nephew Lot captive (see Genesis 14:12) and planned to harm Abraham as well.
44. In this vision, Abraham received the tidings about the exiles of his descendants, particularly the Egyptian exile.
45. Undergoing circumcision at Abraham's advanced age is very painful.
46. The ordeal was disinheriting his older son, Ishmael.

The tenth ordeal: "It was after these matters; God tested Abraham" (22:1).[47]

And why did God challenge Abraham with so many ordeals? So that when Abraham our patriarch will come and take his reward, the nations of the world will say: More than any of us, more than everyone, Abraham is worthy of taking his reward. And in Abraham's regard it is stated: "Go, eat your bread with joy, and drink your wine with a good heart" (Ecclesiastes 9:7).

(*Pirkei deRabbi Eliezer* [Higer] 26–30;
Avot deRabbi Natan, version A, chap. 33)

Further reading: For more about Ishmael and his attitude to his brother Isaac, see p. 29.

---

47. This verse introduces the commandment of the binding of Isaac.

Vayera

This Torah portion continues the description of the lives of Abraham and Sarah. It begins with the tidings they receive with regard to the upcoming birth of their son. It continues with the account of the city of Sodom: The despicable conduct of its residents, and a depiction of the destruction of Sodom and its environs, of which Lot and his daughters were the sole survivors. Thereafter, the Torah tells of Sarah's abduction to Avimelekh's palace and her release, the birth of Isaac and the banishing of Hagar and Ishmael, and the covenant established between Avimelekh king of Gerar and Abraham. The portion concludes with the episode of the binding of Isaac.

The chapter that follows presents statements of the Sages pertaining to Abraham's attribute of kindness, the sins of the people of Sodom, the birth of Isaac, the expulsion of Ishmael, and several matters related to the narrative of the binding of Isaac.

Abraham, the Angels, and Hospitality

At the beginning of the Torah portion, Abraham, sitting outside his tent, sees three guests whom he invites to his home. They inform him of the future birth of Isaac. The Sages depict the incident, emphasizing the extent to which Abraham sought the opportunity to fulfill the mitzva of hospitality.

"The Lord appeared to him in the plains of Mamre, and he sat at the entrance of the tent as the day grew hot" (Genesis 18:1). What is the meaning of the phrase, "as the day grew hot"? Rabbi Hama son of Rabbi Hanina said: That day was the third day after Abraham's circumcision, [a particularly painful day], and the Holy One, blessed be He, came to inquire about the well-being of Abraham. The Holy One, blessed be He, took the sun out of its sheath so that its heat would be felt more intensely so as not to burden the righteous one, Abraham, with caring for guests, [as people would refrain from traveling in the heat]. Abraham sent Eliezer his servant to go outside to look for guests. He went out but did not find any. Abraham said: I don't believe you…. He went out himself; He saw the Holy One, blessed be He, who was standing at the entrance. That is what is written: "Please do not depart from upon your servant" (18:3).[48] Who were the "three men" who then approached? Mikhael, Gavriel, and Raphael, three angels. Mikhael – who

---

48. Abraham requested that the Divine Presence not depart from him, even though he was going out to search for guests.

came to bring tidings to Sarah about Isaac's upcoming birth; Raphael – who came to heal Abraham; Gavriel – who was going to destroy Sodom.

(Bava Metzia 86b)

📖 **Further reading:** For the halakhot relating to hospitality, see A Concise Guide to Halakha, p. 606.

Sodom, City of Sin

The Torah states that the people of Sodom were "exceedingly wicked and sinful" (Genesis 13:13), but it does not state precisely how their wickedness was manifest. The Sages elaborate on the matter, particularly the societal depravation of the city's residents.

The people of Sodom would set their sights on property owners, place a property owner alongside an inclined wall about to fall, push it upon him to kill him, and then seize his property.

There were four judges in Sodom: Liar, Habitual Liar, Forger, and Perverter of Justice. In the case of one who strikes the wife of another and causes her to miscarry, they would say to the victim's husband: Give her to the assailant, so that he will impregnate her for you. In the case of one who would sever the ear of another's donkey, they would say to the owner of the donkey: Give it to the assailant until the ear grows back. In the case of one who would wound another, they would say to the victim: Pay the assailant a fee, as he let your blood.[49]

The residents of Sodom had beds of a fixed size on which they would lay their guests; the tall one, they would cut him, the short one, they would stretch him [so that they would fit the size of the beds].

When a poor person would happen to come to them, each one would give him a dinar with his name written on it as if to help him. But they would not give or sell bread to him. When the poor person would die of starvation, each one would come and take back his dinar.

Rabbi Yehuda says: They proclaimed in Sodom: Anyone who supports the poor, the stranger, or the destitute with a portion of bread will be burned in fire. Pelotit, Lot's daughter, was married to one of the prominent residents of Sodom. She saw a miserable, poor person in the city plaza, and was pained by the sight of him. What did she do? When she went to draw water she placed items from all the food in her house in her jug, and supported that poor person. The people of Sodom said: This poor person, how does he

---

49. Bloodletting was considered medically beneficial.

survive? [Who is providing him with food?] Once they discovered the matter, they took her out to be burned. She said: Eternal God, exact justice and
law for me from the people of Sodom. Her cry ascended before the Throne
of Glory of God. The Holy One, blessed be He, said: "I will descend now
and see if they have acted in accordance with the outcry that has reached
Me" (18:21). If the people of Sodom acted in accordance with the cry of this
young woman, and indeed are threatening to kill her for assisting a poor person, I will overturn it, placing its foundations above and its exterior below.
[The allusion to this is that the phrase:] If in accordance with their outcry
[in the plural], is not written; rather, [it is written in the singular:] "In accordance with her outcry," and therefore I will overturn the city.

(Sanhedrin 109a; *Pirkei deRabbi Eliezer* 25)

He Has Made Laughter for Me

After Isaac was born, Sarah commented that the birth of Isaac was so joyful that
anyone who heard about it would laugh with happiness. The Sages explain what
type of joy other people experienced in the wake of Isaac's birth.

"Sarah said: God has made laughter for me; everyone who hears will laugh
for me" (Genesis 21:6). If Reuben is rejoicing, why would Simeon care?
Likewise, Sarah was remembered;[50] why would others care? The reason is
that at the moment that Sarah our matriarch was remembered, many barren
women were remembered with her, many deaf people were cured and could
hear, many blind people were cured and could see, many insane people became sane. That is why all were joyous with her.

(Bereshit Rabba 53)

Against the Scoffers

The marvel of the birth of Isaac to his parents when they were of such an advanced
age, Abraham when he was one hundred years old and Sarah ninety, led to skepticism
and gossip among the people, until it was clearly proven that Isaac was the son of
Abraham and Sarah.

"[Sarah] said: Who would have said of Abraham that Sarah would nurse
children?" (Genesis 21:7).[51] Why is "children" written in plural; how many

---

50. Conceived and gave birth.
51. After Isaac was born, Sarah expressed her amazement that Abraham had fathered a child and that
    she gave birth to the baby and nursed him.

children did she nurse? Rabbi Levi said: On the day that Abraham celebrated the weaning of his son Isaac, he made a great feast. All the nations of the world were gossiping and saying: Did you see the old man and old woman who brought a foundling from the street and claim: He is our son? Moreover, they make a great feast to bolster their claim. What did Abraham our patriarch do? He went and invited all the prominent men of the generation, and Sarah invited their wives. Each and every one brought her baby with her, but did not bring her wet nurse. A miracle befell Sarah our matriarch and her breasts opened like two springs. Milk flowed from them and she nursed all of them. But they were still gossiping and saying: Even if Sarah, at the age of ninety, could give birth, could Abraham, at the age of one hundred, father a child? Immediately, the countenance of Isaac's face was transformed and he resembled Abraham. All of them began to say: "Abraham begot Isaac" (25:19).

(*Bava Metzia* 87a)

The Banishing of Hagar and Ishmael

After the birth of Isaac, Sarah saw Ishmael son of Hagar engaged in an action described by the verse as *metzahek*, literally, laughing or playing. Therefore, she requested that Abraham banish him and his mother. What precisely did Sarah see, and what is the meaning of the term *metzahek*? The Sages provide several explanations.

Rabbi Akiva taught: "Sarah saw the son of Hagar the Egyptian, whom she bore to Abraham, *metzahek*" (Genesis 21:9). *Tzehok* stated here means nothing other than idolatry, as it is stated: "And the people sat to eat and drink, and they rose to frolic [*letzahek*]" (Exodus 32:6).[52] This teaches that our matriarch Sarah saw Ishmael building altars, trapping grasshoppers, and offering and burning the grasshoppers for idol worship.

Rabbi Eliezer son of Rabbi Yosei HaGelili says: *Sehok* stated here means nothing other than forbidden sexual intercourse, as it is stated: "The Hebrew slave whom you brought to us came to me to mock [*letzahek*] me" (Genesis 39:17).[53] This teaches that our matriarch Sarah would see Ishmael engaging in homosexual intercourse and raping women.

Rabbi Yishmael says: The term *sehok* means nothing other than bloodshed, as it is stated: "Avner said to Yoav: Let the lads rise now and play [*veyisahaku*] before us…. Each man grabbed the head of his counterpart, and

---

52. After they crafted the Golden Calf, they ate, drank, and worshipped the calf.
53. This is what the wife of Potiphar told him when accusing Joseph of sexually assaulting her.

his sword into the side of his counterpart, and they fell together" (II Samuel 2:14, 16) to their deaths. This teaches that our matriarch Sarah would see Ishmael taking a bow and arrows and shooting them toward Isaac, as it is stated: "Like the prankster who shoots firebrands, arrows, and death, so is a man who deceives his friend, and says: Am I not joking [*mesahek*]?" (Proverbs 26:18–19).

But I, Rabban Shimon ben Yohai, say: Heaven forfend that it would be so in the house of that righteous man, Abraham. Is it possible for one about whom it is stated: "For I love him, so that he shall command his children and his household after him, and they will observe the way of the Lord, to perform righteousness and justice" (Genesis 18:19),[54] that there will be idol worship, forbidden sexual intercourse, or bloodshed in his house? Rather, *tzehok* stated here pertains to nothing other than the matter of inheritance, as when Isaac was born to Abraham our patriarch, everyone was joyful and would say: A son was born to Abraham! A son was born to Abraham! He will inherit the world and take a double portion, as does a firstborn son. Ishmael would scoff [*metzahek*] in his mind, saying: Don't be fools, don't be fools! I am the firstborn and I will take a double portion. You learn this from Sarah's response to the matter. She said: "For the son of this maidservant shall not inherit with my son, with Isaac" (21:10), [indicating that her complaint was connected to the matter of inheritance].

(*Tosefta* [Lieberman], *Sota* 6:6)

On the Way to the Binding of Isaac

The story of the binding of Isaac is one of the foundational narratives in the history of the Jewish people. Almost nothing is stated in the Torah about the journey of Abraham and his entourage to the binding. The Sages describe a path that was full of challenges.

Why does the verse teach that Abraham arose early? It is because the vigilant are quick to perform mitzvot. Satan preceded him on the way and appeared to him in the image of an older man. Satan said to him: Where are you going? Abraham said to him: I am going to pray. Satan said to him: And does one who is going to pray carry equipment to build a fire, and a knife in his hand and wood on his shoulder? Abraham said to him: Perhaps we will stay there one or two days, and we will slaughter animals, bake, and eat.

---

54. God attested to the fact that Abraham educated the members of his family to follow His path, the path of righteousness and justice.

Satan said to him: Old man, wasn't I there when the Holy One, blessed be He, said to you: Take your son? Will an old man like you go and kill a son that was given him at the age of one hundred years? Haven't you heard the parable: He lost what was in his possession, and he seeks from others? Even if you say: I will have another son, still, will you listen to the Accuser and eliminate a soul, for which you will be legally liable? Abraham said to him: It was not the Accuser who instructed me; rather, it was the Holy One, blessed be He. I will not listen to you.

Satan went, and reappeared like a lad, and stood to the right of Isaac. He said to Isaac: Where are you going? Isaac said to him: To study Torah. Satan said to him: During your lifetime or after your death? Isaac said to him: Is there a person who studies after his death? Satan said to him: Wretched son of a wretched mother; how many fasts did your mother fast before you were born to merit to have you, and the old man has gone insane and he is going to slaughter you. Isaac said: Nevertheless, I will not transgress the wisdom of my Creator or the command of my father.

"On the third day…" (Genesis 22:4).[55] Since the way to the site was short, why was Abraham delayed three days? Once Satan saw that they did not accept his claims, he went and became a great river before them. Immediately Abraham descended into the water and it reached his knees. Abraham said to his lads: Follow me. They descended after him. When he reached halfway through the river, the water reached up to his neck. At that moment, Abraham directed his eyes to the heavens, and he said before God: Master of the Universe: You chose me and revealed Yourself to me, and You said to me: I am one and you are one; through you My name will become known in the world, and offer your son Isaac before Me as a burnt offering. I did not delay, and I am engaged in fulfilling your command, and now the water has come up to my neck. If I or my son Isaac drowns, who will fulfill Your words? Upon whom will the Oneness of Your name be proclaimed?

The Holy One, blessed be He, said to him: By your life, I promise that the Oneness of My name will be proclaimed in the world through you. Immediately, the Holy One, blessed be He, rebuked the spring from which the water flowed. The river dried and they stood on dry land…. At that moment, great fear and terror fell over Isaac, as he did not see anything in Abraham's hand to be sacrificed, and he sensed what was intended to be. He started to say: "Where is the lamb for a burnt offering?" (22:7). Abraham said: Since

---

55. The Torah states that it was only on the third day that Abraham and his entourage reached Mount Moriah.

you said it, the Holy One, blessed be He, has chosen you. Isaac said: If He has chosen me, my soul is given to Him; but I am greatly distressed over my blood, i.e., my death. Nevertheless: "And the two of them went together" (22:8), with certitude, this one to slaughter and that one to be slaughtered. Isaac was thirty-seven years old at the time of his binding.

(*Tanḥuma, Vayera*)

📖 **Further reading:** For more about the preparedness for self-sacrifice, see *A Concise Guide to Mahshava*, p. 198.

The Binding of Isaac – the Angels' Tears

The Sages describe the great sadness of Abraham and Isaac in the moments preceding the binding, and also the shock and weeping of the heavenly angels.

Abraham's eyes were focused on Isaac's eyes, and Isaac's eyes were focused on the heavens of the heavens, and tears were dropping and falling from Abraham's eyes until [Isaac] was entirely flooded with tears. Abraham said to him: Since you began with a quarter *log* of your blood,[56] your Creator will arrange for you a different offering in your stead. At that moment [Isaac][57] opened his mouth wide, crying, and bellowed a great roar. His eyes were blinking intensely and were looking to the Divine Presence, and he raised his voice, and said: "I lift my eyes to the mountains; from where will my help come? My help is from the Lord, Maker of heaven and earth" (Psalms 121:1–2).

At that moment there was a fulfillment of the verse: "Behold, their angels cry out outside, the messengers of peace weep bitterly" (Isaiah 33:7). The ministering angels stood in rows in the sky, and said to one another: See, the individual is slaughtering and the individual is being slaughtered. The angels said to God: If Isaac is killed who will recite before You on the sea: "This is my God and I will glorify Him" (Exodus 15:2)? And what will You do with regard to the oath You made to Abraham: "So shall be your descendants" (Genesis 15:5)? Immediately Abraham heard a call: "Do not extend your hand to the lad" (22:12).

(*Yalkut Shimoni, Vayera* 1:101)

---

56. i.e., since you came willingly to be sacrificed.
57. Alternatively, Abraham.

The Binding of Isaac – the Ram Entangled in the Thicket

After Abraham was commanded not to slaughter Isaac, he saw a ram whose horns were entangled in branches, and he sacrificed it to God in place of Isaac. The Sages explain that this ram symbolizes the future fate of Israel in enslavement and redemption.

Throughout that day, Abraham would see a ram entangled in a tree then untangled itself and escape, entangled in a thicket then untangled itself and escape. The Holy One, blessed be He, said to him: Abraham, your children are destined to be so. They will be entangled in their iniquities and enmeshed, or enslaved, with the gentile kingdoms, from Babylonia to Media, from Media to Greece, and from Greece to Edom, Rome. Abraham said before Him: Master of the Universe, will it be so forever? God said to him: Ultimately, they will be redeemed with the horns of this ram [as the verse states with regard to the future redemption]: "And the Lord God will sound the shofar, and He will go with the storms to the south" (Zechariah 9:14).

(Jerusalem Talmud, *Ta'anit* 10:2)

📖 **Further reading:** On Rosh HaShana we remember and mention the binding of Isaac. See *A Concise Guide to Mahshava*, p. 61; *A Concise Guide to Halakha*, p. 143, 146.

Hayei Sara

The bulk of the Torah portion of *Hayei Sara* addresses the story of the marriage of Isaac, the spiritual heir of Abraham. The portion begins with the death of Abraham's wife Sarah and her interment in Hebron, and continues with a detailed account of the journey of Abraham's servant, identified by the Sages as Eliezer, to find a wife for Isaac. The young woman chosen is Rebecca, daughter of Isaac's cousin Betuel. Eliezer brings her to the land of Canaan and Isaac marries her. The portion concludes with the death of Abraham and his interment in the Cave of Makhpela.

The chapter that follows presents a selection of the statements of the Sages concerning Sarah's burial plot, the arrival of aging in the world, the connection and continuity between Sarah and Rebecca, the woman whom Abraham married in his old age, and the general mourning that took place in the wake of his passing.

Kiryat Arba

From among the four names of the city of Hebron, the Torah chooses the name Kiryat Arba when referring to the burial place of Sarah. The Sages explain that this name contains an allusion to the uniqueness of the place.

"Sarah died in Kiryat Arba" (Genesis 23:2). This location was called by four names: Eshkol, Mamre, Kiryat Arba, and Hebron. Why did the verse call it Kiryat Arba [literally, Town of the Four]? Because four righteous men resided there: Aner, Eshkol, Mamre, and Abraham, and four righteous men were circumcised there: Abraham, Aner, Eshkol, and Mamre. Alternatively, the verse refers to it as Kiryat Arba because four patriarchs of the world were ultimately buried there: Adam the first man, Abraham, Isaac, and Jacob. Alternatively, the verse refers to it as Kiryat Arba because ultimately four matriarchs were buried there: Eve, Sarah, Rebecca, and Leah.

(*Bereshit Rabba* 58)

> **Further reading:** For more about Aner, Eshkol, and Mamre, see *A Concise Guide to the Torah*, p. 29.

Aging

According to the Sages, the first person in the world who experienced the phenomenon of aging was Abraham, and that occurred in the wake of his explicit request. Phenomena like pain and illness are also tied to requests of the patriarchs.

Abraham demanded aging. He said before God: Master of the Universe, when a person and his sons enter the same place, no one knows whom to honor.[58] By adorning the father with old age and white hair, a person knows whom to honor. The Holy One, blessed be He, said to him: By your life, you have demanded properly and it begins with you. From the beginning of the book of Genesis until here, there is no mention of a person aging. Once Abraham our patriarch stood, God granted him aging, and that is what is stated: "Abraham was old" (Genesis 24:1).

Isaac demanded afflictions. He said before God: Master of the Universe, when a person dies without afflictions, the attribute of justice is set against him when he dies.[59] If You bring afflictions upon him, the attribute of justice would not be set against him. The Holy One, blessed be He, said to him: By your life, you have demanded properly and it begins with you. From the beginning of the book of Genesis until here, there are no afflictions written. Once our patriarch Isaac stood, God afflicted him, as it is written: "It was when Isaac was old, and his eyes dimmed from seeing" (27:1), afflicting him with blindness.

Jacob demanded illness. He said before God: Master of the Universe, when a person dies without illness, he cannot settle matters between his children. When a person is ill for two or three days, he can settle matters between his children. God said to him: By your life, you have demanded properly and it begins with you. And it is with regard to this that it is stated in the verse: "And one said to Joseph: Behold, your father is ill" (48:1).

(*Yalkut Shimoni, Hayei Sarah* 1:105)

An Improper Request

The manner in which Eliezer chose to locate a wife for Isaac – searching for a young woman who will demonstrate hospitality – was risky. The Sages criticize him for this, and note other times in the history of Israel where similar tactics were employed.

Eliezer, the servant of Abraham, said to God: "Behold, I stand by the spring of water and the daughters of the men of the city come out to draw water. It shall be that the young woman to whom I will say: Please tilt your jug and I will drink, and she will say: Drink, and I will also give your camels to drink; it is she You have confirmed for Your servant, for Isaac, and through

---

58. Because they are unable to determine who is the father and who is the son.
59. His sins are not atoned for while he is still alive. When afflictions befall him, they atone for his sins before he dies.

her I will know that You have acted with kindness with my master" (Genesis 24:13–14).

They are four people who made improper requests. To three of them, their requests were granted properly, and to one it was granted improperly. And these are the people: Eliezer the servant of Abraham, Caleb, Saul, and Yiftah. Abraham's servant Eliezer said: "It shall be that the young woman to whom I will say…" (24:14). I wonder: Had some maidservant come forth and given him to drink, would he have married her to the son of his master? Nevertheless, the Holy One, blessed be He, arranged it for him properly and an appropriate girl came forth, as the verse states: "It was before he concluded to speak; behold, Rebecca was coming out" (24:15).

Caleb said [during the war to conquer the Land of Israel]: "He who smites Kiryat Sefer and captures it, I will give him Akhsa my daughter as a wife" (Judges 1:12). Had some slave captured it, would Caleb have given him his daughter? Nevertheless, the Holy One, blessed be He, arranged it for him properly, and an appropriate man smote the city, as it is stated: "Otniel son of Kenaz, Caleb's younger brother, captured it; and he gave him Akhsa his daughter as a wife" (Judges 1:13).

Saul said [during the standoff against Goliath]: "It shall be that the man who smites him, the king will enrich him with great wealth, and he will give him his daughter" (I Samuel 17:25). Had some Kushite, some idolater, or some slave come forth and smote Goliath, would Saul have given him his daughter? Nevertheless, the Holy One, blessed be He, arranged it for him properly, and an appropriate man killed Goliath, as it is written: "David was the son of a nobleman" (I Samuel 17:12).

Yiftah [said, before leaving to battle with the Amonites]: "It shall be that that which emerges from the doors of my house to meet me when I return in peace from the children of Amon, it shall be for the Lord, and I will present it as a burnt offering" (Judges 11:31). Had a donkey, some dog, or some cat come forth, would Yiftah have presented it as a burnt offering? The Holy One, blessed be He, arranged it for him improperly as his daughter, who cannot be brought as an offering, was first to emerge from his house, as it is stated: "Yiftah came to the Mitzpa, to his house, and behold, his daughter was coming out to meet him" (Judges 11:34).

(*Bereshit Rabba* 60)

Sarah and Rebecca

Rebecca, the wife designated for Isaac, was fit to be Sarah's spiritual heir as one of the matriarchs of the Jewish people. Immediately upon her arrival, she continued the legacy of Sarah.

"Isaac brought her into the tent of his mother Sarah" (Genesis 24:67). As long as Sarah was alive, a cloud, the symbol of the Divine Presence, hovered over the entrance to her tent. When she died, the cloud was no longer there. Once Rebecca arrived, that cloud returned. As long as Sarah was alive, the doors to her tent were wide open to enable guests to enter. When Sarah died, the doors were no longer wide open. Once Rebecca arrived, the doors were once again wide open. As long as Sarah was alive, there was a blessing present in the dough she made. When Sarah died, that blessing ceased. Once Rebecca arrived, it returned. As long as Sarah was alive, the light miraculously remained lit from Shabbat eve to Shabbat eve. When Sarah died, that light ceased. Once Rebecca arrived, it returned.

(*Bereshit Rabba* 60)

Isaac Was Consoled over the Passing of His Mother

Isaac's marriage to Rebecca brought him tranquility and consolation after mourning the death of his mother. The Sages draw insight concerning the emotional growth that one undergoes upon his marriage.

"Isaac was comforted after his mother" (Genesis 24:67). Rabbi Yosei says: He mourned for his mother for three years. After three years, he took Rebecca and forgot the mourning over his mother. From here you learn: Until a man takes a wife, his love is directed toward his parents. Once a man marries, his love is redirected toward his wife, as it is stated: "Therefore, a man shall leave his father and his mother, and he shall cleave to his wife" (2:24).

Does a man leave the mitzva of giving honor to his parents? He is still obligated to honor his parents, but his profound love cleaves to his wife, as it is stated: "And he shall cleave to his wife" (2:24).

(*Yalkut Shimoni, Vayetze* 109)

Ketura

The Torah portion discusses Abraham's marriage to a woman named Ketura. Who was she?

"Abraham took another wife, and her name was Ketura" (Genesis 25:1). Rabbi Yehuda says: This is in fact Hagar[60]...But isn't it written: "And her name was Ketura"? It is because she attached herself [*shekatra*] to mitzvot and good deeds.

(*Yalkut Shimoni, Vayetze* 109)

The Death of Abraham

Leaders of the entire world mourned the death of Abraham.

Rav Hanan bar Rava said that Rav said: On the day that Abraham our patriarch passed from the world, all the prominent leaders of the nations of the world stood in a row and said: Woe to the world that has lost its leader, and woe to the ship that has lost its captain.

(*Yalkut Shimoni, Hayei Sarah* 1:110)

Further reading: The custom of covering the bride's face with a veil is connected to the marriage of Isaac and Rebecca. See *A Concise Guide to Halakha*, p. 59.

---

60. The mother of Ishmael, whom Abraham had previously married and banished.

Toledot

There are three primary topics in the Torah portion of Toledot: The first is an account of the pregnancy, birth, and development of Jacob and Esau, including Esau's sale of the birthright to Jacob. The second is Isaac's successful endeavors in the economic realm and his ultimately successful attempts to dig wells. The third is the account of Isaac's blessings and the subterfuge employed by Rebecca and Jacob to ensure that Jacob received those blessings.

The chapter that follows presents a selection of the statements of the Sages concerning the personalities and conduct of Jacob and Esau, Isaac's extraordinary prosperity, elaboration upon the episode of Isaac's blessings, and a discussion about the matter of fulfillment of the mitzvot before the giving of the Torah.

Jacob and Esau

The Torah discusses Rebecca's pregnancy and the birth of the twins, Esau and Jacob. The Sages elaborate on the differences between the two in terms of their actions.

"The children were agitated within her" (Genesis 25:22). They ran within her: Rebecca would pass near a house of idol worship, and Esau would twitch to emerge… She would pass near synagogues and study halls, and Jacob would twitch to emerge. In that regard it is stated: "Before I formed you in the womb, I knew you…" (Jeremiah 1:5). "The lads grew" (Genesis 25:27). Rabbi Pinhas said in the name of Rabbi Levi: The development of Jacob and Esau is comparable to the growth of a myrtle bush and a thorn bush [which are similar in appearance in their early states of growth] that grew adjoining each other. When they grew, they blossomed, this one with its fragrance and that one with its thistles, and the difference between them was apparent. Similarly, all thirteen years the two of them would go to and come from school and engage in similar conduct. After thirteen years, this one would go to study halls and that one would go to houses of idol worship.

(*Bereshit Rabba* [Theodor-Albeck] 63)

📖 **Further reading:** For the spiritual experience of the fetus in the womb, see p. 407; *A Concise Guide to Mahshava*, p. 4.

Fulfillment of Mitzvot before the Giving of the Torah

The Sages teach that Abraham fulfilled the mitzvot even before the Torah was given at Sinai.

We find that Abraham our patriarch observed the entire Torah before it was given, as it is stated: "Because Abraham heeded My voice, and observed My commission, My commandments, My statutes, and My laws" (Genesis 26:5). Rava, and some say Rav Ashi, said: Abraham our patriarch fulfilled even the rabbinic ordinance of joining of cooked foods,[61] as it is stated: My laws, in the plural; both the Written Law and the Oral Law.

(Mishna *Kiddushin* 4:14; *Yoma* 28b)

Esau's Conduct

Though there is a reference to women that Esau married who did not find favor in the eyes of his parents, the Torah does not write extensively about his negative conduct. The Sages address this matter at great length in the Midrash.

Esau went out to the field at the age of fifteen and engaged in intercourse with a betrothed young woman[62] and shed blood…Once he did so, Abraham passed away. Why? The Holy One, blessed be He, said: I said to Abraham: "You will come to your fathers in peace; you will be buried at a good old age" (Genesis 15:15). What kind of good old age is this, that Abraham will see his grandson engaging in forbidden sexual intercourse and shedding blood? Therefore, God acted immediately, and Abraham departed from this world.

Jacob was sitting and cooking lentils. Esau came and said to him: Why are you sitting and cooking lentils? Jacob said to him: Because my grandfather Abraham died and I am sitting, mourning,[63] and lamenting so that he will know how I lamented for him, and when the dead are revived in the future my grandfather will love me. Esau said to him: Fool! Is that what you think? That after a person dies and deteriorates in the grave, he is destined to live? By saying this, Esau denied the revival of the dead. He then said: "Behold, I am going to die; for what do I need a birthright?" (25:32). Esau said to Jacob: Moreover, do you believe that the birthright has any value?

---

61. This is the *eiruv tavshilin*, performed when a festival occurs on a Friday.
62. Whose halakhic status is one of a married woman in this regard.
63. Traditionally, lentils are eaten by mourners.

Give me one bowl of these lentils and I will give it to you. "And Jacob gave Esau bread and a stew of lentils...and Esau scorned the birthright" (25:34).

(*Pesikta Rabbati* [Ish Shalom] 12)

📖 Further reading: Today too, lentils are food of mourners. See *A Concise Guide to Halakha*, p. 107.

Esau's Honor for His Father

In order that Jacob would resemble his twin, Rebecca clothed Jacob in "the fine garments of Esau" (Genesis 27:15), which were the garments that Esau would wear when he would appear before Isaac. The Sages learn from here the exceptional manner in which Esau honored his father.

"Rebecca took the fine garments of Esau,[64] her elder son" (27:15). Rabban Shimon ben Gamliel said: I would serve and honor my father all my days, but I did not serve him one-hundredth of how Esau served his father. When I would serve my father, I would serve him wearing dirty garments, but when I would leave to travel, I would leave wearing clean garments. But Esau, when he would serve his father, he would serve him only while wearing regal garments. Esau said: It is not befitting the honor due my father to serve him wearing anything other than regal garments.

(*Bereshit Rabba* 65)

📖 Further reading: For more about the mitzva of honoring parents, see *A Concise Guide to Halakha*, p. 609.

Jacob Coming before Isaac

The Sages elaborate on the events and conversation that took place between Isaac and Jacob, and the great fear that overcame Jacob at the moment his father sought to ascertain if he was indeed Esau.

Rabbi Yohanan said: At the moment that Jacob said in response to Isaac: "Because the Lord your God set it before me" (Genesis 27:20), Isaac said: This wording employing the name of God is not the wording used by Esau; rather, it is the wording used by Jacob, as it is stated: "The voice is the voice of Jacob" (27:22).[65] Isaac first said to Jacob: "Please approach, and I will feel you" (27:21). Rabbi Yehoshua says: When Isaac said: "Please approach," Jacob's body trembled and he was stooped like melting wax. What did the

---

64. Beautiful and distinguished garments, which Esau would wear when bringing food to his father.
65. Not only the tone of voice, but the style of speech.

Holy One, blessed be He, do? He told two angels, Gavriel and Mikhael, to help Jacob, and they assisted him; Mikhael to his right and Gavriel to his left. And He, may His name be blessed, in His glory, supported Jacob from behind him. God said to him: Jacob, why are you afraid and your body is stooped? I am God, and My host is in your assistance and supporting you, and you are afraid?

Immediately, Isaac said to him: "The voice is the voice of Jacob, but the hands are the hands of Esau" (27:22). Your strength is greater than his. Concerning Esau, if he apprehends a person, that person is in his custody, but if that person flees, Esau is unable to do anything to him. But concerning you, even if a person flees from one end of the world to the other end, still: "The voice is the voice of Jacob"; you say words of prayer in the synagogue and he comes on his own.

(*Tanḥuma* [Buber], *Toledot*)

Esau Coming before Isaac

The Sages describe the encounter between Esau and Isaac immediately after Jacob received the blessing from Isaac, and the reaction of Esau and Isaac after they realized that it was Jacob who was blessed.

"And Jacob had just departed from the presence of Isaac his father" (Genesis 27:30). This one, Jacob, exited and that one, Esau, entered. How could that matter have transpired?[66] One who is located in the light does not see one who is located in the relative darkness, but one who is located in the relative darkness sees one who is located in the light. Esau came from outside and did not see Jacob, who was inside the house; but Jacob saw Esau from inside and hid behind the door. Once Esau entered, Jacob emerged from his hiding place and left, as it is stated: "And Jacob had just departed from the presence of Isaac his father and Esau his brother came from his hunt" (27:30).

Did Jacob estimate the hours so precisely that Esau would not come and take the blessings? When Esau went out to hunt, the Holy One, blessed be He, sent an obstructer against him and did not enable him to trap until Jacob came and took the blessings…. How so? Esau would run and trap a deer and tie it and leave it, and would run and trap another and tie it and leave it, and the obstructer would untie them and release them, and Esau would come and would not find either of them. Thus the obstructer did two

---

66. How did Esau not notice Jacob leaving?

or three times … and the obstructer delayed Esau until Jacob came and took the blessings.

At that moment that Esau arrived to receive his father's blessing, Isaac recognized Esau's voice and began trembling. Isaac said to him: Who are you? Because at the moment that Jacob entered, the pleasing aroma of the Garden of Eden entered with him, and the mind of that righteous man Isaac was relaxed, as it is stated: "See, the scent of my son is as the scent of a field that the Lord blessed" (27:27). Therefore, Isaac began blessing Jacob. But when Esau entered, Gehenna opened before Isaac;[67] therefore, "Isaac was overcome with great trembling" (27:33). Isaac was asking in his heart: I see Gehenna with Esau igniting it. "And he said:[68] Who is it then who hunted game [*hatzad tzayid*]?" (27:33).[69] Why is the term for trapping, *tzad*, employed twice? Isaac said to Esau: You went to trap – and you were trapped, as Jacob received your blessings.

(*Tanḥuma* [Buber], *Toledot*)

📖 **Further reading:** For more about the Garden of Eden and Gehenna, see *A Concise Guide to Mahshava*, p. 165.

---

67. Isaac felt as though he was in Gehenna.
68. The verse recounts Isaac's next question.
69. The phrase "hunted game" is written in Hebrew with a doubled word: "*Hatzad tzayid.*"

Vayetze

This Torah portion focuses on Jacob from his departure from the land of Canaan to Haran until his return to the land of Canaan. It includes Jacob's dream of the ladder and the angels ascending and descending it; Jacob's arrival in Haran and his encounter with Rachel; Jacob's work for Laban and his marriage to his daughters, Leah and Rachel; and the birth of Jacob's sons and daughter. It concludes with Jacob's departure – a departure that was accompanied by a dispute with Laban, at the conclusion of which they make a peace treaty.

The chapter that follows presents a selection of the statements of the Sages concerning Jacob in Beit El and God's revelation to him there, Laban's character, Jacob's marriages to Leah and Rachel, Leah's suffering and Rachel's barrenness, and Rachel's theft of the teraphim.

The Departure of a Righteous Person

The impact of a righteous person on his surroundings is perceptible, and when he departs from his place, his departure is profoundly felt.

[After discussing a verse concerning Naomi and Ruth, the midrash continues:] Likewise you find with Jacob our patriarch when he departed from Beersheba. Was he the only one who departed from there? Didn't several camel drivers depart and several donkey drivers depart from there also? And yet you say: "Jacob departed" (Genesis 28:10), indicating that only he departed. The explanation is that when a righteous person is in a city, he is its radiance, he is its glory, he is its splendor; when he departs from there, its radiance leaves, its glory leaves, its splendor leaves, its praiseworthiness leaves.[70]

(*Rut Rabba* 2)

Jacob in Beit El

When Jacob reached Beit El and went to sleep, he dreamed of a ladder, the top of which reached the heavens, and upon which angels were ascending and descending. Then God appeared to him, blessed him, and promised him that his descendants

---

70. Therefore, specifically Jacob's departure was especially conspicuous.

would inherit the land upon which he was resting. The Sages describe the events that transpired on that occasion, which underscore God's love for Jacob.

["He came upon the place, and stayed the night there,] because the sun had set" (Genesis 28:11). "Because the sun had set": This[71] teaches that the Holy One, blessed be He, had the sun set not at its designated time [i.e., it set earlier], in order to speak with Jacob our patriarch in private. This is comparable to the beloved friend of the king who would come to visit him on occasion. The king said: Extinguish the lights, extinguish the lanterns, as I would like to speak with my beloved in private. So, too, the Holy One, blessed be He, had the sun set not at its designated time, in order to speak with Jacob our patriarch in private.

It is written concerning Jacob: "He took of the stones of the place" (28:11), in preparing for sleep, and it is then written: "He took the stone that he had placed beneath his head" (28:18). Were there many stones or just one stone? Rabbi Yitzhak said: It teaches that all those stones gathered in one place, and each and every one of them said: Let this righteous person place his head on me. The Sages taught: They were all incorporated into one stone.

"He dreamed, and behold, a ladder was set on the earth" (28:12). The Sages taught: How wide was the ladder? Eight thousand parasangs[72] .... The angels sought to endanger Jacob. Immediately the verse states: "And behold, the Lord stood over him" (28:13) to protect him. Rabbi Shimon ben Lakish said: Were the verse not written, it would be impossible to say [that God protected Jacob like a person waving over his son.[73]

God told Jacob: "The land upon which you lie, to you I will give it, and to your descendants" (28:13). What is so great [about this promise? Jacob was lying on a small amount of land]. Rabbi Yitzhak said: It teaches that the Holy One, blessed be He, folded the entire Land of Israel and placed it beneath Jacob our patriarch, so that it would be easier for his descendants to conquer it.

(*Bereshit Rabba* 68; *Ḥullin* 91b)

---

71. The verse states, *"ki va hashemesh,"* meaning "because the sun had set." The Sages interpret it as though it said: "Extinguished [*kiba*] the sun."
72. A parasang is approximately 4 km.
73. He waves a fan over his child to keep away flying creatures.

Laban's Avarice

When Jacob arrived at the home of Laban his uncle, Laban hurried to meet him, embraced him, and kissed him. According to the Sages, Laban's motivation was not pure; in fact, he was interested in the possessions that he assumed Jacob brought with him.

"It was when Laban heard the news of Jacob, his sister's son, he ran to meet him" (Genesis 29:13). Laban said to himself: Eliezer[74] was one with flawed lineage in the house of Abraham, and it is written concerning him: "The servant took ten camels" (24:7). This one, who is his beloved of the house of Isaac, all the more so that he will have possessions with him. When Laban did not see Jacob's satchel, "he embraced him" (29:13). He said to himself: Perhaps he has dinars stored in his belt, and embraced him to check. When Laban did not find anything, "he kissed him" (29:13). He said to himself: Perhaps he has gems stored in his mouth, and kissed him to check.

(*Bereshit Rabba* [Theodor-Albeck] 70)

Leah's Tears

The Sages relate that initially, the two sisters, Leah and Rachel, were designated for their two cousins, Esau and Jacob. Because Leah prayed to avoid her fate of marrying Esau, this did not occur.

Leah was intended to be married only to Esau, and Rachel to Jacob. Leah would sit at the crossroads and ask, concerning Esau, what his actions were. Passersby would tell her: He is a nefarious man, a shedder of blood. He robs passersby, he is covered with a cloak of red hair, he is wicked, he has performed all actions that are abominations to God. When Leah would hear that, she would weep and say: I and my sister Rachel emerged from the same womb; will Rachel be married to Jacob the righteous and I to Esau the wicked? She would weep and fast until her eyes grew tender; therefore, it is written: "Leah's eyes were tender" (Genesis 29:17).

"The Lord saw that Leah was hated" (29:31). He saw that Esau's actions were hateful before her.[75] But when Rachel would hear that she would be married to Jacob, her heart was glad and proud. After both of them were married to Jacob, the Holy One, blessed be He, said: Concerning Leah, who was crying and fasting and despised Esau's actions and was praying before Me, it is only right that she should not be distanced from that righteous man

---

74. Abraham's servant, who had come years earlier to find a wife for Isaac.
75. The Sages interpret the verb "hate" as referring to what Leah hated, not that she herself was hated.

Jacob. I will grant her children first so as to bring Leah and Jacob closer. Therefore it is stated: "The Lord saw that Leah was hated, and He opened her womb (29:31).

(*Tanḥuma, Vayetze*)

Rachel's Magnanimity

The Torah portion tells of Laban's act of deceit, in which he promised his daughter Rachel to Jacob but then substituted Leah. The Sages relate that Rachel knew about the plan and acted with magnanimity to avoid her sister's humiliation.

Upon meeting Rachel, "Jacob told Rachel that he was her father's brother" (Genesis 29:31). Was Jacob in fact her father's brother? Wasn't he the son of her father's sister Rebecca? He was not her father's brother, but when Jacob said to Rachel: Will you marry me? She said to him: Yes, but my father is a man of deceit, and you will not prevail against him. Jacob said to her: I am his brother, [I can contend with him,] in deceit. Rachel said to him: Is it permitted for the righteous to engage in deceit? Jacob said to her: Yes, as the verse teaches, "With the scoundrel act like a scoundrel, and with the perverse act perversely" (II Samuel 22:27). Jacob said to her: What is his method of deceit? Rachel said to him: I have a sister who is older than I, and he will not marry me off before she is married. Jacob gave her signs to prove her identity to him at their wedding. When the night arrived, Rachel said to herself: Now my sister will be shamed. Rachel gave the signs to Leah, and that is what is written: "It was in the morning and, behold, she was Leah" (Genesis 29:25). Is that to say that until now she was not Leah? The explanation is that because of the signs that Rachel gave to Leah, Jacob did not know until now, when the sun rose and he could see her, that he was with Leah. Therefore, due to her magnanimity, Rachel was rewarded, and Saul the first king of Israel came from her. [The verse relates that later, Rachel also married Jacob.] "God remembered Rachel, and God heeded her, and He opened her womb" (30:22) after a period of barrenness. Which memory did God remember for her? God remembered her silence for her sister at the moment that they were giving Leah to Jacob in marriage. She knew and she was silent.

(*Megilla* 13b; *Bereshit Rabba* 73)

Rachel's Barrenness

While Leah was blessed with many children, Rachel remained barren. She demanded from Jacob: "Give me children, and if not, I am dead" (Genesis 30:1). The Sages describe the dialogue between them and Jacob's suggested solution.

Jacob responded to Rachel: "Am I in place of God who withheld from you fruit of the womb? (30:2). He withheld children from you; He did not withhold children from me [as I have several children from Leah]. Rachel said to him: Is that what your father, Isaac, did to your mother? Didn't he gird his loins [i.e., pray vigorously] across from her? Jacob said to her: My father did not have children, but I have children. Rachel said to him: But didn't your grandfather, Abraham, already have children from Hagar and he girded his loins across from Sarah?

Jacob said to her: You can do what my grandmother Sarah did. Rachel said to him: What did she do? Jacob said to her: She introduced her rival into her household by having Abraham marry Hagar. Rachel said to him: If that is the hindrance to my conceiving, I agree. "She said: Here is my maid Bilha, consort with her… and I will be built through her" (30:3). Just as this one, Sarah, was built through her rival, so too, that one, I, will be built through my rival.

(*Bereshit Rabba* 71)

An Additional Son

When Joseph, Rachel's first son, was born, Rachel requested that God grant her an additional son. The Sages relate that God received her prayer, but it was at the expense of the other matriarchs.

The initial formation of the child that was to become Dina, Jacob's daughter from Leah, was male. After Rachel's prayer, when she said: "May the Lord add another son for me" (Genesis 30:24), that child became female.[76] All the matriarchs were prophets, and Rachel was one of the matriarchs. In recounting Rachel's prayer, it is not written in the verse: May the Lord add more sons; rather: "Another son." She said: Jacob is destined to produce one more son. I wish it will be from me. Rabbi Hanina said: The other mothers of Jacob's children, i.e., Leah, Bilha, and Zilpa] convened and said: We have

---

76. Since the number of sons that would be born to Jacob was predetermined, for Rachel's prayer for another son to be realized, Dina was transformed into a female in her mother's womb.

enough males, let Rachel be remembered by God and conceive another child.

(*Bereshit Rabba* [Theodor-Albeck] 72)

The Theft of the Teraphim

When Jacob and his family departed from Haran, Rachel stole teraphim (objects of idol worship) from her father, Laban. The Sages address Rachel's motive for this.

"Rachel stole the teraphim" (Genesis 31:19). Her intent was entirely for the sake of Heaven. She said: We are departing from Haran; will we leave the old man in his state of sin?

(*Bereshit Rabba* [Theodor-Albeck] 74)

Further reading: For more about the power of prayer, see p. 457; *A Concise Guide to Mahshava*, p. 304.

Vayishlah

At the center of this Torah portion is the story of the return of Jacob and his family to the land of Canaan. It recounts Jacob's preparations for his encounter with his brother, Esau; Jacob's struggle with the angel; the encounter between Jacob and Esau after many years of estrangement; Jacob's settlement in the land; the rape of his daughter Dina and its repercussions; Benjamin's birth and Rachel's death; and finally, an account of the lineage of Esau's family and of the kings of the land of Edom.

The chapter that follows presents a selection of the statements of the Sages concerning Jacob's encounter with Esau, Jacob's struggle with the angel, the purchase of the field in Shekhem, and the burial of Rachel.

Jacob's Forces

The Torah relates that when Jacob was on his way to meet Esau, he encountered angels of God. The Sages explain that these angels assisted Jacob – who feared the vengeance of his brother – and intimidated Esau's camp.

"Jacob said when he saw them:[77] This is the camp of God" (Genesis 32:2). How many were in a camp of God? Twenty million ministering angels.... "He called the name of that place Mahanayim" (32:2) – two camps.[78] Why? The verse teaches that Jacob was provided with forty million ministering angels, who appeared like a king's soldiers. Among them were wearers of armor, among them cavalry, and among them charioteers. Esau encountered the wearers of armor; he said to them: Whose are you? They said to him: We are Jacob's. Esau encountered the cavalry; he said to them: Whose are you? They said to him: We are Jacob's. Esau encountered the charioteers; he said to them: Whose are you? They said to him: We are Jacob's. As it is stated [that Esau said to Jacob when they met]: "He said: For whom do you intend this entire camp that I met?" (33:8).

Jacob would also mention the name of the Holy One, blessed be He, to Esau, to intimidate him and to cause him to panic, as it is stated: "For therefore, I have seen your face, as the sight of the face of God" (33:10). To what can this matter be compared? It can be compared to one who invited another to a meal, and the guest recognized that the host was seeking to

---

77. When Jacob saw the angels of God whom he encountered after he took his leave of Laban.
78. *Mahanayim* is the plural form of the word for camp.

kill him. The guest said: The taste of this cooked dish is like the taste of that cooked dish that I ate in the king's palace. The host said to himself: My guest knows the king. The host was afraid and did not kill his guest. Likewise, once Jacob said to Esau: "For therefore, I have seen your face, as the sight of the face of God," Esau the wicked said: The Holy One, blessed be He, accorded him that honor [i.e., that he saw the face of God]; I can no longer prevail over him.

(Bereshit Rabba 75)

Jacob's Concern

As Esau approached, Jacob was dismayed. The Sages explain the precise nature of Jacob's dismay.

"Jacob was very frightened and distressed" (Genesis 32:8). Rabbi Yehuda son of Rabbi Ilai said: Isn't fright the same as distress? Why the two terms? "He was frightened," lest he kill; "he was distressed," lest he be killed. Jacob said: If Esau overcomes me, he will kill me, and if I overcome him, I will kill him. That is the meaning of: "He was frightened"; he was frightened lest he kill, and "he was distressed" lest he be killed.

(Bereshit Rabba 76)

Jacob's Opponent

The Torah describes the episode of a "man" who wrestled with Jacob until dawn and even injured the joint of his thigh. Ultimately, Jacob overcame him, and in exchange for the latter's release, he was forced to bless Jacob. The Sages explain that this man was in fact an angel of God, and describe what transpired during the struggle.

"A man wrestled with him" (Genesis 32:25). Some say he was the angel Mikhael. Mikhael said to Jacob: If you defeated me, one of the primary officials of God, why do you fear Esau? Rabbi Tarfon said: Mikhael did not have permission to move from his place until Jacob gave him permission, as it is stated that he requested of Jacob: "Release me, for dawn has broken" (32:27). Jacob said to him: Are you a thief or a gambler in debt to others that you fear dawn? Several groups of ministering angels came, who said to Mikhael: Mikhael, ascend to heaven, because the time has arrived to recite the song of praise to God. If you do not initiate the song, the song will be canceled. Mikhael began pleading with Jacob. He said to him: I beg of you,

release me, so that the ministering angels in the *Aravot*[79] will not burn me due to the delay of the song. Jacob said to him: "I will not release you unless you bless me" (32:27). Mikhael said to him: Which is more precious, the attendant or the child? I am the attendant of God and you are the child, and you require my blessing? Jacob said to him: Nevertheless, I desire that you bless me. Immediately Mikhael said to him: "No more shall Jacob be said to be your name; rather, Israel" (32:29). Mikhael said to him: Blessed are you, one born of a woman, as you entered the palace on High and were rescued.

(*Yalkut Shimoni, Vayishlah* 1:132)

Esau's Kiss

When Jacob and Esau finally met, Esau kissed Jacob. The Sages ascribe different motives to Esau.

"Esau ran to meet him and he kissed him" (Genesis 33:4). Rabbi Shimon ben Elazar said…this teaches that Esau's pity was aroused at that moment and he kissed Jacob sincerely. Rabbi Yannai said to Rabbi Shimon ben Elazar: If so, why is the term "and he kissed him" written in the Torah scroll with dots above it?[80] This teaches that Esau did not plan to kiss Jacob, but to bite him, but the neck of Jacob our patriarch turned to marble, and the teeth of that wicked one, Esau, were damaged. Why does the verse state: "And they wept" (33:4)? This one, Jacob, wept because of his neck, and that one, Esau, wept because of his teeth.

(*Bereshit Rabba* 78)

This World and the World to Come

The Sages relate that while Esau and Jacob were still in their mother's womb, they made an agreement: Esau would receive this world and Jacob would receive Esau's portion in the World to Come, as well as his own. Ultimately, Esau recognized his error.

The Sages said: When Jacob and Esau were in their mother's womb, Jacob said to Esau: Esau my brother, we are two sons to our father, and there are two worlds before us – this world and the World to Come. This world has eating and drinking, commerce, marriage, and fathering children. But the

---

79. One of the levels in the heavens.

80. When words are written with dots in the Torah scroll, they are to be explained not in accordance with their straightforward understanding.

World to Come does not have any of these elements. Do you want to take this world and I will take the World to Come? Immediately, Esau repudiated the concept of the revival of the dead, saying: People who have spirits and souls die. How do you know that those who died will once again live? At that moment, Esau took this world as his portion and Jacob took the World to Come as his portion. When Jacob returned from Laban's house and Esau saw that Jacob had children, slaves, and maidservants, Esau said to Jacob: My brother, didn't you say that you would take the World to Come? From where do you have all this? You benefit from this world like I do. Jacob said to him: It is the property that the Holy One, blessed be He, gave me for my use in this world,[81] as it is stated [that Jacob responded to Esau: These are] "the children with whom God has graced your servant" (Genesis 33:5). At that moment, Esau reckoned, saying: In this world, which is not Jacob's portion, the Holy One, blessed be He, gave him his reward thus. In the World to Come, which is his portion – all the more so that he will receive great reward.

(*Eliyahu Zuta* [Ish Shalom] 19)

Places of Irrefutable Ownership

The Torah portion relates that Jacob purchased a tract of the field adjacent to the city of Shekhem from its residents, where he had pitched his tent when he arrived at the place. Years later, his son Joseph was buried there. This tract of land, as well as two other places in the Land of Israel, are described by the Sages as places whose ownership is irrefutable.

"He purchased a tract of the field [that is in Shekhem]" (Genesis 33:19). This is one of three sites concerning which the nations of the world are unable to defraud the Jewish people and say to them: You stole them. These are: The Cave of Makhpela, Joseph's Tomb, and the Holy Temple. The Cave of Makhpela: The verse relates that "Abraham weighed for Efron the silver… four hundred silver shekels" (23:16). The Holy Temple: The verse relates that "David gave to Ornan for the place six hundred gold shekels by weight" (I Chronicles 21:25). Joseph's Tomb: The verse relates that "he purchased a tract of the field… for one hundred *kesita*" (Genesis 33:19).

(*Yalkut Shimoni, Vayishlah* 1:133)

---

81. God, in His kindness, granted me all this.

Rachel Weeping for Her Children

In the Torah portion, there is an account of the death of Rachel and of Jacob burying her alongside the road. The Sages explain why he did this.

"Rachel died, and she was buried on the path to Efrat" (Genesis 35:19). What did our patriarch Jacob see that caused him to bury Rachel on the path to Efrat? Jacob our patriarch foresaw that the exiles were destined to pass there following the destruction of the Temple. Therefore, he buried her there, so that she would plead for mercy for them. That is what is written: "So said the Lord: A voice is heard in Rama, wailing, bitter weeping; Rachel weeping for her children" (Jeremiah 31:14).

(Bereshit Rabba 82)

📖 **Further reading:** For more about the graves of the righteous and the efficacy of prayer there, see *A Concise Guide to Mahshava*, p. 245.

Vayeshev

This Torah portion deals primarily with the lives of the sons of Jacob. Joseph, the most beloved son of his father, told his brothers of his dreams, which alluded to his superiority, and they hated him as a result. When he went to check upon them in the pasture, they cast him into a pit, and he was sold as a slave and brought to Egypt. Joseph was very successful in the house of Potiphar, his master, but after he refused the advances of Potiphar's wife, she had him incarcerated. Concurrently, the Torah tells of the incident of Judah and Tamar, where Judah's greatness is revealed.

The chapter that follows presents a selection of the statements of the Sages concerning the relationship between Jacob and Joseph, the relationship between Joseph and his brothers; Joseph's being cast into a pit and his being sold; Tamar's nobility, and the ultimate outcome of her encounter with Judah; and Joseph in his master's house – his success, his adherence to God, his conceit, and his righteousness.

Love and Jealousy

Jacob loved Joseph more than he did the rest of his sons, which aroused jealousy among Joseph's brothers. Therefore, Jacob was also subject to criticism by the Sages.

Who caused Joseph to become hated? It was the excessive love of his father, Jacob. "Israel loved Joseph more than all his sons, because he was a son of his old age [ben zekunim]" (Genesis 37:3). Rabbi Yehuda and Rabbi Nehemya explained this:[82] Rabbi Yehuda said that Jacob loved Joseph because Joseph's shining countenance[83] was similar to that of Jacob. Rabbi Nehemya said that Jacob loved Joseph because he transmitted to Joseph all the *halakhot* that Shem and Ever transmitted to him.[84]

"He made him a fine tunic" (Genesis 37:3). One must not favor one child over the rest, as because of the fine tunic that our patriarch Jacob made for Joseph, the verse relates: "And they hated him…" (37:4).

(*Tanḥuma* [Buber], *Vayeshev*; *Bereshit Rabba* 84)

---

82. Both Sages are providing interpretations for the phrase "*ben zekunim,*" literally, "son of [his] old age." This phrase is difficult to understand, as Benjamin was born several years after Joseph.
83. "*Ziv ikanon,*" which looks and sounds similar to "*ben zekunim.*"
84. This interpretation understands "*zekunim*" to connote wisdom.

The Pit

The Sages describe the pit into which the brothers cast Joseph, and their severe spiritual lapse.

"They took him and cast him into the pit; and the pit was empty, there was no water in it" (Genesis 37:24). [Since if the pit were entirely empty, there would be no need to state that it did not contain water, one can infer:] There was no water in it, but there were serpents and scorpions in it. What did Simeon do? Once the brothers placed Joseph in the pit, Simeon commanded his brothers, and they cast large stones upon him in order to kill him. But when Simeon ultimately fell into Joseph's custody in Egypt, Joseph did not exact revenge. Rather, he cast fattened birds upon him [i.e., fed him delicacies].

Rabbi Aha said: "And the pit was empty." Jacob's pit [i.e., his children] was emptied [i.e., they were devoid of wisdom]. The phrase "there was no water in it" teaches that there were no matters of Torah, likened to water, among the brothers. It is written: "If a man is found abducting any of his brethren of the children of Israel, and he enslaved him and sold him, that thief shall die" (Deuteronomy 24:7) – and you are selling your brother?

(*Tanḥuma* [Buber], *Vayeshev*; *Bereshit Rabba* [Theodor-Albeck] 84)

The Brothers' Oath

The brothers did not reveal the truth about Joseph to Jacob. According to the Sages, they forbade anyone, with a severe oath, to reveal it to him; therefore, even God did not reveal the sale of Joseph to Jacob.

The brothers said: Let us impose a decree of excommunication upon ourselves ensuring that none of us will tell this matter to Jacob. Judah said to them: Reuben is not here – excommunication cannot be enacted with only nine people present. What did they do? They included the Omnipresent with them and they enacted the excommunication. They told Reuben that they enacted the excommunication, and he heard the excommunication and was silent, and the Holy One, blessed be He, too was included.... The verse states concerning God: "He tells His matters to Jacob" (Psalms 147:19), but He did not tell Jacob of this matter due to the decree of excommunication.

(*Yalkut Shimoni, Vayeshev* 1:142)

The Light of the Messiah

The Torah interrupts the telling of the tragic episode of the sale of Joseph in order to relate the episode involving Judah and Tamar. The Sages emphasize that the flourishing of the messiah's glory began from this incident, as King David, progenitor of the messiah, was a descendant of Peretz, son of Judah and Tamar.

The tribes were involved in the sale of Joseph; Joseph was involved in his sackcloth and in his fasting over his sorrow at having been sold, Reuben was involved in his sackcloth and in his fasting to repent for his sin (see Genesis 35:22), Jacob was engaged in his sackcloth and in his fasting in mourning over the loss of Joseph, Judah was involved in taking a wife for himself, and the Holy One, blessed be He, was involved in creating the light of the Messianic king descended from Judah and Tamar.... This tells us that before the first enslaver was born,[85] the progenitor of the ultimate redeemer was born.

(*Bereshit Rabba* 85)

Shaming Another Person

Even when Tamar faced execution because she was suspected of harlotry, she did not announce in public who the father of her child was; rather, she merely alluded to his identity, leaving him the choice to identify himself or not. The Sages derive from this the severity of shaming another.

The verse relates concerning Tamar: "She was taken out,[86] and she sent to her father-in-law, saying: By the man whose these are I am with child" (Genesis 38:25). But let her tell Judah that he was the father...Evidently, it is preferable for a person to hurl himself into a fiery furnace than to shame another in public. From where is this derived? From the actions of Tamar, [who preferred to die rather than shame Judah in public].

(*Sota* 10b)

Joseph's Success

Joseph was very successful serving in the house of his new master, Potiphar, and the Torah relates that "the Lord was with him." The Sages tell of Joseph's adherence to God and his success, but also that he acted haughtily and forgot Jacob's home.

You find that once he was in the house of his master, "The Lord was with Joseph, and he was a successful man; and he was in the house of his master, the

---

85. Before the enslavement of the Jewish people in Egypt.
86. To be executed.

Egyptian. His master saw that the Lord was with him, and all that he did, the Lord made his undertaking successful" (Genesis 39:2–3). Did the wicked Potiphar see that the Holy One, blessed be He, was with him?[87] What is the meaning of the phrase "that the Lord was with him"? It means that the name of the Holy One, blessed be He, would not depart from Joseph's mouth. Joseph would enter to serve Potiphar and he would whisper: Master of the Universe, You are my security, You are my patron; grant me grace, kindness, and compassion in Your eyes, in the eyes of all who see me, and in the eyes of Potiphar my master. Potiphar would say to him: What are you whispering? Perhaps you are performing sorcery against me. Joseph answered him: No; I am praying that I will find favor in your eyes.

Once Joseph saw himself succeed as he did, he began eating and drinking, curling his hair, and saying: Blessed is the Omnipresent, who caused me to forget [the sorrow of being banished from] my father's house. The Holy One, blessed be He, said to him: Your father is mourning over you in sackcloth and ashes, and you are eating and drinking and curling your hair? The wife of your master will harass you and will distress you.

(*Tanḥuma, Vayeshev*)

Joseph and Potiphar's Wife

Potiphar's wife attempts to seduce Joseph, who resists her and flees. The Sages describe the circumstances that led to her attempt and how Joseph overcame the temptation.

His master's wife was with him in the house and was verbally enticing him each and every day. She would change her clothing three times each and every day. She would not wear at midday the garments that she wore in the morning, and she would not wear in the afternoon the garments that she wore at midday. Why did she labor over her appearance to that extent? So that Joseph would gaze at her and desire her. One time, the Egyptian women came together to see Joseph's beauty. What did Potiphar's wife do? She took citrons and gave one to each of them, gave a knife to each of them, and called Joseph to come. She stood Joseph before them. When they looked at Joseph's beauty, they cut their hands with the knives due to their distraction at seeing Joseph. She said to them: If this is what happens to you in a brief moment of seeing him, I, who see him all the time, all the more so that I desire him.

---

87. Being that Potiphar was wicked, how did he discern this?

The verse relates: "It was on a certain day; he went into the house to perform his labor, and none of the people of the household were there in the house" (Genesis 39:11). Is it possible that there was no one in a house as large as the house of that wicked man, Potiphar? That day was the day of their festival, and they all went to their house of idolatry. Potiphar's wife told them that she was ill. She said to herself: There is no day available for me like this day that Joseph will consort with me [as the house is otherwise empty]. "She seized him by his garment, saying: Lie with me" (39:12). At that moment, the image of Joseph's father came and appeared to him in the window. Jacob said to him: Your brothers are destined to be written on the stones of the ephod,[88] with your name among them. Would you like your name to be erased from among them and to be called a companion of harlots? As it is written: "And a companion of harlots will lose a fortune" (Proverbs 29:3). Immediately: "His bow sat firm, and the arms of his hands were golden" (Genesis 49:24) [i.e., Joseph withstood the temptation].

(*Tanḥuma, Vayeshev; Sota* 36b)

The Imprisonment of the Butler and the Baker

After Joseph was thrown into prison in the wake of being accused by Potiphar's wife of attempting to rape her, God arranged matters and incited a new scandal in Egyptian high society, so that people would no longer speak of the episode involving Joseph.

"She called to the people of her household, and spoke to them, saying: See, he brought to us a Hebrew man to ridicule us; he came to me to lie with me, and I cried with a loud voice" (Genesis 39:14). She introduced talk of Joseph into everyone's mouth. The Holy One, blessed be He, said: It is preferable that they turn against each other, and not turn to slander this righteous man. That is what is written: "It was after these matters; the butler of the king of Egypt and the baker sinned [against their master]" (40:2) [providing the Egyptians with a new scandal to discuss]. What was the crime of the butler? A fly was found in Pharaoh's drink.[89] What was the crime of the baker? A fly was found in Pharaoh's pastry. That is what is written: "The butler of the king of Egypt and the baker sinned against their master." Their crimes occurred during their service of their master.

(*Yalkut Shimoni, Vayeshev* 1:146)

---

88. The two onyx stones that were on the ephod (one of the vestments worn by the High Priest), on which the names of the twelve tribes were engraved.
89. The drink he would imbibe after bathing.

Miketz

The focus of the Torah portion of *Miketz* is on Joseph in Egypt. It begins with his release from prison in order to interpret Pharaoh's dream, and his appointment as viceroy and finance minister in charge of the entire Egyptian economy. Thereafter, it relates the elaborate narrative of the arrival of Joseph's brothers in Egypt. They came to purchase food, but Joseph manipulates them into ultimately bringing Benjamin with them from the land of Canaan. The Torah portion concludes with the placing of Joseph's goblet into Benjamin's bag. Once it is found there, Joseph demands that Benjamin remain with him in Egypt as his slave.

The chapter that follows presents a selection of the statements of the Sages concerning Joseph as the interpreter of dreams, Joseph's regal comportment, the Egyptian women's admiration of Joseph, and Joseph's encounter with his brothers: both the harsh manner in which he addresses them and his emotional meeting with Benjamin.

The Interpretation of Pharaoh's Dreams

Pharaoh dreams two troubling dreams, one about seven gaunt cows that swallow seven fat cows, and one about seven thin and blighted stalks of grain that swallow seven plump ones. Joseph is summoned to interpret the dreams only after Pharaoh's wise men unsuccessfully attempt to interpret the dreams, and Pharaoh's mood has turned dark. Joseph's interpretation is accepted.

"He sent and called for all the magicians of Egypt, and all its wise men; Pharaoh related his dream to them, but no one could interpret them for Pharaoh" (Genesis 41:8). The wise men would suggest interpretations, but he would not listen to what they said.[90] They suggested: The seven good cows indicate that you will beget seven daughters, and the seven unsightly cows indicate that you will bury seven daughters. Likewise they said: The seven good stalks indicate that you will conquer seven kingdoms, and the seven blighted stalks indicate that seven principalities will rebel against you.... And why did they give Pharaoh so many incorrect interpretations? So that Joseph would ultimately come and acquire greatness. The Holy One, blessed be He, said: Were Joseph to come first and interpret the dream, that would not lead to his being praised. The astronomers could come and say

---

90. Pharaoh thought their interpretations were incorrect.

to Pharaoh: Had you asked us, we would already have interpreted it for you. Rather, God waited for them until they exhausted and depressed Pharaoh's spirit; thereafter Joseph came and restored it.

(Bereshit Rabba 89)

📖 **Further reading:** For more about dreams and their meaning, see p. 415.

Seventy Languages

Joseph becomes the ruler over all of Egypt. The Sages relate that it was necessary for Joseph to receive heavenly assistance to teach him regal comportment – which served to his benefit in the future.

At the moment that Pharaoh said to Joseph: "And without you no man shall lift his hand or his foot in the entire land of Egypt" (Genesis 41:44), Pharaoh's astrologers said: Would you appoint a slave, whose master purchased him for twenty silver shekels, as ruler over us? Pharaoh said to them: I see regal comportment in him. They said to Pharaoh: If so, he should know seventy languages, as kings do. Gavriel came and taught Joseph seventy languages. The next day, no matter what language Pharaoh spoke with Joseph, Joseph responded to him. Joseph spoke in the sacred tongue, Hebrew, and Pharaoh did not know what he said. Pharaoh said to him: Teach me. Joseph taught him but he did not learn. Pharaoh said to him: Take an oath promising me that you will not reveal that you know a language I do not know. Joseph took an oath promising him.

When Joseph later said to Pharaoh, after Jacob's death: "My father administered an oath to me, saying: Behold, I am dying; in my grave that I dug for myself in the land of Canaan,[91] bury me there. I will go up now and bury my father, and I will return" (50:5), Pharaoh said to him: Go and request dissolution of your oath so that you can remain in Egypt. Joseph said to him: I will request dissolution for the oath I made to you as well. Even though Pharaoh was not amenable to Joseph's going to bury Jacob, he said: "Go up and bury your father, in accordance with the oath he administered to you" (50:6).

(Sota 36b)

---

91. In the Cave of Makhpela.

Joseph and the Women of Egypt

Joseph was handsome, and when he was appointed viceroy, the noble young women of Egypt sought to attract his attention, but he did not give it to them. Joseph, who exhibited restraint, was richly rewarded.

Jacob said of Joseph: "Joseph is a fruitful tree…girls stride on the wall" (Genesis 49:22). When Joseph went out to rule over Egypt, the princesses would peek at him through the windows, and they would throw bracelets, and necklaces, and rings toward him so that he would raise his eyes and look at them. Nevertheless, he would not look at them. The Holy One, blessed be He, said to Joseph: You did not raise your eyes and look at them; I take an oath by your life that you will give your daughters a portion in the Torah.[92]

(*Bereshit Rabba* 89)

The Brothers Come before Joseph

When Joseph's brothers descended to Egypt to purchase food, Joseph treated them harshly. The Sages describe the background to these events.

"Joseph's brothers went down" (Genesis 42:3). The verse should have said: The sons of Israel, or: The sons of Jacob. Initially they did not treat Joseph like a brother, and sold him, and ultimately, they regretted it and said: When will we have the opportunity to descend to Egypt and bring our brother back to our father? When their father told them to descend to Egypt to purchase food, they all agreed to bring him back.

Rabbi Yehuda bar Shimon said: Joseph also knew that his brothers would be descending to Egypt to purchase food. What did he do? He positioned sentries at all the entrances to Egypt and told them: See everyone who enters to purchase food, write his name and the name of his father, and bring me the lists. They did so. Once the sons of Jacob arrived, they each entered a different gate and the sentries wrote their names. In the evening, they brought Joseph the lists. This one read: Reuben son of Jacob, and one read: Simeon son of Jacob, and one: Levi, and likewise all the gatekeepers, each wrote his note with a name of one of the sons of Jacob. Immediately, Joseph told them: Seal the storehouses and leave open one storehouse so that they will be forced to go there. Joseph gave the names of his brothers

---

92. This is a reference to the section in the Torah discussing the laws of inheritance, given in response to a matter raised by the daughters of Tzelofhad, from the tribe of Manasseh son of Joseph (see Numbers 27).

to the owner of the storehouse, and told him: When these people approach you, seize them and send them to me.

Immediately when the brothers appeared before Joseph, "he acted as a stranger to them and spoke harshly to them" (42:7). The verse teaches that he acted like a stranger to them. Joseph took his goblet and knocked on it as if to perform divination. He said to them: I see in the goblet that you are spies, which is why you entered through different gates. They said to him: "We are sincere" (42:11), but so our father commanded us: Do not enter in one gate.[93] Joseph released them.

Three days passed, and the brothers did not come back to purchase food. Immediately, Joseph took seventy warriors from the king's palace, and he sent the warriors to seek the brothers in the marketplace. The warriors went and found them in the marketplace of the harlots. What were they doing in the marketplace of harlots? They said: Our brother Joseph is fine of form and fine of appearance; perhaps he is in a brothel. The warriors seized the brothers and brought them before Joseph. Joseph said to them: What were you doing all together in a marketplace of harlots? Aren't you fearful of the evil eye? Isn't that your father's command?

The brothers told him: We lost an item and we were looking for it there. Joseph said to them: What lost item? I see in the goblet that two of you, Simeon and Levi, destroyed the large city of Shekhem, and thereafter you all sold your brother to the Arabs. The brothers were shocked that he knew this information, and said to him: "We, your servants, are twelve brothers, sons of our father" (42:13). Joseph said to them: Where are the missing two brothers? They said to him: "One is gone," i.e., dead; "and the youngest is with our father today" (42:13).[94] Joseph said to them: Bring your youngest brother to me. Joseph took Simeon and incarcerated him in their presence, because Simeon had pushed him into the pit, and he separated Simeon from Levi, so they would not plot against him.

(Bereshit Rabba 91)

📖 **Further reading:** Jacob too, before his death, was concerned about the bond between Simeon and Levi. See *A Concise Guide to the Torah*, p. 126.

---

93. So as not to arouse jealousy among the Egyptians at the sight of such an impressive family, which could arouse the evil eye.
94. This refers to Benjamin, who remained in Canaan with Jacob.

Joseph's Compassion

When Joseph first saw Benjamin when he arrived in Egypt, he felt intense feelings of compassion and longing, and accorded him special honor.

At that moment when the brothers entered with Benjamin, Joseph invited them to a feast. He wanted to seat Benjamin at his side, but he did not know how to do it in a manner that would not arouse the suspicion of the brothers. He took the goblet and knocked on it, and said to them: I thought that Judah was the firstborn because he speaks first. I now see that Reuben is the firstborn and Judah is a spokesman. Reuben sat at the head of those seated.

He again took the goblet and knocked on it. He said: Simeon, come up and sit at his side, as you are second to him; and he said likewise to Levi to sit next to Simeon; and likewise to Judah; and likewise all of the sons of Leah in the order of their birth. Joseph again took the goblet and knocked on it. He said to them: I see in the goblet that all of you are sons of one father, but your father had many wives. He began calling Dan and Naphtali, the sons of Bilha, and he said to them: Come up and sit, until all of them were seated in their order, the order of their birth. Benjamin remained. Joseph said: I see that this one had a brother who was separated from him and that he has no mother. I too had a brother who was separated from me and I have no mother. Let him come and sit by my side. Benjamin sat by his side. That is what is written: "They sat before him, the firstborn according to his seniority and the younger according to his youth" (Genesis 43:33).

Joseph brought portions for the feast. He gave each of them his own portion. He gave Benjamin his own portion; then Joseph took his own portion and gave it to Benjamin. Asenat, Joseph's wife, took her portion and gave it to Benjamin. Joseph's sons Ephraim and Manasseh took their portions and gave them to Benjamin. There were five portions in Benjamin's possession; therefore, it is written: "Benjamin's gift was five times greater than the gifts of all of them" (43:33).

(*Tanḥuma, Vayigash*)

Vayigash

The Torah portion of *Vayigash* begins precisely at the point that the previous Torah portion concluded – at the height of the tension, with Joseph's demanding that Benjamin become his slave and the brothers return to Jacob in Canaan. Judah delivers an impassioned speech, at the conclusion of which Joseph reveals his identity to his brothers. Later, the Torah portion tells of Jacob, who receives the tidings about his living son; about the descent of Jacob and his family to Egypt; and of Jacob's reunion with Joseph. It concludes with the details of how Joseph managed the Egyptian economy and implemented revolutionary reforms in the economic order of the kingdom.

The chapter that follows presents a selection of the statements of the Sages concerning the exchange between Judah and Joseph, Joseph's revealing of his identity to his brothers, the descent of Jacob to Egypt, the Torah study of Jacob and the members of his household, and the presentation of Joseph's brothers before Pharaoh.

Judah and Joseph

After Joseph demands to keep Benjamin with him as punishment for taking the goblet, Judah delivers an impassioned speech in an attempt to prevent the harsh decree. The Sages describe Judah's profound commitment to rescue Benjamin, as well as the willingness of Judah and his brothers to wage an actual battle with Joseph, which ultimately convinces Joseph to reveal his identity.

At the moment that Joseph detained Benjamin and said to his brothers: "The man in whose hand the goblet was found, he shall be my slave, and you, go up in peace to your father" (Genesis 44:17), Judah said to him: If you detain Benjamin, how will there be peace in our father's house?

Immediately, Judah became angry and roared in a great voice. His voice traveled four hundred parasangs,[95] until Hushim son of Dan heard. Hushim hurried from the land of Canaan and came to Judah. Both of them roared, and the land of Egypt was on the verge of being destroyed. Rabbi Yehoshua ben Levi said: Once his brothers saw that Judah became angry, they too were filled with wrath, and they kicked at the ground, rendering it full of ditches. At that moment, Judah was filled with wrath against Joseph. When

---

95. A parasang is approximately 4 km.

Joseph detected the signs of anger in Judah, he was at once alarmed and frightened. Joseph said: Woe is me, lest he kill me. What were the signs of anger that were in Judah? The Sages of the house of Shilo said: His two eyes were dripping blood. And some say: Judah was wearing a type of armor of the mighty, and five garments. There was a hair on his chest; once he became angry, it pierced the armor and the garments.

What did Joseph do at that moment? He kicked the stone pillar upon which he was sitting and rendered it a heap of pebbles. Immediately, Judah was astounded and said: This one is stronger than I am. At that moment, Judah grasped his sword to draw it from its scabbard, but it would not be drawn for him. Judah said: Joseph must be a God-fearing man. Judah said to him: Initially, you came against us with a false accusation. How many countries descended to Egypt to purchase food and you did not ask any of them about their families? Did we come to take your daughter, or are you thinking of marrying our sister that you questioned us about our families? Nevertheless, we did not conceal any information from you.

Joseph said to him: I see that you are a spokesman; there is among your brothers a spokesman like you.[96] Judah said to him: Despite all that you see, that Benjamin is the one in danger, I served as a guarantor to bring him back to our father in Canaan. Joseph said: Why didn't you do so with your brother [i.e., guarantee his well-being] when you sold him to the Ishmaelites for twenty silver shekels, and you tormented your elderly father, and told him: "Joseph was mauled" (37:33)? Once Judah heard this, he shouted and cried in a loud voice. He said: "As how shall I go up to my father?" (44:34).

Judah said to Naphtali, who was especially quick: Go and see how many marketplaces there are in Egypt. He hurried and returned. Naphtali said to him: There are twelve. Judah said to his brothers: I will destroy three of them and each of you take one; and we will not leave even one man alive. His brothers said to him: Egypt is not Shekhem. If you destroy Egypt, you will destroy the entire world. At that moment: "Joseph could not restrain himself" (45:1). Once Joseph saw that they had arrived at a consensus to destroy Egypt, Joseph said in his heart: It is preferable that I reveal my identity to them and not let them destroy Egypt.

(*Bereshit Rabba* 93)

---

96. Why are you speaking in place of Benjamin, who is the one who should be speaking in his own defense?

Torah – Genesis > Vayigash

📖 **Further reading:** For more about Judah's involvement in the sale of Joseph, see *A Concise Guide to the Torah*, p. 93.

Joseph's Revelation

When Joseph revealed his identity to his brothers, he removed all his servants and guards from the room. The Sages disagree whether he acted wisely, and also describe how he convinced his brothers of his true identity.

"And he called: Remove every man from before me" (Genesis 45:1). Rabbi Hama bar Hanina said: Joseph did not act appropriately in removing all of the Egyptians from the room, as had one of the brothers attacked him he would have died. Rabbi Shimon bar Nahman said: He acted properly and appropriately, as he did not shame his brothers before the Egyptians. Joseph knew of his brothers' righteousness. He said to himself: Heaven forfend, my brothers are not suspected of bloodshed. Joseph strengthened himself and sat before them. He said to them: That brother that you say is dead, are you sure that he is dead? They said to him: Yes. Joseph responded: But why are you lying? Didn't you sell him? I will summon him and he will answer me. Joseph was calling him: Joseph son of Jacob. The brothers were looking all over the room for him. Joseph said to them: "I am Joseph your brother" (45:4). They did not believe him until he uncovered himself and showed them his circumcision.

(*Yalkut Shimoni, Vayigash* 1:151)

Jacob Comes to Egypt

When Jacob learned that Joseph is the ruler over Egypt, he accepted Joseph's offer and moved with his entire family to reside there. So began the Egyptian exile, which God had decreed many years earlier. The arrival of Jacob's family in Egypt was inevitable in any case, but God eased the manner in which it transpired.

This can be compared to a cow that people were pulling to the slaughter-house, but it would not allow itself to be pulled. What did they do to it? They pulled its offspring in front of it, and the mother cow followed after it against its will, involuntarily. So too, it would have been fitting for Jacob our patriarch to descend to Egypt even in body chains and in neck chains [i.e., by force]. The Holy One, blessed be He, said: Will I take my firstborn son Jacob down in shame? And if I place the idea to bring Jacob to Egypt in Pharaoh's heart, [that may be carried out in a way that is distasteful to Jacob]. I

will not take him down publicly. Rather, I will draw his son before him, and Jacob will descend after him against his will, involuntarily.

(Bereshit Rabba 86)

📖 Further reading: For the decree concerning the Egyptian exile in the Covenant between the Parts, see *A Concise Guide to the Torah*, p. 31.

Jacob's Family Studies Torah

Jacob regularly studied Torah with his sons. Judah was sent, even before Jacob's descent to Egypt, to establish a study hall. The sign that Joseph sent to Jacob, so that his father would know that it was really he who sent the message that he was still alive, was based on their joint study.

"He sent Judah before him" (Genesis 46:28). The purpose of Jacob's sending Judah was for Judah to prepare a study hall for him, so that he could issue rulings there and so that he could teach the tribes.

Know that it is so that Jacob studied Torah with his children, as when Joseph went from him, Joseph knew which chapter Jacob was teaching him when he left him. When Joseph's brothers came and said to Jacob: Joseph still lives, Jacob's heart was faint because he did not believe them (see 45:26). Jacob said in his heart: I know that Joseph left me when we were studying the chapter of the calf [*egla*] whose neck is broken (see Deuteronomy 21:1–9). Jacob said to them: Let Joseph give you a sign in the study of which chapter he left me and I will believe you. Joseph, too, remembered in which chapter he left his father. What did Joseph do? He gave them wagons [*agalot*].[97] Once Jacob saw the wagons – "The spirit of Jacob their father was revived" (Genesis 45:27).

(Tanḥuma, Vayigash)

From among His Brothers

Joseph presented his brothers to Pharaoh, who asked them about their occupations and habits. Joseph did not choose the strongest among them, so that Pharaoh would not want to recruit them into his army.

"And from among [literally, the edge of] his brothers he took five men, and he presented them before Pharaoh" (Genesis 45:27). Why does the verse say: "From the edge of his brothers"? The verse comes to teach you that the brothers Joseph took to Pharaoh were not the mightiest among the tribes.

---

97. The word for wagons, *agalot*, includes the same Hebrew letters as *egla*, calf.

And who were the five men he took? Reuben, Simeon, Levi, Benjamin, and Issachar.

Why did Joseph the righteous take these five from among his brothers? Because he knew the strength of each one of his brothers, and he spoke wisely, and said: If I present the mighty among them to Pharaoh, he will see them and make them his soldiers. Therefore, Joseph presented these five men, who were not [as] mighty.

(*Bereshit Rabba* [Theodor-Albeck] 95)

📖 **Further reading:** For the portion of the calf whose neck is broken, see *A Concise Guide to the Torah*, p. 480.

Vayhi

In the Torah portion of *Vayhi*, we read of Jacob's final days. It begins with Jacob's blessing of Ephraim and Manasseh, Joseph's sons; Jacob's blessings of each of his sons; and ultimately Jacob's passing, and the eulogy and funeral procession his family performed for him, taking his body from Egypt to the Cave of Makhpela in the land of Canaan. The Torah portion – and with it, the entire book of Genesis – concludes with the passing of Joseph.

The chapter that follows presents a selection of the statements of the Sages concerning Jacob's final instructions to his sons, his desire to be buried specifically in the Land of Israel, the funeral procession, Esau's demand to receive Jacob's burial plot, and the concern of Joseph's brothers after Jacob's death.

Burial in the Land of Israel

Jacob administered an oath to his sons that they take his body up to the Land of Israel and bury him there, and Joseph commanded the same before his death. The Sages explain the significance of burial in the Land of Israel.

Why did the patriarchs desire burial in the Land of Israel? It is because the dead of the Land of Israel come to life first, before those buried elsewhere, in the days of the messiah, and they will enjoy all the years of the messiah. Rabbi Hananya said: One who dies outside the Land of Israel and is buried there undergoes two deaths[98]...therefore, Jacob said: "Please do not bury me in Egypt" (Genesis 47:29).

Rabbi Shimon said to him: If so, the righteous buried outside the Land of Israel suffer, as they will not be resurrected. What does the Holy One, blessed be He, do? He burrows tunnels in the ground for the righteous buried outside the Land of Israel, and renders them like these burial caves, through which they roll until they reach the Land of Israel. Once they reach the Land of Israel, the Holy One, blessed be He, implants a spirit of life in them and they rise, as it is stated: "I will take you up from your graves, My people, and I will bring you to the soil of Israel" (Ezekiel 37:12). And there-

---

98. One when he dies, and the other more of a spiritual death, when those buried in the Land of Israel come to life before he does.

after the verse states: "I will put My spirit into you and you will live" (Ezekiel 37:14).

There was an incident involving Rabbi Yehuda HaNasi and Rabbi Elazar, who were walking near the city gate outside of Tiberias. They saw the coffin of a deceased person from outside the Land of Israel that was brought to be buried in the Land of Israel. Rabbi Yehuda HaNasi said to Rabbi Elazar: What has this person accomplished, whose soul departed outside the Land of Israel, and he comes to be buried in the Land of Israel? I read concerning him the verse: "You rendered My inheritance an abomination" (Jeremiah 2:7). During your lifetime you did not ascend to the Land of Israel, and you came and defiled the land upon your death? Rabbi Elazar said to him: Once he is buried in the Land of Israel, the Holy One, blessed be He, grants him atonement for having resided outside of the Land of Israel during his lifetime, as it is stated: "And His land will atone for His people" (Deuteronomy 32:43).

(Tanḥuma, Vayhi)

📖 **Further reading:** For more about the revival of the dead, see *A Concise Guide to Mahshava*, p. 295.

Hear, Israel: The Lord Is Our God, the Lord Is One

Before his death, Jacob gathered his sons in order to take his leave from them and to convey his final words to each of them. The Sages add that on that occasion, Jacob also sought to assess his sons' faith, and he was overjoyed when he saw they were all steadfast in their faith.

From here,[99] Israel [i.e., the Jewish people] received the recitation of *Shema*. When Jacob our patriarch was passing from the world, he summoned his twelve sons. He said to them: Is the God of Israel in the heavens your Father? Do you believe that the Holy One, blessed be He, is divided, that there is more than one god? The sons said to him: Hear us, Israel [i.e., Jacob] our father: Just as you believe there is no division within the Holy One, blessed be He, so too we believe there is no division. Rather: The Lord is our God, the Lord is one. Jacob then pronounced: Blessed be the name of His glorious kingdom forever and ever. Rabbi Berekhya and Rabbi Helbo said in the name of Rabbi Shmuel: This explains why the Jewish people come early every morning and late every evening, every day, and recite: Hear Israel, our

---

99. From the account of Jacob's parting from his sons before his death.

father from the Cave of Makhpela: The same matter that you commanded us is still practiced among us: The Lord is our God, the Lord is one.

(Bereshit Rabba [Theodor-Albeck] 98)

The Blessings of Each of Jacob's Sons Are Included in the Others

Jacob blessed each son with an individual blessing particularly appropriate for that son. The Sages add that nevertheless, each of the tribes was blessed with the blessings of the others as well.

"All these are the tribes of Israel, twelve, and this is that which their father spoke to them, and he blessed them; each man in accordance with his blessing he blessed them" (Genesis 49:28). The verse does not write: Blessed him, in the singular, rather, it writes: "Blessed them." Why? Because Jacob granted to Judah the strength of a lion (see 49:6), to Joseph the strength of a bull (see 49:22), to Naphtali the fleetness of a deer (see 49:21), and to Dan the bite of a serpent (see 49:17). Would you say that one is greater than the other in these facets? Ultimately, Jacob included them all – "each man in accordance with his blessing he blessed them."[100]

(Tanḥuma, Vayhi)

Jacob's Funeral Procession

The Torah describes the dignified funeral procession that Joseph and his brothers conducted for Jacob. The Sages describe the mourning and the eulogy, and tell of Esau's demand to be buried in the burial plot designated for Jacob.

"They came to the threshing floor of Atad" (Genesis 50:10) – is there a threshing floor for the thorn bush [*atad*], which does not produce anything edible? The verse teaches that those who participated in the procession ultimately surrounded Jacob's coffin with crowns, like a threshing floor that is surrounded by thorn bushes. This happened because the children of Esau, the children of Ishmael, and the children of Ketura, Abraham's wife (see 25:1)…all of them came to wage war against Jacob's family. Once they saw Joseph's crown suspended from Jacob's coffin, each of them took his crown and suspended it from Jacob's coffin. The Sages taught: Thirty-six crowns were suspended from Jacob's coffin.

Once they reached the Cave of Makhpela, Esau came and delayed them from burying Jacob. He said to them: This place is described as "Mamre,

_____
100. The plural term "them" indicates that Jacob included all of them in each blessing.

Kiryat Ha'arba, which is Hebron" (35:27). There were four [*arba*] couples: Adam and Eve, Abraham and Sarah, Isaac and Rebecca, Jacob and Leah. Jacob buried Leah in his plot in the cave, and the one that remains is mine. Jacob's family said to him: You sold your birthright to Jacob (see 25:33). Esau said to them: Although I sold the additional portion of the birthright as a firstborn, did I sell my basic portion? Jacob's family said to him: Yes.... Esau said: Show me the document of sale. Jacob's family said to him: The document is in Egypt. Who will go? Naphtali will go, as he is fleet as a doe, as it is written: "Naphtali is a doe let loose, who provides pleasant sayings" (35:27). Do not read: Pleasant [*shefer*] sayings; rather read: Sayings of a document [*sefer*].

Hushim son of Dan was there, and he was hard of hearing. He said to them: What is this? They said to him: This one, Esau, is delaying Jacob's burial until Naphtali returns from the land of Egypt. Hushim said to them: Will my grandfather be left lying in disgrace until Naphtali comes from the land of Egypt? He took a club and struck Esau on his head. Esau's eyes were detached and they fell on Jacob's legs. Jacob opened his eyes and smiled. At that moment, Rebecca's prophecy was fulfilled, as it is written: "Why should I be bereaved of both of you on one day?" (27:45). Even though their deaths were not on one day, in any case, their burial was on one day.

Had Joseph not tended to Jacob's burial, wouldn't his brothers have tended to it?[101] As it is written: "His sons conveyed him to the land of Canaan" (50:13) [indicating that the brothers were capable of conducting Jacob's burial on their own]. The brothers said: Let Joseph take the initiative; Jacob's honor is with kings such as Joseph more than with commoners.

(*Sota* 13b)

📖 **Further reading:** For more about the laws of the funeral ceremony, see *A Concise Guide to Halakha*, p. 85.

Joseph Returns to the Pit

After Jacob's death, Joseph's brothers were concerned that Joseph would now want to harm them. One event in particular aroused their concern – Joseph's visit to the pit into which they cast him.

"Joseph's brothers saw that their father had died, and they said: Perhaps Joseph will hate us and will repay us for all the evil that we did to him" (Genesis

---

101. Why did Joseph insist to Pharaoh that he must bring Jacob's body to the Land of Israel?

50:15). What did the brothers see then that caused them to become afraid? When they returned from the burial of their father, they saw that Joseph went to recite a blessing at the same pit into which his brothers cast him. He recited a blessing there in accordance with the blessing that one is required to recite at the place where a miracle was performed for him: Blessed is the Omnipresent, who performed a miracle for me at this place. Once they saw that their casting Joseph into the pit was still on his mind, they said: Now that our father died: "Perhaps Joseph will hate us and will repay us for all the evil that we did to him."

(Tanḥuma, Vayhi)

The Importance of Peace

In order to prevent acrimony and rancor, the brothers misrepresented the truth and told Joseph that their father requested that he forgive them. The Sages learn from this episode the importance of peace.

Great is peace, as even Joseph's brothers spoke false matters in order to establish peace between Joseph and the tribes. That is what is written: "They instructed to tell Joseph, saying: Your father instructed before his death, saying: So say to Joseph: Please, forgive the transgression of your brothers and their sin, as they did evil to you" (Genesis 50:16–17). Where did Jacob command them to convey this message to Joseph? We do not find that he issued such a command.[102] The verse then states: "Joseph wept as they spoke to him" (50:17). He said: Do my brothers suspect me of taking revenge?

"He comforted them and spoke to their heart" (50:21). The verse teaches that Joseph spoke to them persuasively. He told them: If ten lights [i.e., the ten of you] were unable to extinguish one light [i.e., me], how can one light extinguish ten lights?

(Tanḥuma, Vayhi)

📖 Further reading: For more about the virtue of peace, see p. 374.

---

102. Evidently, the importance of maintaining peace justified their falsehood.

Torah – Exodus

Shemot

The Torah portion begins by relating how the Egyptians subjugated the children of Israel with oppressive labor. Into this reality Moses is born. He is raised in Pharaoh's palace, and once he matures he emerges from the palace to see the suffering of his people. After he kills an Egyptian taskmaster, he flees to Midyan and marries Tzipora, daughter of Yitro. While in the wilderness, he experiences a divine revelation at the burning bush, and God tasks him with the mission to return to Egypt and lead the Israelites out of there. Later, there is a description of the miracles performed by Moses and Aaron in the presence of the Israelites and in the presence of Pharaoh, to whom they come with a request that he free the Israelites. The Torah portion concludes with a temporary setback: Pharaoh does not grant Moses and Aaron's request to liberate the Israelites; rather, he intensifies the yoke of enslavement upon them.

The chapter that follows presents statements of the Sages concerning Pharaoh's edicts; the resourcefulness of Miriam, Moses' sister; Moses' leadership and sensitivity; the character of Yitro, priest of Midyan; the wondrous revelation at the bush; Moses' staff and the signs that were performed with it; and the elders and the foremen of the children of Israel who endangered themselves to defend the people.

With a Gentle Mouth

The Egyptians subjugated the Israelites with oppressive labor [*befarekh*]. The Sages interpret the term *befarekh* as a contraction of the words *befeh rakh*, with a gentle mouth. Initially, the Egyptians persuaded the Israelites to work by means of positive speech, which then transformed into violent coercion.

This is to teach you that when Pharaoh said to his advisors about the Israelites: "Let us be cunning concerning them" (Exodus 1:10), Pharaoh then assembled all of the Israelites. He said to them: Please, do me a favor today and perform labor. That is what is written: "The Egyptians coerced the children of Israel to work *befarekh*" (1:13), initially *befeh rakh*, with a gentle mouth. Pharaoh took a basket and a rake to gather stalks and straw to make bricks, and anyone who saw Pharaoh taking a basket and a rake and making bricks would do so. The Israelites went with alacrity, and they worked with him all day to the best of their abilities. They produced many bricks because they were powerful and strong. Once it grew dark, Pharaoh appointed taskmasters [who had authority even to strike the Israelites] over them. He said to the taskmasters: Count the bricks the Israelites produced. Immediately,

they stood and tallied them. Pharaoh said to the taskmasters: You will supply me with this amount of bricks every day.

(*Tanḥuma, Behaalotekha*)

📖 **Further reading:** The enslavement in Egypt was decreed on the children of Israel many years before their arrival in Egypt. See *A Concise Guide to the Torah*, p. 31.

Israel Kept Their Faith

The children of Israel kept the faith of their ancestors even when adherence to that faith resulted in onerous enslavement. Even when Pharaoh decreed that every son born to the Israelites would be cast into the Nile, they continued to circumcise their sons.

When the Israelites were in Egypt, they were upstanding…they gathered and sat as one group. They entered a covenant that they would perform acts of kindness with each other; that they would observe in their hearts the covenant God entered with Abraham, Isaac, and Jacob; and that they would not forsake the language of Jacob's house and learn the Egyptian language, due to avoiding the ways of idol worship.

The Egyptians would say to them: Why do you worship your God? If you worship the gods of Egypt, Pharaoh will release you from labor. The Israelites responded and said to them: Did Abraham, Isaac, and Jacob forsake our God who is in heaven, such that it would also be justified for their descendants to forsake Him after them? The Egyptians said to them: No. The Israelites said to them: Just as they did not forsake Him, so we will not forsake Him.

The Israelites would circumcise their sons in Egypt. The Egyptians said to them: What, will that cause Pharaoh to ease the hard labor of enslavement from you? The Israelites responded and said to them: Did Abraham, Isaac, and Jacob forget the covenant of our God who is in heaven, such that it would also be justified for their descendants to forget the covenant after them? The Egyptians said to them: No. The Israelites said to them: Just as they did not forget the covenant of our God who is in heaven, so their descendants after them will not forget.

(*Eliyahu Rabba* [Ish Shalom] 21)

The Egyptians Embittered the Israelites' Lives

The Egyptians embittered the lives of the Israelites with what the verse describes as
"oppressive labor." The Sages explain that the difficulty referenced pertained to the
unstructured timing of the labor, and by forcing people to engage in labor that did
not fit their skills.

In Egypt there were immigrants of seventy languages, but the Egyptians enslaved only the Israelites, as it is stated: "They embittered their lives with
oppressive labor, with mortar and with bricks and with all work in the field"
(Exodus 1:14). What is the meaning of: "And with all work in the field"?
After an Israelite would perform labor with mortar and bricks and would
come to rest in the evening in his home, an Egyptian would come and say
to him: Go out and gather vegetables for me from the garden; or: Chop this
wood for me; or: Fill this barrel with water for me. That is the meaning of:
"And with all work in the field." What is the meaning of: "With all their work
with which they worked for them with travail" (1:14)? It is that they would
give a man's work to a woman and a woman's work to a man. They would say
to the man: Arise! Knead and bake! They would say to the woman: Fill this
barrel! Chop this wood! Go to the garden, bring vegetables!

(*Tanḥuma, Vayetze*)

Miriam's Prophecy and Advice

The Torah mentions Amram, grandson of Levi, who marries Yokheved. Together they
have a son, Moses. The Sages relate that in fact this was their second time married to
each other, as Amram divorced Yokheved due to the Egyptian decree mandating that
all the Israelites' male newborns be thrown into the Nile. They remarried at the advice
of their daughter, Miriam.

[The verse states with regard to Amram:] "A man from the house of Levi
went and he took a daughter of Levi" (Exodus 2:1). Where did he go? Rav
Yehuda bar Zevina said: He followed the advice of his daughter. The Sages
taught: Amram was the spiritual leader of his generation. When Pharaoh
decreed: "Every son who is born, into the Nile you shall cast him" (1:22),
Amram said: We are toiling in raising children for naught. He arose and divorced his wife. All the Israelites arose and divorced their wives.

His daughter Miriam said to him: Father, your decree is more extreme
than Pharaoh's. Pharaoh decreed death only on the males, but you decreed
death on the males and on the females by encouraging the Israelites to stop
procreating. Pharaoh decreed death only in this world [as even if the sons
are killed they will enter the World to Come], and you decreed death in this

world and in the World to Come. Concerning Pharaoh the wicked, there is uncertainty whether his decree will be fulfilled or not [as some sons might survive]; but you are righteous – certainly your decree will be fulfilled... Therefore, Amram arose and remarried his wife; likewise, all the Israelites arose and remarried their wives.

Miriam was prophesying when she was only Aaron's sister, before Moses was born, saying: My mother is destined to bear a child who will redeem Israel. Once Moses was born, the entire house was filled with light. His father Amram stood and kissed Miriam on her head. He said: My daughter, your prophecy has been fulfilled. When they cast Moses into the Nile so that he would not be discovered by the Egyptians, her father stood and tapped her on her head. He said to her: My daughter, where is your prophecy? And that is the meaning of what is written: "His sister stationed herself at a distance, to know what would be done to him" (2:4). Miriam stood there to know what would be at the culmination of her prophecy.

(*Sota* 13a)

Moses in Pharaoh's Palace

Pharaoh's daughter drew Moses from the water and raised him in her father's palace. The Sages describe Moses' charm and relate that his actions as a toddler were a portent of what he was destined to do to Pharaoh.

[The verse teaches concerning the maidservant of Pharaoh's daughter:] "She brought him to Pharaoh's daughter and he was a son to her" (Exodus 2:10). Pharaoh's daughter would kiss, embrace, and treat Moses fondly as though he were her son, and she would not take him out of the king's palace. Because he was beautiful, everyone desired to see him. Anyone who would see him would not be able to look away from him. Pharaoh would kiss him and hug him. He would take Pharaoh's crown and place it on his own head, just as he was destined to do to him when he grew up, [as Moses would cause Pharaoh to lose his kingship].... Thus Pharaoh's daughter raised one who was destined to take vengeance against her father.

The magicians of Egypt were sitting there, and they said: We are afraid of this one, who is taking your crown and placing it on his head, lest he be the one we are saying is destined to wrest your kingdom from you [as they had previously experienced such a vision]. Some of them said to behead Moses; some of them said to burn him. Yitro[1] was sitting among them and

_____
1. One of Pharaoh's advisors, who ultimately fled from Egypt and later became Moses' father-in-law.

said to them: This is just a lad, who may lack intelligence. Test him by bringing before him gold and a coal in a bowl. If he extends his hand to the gold, he has intelligence, and kill him; if he extends his hand to the coal, he lacks intelligence, and he needs no death sentence. Immediately, they brought a bowl before him, and he extended his hand to take the gold. The angel Gavriel came and pushed his hand. He grabbed the coal and placed his hand with the coal into his mouth. From that coal he became cumbrous of speech and cumbrous of tongue.

(*Shemot Rabba* 1)

The Devoted Shepherd

Moses, who was raised as a prince, went out to see his Hebrew brethren and was exposed to their distress. The Sages describe how he aided them by both empathizing with their distress and physically assisting them. Moses' sensitivity to the suffering of others was the reason for God's selecting him as leader.

"Moses grew and he went out to his brethren and he saw their burdens" (Exodus 2:11). What is the meaning of: "And he saw"? It is teaching that he saw their burdens, and would cry and say: I am so sorry for you, if only I could die in your place; as there is no labor more arduous than labor with mortar. Moses would lend a hand and aid each and every one of them.

Rabbi Elazar son of Rabbi Yosei HaGelili says: Moses saw a great burden on a child and a small burden on an adult, and the burden of a man on a woman and the burden of a woman on a man, and the burden of an old man on a young man and the burden of a young man on an old man. He would leave his entourage and go and redistribute their burdens on the pretense that he was aiding Pharaoh. The Holy One, blessed be He, said: You set aside your affairs, went to see the suffering of Israel, and acted with them in a brotherly manner. I will set aside My involvement in the heavenly and the earthly matters and I will speak to you.

Our Sages said: When Moses our teacher, of blessed memory, was herding Yitro's flock in the wilderness, a goat fled from him, and he pursued it until it reached a sheltered area. Once the goat reached the sheltered area, it happened upon a pool of water and began to drink. When Moses reached it, he said: I didn't realize that you were running because you were thirsty; now I see you are thirsty. He carried it on his shoulders and walked with it back to the flock. The Holy One, blessed be He, said: You have the compassion to lead the flock belonging to flesh and blood in this manner. I take an oath by your life that you will shepherd My flock, Israel.

(*Shemot Rabba* 1–2)

📖 **Further reading:** For more about caution regarding vigilance in preventing the suffering of animals, see p. 435; *A Concise Guide to Halakha*, p. 613.

The Bush Was Not Consumed

God revealed Himself to Moses from the midst of a small thorn bush, which burned with fire but was not consumed. The Sages explain the significance of the revelation's coming specifically from the midst of thorns.

Just as with regard to twins, if one's head aches the other feels it, so too, the Holy One, blessed be He, said, as it were: "I am with [the children of Israel] in [their] distress" (Psalms 91:15)[2].... The Holy One, blessed be He, said to Moses: Don't you feel that I am in distress just as Israel is in distress? Know it from the place that I am speaking to you, from the thorns. As it were, I share their distress.

(*Shemot Rabba* 2)

Moses' Staff

God commanded Moses to take to Egypt "this staff…with which you will perform the signs." According to the Sages, this staff was created during twilight on the sixth day of Creation, and was passed on as a legacy from generation to generation, until it reached Yitro.

The staff that was created during twilight of the sixth day of Creation was given to Adam the first man in the Garden of Eden. Adam gave it to Hanokh, Hanokh gave it to Noah, Noah gave it to Shem, Shem gave it to Abraham, Abraham gave it to Isaac, Isaac gave it to Jacob, and Jacob took it down to Egypt and gave it to Joseph his son. When Joseph died, all his property was taken and placed in Pharaoh's palace. Yitro was one of Pharaoh's magicians, and he saw the staff and the markings that were on it indicating its power, and he coveted it. He took it, brought it to Midyan, and embedded it in the garden of his house…no man could approach it any longer [i.e., no one could remove it from the ground]. When Moses arrived at Yitro's house, he entered the garden…. He saw the staff and read the markings that were on it, and he extended his hand and took it. Yitro saw Moses and said: This one is destined to redeem Israel from Egypt. Therefore, Yitro gave Moses his daughter Tzipora as a wife.

(*Pirkei deRabbi Eliezer* 40)

---

2. Just as twins are connected as one, so are God and the children of Israel.

The Israelite Foremen

After Moses requested from Pharaoh to release the Israelites, Pharaoh increased the slaves' workload. The Israelite foremen, who were tasked with ensuring that the slaves met the daily quota, suffered from the Egyptians' beatings. According to the Sages, the sacrifice and devotion of these foremen served them well, as they were later rewarded with honor and prominence.

Pharaoh appointed Egyptian taskmasters over the Israelite foremen, and the foremen were appointed over the rest of the enslaved people. When Pharaoh said to them: "You shall not continue to give straw to the people" (Exodus 5:7), yet the daily quota of bricks remained the same, the taskmasters would come and count the bricks. If their number was found lacking, the taskmasters would strike the foremen, as it is stated: "The foremen of the children of Israel, whom Pharaoh's taskmasters appointed over them, were beaten, saying: Why did you not complete your quota to produce bricks as previously?" (5:14). The foremen were struck for the unmet quota of the rest of the people, but the foremen would not deliver the slaves into the hand of the taskmasters. They would say: It is preferable for us to be flogged, and let the rest of the people not suffer.

Therefore, when the Holy One, blessed be He, said to Moses: "Gather to Me seventy men of the elders of Israel" (Numbers 11:16) to assist you in judging the people, Moses said: I do not know who is worthy and who is unworthy. God said to him: "Whom you know to be the elders of the people, and its foremen" (Numbers 11:16). The same foremen who sacrificed themselves to be flogged on the Israelites' behalf in Egypt concerning the preparation of the bricks will come and take this greatness…. From here you learn that anyone who sacrifices himself on behalf of Israel is rewarded with honor and prominence.

(*Tanḥuma* [Buber], *Behaalotekha*)

📖 Further reading: For more about the appointment of elders, see p. 183.

Va'era

The Torah portion addresses Moses' repeated demand to liberate the children of Israel and Pharaoh's resolute refusal. In response, Egypt suffers harsh plagues. In this portion, the first seven plagues are described: blood, frogs, lice, swarm, pestilence, rash, and hail. The chapter that follows presents statements of the Sages concerning Moses' grievance in light of the increased hardship of the enslavement, the preponderance of sorcery in Egypt, Aaron's staff that was transformed into a serpent, and the plagues afflicting Egypt.

The Faith of the Patriarchs

At the conclusion of the previous Torah portion, Moses laments to God about his initial approach to Pharaoh being counterproductive, causing a deterioration in the working conditions of the Israelite slaves. God responds by contrasting the method of His revelation to the patriarchs with the method of His revelation to Moses. According to the Sages, God sought thereby to make Moses conscious of the fact that the patriarchs did not question His ways, while Moses expressed skepticism.

For this matter [Moses' complaint concerning the suffering of the Israelites], Moses our teacher was punished, as it is stated that Moses complained to God: "And since I came to Pharaoh to speak in Your name, he has harmed this people,[3] and You did not save Your people." (Exodus 5:23). The Holy One, blessed be He, said to him: Woe for those who are gone and can no longer be found. I appeared to Abraham, Isaac, and Jacob several times with the name of God Almighty[4] and they did not question My attributes, and they did not say to Me: What is your name?

I said to Abraham: "Arise, walk in the land to its length and to its breadth, as to you I will give it" (Genesis 13:17). He sought a place to bury Sarah, but he did not find one until he purchased the Cave of Makhpela for four hundred silver shekels [seemingly contradicting the promise that the land would be his], yet Abraham did not question My attributes. I said to Isaac: "Reside in this land, and I will be with you and I will bless you" (Genesis 26:3). His servants sought water to drink and they did not find it [seemingly contradicting the promise that he would be blessed], to the degree that

---

3. By increasing their burden.
4. Not with the Tetragrammaton, and nevertheless, they never wondered what was My name, and they didn't question My ways, as you did.

the people of Gerar started a quarrel with them for digging wells, as it is stated: "And the herdsmen of Gerar quarreled with Isaac's herdsmen saying: The water is ours" (Genesis 26:20), yet Isaac did not question My attributes. I said to Jacob: "The land upon which you lie, to you I will give it" (Genesis 28:13). He sought a place to pitch his tent and he did not find one until he purchased it for one hundred *kesita*[5] [seemingly contradicting the promise that he will receive the land], yet Jacob did not question My attributes. They did not say to Me: What is Your name?

And you, Moses, initially said to Me: What is Your name, and now you say to Me: "And You did not save Your people" (Exodus 5:23). The verse then states: "Now you will see what I will do to Pharaoh" (6:1). You will see the war with Pharaoh, but you will not live to see the war with the thirty-one kings of Canaan, when the Israelites conquer the Land of Israel.

(*Sanhedrin* 111a)

Signs and Wonders in the Land of Egypt

When Moses and Aaron presented before Pharaoh the first sign of God's might, transforming Aaron's staff into a serpent, the Torah relates that Pharaoh called his magicians and wise men, who did precisely the same. The Sages describe how Pharaoh mocked Moses and Aaron, and discuss the greatness of the miracle Aaron performed in the presence of Pharaoh and his servants.

"Pharaoh also summoned the wise men and the sorcerers, and they, the magicians of Egypt, also did so with their artifices" (Exodus 7:11). At that moment, Pharaoh began mocking Moses and Aaron and cackling like a chicken. Pharaoh said to them: Are these the signs of your God? It is the way of the world that people take merchandise to a place where people need it. Does one bring fish brine to Aspamya? Fish to Akko? Don't you know that all sorcery is in my domain? Sorcery is common here. Immediately, Pharaoh sent messengers and brought children from their schools, and they too performed this sorcery. Moreover, he called his wife and she did so.... He called even the four- and five-year-old children and they did so....

At that moment, the Holy One, blessed be He, said: If a serpent would swallow the Egyptian's serpents, that would be the way of the world, as a snake swallows a snake. Rather, the staff will return to its original state and swallow their serpents..."and Aaron's staff swallowed their staffs" (7:12).... It was a miracle within a miracle. The verse teaches that the staff returned to

---

5.   A type of coin.

its original state as a staff and swallowed the staffs in the form of serpents. When Pharaoh saw this, he wondered and said: What would happen if Aaron would say to the staff: Swallow Pharaoh and his throne? Now it would swallow him.... A great miracle was performed with the staff, as even though it swallowed all the staffs that the Egyptians had cast down, numerous enough to make from them ten large piles, it did not become thicker.

(*Shemot Rabba* 9)

📖 **Further reading:** For more about miracles and their significance, see *A Concise Guide to Mahshava*, p. 213.

Tactics of War

The order of the plagues was not random; rather, it was calculated based on shrewd military tactics. There was also an element of punishment administered measure for measure to Egypt.

Our Sages, of blessed memory, said: The Holy One, blessed be He, brought the plagues upon the Egyptians in accordance with the tactics of kings.

In the case of a human king, when one of the states under his rule rebels against him, he sends legions against it and surrounds it. First he dams their aqueduct. If they relent, fine; if not, he brings producers of loud noise to harass them. If they relent, fine; if not, he shoots arrows at them. If they relent, fine; if not, he brings barbarians to attack them. If they relent, fine; if not, he brings chaos upon them. If they relent, fine; if not, he throws naphtha, a flammable fuel, upon them. If they relent, fine; if not, he casts catapult stones upon them. If they relent, fine; if not, he sets masses of soldiers against them. If they relent, fine; if not, he incarcerates them in prison. If they relent, fine; if not, he kills the greatest among them.

So too, the Holy One, blessed be He, came against Egypt with the tactics of kings. First He dammed their aqueduct by turning their water into blood...The Egyptians did not relent. He brought producers of loud noise against them – these are the frogs. Rabbi Yosei bar Hanina said: The frogs' croaking was more difficult for the Egyptians than the damage they caused. The Egyptians did not relent. He shot arrows at them – these are the lice, which would penetrate the bodies of the Egyptians like arrows. The Egyptians did not relent. He brought barbarians against them – this is the swarm. The Egyptians did not relent. He brought chaos upon them – this is the pestilence, which killed their livestock. The Egyptians did not relent. He threw naphtha upon them – this is the rash. The Egyptians did not relent. He cast

catapult stones upon them – this is the hail. The Egyptians did not relent. He set the masses against them – this is the locusts. The Egyptians did not relent. He incarcerated them in prison – this is darkness. The Egyptians did not relent. He killed the greatest among them.

Everything that the Egyptians planned for the Israelites, the Holy One, blessed be He, brought upon the Egyptians themselves. The Egyptians thought the Israelites would be their water drawers. Therefore: "He turned their rivers into blood" (Psalms 78:44). The Egyptians thought the Israelites would carry their merchandise. Therefore, God brought frogs upon them, which would destroy the merchandise. The Egyptians thought the Israelites would till the land for them. Therefore, God filled the land with crawling lice. The Egyptians thought the Israelites would carry them like a caregiver. Therefore, God sent among them the swarm: lions, wolves, tigers, bears, and vultures. If the Egyptian had five children and gave them to the Israelite to take out to the street, a lion would come and take one, a wolf would take one, a bear would take one, a leopard would take one, and a vulture would take one. The Egyptians thought the Israelites would herd their livestock. Therefore, God sent pestilence among them…. The Egyptians thought the Israelites would boil water for them. Therefore, God sent a rash among them. The Egyptians thought to stone the Israelites with stones. Therefore, God brought hail upon them. The Egyptians thought the Israelites would care for their vineyards. Therefore, God brought upon them locusts that consumed their trees: "They consumed all the vegetation of the land and all the fruit of the trees" (Exodus 10:15). The Egyptians thought to incarcerate the Israelites in prison. Therefore, God brought darkness upon them. The Egyptians thought to kill the Israelites. Therefore: "The Lord smote every firstborn" (12:29). The Egyptians thought to drown the Israelites in water. Therefore: "He hurled Pharaoh and his army into the Red Sea" (Psalms 136:15).

(Tanḥuma, Bo)

The Plague of Blood

The first plague was blood. The Sages explain why God began specifically with this plague, and describe how conspicuous the difference was between the Egyptian and Israelite camps while the plague ran its course.

Why were the Egyptians afflicted with the plague of blood first? It is because Pharaoh and the Egyptians worshipped the Nile as a god. The Holy One, blessed be He, said: I will smite their god first, and the people thereafter.

The Israelites became wealthy from the plague of blood. An Egyptian and an Israelite would be in one house with a vat filled with water. The Egyptian would go to fill a jug from the vat. He would remove the jug filled with blood. The Israelite would drink water from the vat. The Egyptian would say to him: Give me a little water with your hand. The Israelite would give it to him, and it would become blood. The Egyptian would say to him: Let you and I drink from the same bowl. The Israelite would drink water and the Egyptian, blood. When the Egyptian would purchase it from the Israelite with money, he would drink water; the Israelites became wealthy from selling water to the Egyptians.

(*Shemot Rabba* 9)

The Plague of Frogs

The Torah refers to the frogs in the singular. The Sages disagree with regard to the reason the Torah uses the singular form of the word. They also speak in praise of the frogs, which endangered their lives to punish the Egyptians.

"The frogs [*hatzefarde'a*, in the singular] arose and covered the land of Egypt" (Exodus 8:2). Rabbi Akiva says: It was one enormous frog that filled the entire land of Egypt. Rabbi Elazar ben Azarya said to him: Akiva, what are you doing involving yourself with *Aggada*?[6] Cease making statements in these matters and go to study *Nega'im* and *Oholot* [complex tractates that discuss *halakhot* of ritual impurity]. It was one frog that whistled for others, and they came.

The verse relates that "the Nile will swarm with frogs, and they will arise and come into your house ... and into your ovens and into your kneading bowls" (7:28). When the Egyptian woman would knead the dough and ignite the oven, the frogs would enter the dough and eat the dough, and enter the oven and cool it, and would stick to the bread.... Hananya, Mishael, and Azarya drew an *a fortiori* inference from the behavior of the frogs for themselves,[7] and they descended into the fiery furnace rather than worship idols (see Daniel 3).

(*Sanhedrin* 67b; *Shemot Rabba* 10)

📖 Further reading: For more about self-sacrifice, see *A Concise Guide to Mahshava*, p. 198.

---

6. Your aggadic explanations are incorrect.
7. The inference was: If the frogs, which were not commanded to sanctify God's name, entered the furnaces, certainly we, who are so commanded, should enter the fiery furnace.

Appreciating the Good

In order for the first three plagues to commence, it was necessary to use a staff to strike Egypt's water and its dust. The Sages relate that because the water and dust of Egypt provided benefit to Moses in the past, it was not he who generated these plagues but rather his brother, Aaron.

Why was the water not struck by Moses to generate the plagues of blood and frogs? The Holy One, blessed be He, said to Moses: Concerning the water that protected you when you were cast into the Nile, it is inappropriate for it to be hit by you. I take an oath by your life that it will be hit only by Aaron.

"The Lord said to Moses: Say to Aaron: Extend your staff and strike the dust of the earth and it will become lice" (Exodus 8:12). Rabbi Tanhum said: The Holy One, blessed be He, said to Moses: Concerning the soil that defended you when you killed the Egyptian and buried him in the sand, it is inappropriate for it to be hit by you. Therefore, these three plagues of blood, frogs, and lice were effected by Aaron.

(Shemot Rabba 10)

The Finger of God

In contrast to the previous plagues, Pharaoh's magicians were unable to replicate the plague of lice. The Sages disagree concerning the reason for this.

"The magicians did so with their artifices to draw out the lice, but they could not" (Exodus 8:14). Rabbi Elazar said: From here one can derive that a demon [through whose power the Egyptians' magic worked] is unable to create an item less than the bulk of a barley kernel. The Rabbis say: It cannot create any item, even one the size of a camel; rather, the magicians can gather together these larger items with their magic but they cannot gather together these smaller items. "The magicians said to Pharaoh: It is the finger of God" (8:15). Once the magicians saw they were unable to generate the lice, they immediately acknowledged that these creatures were the creation of God and not the creation of demons, and they would no longer attempt to liken themselves to Moses and continue replicating the plagues.

(Shemot Rabba [Shinan] 10)

Swarm

The Sages disagree concerning which creatures were involved in the plague of the swarm: birds, animals, or a combination of the two.

From where did the swarm come upon the Egyptians? Some say it came from above in the form of birds, and some say it came from below in the form of land animals. Rabbi Hoshaya says it came from above and from below.

(*Shemot Rabba* [Shinan] 11)

Rash

In order to generate the plague of the rash, Moses threw ashes from a furnace heavenward. The ashes scattered throughout the land of Egypt and caused a rash on the Egyptians' skin. According to the Sages, in addition to the wonder of the rash itself, the throwing of the ashes and their dispersal were also miraculous.

Rabbi Yehoshua ben Levi said: A great miracle was performed in the plague of rash, as when a person shoots an arrow upward it does not fly even one hundred cubits,[8] while Moses threw two handfuls of the ashes of a furnace, an insubstantial substance, and Moses threw it heavenward until it flew so high that it reached the Throne of Glory. There was yet another miracle that was performed in the plague of rash: Moses' one hand held two handfuls of ashes.[9] There was yet another miracle that was performed in the plague of rash: When a person scatters a *kav*[10] of dust, it scatters only four cubits. Moses took two handfuls of ashes and he scattered the ashes over the entire land of Egypt, which was four hundred parasangs[11] by four hundred parasangs, as it is stated: "It will become dust over the entire land of Egypt" (Exodus 9:9).

(*Shemot Rabba* [Shinan] 11)

Hail

In the plague of hail, there was a melding of two contradictory forces, water and fire, in order to punish the Egyptians.

To what can the plague of hail be compared? It can be compared to two forceful legions that were waging war against each other. Eventually, the time for the king's war arrived [i.e., the king waged a war], and the king made peace between the two legions and they executed the king's mission together. So too, fire and hail are antagonistic to each other. Once the time for war

---

8. A cubit is approximately 50 cm.
9. As the verse states: "The Lord said to Moses and Aaron: Take for yourselves handfuls of soot of a furnace and Moses shall throw it heavenward" (Exodus 9:8).
10. A *kav* is approximately 2 L.
11. A parasang is approximately 4 km.

against Egypt arrived, the Holy One, blessed be He, made peace between fire and hail and they struck Egypt. This is the meaning of: "There was hail and fire igniting amid the hail" (Exodus 9:24). What is the meaning of the term "igniting"?... After an Egyptian was struck by the hail, the fire would burn him.

(*Shemot Rabba* 12)

Further reading: For more about miracles, see *A Concise Guide to Mahshava*, p. 213.

Bo

In this Torah portion, the pressure on Egypt reaches its peak. The three final plagues – locusts, darkness, and the death of the firstborn – cause a panic-stricken Egypt to expel the Israelites. Likewise, the first of God's commandments to the Israelites appear in this Torah portion, primary among them the procedure for preparation of the paschal offering and the commandment to mark the exodus throughout the generations. The chapter that follows presents statements of the Sages concerning the final plagues in Egypt; the abundant property with which the Israelites emerged from Egypt; the timing of the exodus from Egypt, in terms of both the time of day and the time of year; the actions of the Israelites while they were in Egypt and why they merited redemption; and the removal of Joseph's coffin from Egypt.

But All the Children of Israel Had Light

The ninth plague was the plague of darkness. The Sages relate that Israelites had light everywhere they went, even in the houses of the Egyptians. Therefore, they were able to locate items of value that they would later get from the Egyptians, and to gain their trust so the Egyptians would agree to give them those items (see below).

The darkness the Egyptians experienced was extremely intense. Our Sages say: There were seven days of darkness. How so? During the first three days, one who was sitting and sought to stand would be able to stand, and one who was standing who sought to sit would be able to sit. Concerning those days, it is stated: "There was pitch darkness in the entire land of Egypt for three days; they did not see one another" (Exodus 10:22–23). For the next three days, one who was sitting was unable to stand, and one who was standing was unable to sit, and one who was crouching was unable to stand upright. Concerning them, it is stated: "Nor did anyone rise from his place for three days" (10:23).

During the first three days of pitch darkness, the Holy One, blessed be He, enabled the Israelites to find favor in the eyes of the Egyptians, so that the Egyptians would later lend items to them. When the Israelites entered the Egyptians' houses during the days of pitch darkness, they saw silver and gold vessels and garments. If the Egyptians would later say to the Israelites, in response to their request for items: We have nothing to lend you, the Israelites would say to them: It is in such and such place. At that moment, the Egyptians would say: Had the Israelites sought to deceive us, they would

have taken the items when they discovered them during the days of darkness and we would have been unaware, as they saw them already. Since they did not touch them without our knowledge, likewise, they will not keep them.

The Egyptians lent the items to them in fulfillment of that which is stated concerning the Israelites, in God's covenant with Abraham: "And afterward they will emerge with great property" (Genesis 15:14). That is what is written: "But all the children of Israel had light in their dwellings" (Exodus 10:23). It is not stated that they had light in the land of Goshen, where they resided. Rather, it is stated "in their dwellings," teaching that anywhere an Israelite entered, light entered and illuminated for him what was in barrels, and in chests, and in closets.

(*Shemot Rabba* 14)

Further reading: Regarding the significance of the sequence of the plagues, see p. 86.

Requesting the Vessels

One of the instructions to the Israelites was to request vessels from the Egyptians prior to their departure from Egypt and to take the vessels with them. The Sages explain that God promised Abraham that after the exile, his descendants would emerge with great wealth, and He must keep His word.

"Speak now [*na*] in the ears of the people and they shall ask each man from his neighbor and each woman from her neighbor, silver vessels and gold vessels" (Exodus 11:2). The Sages said in the study hall of Rabbi Yannai: "*Na*" is an expression of nothing other than entreaty. The Holy One, blessed be He, said to Moses: I entreat you, go and say to the Israelites: I entreat you, request from the Egyptians silver vessels and gold vessels, so that righteous man, Abraham, will not say: You fulfilled concerning them that which You told me: "And they will be enslaved to them and they will oppress them" (Genesis 15:13), but You did not fulfill concerning them that which You told me: "And afterward they will emerge with great property" (Genesis 15:14).

The Israelites said to Moses: It would be enough if we ourselves depart Egypt, [even without wealth]. This can be compared to a man who was incarcerated in prison, and people would say to him: Tomorrow they are releasing you from prison and giving you much property. He says to them: I entreat you, release me today, and I request nothing.

(*Berakhot* 9a)

📖 **Further reading:** God told Abraham that his children would descend into exile and emerge from it with abundant property during the Covenant between the Parts; see *A Concise Guide to the Torah*, p. 31.

Withdraw Your Hands from Idol Worship

The Sages relate that when the Israelites were in Egypt they were completely steeped in idol worship, like their Egyptian neighbors. The first mitzva they were commanded was to take a lamb and slaughter it. This act was a clear departure from their path of idol worship, and is what enabled the redemption.

Likewise, you find concerning Israel that when they were in Egypt, they would worship idols and would not forsake them, as it is stated: "No man cast out the repugnancies of their eyes, and they did not forsake the idols of Egypt" (Ezekiel 20:8). The Holy One, blessed be He, said to Moses: As long as the Israelites worship the gods of Egypt, they will not be redeemed. Go and tell them that they should forsake their evil actions and repudiate idol worship. That is the meaning of what is written: "Select [*mishkhu*] and take for yourselves" (Exodus 12:21); in other words, withdraw [*mishkhu*] your hands from idol worship, and take sheep [which were considered sacred by the Egyptians] for yourselves, and slaughter the gods of Egypt, and perform the rite of the paschal offering [*pesah*]; as through this, the Holy One, blessed be He, will pass over [*pose'ah*] you during the plague of the firstborn.

(*Shemot Rabba* 16)

Male and Female Firstborn

What was the fate of Bitya the daughter of Pharaoh, Moses' savior, during the plague of the firstborn?

The firstborn females also died in the plague of the firstborn, with the exception of Bitya the daughter of Pharaoh, because a good advocate to plead on her behalf was found [i.e., she had performed a meritorious act that made her worthy of being saved]. This is Moses, as it is stated concerning what Moses' mother said upon his birth: "She saw him that he was good" (Exodus 2:2).

(*Shemot Rabba* 18)

📖 **Further reading:** For more about Bitya, Moses' savior, see p. 80; *A Concise Guide to the Torah*, p. 137.

Pharaoh's Haste

When the plague of the firstborn descended upon Egypt, Pharaoh hastened to search for Moses and Aaron in order to expel the Israelites. The Sages relate that he did not find them easily.

"He summoned Moses and Aaron" (Exodus 12:31). Pharaoh walked and called during the night in all the marketplaces, saying: Where is Moses? Where does he reside? The children of the Israelites mocked him and said to him: Pharaoh, where are you going? Pharaoh said to them: I am seeking Moses. They said to him: He resides here [giving an incorrect place of residence]. They mocked Pharaoh until he finally located Moses. Pharaoh said to Moses: "Rise and go out from among my people" (12:31). Moses said to him: Are we thieves, who seek to escape under the cover of darkness? The Holy One, blessed be He, said to us: "And no man shall emerge from the entrance of his house until morning" (12:22). Pharaoh said to him: I entreat you, rise and leave. Moses said to him: Why are you so adamant? Pharaoh said to him: I am a firstborn, and I fear that I will die. Moses said to him: Have no fear from that, you are destined for a much greater punishment than that.[12]

(*Tanḥuma* [Buber], Bo)

Perfect Timing

The exodus of the Israelites from Egypt occurred at a precise moment both in terms of the time of the year and in terms of the time of the day.

[A verse describing the exodus from Egypt states:] "He joyously [*bakosharot*] takes out prisoners" (Psalms 68:7). What is the meaning of *bakosharot*? ... Rabbi Akiva said: He liberated them only during a month fit [*kasher*] for departure: Not during Tammuz, due to the heat, and not during Tevet, due to the cold; rather, during Nisan, which is fit for setting out on a journey, as there is not severe heat nor severe cold.

The Holy One, blessed be He, said: If I take the Israelites out of Egypt at night, the Egyptians will say: Now He acted in the manner of thieves. Rather, I will take them out at midday, when the sun is most powerful, as it is stated: "It was in the midst of that very day, the Lord brought the children of Israel out of the land of Egypt, in their hosts" (Exodus 12:51).

(*Bemidbar Rabba* 3; *Pirkei deRabbi Eliezer* 48)

---

12. Your demise will be in a more glorious incident, at the splitting of the Red Sea.

Like a Lily among the Thorns

The Sages note the virtues of the Israelites for which they merited to be redeemed from Egypt.

Due to four matters the Israelites were redeemed from Egypt: they did not change their names, they did not change their language, they did not slander one another, and no one among them acted licentiously by engaging in forbidden sexual intercourse.

(*Vayikra Rabba* 32)

Joseph's Coffin

During the Exodus, Moses did not forget Joseph's request that his coffin be taken out of Egypt. The Sages describe the manner in which the coffin accompanied the people of Israel during their wanderings in the wilderness.

The Sages taught: Come and see how beloved mitzvot were to Moses our teacher. As while all the Jewish people were involved in taking the plunder from the Egyptians, he was involved in mitzvot by taking Joseph's coffin…. From where did Moses our teacher know where Joseph was buried? They said: Serah daughter of Asher remained alive from Joseph's generation. Moses went to her and said to her: Do you know anything about where Joseph is buried? She said to him: The Egyptians fashioned a metal casket for him and set it in the Nile River so that its water would be blessed.

And all those years that the Israelites were in the wilderness, there were these two chests – one containing the corpse of Joseph and one the Ark of the Divine Presence, traveling with each other. Passersby would say: What is the nature of these two chests? The Israelites would say: One is of a corpse and one is of the Divine Presence. They would ask: And is it the manner of a corpse to travel with the Divine Presence? The Israelites said: This person, Joseph, fulfilled everything that is written in the tablets in that ark.

(*Sota* 13a)

Beshalah

The beginning of this Torah portion tells of the beginning of the Israelites' journey in the wilderness. Pharaoh regretted having emancipated the Israelites from slavery and began to pursue them. When the Israelites reached the Red Sea, the sea split before them and they passed through it unharmed. Immediately afterward, when the Egyptians entered the seabed, the water drowned them. After the splitting of the Red Sea, the Israelites sang the Song at the Sea.

The continuation of the Torah portion tells of the manna – the food that fell from the heavens daily in the wilderness – and the Israelites' war against Amalek. The chapter that follows presents statements of the Sages concerning the Israelites standing at the sea; the splitting of the Red Sea; the taste of the manna, the Israelites' lack of gratitude, and Amalek's attack.

The Dove and the Hawk

When the Israelites stood at the seashore – with the sea before them and Pharaoh's army behind them – they had nowhere to go and no action to take, other than to vociferously cry out to God.

To what were the Israelites comparable when they emerged from Egypt? They were comparable to a dove that fled from a hawk and entered into the crevice of a rock and found a snake nesting there. The dove wanted to enter inside, but it could not enter because the snake was still nesting. It could not retreat, as the hawk was standing outside. What did the dove do? It began screaming and flapping its wings so that the owner of the birdhouse would hear it and come and rescue it.

The Israelites at the sea were similar to that: They were unable to descend into the sea, as the sea had not yet been split for them. They were unable to retreat, as Pharaoh was already approaching. What did they do? "They were very frightened; the children of Israel cried out to the Lord" (Exodus 14:10). Immediately – "The Lord saved Israel on that day from the hand of Egypt" (14:30).

(Shir HaShirim Rabba 2)

The Tribes at the Sea

Nahshon ben Aminadav was the first Israelite to leap into the Red Sea. His self-sacrifice effected the splitting of the sea, and he was rewarded by having King David as one of his descendants.

When the tribes stood at the sea, this one said: I will not descend first into the sea, and that one said: I will not descend first into the sea…. While they were standing and deliberating about what to do, Nahshon leapt and descended into the sea…. Immediately, the Omnipresent said to Moses: My beloved is drowning in the sea, the sea is blocked, and the enemy is in pursuit, and you are merely standing and persisting in prayer. Moses said before Him: Master of the Universe, what am I to do? God said to him: "And you, raise your staff and extend your hand over the sea and split it" (Exodus 14:16)…. The Omnipresent said: As a reward for Nahshon, who initially treated Me as a king by obeying My will at the sea, I will make his descendant, David, king over Israel.

(*Mekhilta deRabbi Yishmael, Beshalah, Mesekhta deVayhi* 5)

My Handiwork Is Drowning in the Sea

God prevented the angels from singing a song of praise when the Egyptians were drowning in the sea, as they, too, are His handiwork.

And Rabbi Yohanan said: What is the meaning of that which is written: "And the one came not near the other all the night" (Exodus 14:20)? The ministering angels wanted to sing their daily song of praise, but the Holy One, blessed be He, said: My handiwork is drowning at sea, and you are singing songs?

(*Megilla* 10b)

The Song of the Children and the Fetuses

The revelation of the Divine Presence at the sea was clear and palpable, to the extent that babies also joined in the song that the Israelites sang at the sea, and some interpret that even fetuses in the womb did so.

When our ancestors were at the sea, the child was lying on his mother's lap and the baby was nursing at his mother's breast. Once they saw the Divine Presence, the child lifted his head from his mother's lap and the baby removed his mouth from his mother's breast. They, too, opened their mouths in song and praise, and said: "This is my God and I will glorify Him" (Exo-

dus 15:2). Rabbi Meir says: Even the fetuses in their mothers' wombs were singing a song, as it is stated: "Among the great assemblies, bless God; the Lord, from the source[13] of Israel" (Psalms 68:27).

(Jerusalem Talmud, *Sota* 5:4)

Miriam's Song

Concurrent with the song led by Moses, Miriam led all the women together in song and music. According to the Sages, while Miriam was still in Egypt she prepared the musical instruments that she would eventually use at the sea.

"Miriam the prophetess, sister of Aaron, took the drum in her hand, and all the women came out after her with drums and musical instruments" (Exodus 15:20). From where did the Israelites have drums and musical instruments in the wilderness? The righteous were certain that the Holy One, blessed be He, would perform miracles and mighty acts when they emerged from Egypt, and they prepared drums and musical instruments for themselves.

(*Mekhilta deRabbi Yishmael, Beshalah, Mesekhta deShira* 10)

The Taste of the Manna

The taste of the manna, the food that God provided for the Israelites in the wilderness, is described in the verses in various ways. The Sages relate that the manna did not have one definitive taste; rather, its taste changed according to the one consuming it and his situation.

"And its taste was like the taste of a cake moist with oil [*leshad hashemen*]" (Exodus 11:8). Rabbi Abbahu said: Just as with regard to milk from the breast [*shad*] a baby tastes several flavors in it, so too the manna. Whenever the Israelites ate it, they would find several flavors in it. Some say: The manna had the characteristic of an actual demon [*shed*]. Just as a demon transforms into several shapes and colors, so too, manna is transformed into several flavors.

(*Yoma* 75b)

---

13. The Hebrew term for "source," *makor*, also means "womb."

The Sun Grew Hot and the Manna Melted

Not only the Israelites enjoyed the manna. They would gather it in the morning, and later in the day the sun would melt all the manna that remained. The animals enjoyed that liquid, and in their wake, other nations enjoyed the manna as well.

"And the sun grew hot and it melted" (Exodus 16:21). Once the sun shone upon the manna, it would gradually liquefy, and streams of it would flow and reach the Mediterranean Sea. The deer, the gazelle, the fallow deer, and all the animals would drink from it. Thereafter, the nations would come and hunt those animals and eat them, and taste in them the taste of manna that would fall for the Israelites.

(*Mekhilta deRabbi Yishmael, Beshalah, Mesekhta deVayisa* 10)

Is the Lord in Our Midst?

Before the description of the Israelites' war with Amalek, it is stated that they asked: "Is the Lord in our midst, or not?" (Exodus 17:7). The Sages liken their conduct to that of a child whose father sees to all his needs, yet still asks: Have you seen my father?

To what were the Israelites comparable? They were comparable to one who was riding on his father's shoulders. He saw an item that he desired, and he said to his father: Acquire it for me. The father acquired it for him. And this occurred a second and third time. As they were walking, the child saw someone. He asked him: Have you seen my father? The father said to his child: You are riding on my shoulders, and everything that you request I do for you, and you say to him: Have you seen my father? The father cast his child from upon his shoulders and a dog came and bit him.

So it was with the Israelites. When they departed from Egypt, the clouds of glory immediately surrounded them; they requested manna, and the Holy One, blessed be He, rained down manna for them; they requested pheasant, He provided them…. He provided them with all their needs. They began contemplating: "Is the Lord in our midst, or not?" (17:7). The Holy One, blessed be He, said to them: I take an oath by your lives! I am informing you, the dog is coming and it will bite you [and then you will realize that I have been caring for you]. Who is that dog? It is Amalek.

(*Tanḥuma* [Buber], *Yitro*)

The Scalding Tub

Amalek was the first nation to harass the Israelites after the great and open miracles they experienced (see Exodus 17:8–16) ; other nations then followed their lead.

The Rabbis say: [When describing the attack of the Amalekites, the verse employs the term: "Encountered you [*karekha*]" (Deuteronomy 25:18). This teaches that the Amalekites cooled you [*hikrekha*] before anyone else. Rabbi Hunya said: To what is the matter comparable? It is comparable to a scalding bathtub into which no creature was able to descend. One ruffian came and leapt into it. Even though he was scalded, he cooled the water for others. Here too, when the Israelites departed from Egypt, the Holy One, blessed be He, split the sea before them, and the Egyptians drowned in it. Fear of the Israelites fell over the nations.... When Amalek came and confronted them, even though the Amalekites received their just deserts through them and lost the battle, their attack cooled the Israelites, [i.e., lessened the fear of them,] before the nations of the world.

(*Tanḥuma, Ki Tetze*)

The Hands of Moses

While the Israelites battled Amalek, Moses climbed to the top of the hill above the battleground and raised his hands heavenward. The Sages explain that he thereby spurred the Israelites to direct their attention to God, and with His assistance, the children of Israel were victorious.

"It was when Moses raised his hand, Israel prevailed, and when he lowered his hand, Amalek prevailed" (Exodus 17:11). Do the hands of Moses wage the war or damage the war effort? The verse serves to tell you that as long as the Israelites were looking upward after seeing Moses' raised hands, and subjected their hearts to their Father in Heaven, they would prevail, but if not, they would fall in battle.

(Mishna *Rosh HaShana* 3:8)

Yitro

The beginning of this Torah portion tells of the arrival of Moses' father-in-law, Yitro, at the Israelite camp, and describes his advice to Moses to appoint judges and magistrates who would assist him in administering the numerous public affairs. The second part of the Torah portion tells of the giving of the Torah: The revelation of God to the entire nation on Mount Sinai, and the Ten Commandments that were stated during that revelation.

The chapter that follows presents statements of the Sages concerning Yitro's arrival, the characteristics of those worthy of being appointed as judges, and the giving of the Torah. It also includes statements about the unity of the Israelites at the giving of the Torah, the eradication of the boundaries between heaven and earth, the connection between the exodus from Egypt and the giving of the Torah, the revelation of God at Sinai and elsewhere, the commandments and the tablets, God's speech, and the nations of the world vis-à-vis the giving of the Torah.

What Did Yitro Hear?

The Torah portion relates that Yitro heard about the good that God performed for the Israelites, as a result of which he came to the Israelite camp in the wilderness. The Sages disagree with regard to what caused him to leave his home and come.

"Yitro, priest of Midyan, father-in-law of Moses, heard all that God had done to Moses and to Israel His people, that the Lord took Israel out of Egypt" (Exodus 18:1). What report did he hear that caused him to come? He heard of the war with Amalek and came, as that is the topic written alongside it [i.e., immediately beforehand]; this is the statement of Rabbi Yehoshua.

Rabbi Elazar HaModa'i says: Yitro heard of the giving of the Torah and came,[14] as at the moment that the Torah was given to Israel, all the kings of the land quaked in terror in their palaces. At that moment, all the kings of the nations of the world assembled before Bilam the wicked. They said to him: Bilam, perhaps the Omnipresent is doing to us [i.e., beginning to destroy the world] as He did to the generation of the flood. Bilam said to them: Fools of the world, the Holy One, blessed be He, already took a vow to Noah that he will never bring another flood .... They said to him: Perhaps He took an oath only that He will not bring a flood of water, but He will

---

14. Even though the chapter of the giving of the Torah is written after the account of Yitro's arrival.

bring a torrent of fire. Bilam said to them: He will not bring a torrent of fire or a flood of water. Rather, the Holy One, blessed be He, is giving a Torah to His beloved people.

Rabbi Eliezer says: Yitro heard of the splitting of the Red Sea, as at the moment that the Red Sea split, the sound of its splitting was heard throughout the world.

(Mekhilta deRabbi Yishmael, Beshalah, Mesekhta deAmalek 1)

The Qualities of a Judge

Moses was constantly occupied with tending to the people's needs and resolving disputes between them. Yitro advised him to establish a wide-ranging, decentralized judicial system. To that end, Moses needed to select people worthy of serving as judges. The Sages explain the qualities of a judge according to Yitro.

"You shall identify from all the people capable men, fearers of God, men of truth, haters of ill-gotten gain" (Exodus 18:21). Capable men means those who are mighty in their striving to understand the Torah…. Fearers of God is in accordance with its straightforward meaning. Men of truth refers to those who insist on the truthfulness of judgment. Haters of ill-gotten gain refers to those who are haters of even their own property; all the more so, the property of others. Such a person should say: Even if he burns my grain pile, even if he cuts down my vineyard, I will judge him justly.

(Tanḥuma, Yitro)

One Heart

The Israelite camp on the eve of the giving of the Torah experienced peace and unity.

[The verse teaches about the nation's encampment around Mount Sinai:] "Israel encamped there next to the mountain" (Exodus 19:2). Every place that the verse states: "They traveled [*vayisu*]," or "they encamped [*vayahanu*]," in the plural, it means that they traveled in dispute and encamped in dispute. But here, all of them shared one unified heart; that is why the verse states: "Israel encamped [*vayihan*, in the singular] there next to the mountain."

(Mekhilta deRabbi Yishmael, Yitro, Mesekhta deBaḥodesh 1)

The Heavenly and the Earthly

Until the giving of the Torah, connection between the heavenly world and this earthly world was not possible. At the giving of the Torah, the borders opened – the heavenly descended below and the earthly ascended above.

To what is this matter comparable? It is comparable to a king who issued a decree and said: The residents of Rome may not travel to Syria, and the residents of Syria may not travel to Rome. Similarly, when the Holy One, blessed be He, created the world, He issued a decree and said: "The heavens are the heavens of the Lord, while He has given the earth to the people" (Psalms 115:16). When He sought to give the Torah, He nullified the original decree, and said: The earthly will ascend to the heavenly, and the heavenly will descend to the earthly; and I am the Initiator, as it is stated: "The Lord descended upon Mount Sinai" (Exodus 19:20), and it is written: "To Moses, He said: Ascend to the Lord" (24:1).

(*Shemot Rabba* 12)

The Exodus from Egypt and the Giving of the Torah

The giving of the Torah and the Ten Commandments are among the fundamentals of the Torah and a seminal event for the children of Israel. Why didn't the Torah begin with them?

"I am the Lord your God, who took you out of the land of Egypt" (Exodus 20:2). Why weren't the Ten Commandments stated at the beginning of the Torah? The Sages stated a parable to explain what this is comparable to. It is comparable to one who entered a region and said: I will reign over you. The people said to him: Have you accomplished anything for us, so that you should reign over us? What did that person then do? He built a wall for them, he streamed in water for them, and he waged wars for them. He then said to them: I will reign over you. They said: Certainly, yes.

So too, the Omnipresent took Israel out of Egypt, split the sea for them, rained manna down for them, raised the well for them, gathered pheasant for them, and waged the war with Amalek for them. God then said: I will reign over you. They said: Certainly, yes.

(*Mekhilta deRabbi Yishmael, Yitro, Mesekhta deBaḥodesh* 5)

I Am at the Sea and I Am at Sinai

The Creator reveals Himself to his people with different techniques and with emphasis on different aspects of divine providence. The Ten Commandments begin with a declaration that all these are merely different manifestations of the one and only God.

"I am the Lord your God, who took you out of the land of Egypt" (Exodus 20:2). Why was that said? Because God was revealed at the sea as a hero waging wars, as it is stated: "The Lord is a warrior" (15:3), and he was revealed on Mount Sinai as an elder filled with compassion…. In order not to provide substantiation for the nations of the world to say: There are two authorities, one who wages war and the other who acts with compassion, to counter that, God stated: "I am the Lord your God." I am the God who acted in Egypt, I am the God who acted at the sea, I am the God who acts at Sinai, I am the God who acted in the past, I am the God who will act in the future, I am the God who acts in this world, I am the God who acts in the World to Come.

(*Mekhilta deRabbi Yishmael, Yitro, Mesekhta deBaḥodesh* 5)

The Ten Commandments and the Tablets

The Ten Commandments were carved on two tablets. The Sages explain that the arrangement of the commandments opposite one another was of great significance.

How were the commandments given? The first five were carved on this tablet and the latter five were carved opposite the first five on that tablet.

It is written on the first tablet: "I am the Lord your God" (Exodus 20:2), and it is written opposite it on the second tablet: "You shall not murder" (20:13). The verse thereby teaches that concerning anyone who sheds blood, the verse ascribes blame to him as though he diminishes the image of God, the King. This can be explained through a parable to a flesh and blood king who entered a region and established icons of himself, and crafted idols of himself, and minted coins of himself. After a while, the people there bent his icons, smashed his idols, invalidated his coins, and diminished the image of the king. So too, concerning anyone who sheds blood [of a person, who is created in the image of God], the verse ascribes him blame as though he diminishes the image of God, the King, as it is stated: "One who sheds the blood of man … as He made man in the image of God" (Genesis 9:6).

It is written on the first tablet: "You shall have no other gods before Me" (Exodus 20:3), and it is written opposite it on the second tablet: "You shall not commit adultery" (20:13). The verse teaches that concerning any-

one who engages in idol worship, thereby choosing another god, the verse ascribes him blame]as though he commits adultery against the Omnipresent.

It is written on the first tablet: "You shall not take the name of the Lord your God in vain" (20:7) when taking an oath, and it is written opposite it on the second tablet: "You shall not steal" (20:13). The verse teaches that anyone who steals ultimately comes to take an oath in vain.

It is written: "Remember the Sabbath day, to keep it holy" (20:8), and it is written opposite it: "You shall not bear false witness against your neighbor" (20:13). The verse teaches that anyone who profanes the Sabbath testifies before He who spoke and the world came into being that He did not create His world in six days and did not rest on the seventh, and anyone who observes the Sabbath testifies before He who spoke and the world came into being that He created His world in six days and rested on the seventh....

It is written: "Honor your father and your mother" (20:12), and it is written opposite it: "You shall not covet" (20:14). The verse teaches that anyone who covets will ultimately beget a son who curses his father and his mother, and will honor one who is not his father.

That is why the Ten Commandments were given with five carved on this tablet and five carved corresponding to them on that tablet.

(*Mekhilta deRabbi Yishmael, Yitro, Mesekhta deBaḥodesh* 8)

Seeing the Thunder

The verse states that the Israelites "saw the thunder" during the revelation of God at Sinai. The Sages disagree as to the meaning of that phrase, and describe how the Israelites stood ready on the occasion of the giving of the Torah, when they were in a state of total perfection in both mind and body.

"All the people were seeing the thunder and the flames and the blast of the shofar and the mountain smoking" (Exodus 20:15). They were seeing the flames and smoking mountain, which are usually seen, and hearing the thunder and shofar, which are usually heard; this is the statement of Rabbi Yishmael. Rabbi Akiva says: They were seeing and hearing that which is usually only seen – they would see a speech of fire emerging from the mouth of the Almighty and being carved onto the tablets, as it is stated: "The voice of the Lord hews flames of fire" (Psalms 29:7).

Rabbi Eliezer says: The verse serves to notify us of the praise of Israel, as when they all stood before Mount Sinai to receive the Torah, it relates that

there were no blind people among them, as it is stated: "All the people were seeing" (Exodus 20:15); it relates that there were no mutes among them, as it is stated: "All the people answered together" (19:8); and it teaches that there were no deaf people among them, as it is stated: "Everything that the Lord has spoken we will perform and we will heed" (24:7). From where is it derived that there were no cripples among them? As it is stated: "They stood at the foot of the mountain" (19:17). And the verse teaches that there were no simpletons among them, as it is stated: "You have been shown in order to know" (Deuteronomy 4:35) [indicating that they all had wisdom].

(*Mekhilta deRabbi Yishmael, Yitro, Mesekhta deBaḥodesh* 9)

My Soul Had Departed with His Speaking

The Israelites were unable to withstand the intensity of the direct revelation, and their souls left them. God then spoke to them pleasantly and lovingly, and their souls returned.

This is comparable to a king who spoke harshly to his son, and the son was afraid and his soul almost departed from him. When the king saw his soul had departed, he began to caress and kiss him and to comfort him, telling him: What is the matter? Aren't you my only son? Am I not your father?

So too, when the Holy One, blessed be He, spoke and said: "I am the Lord your God" (Exodus 20:2) – immediately the Israelites' souls left them. When they died, the angels began caressing and kissing them, and told them: What is the matter? Do not fear, "you are children to the Lord your God" (Deuteronomy 14:1). The Holy One, blessed be He, spoke sweetly to them, telling them: Aren't you My children? I am the Lord your God. You are My people. You are beloved before Me. He began comforting them until their souls returned and they began requesting an additional revelation from Him....

When their souls left them, the Torah began asking for mercy for Israel from the Holy One, blessed be He. It said before Him: Master of the Universe, is there a king who marries off his daughter and concurrently kills a member of his household? I am likened to Your daughter, and the entire world is joyful on my account. Yet Your children are dying. Immediately, the Israelites' souls returned. That is what is written: "The Torah of the Lord is perfect, restoring the soul" (Psalms 19:8).

(*Shir HaShirim Rabba* 6)

The Nations of the World and Acceptance of the Torah

Before God gave the Torah to Israel, He offered it to the rest of the nations of the world. They refused to accept it, each nation for its own reason.

When the Holy One, blessed be He, revealed Himself to give the Torah to Israel, it was not to Israel alone that He revealed Himself, but to all the nations.

First He approached the children of Esau. He said to them: Do you accept the Torah? They said to Him: What is written in it? He said to them: "You shall not murder" (Exodus 20:13). They said: The very essence of those people [i.e., themselves] and their ancestor is murder, as it is stated in Isaac's blessing to Esau: "By your sword you shall live" (Genesis 27:40).

He approached the children of Amon and Moav. He said to them: Do you accept the Torah? They said to Him: What is written in it? He said to them: You shall not commit adultery (Exodus 20:13). They said: Our very essence is illicit relations.[15]

He approached the children of Ishmael. He said to them: Do you accept the Torah? They said to Him: What is written in it? He said to them: "You shall not steal" (20:13). They said: Our very essence is robbery. Their ancestor was a highwayman, as it is stated concerning Ishmael: "He shall be a wild man. His hand shall be against everyone" (Genesis 16:12).

Likewise, God approached each and every nation. He asked them if they would accept the Torah … could it be that they listened and accepted?… Not only did they fail to listen, they were unable to uphold even the seven commandments that the sons of Noah accepted upon themselves, and they abandoned the observance of those commandments.

Once the Holy One, blessed be He, saw this, He gave the Torah to Israel. This can be explained by a parable of one who sent his donkey and his dog to the threshing floor. He loaded his donkey with a half-*kor* of produce [a relatively heavy amount], and his dog with three *se'a* of produce [a relatively light amount]. The donkey was walking and the dog was panting from exertion. He unloaded one *se'a* from the dog and placed it on the donkey, and likewise the second and likewise the third. So too, Israel accepted the Torah with its explanations and details, even those seven commandments that the sons of Noah were unable to uphold and which they abandoned. Israel came and accepted them.

(*Sifrei Devarim* 343)

📖 Further reading: For additional descriptions of the revelation at Mount Sinai, see p. 309.

---

15. Amon and Moav themselves were born from the incestuous relations between Lot and his daughters.

Mishpatim

The first section of this Torah portion focuses in great detail on civil law – torts, loans, and other aspects of monetary law. The second section discusses mitzvot relating to many different areas of life – idolatry; *halakhot* pertaining to food, festivals, and the pilgrimage to the Temple; and *halakhot* governing interpersonal relationships. In the next section, the verses relate God's promise with regard to entry into the Land of Israel and the nature of that entry. The portion concludes with a detailed description of the event, reported in the previous Torah portion, wherein God established His covenant with the Israelites at Mount Sinai following the giving of the Torah.

The chapter that follows presents statements of the Sages concerning God's civil statutes formulated specifically for the Israelite people, and some of the commandments and principles that appear in the Torah portion: the laws concerning one who steals an ox or a sheep and one who kills a human being unwittingly; the mitzva to assist another while he is traveling; the mitzva to treat strangers respectfully; and the principle of "an eye for an eye" – which refers to payment, not bodily punishment.

God's Statutes and Laws for Israel

The detailed ordinances of the Torah are bestowed directly from God to Israel. These are God's statutes and laws that He Himself observes and fulfills.

"These are the ordinances that you shall place before them" (Exodus 21:1). That is the meaning of what is written: "He declares His words to Jacob" (Psalms 147:7) – these are the Ten Commandments; "His statutes and His laws to Israel" (Psalms 147:7) – these are the rest of the ordinances, [particularly those relating to civil law]. The attributes of the Holy One, blessed be He, are not like the attributes of people. The attribute of a person is that he instructs others to act but he himself does nothing. But the Holy One, blessed be He, is not so; rather, what He does, He instructs others to perform and observe, [as the verse refers to "His statutes" and "His laws," indicating that God Himself observes them] ....

Rabbi Abbahu said in the name of Rabbi Yosei son of Rabbi Hanina: This can be explained by way of a parable of a king who had an orchard. He would plant all types of trees in it, but he would not enter it; rather, he would guard it. When his children grew up, he said to them: My children, I guarded this orchard, and I did not allow any person to enter it. Guard it

in the manner that I guarded it.[16] So God said to Israel: Before I created this world, I prepared the Torah … I did not give it to any of the idol worshippers, only to Israel …. He gave only a few commandments to the nations of the world: He gave Adam six commandments;[17] He added one, the prohibition against eating the limb of a living animal, to Noah; to Abraham He gave an eighth, circumcision; to Jacob, a ninth, the prohibition against eating the sciatic nerve; but He gave everything to Israel.

Rabbi Simon said in the name of Rabbi Hanina: This can be explained by way of a parable of a king with a set table and all kinds of dishes before him. When his servant entered, the king gave him a piece of meat; a second entered, the king gave him an egg; a third entered, the king gave him a vegetable; and likewise to each and every one. When his son entered, the king gave him the entire meal that was before him. The king said to him: I gave a portion to each of those people, but I gave everything into your possession. So too, the Holy One, blessed be He, gave the idol worshippers only a few commandments. But when Israel stood at Mount Sinai, He said to them: The entire Torah is yours.

(*Shemot Rabba* 30)

Fourfold and Fivefold Payments

One who steals an ox or a sheep and then slaughters it or sells it to others pays five times the value of the ox or four times the value of the sheep to the owner. The Sages disagree as to the rationale for the difference in payment between the two animals.

Rabbi Meir said: Come and see how precious labor is before He who spoke and the world came into being: For stealing and then slaughtering or selling an ox, which performs labor, one pays five times its value; for stealing and then slaughtering or selling a sheep, which does not perform labor, one pays only four times its value.

Rabban Yohanan ben Zakkai says: The Holy One, blessed be He, is concerned with human dignity. For stealing and then slaughtering or selling an ox, because it walks on its feet when the thief leads it away, he pays five times its value; for stealing and then slaughtering or selling a sheep, because the thief carries it on his shoulder [which causes him embarrassment], he pays only four times its value.

(*Mekhilta deRabbi Yishmael, Mishpatim, Mesekhta deNezikin* 30)

---

16. Similarly, God observed the Torah, as it were, until He gave it to the Israelites.

17. The first six of the seven Noahide commandments: the prohibitions against idol worship, illicit sexual intercourse, bloodshed, cursing the Creator, and robbery; and the commandment to establish courts.

All Its Paths Are Peace

In this Torah portion we find the mitzva not to disregard the donkey of one's enemy that is stuck while transporting a burden, unable to proceed and bear the burden that is upon it. The Sages demonstrate how this *halakha* can help enemies to reconcile.

Rabbi Alexandri said: Two donkey drivers who hated each other were proceeding on the way. The donkey of one of them crouched. The other passed and saw that the donkey was crouched due to the weight of its burden. He said: Isn't it written in the Torah: "If you see the donkey of your enemy crouching under its burden…you shall assist with him" (Exodus 23:5)? What did he do? He went to load the donkey in a manner that it could bear its burden and thus joined the owner in loading the donkey. The owner began speaking with him: Assist a bit from here, lift from here, loosen here. While they loaded the donkey together, they made peace between them. The other one said: Didn't I believe he was my enemy? Look how he had compassion on me when he saw me and my donkey in distress. Consequently, they entered an inn, ate and drank together, and came to love one another.

(Tanḥuma, Mishpatim)

From Evil People Will Evil Emerge

The punishment for a person who inadvertently kills another person is being exiled to a city of refuge. The Sages note the language of the verse that describes that *halakha*: "God caused it to come to his hand," and derive that it indicates that God caused the person to inadvertently kill the victim.

"But for one who did not have intent and God caused it to come to his hand, I will provide you a place where he shall flee" (Exodus 21:13). What is the verse speaking about? It is speaking about two people who killed other people: One killed unintentionally [and should be exiled to a city of refuge], and one killed intentionally [and should be executed]; but there are no witnesses to either act, [so they will not receive their due punishments]. The Holy One, blessed be He, arranges for them to be in one inn. This one, who killed intentionally, sits beneath a ladder; and that one, who killed unintentionally, descends the ladder, and falls upon the intentional killer and kills him. That one who killed intentionally is killed, and that one who killed unintentionally is now exiled, [so ultimately each of them receives his due punishment].

(Makkot 10b)

The Deer and the Flock

In the Torah portion, we are commanded not to aggrieve converts and to treat them appropriately, because "you were strangers in the land of Egypt." The Sages liken the convert joining the Jewish people to an undomesticated animal that, of its own volition, joins a farm of domesticated animals, and is therefore worthy of abundant love.

"The Lord protects strangers" (Psalms 146:9). The Holy One, blessed be He, loves converts very much. To what is this matter comparable? It is comparable to a king who had a flock that would emerge and graze in the field and return to the pen each evening. One time, a deer joined the flock. It went near the goats and the sheep and was grazing with them. It entered the pen with the flock. When the flock would go out to graze, the deer went out with it. The shepherds told the king: The deer goes with the flock and grazes with them. Each day, it goes out and enters with them. The king loved the deer very much. When it went out to the field, he would command the shepherd, saying to him: Be careful with this deer, and ensure that no man will strike it. When it entered with the flock, he would command his beloved in its regard: Give it to eat and drink. He loved the deer very much.

The shepherd said to him: My master, the king: You have so many male goats, and so many female goats, and so many sheep, and so many kids, and you do not caution me to protect them, but the deer, you command me every day concerning it. The king said to him: As for the flock, it is its manner to graze. But deer, they live in the wilderness, and it is not their manner to enter the settled area, among the people, and this deer entered and lived among us. Shouldn't we give it credit that it left the great, broad wilderness, a place where the male and the female deer graze, and left them and came to us? Therefore, we must give it credit.

So too, the Holy One, blessed be He, said: I must give great credit to the convert, who left his family and his father's house, and came to Me. Therefore, I command concerning him: "You shall love the stranger" (Deuteronomy 10:19); "You shall not mistreat and you shall not oppress him" (Exodus 22:20). That is why it is stated: "The Lord protects strangers" (Psalms 146:9).

(*Midrash Tehillim* [Buber] 148)

📖 Further reading: The command to honor converts and to not aggrieve them appears in several places in the Torah. See *A Concise Guide to the Torah*, pp. 190, 303, 306, 317, 460, 469, 472, 489, 494.

An Eye for an Eye – Money

In the Torah portion, the principle concerning monetary law is cited: "An eye for an eye, a tooth for a tooth, a hand for a hand, a foot for a foot, a burn for a burn, a wound for a wound, an injury for an injury." The Sages taught that this verse should not be understood in accordance with its straightforward meaning. They established that in the case of bodily harm, the punishment is not corporal; rather, the reference is to payment. Presented here are two reasons from among many that were given for this explanation of the verse.

Rabbi Dostai ben Yehuda says: When the verse states: "An eye for an eye" (Leviticus 24:20), it means that the assailant pays money. The Gemara asks: Do you say the assailant pays money, or is the phrase: "An eye for an eye" a reference to the removal of his actual eye? You can say in response: If the eye of the victim is large and the eye of the assailant is small, how can I read in this case: "An eye for an eye"? [Since the eyes are not equal, it would not be a just punishment.] And if you would say: In all cases like this [where their eyes are not of equal size] take money from the assailant, [but if their eyes are of equal size the assailant's eye is removed, that cannot be correct, as] the Torah stated: "You shall have one manner of law" (Leviticus 24:22), teaching that you must have a law equal for all of you.

Rabbi Shimon ben Yohai says: When the verse states: "An eye for an eye" (Leviticus 24:20), it means that the assailant pays money. Do you say he pays money, or is it a reference to the removal of an actual eye? If one is blind and he blinded another, or one is an amputee and he severed the limb of another, or one is lame and he caused one to be lame – in this case, how can I fulfill "An eye for an eye"? And the Torah stated: "You shall have one manner of law" (Leviticus 24:22) – a law equal for all of you. [Therefore, the punishment must be the payment of money in all cases.]

(*Bava Kamma* 83b)

Teruma

The primary focus of this Torah portion is the mitzva to construct the Tabernacle. It includes a precise enumeration of the Tabernacle's dimensions and form, as well as a detailed discussion of its courtyard and the sacred vessels that were placed in it.

The chapter that follows presents statements of the Sages concerning the Tabernacle and the atonement provided by the performance of its service; the Tabernacle as the House of God; the question as to how it is at all possible to build a house for God; the nature of the *taḥash*, whose hide was used in the construction of the Tabernacle; and the source of the boards used in the construction of the Tabernacle.

A Remedy for the Sin

The Tabernacle demonstrates God's forgiving the Israelites for the sin of the Golden Calf.

"They shall make for Me a sanctuary, and I will dwell among them" (Exodus 25:8). When was this passage concerning the Tabernacle said to Moses? It was said on Yom Kippur itself [when the second tablets were given to Moses in place of the tablets that he shattered in the wake of the sin of the Golden Calf]. This is so even though the recording of the passage about the Tabernacle in the Torah precedes the recording of the event of the Calf. Rabbi Yehuda son of Rabbi Shalom said: The verses of the Torah are not ordered chronologically.

[The following explains] why the Tabernacle is called: "The Tabernacle of testimony" (38:21): Because it is testimony for all humankind that the Holy One, blessed be He, rests His presence in the Israelites' Temple, [and forgave them for their sin]. The Holy One, blessed be He, said: Let the gold that is used in the construction and vessels of the Tabernacle come and atone for the gold with which the Calf was formed.

(*Tanḥuma, Teruma*)

📖 **Further reading:** For more about the sin of the Golden Calf, see p. 120.

What Home Could You Build for Me

How is it possible to construct a home for The Master of the Universe? The Sages explain that God asks of people to act to the best of their abilities, even if the task itself is impossible to complete.

This mitzva of building the Tabernacle is one of three matters that Moses heard from the mouth of the Almighty that caused him to recoil. At the moment God said to him in instructing each Israelite to contribute a half-shekel: "Each man shall give a ransom for himself" (Exodus 30:12), Moses said: Who can give the ransom of his life?[18] The Holy One, blessed be He, said to him: I am not asking according to My capacity, but according to their capacity, [and I will value even this small contribution].

At the moment God said concerning the sacrificial service: "My offering, My food, for My fires, My pleasing aroma, you shall take care to present to Me at its appointed time" (Numbers 28:2), Moses said: Who can provide You with offerings? If we sacrifice all the animals of the forest and all the trees of Lebanon, they would not suffice. God said to him: I am not asking according to My capacity, but according to their capacity, [a sheep in the morning and a sheep in the afternoon].

At the moment God said to him: "They shall make for Me a sanctuary, and I will dwell among them" (Exodus 25:8), Moses said before the Holy One, blessed be He: "Behold, the heavens and the heaven of heavens cannot contain You" (I Kings 8:27), and the verse states: "Do I not fill the heavens and the earth" (Jeremiah 23:24), and the verse states: "The heavens are My throne and the earth is My footstool; what house could you build for Me and what place could be My resting place?" (Isaiah 66:1). Can we make a Sanctuary for Him? The Holy One, blessed be He, said to him: I am not asking according to My capacity, but according to their capacity: "You shall make the Tabernacle of ten sheets" (Exodus 26:1).

When the Israelites heard [that if they act to the best of their abilities, God will rest His presence in the Tabernacle], they arose and contributed and made the Tabernacle. Once they made the Tabernacle, it became filled with God's glory, as it is stated: "Moses was unable to enter the Tent of Meeting because the cloud rested upon it, and the glory of the Lord filled the Tabernacle" (40:35).

(*Tanḥuma* [Buber], *Naso*)

---

18. A life is of infinite value; how can a half-shekel be considered payment for one's life?

The *Taḥash*

One of the materials required in the preparation of the sheets of the Tabernacle was "*taḥash* hides." The Sages discussed the identity of the *taḥash*.

Rabbi Yehuda says: The *taḥash* was a large, kosher animal in the wilderness. It had one horn on its forehead and its hide had six different hues. The Israelites took it and made sheets for the Tabernacle with its hides. Rabbi Neḥemya says: The *taḥash* was a miraculous creation [not a naturally occurring animal], and it was concealed as soon as it was created until it was to be used in the construction of the Tabernacle.

(*Tanḥuma, Teruma*)

Boards for the Tabernacle

The Israelites were commanded to construct the Tabernacle while they were in the wilderness. Where did they find large-enough wooden boards with which to build it? Jacob, on his way to Egypt, instructed his sons to plant trees for that eventual purpose.

From where were the boards? Jacob our patriarch planted the trees that produced them when he descended to Egypt. He said to his sons: My sons, in the future you will be redeemed from Egypt, and the Holy One, blessed be He, will say to you in the future, after you will be redeemed, that you shall construct the Tabernacle. Rise and plant cedars even now, so that at the time that He tells you to make the Tabernacle, the cedars will be prepared for you. Immediately, they rose and planted the trees.

(*Tanḥuma, Teruma*)

Tetzaveh

A significant part of *Parashat Tetzaveh* is devoted to the service of the priests in the Tabernacle. First, it details the priestly vestments – the eight vestments of the High Priest and the four vestments of the common priests. Next, the Torah describes at length the seven-day procedure of the Tabernacle's dedication and the investiture of the priests that would take place during that time . The Torah portion concludes with the command to build the incense altar.

The chapter that follows presents statements of the Sages concerning the consecration of Aaron and his sons for the priesthood, the breast piece in which the Urim and the Tumim were placed, and the blessing with which the world was blessed because of the altar.

The Selection of Aaron

When the Israelites sought to craft a god for themselves, they turned to Aaron and he crafted the Golden Calf for them. The Sages explain that Aaron's intentions were proper, to the extent that by virtue of the purity of his intentions he and his sons merited to become priests.

God told Moses: "And you, have Aaron your brother approach you, and his sons with him, from among the children of Israel, to serve as priests to Me" (Exodus 28:1). The Sages said: When Moses descended from Mount Sinai and saw Israel engaged in that action [i.e., worshipping the Golden Calf], he looked at Aaron and saw that he was striking the idol with a hammer to form it. Aaron intended only to delay the people to prevent them from sinning until Moses would descend, but Moses thought that Aaron was complicit in their sin and he was angry with him. The Holy One, blessed be He, said to Moses: I know how proper Aaron's intentions were. This can be explained by means of a parable of a prince who grew arrogant and took an iron spike to dig beneath his father's palace. His mentor said to him: Do not exert yourself. Give it to me and I will dig beneath it. The king looked at the mentor and said to him: I know that your intentions were to slow the digging. I take an oath by your life that I will not appoint any person over my palace other than you.

So too, when the Israelites said to Aaron: "Rise, make us a god" (32:1), he said to them: "Remove the gold rings" (32:2) and give them to me to fashion the calf. Aaron said to them: I am a priest; I will fashion it and will

sacrifice offerings before it. But in truth, he engaged with them only to delay them until Moses came. The Holy One, blessed be He, said to him: Aaron, I know what your intentions were. I take an oath by your life that I will not appoint anyone over the offerings of My children other than you, as it is stated that God said to Moses: "And you, have Aaron your brother approach you" (28:1) to perform the service in the Tabernacle.

(*Shemot Rabba* 37)

Woven Garments

The phrase: "Woven garments," appears for the first time in the context of the priestly vestments. The Sages explain why priestly vestments are characterized as "woven garments."

What is the meaning of what is written: "The woven garments [*bigdei haserad*] to serve in the Sanctuary" (Exodus 35:19)? Were it not for the priestly vestments, no remnant [*sarid*] would have remained from the enemies of Israel [a euphemism for Israel itself].

(*Yoma* 72a)

The Stones of the Breast Piece

The High Priest always wore the breast piece of judgment on his chest. There were twelve precious stones embedded in the breast piece, and each was inscribed with the name of one of the tribes. These items were the Urim and the Tumim, through which it was possible to ask questions of God and receive a response from God, as explained by the Sages.

The Sages taught: How do they ask questions of God with the help of the breast piece? The questioner faces the questioned [i.e., the High Priest], and the questioned faces the Divine Presence present in the Urim and the Tumim…. One does not ask aloud and does not contemplate in his heart. Rather, he asks in the manner that Hannah spoke in her prayer [by forming the words with his mouth, but without saying them out loud]…. One does not ask about two matters together, and if he asked about two matters, God responds to only one…. Why are they called the Urim and the Tumim? Urim – because they illuminate [*me'irin*] their words. Tumim – because they complete [*tam*] their words…. How is it accomplished?[19] Rabbi

---

19. How do the words that answer the question appear in the names of the tribes inscribed upon the Urim and the Tumim?

Yohanan says: The letters that provide the answer protrude. Reish Lakish says: The letters that provide the answer connect to each other.

(*Yoma* 72a; *Shemot Rabba* 38)

The Altar

In the Hebrew term for altar, *mizbe'ah*, the Sages found an allusion to the great blessing that the sacrificial service brings to the people of Israel.

Why is the altar called *mizbe'ah*, [spelled *mem-zayin-bet-ḥet*]? *Mem* – because it forgives [*mohel*] the iniquities of Israel; *zayin* – because it serves as a good remembrance [*zikaron*] for Israel; *bet* – because it brings a blessing [*berakha*] for Israel; *ḥet* – because it is life [*ḥayim*] for Israel.

(*Tanḥuma* [Buber], *Tetzaveh*)

Ki Tisa

This Torah portion opens with the continuation of the commands concerning the Tabernacle: the contribution of the half-shekel, crafting the basin, and preparing the incense. The rest of the Torah portion addresses mainly the sin of worshipping the Golden Calf and its consequences. This includes God's anger and the punishment of the worshippers of the calf, Moses' prayers and his request for revelation, God's forgiveness and His revelation to Moses in the crevice of the rock, and the giving of the second tablets on Mount Sinai. The portion concludes with a description of the forty additional days that Moses stayed on Mount Sinai, at the conclusion of which he descended with the new tablets. From that point on, his face shone with a divine radiance.

The chapter that follows presents statements of the Sages concerning the episode of the calf, Moses' request for mercy and his coming to the defense of the Israelite people, Moses' shattering of the first tablets upon his descent from the mountain, and the prayer that he prays on behalf of the people.

The Sin of Worshipping the Calf

The calf was formed because the Israelites sought a replacement for Moses. His perceived delay in descending Mount Sinai caused them to fear they would be leaderless. The Sages add many details, not found in the verses, concerning different elements of this episode: the Israelites' apprehension, Aaron's role, Moses' reaction, and Moses' request for mercy on the children of Israel.

What is the meaning of what is written: "The people saw that Moses tarried [*boshesh*] in descending from the mountain" (Exodus 32:1)? Do not read *boshesh*; rather, read, *ba'u shesh* [meaning that six hours had passed].

Before Moses ascended to heaven to receive the Torah, he told the Israelites: I will return at the conclusion of forty days, at the beginning of the sixth hour from sunrise. At the conclusion of forty days, Satan came and brought confusion to the world so that the Israelites could not ascertain the precise hour. Satan said to the Israelites: Where is your master Moses? They said to him: He ascended to heaven. Satan said to them: Six hours have passed and he has yet to return. They ignored him. Satan said: He is dead. They ignored him. Satan showed them the image of [Moses dead on] a cot. That is the meaning of what they said to Aaron: "Because this [*zeh*][20] man

---

20. The connotation of the word "this," *zeh*, is that they were pointing at him.

Moses, who brought us up from the land of Egypt, we do not know what became of him" (32:1).

Forty days after Israel received the Ten Commandments, they forgot their God and said to Aaron: The Egyptians would take their god in their hands and lift it; they would sing and play music before it, and would keep it before them. Craft a god for us like the god of Egypt so we will be able to keep it before us…. They went to Moses' colleagues: Aaron and Hur the son of his sister…. Because Hur was from the tribe of Judah and among the luminaries of the generation, he began to harshly reprove the Israelites, and the contemptible among Israel rose against him and killed him.

Aaron saw that Hur was killed, so he built an altar, as it is stated: "Aaron saw, and he built an altar" (32:5). What did Aaron see? He saw the killing of Hur the son of his sister… Aaron reasoned with himself and said: If I tell them: Give me your silver and gold, they will give it to me immediately. Instead, I will tell them: Give me the rings of your wives and your children, and the matter of crafting the idol will be nullified [as presumably the women and children would not want to part with their jewelry].

The women heard the request, and they did not want to participate and did not agree to give their rings to their husbands…. The Holy One, blessed be He, gave them their reward…. The men saw that the women did not listen to them and give their rings to their husbands. What did the men do? Until that point, there were rings in the men's ears, in the manner of the Egyptians and in the manner of the Arabs. They removed the rings that were in their ears and gave them to Aaron.

Aaron found a diadem of gold among the rings, upon which the sacred name of God was written and the form of a calf was engraved. He threw that diadem alone into the crucible of fire…. A lowing calf emerged and all Israel saw. Rabbi Yehuda says: Satan entered into the calf and he was lowing in order to mislead Israel [to convince them that the calf had powers].

All Israel saw the calf, kissed it, prostrated themselves before it, and sacrificed offerings to it. The Holy One, blessed be He, said to Moses, who was in heaven: Moses, Israel has forgotten the power of My majesty that I displayed for them in Egypt and at the Red Sea, and they crafted for themselves an idol…. He said to Moses: "Go descend, for your people…have acted corruptly" (32:7), meaning: Go descend from your greatness. Moses said before God: Master of the Universe, before the Israelites sinned before You, You would call them My people…now that they sinned before You, You say to me: "Go descend, for your people…have acted corruptly"! They

are not my people, "they are Your people and Your inheritance" (Deuteronomy 9:29).

Moses took the two tablets and was descending, and the verses of the Ten Commandments on the tablets were carrying the tablets and Moses with them. When they saw the Israelites with drums, dances, and the calf, the verses fled and flew from the tablets, which then became heavy in Moses' hands. Moses was unable to bear himself or the tablets, and he cast the tablets from his hands and they shattered....

Moses said to Aaron: What have you done to this people?... Aaron said to him: I saw what they did to Hur and I was extremely frightened.

Rabbi Yehuda HaNasi says: None of the princes of the tribes participated in the episode of the calf... Rabbi Yehuda says: The tribe of Levi, too, did not participate in the episode of the calf.... When Moses saw that the tribe of Levi did not participate with the rest of the Israelites, he immediately recovered and grew stronger. He took the calf, burned it in fire, and ground it like the dust of the earth, and Moses cast its dust on the surface of the water....

He had the Israelites drink that water, and the lips of anyone who kissed the calf with all his heart would turn gold, and the members of the tribe of Levi would kill him, until approximately three thousand Israelite men died.

The Holy One, blessed be He, sent five angels to destroy all of Israel, and these five are: fury, anger, ire, destruction, and wrath. Moses heard, and he went to meet Abraham, Isaac, and Jacob. Moses said: If you reside in the World to Come, stand before me at this moment, as your children are like sheep subject to slaughter. The three patriarchs stood before him.

Moses said before God: Master of the Universe, didn't You take an oath to these three people to increase their descendants like the stars of the heavens?...

Based on the merit of the three patriarchs, three of the angels, specifically fury, anger, and ire, were prevented from harming Israel, and two remained. Moses said before God: Master of the Universe, for the sake of the oath that You took to them, prevent the destruction of Israel. The angel called destruction was prevented from harming Israel.

In addition, Moses said before God: For the sake of the oath that You stated to me, prevent the angel called wrath from harming Israel, as it is stated: "Relent from your enflamed wrath" (Exodus 32:22).

(*Shabbat* 89a; *Pirkei deRabbi Eliezer* 45)

📖 Further reading: Even today we remember the sin of the Golden Calf; see *A Concise Guide to Halakha*, pp. 157, 374.

Egyptian Influence

When Moses pleaded for mercy for the children of Israel in the wake of the sin of the Golden Calf, he mentioned the exodus from Egypt. He sought thereby to defend Israel by noting that in Egypt, whence they came, the worship of animals was pervasive.

Moses said to God: "Why shall Your wrath be enflamed against Your people, whom You took out of the land of Egypt?" (Exodus 32:11). What led Moses to mention the exodus from Egypt in this context? Moses said: Master of the Universe, from where did You take the Israelites out? You took them out from Egypt, where the Egyptians all worshipped lambs.

Rav Huna said in the name of Rabbi Yohanan: This can be explained by means of a parable of a wise man who opened a perfume shop for his son in a marketplace of prostitutes. The street had its impact, the profession [which perforce involves interactions with women] had its impact, and the fact that the lad was a young man had its impact – he went astray. His father came and caught him with prostitutes. The father began to shout, and said: I am going to kill you. The father's close friend was there, and said to the father: It is you who led the lad astray, and yet you are shouting at him! You forsook all professions and you taught him only perfumery. You forsook all the streets and you opened a shop for him specifically in a marketplace of prostitutes.

So said Moses: Master of the Universe, You forsook the entire world, and You enslaved Your children specifically in Egypt, who worshipped lambs. Your children learned from them, and they too crafted the calf. Therefore, Moses said: "Whom You took out of the land of Egypt" – know from where You took them out.

(*Shemot Rabba* 43)

Moses' Prayer

In the wake of the sin of the Golden Calf, God sought to destroy Israel and perpetuate the people of Israel through Moses. Moses pleaded for mercy for them and God relented. According to the Sages, God even implied to Moses that he should pray on the Israelites' behalf.

"The Lord spoke to Moses: Go descend, for your people … have acted corruptly" (Exodus 32:7). What is the meaning of: "Go descend"? Rabbi Elazar said: The Holy One, blessed be He, said to Moses: Moses, descend from your greatness. Isn't it only for the sake of Israel that I granted you prominence? Now that Israel has sinned, why do I need you? Immediately, Moses' strength waned and he was powerless to speak. When God said to Moses:

"Leave Me be, and I will destroy them" (Deuteronomy 9:14), Moses said to himself: [By stating that He will destroy the Israelites only if I leave Him be, I can infer that] this matter is dependent upon me. Immediately Moses stood and marshaled his strength in prayer, and pleaded for mercy.

This can be explained by means of a parable of a king who became angry with his son and beat him severely. A well-wisher of the king was sitting before the king, but was afraid to say anything to the king. The king said to his son: Were it not for this well-wisher of mine who is sitting before me, I would kill you. The well-wisher said to himself: This matter is dependent upon me. Immediately, he stood and rescued the king's son.

God said to Moses: "Now leave Me be, and My wrath will be enflamed against them … and I will make you into a great nation" (Exodus 32:10). Rabbi Abbahu said: Had the verse, which indicates that Moses grabbed hold of God, not been written, it would have been impossible to utter it [as it speaks of Moses' treating God in a manner that seems disrespectful]. The verse teaches that Moses grabbed the Holy One, Blessed be He, like a person who grabs his friend by his garment. Moses said before God: Master of the Universe, I will not leave You be until You forgive and pardon them.

God said to Moses: "And I will make you into a great nation" (32:10). Rabbi Elazar said: Moses said before the Holy One, Blessed be He: Master of the Universe, if a chair with three legs [i.e., the Israelites, who descend from the three patriarchs] is unable to stand before You in Your moment of wrath, all the more so a chair with one leg [i.e., Moses]. Moreover, I would have been ashamed before my forefathers. Now they will say: See the leader whom God placed over Israel; he requested greatness for himself but did not request mercy for them.

(*Berakhot* 32a)

📖 **Further reading:** For more about the power of prayer, see p. 457; *A Concise Guide to Mahshava*, p. 300.

Vayak'hel

The portion of *Vayak'hel* continues elaborating on the construction of the Tabernacle. It is almost entirely devoted to the practical implementation of the commands concerning its construction, which were enumerated in the previous Torah portions.

The chapter that follows presents statements of the Sages concerning the importance of studying about Shabbat and the festivals on the days on which they occur, and the choice of the craftsmen who constructed the Tabernacle.

To Assemble and to Study

At the beginning of the portion, before the Torah resumes its discussion of Tabernacle–related matters, Moses is told to assemble the entire people and command them once again not to perform labor on Shabbat. The Sages derive from here that on every Shabbat and festival, there is a requirement to teach and publicly engage in the study of matters relevant to the day.

"Moses assembled" (Exodus 35:1). Our Sages, experts in homiletics, said: From the beginning of the Torah through its conclusion, this is the only Torah portion that begins with the term *vayak'hel* [he assembled]. The Holy One, blessed be He, said: Convene great assemblies for yourself and publicly teach them the laws of Shabbat. Do this so that future generations will learn from you to convene assemblies each and every Shabbat and to gather in study halls to teach and instruct Torah matters and ritual matters to the people of Israel, so that My great name will be acclaimed among My children.

From here the Sages said: Moses enacted for the Jewish people that the Israelites should teach the matter of the commemorative day on the day itself: The *halakhot* of Passover on Passover, the *halakhot* of *Shavuot* on *Shavuot*, and the *halakhot* of *Sukkot* on *Sukkot*. Moses said to Israel: If you do this, the Holy One, blessed be He, will ascribe credit to you as though you crowned Him over His world.

(*Yalkut Shimoni, Vayak'hel* 1:408)

📖 Further reading: For more about Shabbat and festivals as an appropriate time for public Torah study, see *A Concise Guide to Mahshava*, pp. 35, 53.

Betzalel

The craftsman Betzalel son of Uri was installed as supervisor over the construction of the Tabernacle. The Sages learned from the manner of his appointment that it is necessary to consult the public when appointing a public figure. They also expand on Betzalel's wisdom and understanding.

Rabbi Yitzhak said: One may appoint a leader over the public only if he consults with the public, as it is stated: "See, the Lord has called by name Betzalel" (Exodus 35:30). The Lord said to Moses: Moses, is Betzalel suitable in your eyes? Moses said to Him: Master of the Universe, if he is suitable in Your eyes, all the more so in my eyes. God said to him: Nevertheless, go and tell Israel. Moses went and said to Israel: Is Betzalel suitable in your eyes? They said to him: If he is suitable in the eyes of the Holy One, Blessed be He, and in your eyes, all the more so is he suitable in our eyes.

Rabbi Shmuel bar Nahmani said that Rabbi Yonatan said: Betzalel was called by that name because of his wisdom. When the Holy One, Blessed be He, said to Moses: Go tell Betzalel: "Make a Tabernacle, an ark, and vessels" (see 31:7–11), Moses went and reversed the order and said to Betzalel: "Make an ark, and vessels, and a Tabernacle" (see 31:25–26). Betzalel said to Moses: Moses our teacher, the standard practice throughout the world is that a person first builds a house and only afterward places the vessels in the house, and you say to me: Make an ark, and vessels, and a Tabernacle. If I do so in the order you have commanded, where shall I place the vessels that I make? Perhaps God told you the following: "Make a Tabernacle, an ark, and vessels" (see Exodus 36). Moses said to Betzalel: Perhaps you were in God's shadow [*betzel El*], and you knew precisely what He said. Rav Yehuda said that Rav said: Betzalel knew how to join in mystical fashion the letters with which God created the heavens and earth.

(*Berakhot* 55a)

Betzalel and Oholiav

Alongside Betzalel, who was from the tribe of Judah, Oholiav son of Ahisamakh from the tribe of Dan was appointed to assist Betzalel in the construction project. Representatives of these two tribes specifically – the most and least significant among them – were chosen so that no person would be arrogant on the basis of his origins.

Rabbi Hanina ben Pazi said: There is no tribe superior to the tribe of Judah, and there is no tribe inferior to the tribe of Dan, who was born from Bilha,

one of the maidservants; and what is written in his regard? "And the sons of Dan: Hushim" (Genesis 46:23).[21] The Holy One, blessed be He, said: Let the tribe of Judah come and join the tribe of Dan, so the Israelites will not demean him, and so that no man will be arrogant, because great and small are equal before the Omnipresent. Betzalel was from Judah and Oholiav from Dan, and [yet Oholiav] joined Betzalel.

(*Shemot Rabba* 40)

📖 Further reading: For more about public appointments, see pp. 103, 183, 211, 243.

---

21. Dan had only one child, and in that sense, too, Dan was the least significant of the tribes.

Pekudei

This Torah portion concludes the extensive discussion pertaining to the construction of the Tabernacle. The beginning of the portion tells of the preparation of the priestly vestments, in accordance with the command to prepare them elaborated in *Parashat Tetzaveh*. After that, the Torah describes the actual assembly of the Tabernacle: The assembling of its structural parts and the placing of each item where it belonged within the structure. Ultimately, the Divine Presence rested in it, as the verse states: "And the glory of the Lord filled the Tabernacle."

The chapter that follows presents statements of the Sages concerning the reckoning Moses conducted of the donations given for the Tabernacle and the outlays in its construction, as well as the actual erecting of the Tabernacle that was performed by Moses exclusively.

To Prevent Suspicion

The Torah portion begins with an accounting of the Israelites' contributions that were earmarked for construction of the Tabernacle, and precisely how those funds were utilized in practice. The Sages explain that it was necessary to prepare a detailed reckoning because there were those who maligned Moses, accusing him of misappropriating some of those funds.

"These are the reckonings of the Tabernacle" (Exodus 38:21). Why did Moses prepare a reckoning for them? The Holy One, blessed be He, trusted Moses, as it is stated: "Not so My servant Moses; in all My house he is trusted" (Numbers 12:7), and Moses said to the people: Come and prepare a reckoning with me!

Moses heard the Israelites speaking behind his back, as it is stated: "It would be, upon Moses' going out to the tent, that all the people would rise, and each would stand at his tent's entrance; they would gaze after Moses" (Exodus 33:8). What were they saying? Rabbi Yitzhak says: They were speaking words of praise. They would say: Happy is the one who gave birth to him. All his days, the Holy One, blessed be He, speaks with him. All his days he is perfect in the eyes of the Holy One, blessed be He…. Rabbi Hama said: They were speaking words of deprecation. They would say: Look at the thickness of his neck, look at the girth of his thighs. He eats at the expense of the Israelites and he drinks at the expense of the Israelites, and everything that he has is from the Israelites. His counterpart would answer him:

Wouldn't you expect a person who controlled the Tabernacle project to be wealthy?

When Moses heard that, he said to them: By your lives, once the Tabernacle is completed, I will prepare an accounting for you.

(*Tanḥuma* [Buber], *Pekudei*)

Erecting of the Tabernacle

After all the component parts of the Tabernacle were crafted, it was necessary to assemble the structural parts together and put each vessel in its place. Only when the Tabernacle stood ready could the Divine Presence rest in it. The Sages relate that Moses was the only one who was able to assemble the Tabernacle.

Once the Israelites completed the labor of the Tabernacle, they sat and awaited the Divine Presence to come and rest in it. They were all disappointed because the Divine Presence had not yet rested upon it. What did they do? They went to the wise [craftsmen who participated in the preparation of the Tabernacle] and said to them: Why are you sitting there? Erect the Tabernacle so the Divine Presence will rest among us! The craftsmen attempted to erect it, but they did not know how and they were unable to put it up, and when they attempted to erect it – it would collapse.

Immediately, they went to Betzalel and Oholiav. They said to them: You come and erect the Tabernacle, as you are the ones who crafted it. Perhaps through your efforts, it is fit to be erected. Betzalel and Oholiav immediately began to erect it, but were unable to do so. The Israelites began speaking, defaming, and saying: Look what Moses the son of Amram has done to us! He spent all our money on this Tabernacle, and he involved us in all this effort. He told us that the Holy One, blessed be He, would descend from on High and rest in the sheets of goat's hair.

Why were the Israelites unable to erect it? It was because Moses was pained that he had not participated with them in the Tabernacle project. How so? The donations were provided by the Israelites, and the labor was performed by Betzalel and Oholiav and the wise craftsmen. Because Moses was pained, the Holy One, blessed be He, concealed from them what to do and they were unable to erect the Tabernacle.

All Israel approached Moses. They said: Moses our teacher, we have done everything that you told us, and we gave everything that you commanded us to give and to expend. All the work we performed is before you. Have we neglected anything? Did we add anything beyond what you said to

us? Look, everything is before you. And they showed him each and every item…. They said to Moses: Didn't you tell us to do this and that? Moses said to them: Yes. And likewise they had this exchange regarding each and every item. They said to him: If so, why doesn't the Tabernacle stand? Moses was pained by this situation, until the Holy One, blessed be He, said to Moses: Because you were pained that you took no action and you took no part in the Tabernacle project, that is why those wise men were unable to erect it. It is for your sake, so that all Israel will know that if it does not stand through your actions, it will never stand.

Moses said: Master of the Universe, I do not know how to erect it. God said to him: Engage with your hands and go through the motions of erecting it, and it will stand on its own, but I will write about you that you erected it.

(*Tanḥuma, Pekudei*)

Torah – Leviticus

Vayikra

The bulk of the book of Leviticus is devoted to the service in the Sanctuary. *Vayikra*, the first Torah portion of Leviticus, enumerates the procedure of presenting various offerings. It opens with an explanation of the laws of the gift offerings: the burnt offering, the meal offering, and the peace offering. The burnt offering is brought from living beings and burned on the altar in its entirety. The meal offering is brought from plants. Part of it is burned on the altar, with the rest eaten by the priests. The peace offering is brought from living beings. Part of it is burned on the altar, although most of it is eaten by the priests and the one who brought the offering.

After the laws of the gift offerings are enumerated, the laws of offerings brought to effect atonement for transgressions are then described. These are the sin offering and the guilt offering.

The chapter that follows presents statements of the Sages concerning the importance of studying the book of Leviticus, the offerings of the wealthy and the indigent, and the intent of the one bringing the offering.

Let the Pure Come and Engage in the Act of the Pure

There is an ancient custom for children to begin their Torah study with the book of Leviticus, which addresses the laws of the offerings, consecrations, and ritual purity and impurity. The Sages explain that there is no one more appropriate to engage in these matters than children.

Rabbi Asya said: Why do young students begin their studies with the book of Leviticus? It is because all the offerings are written there, and because the children are still pure, as they have not yet tasted sin. Therefore, the Holy One, blessed be He, said that children should begin their studies with the order of the offerings – let the pure come and engage in the act of the pure [i.e., offerings, brought by those who are ritually pure].

Therefore, I ascribe credit to them as though they are standing and sacrificing offerings before Me. And the verse informs you that now that the Holy Temple was destroyed and the rite of the offerings is not performed, leaving the world without their merit, were it not for the young children who read the order of the offerings as a substitute for bringing them, the world would not endure.

(*Tanḥuma, Tzav*)

📖 Further reading: For more about the Torah study of children, see p. 404; *A Concise Guide to Halakha*, p. 512; *A Concise Guide to Mahshava*, p. 186.

The Offerings of the Wealthy and the Indigent

Not only expensive animals are sacrificed on the altar, but also inexpensive birds and even low-priced wheat flour. Even the simple offering of a poor person is no less pleasing before God than any other offering, and when he sacrifices something that is dear to him, it is considered as though he sacrificed his soul.

Rabbi Yohanan said: Any ordinary person who smells the odor of the burning wings of a bird is repulsed, and you say that it should be sacrificed on the altar? Why? So that the altar will be glorified with every part of the offering of a poor person [who cannot afford more than a bird].

There was an incident involving a certain woman who brought one handful of fine flour for a meal offering, and the priest belittled her and said: Look what they are sacrificing! Is there enough here to eat? Is there enough here to sacrifice? The priest saw a message in a dream: Do not belittle her. It is as though she is sacrificing her soul.

(*Vayikra Rabba* 3)

The Intent of the Heart

The primary importance of an offering is not in its monetary value, but rather in the intent of the person bringing it.

It is stated regarding a burnt offering brought from one's livestock: "A fire offering, an aroma pleasing to the Lord" (Leviticus 1:9), and it is stated regarding a bird burnt offering: "A fire offering, an aroma pleasing to the Lord" (1:17), and it is stated regarding a meal offering: "A fire offering, an aroma pleasing to the Lord" (2:2). This usage of the same terminology regarding all three offerings serves to teach you that one who brings a substantial [i.e., an animal] offering and one who brings a meager [i.e., a bird or meal] offering are equal – provided that the one bringing the offering focuses his intent to do so for the sake of Heaven.

(Mishna *Menaḥot* 13:11)

God Seeks the Good of Those That Are Pursued

The animals fit for an offering are from among those that are prey, not from among the predators.

A bull is pursued by a lion, a lamb is pursued by a wolf, a goat is pursued by a leopard. Therefore, the Holy One, blessed be He, said: Do not sacrifice the pursuers before Me, but rather the pursued. "A bull, or a sheep, or a goat, when it is born ... it shall be accepted as a fire offering to the Lord" (Leviticus 22:27).

(Vayikra Rabba [Margaliyot] 27)

📖 **Further reading:** On the inner meaning of the offerings, see *A Concise Guide to Mahshava,* p. 163.

Tzav

The Torah portion of *Tzav* continues the discussion of the laws of the offerings, while introducing and underscoring the details of some laws that relate primarily to the priests themselves. Later in the portion, the verses describe the procedure of the Tabernacle service during the seven days of the Tabernacle's inauguration, during which both the Tabernacle and the priests were consecrated.

The chapter that follows presents statements of the Sages concerning the importance of studying the laws of the offerings, the connection between honesty and the offerings, the fire of the arrangement of wood that was always burning, and the thanks offering.

As Though You Sacrificed

Studying the laws of offerings is tantamount to bringing the offerings themselves.

The Holy One, blessed be He, said to Israel: Even though the Temple is destined to be destroyed and the offerings will be abolished, do not forget the order of the offerings. Instead, take care to read and study them. If you engage in their study, I will ascribe credit to you as though you are engaged in the actual sacrifice of the offerings.

Rabbi Yitzhak said: What is the meaning of that which is written: "This is the law of the sin offering" (Leviticus 6:18) and "this is the law of the guilt offering" (7:1)? This teaches that for anyone who engages in the study of the laws of the sin offering, it is as though he sacrificed an actual sin offering, and for anyone who engages in the study of the laws of the guilt offering, it is as though he sacrificed an actual guilt offering.

(*Tanḥuma, Tzav; Menaḥot* 110a)

An Honest Person

The juxtaposition of the laws of a robber to the continued enumeration of the laws of the offerings led the Sages to underscore the significance of honesty and refraining from engaging in robbery as a fundamental prerequisite for the Temple service and the offerings.

"Command Aaron and his sons, saying: This is the law of the burnt offering" (Leviticus 6:2). The Holy One, blessed be He, said: Fulfill what is written just before this matter, [the prohibition against robbery], and then: "This is

the law of the burnt offering." Why? "For I am the Lord, who loves justice, hates robbery with iniquity [*be'ola*]" (Isaiah 61:8) – I hate robbery even if one steals in order to bring a burnt offering [*be'ola*].

What is written just before this matter? "It shall be when he shall sin and is guilty, he shall restore the robbed item that he robbed" (Leviticus 5:23); and thereafter the verse states: "This is the law of the burnt offering." When do you offer a burnt offering that I accept? When you cleanse your hands from robbery....

And you learn this idea from the beginning of the commands concerning the offerings. The verse states: "Speak to the children of Israel, and say to them: When any man [*adam*] of you brings an offering" (1:2). Why does the verse use the term "*adam*" [when referring to a person, as opposed to the term "*ish*"]? The Holy One, blessed be He, said: When you are sacrificing offerings before Me, be like Adam the first man, who did not steal from others, as he was alone in the world and everything was his. Similarly, you shall not steal from any person. Why? "For I am the Lord, who loves justice, hates robbery with iniquity [*be'ola*]" (Isaiah 61:8).

(*Tanḥuma, Tzav*)

The Altar Fire

At the climax of the Tabernacle's dedication ceremony, described in *Parashat Shemini*, fire descends from the heavens and kindles the wood arrangement on the bronze altar. Even though that fire burned perpetually, there is a commandment to add fire kindled by a person to it.

"The sons of Aaron the priest shall place fire upon the altar" (Leviticus 1:7). Even though the fire on the altar descends from the heavens, there is a commandment to place fire from an ordinary source. The fire that descended during the days of Moses did not leave the bronze altar where offerings were sacrificed until the Israelites arrived at [i.e., built] the eternal Temple. The fire that descended during the days of Solomon did not leave the altar of the burnt offering until it left hundreds of years later during the days of Menashe [a king from the house of David who sinned excessively].

(*Sifra, Vayikra Dibbura diNedava* 4)

The Thanks Offering

The thanks offering is particularly beloved because it is offered voluntarily, out of a desire to give thanks to God.

And the sin offering would come to atone for specific unwitting actions… a burnt offering would come to atone for improper thoughts…but when the thanks offering comes, it comes for no particular reason. The Holy One, blessed be He, said: This thanks offering is more beloved to Me than all the other offerings.

(*Tanḥuma* [Buber], *Tzav*)

Further reading: For more on gratitude, see p. 89.

Shemini

The Torah portion begins with the dedication of the Tabernacle. After the seven days of inauguration, a ceremony was held, at whose climax a fire descended from the heavens and ignited the arrangement of wood that was on the altar. In the meantime, a tragic incident transpired, when the two sons of Aaron, Nadav and Avihu, offered a "strange fire" in the Tabernacle and died. The portion also addresses how Aaron and his remaining sons coped with and reacted to this tragedy. In the second part of the Torah portion, the extensive treatment of the laws of ritual purity and impurity begins. The last section of this Torah portion details which creatures are permitted for consumption, and likewise which are prohibited.

The chapter that follows presents statements of the Sages concerning the selection of Aaron to the position of the priesthood, the sin of Nadav and Avihu, the evils of intoxication, and the dietary laws that are unique to the Jewish people.

Moses and Aaron

It was specifically Aaron, not Moses, who merited the crown of the priesthood. The Sages explain that this is because of Moses' earlier hesitation to accept the mission with which God tasked him when he was in Midyan. Despite this, Moses rejoiced in the joy of his brother and was not envious.

[After the seven days of inauguration, on the day of the dedication of the Tabernacle, the verse states:] "It was on the eighth day that Moses summoned Aaron and his sons, and the elders of Israel" (Leviticus 9:1). Our Sages said: On all seven days that Moses was at the burning bush, the Holy One, blessed be He, said to him: Go as My emissary. Moses said to Him: "Please send by means of whom You will send" (Exodus 4:13). So it was on the first and second days. The Holy One, blessed be He, said to Moses: I tell you: Go, and you say to Me: "Please send by means of whom You will send"? I take an oath by your life that in the future, I will repay you. When the Tabernacle will be built, you will believe that you will serve in the High Priesthood, but I will tell you: Call Aaron so that he can serve. Therefore, it is stated: "Moses summoned Aaron and his sons" (Leviticus 9:1).

Moses said to Aaron: This is what the Holy One, blessed be He, told me: To appoint you as the High Priest. Aaron said to him: You exerted yourself in building the Tabernacle, and I will become the High Priest? Moses responded: I take an oath by your life that even though you are becoming

the High Priest, it is as though I am being appointed. Just as you rejoiced with my ascent to greatness when I was chosen to lead the Israelites, I rejoice with your ascent to greatness.

Why did Moses summon the elders of Israel? He did so in order to promote Aaron in the presence of the elders. The Holy One, blessed be He, said: Summon the elders and anoint Aaron, and I will confer greatness upon him in their presence, so they will not say: He became High Priest at his own initiative.

(*Tanḥuma, Shemini*)

📖 **Further reading:** For the story of Moses' appointment as leader of the nation, see *A Concise Guide to the Torah*, p. 139.

The Sons of Aaron

At the climax of the Tabernacle's dedication, the two elder sons of Aaron, Nadav and Avihu, died because they offered "a strange fire that [God] had not commanded them." The Sages explain what exactly their sin was.

Aaron's sons died due to four matters: for the approach, for the sacrifice, for the strange fire, and for not consulting with each other. For the approach – this is because they entered into the Holy of Holies … for the sacrifice – this is because they sacrificed an offering that they were not commanded … for the strange fire – this means that they introduced fire from a stove [not from the altar] … and for not consulting with each other – … this means that each of them acted on his own ….

In four places the Torah mentions the death of Aaron's sons, and in all of them it mentions their sin. Why is their sin emphasized to that extent? It is emphasized to inform you that they had committed only that sin. Rabbi Elazar HaModa'i said: Come and see how significant the death of Aaron's sons is before the Holy One, blessed be He. As every place that He mentions their death in the Torah He mentions their sins. Why is their sin emphasized to that extent? It is emphasized to inform you of their sin, so that there will not be room for people to claim: They performed terrible actions in private, and that is why they died.

(*Vayikra Rabba* 20)

Who Buries Whom

Nadav and Avihu were arrogant and coveted authority; ultimately, they died untimely deaths.

Moses and Aaron were walking on their way, and Nadav and Avihu were walking behind them, and all the Israelites were walking behind Nadav and Avihu. Nadav said to Avihu: When will these two old men die so that you and I will lead the generation? The Holy One, blessed be He, said to them: We will see who buries whom.

(*Sanhedrin* 52a)

Wine Enters, a Secret Emerges

After the death of Nadav and Avihu, the priests were commanded not to drink wine or any intoxicating beverage before performing the Tabernacle service. The Sages explain that it is incumbent upon a priest serving in the house of God to maintain his sobriety.

You shall not drink wine or intoxicating drink, neither you nor your sons with you, upon your entry into the Tent of Meeting (Leviticus 10:9) ... Rabbi Yehuda HaLevi son of Rabbi Shalom said: In Hebrew, wine is called *yayin*; in Aramaic, wine is called *ḥamar* – which, in *gematriya*,[1] totals 248 [*ḥet* = 8, *mem* = 40, *resh* = 200], parallel to a person's 248 limbs. The wine enters into each and every limb, and the body grows weak, and the drinker's rationality is undermined. Wine enters and rationality departs. Likewise, Rabbi Eliezer HaKappar taught: Wine enters and a secret emerges. Wine [*yayin*], which in *gematriya* totals seventy [*yod* = 10, *yod* = 10, *nun* = 50], enters, and a secret [*sod*], which totals seventy [*samekh* = 60, *vav* = 6, *dalet* = 4], emerges.

Therefore, Aaron the High Priest was commanded that priests may not drink wine during the service, so that their rationality will not be undermined; rather, they must observe the Torah and maintain rationality.

(*Tanḥuma, Shemini*)

Intoxication

Intoxication is odious, and the Sages illustrate through an anecdote that the craving for alcoholic drink is so powerful that it is apt to overcome any logical considerations.

---

1. *Gematriya* is a system in which each Hebrew letter is given a numerical value. It often highlights connections, sometimes mystical ones, between words.

There was a pious student whose father drank a lot of wine. Whenever he would fall in the street, people would come and pelt him with stones and pebbles, and shout after him: Look, a drunkard!

Whenever his pious son would see this, he would be ashamed and would wish to die. Every day he would say to him: Father, I will send messengers and they will bring you home, away from all the wine that they have in the city, and you will not go drinking wine in the pub, as you are making a mockery of both me and you. The son would tell him this once or twice each day, until his father told him that he would do as his son says and not go drinking wine in the pub. And this is what the pious son did: He would prepare food and drink for his father each day and night, and he would put him to sleep in his bed, and then he would go.

One day it was raining. The pious son went out to the street on his way to the synagogue for prayer, and he saw a drunkard lying in the street with a stream of water falling on him. The young men and the lads were pelting him with stones and pebbles and were casting mud on his face and into his mouth. When the pious son saw this, he said to himself: I will go to my father and bring him here, and I will show him this drunkard and the mockery that the young men and the lads are making of him. Perhaps then he will refrain from drinking wine in the pub and from becoming intoxicated. He did so. He brought his father there and showed him.

What did the elderly father do? He went to the drunkard and asked him in which pub he drank the wine with which he became intoxicated so that he could drink of that same wine. His pious son said to him: Is it for this that I called you? I called you only so you could see the mockery they are making of him, as they do to you when you drink, and perhaps you would refrain from drinking in the pub. His father said to him: My son, I take an oath by my life that I have no pleasure or paradise other than drinking. When the pious son heard this, he went away bitterly disappointed.

(*Tanḥuma, Shemini*)

The Forbidden Foods

This *parasha* enumerates the living beings whose consumption is permitted and those whose consumption is forbidden. These prohibitions apply exclusively to the Israelite people. The Sages explain, by means of a parable, why it is specifically the Israelites who must eat kosher food.

This can be explained by means of a parable. To what is this matter comparable? It is comparable to a doctor who went to visit two ill people. He saw one of them in danger [i.e., close to death]. He said to the members of his household: Give him any food he requests. He saw the other one, who was destined to survive. He said to the members of his household: He may eat this kind of food, but he may not eat that kind of food.

They said to the doctor: What is this? You told this one that he may eat any food that he requests, but you told the other one not to eat such and such. The doctor said to them: Concerning the one who will live, I said: Eat this but do not eat that. But concerning the one who will die, I said to them: Give him anything he requests, because he is going to die soon anyway [so there is no reason to deprive him].

So too, the Holy One, blessed be He, permitted worshippers of stars and constellations to eat repugnant creatures and creeping animals. But to the Israelites, who are destined to live in the World to Come, He said: "This you may eat," and "these you shall not eat." Why? Because they are destined to live in the World to Come, as it is stated: "But you, who cleave to the Lord your God, all of you live today" (Deuteronomy 4:4).

(*Tanḥuma*, Shemini)

Purity and Impurity

The prohibited foods render impure those who eat them, while abstaining from them causes a person to be sanctified. Every minute action of a person carries significant consequences.

The Sages taught: The verse states: "And you shall not be rendered impure by them, and become impure through them" (Leviticus 11:43). [The repetition of the word impure means that] if a person renders himself a little impure, he is rendered extremely impure; if a person renders himself impure from below [at his own initiative], he is rendered impure from above; if a person renders himself impure in this world, he is rendered impure in the World to Come.

The Sages taught: The verse states: "You shall sanctify yourselves and be sanctified" (11:44). [The repetition of a term of sanctity means that] if a person sanctifies himself a little, he is sanctified a lot; if a person sanctifies himself from below, he is sanctified from above; if a person sanctifies himself in this world, he is sanctified in the World to Come.

(*Yoma* 39a)

Tazria

This Torah portion continues addressing the laws of purity and impurity. It begins with the *halakhot* of the impurity of a woman after childbirth. Along with this, the commandment of circumcision is stated. The rest of the Torah portion is devoted to the laws of the impurity of leprosy – leprosy of the body, leprosy of a garment, and other types of marks that appear on the skin or on a garment.

The chapter that follows presents statements of the Sages concerning the creations of people vis-à-vis the creations of the Creator; the beloved status and virtue of the commandment of circumcision; and the importance of guarding one's tongue, which is closely associated with leprosy.

The Creations of the Creator and the Creations of People

At the beginning of the Torah portion, the verse instructs that one must circumcise a newborn boy on the eighth day. The Sages relate an exchange between Rabbi Akiva and Turnusrofus, the Roman prefect who ruled in the Land of Israel, regarding the question: Why do we attempt to improve upon the acts of the Creator?

Turnusrofus asked a question of Rabbi Akiva, saying to him: Which is superior, the creations of the Creator or the creations of people? Rabbi Akiva immediately understood his intent. He said to himself: This cursed one is using subterfuge to confound me concerning circumcision. If I answer him that the creations of people are superior, he will kill me for treating the Creator with contempt. If I answer him that the creations of the Creator are superior, then too, he will kill me, saying: Why are you modifying what the Creator willed by performing circumcision?

Rabbi Akiva said: My lord the king, wait two hours for me until I go home and return. Turnusrofus said to him: Go. Rabbi Akiva went home and said to his wife: I want you to prepare for me now one very fine loaf of bread, sifted of bran and waste, with a little oil, sesame, and nigella seeds. Immediately, his wife prepared for him a loaf of a higher quality than what he had requested. Rabbi Akiva took the loaf and took a little wheat, and came before the king. Rabbi Akiva said to him: My lord the king, by your life! Answer me this question that I will ask you before I answer you the question that you asked me. Turnusrofus said to him: What do you want? Rabbi Akiva said to him: My lord the king, which is finer: This loaf, or these wheat kernels? The king said to him: This loaf is finer.

Rabbi Akiva said: My lord the king, you have answered the question that you asked me, because you just now said that the actions of people are superior. As in this case, the creation of the Creator is the wheat kernel and the creation of people is the loaf. You asked me your question because of circumcision and you were using subterfuge to confound me. But now, you yourself answered, and your own mouth responded to your question.

Turnusrofus said to him: Rabbi Akiva, You have answered well. But if a circumcised male is preferable, why didn't the Holy One, blessed be He, create man circumcised? Rabbi Akiva said to him: If so, why didn't the Holy One, blessed be He, create the umbilical cord cut? Why did He leave it so that the person must cut it? The Creator created this circumstance [that the male child needs completing] in order to refine His creations by their performing His mitzvot.

(*Midrash Aggada* [Buber], *Vayikra, Shemini–Tazria* 12)

Your Covenant That You Stamped in Our Flesh

The commandment of circumcision is especially dear: The result of the mitzva is impressed upon the body of the man himself, and accompanies him everywhere, and at all times.

When David entered the bathhouse and saw himself standing naked, he said: Woe is me that that I am standing naked, without any mitzva. Once he remembered the circumcision in his flesh, his mind was put at ease, as he realized he was still accompanied by this mitzva. After he left the bathhouse, he recited a song about the mitzva of circumcision, as it is stated: "For the chief musician, on the eight-stringed harp [*hasheminit*], a psalm by David" (Psalms 12:1). This is a reference to circumcision, which was given to be performed on the eighth [*bashemini*] day.

(*Menaḥot* 43b)

Who Is the Man Who Desires Life

According to the Sages, the type of leprosy detailed in the Torah is a punishment for malicious speech. In this tale, a merchant offers passersby an elixir of life: Be scrupulous with your speech and your actions.

"This shall be the law of the leper" (Leviticus 14:2) – that is the meaning of what is written: "Who is the man who desires life, loving his days to see good?" (Psalms 34:13). There was an incident involving a peddler circulat-

ing in the towns that were adjacent to Tzipori. He would proclaim: Let anyone who wishes to purchase an elixir of life come and take it. He entered Akhbera and approached the residence of Rabbi Yannai. Rabbi Yannai was sitting and changing clothes in his room, and heard him proclaim: Is there anyone who wishes to purchase an elixir of life? Rabbi Yannai said to him: Come and enter here, sell it to me. The peddler said to him: You and those like you do not need to get it [from me, as you already have it].

Rabbi Yannai implored him to enter, and he entered. The peddler took out a scroll of Psalms, and showed him this verse: "Who is the man who desires life, loving his days to see good?" (Psalms 34:13). What is written after it? "Guard your tongue from evil and your lips from speaking deceit. Turn away from evil and do good; seek peace and pursue it" (Psalms 34:14–15). Rabbi Yannai said: All my days I would read this verse, but I did not know how straightforward it is, until this peddler came and informed me: "Who is the man who desires life." Therefore, Moses cautioned the Israelites and said to them: "This shall be the law of the leper [metzora]," which is an allusion to the law of the slanderer, [as the Hebrew term for slanderer, motzi shem ra, is similar to the Hebrew term for leper, metzora]. Moses thereby warned them of the severity of speaking evil.

(*Vayikra Rabba* 16)

Metzora

The Torah portion continues the discussion of the laws of leprosy, and enumerates the procedure of the leper's purification and the laws of leprosy of the house. The verses then discuss the impurities relating to emissions that secrete from a person's body, the impurity of *ziva* and semen, and the impurity of the menstruant and the *zava*.

The chapter that follows presents statements of the Sages concerning the power of speech, the purification ceremony of the leper, and the good tidings latent in leprosy of the house.

Their Tongue Is a Sharp Sword

According to the Sages, the leprosy discussed in the Torah was often the punishment for malicious speech. The Sages likened speaking slander to shooting an arrow, which can easily kill even someone far away.

Our Sages said: Leprosy afflicts a person only due to the slander that emerges from his mouth. The verse states: "This shall be the law of the leper" (Leviticus 14:2) – this is consistent with what the verse says: "Death and life are in the power of the tongue" (Proverbs 18:21). Everything is contingent on the tongue: If a person merits – he will merit life, if he does not merit – he will be condemned to death. If a person engaged in Torah with his tongue – he merits life, as the Torah is called life … and Torah study is his cure for slander. If he engaged in slander – he has condemned his soul to die, as slander is more severe than bloodshed. As one who kills, kills only one soul, while one who speaks slander kills three: the one who speaks the slander, the one who accepts it as true, and the one about whom it was spoken.

Who is more dangerous: One who strikes another with a sword or one who strikes him with an arrow? You must say that one who strikes another with an arrow is more dangerous. One who strikes another with a sword can kill another only if the attacker drew near to him and touched him, which is not the case with one who strikes another with an arrow. He shoots the arrow and strikes him anywhere that he sees him. That is why the speaker of slander is likened to one who attacks with an arrow, as it is stated: "A sharpened arrow is their tongue …" (Jeremiah 9:7).

Alternatively: "Death and life are in the power of the tongue" means as follows: Do not say: Since I have been given license to speak, I will speak

anything that I please. The Torah has already cautioned you: "Guard your tongue from evil and your lips from speaking deceit" (Psalms 34:14). Lest you say that as a result of refraining from such speech you will lose, you will only gain. The divine inspiration shouts: "He who guards his mouth and his tongue guards himself from troubles [*mitzarot*]" (Proverbs 21:23). Do not read the verse as it is written; rather, read it as stating that he "guards himself from leprosy [*mitzara'at*]."

(*Tanḥuma* [Buber], *Metzora*)

The Purification Process of the Leper

When the leprosy was no longer present on the person's body, a purification ritual involving two birds, various types of plants, and additional items was conducted. The Sages explain the connection between the components of the ritual and the actions of the leper.

"This shall be the law of the leper on the day of his purification" (Leviticus 14:2). With what is he purified? He is purified with "two living pure birds, and cedar wood, and scarlet wool, and hyssop" (14:4).

Why is his offering different from all the other offerings? Since he spoke slander, therefore the verse says that his offering includes "birds," whose voices are heard at a distance....

"And cedar wood." There is no tree taller than the cedar. Because the slanderer elevated himself like a cedar, he was afflicted with leprosy, as Rabbi Shimon ben Elazar said: Leprosy comes due to haughtiness....

"And hyssop." There are no trees lower than the hyssop. Because he humbled himself [by isolating himself from society while he was a leper], therefore he is cured by means of hyssop.

"And one shall slaughter the one bird" (Leviticus 14:5). Why does one slaughter one bird and send one bird away to fly away freely? It is because [the Torah is teaching the leper]: If you repent, you will not experience leprosy again; but if you do not repent, the leprosy will return to you, just as the living bird could return.

Leprosy of the House

According to the Sages, leprosy that appeared on the walls of the house that was of the type that mandated the dwelling's destruction would occasionally benefit the homeowner.

"When you come to the land of Canaan … I shall place a mark of leprosy on a house in the land of your ancestral portion" (Leviticus 14:34). Rabbi Hiyya taught: Are these good tidings,[2] that leprosy is going to afflict them? Rabbi Shimon ben Yoḥai taught: When the Canaanites heard that the Israelites were coming to do battle against them, they arose and concealed their property in the houses and the fields.

The Holy One, blessed be He, said: I promised the Israelites' ancestors that I will bring their descendants into a land full of everything good, as it is stated: "And houses full of everything good" (Deuteronomy 6:10). What does the Holy One, blessed be He, do to fulfill that promise? He instigates leprosy in an Israelite's house [that was previously resided in by a Canaanite], and when the Israelite demolishes it, he finds a treasure. His field is blighted, and in the course of plowing, he finds a treasure.

(*Vayikra Rabba* 17)

---

2. By stating: "I shall place a mark of leprosy on a house," instead of: If there will be a mark of leprosy on a house, the verse indicates that this is an event they should be looking forward to.

Aharei Mot

The first part of the Torah portion of *Aharei Mot* addresses the detailed procedure of the Temple service of Yom Kippur. After that, there are several commands relating to the procedures of the slaughter of animals. The final section of the Torah portion addresses forbidden sexual relations.

The chapter that follows presents statements of the Sages concerning the giving of one's life to fulfill a commandment of God, the Torah commandments that do and do not have apparent reasons, and "the practices of the land of Egypt…and the practices of the land of Canaan," i.e., forbidden sexual relations.

Self-Sacrifice and the Sanctification of God's Name

In general, a human life is of paramount value from the perspective of the Torah, and one is not required to sacrifice his life in order to fulfill its commandments. But in the context of specific commandments, or under specific circumstances, the sacrifice of one's life constitutes the sanctification of God's name in the world.

The commandments were given to Israel only so they could live by them, as it is stated: "Which a person shall perform and live by them" (Leviticus 18:5). The verse teaches: "And live by them," and not that one should die by observing them. There is nothing that stands in the face of a life-threatening situation except for idol worship, forbidden sexual relations, and bloodshed [where one must refrain from violating these prohibitions even it costs him his life].

In what case is that said? It is said when it is not a time of persecution by the government. But in a time of persecution a person must sacrifice his life even for the observance of the least significant commandment.

(*Tosefta Shabbat* 15:17)

📖 Further reading: For more about the sacrifice of one's life to sanctify the name of God, see *A Concise Guide to Mahshava*, p. 198.

Ordinances and Statutes

There is no difference at all between commandments whose fulfillment is dictated by reason and the commandments that have no apparent logical rationale. Both are statutes of the Lord.

The Sages taught: "You shall perform My ordinances" (Leviticus 18:4). These are matters that even had they not been written, logically they should have been written, and these are: idol worship, forbidden sexual relations, bloodshed, theft, and cursing God.

"And My statutes you shall observe" (18:4). These are matters to which the accuser and the nations of the world object to their relevance, and these are: the prohibition against eating pork, the prohibition against wearing a mixture of wool and linen, the mitzva of freeing of a woman from her levirate bond to allow her to marry a man other than her late husband's brother, the purification ritual of a leper, and the sending of the scapegoat sent to Mount Azazel on Yom Kippur and killed there to atone for the sins of the people.

Lest you say: These mitzvot are meaningless, the verse states: "I am the Lord" (18:4). I, the Lord, legislated them, and you do not have the right to doubt them.

(*Yoma* 67b)

Further reading: For more about Torah being from the heavens, see *A Concise Guide to Mahshava*, p. 269.

The Practices of the Land of Egypt

In introducing forbidden sexual relations, the Torah commands the Jewish people to refrain from engaging in "the practices of the land of Egypt…and the practices of the land of Canaan" (Leviticus 18:3). The Sages explain that this does not mean one should refrain from every practice the Egyptians and Canaanites engaged in, but rather from the statutes that were uniquely theirs.

The verse states: "You shall not do the practices of the land of Egypt…and the practices of the land of Canaan" (18:3). Could it be that the Israelites shall not build buildings and plant saplings as the Egyptians and Canaanites did? The verse states: "And you shall not follow their statutes" (18:3) – I spoke only concerning the statutes that were legislated uniquely for them, and for their fathers, and for their ancestors. What would they do? A man would marry a man, and a woman would marry a woman; a man would marry a woman and her daughter, and a woman would marry two men. Concerning this it is stated: "And you shall not follow their statutes."

(*Sifra, Aharei Mot* 8)

Like a Lily among the Thorns

The Sages teach that both in Egypt and in Canaan, the Israelites were like a beautiful flower growing in thorny surroundings. They were surrounded by sinners steeped in sexual immorality. They also underscore the severity of the sin of promiscuity, which is apt to introduce indiscriminate killing into the world.

Rabbi Berekhya said: The Holy One, blessed be He, said to Moses: Go tell the Israelites: My children, when you were in Egypt, you were like a lily among the thorns. Now you are coming to the land of Canaan [and will again be surrounded by sinners]; continue to be like a lily among the thorns. Be vigilant that you do not perform the actions of these Egyptians or the actions of those Canaanites ....

Rabbi Yishmael taught: "You shall not do the practices of the land of Egypt ... and the practices of the land of Canaan ... I am the Lord your God" (Leviticus 18:3–4). And if not [i.e., if you do engage in those practices], it is as if I am not the Lord your God.

Rabbi Hiyya taught: "I am the Lord your God" is repeated twice (18:2, 4). The repetition serves to say: I am the One who punished in the past the generation of the flood, the people of Sodom and Gomorrah, and the people of Egypt, and I am destined to punish in the future anyone who acts in accordance with the actions of those people. The generation of the flood consisted of dignitaries who were eliminated from the world because they were steeped in lewdness. Rabbi Simlai said: Any place that you find promiscuity, death comes to the world and indiscriminately kills the good and the evil.

(*Vayikra Rabba* [Margaliyot] 23)

Kedoshim

In the Torah portion of *Kedoshim*, there is a broad range of commandments and prohibitions. There are commandments relating to interpersonal relations, prohibitions relating to idol worship, commandments relating to crops, and an extensive treatment of matters relating to forbidden sexual relations. All of these are designed to establish a society characterized by a sacred lifestyle.

The chapter that follows presents statements of the Sages concerning respecting and fearing one's parents, improving the world for the benefit of the person himself and for the benefit of subsequent generations, the prohibition against giving bad advice, and the commandment to rebuke, yet love, one's neighbor.

Honoring One's Father and Fearing One's Mother

The Torah states concerning a person's parents: "Each of you shall fear his mother and his father" (Leviticus 19:3). The Sages teach that the verse first lists the parent whom one naturally fears less.

Rabbi Yehuda HaNasi says: It is revealed and known before the One who spoke and the world came into being that a person honors his mother more than his father, because one's mother persuades him with affectionate speech. Therefore, He gave precedence to the father before the mother in the commandment to honor one's parents (Exodus 20:12). And it is revealed and known before the One who spoke and the world came into being that a person fears his father more than his mother, because one's father teaches him Torah. Therefore, He gave precedence to the mother before the father in the commandment to fear one's parents (Leviticus 19:3).

(Mekhilta deRabbi Yishmael, Yitro, Mesekhta deBaḥodesh 8)

For the Sake of Subsequent Generations

One cannot be satisfied with the world as he received it from those who preceded him; he must seek to improve it so those who succeed him will enjoy it as he did.

"When you shall come into the land and plant" (Leviticus 19:23): The Holy One, blessed be He, said to the Israelites: Even though you will find the Land of Israel filled with everything good, do not say: We will sit idly and will not plant. Rather, be vigilant in your planting, as it is stated: "And plant any food

tree" (19:23). Just as you entered and found trees planted by others, so too, you shall plant trees for the benefit of your children.

In order that a person will not say: I am old and tomorrow I will die; why should I exert myself for others? Solomon said: "He made everything beautiful in its time; He put the world [*ha'olam*] too in their heart" (Ecclesiastes 3:11). [The word *ha'olam* is written without the letter *vav*, so that] concealment [*he'elem*] is written. Why? Had the Holy One, blessed be He, not concealed the day of death from people, a person would not build and he would not plant, as he would say: I will die tomorrow; why should I exert myself for the benefit of others? Therefore, the Holy One, blessed be He, concealed the day of death from people's hearts, so that a person would build and plant. If he merits, what he builds and plants will be for him; if he does not merit, it will be for others.

(*Tanḥuma, Kedoshim*)

You Shall Not Place an Obstruction before the Blind

One of the prohibitions that appear in this Torah portion is the prohibition against causing a blind person to stumble. In addition to its literal meaning, the Sages also understood the specific example written in the verse as a metaphor, prohibiting giving bad advice.

"You shall not place an obstruction before the blind" (Leviticus 19:14). This means not to place an obstruction before someone who is blind concerning a specific matter…. If one is seeking advice from you, do not give him advice that is not appropriate for him…Lest you claim to him, disingenuously: It is good advice that I am giving you, know that intent is determined by the heart, as it is stated in the next clause of the verse: "You shall fear your God, I am the Lord" [and God knows if you intended to give good advice].

(*Sifra, Kedoshim* 2)

Rebuke

This Torah portion records the commandment to rebuke others. According to the Sages, it is no simple matter to issue a proper rebuke, or to wholeheartedly accept words of rebuke.

Rabbi Tarfon said: I take an oath by the Temple service that there is no one in this generation who can give rebuke. Rabbi Elazar ben Azarya said: I take an oath by the Temple service that there is no one in this generation capable

of accepting words of rebuke. Rabbi Akiva said: I take an oath by the Temple service that there is no one in this generation who knows how to rebuke effectively.

(*Sifra, Kedoshim* 2)

You Shall Love Your Neighbor as Yourself

Loving another stems from the fact that all people were created in the image of God. Rabbi Akiva says: "You shall love your neighbor as yourself" (Leviticus 19:18); this is a fundamental principle in the Torah. One should not [think to treat his fellow as himself in all ways and] say: Since I was humiliated, let my fellow be humiliated with me; since I was cursed, let my fellow be cursed with me.[3]

Rabbi Tanhuma said: If you do act in this way, know whom you are humiliating: [A person created in the image of God, and by extension, God. As the verse states:] "In the likeness of God He made him" (Genesis 5:1).

(*Bereshit Rabba* 24)

📖 **Further reading:** For the *halakhot* dictating conduct between people, see *A Concise Guide to Halakha*, p. 597.

---

3. One treats his fellow like himself only with regard to treating him with love.

Emor

The first part of the Torah portion of *Emor* resumes the discussion of the Temple and associated matters, primarily the laws unique to priests, e.g., the prohibition against becoming impure with impurity imparted by a corpse, alongside laws related to offerings and consecrations. An additional lengthy section addresses Shabbat and the festivals, in which the Torah details the appointed times and commandments of Shabbat; Passover – including the laws of the *omer* offering, the counting of the *omer*, and the festival of *Shavuot*; Rosh HaShana; Yom Kippur; and *Sukkot*. At the end of the Torah portion, we read of the commands to kindle the lights in the Temple candelabrum and to place the showbread on the table in the Sanctuary.

The chapter that follows presents statements of the Sages concerning the animal species fit to be presented as offerings, with the ox primary among them; the relationship between the commandments that a person fulfills and the kindness of God that enables their fulfillment; the commandments to reap the *omer*, to present the *omer* offering, and to wave the *omer*; the rejoicing on the festivals; and the episode of the blasphemer.

Ox, Sheep, and Goats

The animals fit to serve as offerings are domesticated farm animals, not wild animals. The reason for this is in order to spare a person the exertion involved in trapping an animal to bring as an offering.

"An ox, or a sheep, or a goat, when it is born … it shall be accepted as a fire offering to the Lord" (Leviticus 22:27). Rabbi Yehuda bar Rabbi Shimon said that the Holy One, blessed be He, said: I have provided you with ten animal species of kosher animals. Three are under your control and seven are not under your control. Three are under your control: "An ox, a sheep, and a goat" (Deuteronomy 14:4), and seven are not under your control: "A deer, and a gazelle, and a fallow deer, and a wild goat, and an oryx, and an aurochs, and a wild sheep" (Deuteronomy 14:5). I did not make matters difficult for you by telling you to exhaust yourselves in the mountains to bring offerings before Me from the animals that are not under your control, but rather from the animals that are under your control – those that feed from your trough. That is the meaning of what is written: "An ox, or a sheep, or a goat" (Leviticus 22:27).

(*Vayikra Rabba* 27)

📖 **Further reading:** To learn more about animals fit for offerings, see p. 134.

The Ox – Primary among the Offerings

The ox is listed first among the animals fit to serve as offerings. The reason is that the ox is associated with the sin of the Golden Calf, and God wanted to indicate that the Israelite people as a whole were innocent of that sin.

What did God see in the ox that led Him to make it primary among the offerings? Rabbi Levi said: This can be explained by means of a parable of a matron, about whom rumors circulated that she had an affair with one of the prominent men of the kingdom. The king investigated the matter and discovered that it was without basis. What did the king do? He made a feast and seated that man at the head of the table, to inform everyone that the king investigated and discovered that the rumors were without basis.

Similarly, the nations of the word were saying to the Israelites: You made and worshipped the Golden Calf. The Holy One, blessed be He, investigated and discovered that their allegations were without basis [as the primary actors in that sin were outsiders who appended themselves to the Israelite people]; therefore, the ox was made primary among the offerings.

(*Tanḥuma, Emor*)

Who Surpasses Me I Will Pay

People would not be able to give anything to God if He did not first provide them with the wherewithal to do so.

Rabbi Yirmeya ben Elazar said: A divine voice [*bat kol*] is destined to resonate on the mountain peaks and say: Let anyone who worked in cooperation with the Holy One, blessed be He, come and collect his reward. The divine spirit will proclaim: "Who surpasses Me? I will pay; everything beneath the heavens is Mine" (Job 41:3). Who praised Me before I instilled a soul in him? Who performed a circumcision before Me before I gave him a son? Who prepared fringes before Me before I gave him a garment? Who built a parapet before I gave him a roof? Who built a *sukka* before I gave him a place to build it? Who separated *pe'a* before I gave him a field? Who separated *teruma* and tithes for Me before I gave him a granary? Who presented an offering before Me before I gave him an animal?

(*Tanḥuma, Emor*)

From "the Day after the Sabbath"

The Torah states that the *omer* offering is sacrificed on "the day after the Sabbath." In this context, "Sabbath" means the first festival day of Passover. Therefore, the *omer* must be cut and sacrificed on the sixteenth of Nisan. Because there was a sect that adopted an alternative interpretation, the Sages were insistent that the cutting of the *omer* take place publicly and festively.

How would they perform the rite of the *omer* harvesting? Emissaries of the court would emerge on the eve of the festival of Passover and fashion the stalks of barley into sheaves while the stalks were still attached to the ground, so that it would be easier to reap them. The residents of all the adjacent towns would assemble there, so that the barley for the *omer* offering would be harvested with great fanfare.

Once it grew dark, the court emissary would say to those assembled: Did the sun set? The assembly would say: Yes. He would again ask: Did the sun set? They would say: Yes. He would then ask: Shall I reap the sheaves with this sickle? They would say in response: Yes. He would again ask: With this sickle? They would say: Yes. He would ask: Shall I place the gathered sheaves in this basket? They would say: Yes. He would again ask: In this basket? They would say: Yes.

If the day for harvesting the *omer* would occur on Shabbat, the court emissary would say to those assembled: Shall I cut the sheaves on this Shabbat? The assembly would say in response: Yes. He would again ask: On this Shabbat? They would say: Yes. He would ask: Shall I cut the sheaves? They would say to him: Cut. He would again ask: Shall I cut the sheaves? They would say to him: Cut. The emissary asks three times with regard to each and every matter, and the assembly would say to him: Yes, yes, yes. Why did they need publicity to that extent? It is due to the Boethusians, as they deny the validity of the Oral Law and would say: There is no harvest of the *omer* at the conclusion of the first festival day [of Passover, unless it occurs at the conclusion of Shabbat].

(Mishna *Menaḥot* 10:3)

The Waving of the *Omer*

Before the *omer* meal offering was sacrificed on the altar, a priest would wave the offering in the air. The Sages explain the symbolism of this waving: It served as an acknowledgment of the kingdom of God, who rules over the entire world, and it served as a request that the Jewish people's produce will be blessed and protected from blight.

Rabbi Yehuda said in the name of Rabbi Akiva: For what reason did the Torah say: Bring the *omer* offering on the second day of Passover? It is because Passover is the beginning of the grain harvest season. Therefore, the Holy One, blessed be He, said: Bring the *omer* offering before Me on Passover so that the grain in the fields will be blessed for you.

"He shall wave the sheaf before the Lord" (Leviticus 23:11). How would he wave it? Rabbi Hama son of Rabbi Ukva said in the name of Rabbi Yosei son of Rabbi Hanina: He moves it back and forth and he raises and lowers it. He moves it back and forth in order to eliminate harmful winds, he raises and lowers it in order to eliminate harmful dews.

Rabbi Shimon said in the name of Rabbi Yehoshua ben Levi: He moves it back and forth to dedicate it to He to whom the entire world all four directions belongs. He raises and lowers them to He to whom the entire world all four directions belongs.

(*Rosh HaShana* 16a; *Vayikra Rabba*, 28)

📖 Further reading: For more about the counting of the *omer*, see *A Concise Guide to Halakha*, p. 331.

Rejoicing on the Festivals

In this Torah portion, there is an additional commandment to rejoice on the festival of *Sukkot*, a commandment that is repeated elsewhere in the Torah. The Sages address the question: Why is the rejoicing on the festival of *Sukkot* so great, while it is relatively restrained on the other festivals?

You find three mentions of rejoicing written regarding the festival of *Sukkot*: "You shall rejoice on your festival" (Deuteronomy 15:14), "And you shall be completely joyous" (Deuteronomy 15:15), "You shall rejoice before the Lord your God seven days" (Leviticus 23:40). But on Passover you do not find even one mention of rejoicing written in its regard. Why? You find that on Passover the world is judged concerning grain, and a person does not know whether his land will produce a plentiful grain crop this year or whether it will not produce a plentiful crop.

Alternatively: There is no verse that mentions rejoicing on Passover, because the Egyptians died then. Likewise you find that we recite *Hallel* all seven days of the festival of *Sukkot*, but on Passover we recite *Hallel* only on the first festival day and its preceding night. Why? Due to the idea of: "Do not rejoice at the fall of your enemy" (Proverbs 24:17).

Similarly, you find that only one mention of rejoicing is written concerning *Shavuot*, as it is written: "You shall hold the festival of *Shavuot* to the

Lord your God…you shall rejoice before the Lord your God" (Deuteronomy 16:10–11). Why is one mention of rejoicing written concerning *Shavuot*? It is because of [the joy of] the produce being gathered from the fields. What is the reason that two mentions of rejoicing are not written there? It is because the joy is tempered, as the world is judged on *Shavuot* concerning the fruit of the trees.

But concerning Rosh HaShana not even one mention of rejoicing is written. This is because all people are judged, and a person beseeches for his soul more than he does for his property.

Three mentions of rejoicing are written concerning the festival of *Sukkot*, since the souls receive their writ of release on Yom Kippur, as it is stated: "For on that day He will atone for you" (Leviticus 16:30); moreover, by the time *Sukkot* arrives, the grain and the fruits of the tree are already gathered inside the storehouses.

What is the meaning of: "Completely [*akh*][4] joyous"? You find that although a person is joyous in this world, his joy is not complete. How so? If children are born to him, he is concerned about them lest they are not viable. But in the future, the Holy One, blessed be He, will eliminate death forever; then the joy will be complete, as it is stated: "Then our mouths will be filled with laughter" (Psalms 126:2).

(*Yalkut Shimoni, Emor* 1:654)

📖 **Further reading:** For more about the special rejoicing on the festival of *Sukkot*, see p. 292; *A Concise Guide to Halakha*, p. 213.

The Blasphemer

The Torah relates the incident involving the son of an Israelite woman and an Egyptian man who blasphemed the name of God and was sentenced to death. The Sages explain that his harsh treatment by other Israelites due to his ancestry caused him to blaspheme.

As when this man came to establish his tent in the camp of Dan, his mother's tribe, [the people of the tribe of Dan] rejected him, saying to him: You are the son of an Egyptian, and it is written: "Each at his banner, with the insignias of their patrilineal houses" (Numbers 2:2) – and not of their matrilineal houses. Immediately, he began to blaspheme the name of God and to curse Him.

(*Tanḥuma, Emor*)

---

4. The standard connotation of the word *akh* is limitation and restriction.

Behar

In this Torah portion, there are a series of commandments relating to the relationship between people and their property and to economic interaction between people. At the beginning of the Torah portion, there is a discussion of the commandments relating to the Sabbatical Year and the Jubilee Year – the fiftieth year, during which slaves are freed and land returns to the original owners of the ancestral holdings. Likewise, the laws governing the sale of ancestral fields and houses are addressed, as are the laws of aiding and supporting the indigent, and the appropriate conduct toward one who is forced to sell himself into slavery.

The chapter that follows presents statements of the Sages concerning the commandment of the Sabbatical Year, the supporting of a person who became impoverished, the connection between the life of a person and the life of another, and the prohibition against tormenting someone with hurtful speech.

The Commandment of the Sabbatical Year

The commandment to observe the Sabbatical Year, i.e., the prohibition against working the land during the seventh year of the agricultural cycle, appears in this Torah portion. The Sages provide a rationale for this commandment, and characterize as mighty those who observe the Sabbatical Year.

A certain student came and said to Rav Huna: What is the reason for the Sabbatical Year? Rav Huna said to him … The Holy One, blessed be He, said to the Jewish people: Sow for six years and refrain during the seventh, so that that you will know that the land is Mine.

"Mighty in strength, who do His bidding, heeding His word" (Psalms 103:20) …. Rabbi Yitzhak said: This verse is speaking of those who observe the Sabbatical Year. Typically, a person observes a commandment for an hour or for a day, but is one ever asked to observe a commandment for a year? And the Israelites observe this commandment for a year.

(*Sanhedrin* 39a; *Midrash Tehillim* [Buber] 103)

You Shall Support Him

The Torah commands us to support those whose financial situation deteriorates. The Sages underscored that one should assist him even before he loses everything.

"And if your brother should become poor, and his means fail with you, you shall support him" (Leviticus 25:35) – do not allow him to collapse. To what is the poor person comparable? He is comparable to a heavy burden on a donkey. While the burden is still in place, one can hold it and stabilize it. If it falls to the ground, even five people will be unable to lift it. [Similarly, as long as a poor person remains solvent, it is possible to support him with relative ease. But once he loses everything, it will be much more difficult to provide him with the support that he needs.]

(*Yalkut Shimoni, Behar* 1:665)

Your Brother Shall Live with You

The Sages disagreed with regard to how one should conduct himself in a situation in which only one person can be saved. How should the individual weigh the possibilities of saving one or both of them?

The verse states: "And your brother shall live with you" (Leviticus 25:36). This is what ben Petori expounded: There is the case of two individuals who were walking in the wilderness and one of them has only one jug of water. If one of them drinks it, he, but not his fellow, will reach a settled area, but if the two of them share it and drink it, both of them will [likely] die without reaching a settled area. Ben Petori expounded: "And your brother shall live with you," and they must share the water. Rabbi Akiva said to him that the verse states: "And your brother shall live with you," indicating that your life takes precedence over the life of your fellow[5] [and the one with the jug shall drink all the water so that at least he will definitely survive].

(*Sifra, Behar* 5)

Verbal Mistreatment

The prohibition against mistreating another appears in this Torah portion. The Sages taught that in addition to the prohibition against monetarily exploiting another, it is forbidden to torment another with words as well.

The verse states: "And you shall not wrong one another" (Leviticus 25:17); this is a reference to verbal mistreatment. Could it perhaps be a reference to monetary exploitation? No, because when the verse states: "And if you sell a sale item to your counterpart, or acquire from the hand of your counterpart,

---

5. Rabbi Akiva understands the verse as teaching that the obligation to save the life of another begins only after one's own life is secured. If one saves his fellow's life at the expense of his own, the fellow is not "living *with* him," as the one who saved him is himself no longer alive.

you shall not exploit one another" (25:14), monetary exploitation is already stated, [and there is no need for another verse to state this command. Therefore,] how do I explain the meaning of: "And you shall not wrong one another"? It is referring to verbal mistreatment.

How so? [What are some examples of verbal mistreatment?] If one was a penitent, a person should not say to him: Remember your previous actions. If one was the son of converts, a person should not say to him: Remember the actions of your ancestors.

How so? If one was afflicted with illnesses or if he was burying his children, a person should not speak to him in the manner that Job's comrades spoke to him: "Shouldn't your reverence be your security, your hope and the virtuousness of your way? Please remember, who is the innocent who perished and where are the upright who were destroyed?" (Job 4:6–7).[6]

(*Sifra, Behar* 3)

Gentle Speech

A person's tongue is an instrument. He can utilize it in a positive manner, or he can utilize it negatively.

Rabbi Yehuda HaNasi made a feast for his students. He brought before them soft tongue meat and coarse tongue meat. They began selecting the soft ones and forsaking the coarse ones. Rabbi Yehuda HaNasi said to them: Be aware of what you are doing. Just as you are choosing the soft tongues and forsaking the coarse ones, so too, you should speak to each other with a gentle tongue.

(*Vayikra Rabba*, 33)

Further reading: For more about appropriate speech, see p. 147, 445; *A Concise Guide to Halakha*, p. 598.

6. They sought to console him for his suffering by telling him that he must have sinned, as had he not sinned, these tragedies would not have befallen him.

Behukotai

The first part of this Torah portion details the blessings and curses. The Torah tells of a series of blessings with which the Israelites will be blessed if they follow the commandments of God, and a series of curses that will befall them if they do not follow that path. The second part of the Torah portion, with which the book of Leviticus concludes, discusses the laws of valuations. This is the sum of money that one is required to contribute for Temple maintenance upon taking a vow to donate the monetary value of a specific person. The Torah portion also speaks of the laws of substitution: The prohibition against substituting another animal for a consecrated animal, and what is the law when a person does so nevertheless.

The chapter that follows presents statements of the Sages with regard to following the statutes of the Lord and engaging in Torah study, and some of the blessings enumerated in the Torah portion as a reward for observance of the Torah; the resting of the Divine Presence among the Israelites; the blessing of rain; the blessings of produce and peace; and the banishment of wild beasts.

Toiling in Torah Study

In addition to fulfilling the commandments, there is special significance accorded to engaging in Torah study with the objective of fulfilling what is written in it.

The verse states: "If you follow My statutes and observe My commandments" (Leviticus 26:3). This teaches that the Omnipresent desires the Israelites to toil in Torah study. [The phrase "and observe My commandments" is understood as referring to Torah study because the performance of mitzvot is included in the phrase, "If you follow My statutes."]

"If you follow My statutes and observe My commandments and perform them" (26:3). This refers to one who studies Torah in order to fulfill its commandments, not one who studies Torah with the intention not to perform them. Concerning one who studies Torah with the intention not to perform its commandments, it would have been preferable for him not to have been created.

(*Sifra, Behukotai* 1)

The Statutes of the Heavens and Earth

According to the Sages, the mitzvot of the Torah are also the foundation on which the entire natural world exists. From the time of Creation, reward and punishment have been contingent on the Torah and the commandments: If Israel will observe the commandments, they will merit reward; and if not, they will receive punishment.

"If you follow My statutes" (Leviticus 26:3). These are the statutes on whose basis I established the heavens and the earth, as it is stated: "If not My covenant of day and night, I would not have set the statutes of heaven and earth" (Jeremiah 33:25).

The Sages taught in the name of Rabbi Elazar: The sword and the scroll were given from Heaven intertwined. The Holy One, blessed be He, said to the Israelites: If you observe what is written in this book, you will be spared from the sword. But if not, it will ultimately kill you. Where does He pronounce these matters to them? As it is stated with regard to Adam the first man after his sin of eating from the tree of knowledge: "He banished the man, [He stationed the cherubs east of the Garden of Eden] and the blade of the ever-turning sword to guard the path to the tree of life" (Genesis 3:24)…"tree of life" – this is the Torah.[7]

The Sages taught in the name of Rabbi Shimon bar Yohai: The loaf and the rod were given from Heaven intertwined. God said to them: If you observe the Torah, here is a loaf to eat. But if not, here is a rod with which to be flogged. Where does He pronounce these matters to them? "If you are willing, and heed, the goodness of the land you will eat. But if you refuse and are defiant, you will be devoured by the sword" (Isaiah 1:19–20).

(*Vayikra Rabba* 35)

The Resting of the Divine Presence

The essence of all the blessings enumerated in this Torah portion is ultimately the expression of the Divine Presence residing in the midst of the children of Israel.

"If you follow My statutes" (Leviticus 26:3). What is written there, in the blessings that follow this statement? "I will place My dwelling in your midst" (26:11). If you fulfill My commandments, I will abandon the world above and I will rest among you, as it is stated: "And I will dwell among the children of Israel" (Exodus 29:45). It was for that purpose that the Israelites left Egypt, in order that they would build the Tabernacle and the Divine Presence would rest in their midst….

---

7. The sword ensures that people will observe the commandments of the Torah.

If they perform My will, My Divine Presence will not move from their midst. Why? Rabbi Ami said: The Holy One, blessed be He, desired that just as He has a residence above, He would have a residence below.

(*Tanḥuma, Behukotai*)

📖 **Further reading:** For more about reward and punishment, see *A Concise Guide to Mahshava*, p. 256.

Rains in Their Season

One of the blessings promised to the Jewish people as a reward for following the Torah is: "I will provide your rains in their season." The Sages explain that this means rain will fall at a time when it will not interrupt life's routine, while at the same time it will water the crops.

When the verse states: "I will provide your rains in their season" (Leviticus 26:4), this means that it will rain at night. In the days of King Herod, rain would fall at night, and in the morning the sun shone and the wind blew, the clouds scattered and the land dried. The workers went out and engaged in their labor and knew that their actions accorded with the will of their Father in Heaven [since it rained in a manner that did not impede their routines].

Alternatively, when the verse states: "I will provide your rains in their season" (26:4), this means that it will rain on the night of Shabbat [i.e., Friday night, a time when people are inside their homes]. There was an incident in the days of Shimon ben Shatah and Queen Shlomtzion when rain would fall every Shabbat night, to the extent that wheat kernels grew to the size of kidneys, barley kernels grew to the size of olive pits, and lentils grew to the size of gold dinars. The Sages collected them and stored them for future generations to see. Why did the Sages go to such effort? To inform [the Jewish people in the future who will not observe the commandments] to what degree the sin has an effect, in fulfillment of what is stated: "Your iniquities have diverted these, and your sins have withheld good from you" (Jeremiah 5:25).

(*Vayikra Rabba* 35)

He Has Made His Wonders a Lasting Memory

When the promised blessing will be completely fulfilled, the plants will produce fruit rapidly, as it was at the time of Creation.

"The land will yield its produce" (Leviticus 26:4). Not in the manner that it does now, but rather in the manner that it did in the days of Adam the first man.... The verse teaches that on the same day that the plants were sown, they yielded produce.

"The tree of the field will yield its fruit" (26:4). Not in the manner that it does now, but rather in the manner that it did in the days of Adam the first man.... The verse teaches that on the same day that a tree was planted, it yielded fruit.

From where is it known that the tree, too, is destined to be edible? As it is stated: "A fruit tree bearing fruit" (Genesis 1:11). If the verse means to teach that the tree will yield fruits, it already says "bearing fruit." If so, why does it say "a fruit tree"? The verse teaches that just as the fruit is edible, the tree, too, is destined to be edible.

From where is it known that even non-fruit-bearing trees are destined to bear fruit? The verse states: "The tree of the field will yield its fruit" (Leviticus 26:4).

(*Yalkut Shimoni, Behukotai* 1:672)

📖 Further reading: According to the Sages, some of these blessings will be realized only with the coming of the messiah. For more about the coming of the messiah, see p. 391; *A Concise Guide to Mahshava*, p. 145.

The Blessing of Food and the Blessing of Peace

The Sages explain the verses that speak of the blessing of produce and food, but emphasize that the blessing of peace surpasses them all.

When the verse states: "Your threshing shall reach until grape harvest" (Leviticus 26:5), this means that you will be engaged in threshing in the spring until the time for the grape harvest arrives at the end of the summer. When it states: "And grape harvest shall reach until sowing" (26:5), this means that you will be engaged in the grape harvest until the time for sowing arrives in the autumn.

When the verse states: "You shall eat your food to repletion" (26:5), there is no need to say that a person will eat a lot and be sated. It means that one eats a little and the food is blessed within him to satiate him, similar to what is written: "And you shall serve the Lord your God and He will bless your bread and your water" (Exodus 23:25).

Lest you say: There is food and there is drink, but if there is no peace there is nothing; the verse states: "I will grant peace in the land" (26:6). It

tells you that peace is the equivalent of everything good. Likewise the verse states: "Who makes peace and creates evil" (Isaiah 45:7). This tells you that peace is the equivalent of everything good [as it is the opposite of evil].

(*Sifra, Behukotai* 1)

Further reading: For more about the virtue of peace, see pp. 179, 226, 374.

Banishing Wild Animals

The Torah promises that when the Israelites observe the commandments, God will banish wild beasts from the land. The Sages disagreed with regard to how this banishment will take effect: Will it be the elimination of the destructive beasts, or a change in their nature?

The verse states: "I will banish wild beasts from the land" (Leviticus 26:6). Rabbi Yehuda says: God will eliminate the wild beasts from the land. Rabbi Shimon says: God will restrain them so that they will not cause harm. Rabbi Shimon says: Which would be greater praise of the Lord: When there are no harmful beasts, or when there are harmful beasts that no longer cause harm? Say that it is a greater praise in a time when there are harmful beasts that no longer cause harm. Likewise, the verse states: "A psalm, a song for the Sabbath [*Shabbat*] day" (Psalms 92:1). This refers to the One who eliminates [*mashbit*][8] harmful creatures from the world, meaning eliminates them, in the sense that they will no longer cause harm. Likewise, the verse states: "Wolf will reside with sheep, and leopard will lie down with kid" (Isaiah 11:6).

(*Sifra, Behukotai* 1)

---

8. The term *mashbit* is from the same Hebrew root as *Shabbat*.

Torah – Numbers

Bemidbar

The Torah portion of *Bemidbar* begins by describing the configuration of the encampment and travel of the children of Israel in the wilderness, each tribe under its banner and in its fixed location. In this context, Moses conducts a census of the people. He counts each Israelite tribe alone and then tallies the entire body of Israelites. Thereafter, the Torah addresses the Levites and their separate census, and enumerates the specific tasks of each Levite family.

The chapter that follows presents statements of the Sages concerning the children of Israel in the wilderness, the census of the Israelite tribes, and the configuration of the encampment and travel of the Israelites.

Israel in the Wilderness

Unlike the nature of a typical sojourn in the wilderness, God led the children of Israel there in extreme comfort, like princes, with no worries and no pain.

When a flesh-and-blood king goes out to the wilderness, would he typically find tranquility there like he would in his palace? Would he find comparable food and drink?

You were slaves in Egypt and I took you out of there, and I lay you on cushioned divans, as it is stated: "God led the people circuitously [*vayasev*] via the wilderness" (Exodus 13:18). What is *vayasev*? It teaches that he lay them the way that kings recline [*mesubin*],[1] lying on their divans. I did not expose them to even three fleas to irritate them.

I even provided you with three saviors to serve you, as it is stated: "I sent before you Moses, Aaron, and Miriam" (Micah 6:4). Due to the merit of Moses, you ate the manna … and due to the merit of Aaron, I surrounded you with clouds of glory.… There were seven clouds protecting the Israelites: one from above; one from below; one on each of the four directions; and one that proceeded before them and killed snakes and scorpions, and leveled the mountains and the valleys, and burned the thistles and the thorn bushes, and produced smoke that all the kings of the east and the west could see. And it is written: "Your garment did not grow worn from upon you" (Deuteronomy 8:4). The verse teaches that a baby, as he grew, his inner garments and his outer garments would grow with him.

---

1. The Hebrew root of *mesubin* is similar to the Hebrew root of *vayasev*.

The well was due to the merit of Miriam, who recited a song at the sea…. How was the well fashioned? It was stone, like a round basket or a ball, and it would roll with them on their travels. When the tribes would encamp in their formations, and the Tabernacle was erected, the stone would come and settle in the courtyard of the Tent of Meeting. The princes of the tribes would come and stand on it and would say: "Rise well; give voice for it" (Numbers 21:17), and it would rise.

(Tanḥuma, Bemidbar)

Further reading: For the connection between the clouds of glory and the *sukka* on the festival of *Sukkot*, see p. 290.

Precious Merchandise

The Israelite people were counted several times in the wilderness. According to the Sages, this was done because they are greatly beloved in the eyes of God, who therefore repeatedly counted them.

Come and see how beloved the Israelites are before the Omnipresent. As the Holy One, Blessed be He, wrote the number of the Israelites four times in the encampment and travels of each tribe in its grouping:[2] twice writing the total of each individual tribe and twice writing the tally of all the tribes together. In addition, He counted for each and every grouping the total of each individual tribe and the total of each grouping. This is to inform you how beloved the Israelites are before Him, as they are His multitude and He wishes to count them all the time.

This is like a person who has merchandise that is very precious to him, who counts it and counts it again, many times, so that he will know its tally and he will rejoice over it for each and every tally. Likewise, the Holy One, Blessed be He, rejoiced at the mention of the tally of the Israelites, saying: Such a great multitude I have in My world who perform My will, and He takes solace in them.

(Bemidbar Rabba 2)

The Banners of the Wilderness

In this Torah portion, the configuration of the encampment of the tribes is described in great detail. Each tribe is situated under its banner in its fixed place, both in the

---

2. There were three tribes in each camp, with each camp stationed on one of the four sides of the Tabernacle.

encampment and in travel. The Sages relate that this configuration was determined back in the days of Jacob, who commanded his sons how to convey his coffin from Egypt on the way to his burial in the Land of Israel.

When Jacob our patriarch was passing from this world, he told his sons: "I will lie with my fathers and you will carry me from Egypt and bury me in their burial place" (Genesis 47:30). How did he command them to transport his body? He said to them: Judah, Issachar, and Zebulun will carry my coffin on the eastern side. Reuben, Simeon, and Dan will carry it from the southern side. Dan, Asher, and Naphtali will carry it from the northern side. Benjamin, Ephraim, and Manasseh will carry it from the western side. Joseph will not carry it. Why? Because he is a king and you are required to pay him respect. Levi will not carry it. Why? Because they are destined to carry the ark, and one who carries the ark of He who gives life to the world will not carry the coffin of a corpse. If you carry my coffin as I commanded you, the Holy One, Blessed be He, is destined to rest His Divine Presence among you when you are divided into camps. Once Jacob died, they carried him as he commanded them to carry him....

When the Israelites left Egypt, the Holy One, Blessed be He, said: The time has arrived for them to be divided into camps in the manner that their forefather informed them that they are destined to be divided into camps. Immediately, the Holy One, Blessed be He, said to Moses: Moses, divide them into camps in My name. Moses began to be concerned: Now disputes between the tribes are going to begin. If I say to the tribe of Judah to encamp to the east, it will say to me: I want only to the south. Likewise, the others will do the same, each and every tribe.

The Holy One, Blessed be He, said to Moses: Moses, why are you concerned? They do not need you in this matter, as they are familiar with their proper locations on their own. Why? Because they possess their forefather's instructions determining where their camps shall be stationed. I am not introducing anything novel to them, as they already have protocols from Jacob their forefather. In the manner that they surrounded his coffin, so will they surround the Tabernacle.

(*Tanḥuma, Bemidbar*)

The Banners

The Sages describe the unique banners that each tribe possessed, the distinctive color of each banner, and the drawing that adorned it.

Each and every prince had an emblem and a banner. The color on each and every banner corresponded to the color of the gems that were on Aaron's heart, on the breast piece worn by the High Priest. It is from these banners that kingdoms throughout the world learned to prepare national banners with unique colors on each and every banner....

The tribe of Reuben's stone was a ruby, its banner was red, and mandrakes were drawn on it (see Genesis 30:14). Simeon's stone was a topaz, its banner was green, and Shekhem was drawn on it (see Genesis 34:25). Levi's stone was an emerald; its banner was one-third white, one-third black, and one-third red; and the Urim and the Tumim was drawn on it (see Exodus 28:30).

Judah's stone was a carbuncle, the color of its banner was an image of the heavens, and a lion was drawn on it (see Genesis 49:9). Issachar's stone was a sapphire, its banner was midnight blue, and the sun and the moon were drawn on it, based on the verse: "From the children of Issachar, possessors of understanding of the times" (I Chronicles 12:33). Zebulun's stone was a clear quartz, the color of its banner was white, and a ship was drawn on it, based on the verse: "Zebulun shall dwell at the shore of seas" (Genesis 49:13).

Dan's stone was a jacinth, the color of its banner was like a sapphire, and a snake was drawn on it, based on the verse: "Dan shall be a serpent" (Genesis 49:17). Gad's stone was an agate, the color of its banner was not white and not black but a blend of black and white, and a military camp was drawn on it, based on the verse: "Gad, a troop shall slash his enemies" (Genesis 49:19). Naphtali's stone was an amethyst, the color of its banner was like unclouded wine that is red but not dark red, and a doe was drawn on it, based on the verse: "Naphtali is a doe let loose" (Genesis 49:21).

Asher's stone was a beryl, the color of its banner was similar to a gem with which women adorn themselves, and an olive tree was drawn on it, based on the verse: "From Asher, his bread is fat" (Genesis 49:20).[3] Joseph's stone was an onyx, the color of its banner was a very deep black.... A bull was drawn on the banner of Ephraim, based on the verse: "A firstborn bull is his majesty" (Deuteronomy 33:17), which is a reference to Joshua, who was from the tribe of Ephraim. An aurochs was drawn on the banner of the tribe of Manasseh, based on the verse: "And his horns are the horns of an aurochs" (Deuteronomy 33:17), which is a reference to Gideon son of Yoash,

---

3. The term for "fat," *shamen*, is similar to the term for oil, *shemen*.

who was from the tribe of Manasseh. Benjamin's stone was a chalcedony, the color of its banner is similar to the twelve colors of the other tribes' banners, and a wolf is drawn on it, based on the verse: "Benjamin is a wolf that mauls" (Genesis 49:27).

(Bemidbar Rabba 2)

Like Angels

The positioning of all the tribes in the framework of the different camps is similar to the configuration of the administering angels, which are also identifiable in their places and in their unique camps.

When the Holy One, Blessed be He, revealed Himself on Mount Sinai, 22,000 chariots of angels descended with Him, as it is stated: "The chariots of God are myriads, thousands upon thousands of companies" (Psalms 68:18),[4] and they were all divided into camps [*degalim*], as it is stated: "My beloved is clear and ruddy, more eminent [*dagul*] than a myriad" (Song of Songs 5:10).

Once the Israelites saw that the angels were divided into camps, they began desiring camps of their own. They said: If only we could divide into camps like them…. If only He will bestow love upon us…. The Holy One, Blessed be He, said: What did you desire, to be divided into camps? By your lives, I will fulfill your wishes…. Immediately, the Holy One, Blessed be He, pronounced His love for Israel and said to Moses: Go divide them into camps as they desired.

(Bemidbar Rabba 2)

Further reading: For more about the angels that descended during the revelation at Sinai, see p. 107.

---

4. The Hebrew word *revava*, translated as myriad, generally refers to ten thousand people. The Sages explain that the minimum number for any plural is two. Consequently, the word *myriads* in the verse from Psalms comes to mean 20,000, and the word *thousands* in the same verse is understood as 2,000.

Naso

The beginning of *Parashat Naso* continues the Torah's discussion of the Levite families and their respective duties. Several topics are then addressed, among them the *sota*, a woman whose husband suspects her of adultery, and the rite she undergoes to determine her guilt; the nazirite and the situation of one who takes a vow of naziriteship; and the priestly blessing. The second half of the Torah portion describes the contributions of the princes and their offerings during the dedication of the Tabernacle.

The chapter that follows presents statements of the Sages concerning the water that is part of the *sota* ritual; God's treatment of a person with the attribute of measure for measure; abstinence; living a life of sanctity; the priestly blessing, and the blessing of peace in particular; and the resting of the Divine Presence in the Tabernacle.

To Institute Peace between a Man and His Wife

In the preparation of the *sota* water, it was necessary to erase into the water the writing from a parchment on which verses from the section in the Torah that discuss the *sota* are written. Doing so involves erasure of the name of God. Nevertheless, they would erase God's name in order to promote marital peace.

Great is peace, as the name of God that is written in sanctity is erased in the water of the *sota* in the interest of peace, in order to institute peace between a man and his wife.

(*Sifrei Bemidbar, Naso* 42)

Sota Water

They gave the *sota* "bitter water" to drink. If she in fact had committed adultery, she would die an unusual death. If she had not committed adultery, she would be blessed. The Sages describe the potency of the water, as its mere vapor was enough to check if the woman had committed adultery.

There was an incident involving two sisters who resembled each other. One was married and living in one city, and the other was married and living in another city. The husband of one suspected his wife of adultery and sought to warn her, then have her drink the bitter [*sota*] water in Jerusalem. She went to that city in which her married sister was living. The latter said to her sister: Why did you come here? The visiting sister said to her: My husband

wants me to drink the bitter *sota* water. Her sister said to her: I will go in your stead and drink. She said to her: Go.

The other sister donned her sister's garments and went in her stead. She drank the bitter *sota* water and was found to be pure, and she returned to her sister's house. She went out to greet her sister retuning from Jerusalem, hugged her, and kissed her on the mouth. When they kissed each other, she breathed in the bitter *sota* water and immediately died.

(Tanḥuma, Naso)

Measure for Measure

The *sota* rite is structured measure for measure, with the woman's punishment in line with her sin. The Sages detail additional cases where this principle is manifest, for good and for bad.

With the measure that a person measures, he himself is measured. The *sota* adorned herself to perform a transgression; therefore, the Omnipresent decreed that she be rendered unattractive. She exposed herself to perform a transgression, as she stood in places where she would be noticed by potential adulterers; therefore, the Omnipresent decreed that her body be publicly exposed. She began her transgression with her thigh and afterward with her stomach [i.e., her sexual organs]; therefore, the thigh is smitten first and then the stomach, and the rest of her entire body does not escape punishment.

Samson followed his eyes [by marrying unsuitable women because he was taken by their appearance]; therefore, the Philistines gouged out his eyes.... Absalom was exceedingly proud of his hair; therefore, he was hanged by his hair (see II Samuel 18)....

Likewise with regard to good deeds. Miriam waited for the baby Moses for one hour; therefore, the Israelites delayed their travels in the wilderness for seven days [to wait for her to be healed from her leprosy].

(Mishna Sota 1:7–9)

Further reading: For more about punishment measure for measure, see p. 86; *A Concise Guide to Mahshava*, p. 259.

Sinner or Saint

It is forbidden for a nazirite to drink wine. The Sages disagree whether abstinence from eating and drinking in general and from wine in particular is fundamentally positive, or whether it is a matter for which one is deserving of punishment.

Shmuel said: Anyone who fasts is called a sinner. Shmuel holds in accordance with the opinion of the following *tanna*, as it is taught in a *baraita*: Rabbi Elazar HaKappar the Great says: What is the meaning when the verse states: "And atone for him for that which he sinned regarding the soul" (Numbers 6:11)? But regarding which soul did this nazirite sin? [Whom did he sin against?] This means that he sinned in causing himself to suffer when he abstained from wine. Aren't these matters inferred *a fortiori*? If this nazirite, who caused himself to suffer by abstaining from wine alone is called a sinner, then with regard to one who causes himself to suffer by abstaining from each and every type of food and drink by fasting, all the more so is he considered a sinner.

Rabbi Elazar says: One who fasts is called holy, as it is stated concerning the nazirite: "He shall be holy, the hair of his head shall be grown out" (Numbers 6:5). [Here too, it can be inferred *a fortiori*:] And if one who caused himself to suffer by abstaining from only one matter, wine, is called holy, then with regard to one who caused himself to suffer by abstaining from everything, all the more so is he considered holy.

(*Ta'anit* 11a)

Who Blesses

God informed the priests, who bless the Israelites, that it is in fact He who blesses them; the priests are merely His intermediaries who convey His blessings.

"So shall you bless the children of Israel" (Numbers 6:23). The Holy One, Blessed be He, said: Initially I would bless My creations. From now on, the blessings are given to you, the priests; you will bless My children. Therefore, the Holy One, Blessed be He, told Moses that he should notify Aaron and his sons to bless the Israelites ….

The assembly of Israel said before the Holy One, blessed be He: Master of the Universe: Are You telling the priests to bless us? We need only Your blessing, and to be blessed from Your mouth, as it is stated: "Look from Your holy abode, from the heavens, and bless Your people Israel" (Deuteronomy 26:15). The Holy One, Blessed be He, said: Even though I told the priests to bless you, I stand with them and bless you.

(*Tanḥuma, Naso*)

The Importance of Peace

The priestly blessing concludes with the blessing of peace: "And grant you peace." The Sages are expansive in describing the virtue and the significance of peace.

Rabbi Elazar says: Great is peace, as it was only peace that the prophets implanted in the mouths of the people.

Rabbi Shimon ben Halafta says: Great is peace, as peace is the only receptacle that receives blessing.

Rabbi Elazar HaKappar says: Great is peace, as it is only peace that concludes all the blessings, as it is stated: "The Lord shall bless you, and keep you. The Lord shall shine His countenance to you, and be gracious to you. The Lord shall lift His countenance to you, and grant you peace" (Numbers 6:24–26).

Rabbi Elazar son of Rabbi Elazar HaKappar says: Great is peace, as even if Israel is worshipping idols, as long as there is peace between them, the Omnipresent says, as it were: The adversary cannot touch them....

Great is peace, and dispute is reviled. Great is peace, as even at a time of war, peace is necessary, as it is stated: "When you approach a city to wage war against it, you shall call to it for peace" (Deuteronomy 20:10)....

Great is peace, as the name of the Holy One, blessed be He, is peace, as the verse states: "Gideon built an altar there to the Lord, and he called it: The Lord is peace" (Judges 6:24).

(Sifrei Bemidbar, Naso 42)

The Restoration of the Divine Presence to This World

The Torah portion tells of the dedication of the Tabernacle and the bringing of the offerings donated by the princes of Israel.

According to the Sages, in the wake of human sin, the Divine Presence ascended to the upper heavens. It then gradually returned to the lower world thanks to the actions of the righteous. The establishment of the Tabernacle was the climax of its process of return to this world.

Rabbi Shmuel bar Nahman said: When the Holy One, Blessed be He, created the world, He desired to have a residence in the world below just as there is [one for Him] in the world above.

He created man and commanded him: "The Lord God commanded the man, saying: From every tree of the garden you may eat. But of the tree of the knowledge of good and evil, you shall not eat of it" (Genesis 2:16–17), but Adam violated His command. The Holy One, Blessed be He, said to

entarnish

him: I so much desired to have a residence in the world below like I have in the world above, and I commanded you one matter and you did not observe it.

Immediately, the Holy One, Blessed be He, raised His Divine Presence to the first heaven…. Cain went and killed Abel; immediately He raised His Divine Presence to the second heaven [and so forth, after further sins of humanity, until the Divine Presence was in the seventh, highest, heaven]…. Once He brought Abraham to the world, Abraham accumulated good deeds, and the Holy One, Blessed be He, descended from the seventh heaven to the sixth. Isaac extended his neck atop the altar when he was bound, and He descended from the sixth to the fifth [and so forth, after further righteous acts of humanity, until the Divine Presence was in the first, lowest, heaven]. Moses brought the Divine Presence down to this world…when the Tabernacle was established.

(*Tanḥuma, Naso*)

Behaalotekha

The first part of the Torah portion continues the discussion of the Tabernacle service: the command to kindle the lamps of the candelabrum, the consecration of the Levites for service, a description of the traveling and encampment of the camp with the Tabernacle, and the use of the trumpets in the Tabernacle for assemblies and other events. The section addressing the second *Pesah* appears among those topics. Thereafter, the Torah relates the narrative of the Israelites who expressed a craving for meat. Moses had difficulty coping with the troubles of the people and their complaints, and on the basis of a command from God, gathered seventy elders, upon whom God rested His spirit, to ease his burden. At the conclusion of the Torah portion we read the story of the gossiping that Miriam and Aaron engaged in concerning Moses, due to which Miriam was afflicted with leprosy.

The chapter that follows presents statements of the Sages concerning the crafting of the candelabrum and the kindling of the lamps; the difference between the standard *Pesah* and the second *Pesah*; those who craved meat; the appointment of the elders, and Eldad and Meidad who prophesied alongside them; and the conversation between Miriam and Aaron about Moses.

The Crafting of the Candelabrum

The Torah portion begins with the command pertaining to kindling the candelabrum in the Tabernacle. The Sages relate the difficulty in crafting the candelabrum, until ultimately it was formed on its own, in a miraculous manner.

"This is the craftsmanship of the candelabrum: Hammered gold [*miksha*]" (Numbers 8:4). In other words, the verse means to allude to how difficult[5] it was for Moses to craft it. Moses exerted much effort trying to understand how to craft it. When he had difficulty, the Holy One, Blessed be He, said to Moses: Take a talent of gold and cast it into the fire and remove it, and it will craft itself, as it is stated: "Its base and its shaft; its cups, its knobs and its flowers, were from it" (Exodus 37:17). The term "from it" indicates that Moses strikes with the hammer, and it is crafted from itself. Therefore, the verse states: "The candelabrum shall be made [*te'aseh*] hammered" (Exodus 25:31), written with [the Hebrew letter] *yod*. "Shall make [*ta'aseh*]" is not written, as if to say that it will be crafted on its own.

---

5.   The Sages extrapolated this meaning by splitting the Hebrew word *miksha* into the two-word term *ma kasheh*, meaning "how difficult."

Moses took the talent of gold and cast it into the fire. Moses said: Master of the Universe! The talent is in the fire. Just as You want, so shall You do. Immediately, the candelabrum emerged, crafted in accordance with its specifications.

(*Bemidbar Rabba* 15)

📖 Further reading: For an illustration of the candelabrum, see *A Concise Guide to the Torah*, p. 523.

Illuminate before Me

God is all light. If so, what is the value of the lamps of the candelabrum that the priests kindled in the Tabernacle?

To what can this matter of kindling the candelabrum be compared? It can be compared to a king who had an admirer. The king said to him: Know that I will be dining with you; go and prepare for me. His admirer went and prepared a couch fit for a commoner, a candelabrum fit for a commoner, and a table fit for a commoner. When the king arrived, servants accompanied him who surrounded him on all sides and carried a candelabrum of gold before him. When his admirer saw all the splendor, he was ashamed, and he hid everything that he had prepared, all of which were fit for a commoner.

The king said to him: Didn't I tell you that I will be dining with you? Why didn't you prepare anything for me? His admirer said to him: I saw all the splendor that accompanied you, and I was ashamed and hid everything that I had prepared for you, all of which was fit for a commoner. The king said to him: I take an oath by your life that I am setting aside all the vessels that I brought, and because of your love, I will use only yours.

Similar to this, the Holy One, Blessed be He, is all light, as it is stated: "And the light rests with Him" (Daniel 2:22), but He said to Israel: Prepare for Me a candelabrum and lamps.

(*Bemidbar Rabba* 15)

Second *Pesah*

People who were unable to bring the paschal offering at its appointed time requested from Moses that they also be given an opportunity to perform the mitzva. In response, God provided a second *Pesah*, giving the opportunity to bring the offering a month later, on the fourteenth of Iyar. The Mishna enumerates the distinctions between the offering brought on the standard *Pesah* and the one brought on the second *Pesah*.

What is the difference between the paschal offering brought on the first *Pesah* and the one brought on the second *Pesah*? On the first *Pesah*, owning leavened bread is prohibited due to: "It shall not be seen," and: "It shall not be found." On the second *Pesah* it is permitted to have both leavened bread and matza with him in the house. The first *Pesah* requires the recitation of *Hallel* as the offering is eaten and the second *Pesah* does not require the recitation of *Hallel* as it is eaten. But both require the recitation of *Hallel* as the offerings are sacrificed, and for both, the offerings are eaten roasted with matza and bitter herbs, and their sacrifice overrides Shabbat.

(Mishna *Pesaḥim* 9:3)

Those Who Craved Meat

The Israelites craved meat and complained about not having it. God granted their request and provided them with meat "until it comes out of your nose and it will be loathsome for you." The Sages explain what was behind their complaint and what was the punishment described in the Torah.

Rabbi Shimon ben Yohai said: Was it meat that they were requesting? Couldn't they taste all of the delicacies in the world in the manna? When eating the manna, anyone who craved meat would taste it; anyone who craved fish would taste it; anyone who craved rooster, pheasant, or peacock would taste it; so he would taste anything that he wished to taste. Why were they complaining? They were seeking a pretext to return to Egypt. Nevertheless, so said the Holy One, Blessed be He, to Moses: What are they requesting, meat? Tell them that I will give them meat....

Anyone who did not complain before the Lord would eat and enjoy the meat. Anyone who reviled the Lord would eat the meat and it would examine him to see if he had reviled the Lord, and it would come out of his nose, as it is stated: "Until it comes out of your nose and it will be loathsome for you" (Numbers 11:20).

(*Bemidbar Rabba* 7)

Seventy Elders

Moses told God that he was no longer able to bear the burden of the people and their complaints alone. God commanded him to choose seventy elders to bear the yoke of the people with him. From this episode, the Sages learn how to convince a judge to accept the position.

God told Moses to approach those "whom you know to be the elders of the people" (Numbers 11:16). This teaches that there is no person who sits in a position of authority over the multitudes unless he is accepted among the elite upper classes of the people to the degree that when people speak about him, they say: So-and-so is decent, pious, and fit to be a wise leader.

God instructed Moses: "And you shall take them" (11:16). This means that Moses must convince them with words. First, say words of praise to them: Happy are you that you were appointed; and only then say to them harsh words about the task ahead: Know that the people are libelous and obstinate. Accept this position in full knowledge that they will curse you and stone you.

(*Sifrei Bemidbar, Behaalotekha* 92)

Eldad and Meidad

After the spirit of God rested on the seventy elders and they began prophesying adjacent to the Tent of Meeting, two men, Eldad and Meidad, remained in the camp and also began prophesying. It is stated in their regard: "Two men remained." To what does the term "remained" refer?

"Two men remained in the camp" (Numbers 11:26). Some say that they remained from the receptacle [from which both of them drew blank notes in the lottery appointing the elders]. This is because the Holy One, Blessed be He, told Moses to choose for himself seventy elders. Moses said: What should I do? The seventy elders will be divided as six each from each tribe and five each from two tribes. What tribe would volunteer to have only five elders selected from them?

Moses implemented a solution. He took seventy notes and wrote "elder" on them and he took two blank notes. Moses mixed them and cast them into the receptacle. He said to them: Come and take your notes. To anyone who took a note on which "elder" was written, Moses would say to him: The Omnipresent has already sanctified you. To anyone who took a note on which "elder" was not written, Moses said to him: It is from Heaven, what can I do for you?...

Rabbi Shimon says: They remained in the camp so that they would not be selected. When they saw that Moses was choosing elders, they said: We are not worthy of this prominence, so they went and hid. The Omnipresent said to them: You lowered yourselves; I will elevate you beyond them all. Concerning the seventy elders the verse states: "They prophesied but they

did not continue" (11:25). This teaches that they prophesied for a time and then stopped. Concerning Eldad and Meidad the verse states: "They prophesied in the camp" (11:26). This teaches that they continued prophesying until the day of their death.

(*Sifrei Bemidbar, Behaalotekha* 95)

Miriam, Aaron, and Moses

At the conclusion of *Parashat Behaalotekha*, the Torah relates that Miriam and Aaron spoke about the Kushite woman whom Moses had married. What was the topic of their discussion? Why is Miriam mentioned first, and why was it specifically she who was afflicted with leprosy?

Why did the verse mention Miriam before Aaron in recording their conversation (see Numbers 12:1)? The verse teaches that Tzipora, Moses' wife, went and told Miriam that Moses had separated from her, and Miriam went and told Aaron. The two of them rose and spoke against that righteous man. Because the two of them rose and spoke against the righteous man, punishment came upon them, as it is stated: "The wrath of the Lord was enflamed against them and departed" (12:9). What is the meaning of the term "and departed"? It teaches that the wrath of the Lord left Aaron and clung to Miriam, because Aaron was not the one who initiated the speech. But Miriam, who was the initiator of the speech, was immediately punished more severely than Aaron.

Miriam said: God spoke to me, and I did not separate from my husband. Aaron said: And God spoke to me, and I did not separate from my wife. The same is true of our early ancestors, to whom God spoke, and yet they did not separate from their wives. But Moses, because he is arrogant, separated from his wife.

Miriam and Aaron did not discuss the matter in Moses' presence, [but] rather not in his presence [in order not to humiliate him]. They were not discussing it as a certainty but rather as a possibility; they were saying it was possible he was motivated by arrogance and possible he was not motivated by arrogance. [One can draw an *a fortiori* inference from the matter:] If Miriam, who spoke only against her brother and spoke only not in the presence of Moses, was punished, then an ordinary person who speaks derogatory matters in the presence of another and humiliates him, all the more so will his punishment be great.

(*Avot deRabbi Natan*, version A, chap. 9)

Further reading: For more about the prohibition of malicious speech and its severity, see pp. 145, 147, 385; *A Concise Guide to Halakha*, p. 598.

Shelah

The Torah portion of *Shelah* opens with the narrative of the sin of the spies. Twelve spies were sent to gather information about the land of Canaan. Upon their return, they instilled fear into the hearts of the Israelites, who then refused to attempt to conquer the land. The Israelites' punishment was severe: Forty years of wandering in the wilderness. Some of the Israelites did not accept that decree and were killed in an offensive war.

After the incident of the spies, the Torah portion enumerates a series of commandments: bringing wine libations with offerings, separating a portion of dough for the priest, bringing an offering for unwitting transgressions by the public or by an individual, and the mitzva of ritual fringes.

The chapter that follows presents statements of the Sages concerning the appointment of the spies, Caleb's visit in Hebron, and the duration of the spies' expedition; the destructiveness of malicious speech; the spies' allegations about the land of Canaan and the responses of Joshua and Caleb; the terrible cry that the Israelites wept due to their fear of entering the land; and the commandment of ritual fringes.

The Selection of the Spies

In the Torah portion of *Shelah*, it is related that Moses chose the spies on the basis of God's command. By contrast, when Moses describes the incident in the Torah portion of *Devarim*, it appears that he chose the spies himself. The Sages resolve the contradiction between the verses.

These men were chosen from the entire people of Israel at the directive of the Holy One, Blessed be He, and at the directive of Moses, as the verse states: "The matter was good in my eyes and I took from you twelve men, one man for each tribe" (Deuteronomy 1:23). From where do you say that the men selected were righteous? For Moses did not want to send them at his own initiative, and he consulted with the Holy One, Blessed be He, concerning each one. Moses said: Shall I send so-and-so from such and such tribe? God told him: They are worthy.

From where is it derived that the Holy One, Blessed be He, told Moses that the spies are worthy? As it is stated: "Moses sent them from the wilderness of Paran according to the directive of the Lord" (Numbers 13:3). Thereafter, at the conclusion of their mission, after forty days, they under-

went a transformation and they caused this entire tragedy, and they caused that generation to be stricken with that calamity.

(Tanḥuma, Shelah)

The Graves of the Patriarchs

The Torah relates that the spies reached Hebron. The Sages infer from the verses that Caleb alone went there, to pray for mercy so that he would not be tempted to follow the evil advice of his fellow spies.

"They ascended in the South, and they came [*vayavo*] until Hebron" (Numbers 13:22). The verse should have stated: *Vayavo'u* [in the plural. Why does it state "*vayavo*" in the singular?]. Rava says: This teaches that Caleb separated himself from the advice of the spies and he went and prostrated himself at the graves of the patriarchs. He said to them: My forefathers, pray for mercy for me so that I will be saved from the advice of the spies.

As for Joshua, Moses had already prayed for mercy for him, as it is stated: "Moses called Hoshe'a son of Nun, Joshua [*Yehoshua*]" (13:16), as if to say: May God deliver you from the advice of the spies.[6]

(Sota 34b)

Shortening the Way

The spies executed their mission faster than expected because God had mercy on the Israelites and sought to abbreviate the duration of their punishment.

The verse states concerning the spies: "They returned from scouting the land at the conclusion of forty days" (Numbers 13:25). But don't you find that they traveled south to north in forty days? How did the entire mission last forty days? It was revealed before the Holy One, Blessed be He, that they would come and slander the land, and it would be decreed against that generation that they would endure years of suffering, "each day for a year" (14:34). And the Holy One, Blessed be He, shortened the way before them.

Amalek

When the spies mentioned the Canaanite peoples, they mentioned Amalek first. According to the Sages, the purpose of this was to instill fear in the hearts of the Israelites.

---

6. The name Yehoshua means "God will deliver."

"Amalek lives in the southern region and the Hitites, and the Yevusites, and the Emorites...and the Canaanites" (Numbers 13:29). Why did the spies begin their report with Amalek? This can be explained by means of a parable of a student who misbehaved and was flogged with a strap. When they seek to frighten him, they mention the strap with which he was flogged. Amalek was the evil strap for Israel.

(*Bemidbar Rabba* 16)

The Spies' Claims

The spies presented a series of claims against entering the land, and Joshua and Caleb disputed their account. The Sages described their exchange.

"Caleb silenced [*vayahas*] the people toward Moses" (Numbers 13:30). Rabba said: He enticed them [*hesitan*] with words.[7] Joshua began to respond to the other spies. While he was speaking, they said to him: Will this man with a severed head [i.e., Joshua, who does not have any children that will inherit the land] speak? Caleb said: If I attempt to speak they will say something about me and stop me. Caleb said to them: Is this all that Moses the son of Amram has done to us? The other spies thought he wanted to speak to discredit Moses, and they were silent. Caleb then said to them: He took us out of Egypt, and split the sea for us, and fed us the manna. If he tells us: Build ladders and climb to the heavens, wouldn't we listen to him? "We shall ascend and inherit it; for we can do it" (13:30).

"But the men who ascended with him said: We will not be able to ascend against the people; for they are stronger than we are [*mimenu*]" (13:31). Rabbi Hanina bar Pappa says: The spies made a significant statement at that moment. When the spies said about the Canaanites: "They are stronger *mimenu*," do not read it as their saying that the Canaanites were stronger than us, but rather as their saying that the Canaanites were stronger than Him,[8] meaning that even the One in charge, God, is unable to remove His belongings from there and evict them....

"The entire congregation raised and sounded their voice...and wept that night" (14:1). Rabba says that Rabbi Yohanan says: That night was the eve of the ninth of Av. The Holy One, Blessed be He, said: They wept a gratuitous weeping, so I will establish for them a day of weeping for the gen-

---

7. The Sages are drawing a parallel between *vayahas* and *hesitan* based on their shared root.
8. The Hebrew term *mimenu* can be either first-person plural or third-person singular.

erations, [as both of the Temples were destroyed on the ninth day of the Hebrew month of Av].

(Sota 35a)

📖 **Further reading:** For more about the ninth of Av and the additional calamities that transpired that day, see *A Concise Guide to Halakha*, p. 365.

Weeping

How did the spies succeed in instilling fear in the hearts of the Israelites to the extent that the entire people cried bitterly?

Once the spies returned from scouting the land, they got up and spread out among all the tribes of Israel, each spy to his tribe. He would fall in each corner of his house, distraught, and his sons and daughters would come and say to him: What is it, my master? While attempting to stand, he would feign falling before them. He would say to them: Woe is me over you, my sons, daughters, and daughters-in-law. How those Emorites are going to mock you; how they are going to rule over you; who can withstand them?...

Immediately, they would all begin weeping loudly, their sons, their daughters, and their daughters-in-law, until the neighbors heard it. And they too would cry, until each family would be heard by the next, and until the entire tribe was weeping. Likewise, each spy would cause his tribe to weep, and each and every one did the same until all 600,000 men became one unit, and they wept bitterly and cried out to the heavens.

(Yalkut Shimoni, Shelah 1:743)

Ritual Fringes

At the conclusion of the Torah portion, the Israelites are commanded to attach fringes to the corners of their garments in order to remember the commandments. The Sages expanded upon the value of ritual fringes, teaching that wearing them is equivalent to keeping all the Torah's commandments, and by seeing them one receives the Divine Presence.

Why are these fringes called *tzitzit*? It is because they commemorate the time that the Holy One, Blessed be He, peered [*hetzitz*] at the houses of our fathers in Egypt [at the time of the plague striking the firstborn], as it is stated: "Behold, he is standing behind our wall, watching from the windows, peering through the cracks" (Song of Songs 2:9).

Rabbi Hanina ben Antigenos says: Concerning anyone who fulfills the commandment of ritual fringes, what does the verse state? "In those days,

ten men of all the languages of the nations will take hold; they will take hold of the corner of the garment of a Judean man, saying: Let us go with you" (Zechariah 8:23), and concerning anyone who fails to fulfill the commandment of the corner [*kanaf*] of the garment, what does the verse state? "To seize the ends [*kanfot*] of the earth, and the wicked will be shaken from it" (Job 38:13).

Rabbi Meir says: And you shall see them [*otam*], is not written here in the verse concerning ritual fringes. Rather, "And you shall see it [*oto*]" (Numbers 15:39).[9] The verse tells us that for anyone who fulfills the commandment of ritual fringes, it is ascribed to him as though he received the Divine Presence, as the blue string on the fringes evokes the sea, and the sea evokes the sky, and the sky evokes God's Throne of Glory.

(*Sifrei Bemidbar, Shelah* 115)

A Lifeline

The commandments are compared to a lifeline at sea. Grasping them is tantamount to grasping life; forsaking them is like forsaking life.

"You shall not rove after your heart and after your eyes" (Numbers 15:39). The heart and the eyes are agents for the body; they cause the body to stray. Therefore, the verse states [immediately afterward]: "So that you shall remember, and perform all My commandments" (15:40).

This can be explained by means of a parable of one who was cast into the water, and the captain extended a lifeline to him. The captain told him: Seize this rope with your hand and do not release it, for if you release it, you will have no life. Here too, the Holy One, Blessed be He, said to Israel: As long as you cleave to the commandments, it is stated concerning you: "But you, who cleave to the Lord your God, all of you live today" (Deuteronomy 4:4). Likewise the verse states: "Hold fast to admonition, do not let go; safeguard it, as it is your life" (Proverbs 4:13).

"And be holy" (Numbers 15:40). When you perform the commandments, you are sanctified and dread of you is cast over all the nations. When you abandon the commandments and transgress, you are immediately desecrated and dishonored.

(*Tanḥuma, Shelah*)

📖 **Further reading:** With regard to how one fulfills the commandment of ritual fringes, see *A Concise Guide to Halakha*, p. 580.

---

9.   *Oto* can also mean "him," in this case a reference to God.

Korah

The bulk of this Torah portion addresses the dispute of Korah and his people with Moses, along with its attendant matters. Korah, supported by many others, alleged that Moses and Aaron took the leadership and priesthood for themselves despite the fact that "the entire congregation, all of them are holy."

The punishment for this contention against Moses and Aaron was severe: Korah and his cohorts were swallowed into the ground, and two hundred and fifty of their supporters, who attempted to perform the rite of burning the incense, were killed by a heavenly fire. Later, the Israelites were harshly punished when they complained about the fate of Korah's followers, and it was only Aaron who prevented the outbreak of a greater plague.

The end of the Torah portion focuses on the structure of the obligations and gifts that are to be given to priests and members of the tribe of Levi, i.e., *teruma* and tithes, and the details of their laws.

The chapter that follows presents statements of the Sages concerning Korah's dispute; details about Datan and Aviram, Korah's neighbors; the punishment of Korah and his congregation; and the blossoming of Aaron's staff, which was a sign indicating that God had chosen him.

A Dispute for the Sake of Heaven

Korah's dispute with Moses is an example of a dispute with inappropriate motivation; consequently, there was no justification for it.

Any dispute for the sake of Heaven will ultimately endure, and one not for the sake of Heaven will not ultimately endure. What is a dispute that is for the sake of Heaven? These are the halakhic disputes between Hillel and Shammai and their disciples. What is one that is not for the sake of Heaven? This is the dispute of Korah and his congregation.

(Mishna *Avot* 5:17)

Woe unto the Wicked and Woe unto His Neighbor

Datan and Aviram, members of the tribe of Reuben, were among the first to join Korah in his rebellion against Moses. The Sages explain that the physical proximity between the location of the tribe of Reuben and Korah's family caused them to follow in Korah's path.

"And Datan and Aviram" (Numbers 16:1). From here the Sages said: Woe unto the wicked and woe unto his neighbor. Datan and Aviram joined Korah first because they were neighbors of Korah, whose family encamped to the south of the Tabernacle, as it is written: "The families of the sons of Kehat shall encamp on the side of the Tabernacle to the south" (3:29). And the camp of Reuben was adjacent to them, as it is stated: "The banner of the camp of Reuben is to the south according to their hosts" (2:10)…and Datan and Aviram, who were neighbors of the disputant, were stricken with him and were eliminated from the world.

(Bemidbar Rabba 18)

📖 **Further reading:** For a diagram of the tribal configuration within the Israelite camp, see *A Concise Guide to the Torah*, p. 529.

Morning

When Korah and his congregation complained about the status of Moses and Aaron, Moses instructed them to wait until morning, at which time God would disclose whom He selected. The Sages provide reasons for Moses' postponing the matter until the next morning.

"He spoke to Korah and to his entire congregation, saying: In the morning the Lord will disclose who is His, and who is holy; and will bring him near to Him" (Numbers 16:5). What did Moses see that led him to say "morning"? Moses said: Perhaps they said this matter as a result of eating and drinking. Moses said to himself: Perhaps in the meanwhile [the effects of the food and drink will subside and] they will repent. Therefore, the verse states: "In the morning the Lord will disclose." Moses told Korah: I do not have license to enter before Him now. It is not that there is eating and drinking before Him [and therefore He is too occupied to hear our claims now]. But we may not enter on our account, because we ate and drank.

Alternatively, Moses said to them: The Holy One, Blessed be He, established boundaries in His world; can you mix day and night?…. Just as He distinguished between light and darkness for the constant function of the world, so He distinguished between Israel and the nations…and so He designated Aaron as High Priest, as it is stated: "Aaron was set apart to sanctify him as most holy" (I Chronicles 23:13). If you can nullify that distinction between light and darkness, you can nullify this distinction between Aaron and his sons, the priests; and the rest of the people.

(Bemidbar Rabba 18)

Further reading: For more about the selection of Aaron as High Priest, see above, pp. 117, 139.

The Earth's Opening

Korah's punishment was extraordinary: The earth opened and swallowed Korah, his cohorts, and their property. The Sages disagree with regard to how exactly this transpired, and concerning whether one breach or several opened in the earth.

"The earth opened its mouth" (Numbers 16:32). Rabbi Yehuda said: At that moment, several mouths opened in the earth, as it is stated: "That the earth opened its mouth, and swallowed them ... in the midst of all Israel" (Deuteronomy 11:6).[10]

Rabbi Nehemya said: But isn't it written: "The earth opened its mouth" [in the singular]? Rabbi Yehuda said to him: How do I realize the meaning of: "In the midst of all Israel"? This means that the earth became like a funnel, and wherever in the camp any of them was, he would roll and descend and come with Korah. In that way you have realized the meaning of: "In the midst of all Israel," and you have realized the meaning of: "The earth opened its mouth."

(*Bemidbar Rabba* 18)

The Wise among Women Builds Her House

At the beginning of the Torah portion, On son of Pelet is listed as one of the adherents of Korah, but in the account of the disputants' punishment his name is not mentioned. According to the Sages, the wife of On son of Pelet convinced him to withdraw from the dispute, thereby saving him with her actions.

Rav said: The wife of On son of Pelet saved him. She said to him: How will you benefit from being part of Korah's group? If Moses is the master, you are the disciple, and if Korah is the master, you are the disciple. He said to her: What can I do? I was part of the plot and I took an oath to stay with them. She said to him: I know that the entire congregation is holy, as it is written: "The entire congregation, all of them are holy" (Numbers 16:3). She said to him: Sit, and I will save you. She gave him wine, got him drunk, and lay him down inside. She sat at the entrance and loosened her hair [as though she were getting ready to bathe]. Anyone who came saw her and turned back in modesty. In the meantime, before On awoke, they were swallowed....

---

10. Indicating that the earth opened numerous openings in the entire area of the Israelite camp.

That is the meaning of what is written: "The wise among women builds her house" (Proverbs 14:1). This is a reference to the wife of On son of Pelet.

(*Sanhedrin* 109b)

Aaron's Staff

In order to permanently quash the Israelite complaints about the selection of Aaron for the priesthood, Moses took twelve staffs, one staff for each tribe, and placed them before God. Only from Aaron's staff, the staff of the tribe of Levi, almond leaves blossomed. The Sages provide details of the process and the attendant miracles.

Rabbi Hanina said: Moses took a beam and sawed it into twelve boards. He told the princes: Each of you take one staff. They took the staffs and wrote the names of the tribes, each one the name of his tribe. Aaron wrote his name at the top of his staff and the name Levi below it, and he placed a ring between his name and the name Levi. Moses took Aaron's staff and placed it among the staffs. He tied them together and sealed them, and placed them in the inner sanctum, as it is stated: "Moses placed the staffs [*hamatot*] before the Lord" (Numbers 17:22). The term *hamatot* is written [without the letter *vav*, indicating the singular]. This teaches that all the staffs were as one staff.

In the morning, Moses entered the Tent of Meeting in front of all the Israelites, and he saw that Aaron's staff had blossomed. But it did not blossom in its entirety; rather, the Holy One, Blessed be He, performed a miracle within a miracle: The place where Aaron's name was written blossomed and bore fruit, and the place where the name Levi was written was dry....

What is the meaning of what the verse states concerning Aaron's staff: "And has sprouted a bud [*vayatzetz tzitz*]" (17:23)? Just as the diadem [*tzitz*] was placed on Aaron's head, so too the Holy One, Blessed be He, placed the bud as a crown at the top of the staff. The verse also states: "And had produced almonds [*vayigmol shekedim*]." Rabbi Levi said: God punished [*gamal*] those who had been plotting evil [*shakdu*] against Aaron, and they died that night.

(*Yelamdenu* [Mann], *Yalkut Talmud Torah, Korah*)

📖 Further reading: For a drawing of the diadem, see *A Concise Guide to the Torah*, p. 526.

Hukat

The Torah portion begins with the laws of purification from ritual impurity imparted by a corpse, which is effected by means of the red heifer. The Torah then proceeds to describe the final year of the Israelites' sojourn in the wilderness, including the death of Miriam; the episode of the "waters of dispute," for which Moses and Aaron were punished by not entering the Land of Israel; and the death of Aaron. At the same time, we read of the Israelites' advance toward the Land of Israel. They travel in a roundabout manner to avoid battling the children of Edom, but they wage war with the Emorites and conquer their land east of the Jordan. The Torah portion also includes the account of the bronze serpent, and the brief paean honoring the spring from which the Israelites drew water.

The chapter that follows presents statements of the Sages concerning the red heifer and the hidden reason for that rite, the sin of Moses and Aaron and the decree that they would not enter the land, the death of Aaron, the bronze serpent, the special miracle that took place in the channel of the Arnon ravine, and Moses' apprehension before the war with Og king of Bashan.

I Enacted a Statute

The laws of the red heifer are unclear and contradictory: While its ashes purify the impure, those involved in the purification of the impure become impure themselves. The Sages referenced the red heifer as the most distinctive paradigm of a mitzva whose rationale is unclear.

King Solomon said: All of these I have solved, but the section of the red heifer I investigated, and asked, and searched; "I said: I will become wise, but it is distant from me" (Ecclesiastes 7:23).

The verse states that God told Moses: "[This is the statute of the Torah]... And they shall take to you an unflawed red heifer" (Numbers 19:2). Rabbi Yosei bar Hanina said: The Holy One, Blessed be He, said to Moses: I will reveal the rationale for the heifer to you, but for others, it is a statute.

There was an incident involving a certain non-Jew who asked Rabban Yohanan ben Zakkai: You perform several actions that appear like witchcraft: You bring a heifer, burn it, crush it, and take its ashes. If one of you becomes impure with impurity imparted by a corpse, one sprinkles two or three drops upon him and you say to him: You are purified.

Rabban Yohanan ben Zakkai said to him: Has an evil spirit ever entered you? The man said to him: No. Rabban Yohanan ben Zakkai said to him: Have you ever seen a person into whom an evil spirit entered? The man said to him: Yes. Rabban Yohanan ben Zakkai said to him: What do you do to him? The man said to him: We bring medicinal roots, burn them beneath the afflicted person, and we sprinkle water on him; then the spirit flees. Rabban Yohanan ben Zakkai said to him: Let your ears hear what your mouth is saying. Likewise, this spirit is the spirit of impurity, as it is written: "I will remove … the spirit of impurity from the land" (Zechariah 13:2); one sprinkles the waters of sprinkling upon it, and it flees.

After the non-Jew exited, his students said to him: Our teacher, you dismissed that one with a reed [i.e., with a perfunctory answer]. What do you say to us? Rabban Yohanan ben Zakkai said to them: By your lives, it is not the corpse that renders impure and it is not the water that purifies. Rather, the Holy One, Blessed be He, said: I enacted a statute, I issued a decree. You may not violate My decree, as it is written: "This is the statute of the Torah" (Numbers 19:2).

(*Bemidbar Rabba* 19; *Tanḥuma, Hukat*)

📖 Further reading: For more about Torah statutes that transcend logic, see above, p. 150.

Let the Heifer Come and Atone for the Act of the Calf

One uses specifically the ashes of a heifer, not a bull, in order to remove the impurity imparted by a corpse. The Sages compare this to a mother who cleans the filth generated by her baby.

Why are all the offerings male while this one is female? Rabbi Aivu said: This can be explained by means of a parable of the son of a maidservant who sullied the palace of a king. The king said: Let his mother come and clean the excrement. So said the Holy One, Blessed be He: Let the heifer [i.e., the mother cow] come and atone for the sin of the calf.

(*Bemidbar Rabba* 19)

The Greedy Man's Heifer

A red heifer that meets all the criteria established by the Torah is very rare; therefore, it is very expensive. The Sages relate an incident with a gentile, who, due to his greed, demanded an exorbitant price for his heifer. His desire to exploit the Jews ultimately caused him to lose everything.

There was an incident where the Israelites required a red heifer but they could not find one. They then found one in the possession of a certain gentile. They went and they said to him: Sell us the heifer that you have, as we need it. He said: Pay its price and take it. They asked: And how much does it cost? He responded: Three or four gold pieces. They said to him: We are willing to pay.

While they went to bring the money, that gentile learned why they needed the heifer. When they came and brought the money, he said to them: I will not sell it to you. They said to him: Do you want to raise its price? If you ask, we will pay you whatever you ask. The more anxious the evil person saw they were, the more he would abuse them. They said: Take five gold pieces, but he would not consent; take ten, take twenty, until they reached one hundred, but he would not consent....

When he committed to giving it to them for one thousand gold pieces and they agreed and went to bring him gold pieces, what did that wicked one do? He said to his fellow, another gentile: Come and see how I am mocking these Jews. The reason that they are seeking the heifer and are willing to pay me all this money is only because no yoke has been placed upon it [as performing labor with the heifer disqualifies it]. I am going to take the yoke and place it on the heifer, and I will fool them and take their money. He did so, and took the yoke and placed it on the animal all night.

This is the sign of a heifer upon which a yoke had not been placed: There are two hairs on the neck where a yoke is placed. Until the yoke is placed upon it, the two hairs remain erect. If a yoke is placed on it, the two hairs immediately bend. There is one additional sign in the heifer: Until the yoke is placed upon it, its eyes are straight. Once a yoke is placed on it, its eyes look to and fro and it is cross-eyed from looking back at the yoke.

When the Jews came with their gold to purchase the heifer from him, they showed him the gold. He immediately went and removed the yoke from upon the heifer and took it out to them. Once he took it out to them, they began examining it, looking for the signs. They saw that those two erect hairs were bent, and in addition, the yoke had caused it to move its eyes. They said to him: Take your heifer, we do not need it; go fool your mother. Once that wicked one saw that they returned his heifer to him and he was denied all the gold pieces, the same mouth that said: I am mocking them, began saying: Blessed is He who chose this nation. He entered his house, hung a rope, and strangled himself.

(*Pesikta Rabbati* [Ish Shalom] 14)

Before the Eyes of the Children of Israel

When God instructed Moses to speak to the rock to draw out its water, Moses did not do precisely what God instructed. Rather, he struck the rock twice. According to the Sages, his doing so in public exacerbated the severity of the matter. Therefore, Moses was severely punished.

"The Lord said to Moses and Aaron: Because you did not have faith in Me, to sanctify Me before the eyes of the children of Israel; therefore, you shall not bring this assembly into the land that I have given them" (Numbers 20:12). Hadn't Moses once said something more egregious than this? [After God told Moses that He would provide meat for the Israelites,] he said: "Will flocks and cattle be slain for them and it suffice for them? If all the fish of the sea will be gathered for them, will it suffice for them?" (11:22). There too, there is a lack of faith, and it is a greater offense. Why didn't God decree a punishment upon him then?

To what can this matter be compared? It can be compared to a king who had a beloved friend who would rebuke the king with harsh words between the two of them, and the king did not get angry at him. At a later date, he rebuked the king in the presence of the legions and the king decreed that he be executed. Here too…the Holy One, Blessed be He, said to Moses: The first offense that you performed was just between the two of us. Now, it was in the presence of the multitudes; it is impossible to overlook it.

(*Bemidbar Rabba, Parasha* 19)

The Shepherd in the Wake of His Flock

Moses' punishment was that he would not enter the Land of Israel, but rather, he would die and be buried in the wilderness. According to the Sages, it is inconceivable that the entire generation that Moses led out of Egypt would not enter the land, and only the leader, Moses, would enter.

A parable, to what can this matter be compared? It can be compared to a shepherd who went out to herd the flocks of the king, and the flocks were taken. [After this incident,] the shepherd sought to enter the king's palace. The king said to him: They will say that it was you who took the flocks.

Here too, the Holy One, Blessed be He, said to Moses: Is it considered praiseworthy for you to take out 600,000 men fit for battle and bury them in the wilderness, and [then] take another generation into the land? Now they will say that those who died in the wilderness have no portion in the World

to Come as part of their punishment. You will be buried alongside them, and will accompany them into the World to Come.

(*Tanḥuma, Hukat*)

Lover of Peace

After Aaron dies, the verse states that "the entire house of Israel" cried over him. According to the Sages, Aaron would facilitate peace between people; that is why he was so beloved.

[The mishna writes that one should act like Aaron, and be a] "lover of peace." How so? This teaches that a person should love and facilitate peace in Israel among all, just as Aaron would love and facilitate peace in Israel among all. As it is stated: "The Torah of truth was in his mouth, and injustice was not found on his lips; he walked with Me in peace and honesty and he returned many from iniquity" (Malachi 2:6). Rabbi Meir says: What is the meaning of the verse: "And he returned many from iniquity"? When Aaron would proceed along the way and he encountered a bad or wicked person, Aaron would greet him. The next day, when that man would seek to violate a prohibition, he would say: Woe is me; how will I later be able to look Aaron in the eye if I do this? I would be embarrassed, after he greeted me. The result is that this person would prevent himself from transgressing.

Moreover, when two people would engage in a quarrel with each other, Aaron would go and sit with one of them, and would say to him: My son, see your fellow. What is he saying? He is sorrowful and rending his garments. He is saying: Woe is me; how will I be able to look my fellow in the eye? I am embarrassed before him, because it is I who wronged him. Aaron would sit with the first person until he removed all the enmity from his heart.

Aaron would then go and sit with the other, and would say to him: My son, see your fellow. What is he saying? He is sorrowful and rending his garments. He is saying: Woe is me; how will I be able to look my fellow in the eye? I am embarrassed before him, because it is I who wronged him. Aaron would sit with the second person until he removed all the enmity from his heart.

When the two individuals would meet each other, they would hug and kiss one another. Therefore, it is stated: "They wept for Aaron thirty days, the entire house of Israel" (Numbers 20:29).

(*Avot deRabbi Natan*, version A, chap. 12)

Aaron's Passing

Aaron's death was without prior illness or suffering; it took place calmly, under the direction of God. Moses, too, desired a pleasant death like that, and was granted his wish.

"The Lord spoke to Moses and Aaron…. Take Aaron and Elazar his son, and take them up Hor Mountain. Undress Aaron of his vestments, and dress Elazar his son in them; Aaron will be gathered, and die there. Moses did as the Lord commanded" (Numbers 20:23–27). This serves to teach you that even though God told Aaron of the harsh decree against him, he did not delay Moses from acting.

"Undress Aaron of his vestments." Moses removed a priestly vestment from him and dressed Elazar in it, and likewise the second vestment, and likewise the third. Moses told Aaron: Enter the cave, and he entered the cave. Moses told him: Climb onto the bed and extend your hands, and he [climbed onto the bed and] extended his hands. Moses told him: Close your mouth, and he closed it. Moses told him: Close your eyes, and he closed them.

At that moment, Moses said: Happy is one who dies with this death. Therefore it is stated when Moses was to die: "As Aaron your brother died" (Deuteronomy 32:50) – the death that you coveted.

(*Yalkut Shimoni, Hukat* 1:764)

The Entire Congregation Saw

According to the Sages, the Israelites did not believe that Aaron died until God was forced to prove that he had.

When Moses and Elazar descended from the mountain, the entire assembly gathered around them, and said to them: Where is Aaron? Moses and Elazar told them: He died. They said: How could the angel of death harm him? Aaron is a man who stood against the angel of death and stopped him by burning the incense, as it is written: "He stood between the dead and the living and the plague was stopped" (Numbers 17:13). If you bring Aaron to us, fine; if not, we will stone you.

At that moment, Moses stood in prayer and said: Master of the Universe, clear us of suspicion. Immediately, the Holy One, Blessed be He, opened the cave and showed Aaron to the people.

(*Bemidbar Rabba* 19)

The Bronze Serpent

As punishment for the complaints of the Israelites, God sent poisonous serpents that bit and killed them. Moses prepared a serpent of bronze, and anyone who had been bitten looked at it and was cured. The Sages explain that, obviously, it was not the Israelites' gazing at the snake that provided the cure, but rather their thoughts of repentance caused by their looking at it.

"Craft for yourself a fiery serpent, and place it upon a pole; it shall be that anyone who was bitten, will see it and live" (Numbers 21:8). Does a serpent kill, or does a serpent preserve life? This means that when the Jewish people turned their eyes upward and subjected their hearts to their Father in Heaven, they would be healed, but if not, they would deteriorate.

(Mishna *Rosh HaShana* 3:8)

📖 **Further reading:** The Sages provide an explanation for the effectiveness of the bronze serpent similar to the one provided for Moses' upraised arms in the war with Amalek. See above, p. 101.

The Miracle of the Arnon Ravine Passages

After describing the journey of the Israelites and their encampment adjacent to the Arnon ravine, several vague verses describe a certain event related to the Arnon ravine recorded in the "Book of the Wars of the Lord." According to the Sages, it is a description of a miracle that transpired in the passages of the Arnon ravine, when the Emorites lay in wait to ambush Israel; but they themselves were killed.

"Therefore, it is said in the Book of the Wars of the Lord: Vahev by storm [*et vahev besufa*], and the tributaries of the Arnon, the outpouring of the streams that tended toward the settled area of Ar, and abuts the border of Moav" (Numbers 21:14–15). It was taught: "*Et vahev besufa*"; there were two lepers, named Et and Hev, who were walking at the rear [*sof*] of the camp of Israel. As Israel passed, the Emorites came and prepared caves for themselves and hid in them. They said: When Israel passes here we will kill them. But they did not know that the Ark of the Covenant preceded the children of Israel and would flatten mountains before them.

When the Ark came, the mountains adhered one to another and killed the Emorites and their blood flowed down to the streams of Arnon. When Et and Hev arrived, they saw the blood that was emerging from between the mountains and they came and told Israel, who recited a song of praise.

(*Berakhot* 54a)

Og King of Bashan

The Torah states that God bolstered Moses' spirit in preparation for the war with Og king of Bashan. The Sages explain why Moses was concerned specifically about this confrontation.

What is the difference between Og and Sihon, that Moses feared Og but did not fear Sihon? … Moses said: Perhaps the merit of assisting Abraham our patriarch will help Og, as it is stated (Genesis 14:13): "The survivor came and told Abram the Hebrew" [that Lot, Abraham's nephew, had been captured in battle]. And Rabbi Yohanan said: This survivor is Og, who survived the generation of the flood.

(*Nidda* 61a)

Balak

The Torah portion of *Balak* deals with the episode of Balak and Bilam. Balak king of Moav feared the Israelites would defeat his kingdom in battle, and hired Bilam, a renowned prophet and sorcerer, to curse them. Bilam was compelled to say the words that God placed in his mouth, and instead he blessed the Israelites. Bilam also prophesied about the fate of other nations in the future. At the conclusion of the Torah portion, the grave transgression of the Israelites, engaging in lewdness with Moavite women and worshipping their gods, is described. The roots of this sin were in the counsel of Bilam, who suggested that the Moavites tempt the Israelites. The Torah portion concludes with Pinhas's act of zealotry, killing the Israelite man who publicly sinned with a Midyanite woman, and thereby calmed God's wrath.

The chapter that follows presents statements of the Sages concerning the cooperation between Balak and Bilam, Bilam's personality, his journey to curse the Israelites and his donkey who began to speak, Bilam's blessings, and his evil counsel to cause the Israelites to sin.

The Dogs and the Wolf

When the Moavites were overcome with fear of the Israelites, they turned to Midyan in the hope of finding a solution. The Sages explain how these two nations cooperated here despite their long history of enmity, and they also explain the unique imagery that the Moavites employed in describing their fear of Israel.

But don't you find that Midyanites battle the Moavites … and the enmity between them is eternal? This can be explained by means of a parable. To what can this matter be compared? It can be compared to two dogs who were fighting each other and a wolf came and attacked one of them. The dog not being attacked said: If I do not help the other dog, today the wolf will kill it, and tomorrow it will attack me. Therefore, Moav joined together with Bilam [who was a Midyanite].

Balak said about the Israelites: "Now this assembly will lick clean all our surroundings, as the ox licks clean the grass of the field" (Numbers 22:4). Just as the might of an ox is in its mouth, so too, the might of these Israelites is in their mouths [with their prayers]. Just as there is no sign of blessing from anything an ox chews [as the ox eats the produce with its roots,] so too these; any nation they touch, there is no sign of blessing from it. And just as an ox gores with its horns, so too, these gore with their prayers.

(*Tanḥuma, Balak*)

📖 **Further reading:** For more about the power of prayer, see p. 457; *A Concise Guide to Mahshava*, p. 300.

Bilam and Abraham

The Sages saw Bilam as a symbol and a paradigm of moral turpitude, and presented his corrupt qualities as the polar opposite of the elevated character traits of Abraham our patriarch.

Anyone who possesses these three attributes is among the disciples of Abraham our patriarch, and anyone who possesses these three other attributes is among the disciples of the wicked Bilam. One who possesses contentedness with his lot, humility, and the absence of hedonism is among the disciples of Abraham our patriarch. One who possesses a lack of contentedness with his lot, arrogance, and hedonism is among the disciples of the wicked Bilam. What is the difference between disciples of Abraham our patriarch and disciples of the wicked Bilam? Disciples of Abraham our patriarch enjoy this world and inherit the World to Come…but disciples of the wicked Bilam inherit Gehenna and descend into the pit of destruction.

(Mishna *Avot* 5:19)

📖 **Further reading:** For an example of Abraham's humility, see *A Concise Guide to the Torah*, p. 38.

Knows the Knowledge of the Most High

One of Bilam's unique qualities was his ability to determine the precise moment that the anger of God is aroused. Bilam sought to exploit that moment in order to curse the Israelites. However, God deviated from His routine and did not become angry at the designated moment, so that Bilam's plan would not succeed.

And is there anger before the Holy One, Blessed be He? Yes, as it was taught: "God is furious every day" (Psalms 7:12). For how much time is His anger in force? For one moment. And how long is a moment? For 158,888th of an hour; that is a moment. And no creature can determine that precise moment except for Bilam the wicked, about whom it is written: "He knows the knowledge of the Most High" (Numbers 24:16). Bilam did not understand his animal; did he understand the Most High? This teaches that Bilam was able to determine the precise time that the Holy One, Blessed be He, is angry.

Rabbi Elazar said that the Holy One, Blessed be He, said to Israel: Know how many acts of kindness I performed on your behalf, that I did not

become angry during the days of Bilam the wicked. As, had I become angry, there would have been no remnant or survivor remaining among the enemies of Israel, [i.e., among Israel]. That is what Bilam said to Balak: "How will I curse what God has not cursed? How will I censure those the Lord has not censured?" (23:8). This teaches that all those days, God was not angry.

(*Berakhot* 7a)

Bilam Goes to Curse Israel

When the princes of Moav asked Bilam to curse Israel, he informed them that he would wait for instructions from God. Indeed, God instructed him not to go. When they insisted he come, God agreed he could accompany them, provided that he would say only the prophecies that God would give him. An angel of God impeded the progress of his donkey. Bilam, unaware of the angel, tried to force the donkey to continue, and the donkey spoke with Bilam and rebuked him. The angel, too, repeated the message that Bilam would be compelled to repeat with precision the prophecies he would receive from God. The Sages describe this episode.

"God said to Bilam: You shall not go with them" (Numbers 22:12). Bilam said to Him: If so, I will curse them from my place. God said to him: "You shall not curse the people" (22:12). Bilam said to Him: If so, I will bless them. God said to him: They do not need your blessing, "as it is blessed" (22:12). As people say to the wasp: We want not from your honey and not from your sting....

[The verses recount the conversation between Bilam and the donkey:] "It said to Bilam: What did I do to you that you struck me these three times?" (22:28). [By mentioning three, the donkey] alluded to him: You are seeking to uproot a nation that celebrates three festivals.

Bilam responded: "If only there were a sword in my hand, I would have killed you now" (22:29). This can be explained by means of a parable of a doctor who came to cure someone with a snakebite using the speech of his tongue. On the way, he encountered a certain large lizard. He began looking for a stick to kill it. People said: You are unable to kill this lizard without a stick; how do you come to cure one with a snakebite using your tongue? Likewise, the donkey said to Bilam: You are unable to kill me without a sword in your hand; how do you hope to uproot an entire nation? Bilam was silent and did not find an answer. The princes of Moav began doubting him, as they saw an unprecedented miracle [that the donkey spoke].

(*Bemidbar Rabba* 20)

Places Where Israel Falls

Bilam did not know exactly where to go to observe the Israelite camp from above and attempt to curse them. Balak took him to several places. According to the Sages, Balak especially sought those places where Israel was destined to sin in the future, in order to arouse an indictment against them before God.

"Balak took Bilam and brought him up to the heights of Baal" (Numbers 22:41). Balak was a greater sorcerer and diviner than Bilam, and Bilam was drawn after him like a blind man. To what could the two of them be compared? They could be compared [to two people who wanted to cut up a piece of meat]. One had a knife in his hand but did not recognize the joints where the meat needed to be cut, while the other recognized the joints but did not have a knife in his hand. Balak would see the places where the Israelites were destined to sin. The verse states: "And brought him up to the heights of Baal"; this is a reference to Baal Peor [where the Israelites sinned with the Moavite women and worshipped Baal Peor, the god of the Moavites], as he saw that Israelites would die there.

(*Tanḥuma* [Buber], *Balak*)

Bilam's Blessings

Bilam sought to curse the Israelites three times; instead, he was compelled to bless them those three times. The Sages explain the meaning of some of these blessings.

Bilam said: "Who has counted the dust of Jacob?" (Numbers 23:10). Who can count the mitzvot that the Israelites perform with the dust: "You shall not plow with an ox and a donkey together" (Deuteronomy 22:10); "You shall not sow your vineyard with diverse kinds" (Deuteronomy 22:9)…. Bilam said: "Or tallied one-quarter [*rova*] of Israel" (Numbers 23:10). This is a reference to their pregnancies [*reviiyot*]: Who can tally the population that emerged because the Israelite women cleaved to and treasured the mitzva to bear children, even when slaves in Egypt…. He continued: "He did not see evil in Jacob" (23:21). Bilam said: God does not look at the transgressions that they perform, but looks only at their good deeds.

Bilam said: "The Lord his God is with him" (23:21). You, Balak, told me: "Go curse Jacob for me" (23:7). A thief cannot harm an orchard that has a guard, but if he sleeps, the thief enters. But concerning these people: "Behold, the Guardian of Israel neither slumbers nor sleeps" (Psalms 121:4), how will I be able to harm them? Balak said to him: Since you cannot touch them because of Moses, who serves them, see what will be with the one who

will serve as leader after him. Bilam responded: Joshua, too, is tough like Moses. Bilam continued: "And the blast of the King is in its midst" (23:21); Joshua sounds a *tekia* and sounds a *terua* and flattens the walls of Jericho.

(*Bemidbar Rabba* 20)

How Goodly Are Your Tents

The modesty of the Israelites in their residences caused Bilam to praise and exalt them.

"Bilam raised his eyes, and he saw Israel dwelling according to its tribes" (Numbers 24:2). What did he see? He saw that the entrances of their tents were not aligned opposite each other [so one could not see into his neighbor's tent]. He said: These people are worthy of having the Divine Presence rest upon them.

(*Bava Batra* 60a)

Bilam's Advice

At the conclusion of the Torah portion, there is the account of the Israelites' sin with the Moavite and Midyanite women, who seduced the Israelites to engage in forbidden sexual relations and worship idols. The Torah relates that these sins came about "by the word of Bilam," through his advice. The Sages explain the nature of that advice: He told them that it is impossible to overcome Israel by force, but it is possible to cause them to stray from the virtuous path.

The verse states concerning the women of Midyan: "Behold, they were for the children of Israel, by the word of Bilam" (Numbers 31:16). What was the word of Bilam? He told them: Even if you advance against the Israelites with all the multitudes in the world you will not prevail against them. Are you more numerous than the Egyptians, as it is stated concerning them: "He took six hundred select chariots" (Exodus 14:7)? Come and I will advise you what you shall do: The God of these people hates licentiousness. Provide them with your wives and your daughters for licentiousness.

(*Sifrei Bemidbar, Matot* 157)

Pinhas

The Torah portion begins with the reaction of God to the zealous act of retribution performed by Pinhas against Zimri, with which the Torah portion of *Balak* concluded. God promises Pinhas an eternal covenant of peace. Thereafter, there is a detailed census of the Israelite males. The Torah then presents the request of the daughters of Tzelofhad that the portion their father would have received in the Land of Israel be given to them, and God's approval of their request. Moses asks that a leader be appointed to succeed him, and Joshua is chosen. At the conclusion of the Torah portion, the procedures of the fixed offerings – daily, Shabbat, New Moon, and festivals – are enumerated.

The chapter that follows presents statements of the Sages concerning Pinhas's zealotry, the righteousness of the Israelite women, Tzelofhad's daughters, and the appointment of a leader.

Pinhas

The Israelites were engaging in licentious intercourse with the women of Moav and Midyan. This reached a nadir when Zimri, the prince of the tribe of Simeon, publicly consorted with a princess of Midyan. Pinhas was zealous on behalf of God and killed them. The Sages describe the contempt that Pinhas was subjected to by the people, and God's reaction to his deed.

The tribes began to demean Pinhas: Did you see this son of Puti, [called such] because the father of his mother, Yitro, fattened [*pitem*] calves for idol worship, who killed the prince of a tribe of Israel? The verse comes and provides his lineage: "Pinhas son of Elazar son of Aaron the priest" (Numbers 25:11).

The Holy One, Blessed be He, said to Moses: Be the first to greet Pinhas with a blessing of peace, as it is stated: "Therefore say: Behold I am giving him My covenant of peace" (25:12), and the atonement [engendered by the act of Pinhas] is worthy of continuing to atone forever.

(*Sanhedrin* 82a)

The Virtue of the Women

While the men were remiss and sinned in several episodes, the Israelite women followed the proper path. That was true in the case of the Golden Calf, and the same is true with regard to exhibiting love for the Land of Israel.

In that generation, the women would repair what the men would breach, as you find that Aaron said to the Israelite men who asked Aaron to fashion a god for them: "Remove the gold rings that are in the ears of your wives" (Exodus 32:2); but the women refused and protested to their husbands, as it is stated: "All the people removed the gold rings that were in their ears (Exodus 32:3),"[11] but the women did not participate in the act of the Golden Calf.

Likewise, in the case of the spies who slandered, it was the men who sinned…but the women were not with them in their counsel, as it is written just prior to the matter of the daughters of Tzelofhad: "As the Lord said of them: They will die in the wilderness. No man was left of them" (Numbers 26:65). No man was left, but the punishment for the sin of the spies did not apply to the women. Why? Because the men did not want to enter the land. But the women approached to request an inheritance in the land, as the verse states: "The daughters of Tzelofhad approached" (27:1).

(*Tanhuma, Pinhas*)

Moses Brought Their Case before the Lord

When the daughters of Tzelofhad presented their request before Moses, he did not respond immediately, but rather he turned to God. The Sages take two approaches to this matter. One is that Moses did not know how to respond to their request. The other is that he did know how to respond, but asked out of humility.

There are righteous people who were haughty with regard to a commandment and the Holy One, Blessed be He, enfeebled their minds…He did so with Moses, because Moses said: "And the matter that is too difficult for you, you shall bring near to me, and I will hear it" (Deuteronomy 1:17). Therefore, God enfeebled his mind. This can be explained by means of a parable of a money changer who told his apprentice: If customers bring you *sela* coins, change them; if they bring you gems, bring them to me. A glass necklace was brought to the apprentice. He took it to his master, and his master [did not know its value and] went to show it to another, more expert money changer.

So too, Moses told the judges: "The matter that is too difficult for you, you shall bring near to me." Tzelofhad's daughters came, and the resolution of their question was beyond him: "Moses brought their case before the Lord" (Numbers 27:5). God told him: "The daughters of Tzelofhad speak justly" (27:7), the law is that they shall receive a portion of the land. The

---

11. The Hebrew term for "their ears" is written in the masculine.

Holy One, Blessed be He, said to Moses: Didn't you say: "The matter that is too difficult for you, you shall bring near to me"? The law that you do not know, the women know.

Alternatively: "Moses brought their case before the Lord." Reish Lakish said: Moses our teacher knew this law. The daughters of Tzelofhad first approached the leaders of tens [i.e., those appointed to serve as judges over ten families each]. Those leaders said: This is a law of inheritance, and this is not for us to adjudicate, but for those greater than we. The daughters of Tzelofhad came to the leaders of fifties. Those leaders saw that the leaders of tens treated the women with respect, and the leaders of fifties said: We too will not answer this question; there are others greater than we. It was likewise with the leaders of hundreds, and likewise with the leaders of thousands, and likewise with the princes. All of them responded in a similar manner that they did not want to begin adjudicating [the case] before one who was greater than they. The daughters of Tzelofhad went before Elazar, who said to them: Here is Moses our teacher.

All of these: leaders, princes, and Tzelofhad's daughters, came before Moses. Moses saw that each and every one of them deferred to one greater than they. He said: If I tell them the ruling, I will be taking the prominence for myself. He said to them: I, too, have One who is greater than I. Therefore, "Moses brought their case before the Lord."

(*Bemidbar Rabba* 21)

📖 Further reading: For more about humility and arrogance, see p. 432.

God of the Spirits of All Flesh

Moses requested from God that He appoint a leader capable of addressing the needs of each and every member of the nation.

"Moses spoke to the Lord, saying: May the Lord, God of the spirits of all flesh, appoint a man over the congregation" (Numbers 27:15–16). This serves to inform you of the praise of the righteous, who, when they take leave of the world, they set aside their own needs and attend to the needs of the community.…

Moses said to God: Does the person whom You will install over them have a spirit capable of accepting 600,000 different people, so that he can speak to each and every one of them in accordance with his character? The Holy One, Blessed be He, said to him: Moses, you have spoken well….

Know that this is what Moses requested from the Holy One, blessed be He: Master of the Universe, the character of each and every one is known and revealed before You, and the children's characters are not all alike. Therefore, when I leave You, I implore You: If You seek to appoint a leader over them, appoint a person who will tolerate each and every one of them according to his character, as it is stated: "May the Lord, God of the spirits [of all flesh," with "spirits" written in the plural].

(*Yalkut Shimoni, Pinhas* 1:776)

Who Will Go Out before Them

A true leader leads his soldiers into battle and does not remain at the rear.

[Among the traits required in a leader, Moses states:] "Who will go out before them" (Numbers 27:17). This means that he will not conduct himself in the manner of the kings of the nations of the world, who send out the lowly people to war while they sit in their palaces; rather: "Who will go out before them, who will come before them" (27:17).

(*Sifrei Zuta* 27)

Further reading: For more about leaders and leadership, see pp. 81, 103, 126, 211, 243.

The Guardian of a Fig Tree Will Eat Its Fruit

The Sages teach that Moses thought his sons would take his place leading the people, but God informed him that Joshua would be his replacement.

Moses believed that his sons would inherit his place and assume his position of leadership, so he requested from the Holy One, blessed be He: "May the Lord appoint a man over the congregation" (Numbers 27:16) who has leadership qualities. The Holy One, Blessed be He, said: Moses, it is not as you believe. Your sons will not inherit your position. You know that Joshua served you and accorded you great respect, and he would rise early and remain late in your study hall to arrange the benches and lay out the mats. He will assume the leadership, to fulfill what is stated: "The guardian of a fig tree will eat its fruit" (Proverbs 27:18).

(*Yalkut Shimoni, Pinhas* 1:777)

Further reading: For more about the succession from Moses to Joshua, see p. 262.

Matot

The Torah portion begins with the laws of vows and their nullification. Afterward, Moses commands the Israelites to take vengeance against Midyan for their plot to cause the Israelites to sin in order to arouse God's anger against them. The Torah describes at length the war with Midyan, the victory, and the division of the spoils. The Torah portion concludes with the request of the members of the tribes of Reuben and Gad to remain east of the Jordan River, as that region was ideal for raising their flocks of sheep and herds of cattle. Moses accedes to their request, provided that the men go with the rest of the Israelites to wage war and conquer the land west of the Jordan River.

The chapter that follows presents statements of the Sages concerning the severity of vows and oaths, the war between Israel and Midyan, the killing of Bilam, the laws of utensils received from gentiles, and the erroneous priorities of the tribes of Reuben and Gad.

Oath in the Name of God

Vows and oaths that a person utters are especially severe. Only people of great virtue are permitted to take an oath invoking the name of God, even if their statements are absolutely true.

The Holy One, Blessed be He, said to Israel: Be very cautious concerning vows and do not become lax in their regard, as anyone who is lax concerning vows will ultimately take false oaths. And anyone who takes false oaths denies My existence, and he will never gain atonement, as it is stated: "As the Lord will not absolve one who takes His name in vain" (Exodus 20:7)....

The Holy One, Blessed be He, said to Israel: Do not think that it is permitted for you to take an oath in My name. You are not permitted to take an oath in My name even in truth unless you have all these attributes: "The Lord your God you shall fear, Him you shall serve, and to Him you shall cleave, and in His name you shall take an oath" (Deuteronomy 1:17). You must be like these three who were called God-fearing: Abraham, Job, and Joseph.... If you have all these attributes, you may take an oath, but if not, you may not take an oath.

(*Tanḥuma, Matot*)

Vows

The Sages disagreed with regard to what is preferable: To state vows and fulfill them, or to refrain from stating vows altogether.

["That which you vow, pay;] it is better that you not vow than that you vow and not pay" (Ecclesiastes 5:3–4). Better than both this and that [one who vows and pays and one who vows and does not pay] is one who does not vow at all; this is the statement of Rabbi Meir. Rabbi Yehuda says: Better than both this and that [one who does not vow and one who vows and does not pay] is one who vows and pays.

Rav Dimi brother of Rav Safra teaches: With regard to anyone who states a vow, even if he fulfills it, he is called a sinner. Rav Zevid said: What verse teaches this? "If you will refrain from vowing, there will be no sin in you" (Deuteronomy 23:23). One can infer: If you did not refrain from stating vows, there is sin.

(*Nedarim* 9a, 77b)

📖 Further reading: There is a dispute among the Sages whether it is appropriate to take a vow of naziriteship; see p. 178.

Israel's Vengeance against Midyan

Moses was commanded to wage war against the Midyanites before his death, because they were complicit in Bilam's plot to seduce the Israelites to engage in forbidden sexual activity and to worship idols. Although Moses could have delayed carrying out the mission, thereby postponing his death, he did not delay; he immediately commanded the Israelites to go out to battle.

Rabbi Yehuda says: Had Moses sought to live several more years, he could have lived. As the Holy One, Blessed be He, told him: "Avenge the vengeance of the children of Israel on the Midyanites; then you shall be gathered to your people" (Numbers 31:2). The Holy One, Blessed be He, made Moses' death contingent on taking vengeance against Midyan.

The verse serves to inform you of the praise of Moses, who did not say: So that I will live longer, I will delay the taking of vengeance by the Israelites against the Midyanites. Rather: Immediately, "Moses spoke to the people, saying: Select from among you men for the army, and they shall be against Midyan" (31:3).

"One thousand per tribe from the thousands of Israel were provided, twelve thousand mobilized soldiers" (31:5). The term "were provided" [written in the passive] indicates that it was against their will. Since the verse

made Moses' death contingent upon vengeance against Midyan, the Israelites said: Will we go to attack Midyan and have Moses die? They refrained from going. The Holy One, Blessed be He, said to Moses: Draw lots for the tribes to determine who should go to battle, and the soldiers will be provided against their will.

(*Tanḥuma, Matot*)

Moses and Pinhas

Moses himself did not go out to battle the Midyanites; he sent Pinhas the priest at their head. The Sages suggest a reason for this.

"Moses sent them" (Numbers 31:6). The Holy One, Blessed be He, told Moses: "Avenge the vengeance" (31:2) – you yourself. And yet, he is sending others? Because Moses had lived in the land of Midyan, he said: It is inappropriate for me to harm those who treated me well. The parable says: Do not cast a stone into a well from which you drank.

(*Bemidbar Rabba* 22)

The Killing of Bilam

In the course of the war with Midyan, the Israelites killed the five Midyanite kings, and likewise Bilam, in accordance with whose advice the Midyanites acted. The Sages describe how Bilam attempted to utilize his supernatural powers to save himself, but ultimately failed.

When Pinhas and all the military units that accompanied him went to Midyan, upon seeing Pinhas the wicked Bilam transformed his two arms into stone boards and he flew and ascended upward by using the ineffable name of God. When Pinhas saw that Bilam was flying and ascending, he made his own two arms into two stone boards and flew and ascended, pursuing him, until Pinhas found Bilam prostrating himself before the Throne of Glory. Immediately, Pinhas donned the diadem of the Holy One, blessed be He [worn by the High Priest, upon which the words "sacred to the Lord" were written], and he seized Bilam and brought him before Moses. The Israelites judged Bilam in the Sanhedrin and killed him.

(*Yalkut Shimoni, Matot* 1:785)

Rendering a Gentile's Utensils Kosher

In the war with Midyan, the Israelites seized considerable spoils, among them utensils used with food. The Torah provides methods of rendering utensils kosher, based on their previous uses. According to what is written in the Torah portion, the Sages established fundamental principles concerning how to render utensils kosher.

In the case of one who acquires utensils from a gentile, if he acquires those utensils whose manner is to immerse them in a ritual bath,[12] he must immerse them accordingly. If he acquires those whose manner is to purge them, he must purge them accordingly.[13] If he acquires those whose manner is to heat in the fire until white-hot,[14] he must heat them in the fire until white-hot. If he acquires a spit or a grill, he must heat them in the fire until white-hot. If he acquires a knife, he rubs it and it is purified.

The Sages taught: And all these utensils acquired from a gentile require immersion in forty *se'a* of water. From where is this matter derived? Rava says: From what the verse states: "Everything that may come through the fire, you shall pass through the fire, and it shall be purified" (Numbers 31:23). By writing "and it shall be purified," the verse added for you another act of purification [immersion].

(*Avoda Zara* 75b)

📖 **Further reading:** For more about the laws of immersion of utensils, see *A Concise Guide to Halakha*, p. 560.

The Error of the Members of the Tribes of Reuben and Gad

At the conclusion of the Torah portion, the members of the tribes of Reuben and Gad request to remain east of the Jordan, claiming that the place is compatible with their economic needs. Initially, Moses harshly criticizes them, especially because their words evoke the events of the sin of the spies. The Sages find in Moses' words an allusion to an additional critique of their priorities.

The members of Reuben and Gad made the primary secondary and the secondary primary. How so? They valued their property more than their bodies, as they said to Moses: "We will build sheep enclosures for our livestock here" (Numbers 32:16) first, and only then: "And cities for our children" (32:16).

---

12. Because they were used with only cold non-kosher food items.
13. Because they were used with hot non-kosher food, he must purge them accordingly.
14. Because they came into contact with non-kosher food while on the fire.

Moses said to them: Do not do that. Do the primary task first: "Build cities for your children" (32:24); and only then: "And enclosures for your flocks" (32:24).

The Holy One, Blessed be He, said to those tribes: You valued your property more than your lives. I take an oath by your lives, your property will not be blessed.

(*Tanḥuma, Matot*)

Masei

This Torah portion, which concludes the Israelites' wandering in the wilderness, opens with a chronological list of the journeys and the places through which the people passed during their forty years in the wilderness. The Torah portion continues by addressing the preparations for entry into the Land of Israel and the distribution of the tribal inheritances: the command to conquer the entire land; establishment of each tribe's borders as well as who would be in charge of dividing those inheritances; the command to designate cities for the Levites, who are not entitled to a regular inheritance, among them the cities of refuge where an unwitting murderer is exiled; and the request of members of the tribe of Manasseh that they not suffer a loss from the laws of inheritance instituted in the wake of the request of Tzelofhad's daughters.

The chapter that follows presents statements of the Sages concerning the list of the Israelites' journeys, the cities of refuge, and the preciousness of the Land of Israel and its appropriateness for the children of Israel.

The Israelites' Journeys

The detailed list of the journeys was designed to remind the Israelites of all the kindness God bestowed on them and all the miracles He performed on their behalf during all their years in the wilderness. The list was also intended to remind them of their conduct that angered God time after time.

The Holy One, Blessed be He, said to Israel: My children, be cautious concerning My commandments and observe the Torah, as how many miracles and wonders have I performed for you since the day that you emerged from Egypt? I caused the downfall of your enemies, I took you across the sea, I brought fear and trembling on your enemies, I destroyed the Emorites, Sihon, and Og. All forty years that you were in the wilderness I did not abandon you for even one hour, and how many serpents and scorpions did I kill before you ….

Therefore, the Holy One, Blessed be He, said to Moses: Write of the journeys that the Israelites traveled in the wilderness so that they will know how many miracles I performed on their behalf on each and every journey….

"These are the journeys of the children of Israel" (Numbers 33:1). This can be explained by means of a parable of a king whose son was ill, and he took him to another place to cure him. When they were returning, his father began counting the difficulties they had on the journey on their way to their

destination: Here we slept, here we cooled ourselves, here your head ached. So, too, the Holy One, Blessed be He, said to Moses: Enumerate for them all the places where they angered Me. Therefore, it is stated: "These are the journeys."

(Tanḥuma [Buber], Masei)

He Instructs Sinners in the Way

Cities of refuge were designated to provide protection to unwitting murderers, and it was necessary to clearly mark the roads leading to them. The Sages derive from this the degree to which God accompanies and guides the wicked, and all the more so the righteous.

When Moses stood, the Holy One, Blessed be He, said to him: "You shall designate cities, cities of refuge they shall be for you" (Numbers 35:11). Moses said: Master of the Universe, one who unwittingly kills another in the south or the north, from where will he know where the cities of refuge are so that he can flee there? God said to him: "You shall prepare the way for you" (Deuteronomy 19:3). Direct the path for you so that the one fleeing will not err and the blood redeemer will find him and kill him ….

Moses said to Him: How? God said to him: Position signs for them that direct them to the cities of refuge, so he will know how to go there. Write on each sign: Murderer, flee to a city of refuge…Therefore, David said: "Good and upright is the Lord; therefore He instructs sinners in the way" (Psalms 25:8). If for murderers He prepares a path and a way so they can flee and be saved, all the more so for the righteous: "He guides the humble with justice" (Psalms 25:9).

(Tanḥuma [Buber], Masei)

The Land Is Dear

The Torah portion tells of the preparations for entry into the Land of Israel. The Sages note how precious the Land of Israel is, and how appropriate it is that Israel inherit it.

The Holy One, Blessed be He, said to Moses: This land is precious to Me… and Israel is precious to Me…the Holy One, Blessed be He, said to him: I will bring My children who are precious to Me into a land that is precious to Me.

"This shall be the land that will fall to you as an inheritance" (Numbers 34:2). What is the meaning of "to you"? It is fitting for you. This can be

explained by means of a parable of a king who had slaves and maidservants, and he would marry his slaves to maidservants from another estate. The king arose and thought, and he said: I have slaves and I have maidservants; it is preferable that I marry my slaves to my maidservants. So the Holy One, Blessed be He, said: The land is Mine … and Israel is Mine … It is preferable that I bequeath My land to My servants, to My people. That is why it is stated: "This shall be the land that will fall to you as an inheritance" (34:2).

(*Tanḥuma, Masei; Tanḥuma* [Buber], *Masei*)

Further reading: For more about the Land of Israel and its special virtue, see p. 387; *A Concise Guide to Mahshava*, p. 132.

Torah – Deuteronomy

Devarim

The Torah portion of *Devarim* marks the beginning of Moses' long address to the people prior to his death, an address that extends over the majority of the book of Deuteronomy. Moses' statements in this Torah portion relate, in the main, to the history of the Israelites in the wilderness, with its focus on Moses' difficulties, which led to his appointing judges and magistrates to assist him; the sin of the spies and its consequences; a description of the maneuvering of the Israelite camp before entry into the Land of Israel, circumventing the lands of the Edomites, Amonites, and Moavites; and the wars with the Emorite kings, Sihon and Og, and the conquest of their lands.

The chapter that follows presents statements of the Sages concerning Moses' address: Rebuke given by a beloved person and flattery given by an enemy; the blessing of God and the blessing of Moses; the importance of a just judgment; and the virtue of issuing a call for peace.

Faithful Are the Wounds of a Friend

The Sages consider Moses' address, in which he again mentions the transgressions of the Israelites during their time in the wilderness, a speech with a large component of rebuke. This is particularly true of the opening verse, which alludes to numerous places where Israel sinned. According to the Sages, one who loves another does not refrain from harshly rebuking him, while one who hates another flatters him and speaks smooth talk to him.

It would have been appropriate for rebuke to be voiced by Bilam and blessings to be voiced by Moses. But had Bilam rebuked them, the Israelites would have said: Our enemy is rebuking us, and would have disregarded it. Had Moses blessed them, the nations of the world would have said: He who loves them blessed them, and would have discounted its significance. The Holy One, blessed be He, said: Let Moses, who loves them, rebuke them, and let Bilam, who hates them, bless them, so that the blessings and rebukes will be accepted absolutely, without hesitation.

To what could Moses and Bilam be compared? They could be compared to a prince who had two tutors, one who loved him and one who hated him. The one who loved the prince would caution him and say: My son, be careful not to transgress, because your father is a judge, and if he hears that you transgressed, even though he is your father, he will not treat

you with favoritism. The one who hated the prince said to him: Why are you worried? Your father is a king; do whatever you please and do not fear anything, because your father is not strict with you.

Similarly: The son is Israel, and the two tutors are Moses and Bilam. Moses loved them and said to them: "Beware, lest your heart be seduced, and you stray and serve other gods ...the wrath of the Lord will be enflamed against you" (Deuteronomy 11:16–17). Why? Because God is a judge...But Bilam would say: Fear not, you are His children. Do whatever you please, as He is not strict with you...Therefore, Solomon proclaimed: "Faithful are the wounds inflicted by a friend" (Proverbs 27:6) – this is Moses; "and the kisses of an enemy are onerous" (Proverbs 27:6) – this is Bilam.

(*Devarim Rabba* 1; *Tanḥuma* [Buber], *Devarim*)

Rebuke and Blessing

Since the Israelites accepted Moses' words submissively, they immediately received his blessing.

"These are the words that Moses spoke" (Deuteronomy 1:1). The Sages say: The Holy One, blessed be He, said to Moses: Since they accepted your rebuke, you must bless them. Immediately, Moses blessed them. From where does one see that Moses immediately blessed them? As it is stated: "The Lord, God of your fathers, will add to you one thousand times as you are, and He will bless you" (1:11).

And from where is it derived that anyone who accepts rebuke merits a blessing? It is as Solomon interpreted it: "For the rebukers [*mokhihim*] it will be pleasant, and a blessing of goodness will come upon them" (Proverbs 24:25).[1]

(*Devarim Rabba* 1)

One Thousand Times

Moses blessed the Israelites that they should multiply one thousand times over, but this blessing did not come to limit the blessings that the patriarchs had already received. Moses' blessing was his own personal addition, while the blessings given to the patriarchs remain in effect.

"The Lord, God of your fathers, will add to you one thousand times as you are, and He will bless you, as He spoke to you" (Deuteronomy 1:11). The

---

1. The Sages interpret *mokhihim* as a reference to those who accepted rebuke.

Israelites said to Moses: Moses our teacher: We do not want you to bless us. The Omnipresent promised Abraham our patriarch: "For I will bless you and multiply your descendants as the stars of the heavens, and as the sand that is upon the seashore" (Genesis 22:17), and you impose limits upon our blessings.

This can be explained by means of a parable of a king who had much property and a young son. The king had to travel overseas. He said: If I leave my property in the possession of my son, he will go and squander it. Rather, I will appoint a steward until he grows up. When that son grew up he said to the steward: Give me the silver and gold that my father left me in your possession. The steward went and gave him enough silver and gold to support him from his, the steward's, own possessions. That son began getting upset. He said to the steward: But you have all the silver and gold that my father left me in your possession; why did you give me so little? The steward told him: Everything that I gave you was from my property, and what your father left you is still guarded.

So, too, Moses said to Israel: "The Lord, God of your fathers, will add to you one thousand times as you are"; that is your blessing from me. And your blessing from God is: "And He will bless you, as He spoke to you." Like the sand of the seas, like the plants of the earth, like the fish of the sea, and like the stars of the heavens in abundance.

(*Sifrei Devarim, Devarim* 11)

You Shall Not Give Preference

Moses relates how he appointed ethical judges to assist him in judging Israel, and along with other instructions, he commanded them not to give preference in judgment. The Sages understand this command on two levels: that judges should not give preference to one of the parties for immaterial reasons, and that the appointment of the judges themselves should be for substantive reasons, without favoritism.

When two litigants come before you for judgment, one poor and one wealthy, do not say: How can I find in favor of the poor man and find the wealthy man liable [as that would insult a prominent person], or: How can I find in favor of the wealthy man and find the poor man liable [as that would cause hardship to a needy person]? If I find the poor man liable, the poor man will be my enemy; and if I find in favor of the poor man, the wealthy man will be my enemy. Do not say: How can I take this man's property and

give it to that man? The Torah says: "You shall not give preference in judgment; small and great alike you shall hear" (Deuteronomy 1:17).

"You shall not give preference in judgment." This is directed at the official tasked with appointing judges. Should he say: This person is attractive, I will appoint him as a judge; or: This man is powerful, I will appoint him as a judge; or: This man is my relative, I will appoint him as a judge; or: This man lent me money, I will appoint him as a judge? If he were to appoint a judge for one of those reasons, the judge would thereby find in favor of the guilty and find the innocent liable; not because the judge is wicked, but because he is ignorant. The Torah ascribes guilt to that official as though it was he who gave preference in judgment.

(*Avot deRabbi Natan*, version A, chap. 10; *Sifrei Devarim, Devarim* 17)

Further reading: For more about the appointment of worthy judges, see pp. 103, 211, 243.

Words of Peace

When the Israelites approached the territory of Sihon the Emorite, king of Heshbon, God promised Moses this land would be conquered easily, and He urged him to go out and wage war with him. Nevertheless, Moses dispatched emissaries in order to attempt to peacefully traverse Sihon's territory. It was only after Sihon's refusal that Moses initiated the war. The Sages learn from here the virtue of peace and the importance of initiating an interaction with words of peace and ways of pleasantness.

The Holy One, blessed be He, said: I said: "Provoke war with him" (Deuteronomy 2:24), and you send words of peace? "There is no peace, said the Lord, for the wicked" (Isaiah 48:22). See that matters of peace are great, as Israel violated what God said to them: "Provoke war with him," and He was not angry with them.

Moses said that he sent messengers to offer them peace "from the wilderness of Kedemot" (Deuteronomy 2:26). What is the meaning of "from the wilderness of Kedemot"? Moses said to God: I learned from You, who preceded [*shekidamta*] the world. You could have sent one bolt of lightning and burned the Egyptians, but You did not do so; rather, You sent me to Pharaoh to request that he agree to free the Israelites in peace.

Alternatively, "from the wilderness of Kedemot" – I learned from the Torah, which preceded [*shekadma*] everything. When You came to give the Torah, it was revealed before You that the children of Esau and the children of Ketura would not accept it. Nevertheless, You sought to offer it to them so they would accept it. Therefore, "I sent messengers" [to offer them peace] (2:26).

The Holy One, blessed be He, said: You offer peace? I take an oath by your lives that you will inherit their land in peace, without casualties.

(*Tanḥuma* [Buber], *Devarim*)

📖 **Further reading:** For more about the virtue of peace, see pp. 179, 374.

Va'ethanan

In the Torah portion of *Va'ethanan*, Moses continues with his great speech to the Israelites at the cusp of their entering the Land of Israel. The primary focus of his address is on transmitting spiritual principles of faith and worship of God, including a call to observe God's mitzvot and a delineation of the consequences if the Israelites fail to do so; reminding the Israelites of the miracles that God performed on behalf of the Israelites in Egypt and in the wilderness; and the concept of repentance. Moses also begins enumerating several mitzvot, including a reiteration of the Ten Commandments that were stated at the revelation at Sinai.

At the beginning of the Torah portion, Moses reveals that he will not be entering the land, but rather Joshua will lead them into the land. Toward the end of the Torah portion, the declaration of faith of the verses of *Shema* appears.

The chapter that follows presents statements of the Sages concerning Moses' prayers for himself and for the Israelites; the content and the virtue of the reciting of *Shema*; the source of the statement: Blessed is the name of His glorious kingdom for ever and ever; and the mitzva to love God.

You Will Not Cross This Jordan

Moses implored God to change his punishment and allow him to enter the Land of Israel, even if only after his death. His prayers were not accepted, and he was allowed only to view the land.

Moses said before Him: Master of the Universe, wasn't the decree decreed that I would not enter the Land of Israel … as royalty? I will enter as a commoner. God said to him: A king does not enter as a commoner.

Moses continued standing and posing all these requests. Moses said before the Holy One, blessed be He: Master of the Universe, since the decree was issued that I will not enter the land by crossing the Jordan River, neither as a king nor as a commoner, I will enter it via the Caesarea Philippi tunnel, which is beneath the Banias spring, thus entering under the Jordan River. God said to him: "But there you will not cross" (Deuteronomy 34:4).

Moses said before Him: Master of the Universe, since it was decreed against me that I will not enter, neither as a king nor as a commoner, and not via the Caesarea Philippi tunnel, which is beneath the Banias spring, at least allow my bones to cross the Jordan for burial. God said to him: "As you will not cross this Jordan" (3:27).

Moses said before Him: Master of the Universe, if it is so that I may not cross in any fashion, allow me to see it with my eyes. Regarding that matter, it was stated to him: "Ascend to the top of the peak … and see with your eyes."

(*Mekhilta deRabbi Yishmael, Beshalah, Mesekhta deAmalek* 2)

📖 Further reading: For more about the decree against Moses, see p. 199.

Moses' Entreaties

Although his judgment was decreed and sealed, Moses continued to pray and implore. Because the decree that Moses would not enter the land was based specifically on the letter of the law, he requested entry as a gift from God.

Even though it was decreed upon Moses not to enter the land, he did not stop praying, as it is stated: "I pleaded with the Lord" (Deuteronomy 3:23). It does not say "I prayed," but "I pleaded [*va'ethanan*]," an expression indicating [requesting something for] free [*hinam*].

You find that when Moses ascended up to the Holy One, blessed be He, on Mount Sinai to receive the Torah, he began by saying: "Show me, please, Your glory" (Exodus 33:18), and the Holy One, blessed be He, showed him everything that is in the world above, and the rewards of each and every individual. Moses said to Him: This treasure, whose is it? God said: It belongs to those who engage in Torah study. And this treasure, whose is it? God said: It belongs to those who perform acts of charity. And whose is this? God said: It belongs to those who observe My mitzvot. And whose is this? God said: It belongs to those whose actions are proper.

Then God showed him a great treasure. Moses said to Him: Master of the Universe, whose is this? The Holy One, blessed be He, said to him: This belongs to one who has performed no good deeds, but I give him a reward from this treasure for nothing; as it is stated: "I will favor whom I will favor [*ahon*]" (Exodus 33:19), meaning: I give him from the treasure for nothing [*hinam*].

When Moses came to request from the Holy One, blessed be He, to allow him to enter the Land of Israel, he was pleading, but the Holy One, blessed be He, would not accept his plea. Moses said to Him: Master of the Universe, if I have deeds to my credit, grant it to me for my deeds, and if I have no deeds and no merit, give me from that treasure that I saw that is given for nothing.

Rabbi Hoshaya said: At that moment, the Holy One, blessed be He, said: It is better that a dangerous snake enter your house, and not a person. If I hadn't shown you all My treasures, you would not know what I have.

(*Devarim Rabba* [Lieberman], *Va'ethanan*)

Moses' Intense Love for Israel

After the sin of the Golden Calf, Moses implored God to not destroy the Israelites, and his prayer was answered. But when Moses prayed to enter the Land of Israel, he was told that he could not be granted this request as well. Moses preferred to overlook his own personal benefit.

The Holy One, blessed be He, issued two decrees, one about the Israelites and one about Moses. One about the Israelites: When they performed that action of worshipping the Golden Calf. From where is that derived? It is stated: "Let Me, and I will destroy them" (Deuteronomy 9:14). And one about Moses: When Moses requested to enter the Land of Israel, the Holy One, blessed be He, said to him: "You will not cross this Jordan" (3:27). Moses requested from the Holy One, blessed be He, to abrogate each of those decrees. Moses said before Him after the sin with the Golden Calf: Master of the Universe, "Please pardon the iniquity of this people in accordance with the greatness of Your kindness" (Numbers 14:19). And the Holy One, blessed be He, abrogated His decree, and Moses' request was fulfilled… as it is stated: "I have pardoned in accordance with your word" (Numbers 14:20).

When Moses came to enter the Land of Israel, he began saying: "Please, let me cross, and I will see the good land" (Deuteronomy 3:25). The Holy One, blessed be He, said to him: Moses, I already abrogated My decree and fulfilled your request; I said: "And I will destroy them" (9:14), and you said: Please pardon, and your request was fulfilled. Now, I seek to fulfill My decree and abrogate your request.

The Holy One, blessed be He, said to him: Moses, you do not know what to do. You seek to hold the rope at both ends…. If you want to fulfill the request of "please let me cross," abrogate the request of "please pardon." If you want to fulfill the request of "please pardon," abrogate the request of "please let me cross." Rabbi Yehoshua ben Levi said: Once Moses heard this, he said before God: Master of the Universe, let Moses and one hundred others like him die, and let not even one of their fingernails be damaged.

(*Devarim Rabba* 7)

Remember and Observe

In the Ten Commandments in the Torah portion of **Yitro**, it is stated: "Remember the Sabbath day to make it holy," while in this Torah portion the verse states: "Observe the Sabbath day to make it holy." According to the Sages, God stated both expressions simultaneously.

"Remember" (Exodus 20:8) and "observe" (Deuteronomy 5:12); both were stated simultaneously, something that is impossible for the mouth to speak and impossible for the ear to hear. Likewise, the verse states: "God spoke all these matters" (Exodus 20:1), and it states: "God has spoken once; I have heard it twice" (Psalms 62:12).[2]

(*Mekhilta deRabbi Yishmael* 20:8)

The Lord Is My Portion

The cry: "Hear Israel, the Lord is our God, the Lord is one," is an expression of the direct connection between Israel and God.

"The Lord is my portion, says my soul; therefore I will await Him" (Lamentations 3:24). Rabbi Yitzhak said: To what can this matter be compared? It can be compared to a king who entered a foreign realm, and dukes, prefects, and military governors entered with him. Some of the realm's residents chose a duke to rule over them, some chose a prefect, and some chose a military governor. One who was clever said: I choose only the king. Why? Because all of them will be replaced, and the king will not be replaced.

So too, when the Holy One, blessed be He, descended onto Sinai, many groups of angels descended with Him: Mikhael and his group and Gavriel and his group. Some of the nations of the world chose Mikhael for themselves, and some of them chose Gavriel for themselves, but Israel chose the Holy One, blessed be He, for themselves. They said: "The Lord is my portion, says my soul." That is the meaning of: "Hear Israel, the Lord is our God, the Lord is one" (Deuteronomy 6:4).

(*Devarim Rabba* 2)

In Praise of the Angels

After reciting the verse "Hear Israel," it is customary to add the words: "Blessed is the name of His glorious kingdom for ever and ever." According to the Sages, that is how

---

2. i.e., God spoke at one time what can be heard as two statements.

the angels praise God, and Moses heard it from them and taught the Israelites to say this as well.

"Hear Israel." The Sages say: When Moses ascended on High, he heard the ministering angels saying to the Holy One, blessed be He: Blessed is the name of His glorious kingdom for ever and ever, and he took awareness of this praise down with him and taught it to Israel.

Why don't the Israelites recite: Blessed is the name of His glorious kingdom for ever and ever, out loud, publicly? Rabbi Asi said: To what can this matter be compared? It can be compared to one who stole jewelry from a king's palace. He gave it to his wife and said to her: Do not adorn yourself with it in public, but rather in your house. But on Yom Kippur, when the Jewish people are cleansed of sin and like angels, they recite it out loud: Blessed is the name of His glorious kingdom for ever and ever.

(*Devarim Rabba* 2)

Further reading: For more about reciting "Blessed is the name..." out loud on Yom Kippur, see *A Concise Guide to Halakha*, p. 169. For more about the comparison of people to angels, see *A Concise Guide to Mahshava*, p. 67.

You Shall Love

The Torah commands us: Love God "with all your heart, and with all your soul, and with all your might." The Sages analyze the precise meaning of these phrases and interpret them in several ways.

One is obligated to recite a blessing for the bad just as he recites a blessing for the good, as it is stated: "And you shall love the Lord your God with all your heart, and with all your soul, and with all your might" (Deuteronomy 6:5). "With all your heart" means to serve God with your two inclinations, with your good inclination and your evil inclination. "With all your soul" means that you must serve God even if God takes your soul. "And with all your might" means to serve God with all your money. Alternatively, "with all your might" means that with every measure He metes out to you, good or bad, acknowledge His involvement profusely.

It was taught in a *baraita* that Rabbi Eliezer says: If it is stated: "With all your soul," why does it state: "With all your might"? And if it stated: "With all your might," why does it state: "With all your soul"? The verse should have stated only the more significant of the two. It teaches that if one's body is more precious to him than his property, for such a person it is stated: "With all your soul." And if one's money is more precious to him than his body, for such a person it is stated: "With all your might"....

"And you shall love the Lord your God with all your heart, and with all your soul, and with all your might." What is the meaning of: "With all your soul, and with all your might"? Express your love of God with each and every spiritual ability God created in you. Rabbi Meir said: For each and every breath [*neshima*] that a person takes, one is required to exalt his Maker. From where is this derived? It is derived from a verse, as it is stated: "Let all who breathe [*haneshama*] praise the Lord" (Psalms 150:6).

(Mishna *Berakhot* 9:5; *Berakhot* 61b; *Devarim Rabba* 2)

The Reciting of *Shema*

The reciting of *Shema* is the Jewish declaration of faith, and thereby, in a sense, it encompasses the entire Torah. Reciting it morning and evening is an act of engaging in Torah study day and night, and vigilance in its recitation attests to the fact that one is following the path of uprightness.

This reciting of *Shema*, if a person recites it morning and evening, the Holy One, blessed be He, ascribes to him as though he were immersing himself in Torah study day and night.

The Sages taught in the name of Rabbi Meir: Anyone who resides permanently in the Land of Israel; speaks in the sacred tongue, Hebrew; eats produce in ritual purity; and recites *Shema* morning and evening is informed that he has a place in the World to Come.

(*Midrash Tehillim* 1; Jerusalem Talmud, *Shekalim* 3:3)

📖 Further reading: For more about the reciting of *Shema*, see *A Concise Guide to Halakha*, p. 486.

More than All the Offerings

The words of *Shema* contain allusions to a person's limbs, and reciting it twice a day, morning and evening, is tantamount to sacrificing an offering in the Temple.

Rabbi Mani said: Do not take the reciting of *Shema* lightly, because it contains 248 words, including the statement: "Blessed is the name …," and 248 is equal to the number of a person's limbs.

The Holy One, blessed be He, said: If you observed My 248 words and recited *Shema* in its proper form, I will protect your 248 limbs.

This is what the Holy One, blessed be He, said to Israel: In the past you would bring an offering to Me twice a day: "The one lamb you shall offer in the morning, and the second lamb you shall offer in the afternoon"

(Numbers 28:4). It was revealed and known before Me that the Temple was destined to be destroyed, and from then on you would be unable to sacrifice offerings. But I am asking in exchange for the offerings that you recite *Shema Yisrael* in the morning and *Shema Yisrael* in the evening, and it is considered before Me more valuable than all the offerings.

(*Tanḥuma, Kedoshim; Yalkut Shimoni, Va'ethanan* 1:835)

Proclaiming the Unity of Your Name

In less than perfect circumstances, with the Temple destroyed and Israel exiled among the nations, only the recitation of *Shema*, by which the Jewish people proclaim the unity of the name of God, justifies the continued existence of the world.

When the Holy One, blessed be He, looks at His world and sees theaters and stadiums existing in security, peace, and tranquility, while His Temple is in ruins, He threatens His world with destruction.[3] Once the Jewish people enter synagogues and study halls in the morning and proclaim the unity of His name and say: "Hear Israel, the Lord is our God, the Lord is one" (Deuteronomy 6:4), all the ministering angels gather near the Holy One, blessed be He, and say before Him: You existed before the world was created, You exist since the world was created. You exist in this world and You exist in the World to Come. Sanctify Your name upon those who sanctify Your name. Immediately, the Holy One, blessed be He, is placated and He does not destroy His world, and He calms Himself for the sake of the Jewish people.

(*Yalkut Shimoni, Va'ethanan* 1:835)

Further reading: For more about prayer as a replacement for bringing offerings, see p. 469.

---

3. In the time of the Sages, theaters and stadiums were not merely places of entertainment. In both, actual deaths would occur, either as part of the play or in the course of a competition.

Ekev

In this Torah portion, Moses continues delivering his address. Its main focus in this portion is on essential spiritual matters related to worship of God: reward and punishment, contemplation of the kindnesses that God performed with the Israelites in the wilderness, their preparation for entry into the Land of Israel, and humility before God. In the midst of his discourse about these matters, Moses also recounts the sin of worshipping the Golden Calf and its consequences.

The chapter that follows presents statements of the Sages concerning the minor and major Torah mitzvot, the exacting manner in which the Jewish people relate to reciting Grace after Meals, and the relationship between engaging in Torah study and engaging in labor.

Mitzvot That Are under the Heel

At the beginning of the Torah portion, Moses again presents the fundamental idea that if the Israelites observe God's mitzvot they will receive His blessing. The verse that opens the Torah portion: "It shall be because [ekev] you heed," is expounded by the Sages as an allusion to the meticulous observance of the routine, minor mitzvot that people tend to overlook.

"It shall be because [ekev] you heed these ordinances" (Deuteronomy 7:12). This explains what the verse states: "Why should I fear in days of evil, though the iniquity of my feet [akevai] surrounds me?" (Psalms 49:6).[4] Blessed is the name of the Holy One, blessed be He, who gave Israel the Torah in which there are 613 mitzvot, among them minor ones and major ones. Because there were minor mitzvot among them about which people are not meticulous, but rather they cast them under their heels [ikveihen], ...that is why David feared the day of judgment, and said: Master of the Universe, I do not fear that I was lacking in my observance of the major mitzvot in the Torah, because they are significant, so I was meticulous to observe them properly. What do I fear? That I was lacking in my observance of the minor mitzvot. Lest I violated one of them, whether by doing something I should not have done or by not doing something that I should have done, because it was minor. And You said: Be as meticulous in the observance of

---

4. In other words, I fear that the sins under my feet will surround me.

a minor mitzva as a major one. Therefore, David said: "Why should I fear in days of evil, though the iniquity of my feet surrounds me?"

(*Tanḥuma, Ekev*)

📖 **Further reading:** For more about the ramifications of meticulousness regarding major and minor mitzvot, see p. 403.

And They Are Exacting with Themselves

In this Torah portion, we are commanded to recite a blessing after eating food, provided that we are satiated from it. The Jewish people are exacting and stringent and recite the blessing even if they are not satiated. Just as they go beyond the letter of the law, God, too, tilts the scales of justice in their favor.

The ministering angels said before the Holy One, Blessed be He: Master of the Universe, in Your Torah it is written: "The great, the valorous, and the awesome God, who will not show favor [*yisa panim*], and will not take a bribe" (Deuteronomy 10:17); yet You, nevertheless, show favor to Israel, as it is written: "The Lord shall lift His countenance [*yisa...panav*] to you" (Numbers 6:26). God replied to them: How can I not show favor to Israel? As, I wrote for them in the Torah: "You will eat and be satisfied, and you shall bless the Lord your God" (8:10) [meaning that there is no obligation to bless the Lord until one is satiated]; yet they are exacting with themselves and recite the blessing even if they have eaten as little as an olive-bulk or an egg-bulk.

(*Berakhot* 20b)

📖 **Further reading:** For the laws related to Grace after Meals, see *A Concise Guide to Halakha*, p. 527.

You Will Gather Your Grain

If the Israelites follow in the way of God, He will bless them and their produce. But if not, they will be punished with drought and demise. The Sages disagree concerning the proper relationship between engaging in Torah study and engaging in labor, and whether the statement: "You will gather your grain, and your wine, and your oil," is a blessing or not.

The Sages taught: What is the meaning of what the verse states: "And you shall gather your grain" (Deuteronomy 11:14)? Because it is stated: "This Torah shall not depart from your mouths" (Joshua 1:8) [which seems to contradict the first verse], I might have thought that these matters [in the latter verse] are to be understood as they are written, and one may engage

in nothing other than Torah study, as the verse continues: "And you shall ponder it day and night." Therefore, the verse states: "And you shall gather your grain"; assume in their regard the way of the world, and perform labor as well. This is the statement of Rabbi Yishmael.

Rabbi Shimon ben Yohai says: Is it possible for a person to plow in the plowing season, and sow in the sowing season, and harvest in the harvest season, and thresh in the threshing season, and winnow when it is windy; what will become of Torah? There will be no time to study it. The verse teaches that when Israel performs God's will, their work is performed by others, as it is stated: "And strangers will stand and feed your flocks (Isaiah 61:5). When Israel does not perform God's will, their work is performed by them, as it is stated: "And you shall gather your grain." Moreover, others' work will be performed by them, as it is stated: "You shall serve your enemy" (Deuteronomy 28:48).

Abaye said: Many have acted in accordance with the opinion of Rabbi Yishmael and were successful in both Torah study and their labor. Many have acted in accordance with the opinion of Rabbi Shimon ben Yohai and were not successful in engaging in Torah study not accompanied by labor.

(*Berakhot* 35b)

Re'eh

In the Torah portion of *Re'eh*, Moses continues his speech to the Israelites before they will be entering the land. At the beginning of the Torah portion, he discusses the principle of choosing between good and evil, after which he presents a detailed list of mitzvot that the Israelites will be obligated to fulfill once they enter the land. Among these mitzvot are the command to destroy idols and the laws of those who incite others to engage in idol worship. He then teaches the command to concentrate worship of the Creator around "the place that the Lord will choose," where the offerings shall be presented and to where tithes shall be taken. The laws concerning the consumption of non-sacred meat are specified, and there is a reiteration of the list of kosher and forbidden animals. We then read of the laws of giving tithes to Levites and to the needy, the mitzva of charity, the mitzva of the Sabbatical Year, and the laws of the three pilgrimage festivals.

The chapter that follows presents statements of the Sages concerning the choice between following the good and upright path or its converse; the fact that the Creator gives people the opportunity to sin, especially to continue to engage in idol worship; the mitzva of charity and the blessings of success and wealth that one who is meticulous in its regard will receive; and the obligation not to forget the needy on the festival days.

Two Paths

Moses again relates the concept of freedom of choice to the Israelites. The Sages emphasize that although both paths are open before us, God guides us to follow the proper path. Perhaps it does not always appear pleasant and blessed, but in the long term, it is the preferred path.

"See, I put before you this day a blessing and a curse" (Deuteronomy 11:26). Because it is stated: "I have placed life and death before you, the blessing and the curse" (30:19), perhaps the Israelites will say: Since the Holy One, blessed be He, has placed before us two paths, the path of life and the path of death, we may choose whichever we want. To counter this, the verse states: "You shall choose life" (30:19).

This can be explained by means of a parable of one who was sitting at a crossroads, and there were two paths before him, one whose start is smooth and its end is thorny, and one whose start is thorny and its end is smooth. He would inform the passersby and say to them: Do you see this

path whose start is smooth? For about two or three strides you will be walking on smooth land, but ultimately it will lead to thorns. And do you see that path whose start is thorny? For about two or three strides you will be walking among thorns, but ultimately it will lead to smooth land.

So Moses said to the Israelites: Do you see the wicked who succeed in this world? For about two or three days, i.e., a relatively short time, they succeed, but in the end they will proceed to the ultimate demise…. Do you see the righteous who suffer in this world? For two or three days they suffer, but in the end they will proceed to the ultimate joy….

Rabbi Yehoshua ben Korḥa says: This can be explained by means of a parable of a king who prepared a feast and invited guests, and his friend was reclining among them. The king hinted to his friend to take a fine portion, but his friend lacked the understanding to decipher the hint…. When the king saw that he lacked understanding, he took his friend's hand and placed it on a fine portion. [So too, God guides people and assists them in choosing the proper path.]

(*Sifrei Devarim, Re'eh* 53)

📖 **Further reading:** For more about freedom of choice, see *A Concise Guide to Mahshava*, p. 138.

My Lamp and Your Lamp

The Torah, called the lamp of God, is given to us, and souls, called our lamps, are given to God. If we safeguard His lamp, He will safeguard our lamp.

Bar Kappara said: The soul and the Torah are each likened to a lamp. The soul is likened to a lamp, as it is written: "The spirit of a person is the lamp of the Lord" (Proverbs 20:27), and the Torah is likened to a lamp, as it is written: "For the mitzva is a lamp, the Torah is light" (Proverbs 6:23).

The Holy One, blessed be He, tells a person: My lamp is in your hand and your lamp is in My hand. My lamp is in your hand – that is the Torah. Your lamp is in My hand – that is the soul. If you safeguard My lamp, I will safeguard your lamp. But if you extinguish My lamp, I will extinguish your lamp. From where is this derived? It is derived from a verse, as it is written: "Only beware, and protect yourself [*nafshekha*] greatly" (4:9).[5]

(*Devarim Rabba* 4)

---

5. The verse begins by talking about safeguarding one's *nefesh*, literally, one's soul, and continues by cautioning not to forget or forsake the Torah.

Torah – Deuteronomy > Re'eh _____ SAGES

Torah – Deuteronomy

Should He Destroy His World Because of the Fools?

The prohibition against worshipping idols appears several times in the Torah, among them in the Torah portion of *Re'eh*. Why does God enable the continued existence of idol worship and not destroy the objects of that worship? The fundamental answer of the Sages is that He will not alter the laws of nature in order to discourage the sinners.

Some philosophers asked the Jewish elders who were in Rome: If it is not your God's will that people engage in idol worship, why does He not eliminate it? The Jewish elders said to them: If people were worshipping only objects for which the world has no need, He would eliminate it. But they worship the sun, the moon, the stars, and the constellations. Should He destroy the world because of the fools? Rather, the world follows its course, and the fools who sinned will be judged in the future.

Similarly, if one stole a *se'a* of wheat and planted it in the ground, by right it should not grow. But the world follows its course and the fools who sinned will be judged in the future.

(*Avoda Zara* 54b)

Give Tithes So That You Will Become Wealthy

In this Torah portion, several types of tithes that must be separated from produce are listed: tithes given to Levites; to the poor; and second tithe, which one takes to Jerusalem to eat there. The Sages teach that meticulousness regarding tithes will not decrease a person's property; on the contrary, it will cause one's property to be blessed.

"You shall tithe [*aser te'aser*]" (Deuteronomy 14:22). Give tithes [*aser*] so that you will become wealthy [*titasher*].

Rabbi Yohanan came upon the young son of Reish Lakish, and said to him: Recite for me the verse that you learned today. Reish Lakish's son said to him: "You shall tithe [*aser te'aser*]." The boy asked: And what is the meaning of "you shall tithe"? Rabbi Yohanan said to him: Give tithes [*aser*] so that you will become wealthy [*titasher*]. The boy said to him: From where do you derive that this is so? Rabbi Yohanan said to him: Go and test it.

The boy said to him: Is it permitted to test the Holy One, blessed be He? But isn't it written: "You shall not test the Lord your God" (6:16)? Rabbi Yohanan said to him: Rabbi Hoshaya said: This applies to all matters except for tithes, as it is stated: "Bring all the tithe... test Me now with this, said the Lord of hosts, if I will not open for you the windows of the heavens, and pour out an endless [*ad beli dai*] blessing for you" (Malachi 3:10). What

is the meaning of: "*Ad beli dai*"? Rami bar Hama said that Rav said that it means: The blessing will be so plentiful until [*ad*] your lips will be worn out [*yivlu*, which includes the same Hebrew letters as *beli*] from saying "enough [*dai*]."

(Ta'anit 9a)

Giving a Gift Will Cause a Person to Flourish

The Sages tell of a person who continued to meticulously fulfill the mitzva of giving charity even after he lost almost all his property, and thanks to that conduct, he acquired much greater wealth.

There was an incident involving Rabbi Eliezer and Rabbi Yehoshua, who went out to collect money to fund the Torah study of the Sages. They went to the valley of Antioch. There was a person there called Abba Yudan, who was accustomed to generously donate to the Sages.

That Abba Yudan became impoverished. Rabbi Eliezer and Rabbi Yehoshua saw this when they went to collect there, and he hid from them. He entered his house and remained there for one day or two and did not go to the marketplace. His wife said to him: Why haven't you gone to the marketplace these two days?

Abba Yudan said to her: The Sages came to collect money for the Torah study of those diligently studying Torah, and I do not have the means to give them, and I am therefore embarrassed to go to the marketplace.

His wife, who loved fulfilling mitzvot, said to him: Don't we have one field left? Sell half of it and give the proceeds to them. Abba Yudan went and did so. He sold half the field for five gold pieces and he gave them to the Sages, and he said to them: Pray for me. They prayed for him and said to him: May the Omnipresent restore what you have lost.

The Sages went to collect money elsewhere. Abba Yudan plowed that half-field, found a great treasure there, and became wealthier than he had been previously. When the Sages were returning home at the end of their trip, they passed by that place. They said to someone: Please, arrange a meeting for us with Abba Yudan. That man said to them: Who can arrange a meeting with Abba Yudan? It would be easier to arrange a meeting with the king than with him. The Sages said to him: We are asking to meet him only so that he not hear that we passed here and did not inquire about his well-being.

Abba Yudan found out that the Sages were there and came to them and gave them one thousand gold pieces. He said to them: Your prayer bore fruit. They said to him: We knew about your good deeds, the sacrifice you underwent to give your earlier donation, and we placed you atop our list of contributors even though you gave less than usual.

(*Devarim Rabba* 4)

The Members of Your Household and the Members of My Household

Among the charity obligations mentioned in this Torah portion, there is a special mitzva to give produce to the Levites, who have no agricultural portion in the land, as well as to bring joy on the festivals to the impoverished, the orphans, and the widows. According to the Sages, these are the members of God's household. If we provide for them generously, God will act with us in the same way.

The Holy One, blessed be He, said: You have four members of your household: your son, your daughter, your slave, and your maidservant. I, too, have four members of My household: the Levite, the stranger, the orphan, and the widow. All of them appear in one verse: "You shall rejoice on your festival, you, and your son, and your daughter, and your slave, and your maidservant, and the Levite, and the stranger, and the orphan, and the widow, who are within your gates" (Deuteronomy 16:14). The Holy One, blessed be He, said: I told you that you should bring joy to My household and to yours on the festivals that I gave you. If you do that, I too will bring joy to My household and to yours.

(*Yalkut Shimoni, Re'eh* 1:897)

📖 Further reading: For more about the mitzva of charity and its significance, see *A Concise Guide to Mahshava*, p. 248; *A Concise Guide to Halakha*, p. 615.

Shofetim

In the Torah portion of *Shofetim*, Moses presents a series of mitzvot, most of which relate to communal and governmental protocols: The laws of judges, kings, prophets, and wars. We also find the mitzva to follow the rulings of the central court (the Sanhedrin), the obligation to give certain fixed portions from produce and property to priests and Levites, the laws of an unwitting murderer and the cities of refuge, the laws of conspiring witnesses, and the mitzva of the calf whose neck is broken – a ceremony that is performed when a person was found murdered and the identity of his killer is unknown.

The chapter that follows presents statements of the Sages concerning the desired qualities of judges and the gravity of bribery, the effort required in the performance of charity and kindness, the importance of following the statements of the Sages and especially those who are members of the Sanhedrin, the Jewish people and the heavenly constellations, and a fruit tree that is chopped down.

Incorruptibility

Being a judge demands that one be above suspicion. Moreover, as the Sages illustrate in the following incident, judges must be meticulous in fulfilling the rulings that they themselves issue and instruct others to fulfill.

Judges must be vigorous in the performance of good deeds, as that is what Moses looked for in selecting them: "Moses selected capable men" (Exodus 18:25); men who were capable in Torah, good deeds, and courage.

Judges must be untainted by any suspicion of guilt, such that no person will have any contention against them; like Moses, who said to Israel: "Not one donkey did I take from them, nor did I wrong one of them" (Numbers 16:15), and like Samuel, who said: "Whose ox did I take, whose donkey did I take?" (I Samuel 12:3)....

There was an incident involving Rabbi Hanina ben Elazar, who had a tree planted in his field and its branches extended over the field of another. In addition, someone came and complained before him, and said: The tree of a certain person is extending into my field. Rabbi Hanina said to him: Go away and come back tomorrow. The man said to him: In all the cases that come before you, you issue a ruling immediately, and you delay my case? What did Rabbi Hanina do? Immediately, he sent his workers and had them

chop down the tree that was in his field and extending over the field of another.

The next day, that man came before him for a ruling. Rabbi Hanina said to the other litigant: You must cut down the branches. He said to him: And why are the branches of your tree extending over the field of another? Rabbi Hanina said: Go out and look at it. Just as you see mine, so, do to yours. He went and did so.

(*Tanḥuma, Shofetim*)

Bribery

Judges are cautioned not to take bribes, because bribery will cause even the wisest person to judge wrongly. The Sages relate an incident that underscores how the ties of affection created by receiving a gift from another person, even though it is not bribery at all, influence the recipient in a manner that he cannot control.

"You shall not take a bribe, as the bribe will blind the eyes of the wise" (Deuteronomy 16:19). Once the judge begins thinking of bribery, he becomes blind vis-à-vis the case, and he is unable to adjudicate it correctly....

Rabbi Yishmael ben Elisha said: Come and see how severe bribery is. One time, a certain person came and brought me the first shearing of his sheep [one of the gifts given to a priest]. He had a case before a judge, and I was standing off to one side, and I said: If he advances such and such claim before the judge, he will win his case, and I was hoping for his victory. Even though he gave me only what was mine, as he was required by Torah law to give the wool to a priest, and it was not bribery, nevertheless my heart felt close to him as long as I was watching him. Even after he went to court [sometime after the court case], I asked whether he emerged victorious or not. This informs us how grave bribery is, as it blinds the eyes.

This matter may be inferred *a fortiori*: If in my incident, where he brought me what was mine and I took what was mine, I was hoping for his victory, with regard to one who takes a bribe, all the more so will he support the case of the one who bribed him.

(*Tanḥuma* [Buber], *Shofetim*)

📖 Further reading: For more about the character traits required for a member of the judicial system, see pp. 103, 211.

Justice, Justice You Shall Pursue

One must actively seek opportunities to perform acts of charity and kindness. He must also encourage others to perform them as well, and not be satisfied with what he does on his own.

The verse states: "Justice, justice you shall pursue" (Deuteronomy 16:20). I might have thought that a person does not need to give charity unless the charity collectors come and tell him to give. From where is it derived that even if they do not come and tell him to give charity that one should nevertheless pursue them and give? The verse states: "Justice, justice you shall pursue."…

If one did not encounter the opportunity to perform acts of charity, but rather the charity collectors demanded that he go and request that others perform charity and he did so…he is ascribed credit as though he gave from his own property, as it is stated: "Justice, justice you shall pursue," teaching that one must pursue others to perform acts of charity and kindness.

What reward does he receive for this? "He who pursues righteousness and kindness will find life, righteousness, and honor" (Proverbs 21:21).

(*Midrash Tanna'im, Devarim* 16)

I Support Their Statements

The Torah commands us to obey rulings of the court: "You shall not deviate from the matter that they will tell you" (Deuteronomy 17:11). From here, the Sages derive the general obligation to obey the words of the Sages, as God supports their statements.

A person should not say: I am not fulfilling the ordinances and the decrees of the elders, because they are not Torah law. The Holy One, blessed be He, says to such a person: My son, you are not permitted to say so; rather, everything they decree upon you, you must fulfill, as it is stated: "On the basis of the law that they will instruct you" (17:11). Why? Because I support even their statements, not only their interpretations of the verses.

(*Tanḥuma, Naso*)

You Shall Not Deviate

This Torah portion includes the obligation to resolve in the central court, i.e., the Sanhedrin, disputes relating to Torah laws, and to follow the court's rulings absolutely. There are contrary approaches concerning what to do when the court's ruling is clearly contrary to logic and truth: Must one obey it?

"You shall not deviate from the matter that they will tell you, right or left" (Deuteronomy 17:1). This teaches that even if it seems to you that they ruled about right that it is left and about left that it is right, nevertheless, obey them.

Alternatively: Does this mean that if the Sanhedrin tells you with regard to right that it is left and with regard to left that it is right, you should obey them? The verse states: "To go right or left." Obey the Sanhedrin only when they tell you about right that it is right and about left that it is left.

(*Sifrei Devarim, Shofetim* 154; Jerusalem Talmud, *Horayot* 1:1)

📖 **Further reading:** For more about the significance of the Oral Law, see p. 452; *A Concise Guide to Mahshava*, p. 271.

Two Astrologers

Moses again cautions the Israelites not to be enticed to follow the beliefs of the peoples of the land of Canaan, into which they are entering. This includes faith in sorcery and wizardry, and reliance on constellations to guide them in personal matters. An incident related by the Sages illustrates this concept: The children of Israel are not subject to the control of the celestial bodies.

"For these nations from whom you are taking possession heed soothsayers and sorcerers; but you, not so did the Lord your God give to you" (Deuteronomy 18:14).

There was an incident involving Rabbi Yannai and Rabbi Yohanan, who were sitting at the Tiberias city gate. There were two astrologers there, who saw two Jews going out to work. Those two astrologers said: Those two men are going out to work, but they will not reach their destination; a snake will bite them. Rabbi Yannai and Rabbi Yohanan heard this. What did they do? They sat at the city gate to find out if those two people entered their destination city to perform their labor. They did enter, and Rabbi Yannai and Rabbi Yohanan saw them.

Rabbi Yannai and Rabbi Yohanan said to the astrologers: Didn't you say that these two people will go out but will not reach their destination, as a snake will bite them? The astrologers said to them: Yes. Rabbi Yannai and Rabbi Yohanan said to them: They went out in peace and reached their destination in peace. The astrologers looked at those two men. The astrologers said to them: Tell us, what did you do today? The men told them: We did not do anything special; we did what we are accustomed to doing: We recited *Shema* and we prayed. The astrologers said to them: You are Jews; the

pronouncements of astrologers do not affect you, because you are Jews. The midrash concludes: That is the meaning of what is written: "But you, not so did the Lord your God give to you" [i.e., the Jewish people are not affected by the constellations].

(Tanḥuma, Shofetim)

Further reading: For more about luck and astrology, see p. 423.

The Sound of a Tree

One of the laws of war recorded in this Torah portion is the prohibition against chopping down fruit trees even in the course of laying siege to a city. The Sages describe the extent to which chopping down a fruit tree has an effect on the world.

At the moment that one chops down a fruit-bearing tree, a sound emanates from one end of the world to the other, but the sound is unheard by people.

(Pirkei deRabbi Eliezer [Higer] 33)

Ki Tetze

The Torah portion of *Ki Tetze* has an abundance of mitzvot, relating to all areas of life. Among them are both mitzvot that had already been stated, which Moses reiterates here, and mitzvot that appear for the first time.

The chapter that follows presents statements of the Sages concerning the principle that the performance of one mitzva leads to the performance of another mitzva and the violation of one prohibition leads to the violation of another prohibition, the mitzvot that surround a person wherever he goes, the mitzva of sending away the mother bird and God's compassion, the reward promised to those who fulfill the mitzvot, and the mitzva of remembering what Amalek did to the children of Israel.

One Mitzva Leads to Another Mitzva and One Transgression Leads to Another Transgression

At first glance, the listing of the mitzvot that appear in this Torah portion seems random. The Sages explain that the order is well constructed: It expresses the idea that one transgression will lead to another transgression and to further punishment, and likewise, one mitzva leads to another mitzva and to further reward.

The Sages taught: The performance of one mitzva leads to the performance of another mitzva and the violation of one prohibition leads to the violation of another prohibition. The verse first states: "And you see among the captives a beautiful woman, and you desire her... and she shall shave her head, and she shall do⁶ her nails" (Deuteronomy 21:11–12). She must do this so that she will not find favor in his eyes. What is written after that? "If a man will have two wives" (21:15); when there are two wives in the house, there is contentiousness in the house. Moreover, the result will be that there will be "the one beloved and the one hated" (21:15), or [that] both of them will be hated, but they will not both be loved. What is written after that? "If a man will have a defiant and rebellious son" (21:18).

The ordering of these verses teaches that for anyone who marries a beautiful captive woman, a defiant and rebellious son will emerge from him, as it is written regarding David: Because he desired Maakha daughter of Talmai king of Geshur when he went out to war, Avshalom emerged from him....

---

6. According to most opinions, this means that she should let her nails grow out as a sign of neglect.

The performance of one mitzva leads to the performance of another mitzva. From where is that derived? The verse first states: "If a bird's nest will happen before you…You shall send away the mother, and take the offspring for yourself" (22:6–7). What is written after that? "If you build a new house, you shall make a parapet for your roof" (22:8). You will be privileged to build a new house and make a parapet. What is written after that? "You shall not sow your vineyard with diverse kinds" (22:9). You will be privileged to have a vineyard and to sow a field. What is written after that? "You shall not plow with an ox and a donkey together" (22:10). You will be privileged to acquire oxen and donkeys. What is written after that? "You shall not wear a mixture of fibers, wool and linen together" (22:11). You will be privileged to acquire fine woolen garments and fine linen garments. What is written after that? "You shall make for yourself twisted threads on the four corners of your garment" (22:12). You will be privileged to fulfill the mitzva of ritual fringes. What is written after that? "If a man will take a wife" (22:13). You will be privileged to marry a wife and father children.

We have learned that the performance of one mitzva leads to the performance of another mitzva and the violation of one prohibition leads to the violation of another prohibition; that is why all these passages are juxtaposed to each other.

(*Tanḥuma, Ki Tetze*)

📖 **Further reading:** There is an expression parallel to "a mitzva leads another mitzva": "The reward for a mitzva is a mitzva." See its meaning in *A Concise Guide to Mahshava*, p. 261.

Any Place That You Go, Mitzvot Accompany You

The mitzvot that appear in this Torah portion relate to all areas of a person's life: his house, his garments, his body, and his property. The Sages therefore teach that mitzvot always accompany a person. Everywhere he goes, in any situation in which he is found, he will be surrounded by mitzvot.

Rabbi Pinhas bar Hama said: Anywhere you go, mitzvot accompany you. "If you build a new house, you shall make a parapet for your roof" (Deuteronomy 22:8). If you make a doorway for yourself, mitzvot accompany you, as it is stated: "You shall write them on the doorposts of your house" (6:9). If you wear new garments, mitzvot accompany you, as it is stated: "You shall not wear a mixture of fibers, wool and linen together" (22:11). If you go to

get a haircut, mitzvot accompany you, as it is stated: "You shall not round the edge of your head" (Leviticus 19:27).[7]

If you have a field and go to plow it, mitzvot accompany you, as it is stated: "You shall not plow with an ox and a donkey together" (22:10). If you sow the field, mitzvot accompany you, as it is stated: "You shall not sow your vineyard with diverse kinds" (22:9). If you reap it, mitzvot accompany you, as it is stated: "When you reap your harvest in your field, and you forget a sheaf in the field, you shall not return to take it; for the stranger, the orphan, and the widow it shall be" (24:19).

The Holy One, blessed be He, said: Even if you do not engage in any activity, but merely walk along the way, mitzvot accompany you. From where is that derived? It is derived from a verse, as it is stated: "If a bird's nest will happen before you on the way.... You shall send away the mother, and take the offspring for yourself" (22:6–7).

(Devarim Rabba 6)

Mercy and Decrees

One of the mitzvot in this Torah portion is the mitzva of sending away a mother bird from the nest before taking its eggs or fledglings. In the statements of the Sages we find an approach that views this as a manifestation of God's mercy on His creations, as were the mother to see its eggs or the fledglings taken, it would suffer pain. By contrast, there is an approach that discredits the idea of explaining the mitzvot of the Torah with such a rationale.

Just as in commanding certain mitzvot, the Holy One, blessed be He, extended His mercy to the animals, so He was filled with mercy on the birds. From where is that derived? It is derived from the verse, as it is stated: "If a bird's nest will happen before you" (22:6).[8]

With regard to one who recites: Just as Your mercy is extended to a bird's nest, so too, extend Your mercy to us … he is silenced.

What is the reason? Two *amora'im* in the Land of Israel, Rabbi Yosei bar Avin and Rabbi Yosei bar Zevida, disagreed about this. One said it is because a person who recites this engenders jealousy among God's creations.[9] And one said it is because a person who recites this transforms the attributes and commandments of the Holy One, blessed be He, into mercy, when they are nothing but decrees.

(Devarim Rabba 6; Berakhot 33b)

---

7. It is prohibited to completely shave the hair at the sides of the head near the ears.
8. And requires you to send away the mother bird.
9. As though God plays favorites with some of His creatures.

So That It Will Be Good for You, and You Will Extend Your Days

The Torah promises that one who properly fulfills the mitzva of sending away the mother bird will merit goodness and long life. An incident where this blessing was clearly not fulfilled was a major factor leading to the heresy of Elisha ben Avuya, also known as Aher, a tannaitic Sage.

One time, Elisha ben Avuya was sitting and studying in the Ginosar valley, and he saw a person climb to the top of a palm tree and take the mother bird with its offspring, and he climbed down in peace. The next day, he saw another person climb to the top of a palm tree and take the offspring after sending away its mother, and he climbed down and a snake bit him and he died. Elisha ben Avuya said: It is written: "You shall send forth the mother, and take the offspring for yourself, so that it will be good for you, and you will extend your days" (Deuteronomy 22:7). Where is this person's goodness? Where are this person's extended days?

Elisha ben Avuya did not know that Rabbi Yaakov expounded this verse previously: "So that it will be good for you" means it will be good in the World to Come, which is entirely good. "And you will extend [vehaara-khta] your days" means one will have extended days in the future, in the World to Come, which is entirely long [arokh].

(Jerusalem Talmud, Ḥagiga 2:1)

Further reading: The story of Aher appears on p. 339.

Amalek

The Torah portion concludes with the commandment to remember and destroy Amalek, the nation that initiated a war with the Israelites when they left Egypt. According to the Sages, the commandment to remember the actions of Amalek is, indirectly, a way for God to remind the Israelites of their sin at Refidim (Exodus 17:7), for which they were punished with Amalek's waging war against them.

"Remember that which Amalek did to you" (Deuteronomy 25:17). "Amalek" is an allusion to am lek, meaning a nation [am] that came to lick [lek] the blood of the Israelites, as does a dog. Rabbi Levi said in the name of Rabbi Shimon ben Halafta: To what could the Amalekites be compared? They could be compared to a fly that was eager to get to a bloody wound; so too, the Amalekites were eager to attack Israel, as does a dog.

The Sages taught in the name of Rabbi Natan: Amalek traveled four hundred parasangs[10] to wage war with Israel in Refidim…. The verse states that Amalek attacked "on the way upon your exodus from Egypt" (25:17). Rabbi Levi said: This teaches that Amalek attacked the Israelites from the road, like highwaymen.

This can be explained by means of a parable of a king who had a vineyard and surrounded it with a fence, and placed a biting dog there. The king said: The dog will bite anyone who comes and breaches the fence. Sometime later, the king's son came and breached the fence and the dog bit him. Whenever the king sought to evoke his son's sin of breaching the vineyard, he would say to him: Remember that the dog bit you. So too, anytime the Holy One, blessed be He, sought to evoke the Israelites' sin that they did in Refidim when they said: "Is the Lord among us, or not?" (Exodus 17:7), He would say to them: "Remember that which Amalek did to you."

(*Tanḥuma* [Buber], *Ki Tetze*)

📖 **Further reading:** For more about Amalek and its war with Israel, see p. 100.

---

10. A parasang is approximately 4 km.

Ki Tavo

The Torah portion begins with the mitzva of first fruits and the mitzva of removal of tithes. Following this, the verses describe the renewal of the covenant between God and the Israelites before they enter the Land of Israel. The Israelites are commanded to organize a gathering upon their entry into the land, to construct an altar, and to bless those who follow the way of the Torah and curse those who deviate from it. Moses then describes in great detail the blessing that the Israelites are destined to receive if they follow the way of Torah, and, Heaven forfend, the evil and the curse if they fail to follow that path.

The chapter that follows presents statements of the Sages concerning the bringing of the first fruits up to Jerusalem, the need to always experience observing the Torah in a fresh way, and the gathering where the blessings and the curses upon entering the land were stated.

First Fruits

Parashat Ki Tavo opens with the mitzva of first fruits. An individual takes the fruits that grew first and brings them to the Temple. There, he is obligated to thank God for His acts of kindness in the past and in the present. The Sages describe the impressive ceremony of the bringing of the first fruits up to Jerusalem.

How does one designate first fruits? He goes down into his field and sees a fig that has begun to grow, a cluster of grapes that has begun to grow, or a pomegranate that has begun to grow. He ties it with a strip of papyrus and says: These are first fruits. Rabbi Shimon says: Even though he designated them at this early stage, he again designates them as first fruits after they are detached from the ground.

How does one bring the first fruits to Jerusalem?...

An ox[11] would walk before the people. Its horns would be plated with gold and it would have a crown of olive branches on its head. The flute would be played before them until they drew near to Jerusalem.

All the craftsman in Jerusalem would stand before them and greet them, saying: Our brethren, residents of such and such place, welcome!

---

11. The ox designated for the sacrificial offering that accompanies the first fruits.

The flute was played before them until they reached the Temple Mount. Once they reached the Temple Mount, everyone, even King Agrippas himself, would take the basket on his shoulder and enter until he reached the Temple courtyard.[12] When the one carrying the fruits reached the courtyard, the Levites would begin reciting their song.[13]

(Mishna *Bikkurim* 3:1–4)

📖 **Further reading:** First fruits were brought exclusively from the seven species. For the list of these species, see *A Concise Guide to the Torah*, p. 456.

This Day

Each and every day it is incumbent upon us to feel as though we received the Torah that very day.

"This day, the Lord your God is commanding you to perform these statutes" (Deuteronomy 26:16). What is the meaning of "this day"? Does it mean that until this day the Holy One, blessed be He, had not commanded the Israelites? Wasn't the year when the verse was stated the fortieth year from the exodus? Why does the verse state: "This day"?

This is what Moses said to Israel: Each and every day the Torah should be precious to you as though you received it that very day at Mount Sinai. And it is written elsewhere: "You shall impart them to your children…The day that you stood before the Lord your God at Horev" (4:9–10).

(*Tanḥuma* [Buber], *Ki Tavo*)

The Gathering of the Blessings and the Curses

The Israelites were commanded to organize a mass gathering upon their entering the Land of Israel, to bless those who will follow the proper path and to curse those who will deviate from it. The curses appear explicitly in the Torah, and the Sages explain that the blessings and curses were formulated in ways parallel to each other. The Sages describe this event.

How did the stating of blessings and curses take place? When the Israelites crossed the Jordan and arrived at Mount Gerizim and Mount Eival in Samaria, alongside Shekhem…. Six tribes ascended to the top of Mount Gerizim and six tribes ascended to the top of Mount Eival, and the priests and the Levites and the ark were standing at the bottom, in the middle. The

---

12. The innermost courtyard on the Temple Mount, where the altar and the Sanctuary were located.
13. Psalm 30.

priests were around the ark and the Levites were around the priests, and all the rest of the Israelites were standing on the mountains on this side and on that side ....

The priests and the Levites then turned to face Mount Gerizim and began with a blessing: Blessed is the man who will not craft an idol or a cast figure, and these people and those people, those standing on both mountains, answered: Amen. Then they turned to face Mount Eival and opened with the curse: "Cursed is the man who will craft an idol or a cast figure" (Deuteronomy 27:15), and these people and those people answered: Amen. The priests and the Levites continued until they completed reciting all the blessings and curses.

(Mishna *Sota* 7:5)

📖 **Further reading:** For more about the constant renewal in receiving the Torah, see *A Concise Guide to Mahshava*, p. 103.

Nitzavim

The Torah portion of *Nitzavim*, too, addresses the renewal of the covenant between God and Israel in the plains of Moav, just prior to their entry into the Land of Israel. Moses and the children of Israel make a covenant between themselves and God, and Moses again exhorts the Israelites to choose the path of Torah and mitzvot, as failure to do so will bring upon them suffering and exile. In this context, Moses introduces the concept of repentance: When Israel returns to God, God will return to them and will bestow goodness upon them. He clarifies that sincere repentance is in fact possible and achievable.

The chapter that follows presents statements of the Sages concerning Israel and suffering; the covenant that was made with all of Israel, with no distinctions, those alive at the time and those destined to live in the future; the three covenants God made with Israel; and the Torah, which is not "in the heavens" and is not "overseas," but is very accessible.

You Are Standing

Parashat Nitzavim is juxtaposed to the series of blessings, and the much more extensive series of curses, recorded at the conclusion of *Parashat Ki Tavo*. According to the Sages, the formulation of the statement of Moses at the beginning of *Nitzavim*: "You are standing," was intended to ease the minds of the Israelites, who were very disturbed after hearing the harsh curses.

Hizkiyya son of Rabbi Hiyya said: Why is this Torah portion juxtaposed to the portion of the curses? Because when the Israelites heard one hundred curses less two in that passage, in addition to the forty-nine curses that were stated in *Torat Kohanim* (Leviticus 26), their faces immediately turned pale, and they said: Who can withstand all these? Immediately, Moses summoned them and comforted them with his words....

If you say, asking: Why is it that the other nations of the world become liable to be eliminated when they sin, but we, the Israelites, continue to exist even after we sin? Because when suffering comes upon the other nations, they completely reject the lessons to be learned from them and do not acknowledge the name of the Holy One, blessed be He.... But Israel, when suffering comes upon them, accept it submissively, as it is stated: "I encounter distress and sorrow and I called in the name of the Lord" (Psalms 116:3–4).

Therefore, the Holy One, blessed be He, said to them: Although curses come upon you, the suffering bolsters you. Likewise the verse states: "In order to afflict you, and in order to test you, to do good for you in your future" (Deuteronomy 8:16). This is what Moses said to Israel: Even though suffering comes upon you, you are able to withstand it. Therefore it is stated here, after the curses were recorded: "You are standing" (29:9).

(Tanḥuma [Buber], Nitzavim)

📖 Further reading: For more about suffering and the proper way to accept it, see *A Concise Guide to Mahshava*, p. 228.

One Union

The covenant in this Torah portion was made between God and the entire Israelite people, "all of you," and therefore is in effect when Israel is all together, bonded and united.

"You are standing today, all of you" (Deuteronomy 29:9). Just like concerning the day, some days are darker and some are lighter, so too, you, Israel: Even when things are darker for you, the Holy One, blessed be He, will illuminate an eternal light for you, as it is stated: "The Lord will be for you an eternal light" (Isaiah 60:19).

When will He do this? Only when you will be all together, as it is stated: "But you, who cleave to the Lord your God, all of you live today" (Deuteronomy 4:4). Typically, if a person takes a bundle of reeds, can he break them all together? He cannot. But if he takes one reed, even a small child can break it.

Likewise, you find that Israel will not be redeemed until they will be all together…when they will be bound together, they will receive the Divine Presence.

(Tanḥuma [Buber], Nitzavim)

Three Covenants

God made a covenant with Israel many years prior to the events of this Torah portion, at the revelation at Sinai. The Israelites violated this covenant with the sin of the Golden Calf, and a second covenant was made when they were forgiven for that sin. Now, at the conclusion of forty years, God and Israel ratify the covenant anew.

"To pass you into the covenant of the Lord your God and into His oath that the Lord your God is making with you today" (Deuteronomy 29:11).

The Holy One, blessed be He, made three covenants with Israel after they emerged from Egypt: One when they stood before Mount Sinai, one at Horev (see Leviticus 26), and one here.

Why did the Holy One, blessed be He, make a covenant with them here? Because Israel abrogated the covenant that He made with them at Sinai, by saying about the Golden Calf: "This is your god, Israel" (Exodus 32:4). Therefore, He again made a covenant with them at Horev, and established a curse for one who reneges on the covenant. The expression "to pass you" means only as a person says to another: Accept that a curse be passed on you if you renege on this matter that you agreed with me...

"But not with you by yourselves do I establish this covenant" (Deuteronomy 29:13), but even the souls of future generations were there at that time, as it is stated: "Rather, with him who is here with us standing today... and with him who is not here with us today" (29:14).

Rabbi Abbahu said in the name of Rabbi Shmuel bar Nahmani: Why is it written: "Rather, with him who is here with us standing today... and with him who is not here with us today"?[14] The verse means that the souls of the future generations were there even though their bodies were not yet created; therefore, "standing" is not written in their regard.

(*Tanḥuma, Nitzavim*)

📖 **Further reading:** For more about unity and its power, see p. 373; *A Concise Guide to Mahshava*, p. 113.

He Who Is Here and He Who Is Not Here

The verse states that the covenant with Israel was made with those present and all their future descendants. In a similar vein, the Sages teach that all future prophecies were already transmitted at Sinai, and moreover that all the novel ideas that Torah scholars have introduced and are destined to introduce throughout the generations were given then.

Rabbi Yitzhak said: What the prophets are destined to prophesy in each and every generation was received at Mount Sinai, as Moses said to Israel: "Rather, with him who is here with us standing today... and with him who is not here with us today" (Deuteronomy 29:14).

Likewise the verse states: "The prophecy of the word of the Lord to Israel in the hand of Malachi" (Malachi 1:1). "In the days of Malachi" is not stated; rather, "in the hand of Malachi." As, the prophecy was in Malachi's

---

14. In other words, why doesn't the word *standing* appear in the second clause?

hand from Mount Sinai, but until that time, permission was not granted him to prophesy to others. Likewise, Isaiah said: "From the time that it was set, there I was" (Isaiah 48:16). Isaiah said: From the day that the Torah was given at Sinai, I was there and I received this prophecy…until now, permission was not granted him to prophesy to others.

It was not only the prophets who received their prophecy from Sinai, but also the Sages who stand in each and every generation; each and every one of them received his interpretations from Sinai.

(*Shemot Rabba* 28)

It Is Not in the Heavens

Moses teaches concerning: "This commandment" (Deuteronomy 30:11), that: "It is not in the heavens…it is not across the sea" (30:11–12). The Sages understand "this commandment" to be a reference to the Torah itself, and they learned from Moses' words that even if the Torah were in the heavens, i.e., distant and hard to reach, the Israelites would nevertheless be obligated to expend the effort to learn it.

And this is what Avdimi bar Hama bar Dosa said: What is the meaning of what is written concerning the Torah: "It is not in the heavens…it is not across the sea"? "It is not in the heavens," as were it in the heavens, you would be obligated to ascend after it, and were it "across the sea," you would be obligated to cross the sea after it.

Rava said: "It is not in the heavens" means that it is not to be found in one who raises himself above it, like the heavens [i.e., relates to it arrogantly], and it is not to be found in one who spreads himself over it, like the sea [i.e., relates to it superficially].

Rabbi Yohanan said: "It is not in the heavens" – it is not to be found in the haughty.[15] "It is not across the sea" – it is not to be found among merchants or traders.[16]

(*Eiruvin* 55a)

The Matter Is Very Near to You

The Torah is not in the heavens or across the sea: "Rather, the matter is very near to you" (Deuteronomy 30:14). The Sages likened this to a princess who was not allowed to meet with any man except for one.

---

15. One who thinks he is as exalted as the heavens.
16. One who travels great distances for trade.

"Rather, the matter is very near to you." Rav Shmuel bar Nahmani said: To what can this matter be compared? It can be compared to a princess whom no one knew. The king had one man whom he loved and who would enter to see him at all hours, even when his daughter was with him. The king said to the man: See how fond I am of you, as there is no one who knows my daughter, yet she is standing before you.

So the Holy One, blessed be He, said to Israel: See how fond I am of you, as in My palace there is no one who knows the Torah, yet I gave it to you, as it is stated: "It is vanished from the eyes of all living and hidden from the birds of the heavens" (Job 28:21), but as for you: "It is not hidden from you" (Deuteronomy 30:11); rather, "the matter is very near to you" (30:14). The Holy One, blessed be He, said to Israel: My children, if you keep the Torah close to you, I will proclaim that you are close to Me.

(*Devarim Rabba* [Lieberman] 7)

📖 **Further reading:** For more about the virtue of Torah and its study, and about the appropriate manner of study, see pp. 449, 454; *A Concise Guide to Mahshava*, p. 269.

Vayelekh

The Torah portion of *Vayelekh* addresses the preparations for the death of Moses: the passage of the leadership from Moses to Joshua and writing the Torah and transmitting it to the Levites. The Israelites are commanded to assemble once every seven years, on **Sukkot** following the conclusion of the Sabbatical Year, for a public reading from a Torah scroll.

The chapter that follows presents statements of the Sages concerning the day of Moses' death and the reason that he died, the relationship between Moses and Joshua at the end of Moses' life, and the mitzva of the assembly of all the Jewish people following the Sabbatical Year [*hak'hel*].

Behold, Your Days Are Drawing Near to Die

Immediately before Moses' death, God told him: "Behold, your days are drawing near to die" (Deuteronomy 31:14). The concept latent in this phrase is that ultimately no person can prevent his own death when the time arrives. This phrase also alludes to the fact that Moses did not die because of his own sins, but rather because of the death that was decreed on the entire human race because of the sin of Adam the first man.

"The Lord said to Moses: Behold, your days are drawing near to die"…this is what the verse said: "There is no man who rules the spirit, to retain the spirit" (Ecclesiastes 8:8).[17] Rabbi Yehuda says: No person has dominion over the angel of death, to eliminate it from him…Rabbi Shimon ben Halafta says: A person cannot craft weapons and be saved from the angel of death. What is the meaning of: "And there is no dominion over the day of death" (Ecclesiastes 8:8)? A person cannot say to the angel of death: Wait for me until I settle my accounts or until I instruct my household, and after that I will come….

Alternatively, Rabbi Levi said: To what can this matter be compared? It can be compared to a pregnant woman who was incarcerated in prison. She gave birth to a son, and the child grew. The king passed in front of the prison and that child began shouting: My lord the king, why am I incarcerated in prison? The king said to him: You are placed there due to the crime of your mother. So Moses said: Master of the Universe, there are thirty-three sins

---

17. A person cannot overcome the angel of death and prevent it from taking his soul.

punishable by excision, and if a person violates one of them he is liable to be killed by Heaven. Did I violate even one of them? Why are you decreeing death upon me? God said to him: You are dying due to the sin of Adam the first man, who introduced death to the world.

(Devarim Rabba 9)

📖 **Further reading:** For additional perspectives about the circumstances that led to Moses' death, see p. 199.

One Hundred Deaths but Not One Jealousy

The Sages relate that just before Moses' death, he requested that God allow him to continue to live, but transfer his position and his authority to his successor, Joshua. God granted his request, but when Moses realized that he was becoming jealous of Joshua, he immediately requested to die.

Moses said before God: Master of the Universe, let Joshua assume my position, and I will remain alive. The Holy One, blessed be He, said to him: Act with him as his attendant, as he acts with you.

Immediately, Moses arose early and went to Joshua's home. Joshua feared what would occur and said: Moses our teacher, come to me. They went for a walk, and Moses walked to the left of Joshua.[18] They entered the Tent of Meeting and the pillar of cloud descended and went between them.[19] When the pillar of cloud ascended, Moses went to Joshua and said: What did the word of God say to you? Joshua said to him: When the word of God was revealed to you, did I know what it would say to you? At that moment, Moses screamed and said: One hundred deaths but not one jealousy.

Solomon elaborates on this: "As love is as intense as death, jealousy is as cruel as the grave" (Song of Songs 8:6). This is a reference to the love that Moses had for Joshua and the jealousy that Moses had of Joshua. Once Moses accepted that he would die, the Holy One, blessed be He, began consoling him. God said to him: I take an oath by your life that just as in this world you led My children, in the future too, after the resurrection of the dead, I will lead them through you.

(Devarim Rabba 9)

---

18. As a show of deference.
19. And God spoke only with Joshua.

To Give Reward to Those Who Bring Them

All the Jewish people, men, women, and children, would come to the assembly of all the Jewish people [hak'hel] staged during the eighth year of the Sabbatical cycle at the conclusion of the festival of *Sukkot*. According to the Sages, even though the children would not understand the Torah that was taught there, their parents fulfill a mitzva and receive reward by simply bringing them.

"Assemble the people, the men and the women and the children" (Deuteronomy 31:12). If men come to learn and women come to hear, why do the children come? They come in order for God to give reward to those who bring them.

(Ḥagiga 55a)

📖 **Further reading:** For more about the Torah study of children, see p. 404; *A Concise Guide to Halakha*, p. 512; *A Concise Guide to Mahshava*, p. 186.

Haazinu

The bulk of this Torah portion is devoted to the song of *Haazinu* – a lyric poem that Moses recited before his death. This poem contains a description of the past and future history of the Israelites: God's selecting them as His people and the good that they merited, and the sins they are destined to commit for which they will receive a harsh punishment. God commands Moses to climb Mount Nevo, in order to die there.

The chapter that follows presents statements of the Sages concerning Moses' addressing the heavens and the earth, why matters of Torah are likened to rain, accepting divine judgment, and the future rebellion of the Israelites that will arise from circumstances of tranquility and well-being.

The Heavens and the Earth as Role Models

In the opening words of the Torah portion, Moses conveys a message to the Israelites: Learn from how the heavens and the earth diligently and consistently fulfill the will of the Creator.

Moses said: "Listen, the heavens" (Deuteronomy 32:1). The Holy One, blessed be He, said to Moses: Tell Israel: Look to the heavens that I created to serve you; have they altered their conduct at all? Or perhaps, did the orb of the sun ever say: I am not rising in the east and illuminating for the entire world?… Not only does it perform its task, but it is happy to perform My will for Me….

Moses continued: "And the earth will hear the sayings of my mouth" (32:1). The Holy One, blessed be He, said to Moses: Tell Israel: Look to the earth that I created to serve you; has it altered its conduct at all? Have you sown in it and it did not grow plants? Have you sown wheat and it produced barley? Or did a cow ever say: I am not threshing or I am not plowing today? Or did a donkey ever say: I am not bearing a burden and I will not walk?…

Can these matters not be inferred *a fortiori*: If these that were made not for reward and not for loss, i.e., if they perform a good deed they do not receive reward and if they sin they do not receive a punishment, and they do not need to have compassion for their sons and daughters, nevertheless did not alter their conduct from what is expected of them, you, who if you perform a good deed you receive a reward and if you sin you receive a punishment, and you must have compassion for your sons and your daughters,

all the more so that you must not alter your conduct from what is expected of you.

(*Sifrei Devarim, Haazinu* 506)

Like Rain Falling on the Grass

Moses likens the words of his song to rain falling on grass. The Sages interpret this as relating to the Torah in general, and explain why it is likened to rain.

"My lesson will fall as rain" (Deuteronomy 32:2). Just as rain falls on the trees and contributes flavors to each and every one of them according to its species – to the vine according to its species, to the olive tree according to its species, to the fig tree according to its species – the same is true for matters of Torah: It is one entity, yet it includes Bible, Mishna, Talmud, *halakha*, and *aggada*.

"Like rainstorms on grass" (32:2). Just as rainstorms fall on vegetation and cause it to grow tall, some red, some green, some black, and some white – the same is true for the Torah: It affects people, and the result is that some are wise, some are honest, some are righteous, and some are pious.

(*Sifrei Devarim, Haazinu* 506)

The Acceptance of Divine Judgment

God's actions are perfect: He conducts the world justly and perfectly. According to the Sages, Moses accepted the judgment that God decreed upon him that he would not enter the Land of Israel.

The Israelites said to Moses: What caused the decree that you would not enter the land? Moses said to them: I caused it. They said to him: Didn't the Holy One, blessed be He, do it to you? Moses said to them: Heaven forfend! Even if you see the Holy One, blessed be He, absolving the wicked and condemning the righteous, nevertheless, "the Rock, His actions are perfect, as all His ways are justice; a faithful God and there is no injustice" (Deuteronomy 32:4).

(*Midrash Tehillim* [Buber] 92)

Rebellion from Circumstances of Tranquility

Moses prophesies about the corruption of Israel after they will enter the land: "Yeshurun grew fat and kicked" (Deuteronomy 32:15). It is specifically the tranquil and satiated person who is apt to rebel against God.

"Yeshurun grew fat and kicked" (32:15). To the degree that there is satiation, there is rebellion.

Likewise you find in the generation of the flood, who rebelled against the Holy One, blessed be He, only from a situation of eating, drinking, and tranquility... Likewise we find with the people of the Tower of Babel, who rebelled against the Holy One, blessed be He, only from circumstances of tranquility... Likewise we find with the residents of Sodom, who rebelled only from a situation of eating... Likewise you find in the generation of the wilderness, who rebelled only from a situation of eating and drinking.

(*Sifrei Devarim, Haazinu* 518)

Vezot HaBerakha

The Torah portion of *Vezot HaBerakha* concludes the five books of the Torah. Most of the Torah portion enumerates the blessings that Moses blessed the tribes of Israel with before his death. At its conclusion, there is a brief description of Moses' ascent to Mount Nevo, his viewing of the Land of Israel, and his death there.

The chapter that follows presents statements of the Sages concerning Moses' blessing of Israel and his virtue, the Torah that is an inheritance for Israel, Moses' words of solace to Israel, Moses the man of God, and Moses' death.

Moses' Blessing

Moses' blessing to the children of Israel is superior to all other blessings bestowed by leaders of previous generations. This is because his is a complete blessing, and because he blessed Israel generously.

"This is the blessing that Moses...blessed (Deuteronomy 33:1). That is the meaning of what the verse states: "Many daughters have performed valiantly, but you have surpassed them all" (Proverbs 31:29). This is a reference to the blessing of Moses, as in previous generations, each and every one blessed his generation, but none of them equaled Moses' blessing.

Noah blessed his sons but made a division in his words; he blessed one and he cursed one: "May God expand Yefet" (Genesis 9:27) by making him wealthy. He said about Canaan, the son of his son Ham: "Cursed is Canaan" (Genesis 9:25). Isaac blessed Jacob and a quarrel ensued, as he said to Esau: "Your brother came with deceit, and he took your blessing" (Genesis 27:35), and it is written: "Esau hated Jacob" (Genesis 27:41). Jacob blessed the tribes and a quarrel ensued, as he said to Reuben: "Impetuous as water, you shall not excel" (Genesis 49:4), and likewise: "Simeon and Levi are brothers; weapons of villainy are their heritage" (Genesis 49:5)....

Moses, who is generous, shall come and bless Israel. Solomon said about him: "A generous eye will be blessed [*yevorakh*]" (Proverbs 22:9). Do not read it as "will be blessed," *yevorakh*, but rather as "will bless," *yevarekh*. This is a reference to Moses our teacher, who was generous when blessing Israel.

(*Tanḥuma* [Buber], *Vezot HaBerakha*)

Further reading: For more about Moses' great love for the Israelite people, see pp. 123, 210, 223.

The Torah Is an Inheritance for Every Jew

The Torah is an inheritance for Israel; and for one who abandons it then returns and engages in studying it, it is as though he is returning to his ancestral home.

"Torah, Moses commanded us, a heritage of the assembly of Jacob" (Deuteronomy 33:4). This teaches that the Torah is a heritage for Israel.

This can be explained by means of a parable. To what can this matter be compared? It can be compared to a prince who was taken captive in a distant country when he was young. If he seeks to return, even after one hundred years have passed, he will not be embarrassed to return, because he says: I am returning to my inheritance. So too, with regard to a Torah scholar who forsook the Torah and went to engage in other matters, if he seeks to return, even after one hundred years have passed, he will not be embarrassed to return, because he says: I am returning to my inheritance. Therefore, it is stated: "A heritage of the assembly of Jacob" (33:4).

(*Sifrei Devarim, Haazinu* 545)

Asking Forgiveness

Just before his death, Moses sought to bless Israel, after having rebuked them often during the course of his life. He asked their forgiveness, and they asked his forgiveness.

The heavenly assembly came to Moses and said: The time has come for you to pass from the world. He said to them: Wait for me until I bless Israel, as they never found respite from me because of all the warnings and reprimands with which I would rebuke them. Moses began blessing each and every tribe individually. When he saw that time was growing short, he included all of them in one general blessing....

Moses said to Israel: I aggrieved you a lot concerning Torah and mitzvot; now forgive me. The Israelites said: Our master, our lord, all is forgiven you. Israel, too, stood before Moses and said to him: Moses our teacher, we greatly angered you and we troubled you greatly; forgive us. He said: All is forgiven you.

(*Tanḥuma, Va'ethanan*)

Man of God

The verse describes Moses as a man of God. The Sages provide several explanations for this term, which expresses different aspects of Moses' personality.

"This is the blessing that Moses, the man of God, blessed the children of Israel with" (Deuteronomy 33:1). Rabbi Tanhuma said: If God, why is he called man; if man, why is he called God?[20] This teaches that at the moment when Moses was cast into the Nile in Egypt, he was vulnerable like a mere man, and at the moment that the Nile was transformed into blood with his staff, he was powerful like God. Alternatively: When he fled from Pharaoh he was like a man, and when he drowned Pharaoh and the Egyptians with his staff, he was like God. Alternatively: When he ascended to heaven to receive the Torah, he was like a man. And what is meant by his being like a man? Relative to the angels, who are all fire. And when he descended from Mount Sinai he was like God. From where is it derived? As it is written concerning the Israelites: "They feared to approach him" (Exodus 34:30). Alternatively: When he ascended to heaven to receive the Torah, he was like an angel of God; just as the angels do not eat and drink, so too, he did not eat and drink.

(*Devarim Rabba* 11)

Return My Soul

Several times, the angel of death sought to take Moses' soul, but Moses survived. Ultimately, he understood that his time had come, and he accepted God's judgment.

"This is the blessing that Moses, the man of God, blessed the children of Israel with before his death" (Deuteronomy 33:1). What is the meaning of "before his death"? The Rabbis said: What did Moses do? He took the angel of death and cast it before him to prevent it from killing him, and he blessed each and every tribe according to its blessing.

Rabbi Meir said: The angel of death went to Moses, and said to him: The Holy One, blessed be He, sent me to you, as you are departing this world today. Moses said to it: Go from here, as I wish to exalt the Holy One, blessed be He … It said to him: Moses, why are you being arrogant?[21] He has those who can exalt him; the heavens and the earth exalt him all the time … Moses said to it: I will silence them and exalt Him ….

The angel of death came to him a second time. What did Moses do? He invoked the ineffable name and it fled … When it came to him a third time,

---

20. Although the straightforward meaning of the verse is that Moses is described as a man of God, Rabbi Tanhuma is taking advantage of the fact that in biblical Hebrew, the word *of* is implicit, and he interprets the verse as if it is ambiguous whether a man or God is performing the blessing.
21. By presuming that only you can exalt God.

he said: Since your coming is from God, I must accept His judgment upon me. From where is this derived: "The Rock, His actions are perfect" (32:4).

(*Devarim Rabba* 11)

Moses' Passing

When Moses' time came, he requested not to be handed to the angel of death. Therefore, God Himself tended to his death and his burial, and collected Moses' soul after it refused to separate from his sacred body.

A divine voice [*bat kol*] emerged and said: The time of your death has arrived. Moses said before the Holy One, blessed be He: Master of the Universe, remember the day that You appeared to me in the bush, and You said to me: "Go, and I will send you to Pharaoh; and take My people, the children of Israel, out of Egypt" (Exodus 3:10). Remember the day that I was standing on Mount Sinai forty days and forty nights. I implore You, do not hand me to the angel of death. A divine voice emerged and said to him: Have no fear; I Myself will tend to you and your burial.

At that moment, Moses stood and sanctified himself like the seraphs, and the Holy One, blessed be He, descended from the highest heavens to take Moses' soul. Three ministering angels were with Him: Mikhael, Gavriel, and Zagzagel. Mikhael prepared Moses' bed, Gavriel spread a garment of fine linen under his head, and Zagzagel spread a garment of fine linen for his legs. Mikhael was on one side and Gavriel was on one side.

The Holy One, blessed be He, said to Moses: Moses, close your eyelids, and he closed his eyelids. He said to Moses: Place your hands on your chest, and he placed his hands on his chest. He said to Moses: Put your legs together, and he put his legs together.

At that moment, the Holy One, blessed be He, called his soul from within his body. He said to it: My daughter, I allocated 120 years for you to be in Moses' body; now the time has come to leave. Leave and do not tarry. Moses' soul said before the Holy One, blessed be He: Master of the Universe, I know that You are the God of all spirits, and all the souls. The souls of the living and the souls of the dead are given in Your hand, and You created me, You formed me, and You placed me in Moses' body for 120 years. Now, is there a body in the world purer than the body of Moses, in which no putrid spirit, lice, or intestinal worms were ever seen? That is why I love him and do not want to leave him.

The Holy One, blessed be He, said to it: Soul, leave and do not tarry, and I will elevate you to the highest heavens and I will place you beneath the throne of My glory with the cherubs, the seraphs, and the troops of angels....

At that moment, the Holy One, blessed be He, kissed Moses and took his soul with a kiss on the mouth. The Holy One, blessed be He, was crying, saying: "Who will rise up for Me against the wicked? Who will take a stand for Me against the evildoers?" (Psalms 94:16). The divine spirit was saying: "And there has not arisen another prophet in Israel like Moses" (Deuteronomy 34:10). The heavens were crying and saying: "The virtuous one is lost from the land" (Micha 7:2). The earth was crying and saying: "And the upright among people is no more" (Micha 7:2).

When Joshua was seeking Moses his master and did not find him, he was crying and saying: "Help, Lord, for the faithful man is no more, for trustworthiness has disappeared from among men" (Psalms 12:2). The ministering angels were saying: "He performed the righteousness of the Lord" (Deuteronomy 33:21), and the Israelites were saying: "And His ordinances with Israel" (33:21).

These and those were saying: "May he depart in peace, may he who walks in his uprightness rest on their resting places" (Isaiah 57:2). "The memory of the righteous is a blessing" (Proverbs 10:7), and his soul is destined for life in the World to Come.

(*Devarim Rabba* 11)

Sages on the Festivals

Shabbat

Shabbat is the foremost and most frequent of the special days in the Jewish calendar. It is the holy day each week on which we rest from labor, just as God rested on the seventh day from the labor of the creation of the world.

The Sages deal extensively with the significance and sanctity of Shabbat. In the chapter that follows, we will study some of their statements on the virtue of Shabbat and learn about the preparations for the special day, the delight on this day, and the ultimate reward that awaits those who observe Shabbat.

Shabbat – Testimony

Resting from work on Shabbat is our way of proclaiming and attesting that God created the world, and that He rested on Shabbat.

It is written: "Remember the Sabbath day, to keep it holy" (Exodus 20:8); corresponding to it, "You shall not bear false witness" (Exodus 20:13) is written.[1] The Torah is stating that whoever profanes Shabbat testifies before the One who spoke and the world came into being that He did not create His world in six days and did not rest on the seventh day. And whoever observes Shabbat testifies before the One who spoke and the world came into being that He did create His world in six days and rested on the seventh day, as it is stated: "You are My witnesses – the utterance of the Lord – and I am God" (Isaiah 43:12).

(*Mekhilta deRabbi Yishmael, Yitro, Mesekhta deBaḥodesh* 8)

A Fine Gift

Shabbat is a fine and special gift that the Holy One, blessed be He, gave to His people Israel.

I have a good gift in My treasure house and Shabbat is its name, and I seek to give it to Israel.

(*Shabbat* 10b)

---

1. Each of the two tablets that Moses brought down from Sinai contained five of the Ten Commandments, and these sets of five correspond to one another. Accordingly, the fourth commandment, "Remember the Sabbath day, to keep it holy" on the first tablet corresponds to the ninth commandment, "You shall not bear false witness against your neighbor."

Partner

Each of the days of the week is considered to be the partner of another day of the week, apart from Shabbat, whose partner is Israel.

Rabbi Shimon bar Yohai taught: Shabbat said to the Holy One, blessed be He: Master of the Universe, each day has a partner,[2] but I do not have a partner. How can that be? The Holy One, Blessed be He, said to it: The congregation of Israel is your partner. When Israel stood before Mount Sinai, the Holy One, blessed be He, said to them: Remember what I said to Shabbat, the congregation of Israel is your partner: "Remember the Sabbath day, to keep it holy" (Exodus 20:8).

(*Bereshit Rabba* [Theodor-Albeck] 11)

The Virtue of Shabbat Observance

The significance of Shabbat is so great that it is equal to all the other mitzvot of the Torah, and its observance entails great reward.

The Holy One, blessed be He, said to Israel: If you are privileged to observe Shabbat, I will consider it as though you have observed all the mitzvot of the Torah; and if you profane it, I will consider it as though you have profaned all the mitzvot. Likewise it is stated: "Who keeps the Sabbath from its desecration and stays his hand from performing any evil" (Isaiah 56:2).

Rabbi Hiyya bar Abba said in Rabbi Yohanan's name: Concerning anyone who observes Shabbat in accordance with its *halakhot*, even if he worships idolatry as in the generation of Enosh,[3] God forgives him his sins.

Rav Yehuda said in Rav's name: Had Israel properly observed the first Shabbat, no nation … would have ruled over them, as it is stated: "It was on the seventh day, some of the people went out to gather" (Exodus 16:27),[4] and it is written afterward: "Amalek came[5] and made war with Israel in Refidim" (Exodus 17:8).

Rabbi Yohanan said in the name of Rabbi Shimon ben Yohai: Were the Jewish people to observe two *Shabbatot* in accordance with the *halakha*, they would immediately be redeemed.

(*Shemot Rabba* 25; *Shabbat* 118b)

---

2. Each day of the week has a partner: Sunday has Monday; Tuesday has Wednesday; Thursday has Friday.

3. Enosh, in whose time people began to worship idols, was a grandson of Adam and Eve.

4. They gathered manna, despite the prohibition against doing so on Shabbat.

5. The Amalekites were successful in launching an attack against Israel, which they would not have been able to had all the Israelites properly observed the first Shabbat.

"Remember" and "Observe"

In the two versions of the Ten Commandments, the Torah stated two different commands about Shabbat: "Remember the Sabbath day, to keep it holy" (Exodus 20:8), and: "Observe the Sabbath day, to keep it holy" (Deuteronomy 5:12). From these commands, the Sages derived several *halakhot* related to the remembrance of Shabbat and the special place that it should be accorded.

"Remember" and "observe:" Remember it before it begins and observe it after it ends. From here the Sages said that one adds from the profane to the sacred…[6]

Further reading: For more on the practical ramifications of adding from the profane to the sacred, see *A Concise Guide to Halakha*, pp. 381, 398.

Elazar ben Hananya ben Hizkiyya ben Hananya ben Garon says: "Remember the Sabbath day, to keep it holy" (Exodus 20:8); one should remember it from the first day of the week; if you happen across a fine portion you should prepare it for the sake of Shabbat.

Rabbi Yitzhak says: One should not count in the manner that others count days, but rather one should count for the sake of Shabbat.[7]

"To keep it holy"; to sanctify it with a blessing. From here they said: One sanctifies it over wine at its start.

(*Mekhilta deRabbi Yishmael, Yitro, Mesekhta deBaḥodesh* 7)

Further reading: For more on *Kiddush*, the sanctification of Shabbat, and how and when this is performed, see *A Concise Guide to Halakha*, p. 386.

Yosef Who Cherished Shabbat

The Sages relate a story about a man who made great efforts to buy choice foods in honor of Shabbat. He eventually merited enormous wealth due to his piety in this regard.

Regarding Yosef who cherished Shabbat: There was a gentile in his neighborhood who owned a great deal of property. The astrologers said to him: Yosef, who cherishes Shabbat, will acquire all your property.

---

6. Some time is added to Shabbat both before its start and after its conclusion. The halakhic status of this time is like that of Shabbat, and no labor may be performed.
7. The days of the week should not be counted as they are in other languages, with each day bearing its own designated name; rather, they should be counted as the first day, the second day, etc., all relative to Shabbat, the focal point of the week. This practice remains in effect in modern Hebrew.

That gentile went and sold all his property, and with the proceeds he purchased a pearl, which he placed in his hat. While he was crossing a river in a ferry, the wind blew the hat into the water and a fish swallowed it. Fishermen removed the fish from the water and brought it ashore at nightfall on Shabbat eve. The fishermen said: Who will buy fish at this hour? The townspeople said to them: Go bring it to Yosef who cherishes Shabbat, as he regularly purchases items for Shabbat even at this hour. They brought it to him. He purchased it, ripped the fish open and inside it he found a pearl, which he then sold for thirteen vessels filled with gold. A certain elderly man encountered him and declared: For one who borrows money to purchase items to honor Shabbat, Shabbat repays him.

(*Shabbat* 119a)

Preparations for Shabbat and Welcoming Shabbat

Just as one expends great effort to prepare for the visit of a distinguished guest, so too must one prepare in honor of Shabbat and welcome it. The Sages relate that many rabbis would themselves be involved in the preparations for Shabbat.

Rabbi Hanina would wrap himself and stand at nightfall on Shabbat eve, and say: Come and we will go out to greet Shabbat the queen. Rabbi Yannai would don his garment before Shabbat and say: Enter, bride. Enter, bride...

Rav Safra would roast an animal head to eat on Shabbat; Rava would salt a *shibuta* fish to eat on Shabbat; Rav Huna would kindle lamps for Shabbat; Rav Pappa would spin the wicks for the Shabbat lamps. Rav Hisda would cut the beets to eat on Shabbat; Rabba and Rav Yosef would cut wood for kindling for Shabbat; Rabbi Zeira would prepare thin sticks for Shabbat.

(*Shabbat* 119a)

The Shabbat Spice

Although there are certain restrictions on the preparation and heating of food on Shabbat, the Sages teach that these limitations do not impair the quality of the food, but on the contrary, they actually serve to enhance its taste.

Rabbi Yehuda HaNasi made a feast on Shabbat for the Roman emperor Antoninus. Rabbi Yehuda HaNasi brought before him cooked dishes that were cold.[8] Antonius ate from them and they were very tasty for him. Rabbi Yehuda HaNasi made a feast for him during the week and brought before

_____
8. It is prohibited to light a fire to warm food on Shabbat.

him hot cooked dishes. Antoninus said to him: Those cold dishes tasted better to me than these hot dishes. Rabbi Yehuda HaNasi said to him: These dishes lack one spice. Antoninus said to him: But is there anything lacking in the king's pantry that I could not have supplied? Rabbi Yehuda HaNasi explained: These dishes are missing Shabbat; do you have Shabbat?

(*Bereshit Rabba* 11)

Delight in Shabbat – Material and Spiritual

There is a mitzva stated by the prophets to delight in Shabbat. The Sages disagree whether the central objective of refraining from labor on Shabbat is for this delight, or whether its primary objective is Torah study, while delighting in Shabbat is secondary. In any case, the proper way to sanctify Shabbat is by delighting in and honoring the day, and one who delights in Shabbat merits a great reward.

Rabbi Hiyya bar Abba says: Shabbat was given only for delight. Rabbi Haggai says in the name of Rabbi Shmuel bar Nahman: Shabbat was given only for Torah study.

They do not disagree: What Rabbi Berekhya said in the name of Rabbi Hiyya bar Abba, that Shabbat was given only for delight, is regarding Torah scholars who immerse themselves in Torah throughout the days of the week, and on Shabbat they come and delight in the holy day. What Rabbi Haggai said in the name of Rabbi Shmuel bar Nahman, that Shabbat was given for Torah study, is regarding laborers who are engaged in their labor all the days of the week, and on Shabbat they come and engage in Torah study.

Rabbi Yehoshua of Sakhnim says in the name of Rabbi Levi: When anyone who delights in Shabbat asks for something from God, the Holy One, blessed be He, grants him his request. What is the reason? "Take pleasure in the Lord, and He will grant you the desires of your heart" (Psalms 37:4).

"Remember the Sabbath day, to keep it holy" (Exodus 20:8): In what way does one keep it holy? One does so through study of Bible and Mishna, through food and drink, and clean garments.

Rabbi Yohanan said in the name of Rabbi Yosei: As for anyone who delights the Shabbat, God gives him a boundless inheritance.

(*Pesikta Rabbati* [Ish Shalom] 23; *Yalkut Shimoni, Va'ethanan* 830;
Shabbat 118a)

Two Angels

In the Friday night prayer, and again later in *Kiddush* over wine, one recites a passage (Genesis 2:1–3) that begins with the word *vaykhulu*, which describes God resting from the labor of Creation on the seventh day and the sanctification of Shabbat. The Sages teach that two angels accompany each person on Friday night, and they bless him when he recites these verses.

Mar Ukva said: Concerning anyone who prays on Shabbat evening and recites *vaykhulu*, the two ministering angels that accompany the person place their hands on his head and say to him: "Your iniquity is removed and your sin atoned" (Isaiah 6:7).

It was taught that Rabbi Yosei bar Yehuda says: Two ministering angels accompany a person on Shabbat evening from the synagogue to his home, one of them good and one of them evil. When he reaches his home and finds a lamp burning, a table set, and his bed made, the good angel says: May it be God's will that it will be like this on another Shabbat, and the evil angel answers against his will: Amen. If his home is not prepared for Shabbat, the evil angel says: May it be God's will that it will be so on another Shabbat, and the good angel answers against his will: Amen.

(*Shabbat* 119b)

A Glowing Face

A person's very appearance is different on Shabbat than it is during the rest of the week.

"God blessed the seventh day, and sanctified it" (Genesis 2:3). This means that He blessed it with the glow of one's face. The glow of a person's face throughout the week is not like its glow on Shabbat.

(*Bereshit Rabba* [Theodor-Albeck] 11)

A Cow That Observed Shabbat

It is not only Jewish people who are commanded to rest on Shabbat; their animals may also not work. The Sages relate a story of a gentile who bought a cow from a Jew. Since it was accustomed to rest on Shabbat, the cow was unwilling to work on Shabbat.

Our Sages said: There was an incident involving a certain Jew who had a particular cow that plowed. His financial situation worsened and he sold it to a certain gentile. When the gentile took it, he plowed with it on the six days of the week. On Shabbat he took it out to plow with him and it crouched under the yoke. He continually struck it, but the cow would not move from its place. When he saw that this was the case, he went and said to the Jew who

had sold it to him: Come, take your cow, perhaps it is ill, as no matter how many times I strike it, it will not move from its place.

That Jew realized that it was because of Shabbat, as the cow was accustomed to rest on Shabbat. He said to the gentile: Come, and I will cause it to stand. When he arrived, he said to the cow in its ear: Cow, cow, you know that when you were in my possession you would plow on the days of the week and you would rest on Shabbat. Now that my sins have caused my poverty and you are in the possession of a gentile, I implore you to stand and plow. Immediately, it stood and plowed.

That gentile said to him… I will not leave you until you tell me what you did to it in its ear. I exhausted myself striking it and it would not stand.

That Jew began placating him, and said to him: I did not perform sorcery or witchcraft. Rather, this is what I said in its ear, and it stood and plowed. Immediately, the gentile grew fearful and said: If a cow, which cannot talk and has no understanding, knows its Creator, I, who was formed by my Maker in His image, and He instilled knowledge in me, shouldn't I go and know my Creator? Immediately, he went and converted, studied and attained the Torah, and they would call him Yohanan ben Toreta,[9] and to this day our Sages cite *halakhot* in his name.

(*Pesikta Rabbati* [Ish Shalom] 14)

The Breach in the Fence

Not only is it prohibited to perform labor on Shabbat, but at times even discussing future plans to perform labor after the conclusion of Shabbat is prohibited. By contrast, it is not prohibited to think about doing labor after Shabbat. The Sages relate a story about a man who adopted a stringency and refrained from performing labor about which he had merely thought about on Shabbat.

There was an incident involving a certain pious individual who went out for a stroll in his vineyard on Shabbat, and he saw there a certain breach in a fence and thought to repair the fence at the conclusion of Shabbat. He said: Since I thought to repair the fence, I will never repair the fence. What did the Holy One, blessed be He, do for him? He arranged for a branch of a caper bush to grow into the breach and repair the fence. All his days, he sustained himself and earned his living from the fruits of the caper bush.

(*Jerusalem Talmud, Shabbat* 15:3)

Further reading: Regarding the deeper meaning of Shabbat, see *A Concise Guide to Mahshava*, p. 33; for the *halakhot* of Shabbat, see *A Concise Guide to Halakha*, p. 379.

_____
9. Based on the Aramaic word for ox – *tora*.

Rosh HaShana

Rosh HaShana, which falls on the first of the month of Tishrei, is called in the Torah "a remembrance day" and "a day of sounding the alarm" (Numbers 29:1). The central mitzva of the day is sounding the alarm with the shofar. The Sages also emphasize that Rosh HaShana is a day of judgment, when all of humanity stands before God for judgment, and their deeds are evoked before Him.

This chapter cites statements of the Sages that deal with the various designated "days of judgment," the prayers of Rosh HaShana and the blasts of the shofar, a ram's horn, and the special characteristics of Israel's Day of Judgment.

Sages on the Festivals

Kivnei Maron

On four occasions each year the Holy One, blessed be He, judges the world and humanity. On Rosh HaShana all people pass before God for judgment, and He judges each person individually and everyone together, in a single glance.

At four times the world is judged: On Passover it is judged concerning grain; on *Shavuot* it is judged concerning fruits of the tree; on Rosh Ha-Shana all creatures pass before Him like *benei maron*, for judgment, as it is stated: "He who fashions all their hearts, who understands all their deeds" (Psalms 33:15); and on the festival of *Sukkot* they are judged concerning water.

What are *benei maron*? Here, in Babylonia, the Sages interpreted it: Like a flock of sheep [*imerana*]. Reish Lakish said: Like the ascent of Beit Maron.[10] Rav Yehuda said that Shmuel said: Like the soldiers of the house of David.[11] Rabba bar bar Hana said that Rabbi Yohanan said: And they are all scanned in a single scan.

(Mishna *Rosh HaShana* 1:2; *Rosh HaShana* 18a)

A Statute for Israel, a Law of the God of Jacob

Israel's Day of Judgment differs from standard trials. Typically, a person is concerned about an impending court case, whereas Israel places its trust in the kindness of the Judge, and even determines and proclaims the date of the trial.

---

10. It was narrow and allowed passage of only one person at a time.
11. The imagery used is of the soldiers who would stand in single file for roll call.

Rabbi Hama ben Rabbi Hanina, and Rabbi Hoshaya; one said: What nation is like this nation! Typically, a person who knows that he has a trial will wear black garments[12] and wrap himself in black robes, and grow his beard, as he does not know the outcome of his trial. But regarding Israel it is not so. Rather, they wear white and wrap themselves in white, and shave their beards, and eat and drink and rejoice, as they know that the Holy One, blessed be He, performs miracles for them.

The other said: What nation is like this nation! Typically, if the authorities say: The trial is today, and the armed robbers say: The trial is tomorrow, to whom do we listen? Don't we listen to the authorities? But regarding the Holy One, blessed be He, it is not so: If the court said: Today is Rosh HaShana,[13] the Holy One, blessed be He, says to the ministering angels: Erect a platform, let the advocates stand, and let the prosecutors stand, as My children have said: Today is Rosh HaShana.

If the court reconsiders to make the previous month full and to postpone Rosh HaShana to the following day,[14] the Holy One, blessed be He, says to the ministering angels: Remove the platform, remove the advocates, and remove the prosecutors, as My children have reconsidered to make the previous month full and to postpone Rosh HaShana to tomorrow.

(Jerusalem Talmud, *Rosh HaShana* 1:3)

Three Ledgers Are Opened

The final verdict concerning the righteous and the wicked is sealed immediately on Rosh HaShana, whereas those whose deeds are balanced receive ten additional days in order to mend their ways.

Rabbi Kruspedai said that Rabbi Yohanan said: Three ledgers are opened in the Heavenly court on Rosh HaShana: one of wholly wicked people, one of wholly righteous people, and one of middling people. Wholly righteous people are immediately written and sealed for life; wholly wicked people are immediately written and sealed for death; and middling people[15] remain suspended from Rosh HaShana until Yom Kippur. If they merit,[16] they are written for life; if they do not merit, they are written for death.

(*Rosh HaShana* 16b)

---

12. Black garments indicate a state of apprehension as to the outcome of the trial.
13. The court has the authority to determine when the new month would start.
14. This would occur if the court decided that Elul would be 30 days, not 29, thereby postponing Rosh HaShana to the next day.
15. This refers to those whose good deeds are more or less equal to their bad deeds.
16. By performing good deeds and repenting.

Kingships, Remembrances, and *Shofarot*

The unique element of the Rosh HaShana prayers are the three special blessings added to the additional prayer [*Musaf*]: Kingships, Remembrances, and *Shofarot*.

Recite before Me on Rosh HaShana the blessings of Kingships, Remembrances, and *Shofarot*: Kingships so that you will crown Me as King over you; Remembrances so that your remembrance will ascend before Me for good; and with what?[17] With the shofar.

Rabbi Abbahu said: Why does one sound the shofar with a ram's horn? The Holy One, blessed be He, said: Sound the shofar before Me with a ram's horn, so that I will remember for you the binding of Isaac[18] son of Abraham, and I will ascribe it to you as though you have bound yourselves before Me.

(*Rosh HaShana* 16a)

---

17. What will help your remembrances ascend before Me?
18. Isaac was bound upon an altar by his father Abraham, but ultimately a ram was offered in his stead.

Yom Kippur

Yom Kippur, which the Sages also called "the great day," "the sacred day," or simply "the day," is the holiest day. On this day, we afflict ourselves, refrain from eating and drinking and other pleasures, and God gives atonement for the sins and transgressions of His people. When the Temple was intact, the High Priest performed a special, complex service regimen on that day, which climaxed with his entry into the most sacred area in the Temple, an entry that was done exclusively on Yom Kippur.

The chapter that follows presents statements of our Sages regarding the prohibitions in effect on the fast, the atonement of sins on Yom Kippur, the mitzva of confession, the virtue of repentance, and honoring the day and the final meal on the day before Yom Kippur.

Yom Kippur – from Time Immemorial

According to tradition, on the first day of the month of Elul, Moses ascended to Mount Sinai, after having broken the first tablets due to the sin of the Golden Calf. Forty days later, on Yom Kippur, he descended with the second tablets. At that point, Yom Kippur became a day of atonement and absolution for iniquity.

Ben Beteira says: Moses remained forty days on the mountain, expounding words of Torah and analyzing its letters. After forty days he took the Torah and descended on the tenth of the seventh month, on Yom Kippur, and he bequeathed the Torah to Israel as an eternal statute, as it is stated: "This shall be an eternal statute for you" (Leviticus 16:34).[19]

Were it not for Yom Kippur the world would not survive, as Yom Kippur atones in this world and in the World to Come…. Even if all the festivals are abrogated, Yom Kippur will not be abrogated, because Yom Kippur atones for minor and major transgressions, as it is stated: "For on this day he shall atone for you, to purify you from all your sins" (Leviticus 16:30). It is not written: "From your sins,"[20] but rather, "from all your sins."

(*Pirkei deRav Eliezer* 47)

---

19. Although the verse is referring to the Yom Kippur service, the Sages expounded it as though the reference is to the entire Torah that was given to Israel a second time that day.
20. Writing "from your sins" rather than "from all your sins" would indicate that only some of the sins are atoned.

📖 **Further reading:** For more about Yom Kippur, see *A Concise Guide to Torah*, p. 318; *A Concise Guide to Mahshava*, p. 66; *A Concise Guide to Halakha*, p. 167.

The Five Prohibitions

The central mitzva of Yom Kippur is: "You shall afflict yourselves" (Leviticus 16:29). The Sages determined that this affliction consists of five prohibitions.

On Yom Kippur one is prohibited from eating, drinking, bathing, smearing oil on one's body, wearing leather shoes, and conjugal relations. But a king, and a bride in the days immediately after her marriage, may wash their faces, and a woman after childbirth may wear shoes; this is the statement of Rabbi Eliezer, but the Rabbis prohibit these.

(Mishna *Yoma* 8:1)

📖 **Further reading:** For elaboration and explanation of each of the prohibitions in effect on Yom Kippur, see *A Concise Guide to Halakha*, p. 163.

Atonement and Purification

On Yom Kippur, God atones for the sins of His children and purifies them. Nevertheless, the Sages explain that there are certain caveats: Someone who has hurt another can achieve atonement only if he first placates his victim. Furthermore, the sins of one who relies in advance on the atonement that will come on Yom Kippur will not be atoned.

Concerning one who says: I will sin and I will then repent, I will sin and I will then repent, he will not be provided with the opportunity to repent. Concerning one who says: I will sin and Yom Kippur will atone, Yom Kippur will not atone.

For transgressions between a person and the Omnipresent, Yom Kippur atones; for transgressions between one person and another, Yom Kippur does not atone until he appeases the other. Rabbi Elazar ben Azarya expounded: "From all your sins before the Lord you shall be purified" (Leviticus 16:30). For transgressions between a person and the Omnipresent,[21] Yom Kippur atones, but for transgressions between one person and another, Yom Kippur does not atone until he appeases the other.

(Mishna *Yoma* 8:9)

---

21. This is based on the words: "From all your sins before the Lord," and not your sins committed against another person.

Confession

There is an obligation to confess one's sins on Yom Kippur. The Sages state that confessing once does not suffice. One must recite the confession several times, in each of the prayers of Yom Kippur.

The Sages taught: The mitzva of confession is just before Yom Kippur when darkness falls. But the Sages said: One should confess before Yom Kippur before he eats and drinks the final meal before the fast, lest he become confused at the meal due to excessive eating and drinking. Even though one confessed before he ate and drank, he confesses again after he eats and drinks, as perhaps something improper transpired during the meal.

Even though one confessed during the evening prayer, he must confess in the morning prayer. And even though he confessed in the morning prayer, he must confess in the additional prayer. And even though he confessed in the additional prayer, he must confess during the afternoon prayer. And even though he confessed in the afternoon prayer, he must confess in the closing prayer.

(*Yoma* 87b)

Great Is Repentance

Although repentance is effective throughout the year, it is especially effective on Yom Kippur. The Sages extolled the virtue of repentance, which reaches God's heavenly Throne, and is capable of transforming even a person's most severe transgressions into mitzvot.

Rabbi Levi said: Great is repentance, as it reaches the heavenly Throne…

Rabbi Yonatan said: Great is repentance, as it engenders the redemption, as it is stated: "A redeemer will come to Zion and to those who repent from transgression in Jacob" (Isaiah 59:20).

Reish Lakish said: Great is repentance, as one's intentional sins are transformed for him into unwitting transgressions…. Is that so? Wasn't it Reish Lakish who said: Great is repentance, as one's intentional sins are transformed for him into merits?… This is not difficult: Here, it is referring to repentance motivated by love of God;[22] there, it is referring to repentance motivated by fear of God.[23]

---

22. His transgressions are credited to him as merits.
23. His transgressions are considered unwitting rather than intentional if his repentance is motivated by fear of God.

Sages on the Festivals

Rabbi Shmuel bar Nahmani said that Rabbi Yonatan said: Great is repentance, as it prolongs a person's life…

It is taught that Rabbi Meir would say: Great is repentance, as on account of one individual who has repented, the entire world is forgiven.

(*Yoma* 86a)

Unlike the Attribute of Flesh and Blood

Repentance is unique; there is nothing comparable in standard social interactions: People do not always forgive one another, and when they do, they do so begrudgingly, while God always accepts the sinner who sincerely returns to Him.

Come and see that the attribute of flesh and blood is unlike the attribute of the Holy One, blessed be He. The attribute of flesh and blood is that when one provokes another verbally, it is uncertain whether the victim will be appeased by him or will not be appeased by him. Even if you say that he will be appeased, it is uncertain whether he will be appeased by words or will not be appeased by words.[24] But concerning the Holy One, blessed be He, if a person commits a transgression in private, He is appeased by him with words. Moreover, He gives him credit as though he did Him a favor…. Moreover, the verse ascribes him credit as though he sacrificed bulls, as it is stated: "And we will substitute our lips for bulls" (Hosea 14:3).

(*Yoma* 86b)

The Pious Man and the Fish

Although we refrain from eating and drinking on Yom Kippur, this does not mean that it is not a festive day. On the contrary, it is the most cherished day of the year. Its festive meal is held on the day before Yom Kippur. The Sages relate the story of a man who spent a fortune to honor the sacred day with this meal.

There was an incident involving a certain pious man in Rome who would honor all the festivals and *Shabbatot*. One evening, and some say that it was the day before the great fast of Yom Kippur, he arrived at the market in order to buy something for the meal, but he found only a single fish. There was a servant of the provincial ruler standing there, and this one bid and raised the price of the fish, and that one bid and raised the price of the fish. The Jew purchased it, a fish weighing one *litra* for one dinar.[25]

---

24. If words do not appease him, he may demand some material compensation.
25. This was an exorbitant price.

At the time of the meal, the provincial ruler said to the servant: There is no fish here! The servant said to him: Only one fish was brought to the market today, and a certain Jew purchased it, one *litra* for one dinar. The ruler said to him: Do you know him? The servant said to him: Yes. The ruler said to him: Go and shout at him, as he possesses a treasure that belongs to the king. The servant went and shouted at him, and the Jew said to him: I am a tailor [and have no illegal income]. The servant said to him: Is there a tailor who eats one *litra* of fish for one dinar? The servant brought the Jew to the ruler.

The Jew said to the ruler: May my lord give me permission, and I will speak before you. The ruler said to him: Speak. The Jew said to him: We have one day in the year that is more cherished for us than all the days of the year. That day absolves us from all the guilt that we incur. For this reason, we honor it more than all the days of the year. The ruler said to him: Since you brought proof for your claim, you are exempt.

How did the Holy One, blessed be He, repay the Jew? He arranged for him to find a precious stone, a pearl, inside the fish, from which he was able to make a living the rest of his life.

(Pesikta Rabbati [Ish Shalom] 23)

📖 Further reading: For more on the final meal before Yom Kippur, see *A Concise Guide to Halakha*, p. 160.

Sukkot

Sukkot is celebrated for seven days, beginning on the fifteenth of Tishrei. The mitzvot of the festival include sitting in the *sukka*, commemorating the *sukkot* in which the Israelites resided when they left Egypt, and the taking of the four species, *lulav*, *etrog*, *hadas*, and *arava*.

The festival is characterized by great rejoicing. While the Temple was standing, on each day of the festival the priests performed a special mitzva of pouring water on the altar, and each evening featured celebrations of great joy. This celebration was known as *Simhat Beit HaSho'eva*, "Celebration of the Place of the Drawing of the Water." The seventh day of the festival is called *Hoshana Rabba*, on which many prayers and supplications are recited, and which includes the special mitzva of "beating the *arava*."

The eighth day of *Sukkot* is a separate festival, *Shemini Atzeret*. On this day, mitzvot unique to *Sukkot*, the *sukka* and the four species, are not observed. Over the generations, this eighth day became linked to celebrations of concluding the cycle of the Torah reading, *Simhat Torah*. Outside of Israel, *Simhat Torah* is the additional festival day of the Diaspora, the day after *Shemini Atzeret*.

In the chapter that follows we cite statements of our Sages regarding matters related to the *sukka* and the laws of sitting in it; the four species and their symbolic meaning; *Simhat Beit HaSho'eva*; and the festival of *Shemini Atzeret*, when the close connection between God and Israel is manifest.

Sukkot

The Sages disagree as to the precise nature of the *sukkot* in which the Israelites resided when they left Egypt, in commemoration of which we are commanded to reside in *sukkot* throughout the festival.

"So that your generations will know that I had the children of Israel live in booths [*sukkot*], when I took them out of the land of Egypt" (Leviticus 23:43). Rabbi Eliezer says: These were actual booths; Rabbi Akiva says: They were booths of clouds of glory.[26]

(*Sifra, Emor* 12)

---

26. The clouds of glory accompanied the children of Israel in the wanderings through the wilderness and provided them shelter, like a booth.

Sitting in a *Sukka*

The mitzva of sitting in a *sukka* is that the *sukka* should serve as one's primary fixed residence for the seven days of the festival.

The Sages taught: For all seven days of *Sukkot*, a person renders his *sukka* his permanent residence and his house his temporary residence. How so? If he has beautiful vessels, he takes them up[27] to the *sukka*. If he has beautiful bedding, he takes it up to the *sukka*. Likewise, he eats and drinks and relaxes in the *sukka*. From where are these matters derived? As the Sages taught that the verse states: "You shall live" (Leviticus 23:43), teaching that you shall live in the *sukka* as you dwell in your permanent home.

(Sukka 28b)

The Four Species

One of the mitzvot of the festival is the taking of four species of plants. Only the palm branch and the willow are named in the Torah. The Sages identified the precise species of the other two based on their description in the Torah.

"The fruit of a pleasant tree [*peri etz hadar*]" (Leviticus 23:40); Rabbi Hiyya taught: This is a tree the taste of whose tree and fruit is the same;[28] this is the *etrog*. "Pleasant [*hadar*]" (Leviticus 23:40); ben Azzai says: A fruit that resides [*hadar*] on its tree from one year to the next. Akiles the convert translated it as *hidor* [Greek for water], as it grows on all types of water.[29] "Branches [*kappot*] of date palms" (Leviticus 23:40); Rabbi Tarfon says: Bound [*kafut*]; if its leaves were separated, one must bind them together. "And a bough of a leafy tree" (Leviticus 23:40); whose branches cover its tree,[30] you must say that this is the myrtle [*hadas*].[31]

(Vayikra Rabba [Margaliyot], Parasha 30)

Four Species – Four Categories of People

The four species represent the entire people of Israel: Torah scholars, performers of good deeds, and even people who possess neither quality. Nevertheless, it is only when they are all joined into a single bundle that the mitzva is fulfilled properly.

---

27. *Sukkot* were typically built on the roof.
28. This teaching is based on the juxtaposition of the words *peri*, fruit, and *etz*, tree.
29. "All types of water" refers to both rainwater and irrigation.
30. The leaves of the myrtle conceal its branch.
31. The fourth of the species is the willow [*arava*].

"The fruit of a pleasant tree" (Leviticus 23:40): This symbolizes Israel: Just as this *etrog* has both a good taste and a pleasant fragrance, so too, Israel includes people who have both Torah and good deeds.

"Branches of date palms" (Leviticus 23:40): These too are symbolic of Israel: Just as this date has a good taste but does not have a pleasant fragrance, so too, Israel includes people who have Torah but do not have good deeds.

"And a bough of a leafy tree" (Leviticus 23:40): This too is symbolic of Israel: Just as this myrtle has a pleasant fragrance but does not have a good taste, so too, Israel includes people who have good deeds but do not have Torah.

"And willows of the brook" (Leviticus 23:40): These too are symbolic of Israel: Just as this willow has neither a good taste nor a pleasant fragrance, so too, Israel includes people who have neither Torah nor good deeds.

And what does the Holy One, blessed be He, do with those lacking both Torah and good deeds? To destroy them is impossible. Rather, the Holy One, blessed be He, said: Let them all be bound in one bundle, and they will atone for each other.

(*Vayikra Rabba* [Margaliyot] 30)

📖 Further reading: For how one chooses the four species, see a guide accompanied by charts in *A Concise Guide to Halakha*, p. 180.

Simhat Beit HaSho'eva

On each morning of the festival of *Sukkot*, the people would descend to the Siloam pool, adjacent to the Temple, and draw water for libation onto the altar. This custom is unique to *Sukkot*, and although it is not mentioned in the Torah, it is attributed to a tradition from Moses. The Sages describe the procession to draw the water, and the joyous celebrations of thanksgiving that would continue all night.

The Sages said: One who did not see *Simhat Beit HaSho'eva* never saw a genuine celebration in his days. At the conclusion of the first day of the festival, the priests and the Levites descended from the Israelites' courtyard in the Temple to the women's courtyard, where they would introduce a significant improvement.[32] There were golden candelabra placed atop pillars there, and four basins of gold at the top of each candelabrum, and four ladders for each and every pillar. There were four children from the priesthood trainees, and

---

32. They would see to appropriate partition between men and women.

in their hands were pitchers with a capacity of 120 *log*[33] of oil that they would pour into each and every basin.

They would loosen and tear strips from the worn trousers of the priests and their belts to use as wicks, with which they would kindle the candelabra. There was not a courtyard in Jerusalem that was not illuminated from the light of *Simhat Beit HaSho'eva*. The pious and the men of action would dance before the people, juggling flaming torches in their hands, and those men would recite before the people passages of song and praise. And the Levites would play on lyres, harps, cymbals, and trumpets, and countless other musical instruments. The Levites would stand on the fifteen stairs that descend from the Israelites' courtyard to the women's courtyard …

It is taught: The Sages said about Rabban Shimon ben Gamliel that when he would rejoice at the *Simhat Beit HaSho'eva*, he would take eight flaming torches and toss one and catch another, and they would not touch each other. And when he would prostrate himself, he would insert his two thumbs into the ground, and bow, and kiss the floor and straighten, and there was no other person that could do that. This was the form of bowing called *kidda* mentioned elsewhere.

It is taught that Rabbi Yehoshua ben Hananya said: When we would rejoice at *Simhat Beit HaSho'eva*, we did not sleep. How so? In the first hour of the day, the daily morning offering was sacrificed. From there we proceeded to prayer; from there, to the additional offerings; and from there to the additional prayer; from there to the study hall; from there to eating and drinking in the *sukka*; from there to the afternoon prayer; and from there to the daily afternoon offering. From this point onward, we returned to the *Simhat Beit HaSho'eva*.

Is that so? But didn't Rabbi Yohanan say: In the case of one who took an oath: I will not sleep three days, the court flogs him, and he may sleep immediately?[34] Rather, this is what Rabbi Yehoshua is saying: We did not experience the sense of actual sleep; as they would merely doze on each other's shoulders.

(Mishna *Sukka* 5:1; *Sukka* 53a)

Further reading: For more about the special rejoicing on the festival of *Sukkot*, see p. 159.

---

33. At least forty liters.
34. One who takes an oath that he will not sleep for three days is flogged for taking an oath in vain, as it is impossible to fulfill such an oath. Therefore, how did Rabbi Yehoshua claim that they did not sleep throughout the entire festival?

The Yearly Rainfall

The celebrations of *Simhat Beit HaSho'eva* would continue all night in anticipation of the drawing of the water at dawn and the libation of the water upon the altar. The Sages explained why this mitzva was performed specifically on the festival of *Sukkot*.

And for what reason did the Torah say: Pour a libation of water upon the altar in the Temple on the festival of Sukkot? The Holy One, blessed be He, said: Pour a libation of water before Me on the festival so that the rains of the year, which begin to fall after Sukkot, will be blessed for you.

(*Rosh HaShana* 16a)

Shemini Atzeret

The unique mitzvot of *Sukkot* are not observed on *Shemini Atzeret*. Furthermore, unlike *Sukkot*, when numerous offerings were sacrificed each day in the Temple, on *Shemini Atzeret* only one bull and one ram were offered. The Sages see this as an expression of the close ties between God and the people of Israel.

"You shall present a burnt offering…to the Lord: one bull, one ram" (Numbers 29:36). This is comparable to a king who made a feast for seven days and invited all his people for the seven days of the feast. When the seven days of the feast had passed, he said to his beloved servant: We have fulfilled our obligation to the people, let you and I suffice with whatever you find:[35] A *litra*[36] of meat or fish or vegetables. Similarly, the Holy One, blessed be He, said to Israel: All the offerings that you brought over the seven days of the festival of *Sukkot*, you brought them on behalf of the nations of the world,[37] but "on the eighth day it shall be an assembly for you" (Numbers 29:36); suffice with what you find, one bull and one ram.

To what do these seventy bulls that are brought over the seven days of *Sukkot* correspond? They correspond to the seventy nations. Why is a single bull brought on *Shemini Atzeret*? It corresponds to the single nation of Israel. This can be explained by means of a parable of a flesh-and-blood king who said to his servants: Prepare for me a great feast. On the last day, he said to his beloved servant: Prepare for me a small feast so that I can enjoy your company alone.

(*Tanḥuma* [Buber] 15; *Sukka* 55b)

📖 **Further reading:** For more on *Shemini Atzeret* and the manner in which it is celebrated today, see *A Concise Guide to Halakha*, p. 221.

---

35. In other words: We are so fond of each other, there is no need for a great feast.
36. A small amount.
37. During *Sukkot* seventy bulls were offered, corresponding to the seventy archetypal nations of the world.

Hanukkah

Hanukkah is celebrated for eight days, beginning on the 25th of Kislev. It is celebrated because the Hellenistic government that ruled the Land of Israel sought to nullify the uniqueness of the Jewish people and force them to transgress the laws of the Torah, and the Hasmoneans led a revolution against those decrees. The holiday is observed in commemoration of the rededication of the Temple after it was liberated by the Hasmoneans, and the renewed kindling of the candelabrum in the Temple. The central mitzva of the holiday is the candle lighting each evening.

The Sages spoke relatively little about Hanukkah. This chapter contains some of their statements on the nature of this holiday; the order and number of the Hanukkah candles; and the relationship between the Hanukkah candles, the Shabbat candles, and the mitzva of *Kiddush*.

The Hanukkah Miracle

The Sages explained why the holiday of Hanukkah was instituted, and why it is celebrated for eight days.

On the twenty-fifth in the month of Kislev is Hanukkah, for eight days, during which one may not eulogize[38] .... When the Greeks entered the Sanctuary they defiled all the oil that was in the Sanctuary. When the house of the Hasmoneans overcame them and emerged victorious over them, they searched and found only one cruse of undefiled oil that was resting there with the seal of the High Priest. It had enough oil to kindle the candelabrum for only one day. But a miracle was performed, and the priests kindled from it for eight days. The next year the Sages instituted them as eight days of festivity....

What did the Sages see that led them to make Hanukkah eight days? In the days of the Greek kingdom, the Hasmoneans entered the Sanctuary and rebuilt the altar and whitewashed it with lime. For all seven days the Hasmoneans dedicated the altar by presenting offerings on it utilizing service vessels.

The dedication by the Hasmoneans is commemorated throughout the generations. Why is it observed throughout the generations? Because they performed the dedication of the altar when they were redeemed from dis-

---

38. One does not eulogize on days of rejoicing.

tress to relief, and they then recited psalms of praise, *Hallel*, and thanksgiving, and they kindled lamps in purity.

Since the Greeks entered the Sanctuary and defiled all the vessels, there was nothing on which to kindle the lamps.[39] When the house of the Hasmoneans overcame them, they brought seven iron skewers, and they plated them with tin, and began to kindle them…

(Megillat Ta'anit 9)

📖 Further reading: For more on the holiday of Hanukkah, its essential meaning and its laws, see *A Concise Guide to Mahshava*, p. 79; *A Concise Guide to Halakha*, p. 244.

The Hanukkah Lights

The Sages detailed the number of Hanukkah lights one must kindle and where they should be placed. They disagreed whether one light should be added each day, or one light should be subtracted each day.

The basic mitzva of Hanukkah is to have one light kindled by a person for himself and his household each day. And the *mehadrin*, those who are meticulous in the performance of mitzvot, kindle a light for each person in the household. And the *mehadrin min hamehadrin*, those who are even more meticulous, add a light for each and every person on each night.

Beit Shammai say: On the first day one kindles eight lights and, from then on, one gradually decreases the number of lights by one each day. And Beit Hillel say: On the first day one kindles one light, and from then on, one gradually increases the number of lights until, on the last day, he kindles eight lights.

There were two elders in Tzaidan. One acted in accordance with the opinion of Beit Shammai, and one acted in accordance with the opinion of Beit Hillel. Each gave a reason for his claim. One said it is like the bulls of the festival of *Sukkot*,[40] and one said: One elevates in matters of sanctity and one does not downgrade.

The mitzva of kindling the Hanukkah lights is from sunset until traffic in the marketplace ceases. And it is a mitzva to place the Hanukkah lights at the entrance to one's house on the outside. If one lives upstairs, he places it at the window near the public domain. If he is afraid of the gentiles, he puts it at the entrance to his house on the inside. In time of danger, he places it on the table and that is sufficient to fulfill his obligation.

(Megillat Ta'anit 9)

---

39. It was forbidden to kindle lights on a defiled candelabrum.
40. On each day of Sukkot, the number of bulls sacrificed is one fewer than on the preceding day.

Publicizing the Miracle

The Sages established the order of priority for one who cannot afford to fulfill the mitzva of Hanukkah lights and the mitzvot of Shabbat: lighting the Shabbat candles and reciting *Kiddush* over wine.

Rava said: It is obvious to me that if one must choose between purchasing oil to kindle a Shabbat lamp for his home or oil for a Hanukkah lamp, oil for the Shabbat lamp for his home takes precedence, due to harmony in his home.[41] If there is a conflict between buying oil for a lamp for his home and wine for *Kiddush*, sanctification of the day, oil for the lamp for his home takes precedence, due to harmony in his home.

Rava raised a dilemma: When the conflict is between oil for a Hanukkah lamp and wine for *Kiddush* of the day, what is the *halakha*? Does wine for *Kiddush* of the day take priority because it is frequent,[42] or perhaps oil for the Hanukkah lamp takes precedence, due to the requirement for publicizing the miracle? After he raised the dilemma, he then resolved it: Oil for the Hanukkah lamp takes precedence due to publicizing the miracle.

(*Shabbat* 23b)

📖 Further reading: For how one kindles the Hanukkah lights, see *A Concise Guide to Halakha*, p. 244.

---

41. The purpose of the Shabbat lights is to facilitate eating the Shabbat meal, and to create a pleasant and harmonious atmosphere in the home.
42. When a frequent practice and an infrequent practice clash, the frequent practice takes precedence.

Purim

Purim is celebrated on the fourteenth day of the month of Adar (and in certain cities on the fifteenth). It marks the salvation of the Jews from the decree of Haman, King Ahashverosh's prime minister, who sought to destroy them. Ultimately, the tables were turned: Haman was hanged, and the Jews were given permission to fight back. The heroes of the tale are Queen Esther, whom King Ahashverosh selected as his queen, and who initiated and manipulated maneuvers that led to Haman's execution; Mordekhai, her cousin, whose belated reward for thwarting the attempted assassination of the king marked the reversal of fortunes that culminated in Haman's downfall and frustration of his plot.

The primary mitzvot of Purim are the reading of the Scroll of Esther, giving gifts to the poor, sending portions of food one to another, and enjoying a festive meal. The holiday is exemplified by great rejoicing. In the chapter that follows we cite statements of our Sages regarding the month of Adar, the special mitzvot of the holiday, and details of the story of the scroll of Esther: Ahashverosh's feast; Queen Esther, who found favor in the eyes of all; the plot to assassinate King Ahashverosh; Haman's decree; the fast and prayer of the Jews; and the honor that Haman was forced to grant Mordekhai in the city streets.

Increasing Joy

It is not only the days of Purim that are days of rejoicing; rather, throughout the entire month of Adar, "the month that was transformed for them from sorrow to joy" (Esther 9:22), one should increase his rejoicing.

Rav Yehuda, son of Rav Shmuel bar Sheilat, said in the name of Rav: Just as when the month of Av begins one decreases his rejoicing, so too, when Adar begins, one increases his rejoicing...

Rav Pappa said: Therefore, in the case of a Jew who has litigation with a gentile, let him avoid it in Av, when his fortune is bad, and make himself available in Adar, when his fortune is good.

(*Ta'anit* 29a)

Further reading: For more on the joy unique to the month of Adar, see *A Concise Guide to Mahshava*, p. 48. For an innovative explanation of the decrease in joy in Av, see *A Concise Guide to Mahshava*, p. 50.

The Temple Vessels

King Ahashverosh held a huge feast, which lasted for one hundred and eighty days, for all his government officials. At the conclusion of this period, he added a week-long banquet for all the residents of the capital city of Shushan. According to the Sages, at this magnificent banquet Ahashverosh made use of the Temple vestments and vessels, and some of the Sages considered the enjoyment of the Jews at this feast as the spiritual cause of the harsh decree that Haman issued against them.

"In those days, when King Ahashverosh sat on the royal throne...he made a banquet" (Esther 1:2–3). He took out Temple vessels and used them.

"With his showing the riches of his glorious kingdom, and the honor of his splendid [*tiferet*] majesty" (Esther 1:4). Rabbi Yosei bar Hanina said: This teaches that Ahashverosh donned the priestly vestments, as it is written here: "The honor of his splendid majesty," and it is written there, regarding the priestly vestments: "For glory and for splendor [*tifaret*]" (Exodus 28:2).

The students of Rabbi Shimon bar Yohai asked him: For what reason were the enemies of the Jewish people[43] in that generation deserving of annihilation? Rabbi Shimon bar Yohai said to them: Say the answer yourselves. They said to him: It is because they enjoyed themselves at the feast of that wicked Ahashverosh. Rabbi Shimon said to them: If so, those in Shushan, who participated in the feast, should have been killed; those in the rest of the world should not have been killed.

They said to him: You say the answer. Rabbi Shimon bar Yohai said to them: It is because they prostrated themselves before the idol. They said to him: Is there favoritism in that matter?[44] Rabbi Shimon bar Yohai said to them: They did so only for appearances.[45] So too, the Holy One, blessed be He, acted with them only for appearances.[46]

(*Megilla* 12a)

📖 Further reading: "They did so only for appearances" is cited as a reason for the custom of masquerading on Purim, see *A Concise Guide to Mahshava*, p. 90.

Esther

After Ahashverosh removed Vashti from her position as queen, the king searched for a long time for a suitable replacement. Eventually he chose Esther, who "found favor

---

43. This is a euphemism for the Jewish people themselves.
44. If they engaged in idol worship, why weren't they destroyed?
45. They created the impression that they were worshipping the idol because they feared the king.
46. He merely threatened them with destruction.

in the eyes of everyone who saw her" (Esther 2:15). The Sages explain the meaning of this phrase.

"Esther found favor in the eyes of everyone who saw her" (Esther 2:15). Rabbi Yuda says: She was like this fine portrait that is viewed by one thousand people and is liked by all. Rabbi Nehemya says: They positioned Median woman on one side and Persian women on the other side, and Esther was more beautiful than all of them.

And the Rabbis say: "Esther found favor in the eyes of everyone who saw her"; in the eyes of the upper worlds [God and His angels] and in the eyes of the lower worlds [people], as the verse states: "And you will find grace and high favor in the eyes of God and man" (Proverbs 3:4).

(*Esther Rabba 6*)

Bigtan and Teresh

Two of the king's officials, Bigtan and Teresh, sought to assassinate Ahashverosh, but Mordekhai exposed their plot and saved him.

Rabbi Yohanan said: Bigtan and Teresh were two Tarsians,[47] and they would converse in the Tarsian language. They said: From the day that Esther arrived we have not slept.[48] Come, let us put poison into his goblet so that he will die. But they did not know that Mordekhai, as a member of the Sanhedrin, was one of those who sat in the Chamber of Hewn Stone, and that he knew seventy languages.[49]

(*Megilla 13b*)

Haman and Ahashverosh

Haman offered King Ahashverosh a considerable sum for permission to kill all the Jews in his kingdom, but the king acquiesced immediately and without payment. The Sages portray this agreement with a parable about a person who was very glad for the opportunity to be rid of an item that he did not need.

"The king said to Haman: The silver is given to you, and the people, to do with them as it is pleasing in your eyes" (Esther 3:11). Rabbi Abba said: The actions of Ahashverosh and Haman can be understood by means of a

---

47. From the city of Tarsus.
48. Because Ahashverosh was constantly bothering them with requests throughout the nights that he was consorting with his new queen.
49. Knowing seventy languages is a prerequisite for membership in the Sanhedrin.

parable; to what is the matter comparable? It is comparable to two individuals, one who had a mound in the middle of his field and the other had a ditch in the middle of his field. The owner of the ditch said: Who will give me for money this mound with which to fill my ditch? The owner of the mound said: Who will give me for money this ditch into which I can move my mound? One day, they met one another. The owner of the ditch said to the owner of the mound: Sell me your mound. He said to him: Take it for free; would that it would be so.[50]

(*Megilla* 13b)

Removal of the Ring

The story of the book of Esther teaches us that suffering or tangible danger can be far more effective motivators for repentance than reprimands and reproof, vigorous though they may be.

"The king removed his ring from his hand and he gave it to Haman" (Esther 3:10). Rabbi Abba bar Kahana said: Removal of the king's ring to affix a seal to Haman's decree was more effective than the rebukes of forty-eight prophets and seven prophetesses who prophesied on behalf of the Jewish people, as they were all unable to return them to the right path, but the removal of the ring returned them to the right path.[51]

(*Megilla* 14a)

📖 **Further reading:** For more on the holiday of Purim, see *A Concise Guide to Mahshava*, p. 86; *A Concise Guide to Halakha*, p. 262.

Esther's Prayer

After the seal was affixed to the decree of the Jews' destruction, Esther was sent to the king to plead on behalf of her people. The Sages portray Esther's feelings at the time, and describe her emotional prayer.

At that time, Esther was very frightened because of the evil that overshadowed Israel. She removed her royal garments and her splendor, and donned sackcloth and loosened the hair on her head and covered it with dust and ashes. She afflicted herself by fasting, and fell on her face before God.

---

50. Ahashverosh wanted to be rid of the Jews, but had no one to do it for him. When he found Haman, he rejoiced and requested no payment.
51. When the decree was issued, the Jews immediately engaged in fasting and prayer.

She prayed and she said: Lord, God of Israel, who has ruled from ancient days and who created the world. Please help Your maidservant, as I have been left an orphan without father or mother. I am comparable to a poor woman who goes from house to house asking for alms, as I am asking for Your compassion while going from window to window in the house of Ahashverosh. And now, God, please grant success to this poor maidservant of Yours, and rescue the sheep of Your flock from these enemies that have risen against us, as nothing prevents You from saving with a great or minor salvation. And now, Father of orphans, please stand to the right of this orphan who has relied on Your kindness, and let me receive mercy from this man, for I fear him; and humble him before me, as You humble the proud.

(*Esther Rabba* 8)

The Prayer of the Children

The Sages state that Jewish schoolchildren were diligently engaged in Torah study and prayer, while fasting, throughout the three days that preceded Esther's entry to the king. Their cries reached the heavenly Throne and ultimately abrogated Haman's wicked decree.

After Haman made the gallows, he went to Mordekhai and found him sitting in the study hall, and children were sitting before him, with sackcloth on their loins, and they were engaged in Torah study, and screaming and crying. Haman counted them and found that there were twenty-two thousand children there. He threw iron chains over them, and appointed guards over them, saying: Tomorrow I will kill these children first, and then I will hang Mordekhai.

Their mothers brought them bread and water, and said to them: Our children, eat and drink before you die tomorrow, so you will not die hungry.

Immediately the children placed their hands upon their books and took oaths on Mordekhai's life: Our Master, we will neither eat nor drink, but rather we will die while in the midst of our fast. They all burst into tears until their cries rose to the heavens, and the Holy One, blessed be He, heard the sound of their cries in the second hour of the night.

At that hour the mercies of the Holy One, blessed be He, were awakened, and He arose from upon the Throne of judgment and said: What is this great noise that I hear, which is like the bleating of goats and lambs? Moses our Master stood before the Holy One, blessed be He, and said: Master of the Universe, they are neither goats nor lambs, but rather they are the

young of Your people who have been fasting for three days and three nights, and tomorrow the enemy wants to slaughter them like goats and lambs. At that moment, the Holy One, blessed be He, took hold of those letters that he decreed on them, which were sealed with a seal of mud, and He tore them. He caused Ahashverosh to become confused that night, and that is the meaning of what is written: "On that night, the king's sleep was disrupted" (Esther 6:1).

(Esther Rabba 9)

📖 **Further reading:** For more on the children's prayer, see p. 357.

Mordekhai on the Horse

At the height of Haman's success, when he came to ask the king to hang Mordekhai, his fortune was reversed. The king asked him how it would be appropriate to honor a person who had performed kindness for the king. Haman was convinced that Ahashverosh was talking about him, but it soon became clear to him that the king was referring to Mordekhai, and that it was incumbent upon him to honor Mordekhai in public. The Sages described and elucidated at length the relevant events cited in the book of Esther.

"On that night, the king's sleep was disrupted" (Esther 6:1). Rabbi Tanhum said: The sleep of the King of the Universe was disturbed. And the Sages said: The sleep of the King of the upper ones, God, was disturbed, and the sleep of the king of the lower ones, Ahashverosh, was disturbed. Rava said: It was actually the sleep of King Ahashverosh that was disturbed. A thought occurred to him and he said to himself: What is this that is before us that Esther has invited Haman? Perhaps they are conspiring against that man[52] to kill him. King Ahashverosh said again: If this is so, is there no man who loves me who would inform me? He said again: Perhaps there is some man who has done me a favor and I have not rewarded him, and for that reason, because they stand to gain nothing, people refrain from revealing it to me. Immediately: "He said to bring the book of records, the chronicles, and they would be read before the king" (Esther 6:1).

"And do so[53] to Mordekhai" (Esther 6:10). Haman said to the king: Who is Mordekhai? Ahashverosh said to him: "The Jew" (Esther 6:10). Haman said to him: There are several Mordekhais among the Jews. He said to

---

52. He was referring to himself.
53. Dress him in royal garments, place him on a horse, and lead him through the city streets, while calling out: "So shall be done to the man whose honoring the king desires" (Esther 6:9).

him: Mordekhai "who sits at the king's gate" (Esther 6:10). Haman said to him: It would be enough for him if you gave him one village or one river. Ahashverosh said to him: Give him that too; "do not omit any matter from all that you have spoken" (Esther 6:10).

"Haman took the garments and the horse" (Esther 6:11). He went and found Mordekhai with the Sages sitting before him, and he was demonstrating to them the *halakhot* of the handful.[54] When Mordekhai saw Haman coming toward him with the reins of his horse held in his hands, he became frightened, and he said to the Sages: This evil man has come to kill me. Go away from him so that you should not be burned by his coals.

At that moment, Mordekhai wrapped himself in his prayer shawl and stood to pray. Haman came and sat down before them and waited until Mordekhai finished his prayer.

Haman said to the Sages: With what were you occupied? They said to him: When the Temple is standing, one who pledges a meal offering would bring a handful of fine flour and achieve atonement with it. Haman said to them: Your handful of fine flour has come and overridden my ten thousand silver pieces[55] ....

Haman said to Mordekhai: Rise, don these garments, and ride this horse; the king wants to honor you. Mordekhai said to him: I cannot do so until I enter the bathhouse and trim my hair, as it is not proper conduct to use the king's garments in this state.

Esther sent a directive and closed all the bathhouses and all the bloodletters and barbers. Haman took Mordechai into the bathhouse and bathed him, and Haman went and brought scissors from his house and trimmed Mordekhai's hair with them. While Haman was trimming he injured himself and groaned. Mordekhai asked him: Why are you groaning? Haman said to him: The man whom the king had regarded above all his ministers is now made a bathhouse attendant and a barber. Mordekhai said to him: Wicked one, weren't you the barber of the village of Kartzum? As it was taught by the Sages: Haman was the barber of the village of Kartzum for twenty-two years....

"And he proclaimed before him: So shall be done to the man whose honoring the king desires" (Esther 6:11). As Haman was taking Mordekhai along the street of Haman's house, Haman's daughter was standing on the roof and saw the spectacle. She thought that the one who was riding was her

---

54. The handful was an exact measure taken from meal offerings and burned on the altar.
55. Haman offered ten thousand silver pieces to Ahashverosh to kill the Jews.

father, and the one walking before him was Mordekhai. She took a chamber pot and cast it onto her father's head. Haman lifted his eyes; she saw that it was her father. She fell from the roof to the ground and died.

(*Megilla* 15b)

The Mitzvot of the Holiday

In addition to the reading of the book of Esther, there are other mitzvot on Purim: having a joyous feast, sending portions of food to each other, and giving gifts to the poor. The Sages derived the details of these mitzvot from the verses of the book of Esther.

Rav Yosef taught: "Sending portions of food one to another [*lere'ehu*]" (Esther 9:22), meaning two portions to one person.[56] The verse continues: "And gifts to the indigent [*evyonim*]" (Esther 9:22), meaning two gifts to two people[57].... Rava said: A person is obligated to become intoxicated on Purim until he does not know to distinguish between "cursed is Haman" and "blessed is Mordekhai."

(*Megilla* 7a)

---

56. This is learned from the fact that the word "portions" is plural, whereas the word "another" is singular.
57. Here the word "indigent" appears in the plural form.

Passover

The festival of Passover is observed for seven days, beginning on the fifteenth of Nisan. On the first night of the festival, the Seder night, one festively recounts the exodus from Egypt, and eats matza and bitter herbs [*maror*] and drinks four cups of wine. In the Diaspora, the festival is observed for eight days and there are two Seder nights. Throughout the seven, or in the Diaspora, eight, days of the festival, no leavened bread [*hametz*] may be eaten. When the Temple was standing, all the people would bring a special offering on the fourteenth of Nisan, the paschal offering, whose consumption was the climax of the Seder.

In the chapter that follows we cite statements of the Sages regarding the search for *hametz* before the festival; recounting the story of the exodus to children, each according to his ability; and the mitzva of drinking four cups of wine at the Seder.

Candlelight

The search for *hametz* in one's house before Passover should be performed by candlelight.

Mishna: On the evening of the fourteenth, one searches for leavened bread with the light of a lamp.

Gemara: The Sages taught: One searches neither by the light of the sun, nor by the light of the moon, nor by the light of a torch with multiple wicks, but rather, by the light of a lamp, because the light of a lamp is effective for searching.... A lamp but not a torch? Rav Nahman bar Yitzhak said: One can put this lamp into holes and crevices, and one cannot put that torch into holes and crevices, as it has a large flame. Rav Zevid said: This lamp projects its light before it, and that torch projects its light behind it. Rav Pappa said: When using this torch, one fears starting a fire, and when using that lamp he does not fear starting a fire. Ravina said: Concerning this lamp, its light is drawn[58] and steady, but the light of that torch is unstable and jumps.

(Mishna *Pesaḥim* 1:1; *Pesaḥim* 7b)

---

58. The wick draws the oil smoothly.

The Four Sons

In the verses that deal with the obligation to tell the story of the exodus from Egypt, one can find four paradigmatic children, each of whom receives a response specifically tailored for him.

The Torah spoke corresponding to four sons: a wise son; a wicked son; an unintelligent son; and a son who does not know to ask.

What does the wise son say? "What are the testimonies, and the statutes, and the ordinances that the Lord our God commanded you" (Deuteronomy 6:20). You too say to him: "With strength of hand, the Lord took us out from Egypt, from the house of bondage" (Exodus 13:20).

What does the wicked son say? "What is this service to you" (Exodus 12:26); what is this burden that you impose on us each and every year? Since he removed himself from the community, you too say to him: "It is because of this that the Lord did this for me" (Exodus 13:8), God did it for me but not for that man [for you, the wicked son]: Had that man been in Egypt, he would never have been worthy of being redeemed from there.

What does the unintelligent son say? "What is this" (Exodus 13:14). You too should teach him the laws of the paschal offering: That one may not have afikoman[59] after the paschal offering; and that one may not rise from one group and join another group.

For the son who does not know how to ask, you must first initiate the dialogue with him. Rabbi Yosa says: Our Mishna too says so: If the son has no understanding, his father teaches him.

(Jerusalem Talmud, *Pesaḥim* 10:4)

In Each and Every Generation

It is not only our ancestors that God redeemed from Egypt, but each and every one of us as well.

In each and every generation a person must view himself as though it was he who went out of Egypt, as it is stated: "You shall tell your son on that day, saying: It is because of this that the Lord did for me[60] upon my exodus from Egypt" (Exodus 13:8).

(Mishna *Pesaḥim* 10:5)

---

59. There are several explanations of this statement. One is that one may not eat dessert after having eaten the paschal offering.

60. The emphasis is on the word "me." Even one who was not in Egypt recounts the experience to his son in the first person.

Four Cups

The Sages instituted that on Seder night one drinks four cups of wine. Why?

From where is the obligation to drink four cups on Passover derived? Rabbi Yoḥanan says in the name of Rabbi Benaya: The four cups correspond to four expressions of redemption: "Therefore, say to the children of Israel: I am the Lord and I will take you out from under the burdens of Egypt and I will deliver you from their work and I will redeem you with an outstretched arm and with great punishments" (Exodus 6:6). The four expressions are: "I will take you out," "I will deliver you," "I will redeem you," and "I will take you" (Exodus 13:15).

Rabbi Levi says: The four cups correspond to the four kingdoms[61] that subjugated Israel.

The Rabbis say: The four cups correspond to the four cups of retribution that the Holy One, blessed be He, is destined to have the nations of the world drink … and corresponding to them the Holy One, blessed be He, will have Israel drink four cups of consolation.

(Jerusalem Talmud, *Pesaḥim* 10:1)

Further reading: For more on the enslavement in Egypt and the exodus, see p. 77. On the festival of Passover, its inner meaning and its laws, see *A Concise Guide to Mahshava*, p. 93; *A Concise Guide to Halakha*, from p. 274.

---

61. The four kingdoms are Babylonia, Persia, Greece, and Rome.

Shavuot

The appointed time of the festival of *Shavuot* is fifty days from the second day of Passover. *Shavuot* marks the conclusion of the period of the counting of the *omer* and the sacrifice of the offering of the "two loaves" in the Temple. In addition, the Sages noted that based on the Torah account, the Torah was given on or around that day. Ever since, *Shavuot* is characterized primarily by its close connection to the Torah and the revelation at Sinai. Today, when the annual calendar and the number of days in each month are determined in advance, *Shavuot* always coincides with the sixth day of Sivan.

In the chapter that follows, we cite statements of the Sages regarding the sublime occasion of the revelation at Sinai and the events that preceded it.

We Will Perform and We Will Heed

"Everything that the Lord has spoken we will perform and we will heed" (Exodus 24:7). This concept, that the obligation to obey ("we will perform") precedes hearing and understanding the details of the Torah ("we will heed"), is considered by the Sages to be an exalted principle, comparable to the conduct of the celestial angels. Because of this, the Israelites were worthy of distinction and majesty.

Reish Lakish said: What is the meaning of what is written: "It was evening and it was morning, the sixth day [*hashishi*]" (Genesis 1:31)? Why do I require the superfluous *heh*?[62] It teaches that the Holy One, blessed be He, made a condition[63] with the act of Creation, and said to them: If Israel accepts the Torah on the sixth day of Sivan you will continue to exist; but if not, I will return you to the primordial state of chaos and disorder.

Rabbi Simai taught: When Israel pronounced the declaration: "We will perform" before the declaration: "We will heed," 600,000[64] ministering angels came and tied two crowns to each and every member of the Israelites, one corresponding to "we will perform" and one corresponding to "we will heed." And when Israel sinned [with the Golden Calf], 120,000 angels of destruction descended and removed them…

---

62. All the other days of Creation are written without the definite article [*heh*], e.g., *sheni*.
63. The continued existence of creation is contingent on Israel accepting the Torah at Sinai on "the sixth day" of Sivan.
64. The number of angels corresponds to the number of Israelite males between 20 and 60 (see Exodus 12:37).

Reish Lakish said: In the future, the Holy One, blessed be He, will return them to us...

Rabbi Elazar said: When Israel pronounced "we will perform" before "we will heed," a Divine Voice emerged and said to them: Who revealed to My children this secret used by the ministering angels? As it is written: "Bless the Lord, His angels, mighty in strength, who do His bidding, heeding His word" (Psalms 103:20). Initially, the angels do His bidding, afterward they heed.

(Shabbat 88a)

Though the Lord Is Exalted, He Sees the Lowly

God selected Mount Sinai as the site for the giving of the Torah not because it is the tallest and grandest of all mountains; on the contrary, because it is small and relatively short.

When the Holy One, blessed be He, sought to give the Torah to Israel, Mount Carmel came from Spain and Mount Tavor came from Beit Eilim.... This one said: I am called Mount Tavor, and the Divine Presence should rest upon me, as I am taller than all the mountains, and the waters of the flood did not fall upon me and cover me. This one said: I am called Mount Carmel, and the Divine Presence should rest upon me, as I lowered myself in the middle, and they passed through the sea[65] over me.

The Holy One, blessed be He, said: You are already disqualified before me due to your haughtiness; you are all disqualified before me... I want none other than Sinai, for it is more humble than all of you, as it is stated: "Exalted and holy I will dwell and I will be with the downtrodden and humble" (Isaiah 57:15), and it is stated: "Though the Lord is exalted, He sees the lowly" (Psalms 138:6).

(Midrash Tehillim [Buber] 68)

The Speech of God

At the giving of the Torah, the Israelites heard the voice of God Himself. The Sages depict the tremendous effect of the speech of God.

Rabbi Yehoshua ben Levi said: Each and every utterance that emerged from the mouth of the Holy One, blessed be He, caused the entire world to be filled with fragrant spices....

---

65. During the splitting of the Red Sea.

And Rabbi Yehoshua ben Levi said: Each and every utterance that emerged from the mouth of the Holy One, blessed be He, caused the souls of the Israelites to depart from their bodies, as it is stated: "My soul had departed with His speaking" (Song of Songs 5:6). Since their souls left from the first utterance, how did they receive the second utterance? God rained the dew upon them that, in the future, will revive the dead, and it revived them.

The Holy One, blessed be He, may His name and might be blessed, when He pronounced His speech, the voice was divided into seven voices, and from seven it split into the seventy languages of the seventy archetypal nations, so that everyone would understand.

(*Shabbat* 88a; *Midrash Tehillim* [Buber] 68)

Moses and the Ministering Angels

The exalted Torah of God was written specifically for humans, here, in this world. The Sages expressed this idea in their story about Moses our Master, who was forced to quarrel with the ministering angels until they relented and allowed him to take the Torah down to earth.

When Moses ascended on High to receive the Torah, the ministering angels said before the Holy One, Blessed be He: Master of the Universe, what is one born of a woman doing among us? God said to them: He came to receive the Torah. The angels said before Him: The Torah is a hidden treasure that was concealed for You for 974 generations[66] before the creation of the world, and You seek to give it to flesh and blood? "What is a mortal that You remember him, a man that You take him into account?" (Psalms 8:5). Rather, "Lord, our Master, how mighty is Your name throughout the world! You place Your glory in the heavens" (Psalms 8:2).[67] The Holy One, blessed be He, said to Moses: Provide them with an answer. Moses said before Him: Master of the Universe, I am afraid that they might burn me with the breath of their mouths. God said to him: Hold onto My Throne of Glory and provide them with an answer....

Moses said before God: Master of the Universe, the Torah that You are giving me, what is written in it? God said: "I am the Lord your God, who took you out of the land of Egypt" (Exodus 20:2). Moses said to the angels:

---

66. Including the twenty-six generations since Creation results in a total of 1,000 generations.
67. Therefore, Your glory and Your Torah should be given to the residents of the heavens.

Did you go down to Egypt? Were you enslaved to Pharaoh? Why should the Torah be yours?

Moses said before God: What else is written in it? God said: "You shall have no other gods" (Exodus 20:3). Moses said to them: Are you among the nations who worship idols?[68]

Again, Moses asked: What else is written in it? God said: "Remember the Sabbath day, to keep it holy" (Exodus 20:8). Moses asked the angels: Do you perform labor that you require rest?

Again, what else is written in it? "You shall not take the name of the Lord your God in vain" (Exodus 20:7).[69] Moses asked: Do you conduct business with one another?[70]

Again, what else is written in it? God said: "Honor your father and your mother" (Exodus 20:12). Moses asked: Do you have a father or a mother?

Again, what else is written in it? God said: "You shall not murder. You shall not commit adultery. You shall not steal" (Exodus 20:13). Moses asked: Is there jealousy among you? Is there an evil inclination within you? Immediately, they conceded to the Holy One, Blessed be He.

(*Shabbat* 88b)

Further reading: For more on the festival of *Shavuot*, its inner meaning and laws, see *A Concise Guide to Mahshava*, p. 99; *A Concise Guide to Halakha*, p. 340.

Moses and Rabbi Akiva

The Sages relate that Moses was granted a glimpse into the future, and that he was enthused to see the development of the Torah and the novel ideas stated in it.

When Moses ascended on High, he found the Holy One, blessed be He, sitting and attaching crowns to the letters of the Torah. Moses said before Him: Master of the Universe, who is preventing You?[71] God said to him: There is a man who is destined to live after several generations, and Akiva ben Yosef is his name; he is destined to derive from each and every stroke of these crowns mounds and mounds of *halakhot*. Moses said before Him: Master of the Universe, show him to me. God said to him: Take a step back and look into the future.

---

68. Is there a danger that you will be influenced by them and worship idols?
69. It is prohibited to take a false oath.
70. Often in the course of conducting business, disputes, which require one of the parties to take an oath, arise.
71. Who is preventing You from giving the Torah as it is? Why do You need to enhance it?

Moses went and sat behind eight rows of students[72] in Rabbi Akiva's study hall and did not understand what they were saying. Moses felt weak. When Rabbi Akiva reached a certain matter, his students said to him: My teacher, from where do you derive this? Rabbi Akiva said to them: It is a *halakha* transmitted to Moses from Sinai. Moses' mind was put at ease.[73]

Moses returned and came before the Holy One, blessed be He; he said before Him: Master of the Universe, You have a man like this and You give the Torah through me? God said to him: Be silent; this is My will that arose before Me.

Moses said before Him: Master of the Universe, You have shown me Rabbi Akiva's Torah, show me his reward. God said to him: Take a step back. Moses saw that the Romans were weighing Rabbi Akiva's flesh in a butcher shop after killing him. Moses said before God: Master of the Universe, this is Torah and this is its reward? God said to him: Be silent; this is My will that arose before Me.

(*Menaḥot* 29b)

📖 **Further reading:** For the fascinating biography of Rabbi Akiva, see p. 335; about his tragic death, see p. 364.

The Two Loaves

On *Shavuot* the priests bring the "two loaves," an offering made from leavened bread, unlike most meal offerings, which may not be brought from leavened bread. The Sages explain why *Shavuot* is the time for this offering.

For what reason did the Torah say: Bring the two-loaves offering on *Shavuot*? Because *Shavuot* is the beginning of the time of the ripening of fruits that grow on a tree. The Holy One, blessed be He, said: Bring the two loaves before Me on *Shavuot* so that the fruits of the tree will be blessed for you.

(*Rosh HaShana* 16a)

---

72. The beginners sat toward the back of the hall.
73. He saw that ultimately the core of the Torah of the Sages is based on a tradition that he transmitted.

Stories from the Sages

The Kings of Israel

The Sages elaborated on the lives of the kings of Israel. These accounts illuminate aspects that were not mentioned in the verses or were cited only in passing. These portrayals shed new light on the personalities and lives of the kings.

King David's Way of Life

The Sages describe the daily routine of David king of Israel; his engagement in Torah study; and his dedication to judging and instructing the people and seeing to their needs.

A lyre was suspended over David's bed, and when midnight arrived, a northern wind would come and blow on it and cause the lyre to play on its own. David would immediately rise and study Torah until the first rays of dawn. When dawn arrived, the Sages of Israel entered and said to him: Our lord the king, your nation requires sustenance. He replied: Go and sustain one another [by trading with each other]. They responded with a parable: A single handful of food does not satisfy a lion, and a pit will not be filled from its own dirt.[1] David instructed them: Go and take up arms with the troops.[2] The Sages immediately sought advice from Ahitofel [an advisor to King David], consulted the Sanhedrin, and inquired of the Urim and the Tumim....[3]

The verse states: "A prayer by David...Watch over me, for I am pious" (Psalms 86:1–2). Levi and Rabbi Yitzhak disagreed as to how David's piety was manifest. One said: This is what David said before the Holy One, blessed be He: Master of the Universe, am I not pious? All the kings of the East and the West sleep until the third hour of the day, but I, "at midnight, I rise to give thanks to You" (Psalms 119:62).

---

1. Just as a lion is not satisfied by a small portion and a pit cannot be filled by the dirt that was dug from it, so too, the people of Israel alone are incapable of supporting themselves.
2. A military campaign would expand borders and economic opportunities.
3. The Urim and the Tumim were on the breast piece of the High Priest, who would consult them to determine whether God had sanctioned the decision to wage war.

And the other Sage said: This is what David said before the Holy One, blessed be He: Master of the Universe, am I not pious? All of the kings of the East and the West sit in groups [with other members of the royal and aristocratic classes] befitting their honor, but my hands become soiled with blood to determine whether it is menstrual blood, with a miscarried fetus, and with a placenta,[4] in order to render a woman ritually pure and consequently be permitted to her husband. Moreover, I consult my teacher, Mefivoshet [a grandson of King Saul], with regard to everything that I do. I say to him: Mefivoshet my teacher, did I decide properly? Did I judge as liable properly? Did I judge as exempt properly? Did I rule that an item is ritually pure properly? Did I rule that an item is ritually impure properly? I was not embarrassed to seek counsel.

(*Berakhot* 3b–4a)

Further reading: For how one would receive answers from the Urim and the Tumim, see p. 118.

Death of David

David requested from God to inform him of the day of his death. He attempted to prevent the angel of death from harming him, but he was ultimately unsuccessful and passed away.

Rav Yehuda said that Rav said: What is the meaning of what David said: "Lord, let me know my end and what will be the measure of my days. Let me know when I will cease to be" (Psalms 39:5)? David said before the Holy One, blessed be He: Master of the Universe, "Lord, let me know my end," when I will die. God said to him: It is a decree before Me that I do not reveal the end of the life of flesh and blood. David continued: "And what will be the measure of my days" [the day of the year that I will die]? God responded: It is a decree before Me not to reveal the measure of a person's days. David persisted: "Let me know when I will cease to be," [the day of the week on which I will I die]. God said to him: You will die on Shabbat. ...

Every Shabbat, David would sit and study Torah all day.[5] On the day he was supposed to die, the angel of death stood before him, but was unable to overcome him, as David's mouth did not pause from study. The angel of death said to himself: What shall I do to him? David had a garden behind his

---

4. Examining the placenta would determine whether a miscarried fetus was sufficiently developed to render the mother impure with the status of a woman after childbirth.
5. He studied so that in the merit of Torah study he would be protected from the angel of death.

house; the angel of death came, ascended, and shook the trees. David went out to see. He was climbing the stairs, a stair broke beneath him. He was startled and was silenced from his studies, and he passed away.

(Berakhot 30a–b)

Hizkiyahu's Prayer

The verses relate that when Hizkiyahu king of Judah was very ill, the prophet Isaiah came to inform him that he would soon die. The Sages elaborate on this narrative, and describe the exchange between Hizkiyahu and Isaiah and the resolute faith of the king, who continued to pray to God despite the decree. Ultimately, his prayer was accepted.

"In those days, Hizkiyahu became deathly ill, and Isaiah son of Amotz the prophet came to him. He said to him: So said the Lord: Instruct your household, as you are dying and will not survive" (Isaiah 38:1). What is the meaning of "you are dying and will not survive"? [Why the redundancy?] You are dying in this world, and you will not survive in the World to Come. Hizkiyahu said to him: What is all this? [What did I do to deserve this punishment?] Isaiah said to him: It is because you did not engage in procreation. Hizkiyahu explained: I did not engage in procreation because I envisaged through divine inspiration that the children who emerge from me will not be virtuous. Isaiah said to him: Why do you involve yourself with the secrets of the Holy One, blessed be He? What you have been commanded, to beget children, you are required to perform, and what is acceptable to the Holy One, blessed be He, He will perform.

Hizkiyahu said to him: Now give me your daughter as a wife; perhaps my merit and your merit will cause virtuous children to emerge from me. Isaiah said to him: The decree that you will die has already been issued against you. Hizkiyahu said to him: Son of Amotz, cease your prophecy and leave. I have a tradition from the house of my father's father [King David]: Even if a sharp sword is placed against a person's neck, he should not desist from praying for mercy. Immediately: "Hizkiyahu turned his face to the wall and he prayed to the Lord" (Isaiah 38:2).[6]

(Berakhot 10a)

Stories from the Sages

---

6. In fact, Hizkiyahu recovered, after which he married Isaiah's daughter and she bore him children.

Nikanor's Doors

Nikanor was an Alexandrian Jew who risked his life to protect the doors he had donated to the Temple. While he was transporting them by sea to the Land of Israel, a storm arose. A miracle was performed on his behalf, and his doors did not sink into the sea.

Miracles were performed on behalf of Nikanor's doors. The Sages taught: What miracles were performed on behalf of his doors? They said: When Nikanor went to bring doors for the eastern gate of the Temple from Alexandria in Egypt, a giant wave arose in the sea on his return voyage and threatened to drown him. The passengers took one of the doors and cast it into the sea. But the sea still did not rest from its rage. They sought to cast the other door into the sea as well. Nikanor stood and embraced it. He said to them: Cast me into the sea with it. Immediately, the sea rested from its rage, and for the rest of voyage he was pained about the other door [that it had been cast into the sea].

When they arrived at the port of Akko, the door that had been thrown into the sea was protruding under the sides of the ship. Some say that a sea creature had swallowed it and spewed it onto the land...All the gates in the Temple were replaced and became gold, except for the doors of the Gate of Nikanor [which remained bronze], because miracles had been performed on their behalf. Some say [they were left as bronze] because their bronze was brightly colored. Rabbi Eliezer ben Yaakov says: It was bronze made from refined copper, and it illuminated like gold.

(*Yoma* 38a)

📖 **Further reading:** For more on the Temple, see *A Concise Guide to Mahshava*, p. 160.

Herod's Temple

Many years after the construction of the Second Temple, it was completely renovated by Herod king of Judea. The Sages relate how Herod, an Edomite slave, came to power, and how he destroyed the Torah centers and killed the Sages of Israel, and that he sought to atone for his deeds by establishing a new, magnificent structure.

Herod, who was a slave in the house of the Hasmoneans, set his eyes upon a certain young Hasmonean girl. One day, that man, Herod, heard a divine voice saying: Any slave who rebels now will succeed. He rose and killed all his masters, but spared that girl. When that girl saw that he wanted to marry her, she went up to the roof and raised her voice; she said: Anyone who comes and says: I come from the house of the Hasmoneans, is actually a

slave, as only this girl [I] remained from them. That girl fell from the roof to the ground and died....

Herod said to himself: Who is it who expounds: "From among your brethren you shall place a king over you" (Deuteronomy 17:15)? It is the Sages. He rose and killed all the Sages. He spared Bava ben Buta in order to consult with him.

Herod placed a garland of porcupine quills on Bava ben Buta's head, which poked his eyes out, blinding him. One day Herod came and sat before Bava ben Buta without identifying himself, in order to test him. Herod said: See, Master, what this evil slave [i.e., Herod] is doing. Bava ben Buta said to him: What should I do to him? Herod said to him: The Master should curse him. Bava ben Buta said to him: It is written: "Even in your thought do not curse a king" (Ecclesiastes 10:20). Herod said to him: He is not a legitimate king. Bava ben Buta said to him: Even if he were merely wealthy, it is written: "And in your bedrooms do not curse the rich" (Ecclesiastes 10:20). Even if he were only a leader, it is written: "And a prince among your people you shall not curse" (Exodus 22:27).

Herod said to him: That applies only to one who performs the deeds of your people [acts in accordance with Torah law], and this one does not perform the deeds of your people. Bava ben Buta said to him: I fear him. Herod said to him: There is no one who will go and tell him, as it is only you and I who are sitting here. Bava ben Buta said to him: It is written: "As a bird of the heavens will carry the voice, and a winged creature will tell a matter" (Ecclesiastes 10:20). Herod said to him: I am he. Had I known that the Sages were so cautious, I would not have killed them. Now, what is that man's [my] remedy? [How can I atone for my sinful actions?]

Bava ben Buta said to him: He who extinguished the light of the world, as it is written: "For the commandment is a lamp, and the Torah is light" (Proverbs 6:23), should go and occupy himself with the light of the world, the Temple, as it is written: "And all nations will stream [venaharu][7] to it" (Isaiah 2:2). Some say that this is what Bava ben Buta said to him: One who blinded the eye of the world, as it is written: "It shall be, if from the eyes of the congregation" (Numbers 15:24),[8] should go and occupy himself with the eye of the world, the Temple, as it is written: "I am profaning My Sanctuary, the pride of your strength, the delight of your eyes" (Ezekiel 24:21).

---

7. *Venaharu* is an allusion to *nehora*, meaning light.
8. "The eyes of the congregation" is a reference to the Sages of Israel.

Herod said to him: I fear the Roman monarchy. Bava ben Buta said to him: Send a messenger and he will travel there one year, and remain there one year, and travel back one year. Meanwhile, you can demolish the existing Temple and rebuild a grander structure. He did so. Eventually, the Romans sent a message to Herod: If you have not demolished it, do not demolish it; and if you have demolished it, do not rebuild it; and if you have demolished it and rebuilt it, you are one of the wicked slaves who seek counsel after they have taken action. Even if you are armed and have an army at your command like a king, your book of genealogy is here. You are not a king and not the son of a king. You are Herod the slave who made himself a free man.

The Sages said: One who has not seen Herod's building has never seen a beautiful building in his life. With what did he build it? Rabba said: He built it with stones of white and green marble. Some say that it was with stones of blue, white, and green marble.

He extended the edge of one row and indented the edge of one row, so that they would receive and hold the plaster. He sought to plate it with gold, but the Sages said to him: Leave it, as it is more beautiful this way, because it looks like the waves of the sea.

(*Bava Batra* 3b–4a)

Kamtza and Bar Kamtza

The Sages assert that the First Temple was destroyed due to the grave transgressions of idolatry, bloodshed, and forbidden sexual relations. By contrast, the destruction of the Second Temple was due to a single sin: Gratuitous hatred.

Jerusalem was destroyed on account of Kamtza and bar Kamtza. As there was a certain man whose friend was Kamtza and whose enemy was bar Kamtza. That man made a feast and said to his servant: Go bring me Kamtza. He went and brought him bar Kamtza instead.

The host came and found bar Kamtza sitting at his feast. He said to bar Kamtza: This man [referring to himself] is the enemy of that man [you]. What do you seek here? Bar Kamtza said to him: Since I came, let me stay, and I will pay you for the cost of what I eat and drink.

The host said to him: No. Bar Kamtza said to him: I will give you half the cost of the feast. The host said to him: No. Bar Kamtza said to him: I will give you the cost of the entire feast. He said to him: No. The host seized bar Kamtza by the hand, stood him up, and took him outside.

Bar Kamtza said to himself: Since the Sages were sitting there and did not protest the host's actions, they apparently were comfortable with his

conduct. I will go and inform against them at the palace. Bar Kamtza went and said to the emperor: The Jews have rebelled against you. The emperor said to him: Who says so? Bar Kamtza said to him: Send them an offering to be brought on your behalf, and see whether they sacrifice it.

The emperor sent a choice calf with him. As bar Kamtza was en route to the Temple, he inflicted a blemish on the calf's upper lip. Some say it was on its eyelids, a place that for us is considered a blemish; but according to them it is not a blemish.[9]

The Sages thought to sacrifice the calf despite the blemish due to the obligation to maintain peaceful relations with the government. Rabbi Zekharya ben Avkolas said to them: People will say that blemished animals may be offered on the altar. The Sages thought to kill bar Kamtza so that he would not go and tell the authorities. Rabbi Zekharya said to them: People will say that one who inflicts a blemish on consecrated animals is liable to be executed.

Rabbi Yohanan said: The humility[10] of Rabbi Zekharya ben Avkolas destroyed our Temple, burned our Sanctuary, and exiled us from our land.

(*Gittin* 55b–56a)

Rabban Yohanan Ben Zakkai and the Emperor

When the Roman emperor decided to destroy the Temple, he sent his chief of staff to carry out the mission. The Sages reveal what happened in Jerusalem at that time, including the disputes between the various factions among the people, the attitude of the Sages, and Rabbi Yohanan ben Zakkai's attempt to abolish the evil decree.

The emperor sent Vespasian Caesar against the Jews. He came and laid siege to Jerusalem for three years. There were three wealthy men there: Nakdimon ben Guryon, ben Kalba Savua, and ben Tzitzit HaKasat....

One of them said to the other two: I will sustain the residents with wheat and barley; and one said to them: I will sustain them with wine, salt, and oil; and one said to them: I will sustain them with wood. They had enough to sustain the residents for twenty-one years.

There were zealots among the Jews in Jerusalem. The Sages said to them: Let us go out and make peace with the Romans. But the zealots did not allow them to do so. They said to the Sages: Let us go out and wage war

---

9. The *halakha* is that an animal with a blemish on its eyelid is disqualified for sacrifice as an offering. According to gentile practice, the animal is fit for sacrifice.
10. Here the term is used in the sense of fear of God that led to improper excessive righteousness.

against the Romans. The Sages said to them: The matter will not be successful. The zealots rose and burned those storehouses of wheat and barley, and there was a famine. …

Abba Sikara was the leader of the zealots of Jerusalem and the son of Rabban Yohanan ben Zakkai's sister. Rabban Yohanan ben Zakkai sent a message to him: Come to me in secret. He came, and Rabban Yohanan said to him: Until when will you act in this manner, and kill everyone through starvation? Abba Sikara said to him: What can I do? If I say something to the zealots they will kill me. Rabban Yohanan ben Zakkai said to him: See if you can find a way for me to leave the city, and perhaps there will be a small salvation for the people.

Abba Sikara said to him: Pretend to be sick, so that everyone will come and ask about you. Next, bring something putrid and place it near you, and people will say that you have died. Then, have your students come to take you to burial, and let no one else enter, so that the zealots will not notice that you are light, as they know that a living person is lighter than a dead person.

Rabban Yohanan ben Zakkai did so. Rabbi Eliezer came from one side and Rabbi Yehoshua from another side to take him out. When they arrived at the entrance of the city, the guards posted by the zealots wanted to stab Rabban Yohanan ben Zakkai to ensure that he was really dead. Abba Sikara said to them: The Romans will say that the Jews stabbed their teacher. The guards wanted to push Rabban Yohanan ben Zakkai to see if there would be any reaction. Abba Sikara said to them that the Romans will say that the Jews pushed their teacher. The guards opened the gate for him and he left the city.

When Rabban Yohanan ben Zakkai reached the Roman camp, he said: Greetings to you, king. Vespasian said to him: You are liable to be executed on two counts; one because I am not a king, yet you call me king. Furthermore, if I am king, why didn't you come to me until now? Rabban Yohanan ben Zakkai said to him: Concerning what you said: I am not a king, in fact, you are a king, as were you not a king, Jerusalem would not be given into your hand, as it is written: "And the Lebanon will fall by a mighty one" (Isaiah 10:34). "Mighty one" means nothing other than a king, and "Lebanon" means nothing other than the Temple. … Concerning what you said: If I am king, why didn't you come to me until now, the zealots among us did not allow me to do so.

Vespasian said to him: If there is a barrel of honey and a snake is wrapped around it, wouldn't people break the barrel to kill the snake?[11] Rabban Yohanan ben Zakkai remained silent. Rav Yosef read this verse in his regard, and some say it was Rabbi Akiva: "I am the Lord…. who turns around the wise and makes their knowledge foolishness" (Isaiah 44:24–25). Rabban Yohanan ben Zakkai should have said to him: We take tongs, remove the snake and kill it, and leave the barrel intact.

Meanwhile, a messenger arrived from Rome and said to Vespasian: Rise, as the emperor has died, and the noblemen of Rome want to install you as the leader. Vespasian was wearing one shoe then. He sought to put on the other one, it did not fit. He sought to remove the other shoe, but it would not come off. He said: What is this?

Rabban Yohanan ben Zakkai explained to him: Do not be troubled, as good tidings have reached you, as it is written: "Good news fortifies bones" (Proverbs 15:30). But what is its remedy? Have someone with whom you are displeased come and pass before you, as it is written: "A depressed spirit dries bones" (Proverbs 17:22). He did so, and his shoe went on his foot. Vespasian said to him: Since you are so wise, why did you not come to me until now? Rabban Yohanan ben Zakkai said to him: Didn't I tell you already? Vespasian said to him: I, too, told you my response.

Vespasian then said to him: I am going to Rome, and I will send another person to continue the siege. But request something of me that I will grant you. Rabban Yohanan ben Zakkai said to him: Give me [spare] Yavne and its Sages and the dynasty of Rabban Gamliel the *Nasi*, a descendant of King David; and provide doctors to heal Rabbi Tzadok.[12] Rav Yosef read this verse in Rabban Yohanan ben Zakkai's regard, and some say it was Rabbi Akiva: "Who turns around the wise and makes their knowledge foolishness" (Isaiah 44:25). Rabban Yohanan ben Zakkai should have said to him to leave the Jews alone this time. But Rabban Yohanan ben Zakkai maintained that Vespasian would not grant that request, and in that case there would not be even a small measure of salvation.

(*Gittin* 56a–b)

---

11. Similarly, the city should be destroyed in order to kill the zealots.
12. Rabbi Tzadok fasted for forty years in an attempt to prevent the destruction of the Temple, and as a result became gravely ill.

Titus

The general who was sent in Vespasian's place successfully completed his mission and destroyed the Temple and Jerusalem, but ultimately, he was punished for his actions.

Vespasian went to Rome and sent Titus in his place…Titus taunted and blasphemed God on High.

What did he do? He took a prostitute by the hand, and entered the Holy of Holies. He spread a Torah scroll underneath them and committed the sin of sexual intercourse upon it. He then took a sword and stabbed the curtain that partitions the Holy of Holies from the Sanctuary. A miracle occurred and blood spurted from it. He foolishly thought that he had killed God Himself. …

Abba Hanan says: "Who is mighty like You, Lord?" (Psalms 89:9). Who is mighty and resistant like You? As You hear the scorn and the blasphemy of that wicked man, yet remain silent. Similarly, the school of Rabbi Yishmael taught: The verse: "Who is like You among the powers [elim], Lord?" (Exodus 15:11), should be expounded as: Who is like You among the mute [ilemim], who remain silent in the face of blasphemy?

What did Titus do? He took the curtain and fashioned it into a large basket of sorts, and brought all of the sacred Temple vessels, placed them in it, and put them on a ship to be taken so he could be acclaimed in his city. … En route, a wave in the sea rose against him to drown him. Titus said: It seems to me that the might of their God is manifest only in water: Pharaoh came and He drowned him in water. Sisera came and He drowned him in water. He stands against me as well, to drown me in water. If He is mighty, let Him ascend to dry land and wage war against me there. A divine voice emerged and said to him: Wicked one, son of a wicked one, descendant of Esau the wicked, I have a lowly creature in My world and it is called a gnat… ascend to dry land and wage war with it. He ascended to dry land, and a gnat came, entered his nostril, and picked at his brain for seven years. One day he passed by the gate of a blacksmith's workshop. The gnat heard the sound of the blacksmith's hammer and was silenced. Titus said: There is a remedy for my pain. Each day they would bring a blacksmith and they would hammer before him. Titus would give four dinars to a gentile blacksmith, but to a Jew he would say to him: It is payment enough for you that you saw your enemy suffering. He did this for thirty days with similar results. From that point forward, once the gnat grew accustomed to the sound, it grew accustomed, and resumed picking at Titus's brain.

The Sages taught that Rabbi Pinhas ben Arova said: I was among the noblemen of Rome, and when Titus died they split open his head and found that the gnat had grown to the size of a sparrow weighing two *sela* coins. It was taught in a *baraita*: It was like a one-year-old pigeon weighing two *litra* [approximately 650 g].

Abaye said: We have a tradition that the gnat's mouth was copper and its claws were iron. When Titus was dying, he said to his attendants: Burn that man [me], and scatter his ashes across the seven seas, so that the God of the Jews will not find him and subject him to judgment.

(Gittin 56b)

For These I Weep

In the wake of the destruction of the Temple, the most exceptional children of Jerusalem were led into exile. The Sages relate the following tragic story of a brother and sister who were taken into captivity.

There was an incident involving the son and the daughter of Rabbi Yishmael ben Elisha the High Priest, who were taken captive and sold to two masters. After some time, the two masters met in a certain place. This one said: I have a male slave whose beauty is unmatched in the entire world, and that one said: I have a maidservant whose beauty is unmatched in the entire world.

They said to each other: Come, let us marry them to one another and divide their offspring between us. They secluded them in a room to engage in intercourse. This slave sat in this corner, and that maidservant sat in that corner. He said: I am a priest, a descendant of High Priests; shall I marry a maidservant? And she said: I am the daughter of a priest, a descendant of High Priests; shall I marry a slave? They wept all night.

At dawn they recognized each other. They fell on each other and burst into bitter tears until their souls departed. With regard to them, Jeremiah lamented: "For these I weep; my eye, my eye sheds water" (Lamentations 1:16).

(Gittin 57b)

Akiva, You Have Comforted Us

Despite the difficulties and suffering that were Israel's lot after the destruction of the Temple and the exile of the people, Rabbi Akiva was able to find a source of comfort and hope within the destruction itself.

Stories from the Sages

Rabban Gamliel, Rabbi Elazar ben Azarya, Rabbi Yehoshua, and Rabbi Akiva were walking along the road in the Roman Empire, and they heard the sound of the multitudes of the city of Rome from the main hill of the city at a distance of one hundred and twenty *mil* [about 120 km]. The other Sages began weeping, but Rabbi Akiva was laughing. They said to him: For what reason are you laughing? Rabbi Akiva said to them: And you, for what reason are you weeping? They said to him: These gentiles, who prostrate themselves to false gods and burn incense to idols, dwell securely and tranquilly, but for us, the House of the footstool of our God, the Temple, is burned in fire; shall we not weep? Rabbi Akiva said to them: That is why I am laughing: If for those who violate His will it is so, for those who perform His will [the Jewish people], all the more so will they be rewarded.

On another occasion, those Sages were ascending to Jerusalem. When they arrived at Mount Scopus, from where they could see the site of the destroyed Temple, they rent their garments in mourning. When they arrived at the Temple Mount, they saw a fox emerging from the site of the Holy of Holies. They began weeping, and Rabbi Akiva was laughing. They said to him: For what reason are you laughing? Rabbi Akiva said to them: For what reason are you weeping? They said to him: [This is] the place about which it is written: "And the stranger who approaches shall be put to death" (Numbers 1:51), and now "foxes walk on it" (Lamentations 5:18); shall we not weep?

Rabbi Akiva said to them: This is why I am laughing, as it is written: "I had trustworthy witnesses testify for me: Uriya the priest and Zecharyahu son of Yeverekhyahu" (Isaiah 8:2). Now what is the connection between Uriya and Zechariah? After all, Uriya prophesied during the First Temple period, and Zechariah prophesied during the Second Temple period. Rather, the verse established that the fulfillment of the prophecy of Zechariah is dependent on the fulfillment of the prophecy of Uriya. In the prophecy of Uriya it is written: "Therefore, due to you, Zion will be plowed as a field… and the Temple Mount into forested heights" (Micah 3:12), and in the prophecy of Zechariah it is written: "Old men and old women will again sit in the squares of Jerusalem" (Zechariah 8:4). Until the prophecy of Uriya was fulfilled, I feared that the prophecy of Zechariah would not be fulfilled. Now that the prophecy of Uriya has been fulfilled, it is evident that the prophecy of Zechariah will likewise be fulfilled. The Sages said to him in this formulation: Akiva, you have comforted us; Akiva, you have comforted us.

(*Makkot* 24a–b)

📖 **Further reading:** The belief in the ultimate redemption and the building of the Third Temple is one of the fundamental principles of Jewish faith; see *A Concise Guide to Mahshava*, p. 145; for more on the redemption, see p. 391.

The Lion and the Crane

A few decades after the destruction of the Temple, an opportunity arose to rebuild it once again, but it was missed due to a change in governmental policy. Rabbi Yehoshua ben Hananya somewhat eased the people's great disappointment using an apt parable.

In the days of Rabbi Yehoshua ben Hananya, the Roman Empire decreed that the Temple should be built. Papus and Lulyanus therefore arranged money-changing tables to be placed from Akko to Antioch to tend to the needs of the pilgrims who came from the exile.

The Samaritans went and said to the emperor: "Now let it be known to the king that if this city is built, and its walls finished, they will not pay property tax, poll tax, or toll" (Ezra 4:13).... The emperor said to them: What can we do; I have already decreed that they may rebuild the Temple. They said to him: Send a message and say to them: Either change the site of the Temple, or add five cubits to it, or remove five cubits from it; and they will change their minds on their own.[13] The Jewish communities were gathered in the valley of Beit Rimon. When the missives from the emperor arrived they began weeping and sought to rebel against the Roman Empire.

They said: Let a wise man enter and placate the public. They said: Let Rabbi Yehoshua ben Hananya enter, as he is exceedingly wise in the realm of Torah. Rabbi Yehoshua entered and preached: A lion ate its prey and a bone became stuck in its throat. It said: If someone comes and removes it, I will give him his reward. An Egyptian heron, whose beak is long, came and inserted its beak into the lion's throat and removed the bone. The heron said to the lion: Give me my reward. The lion said to it: Go, be satisfied with the fact that you can boast and say that you entered the lion's mouth and emerged in peace. Likewise, it is sufficient for us that we entered into dealings with this Roman nation in peace, and emerged in peace.

(Bereshit Rabba [Theodor-Albeck] 64)

📖 **Further reading:** We commemorate the destruction of the Temple even today on the days of mourning designated for that purpose; see *A Concise Guide to Halakha*, p. 359; pp. 35, 48, 65, 66, 499.

---

13. The Jewish people would not agree to any change, but would want the Temple only at its precise location and with its precise dimensions.

Hillel the Elder in the Snow

Hillel the Elder began his path in a state of extreme poverty, yet he refused to forsake daily Torah study. On one occasion, when he did not have money to pay the fee to the guard of the study hall, he climbed onto the roof, and from there he listened intently to the discourse inside the study hall.

The Sages said about Hillel the Elder that each and every day he would work and earn a *tarpe'ik* [a small coin], half of which he would give to the guard of the study hall and half of which went for his sustenance and the sustenance of the members of his household.

One time he did not find employment to earn a wage, and the guard of the study hall did not allow him to enter. He climbed onto the roof, suspended himself, and sat at the edge of the skylight so that he could hear the words of the Torah of the living God from the mouths of Shemaya and Avtalyon.[14]

They said: That day was Friday, and it was the season of Tevet, winter, and snow fell on him from the sky. After dawn on Shabbat morning, Shemaya said to Avtalyon: Avtalyon, my brother, every day at this hour the study hall is light, yet today it is dark; is it perhaps a cloudy day? They glanced upward and saw the form of a man in the skylight. They climbed up and found snow that was three cubits [approximately 1.5 m] high atop him. They extricated him, bathed him, smeared him with oil, and sat him opposite the fire.[15] They said: This man is worthy of us desecrating Shabbat on his behalf.

(*Yoma* 35b)

📖 **Further reading:** For more on Torah study that is acquired through toil and effort, see *A Concise Guide to Mahshava*, p. 277.

Rabbi Yohanan and Reish Lakish

Rabbi Yohanan persuaded Rabbi Shimon ben Lakish, also known as Reish Lakish, to study Torah. He taught him himself until Reish Lakish became a great scholar and a close friend. A halakhic dispute between them developed into an exchange of mutual insult and offense, and ultimately both of their lives ended in tragic circumstances.

One day Rabbi Yohanan was swimming in the Jordan River. Reish Lakish saw him and jumped after him into the Jordan. Rabbi Yohanan said to Reish Lakish: Your strength would be ideally used for Torah study. Reish Lakish

---

14. Shemaya and Avtalyon, who were the *Nasi* and the president of the *Sanhedrin* respectively, were the spiritual leaders of the generation.
15. They kindled the fire to warm him even though it was Shabbat.

said to him: Your beauty is fit for belonging to women. Rabbi Yohanan said to him: If you repent,[16] I will give you my sister, who is more beautiful than I am, as a wife. Reish Lakish committed himself to study Torah. Then, Reish Lakish wanted to return to dry land and retrieve his garments, but was unable to return.[17] Rabbi Yohanan taught Reish Lakish Bible and Mishna, and he rendered him a great man.

One day the Sages disagreed in the study hall: With regard to a sword, knife, dagger, spear, hand sickle, and a harvest sickle, from when are they susceptible to ritual impurity? From the time their manufacture is complete. When is their manufacture complete? Rabbi Yohanan said: From when one fires them in the furnace; Reish Lakish said: From when one scours them in cold water. Rabbi Yohanan said to Reish Lakish: A bandit knows his banditry.

Reish Lakish said to him: How have you benefited me by bringing me close to Torah? There, [when I was leader of the bandits], they called me master; here, too, they call me Master. Rabbi Yohanan said to him: I benefited you, as I brought you near, under the wings of the Divine Presence.

Rabbi Yohanan was offended. Reish Lakish fell ill [as a consequence of Rabbi Yohanan's taking offense]. Rabbi Yohanan's sister [who was married to Reish Lakish] came to Rabbi Yohanan and wept. She said to him: Act [pray for Reish Lakish] for the sake of my children, so they will not be orphaned. Rabbi Yohanan said to her: "Leave your orphans; I will sustain them" (Jeremiah 49:11). She said: Do so for the sake of my widowhood, so that I will not be widowed. He said to her: "And your widows should rely on Me" (Jeremiah 49:11). Rabbi Shimon ben Lakish passed away. Rabbi Yohanan was exceedingly upset over his passing.

The other Sages said: Who will go to settle Rabbi Yohanan's mind in the wake of his loss? They said: Let Rabbi Elazar ben Pedat go, as his statements are sharp. [He will be an appropriate replacement for Reish Lakish.]…Rabbi Elazar ben Pedat went and sat before Rabbi Yohanan. Every matter that Rabbi Yohanan would say, Rabbi Elazar ben Pedat would reply to him: It is taught in a baraita in support of your opinion. Rabbi Yohanan said: Are you like ben Lakish? With ben Lakish, when I would state a matter, he would challenge me with twenty-four difficulties, and I would respond to him with twenty-four responses; consequently, the halakha would become

---

16. Reish Lakish was then a gladiator and a highwayman.
17. Once he made the commitment to study Torah, he was weakened, as Torah weakens a person's strength.

clarified. But you say: It is taught in a *baraita* in support of your opinion; don't I know that what I said is correct?

Rabbi Yohanan would go and rend his garments, weeping and saying: Where are you, ben Lakish? Where are you, ben Lakish? He screamed until he lost his mind and became insane. The Sages prayed for mercy for him to put an end to his suffering, and he died.

(*Bava Metzia* 84a–b)

📖 **Further reading:** For a selection of the scholarly discussions between Reish Lakish and Rabbi Yohanan, see pp. 11, 118, 240, 441.

Rabbi Eliezer Ben Hyrcanus

Rabbi Eliezer ben Hyrcanus was from a wealthy family. He had never studied the Written or Oral Torah, and his father objected to his engaging in Torah study. Nevertheless, his yearning for the Torah was so great that he decided to dedicate his life to its study, until ultimately, his father was very proud of him.

There was an incident involving Rabbi Eliezer ben Hyrcanus, whose father had plowmen who would plow the arable land, while he would plow rocky ground. Rabbi Eliezer sat and wept. His father said to him: Why are you weeping? Perhaps you are distressed that you are plowing rocky ground. Now you will plow the arable land. Rabbi Eliezer sat on the arable land and wept. His father asked him: Why are you weeping? Perhaps you are distressed that you are plowing the arable land? Rabbi Eliezer said to him: No. His father asked: But why are you weeping? Rabbi Eliezer said to him: Because I wish to study Torah. His father said to him: You are twenty-eight years old, yet you wish to study Torah? Rather, take a wife and she will bear you sons and you can take them to school to learn Torah.

For two weeks, Eliezer did not taste anything, until Elijah, of blessed memory, appeared to him and said to him: Son of Hyrcanus, why are you weeping? Rabbi Eliezer said to him: Because I wish to study Torah. Elijah said to him: If you wish to study Torah, ascend to Jerusalem to study with Rabban Yohanan ben Zakkai.

Eliezer stood up and went to Rabban Yohanan ben Zakkai. He sat and was weeping. Rabban Yohanan said to him: Why are you weeping? Rabbi Eliezer said to him: Because I wish to study Torah. Rabban Yohanan said to him: Whose son are you? But he would not tell him. Rabban Yohanan said to him: Have you never learned to recite *Shema*, the *Amida* prayer, or Grace after Meals? Rabbi Eliezer said to him: No. Rabban Yohanan said to

him: Stand, and I will teach you the three of them. He sat and wept. Rabban Yohanan said to him: Why are you weeping? Rabbi Eliezer said to him: Because I wish to study Torah. Rabban Yohanan would tell him two *halakhot* each day of the week, and he would review them and absorb them. He went eight days and did not taste anything until the odor of his mouth reached before Rabban Yohanan ben Zakkai, who distanced him from his presence.

Rabbi Eliezer was sitting and weeping. Rabban Yohanan said to him: Why are you weeping? Rabbi Eliezer said to him: Because you distanced me from your presence, just as a man distances from before him one afflicted with boils [an infectious disease]. Rabban Yohanan said to him: My son, just as the odor of your mouth rose before me, so may the fragrance of the statutes of the Torah ascend from your mouth to Heaven. Rabban Yohanan said to him: My son, whose son are you? He replied: I am the son of Hyrcanus. Rabban Yohanan said to him: If so, then aren't you the son of one of the most prominent men of the world? And you would not tell me. Rabban Yohanan said to him: I take an oath by your life that you shall dine with me today. Rabbi Eliezer said to him: I have already dined with my host. Rabban Yohanan said to him: Who is your host? Rabbi Eliezer said to him: Rabbi Yehoshua ben Hananya and Rabbi Yosei the Priest. Rabban Yohanan sent and asked his hosts, and he said to them: Did Eliezer eat with you today? They said to him: No; in fact he has gone eight days without tasting anything…

The sons of Hyrcanus said to their father: Ascend to Jerusalem and disown your son Eliezer from your possessions because he disobeyed you and went to study Torah. He ascended to Jerusalem to disown him, and he found there a celebration in honor of Rabban Yohanan ben Zakkai, and all the nobles of the state were dining with him…The people said to Rabban Yohanan: Behold, the father of Rabbi Eliezer has arrived. Rabban Yohanan said to them: Set a place for him, and they set a place for him and seated him next to Rabban Yohanan. Rabban Yohanan fixed his gaze on Rabbi Eliezer, and said to him: Tell us a matter from the Torah. Rabbi Eliezer said to him: My Master, I will tell you a parable. To what is this matter comparable? It is comparable to that well that cannot yield more water than what it draws from the earth; likewise, I am unable to speak matters of Torah beyond what I received from you. Rabban Yohanan said to him: I will tell you a parable. To what is this matter comparable? It is comparable to a fountain that is flowing and yielding water, and it has the capability of yielding more water than it receives. Likewise, you are able to speak matters of Torah beyond

what Moses received at Sinai. Rabban Yoḥanan said to him: Are you shy to speak before me? I will stand and leave you.

Rabban Yoḥanan ben Zakkai stood up and went outside, and Rabbi Eliezer was sitting and lecturing. His face radiated like the light of the sun, and rays emitted from him like the rays of Moses [whose face radiated when he descended from Sinai], so that there was no person who knew whether it was day or night. Rabban Yoḥanan ben Zakkai came from behind Rabbi Eliezer and kissed him on his head. He said about him: Happy are you, Abraham, Isaac, and Jacob, that this one has emerged from your loins. Hyrcanus inquired: About whom did Rabban Yoḥanan say that? They said to him: About Eliezer your son. Hyrcanus said to him: Rabban Yoḥanan should not have said that; but rather, Happy am I, Hyrcanus, that this one has emerged from my loins.

While Rabbi Eliezer was sitting and lecturing, his father stood on his feet to show respect. When Rabbi Eliezer saw his father standing on his feet, he was alarmed and he said: Father, be seated, as I cannot speak matters of Torah while you are standing. Hyrcanus said to him: My son, it was not for this reason that I came, but rather to disown you from my possessions. Now that I have come to see you and I have witnessed all this praise; behold, your brothers are disowned from them, and all my possessions are given to you as a gift. Rabbi Eliezer said to him: I am not like any of them [in my aspirations]. Had I requested land from the Holy One, blessed be He, He could have given it to me, as it is stated: "The earth is the Lord's, and all that it holds, the world and all its inhabitants" (Psalms 24:1). Had I requested silver and gold from the Holy One, blessed be He, He could have given them to me, as it is stated: "Mine is the silver, and Mine the gold, the utterance of the Lord of hosts" (Haggai 2:8). But I requested only Torah from the Holy One, blessed be He.[18]

(*Pirkei DeRabbi Eliezer* 1–2)

📖 Further reading: For an additional dramatic event involving Rabbi Eliezer, later in his life, see p. 342. For more on the light that radiated from Moses' face, see *A Concise Guide to the Torah*, p. 225. For more on the hollowness of material possessions relative to Torah study, see p. 451.

---

18. Rabbi Eliezer told his father that he did not want possessions, so it would be preferable for his father to give them to his brothers.

Rabbi Akiva

For many years Rabbi Akiva did not engage in Torah study at all. Once he was drawn to Torah study, he studied with great diligence despite his extreme poverty, and eventually became one of the most prominent Sages of all time. None of this would have been possible without the support and dedication of his wife. This chapter recounts Rabbi Akiva's story as it appears in two rabbinic sources, which present the episode from different perspectives.

Rabbi Akiva was the shepherd of ben Kalba Savua [one of the wealthiest men in late first-century Jerusalem]. The daughter of ben Kalba Savua saw that he was humble and refined, and she said to him: If I agree to be betrothed to you, will you go study Torah in the study hall? He said to her: Yes. She was discreetly betrothed to him, and she sent him to study. Her father heard and expelled her from his house, and he vowed that deriving any benefit from his property would be forbidden to her forever.

Rabbi Akiva went and sat and studied for twelve years in the study hall. When he came home, twelve thousand students accompanied him. As Rabbi Akiva approached his house, he heard an elderly man saying to his [Rabbi Akiva's] wife: How long will you live like a widow [even though your husband is alive]? She said to him: If my husband listened to me, he would sit and study another twelve years. Rabbi Akiva said: I am studying away from home with permission. He went and sat for another twelve years in the study hall. When he returned, twenty-four thousand students accompanied him. His wife heard, and she went out to greet him. Her neighbors said to her: Borrow a fine garment and wear it. She said to them: "The righteous knows the nature of his animal" (Proverbs 12:10) [meaning: We are close, and he will identify me and will appreciate me as I am].

When she reached him she fell on her face and kissed his feet. His attendants [who did not know who she was] were pushing her away. He said to them: Let her be, as my Torah studies and yours are actually hers; they are thanks to her.

Her father heard that a great man had come to the town. He said to himself: I will go to him; perhaps he will nullify my vow [thus allowing me to support my daughter]. He approached Rabbi Akiva, who said to him [to help him find a justification for nullifying the vow]: Would you have vowed had you known that your daughter had married a great man? Ben Kalba Savua said to him: Had I known that he would know even one chapter of the Bible or even one *halakha* I would not have vowed. Rabbi Akiva said to him: I am he. Ben Kalba Savua fell on his face and kissed his feet and gave him half of his possessions.

What was Rabbi Akiva's beginning? The Sages said: He was forty years old and had not learned anything. Once he was standing at the mouth of a well, and he said: Who carved this stone [of the well]? They explained to him: It was the water that regularly falls on it each day. They said to him: Akiva, haven't you read: "Stones are worn away by water" (Job 14:19)?

Immediately Rabbi Akiva applied a logical *a fortiori* inference to himself: If a soft substance [water] carved the hard substance [a stone], then matters of Torah, which are as hard as iron, all the more so will they be etched onto my heart, which is [soft] flesh-and-blood. He immediately returned and began to study Torah.

He and his young son went and sat with a teacher of children. Rabbi Akiva said to him: Rabbi, teach me Torah. Rabbi Akiva held one end of the board and his son one end of the board, and the teacher wrote for him *alef bet*, and he learned it. He wrote *alef* through *tav* [the whole alphabet], and he learned it. He taught him the Book of Priests, Leviticus,[19] and he learned it. He continued studying in this manner until he had studied the entire Torah.

He went and sat before Rabbi Eliezer and Rabbi Yehoshua. He said to them: My rabbis, teach me how to learn Mishna. After they taught him one *halakha*, he went and sat by himself and said: Why was this *alef* written? Why was this *bet* written? Why was this matter stated? He returned to the Sages and asked them, and thereby caused them to clarify their statements....

At the age of forty Rabbi Akiva went to study Torah; thirteen years later he taught Torah in public. The Sages said: He did not pass from the world until he possessed tables of silver and gold, and until he climbed into his bed on golden ladders. His wife would go out wearing shoes and a beautiful golden ornament known as "city of gold." His students said to him: Rabbi, you have shamed us by what you have done for her [as we are unable to purchase such jewelry for our wives]. He said to them: She deserves it, as she underwent much suffering with me for the Torah.

(*Shir HaShirim Rabba* 1)

📖 **Further reading:** For more on Rabbi Akiva's extraordinary greatness, see p. 312. Read about his tragic death on p. 364.

_____

19. Traditionally, children began their studies with the book of Leviticus, as the maxim states: "Let the pure come and engage in the act of the pure" (p. 133).

The Couple from Tzaidan

Rabbi Shimon ben Yohai gave good advice to a couple that had not been blessed with children and wished to separate. This advice rekindled their love for each other, and ultimately they were also blessed with a child.

We learned: If a man married a woman and remained with her for ten years but she did not bear children, he is not permitted to remain idle [from the mitzva of procreation any longer. He must divorce his wife and marry another woman].

Rabbi Idi said: There was an incident involving a certain woman in Tzaidan who remained with her husband ten years but did not bear children. The couple came to Rabbi Shimon ben Yohai and said: We wish to leave each other. He said to them: I take an oath by your lives that just as you were joined to each other at your wedding feast with food and drink, so you will separate from each other only through food and drink.

They followed his advice and arranged a celebration for themselves, and prepared a great feast. The wife intoxicated her husband too much. When the husband came to his senses, he said to his wife: My daughter, [now that we are separating,] see any fine item that I have in the house; take it and go to your father's house. What did she do? After he was already sleeping, she signaled to her servants and maidservants and said to them: Carry him in the bed, and take him to my father's house.

In the middle of the night, he awakened. Since the effects of the wine had dissipated, he said to his wife: My daughter, where am I? She said to him: In my father's house. He said to her: What am I doing in your father's house? She explained: Didn't you say to me in the evening: Any fine item that I have in the house, take it and go to your father's house? There is no item in the world that is as good for me as you.

They went to Rabbi Shimon ben Yohai, and he stood and prayed for them; and they were remembered by God, and had a child. This is to teach you: Just as the Holy One, blessed be He, remembers barren women and blesses them with children, so too the righteous cause barren women to be remembered.

The matters can be inferred *a fortiori*: If a flesh-and-blood person, merely for saying to another flesh-and-blood person: There is no item in the world that is as good for me as you, was remembered by God, then Israel, which awaits the salvation of the Holy One, blessed be He, every day and says to Him: There is no item in the world that is as good for us as You, all the more so will God remember them and have compassion on them.

(*Shir HaShirim Rabba* 1)

337

Rabbi Shimon Ben Yohai and His Son in the Cave

When Rabbi Shimon ben Yohai and his son were pursued by the Roman government, they were forced to hide in a cave for twelve years. During this time they occupied themselves with Torah study. When they eventually emerged, they could not fathom how people could spend time engaged in temporal pursuits. Then, after another year in the cave, and upon seeing how much the Jews loved the mitzvot, they were placated.

Rabbi Yehuda, Rabbi Yosei, and Rabbi Shimon were sitting, and Yehuda the son of converts was sitting beside them. Rabbi Yehuda began, and said: How pleasant are the deeds of this Roman nation, as they established market-places, built bridges, and erected bathhouses. Rabbi Yosei remained silent. Rabbi Shimon ben Yohai responded and said: Everything that they established, they established only for their own purposes. They established marketplaces to place prostitutes there. They established bathhouses to pamper themselves. They built bridges to collect taxes from all who cross them. Yehuda the son of converts went and related their statements to others, and ultimately their statements were heard by the Roman authorities. They said: Yehuda, who elevated the Roman authorities, shall be elevated and appointed head of the Sages. Yosei, who remained silent, shall be exiled to Tzippori [a city in the Galilee]. Shimon, who condemned the Romans, shall be killed.

Rabbi Shimon ben Yohai and his son Rabbi Elazar went and hid in the study hall. Every day, Rabbi Shimon's wife would bring them bread and a jug of water, and they would eat. When the decree intensified, Rabbi Shimon said to his son: Women's minds are pliable. Perhaps the authorities will torture her and she will reveal our whereabouts to them. They went and hid in a cave. A miracle transpired, and a carob tree and a spring of water were created for them. They would remove their garments and sit covered in sand up to their necks, and they would study Torah all day. At the time for prayer they would dress, cover themselves, and pray, and would then remove their garments again so that they would not become tattered.

They remained in the cave for twelve years, until Elijah the prophet came and stood at the entrance to the cave and said: Who will inform ben Yohai that the emperor has died and his decree has been abrogated?

Rabbi Shimon and his son Rabbi Elazar came out and saw people plowing and sowing. They said: These people forsake eternal life [Torah study] and engage in temporal life [to make a living]. Every place that they directed their eyes was immediately burned. A divine voice emerged and said to them: Did you come out to destroy My world? Return to your cave.

They went and returned and remained there for the twelve months of the year…. A divine voice emerged and said: Leave your cave. They emerged. Every place that Rabbi Elazar would destroy, Rabbi Shimon would repair. Rabbi Shimon said to Rabbi Elazar: My son, you and I are sufficient for the entire world.[20]

As the sun was setting on Shabbat eve, they saw an elderly man holding two bundles of myrtle branches and running at twilight. They said to him: Why do you have these? He said to them: In honor of Shabbat. They said: But isn't one sufficient for you? He said: One corresponds to: "Remember the Sabbath day to keep it holy" (Exodus 20:8), and one corresponds to: "Observe the Sabbath day to keep it holy" (Deuteronomy 5:12). Rabbi Shimon said to his son: See how beloved the mitzvot are to Israel. They were placated.

Rabbi Pinhas ben Ya'ir, Rabbi Shimon's son-in-law, heard of his return and went out to greet him. He brought him into the bathhouse and was tending to his flesh [which was chafed after all the years in the cave]. He saw that he had cracks in his skin. He began crying, and the tears from his eyes fell, and the salty tears on his wounds caused Rabbi Shimon pain. Rabbi Pinhas said to his father-in-law: Woe is me, that I have seen you like this. Rabbi Shimon said to him: Happy are you that you have seen me like this, as had you not seen me like this, you would not have found me with this prominence in Torah. For initially, when Rabbi Shimon ben Yohai would raise a difficulty, Rabbi Pinhas ben Ya'ir would respond with twelve explanations. Ultimately, after he emerged from the cave, when Rabbi Pinhas ben Ya'ir would raise a difficulty, Rabbi Shimon ben Yohai would respond with twenty-four explanations.

(*Shabbat* 33b)

📖 **Further reading:** This approach of Rabbi Shimon that advocates dedicating oneself completely and exclusively to Torah study was manifest in several of his halakhic rulings; see p. 236.

Aher

Elisha ben Avuya, known as Aher, "the Other," had been one of the greatest Torah scholars of his generation, but he became a heretic and forsook the way of Torah and

---

20. It is sufficient for the world that we devote all our time to Torah. It is unrealistic to expect others to do the same.

mitzvot. Nevertheless, his loyal student Rabbi Meir continued to study Torah from him and attempted to persuade him to repent.

Aher, after he had gone astray, asked Rabbi Meir: What is the meaning of what is written: "It cannot be valued like gold and glass, or its exchange be vessels of fine gold" (Job 28:17)? He said to him: These are matters of Torah, which are as difficult to acquire as gold vessels and vessels of fine gold but are as easy to lose as glass vessels, which break easily. Aher said to him: Rabbi Akiva, your teacher, did not say so, but rather: Just as concerning golden vessels and glass vessels, even though they broke they can be restored; so too concerning a Torah scholar: Although he has strayed, he can be restored. Rabbi Meir said: Then you too, repent. Aher said to him: I have already heard from behind the heavenly curtain [which serves as a partition between God and the world]: "Return, deviant children" (Jeremiah 3:22) except for Aher.

The Sages taught: There was an incident involving Aher, who was riding a horse on Shabbat, and Rabbi Meir was walking behind him, to study Torah from him. Aher said to him: Meir, turn back, as I have already calculated, and according to the paces of my horse the Shabbat boundary ends here.[21] Rabbi Meir said to him: You, too, turn back. He responded: Haven't I already told you that I already heard behind the heavenly curtain: "Return, deviant children" except for Aher? Rabbi Meir grabbed Aher and took him into the study hall. Aher said to a child in an attempt to divine his fate: Recite your verse that you studied today to me. He said to him: "There is no peace, said the Lord, for the wicked" (Isaiah 48:22). He took him to another synagogue. Aher said to another child: Recite your verse to me. He said to him: "For if you launder with natron, and use much soap, your iniquity is stained before Me" (Jeremiah 2:22). He took him into another synagogue. Aher said to a child: Recite your verse to me. He said to him: "And you, plundered one, what will you do? If you don scarlet, if you ornament yourself with gold jewelry, if you enlarge your eyes with eye shadow, in vain you beautify yourself" (Jeremiah 4:30).

He took him into another synagogue, until he had taken him into thirteen synagogues, and all the children recited verses to him in a similar vein. In the last one, he said to a child: Recite your verse to me. He said to him: "But to the wicked one [velarasha] God says: What right have you to

---

21. It is permitted to go only two thousand cubits beyond the outskirts of the city, and therefore it was prohibited to proceed any farther.

speak of My statutes?" (Psalms 50:16). That particular child stuttered, and it sounded as though he said to him: And to Elisha [*vele'elisha*] God says. Some say that Aher had a knife, and he tore the child open and sent pieces of his body to all thirteen synagogues. Others say that Aher said: If I had a knife, I would tear him open.

When Aher passed away, the members of the heavenly court said: They will not condemn him [as would appear warranted by his actions], but he will not come into the World to Come. He will not be condemned, because he engaged in Torah study; but he will not enter the World to Come, because he sinned. Rabbi Meir said: It is preferable that they condemn him, as then he will receive his punishment and eventually come into the World to Come. When will I die so I can cause smoke to rise from his grave?[22] Indeed, when Rabbi Meir passed away, smoke rose from the grave of Aher.

Rabbi Yohanan said: Is it heroic for Rabbi Meir to burn his teacher? There was one Sage among us who strayed, and yet we are incapable of saving him? If we take him by the hand, who will remove him from our protection; who? Rabbi Yohanan said: When will I die so I can extinguish the smoke from his grave? Indeed, when Rabbi Yohanan passed away, the smoke ceased from the grave of Aher. A certain eulogizer began his eulogy of Rabbi Yohanan: Even the guard at the entrance of Gehenna could not stand before you, our rabbi, [as you succeeded in extricating Aher from Gehenna.]

Aher's daughter came before Rabbi Yehuda HaNasi and said to him: Rabbi, sustain me. He said to her: Whose daughter are you? She replied: I am the daughter of Aher. He retorted: Are there still descendants of his in the world? Isn't it written: "He will have neither son nor grandson among his people, and there will be no remnant in his dwellings" (Job 18:19)? She responded: Remember his Torah study, and do not remember his deeds. Immediately, fire descended and licked the bench on which Rabbi Yehuda HaNasi was sitting. Rabbi Yehuda HaNasi wept and said: If God protects the honor of those who treat the Torah with contempt this way, all the more so will He protect the honor of those who treat it with honor.

(Ḥagiga 15a–b)

📖 Further reading: For a factor that led to Aher's forsaking a life of Torah, see p. 251. For more on punishment in Gehenna and its objective, see *A Concise Guide to Mahshava*, p. 167.

---

22. Rabbi Meir said that when he would die, he would request that the heavenly court condemn him. The smoke rising from his grave would serve as an indication that he was being tried in the heavenly court.

Curses That Were Actually Blessings

Two Torah scholars blessed the son of Rabbi Shimon ben Yohai, but their blessings sounded like harsh curses. Rabbi Shimon explained how these were actually blessings.

Rabbi Shimon ben Yohai said to his son: These people, Rabbi Yonatan ben Asmai and Rabbi Yehuda son of converts, are men of noble form [wise and learned individuals]; go to them so that they will bless you. Those Sages said to him: What do you want here? Rabbi Shimon's son said to them: Father told me: Go to them so that they bless you. They said to him: May it be God's will that you should sow and not reap, you should bring in and not take out, you should take out and not bring in, your house should be destroyed and your lodging place should be inhabited, your table should become confused, and you should not see a new year.

When he came to his father, he said to him: Not only did they not bless me, but they even caused me pain. His father said to him: What did they say to you? He said: They said to me such and such. Rabbi Shimon ben Yohai said to him: These are all blessings: You should sow and not reap means that you should bear children and they should not die. You should bring in and not take out means that you should bring in brides for your sons and your sons should not die, which would cause their wives to leave [and return to their parents' home]. You should take out and not bring in means that you should have daughters and their husbands should not die, causing your daughters to return home to you.

Your house should be destroyed and your lodging place should be inhabited means: This world is your lodging place, and the World to Come is your house. [May you live a long life].... Your table should become confused means that you should be blessed with so many sons and daughters [that there will be much noise and confusion at your table]. You should not see a new year means that your wife should not die and you should not marry another woman.[23]

(*Moed Katan* 9a–b)

It Is Not in the Heavens

An impassioned dispute between Rabbi Eliezer ben Hyrcanus and the other Sages regarding the ritual purity of a specific type of oven led to a profound disagreement

---

23. This is based on the verse: "When a man takes a new wife ... he shall be free for his house one year" (Deuteronomy 24:5). The blessing was that he should never be obligated to be "free for his house one year."

over the manner of halakhic decision-making and the significant role of the Sages in this process.

The Sages taught: On that day of their dispute, Rabbi Eliezer provided all the proofs in the world to support his opinion, but the Sages did not accept it from him.

Rabbi Eliezer said to them: If the *halakha* is in accordance with my opinion, this carob tree will prove it. The carob tree was uprooted one hundred cubits [about 50 m] from its place, and some say four hundred cubits. The Sages said to him: One may not cite halakhic proof from a carob tree. Rabbi Eliezer said to them: If the *halakha* is in accordance with my opinion, the canal will prove it. The water in the canal turned and flowed backward. They said to him: One may not cite halakhic proof from a canal.

Rabbi Eliezer again said to them: If the *halakha* is in accordance with my opinion, the walls of the study hall will prove it. The walls of the study hall leaned inward and began to fall. Rabbi Yehoshua scolded the walls, saying to them: If Torah scholars are contending with each other in matters of *halakha*, what is the nature of your involvement in this dispute? The walls did not fall, out of deference to Rabbi Yehoshua, and they did not become upright, out of deference to Rabbi Eliezer; and they still remain inclined.

Rabbi Eliezer again said to them: If the *halakha* is in accordance with my opinion, the heavens will prove it. A divine voice emerged from the heavens and said: What do you have against Rabbi Eliezer? As, the *halakha* is ruled in accordance with his opinion in every situation.

Rabbi Yehoshua stood on his feet and said: "It is not in the heavens" (Deuteronomy 30:12). What is the meaning of "it is not in the heavens"? Rabbi Yirmeya says: Since the Torah was already given at Mount Sinai, we do not take a divine voice into consideration, as You already wrote at Mount Sinai in the Torah: "Incline after the majority" (Exodus 23:2).[24]

Rabbi Natan encountered Elijah the prophet and said to him: What did the Holy One, blessed be He, do at that time when Rabbi Yehoshua said that? Elijah said to him: He smiled and said: My children have triumphed over Me; My children have triumphed over Me....

The Sages voted regarding Rabbi Eliezer and ostracized him [for not accepting the majority opinion]. They said: Who will go and inform him of this decision? Rabbi Akiva said to them: I will go, lest an unseemly person go and inform him, and he would thereby destroy the entire world.[25]

---

24. The halakhic ruling is determined by the majority of the Sages on the deliberating body.
25. If Rabbi Eliezer is informed callously, his distress might endanger the entire world.

What did Rabbi Akiva do? He wore black and wrapped himself in black, and sat before Rabbi Eliezer at a distance of four cubits.[26] Rabbi Eliezer said to him: Akiva, what is different about today from other days, [that you are conducting yourself in an unusual manner]? Rabbi Akiva said to him: My rabbi, it appears to me that our colleagues are distancing themselves from you. Rabbi Eliezer likewise rent his garments and removed his shoes, and he got off his seat and sat on the ground.

Rabbi Eliezer's eyes shed tears; consequently, throughout the world, one-third of its olives, and one-third of its wheat, and one-third of its barley were afflicted. Some say that even dough being kneaded in a woman's hands spoiled. The Sages taught: There was great anger on that day, as any place where Rabbi Eliezer fixed his gaze was burned.

Even Rabban Gamliel[27] was affected, as he was coming on a boat, and a large wave swelled over him threatening to drown him. Rabban Gamliel said to himself: It seems to me that this is only for the sake of Rabbi Eliezer ben Hyrcanus. Rabban Gamliel stood on his feet and said: Master of the Universe, it is revealed and known before You that neither did I act for my honor, nor did I act for the honor of the house of my father; rather, it was for Your honor, so that disputes will not proliferate in Israel. The sea calmed from its rage.

Imma Shalom, wife of Rabbi Eliezer, was the sister of Rabban Gamliel. From that incident forward, she would not allow Rabbi Eliezer to lower his head in [supplicatory] prayer.[28] A certain day was *Rosh Hodesh*,[29] and she confused a full, thirty-day month for a deficient, twenty-nine-day month [thereby thinking that she need not prevent Rabbi Eliezer from lowering his head]. Some say that a pauper came and stood at the door, and she took bread out to him.

When she returned, she found her husband and saw that he had lowered his head in prayer. She said to him: Rise, as you have killed my brother. Meanwhile, the sound of a shofar emerged from the house of Rabban Gam-

---

26. One is required to maintain a distance of four cubits from one who is ostracized.
27. Rabban Gamliel was the *Nasi* of the Sanhedrin and the leader of the Sages who opposed Rabbi Eliezer.
28. Special supplications are recited with one's head lowered. Imma Shalom feared that were Rabbi Eliezer to plead and cry in such a way, Rabban Gamliel would be punished.
29. *Rosh Hodesh* is the first day of the Hebrew month. When a month has thirty days rather than twenty-nine, then *Rosh Hodesh* is celebrated on the thirtieth day of the preceding month and the first day of the new month. On *Rosh Hodesh* one does not say the supplications recited when lowering the head.

liel, proclaiming that the *Nasi* had died. Rabbi Eliezer asked her: From where did you know that he would die? She said to him: This is the tradition that I received from the house of my father's father: All the gates of Heaven can be locked in the face of prayers, except for the gates of verbal mistreatment.[30]

(*Bava Metzia* 59a)

📖 **Further reading:** For more on *Rosh Hodesh*, the way its date is established, and its special prayers, see *A Concise Guide to Halakha*, p. 237.

It Is All for the Best

It is related about two Sages that no matter what happened, good or bad, they would invariably declare that it too was for the best. Even when they encountered unfortunate situations they did not lose their faith, and merited divine salvation.

Why did they call him Nahum man of Gam Zu? Because any matter that would happen to him, he would say: This too is for the best [*gam zu letova*].

Once, the Jews wished to send a gift to the house of the emperor. They asked: Who should go to deliver this gift? Let Nahum man of Gam Zu go, as he is experienced with miracles.

They sent with him a chest full of precious stones and pearls, and he went and spent the night in a certain inn. During the night, some people staying at the inn arose and took all the contents of the chest, and filled it with earth. The next day, when he saw what had happened, Nahum man of Gam Zu said: This too is for the best. When he reached the palace, they opened the chest and saw that it was filled with earth. The king sought to execute all the members of the Jewish delegation; the king said: The Jews are mocking me. Nahum man of Gam Zu said: This too is for the best.

Elijah the prophet came and appeared to them as one of the Roman officials. He said to the emperor: Perhaps this earth is from the earth of their forefather Abraham, as when he would throw earth, it became swords, and when he threw stubble, it became arrows… There was a certain province that the Romans had been unable to conquer. They tested the earth, and it turned into swords, and they conquered that province. They entered the treasury and filled the chest that had been filled with earth with precious jewels and pearls and sent Nahum man of Gam Zu off with great honor.

When the delegation came to spend the night at that inn, those staying there said to him: What did you bring with you to the emperor that

---

30. The prayers of victims of verbal mistreatment are always accepted.

he bestowed upon you such great honor? Nahum man of Gam Zu said to them: What I took from here, I brought there. They tore down their inn and brought the soil underneath to the emperor's palace, and said to him: That earth that was brought here earlier was from our property. The emperor tested the earth in battle, and did not find it to have miraculous powers, and they executed those people.

A person should always be accustomed to saying: Everything that the Merciful One does, He does for the best.

Like this incident involving Rabbi Akiva, who was walking along the way and reached a certain city. He sought lodging but they did not give him any. He said: Everything that the Merciful One does, He does for the best. He went and spent the night in a field, and he had with him a rooster, a donkey, and a candle. A gust of wind came and extinguished the candle; a cat came and ate the rooster; a lion came and ate the donkey. He said: Everything that the Merciful One does, He does for the best. That night, an army came and captured the city. He said to his students: Didn't I tell you? Everything that the Merciful One does, He does for the best.[31]

(Ta'anit 21a; Berakhot 60b)

Rav Nahman Bar Yitzhak and His Mother

By his nature, Rav Nahman bar Yitzhak had a strong tendency toward theft, but with the help of good education and prayer he did not stray from the upright path. Indeed, when the effects of these positive influences eased slightly it became clear how strongly he could be pulled in the direction of sin.

Chaldean astrologers informed Rav Nahman bar Yitzhak's mother: Your son will be a thief. From that day on, she did not allow him to uncover his head. She said to him: Cover your head so that the fear of Heaven will be upon you, and we will also pray for divine mercy [that you will not become a thief]. He did not know why she said this to him.

One day he was sitting and studying beneath a palm tree that belonged to others and the covering fell off his head. He lifted his eyes and saw the palm tree. He was then overcome by his evil inclination and he climbed the tree and detached a cluster of dates with his teeth.[32]

(Shabbat 156b)

---

31. Had the candle not been extinguished and the animals not been killed, the light of the candle and the noise made by the animals would have revealed Rabbi Akiva's presence to the invading army.

32. His compulsion was so powerful that it caused him to endanger and exert himself in order to steal.

📖 **Further reading:** For more on the influence of education from a very tender age, see *A Concise Guide to Mahshava*, p. 5.

Rabbi Zeira

When the Babylonian *amora* Rabbi Zeira came to Israel, he made an extraordinary effort to accustom himself to the method of Torah study characteristic of the Land of Israel.

When Rabbi Zeira ascended from Babylonia to Eretz Yisrael, he fasted one hundred fasts so that he would forget the Babylonian method of studying the Talmud, so that it would not hinder him [from learning the style of study of the Land of Israel]. He fasted an additional one hundred fasts so that Rabbi Elazar ben Rabbi Shimon would not die during his lifetime, as then the burden of communal matters would fall upon him.[33] Rabbi Zeira fasted yet another one hundred fasts so that the fire of Gehenna would not affect him.

Every thirty days, he would test himself: He would ignite an oven, climb in, and sit inside it, and the fire would not affect him. One day, the Sages gave him the evil eye [because they were jealous], and his legs were singed by the fire. From then on they called him: The short one with singed thighs.

(Bava Metzia 85a)

Rabbi Pinhas Ben Ya'ir

The extraordinary righteousness of Rabbi Pinhas ben Ya'ir, which led him, among other things, to refuse to dine in the house of another, left its mark even on his animal, which refused to eat food from which tithes had not been taken. Moreover, when Rabbi Pinhas set out to fulfill the will of the Creator, the world subjugated itself before him.

Rabbi Pinhas ben Ya'ir was going to fulfill the mitzva of the redemption of captives. He encountered the Ginai River.

He said to the river: Ginai, part your water for me and I will pass through you. The river said to him: You are going to perform the will of your Maker and I am going to perform the will of my Maker [to flow in my course, as I was created to do]. Concerning you, it is uncertain whether you will succeed in performing His will or whether you will not succeed in performing His will. I will certainly succeed in performing His will. Rabbi Pinhas ben Ya'ir

---

33. As long as Rabbi Elazar remained at the head of the academy, Rabbi Zeira was free to study Torah in peace.

Stories from the Sages

responded to the river: If you do not part, I will decree upon you that water will never flow through you. The river parted for him.

There was a certain man who was carrying wheat for the preparation of matza for the festival of Passover. Rabbi Pinhas ben Ya'ir said to the river: Part for this man too, as he is engaged in a mitzva. The river parted for him. There was an Arab who was accompanying them. Rabbi Pinhas ben Ya'ir said to the river: Part for that man too, so that he will not say: Is that any way to treat one who is accompanying him? The river parted for him too.

Rav Yosef said: How much greater is this man, Rabbi Pinhas ben Ya'ir, than Moses and the six hundred thousand Israelites who left Egypt. As there [at the Red Sea], the waters parted once, yet here the waters parted three times. The Talmud challenges: But perhaps here too, the waters parted only once [and all three of them passed through the parted river before it began to flow again]. Rather, he was the equivalent of Moses and the six hundred thousand [but not greater].

Rabbi Pinhas ben Ya'ir happened by a certain inn. His hosts cast barley before his donkey but it did not eat. They sifted the barley, but it did not eat. They separated the chaff from the grain, but it did not eat. Rabbi Pinhas ben Ya'ir said to them: Perhaps the barley is not tithed [and that is why the donkey refuses to eat the barley]. They tithed it, and the donkey ate it. Rabbi Pinhas ben Ya'ir said: This wretched beast is going to perform the will of its Maker, and you are feeding it untithed produce?

(Ḥullin 7a–b)

📖 Further reading: For more on an animal that observed the mitzvot of the Torah, see p. 280.

Rabbi Hanina Ben Dosa

Rabbi Hanina ben Dosa was an extraordinary figure. Although he lived in poverty and great deprivation, miraculous acts routinely accompanied him.

Rabbi Hanina ben Dosa was traveling along a road when it began to rain. He said before God: Master of the Universe, the entire world is comfortable due to the needed rainfall, but Hanina is getting wet and suffering. The rain ceased. When he reached his home, he said before God: Master of the Universe, the entire world is suffering due to the lack of the rain, and

Hanina is comfortable. The rains came. Rav Yosef said: What effect does the prayer of the High Priest have vis-à-vis Rabbi Hanina ben Dosa?...[34]

Rav Yehuda said that Rav said: Each and every day a divine voice emerges and says: The entire world is sustained in the merit of My son Hanina ben Dosa, yet for Hanina My son a *kav* of carobs [a small volume of low-quality food] is enough for him from Shabbat eve to Shabbat eve.

Rabbi Hanina ben Dosa's wife would heat the oven every week before Shabbat and generate smoke, due to her shame.[35] She had a certain evil neighbor who said to herself: I know that they have nothing. What is all this smoke? She went and knocked on the door to investigate. Rabbi Hanina's wife was embarrassed, and entered an inner room. A miracle was performed for her, as her neighbor saw the oven filled with bread and the kneading bowl filled with dough. She said to Rabbi Hanina's wife, calling her: So-and-so, So-and-so, bring a peel,[36] as your bread is burning. Rabbi Hanina's wife said to her: I too went inside for that purpose. The Sages taught: She had indeed entered the inner room to bring a peel, because she was accustomed to miracles [and anticipated that one would be performed to spare her shame].

Rabbi Hanina's wife said to him: Until when will we continue to suffer so much from poverty? He said to her: What can we do? She said to him: Pray for mercy that they will give you something from Heaven. He prayed for mercy and a form like the palm of a hand emerged from the heavens and gave him one leg of a golden table. That night, his wife saw in a dream that the righteous are destined to eat in the World to Come at a golden table that has three legs, but she will be eating at a two-legged table.[37]

She told her husband her dream, and he said to her: Are you content that everyone will eat at a complete table and we will eat at a deficient table? She said to him: But what can we do? Pray for mercy, that they take the leg of the golden table from you. He prayed for mercy, and they took it. The Sages taught: The latter miracle was greater than the former, as we learned that the heavens give but do not retract.[38]

One twilight just before Shabbat, Rabbi Hanina ben Dosa saw that his daughter was sad. He asked her: My daughter, why are you sad? She ex-

---

34. The High Priest would pray that God would ignore the prayers of travelers who pray that rain would not fall.
35. She was ashamed that she had no bread in her house and sought to create the impression that she was baking bread.
36. This is a shovel-like utensil used to take baked items out of an oven.
37. The reward in this world is at the expense of the reward in the World to Come.
38. What Heaven has provided miraculously, it does not retract.

plained to him: I confused a vessel of vinegar for a vessel of oil and I kindled the Shabbat lamp with the vinegar. He said to her: My daughter, what is your concern? He who said to the oil that it should burn, He will say to the vinegar that it should burn. The Sages taught: That lamp burned continuously the entire day, until they brought from it light for *Havdala*.

Rabbi Hanina ben Dosa had goats. His neighbors said to him: Your goats are causing damage by eating in our fields. He said to them: If they are causing damage, let the bears eat them. But if not, let each of them, this evening, bring a bear impaled on its horns. That evening, each and every one of them brought a bear impaled on its horns.

Rabbi Hanina ben Dosa had a certain neighbor who was building a house, but the ceiling beams were too short and did not reach from one wall to the other. She came before Rabbi Hanina ben Dosa and said to him: I built my house, but my beams do not reach from one wall to the other. He said to her: What is your name? She said to him: Aykhu. He declared: If so [*Aykhu*], may your beams reach your walls. The Sages taught: The beams not only reached the walls, but they continued until they protruded one cubit from this side and one cubit from that side. Some say that the beams extended by segments. It is taught that the Sage Peleimo says: I saw that house, and its beams protruded one cubit on this side and one cubit on that side. They said to me: This is the house that Rabbi Hanina ben Dosa roofed with his prayer.

From where did Rabbi Hanina ben Dosa have goats? Wasn't he poor? Moreover, the Sages said: One may not raise small domesticated animals in the Land of Israel [because they damage surrounding fields and the property of others]. Rav Pinhas said: There was an incident involving a certain man who passed near the entrance of Rabbi Hanina's house and left chickens there. Rabbi Hanina's wife found them and tended to them. Rabbi Hanina said to her: Do not eat from their eggs, because they do not belong to us. But they laid many eggs, and chickens hatched. The sheer number of chickens was disturbing them; they sold them and bought goats with their proceeds. Once, the man who had lost the chickens passed and said to his companion: Here is where I left my chickens. Rabbi Hanina heard and said to him: Do you have an identifying sign on them? He said to him: Yes. He gave him the sign and took the goats. Those are the goats that brought the bears impaled on their horns.

📖 **Further reading:** For more on the mitzva of returning lost property, see *A Concise Guide to the Torah*, p. 483; *A Concise Guide to Halakha*, p. 604.

The Sages taught: There was an incident in a certain place where there was an *arod* [a dangerous reptile] that was harming the people. They came and informed Rabbi Hanina ben Dosa. He said to them: Show me its hole. They showed him its hole. He placed his heel over the mouth of the hole and that *arod* came out and bit Rabbi Hanina and it died.

Rabbi Hanina ben Dosa then took the carcass of the *arod* on his shoulder and brought it to the study hall. He said to those assembled there: See, my sons, it is not the *arod* that kills, but rather it is transgression that kills.

At that moment the Sages said: Woe to a person who was met by an *arod*, and woe to the *arod* that was met by Rabbi Hanina ben Dosa.

(*Ta'anit* 24b–25a; *Berakhot* 33a)

Further reading: For more on miracles and their significance, see *A Concise Guide to Mahshava*, p. 213.

Account of the Divine Chariot

Certain Sages were privileged to learn the deepest secrets of the Torah, which deal with God's providence over the upper and lower worlds, the secrets of how God conducts the world, and the appearance of the Divine Presence. This mystical topic is known as the account of the Divine Chariot. When those Sages expounded upon these matters, the entire creation would participate.

There was an incident involving Rabban Yohanan ben Zakkai, who was riding on a donkey and traveling along the way, while his student Rabbi Elazar ben Arakh was leading a donkey behind him. Rabbi Elazar said to him: My teacher, teach me one chapter in the account of the Divine Chariot. Rabban Yohanan ben Zakkai said to him: Haven't I taught you: One may not teach the account of the Divine Chariot to an individual [and all the more so in public], unless he is a Sage who understands on his own?

Rabbi Elazar said to him: My teacher, allow me to say before you one matter that you taught me.[39] Rabban Yohanan said to him: Speak. Immediately, Rabban Yohanan ben Zakkai dismounted from the donkey, and wrapped his cloak on his head in a display of reverence, and sat on a stone beneath an olive tree. Rabbi Elazar said to him: My teacher, for what reason did you dismount from the donkey? He said: Is it possible that while you are expounding on the account of the Divine Chariot, and the Divine Presence is with us, and the ministering angels are accompanying us, that I should ride on a donkey?

_____

39. Rabbi Elazar sought to humbly indicate to his teacher that he understood these matters.

Stories from the Sages

Immediately, Rabbi Elazar ben Arakh began to discuss the account of the Divine Chariot and expounded, and fire descended from heaven and encircled all the trees in the field, which began reciting song. What song did they recite? "Praise the Lord from the earth, sea creatures and all depths…. fruit trees and all the cedars…. Halleluya" (Psalms 148:7, 9, 14). An angel responded from the fire, saying: What you expounded is the essence of the account of the Divine Chariot.

Rabban Yohanan ben Zakkai stood and kissed Rabbi Elazar ben Arakh on his head, and said: Blessed is God, Lord of Israel, who gave our father Abraham a son like you, who knows how to understand, analyze, and expound on the account of the Divine Chariot. There are some who expound on the Torah well but do not fulfill it well, and others who fulfill it well but do not expound on it well, but you expound on it well and fulfill it well. Happy are you, our forefather Abraham, that Elazar ben Arakh emerged from your loins.

And when these matters were recounted before Rabbi Yehoshua, he and Rabbi Yosei the priest were walking along the way. They said: Let us too, expound on the account of the Divine Chariot. Rabbi Yehoshua began expounding. That day was the cloudless day of the summer solstice, yet the heavens became filled with clouds, and a rainbow of sorts appeared in a cloud. The ministering angels assembled and came to listen, like people gathering and coming to see the rejoicing of a groom and bride.

Rabbi Yosei the priest went and related this matter before Rabban Yohanan ben Zakkai, who said to him: Happy are you, and happy are those who gave birth to you; happy are my eyes that saw students like these. In my dream, I saw you and me, seated at Mount Sinai, and a divine voice came to us from heaven: Ascend to here, ascend to here, large halls and fine bedding are arranged for you. You, your students, and the students of your students are invited to the third group of those privileged to receive the Divine Presence.

(Ḥagiga 14b)

Request for Rain: Honi HaMe'agel

Honi HaMe'agel, literally, the circle maker, was a unique individual. Not only did he stand up and pray for rain on behalf of the people of Israel during a drought, but he even began negotiating with God, demanding from Him the precise fulfillment of his request.

Once, most of the month of Adar had passed [the rainy season was almost over], and rain had not fallen. They sent a message to Honi HaMe'agel: Pray, so that rain will fall. He prayed, but rain did not fall. He etched a circle in the dust and stood inside it … and said before God: Master of the Universe, Your children have turned to me to pray for them, as I am like a member of Your household. I take an oath by Your great name that I am not moving from here until you have compassion upon Your children. Rain began to trickle down. Honi HaMe'agel's students said to him: Rabbi, we have seen you as one capable of great wonders, but [this meager rain is not enough to ensure that] we will not die. It seems to us that this rain is falling only to annul your oath.[40]

Honi said to God: I did not ask for this, but for rain to fill our cisterns, ditches, and caves. Rain began to fall torrentially, until each and every drop was as large as the mouth of a barrel, and the Sages estimated that no drop was less than a *log* [approximately 350 cc]. His students said to him: Rabbi, we have seen you call upon God and He performs miracles and we will not die, but it seems to us that rain is falling only to destroy the world.

Honi again said before God: I did not ask for this destructive rain either, but rather for rain of benevolence, blessing, and generosity. The rain fell conventionally, until all the people ascended to the Temple Mount due to the rain.[41]

The people said to him: Rabbi, just as you prayed for the rain to fall, so too, pray that it should stop. He said to them: This is the tradition that I received: One does not pray due to an excess of good. Nevertheless, bring me a bull for a thanks offering. They brought him a bull for a thanks offering. He placed his two hands on its head and said before God: Master of the Universe, Your people Israel, whom You took out of Egypt, is unable to withstand either an excess of good or an excess of troubles. You were angry with them and withheld rain, and they were unable to withstand it. You bestowed upon them good, and they are unable to bear it. May it be Your will that the rain stop and there will be relief for the world.

Immediately, the wind blew, the clouds dispersed, the sun shone, and everyone went out to the fields and gathered for themselves truffles and mushrooms that had sprouted in the rain.

---

40. The meaning of the students' words is that the rain was sufficient for their rabbi to be able to leave the circle, but not to satisfy their needs.
41. The conventional rain accumulated, so all the people sought the highest ground available, the Temple Mount.

Shimon ben Shatah sent a message to Honi HaMe'agel: Were you not Honi, I would have decreed ostracism upon you, as had these years been like the years of Elijah, when the keys of rain were in Elijah's hands [and he took an oath that it would not rain], wouldn't the name of Heaven have been desecrated by your oath not to leave the circle until it rained?[42] But what can I do to you, as you indulge yourself before God and He does your bidding, like a son who indulges himself before his father and he does his bidding. The son says to his father: Father, take me to bathe me in hot water; rinse me with cold water; give me nuts, almonds, peaches, and pomegranates, and he gives them to him. Regarding you, the verse states: "Your father and your mother will rejoice, and she who bore you will be happy" (Proverbs 23:25)....

Rabbi Yohanan said: All the days of that righteous man, Honi, he was distressed over his inability to grasp the meaning of this verse: "A song of ascents. When the Lord brings about the return to Zion [after seventy years of exile in Babylon], we were like dreamers" (Psalms 126:1). He said to himself: Is there anyone who can sleep in a dream for seventy years? [How is it possible to compare seventy years of exile to a dream?]

One day, he was walking along the road and he saw a certain man planting a carob tree. Honi said to him: After how many years will this tree bear fruit? The man said to him: Not until seventy years have passed. Honi said to him: Is it clear to you that you will live seventy years? The man said to him: That man [referring to himself] found a world with carob trees. Just as my ancestors planted trees for me, I too am planting trees for my descendants.

Honi sat and ate his bread. Sleep overcame him and he slept. A rock face formed and surrounded him, and he was obscured from sight and slept for seventy years. When he awoke, he saw a certain man gathering carobs from that tree. Honi said to him: Are you the one who planted that tree? The man said to him: I am his son's son. Honi said to him: It is apparent from this that I have slept for seventy years He saw that his donkey had sired several generations of herds during that interval. Honi went to his house. He said to the members of the household: Is the son of Honi HaMe'agel alive? They said to him: His son is not, but his son's son is alive. He said to them: I am Honi HaMe'agel. They did not believe him.

He went to the study hall, and he heard the Sages say: Our *halakhot* are as enlightening and clear as they were during the years of Honi HaMe'agel, as when he would enter the study hall he would resolve for the Sages any

---

42. Inevitably one of the oaths would be violated.

difficulty that they had. Honi said to them: I am he, but they did not believe him and did not accord him the respect that was due him.

Honi became upset, prayed for mercy, and died. Rava said: This is what people say: Either companionship or death.[43]

(*Ta'anit* 23a)

Request for Rain: Abba Hilkiya and Hanan HaNehba

Two of Honi HaMe'agel's grandsons, Abba Hilkiya and Hanan HaNehba (literally, the one who hides), followed in the path of their righteous grandfather. When the people were in need of rain, they would ask these Sages to pray on their behalf. We can learn a lesson in ethics and virtue from their conduct and way of life.

Abba Hilkiya was the son of Honi HaMe'agel's son. When the world was in need of rain, they would send Sages to him, he would pray for mercy, and rain would fall. On one occasion, the world needed rain, and the Sages sent a pair of Sages to him so that he would pray for mercy and rain would fall. They went to his house but did not find him there. They went to the field and found him hoeing. They greeted him, but he did not welcome them.

In the evening, when he gathered firewood, he placed the wood and hoe on one shoulder and his cloak on the other shoulder. All the way home he did not put on his shoes, but when he reached water he put on his shoes. When he reached thorns he lifted his garments. When he reached the city, his wife came out to greet him, adorned with finery.

When he reached his house, his wife entered first, then he entered, and then the Sages entered. He sat and broke bread, but he did not say to the Sages: Come and break bread. He distributed bread to his children; to the older one he gave one piece and to the younger one he gave two. Abba Hilkiya said to his wife: I know that the Sages have come due to the lack of rain. Let us go up to the roof and pray for mercy before they ask us. Perhaps the Holy One, blessed be He, will be appeased, and it will rain, and we will not take credit for ourselves when it rains.

They went up to the roof. He stood in one corner and she stood in the other corner. Clouds began to form in the corner where his wife stood. When he came down, he said to the Sages: Why have the Sages come? They replied: The Sages sent us to the Master, so that you would pray for mercy, for rain. He said to them: Blessed is the Omnipresent, who did not require you to turn to Abba Hilkiya [as the sky is cloudy and rain is imminent]. They

---

43. Death is preferable to a life of solitude.

said to him: We know that the rain has come on the Master's account. But would the Master please explain to us certain matters that are difficult for us to understand?

What is the reason, when we greeted the Master, that the Master did not welcome us? Abba Hilkiya said to them: I was paid as a day laborer, and I said to myself: I may not interrupt my work to answer you. They asked: What is the reason why the Master carried the firewood on one shoulder and his cloak on the other shoulder? He said to them: It was a borrowed cloak. I borrowed it for this purpose [to wear it], and I did not borrow it for that purpose [to place wood on it. Doing so would have damaged the garment].

What is the reason that the Master did not wear his shoes the entire way, but when he reached water he put on his shoes? He said to them: I am able to see the ground the entire way [so there is no need to wear out my shoes], but I am unable to see the ground in the water. What is the reason why, when the Master reached thorns, he lifted his garments? He said to them: This [my flesh] will heal if it is scratched by thorns, but this [my garment] will not heal if it is torn.

What is the reason, when the Master reached the city, that the Master's wife came out adorned? He said to them: So that when I walk through the city I will not direct my eyes toward another woman. What is the reason she entered first, and then the Master entered, and only then we entered? He explained to them: It is because you have not been vetted by me [and I do not know if I can trust you to walk behind my wife].

What is the reason, when the Master broke bread, that he did not say to us: Come and break bread [as would have been common courtesy toward guests]? He said: Because the bread is not plentiful, and I said to myself: Let me not have the Sages beholden to me for nothing. [So that you would not think that I am offering you food, when in fact I had none for you.] What is the reason that the Master gave the older child one piece of bread and the younger child two? He responded: This older child is at home and can eat when he is hungry, but this younger child sits and studies in the synagogue.

What is the reason why the clouds began to form in that corner where the Master's wife was standing? He said: Because my wife is at home, and she gives bread to the poor, the benefit of which is immediate. I give money to the poor, the benefit of which is not immediate [as the poor person must then take the money and purchase food with it]. Alternatively, certain hooli-

gans were in our neighborhood, and I prayed for mercy that they would die; but she prayed for mercy that they would repent, and they repented.

Hanan HaNehba was the son of Honi HaMe'agel's daughter. When the world was in need of rain, the Sages would send schoolchildren to him, and they would grab him by the hem of his cloak and say to him: Father, Father, give us rain.

Hanan said before the Holy One, blessed be He: Master of the Universe, act on behalf of these children, who are unable to distinguish between God, their Father in Heaven, who provides rain, and me, the father who does not provide rain. Why was he called Hanan HaNehba? Because he would hide [mahbi] himself in the lavatory [so that people would not treat him with deference].

(Ta'anit 23a)

📖 Further reading: Regarding prayers for rain in ordinary times, see A Concise Guide to Halakha, p. 242. For more on the proper work ethic, see A Concise Guide to Halakha, p. 603.

Request for Rain: Nakdimon Ben Guryon

Nakdimon ben Guryon borrowed water for the numerous pilgrims who had ascended to Jerusalem. Just before the repayment deadline his prayers were answered, and in a short while rain filled the many cisterns, repaying his debt. The sun then reemerged from behind the clouds on his behalf.

The Sages taught: One time all the Jewish people ascended for the pilgrimage festival to Jerusalem, and they did not have enough water to drink. Nakdimon ben Guryon went to a certain gentile official and said to him: Lend me twelve cisterns of water for the pilgrims, and I will give you twelve wells of water in return. If I do not give them to you, I will give you twelve talents of silver. The official agreed, and fixed a time limit for him to return the water.

When that time arrived and no rain had fallen, in the morning, the official sent a message to Nakdimon: Send me either the water or the money that you owe me. Nakdimon sent to him: I still have time, as the entire day is mine. [The deadline is at the end of the day.] At noon the official sent the same message to him: Send me either the water or the money that you owe me. Nakdimon sent the same message back to him: I still have time left in the day. In the afternoon, he sent the same message to him: Send me either the water or the money that you owe me. Nakdimon sent the same message

back to him: I still have time left in the day. That official ridiculed him, and said: Rain did not fall throughout the entire year, and now rain will fall?

The official entered the bathhouse joyfully. As this master was joyfully entering the bathhouse, Nakdimon entered the Temple sadly. He wrapped himself in his prayer shawl and stood in prayer.

He said before God: Master of the Universe, it is revealed and known before You that I acted neither for my honor, nor for the honor of the house of my father; rather, it was for Your honor that I acted, so that there would be water for the pilgrims. Immediately the sky became overcast, and rain fell until the twelve cisterns were filled with water, beyond what they had been originally.

As the official left the bathhouse, Nakdimon ben Guryon left the Temple. When they encountered one another, Nakdimon said to him: Give me the money you owe me for the surplus water you received. The official said to him: I know that the Holy One, blessed be He, has brought upheaval to His world and caused rain to fall now only on your behalf. But I still have a claim against you, through which I can collect my money from you, as the sun had already set, and the rain that fell after the deadline had already passed was in my possession.

Nakdimon went back and entered the Temple, wrapped himself in his prayer shawl, and stood in prayer. He said before God: Master of the Universe, let it be known that You have beloved ones in Your world. Immediately, the clouds scattered and the sun shone. At that moment, the official said to him: Had the sun not broken through the clouds, I would have had a claim against you, which would have allowed me to collect my money from you. The Sages taught: Nakdimon was not his real name; rather his name was Buni. Why was he called Nakdimon? It is because the sun broke through [*nikdera*] for him.

(*Ta'anit* 19b–20a)

Further reading: For more on the power of prayer, see p. 457; *A Concise Guide to Mahshava*, p. 300.

Request for Rain: Rabbi Hiyya's Prayer

The prayers of Rabbi Hiyya would always bear fruit. As soon as he asked for something, his request would immediately be granted. Furthermore, only the intervention of Elijah the prophet prevented him from reviving the dead through his prayer.

Elijah was frequently in attendance at the academy of Rabbi Yehuda HaNasi. One day it was *Rosh Hodesh*, and Elijah was late and did not come. Rabbi Yehuda HaNasi said to the prophet: What is the reason that the Master was late? Elijah explained to him: I needed to awaken the patriarch Abraham and wash his hands, and then he prayed, and then I laid him down [to sleep]. I did likewise to Isaac, and likewise to Jacob. Rabbi Yehuda HaNasi suggested: Let him [Elijah] awaken them together. Elijah answered: They believed that were they all awake together they would generate so powerful a prayer that they would bring the messiah prematurely. Rabbi Yehuda HaNasi said to Elijah: Is there anyone in this world who is their equivalent in the effectiveness of his prayers? Elijah said to him: There are, Rabbi Hiyya and his sons.

Rabbi Yehuda HaNasi decreed a fast, and he designated Rabbi Hiyya and his sons to descend and serve as prayer leader. Rabbi Hiyya recited [the phrase from the *Amida* prayer]: He makes the wind blow; and the wind blew. He then recited: And the rain fall, and rain fell. When he sought to recite: Who revives the dead, the world trembled.

The angels in the heavens said: Who revealed secrets in the world? They said: It is Elijah. They brought Elijah to the heavens, and they beat him with sixty fiery rods. Elijah came to earth where they were praying, and he appeared to them as a bear of fire. He entered in their midst and distracted them [so they would not say: Who revives the dead].

(*Bava Metzia* 85b)

📖 Further reading: For more on revival of the dead, see *A Concise Guide to Mahshava*, p. 295.

Virtue And Morality

The Torah also teaches us good manners and virtues, in the spirit of the verse: "Its ways are ways of pleasantness, and all its pathways are peace (Proverbs 3:17). These values are reflected in the stories related about the conduct of the Sages. Through their teaching of Torah and their actions they teach us desired conduct, including the willingness to admit mistakes and remedy matters requiring it.

Stories from the Sages

Rav Huna and the Barrels of Wine

When Rav Huna's wine fermented into vinegar, the other Sages told him that there must be significance in this and that it was apparently due to some prohibition he had violated. Rav Huna took inventory of his actions to determine where he had failed, remedied what required remedy, and the vinegar problem was resolved.

Four hundred barrels of Rav Huna's wine fermented into vinegar [resulting in significant financial loss]. Rav Yehuda, brother of Rav Sala the Pious, and the Sages, and some say it was Rav Adda bar Ahava and the Sages, entered to visit him, and said: The Master should examine his actions. Rav Huna said to them: Am I suspect in your eyes? They said to him: Is the Holy One, blessed be He, suspect of exacting punishment without justice?

Rav Huna said to them: If there is anyone who heard something improper about my conduct, let him say so. They said to him: We heard that the Master does not give a share of his grapevines to his tenant farmer.[44] Rav Huna said to them: Does this tenant farmer leave me anything from the crop? He steals it all. They said to him: That is what people say: One who steals from a thief tastes a taste of theft.

He said to them: I accept upon myself to give my tenant farmer his portion. Some say his vinegar miraculously turned back into wine, and others say that the price of vinegar rose and it was sold at the price of wine.

(*Berakhot* 5b)

---

44. A tenant farmer is entitled to a percentage of the crop as well as to a share of the branches of the grapevine.

Rabbi Elazar ben Rabbi Shimon and the Ugly Man

As a result of significant Torah study and self-approbation, Rabbi Elazar son of Rabbi Shimon became arrogant and severely insulted a passerby. From this episode he learned an important lesson in how to conduct himself when interacting with people.

There was an incident in which Rabbi Elazar son of Rabbi Shimon came from Migdal Gedor, from his rabbi's house, and he was riding on a donkey along the bank of the river. He was greatly rejoicing, and he was very arrogant because he had studied much Torah. A certain person who was exceedingly ugly happened to encounter him.

The man said to him: Greetings to you, my rabbi. Rabbi Elazar did not respond to his greeting. Instead, Rabbi Elazar said to him: Worthless one, how ugly is that man! Are all the people of your city as ugly as you are? The man said to him: I do not know, but go and say to the Craftsman who made me: How ugly is this vessel that You made!

When Rabbi Elazar became aware that he had sinned, he dismounted from his donkey and prostrated himself before the man, and said to him: I have sinned against you; forgive me. He said to him: I will not forgive you until you go to the Craftsman who made me and say: How ugly is this vessel that You made.

He was following the man, trying to placate him, until they reached Rabbi Elazar's city. The people of his city came out to greet him, saying to him: Greetings to you, my rabbi, my rabbi, my Master, my Master. The man said to them: Who are you calling my rabbi, my rabbi? They said to him: This man, who is walking behind you. He said to them: If this man is a rabbi, may there not be many like him among the Jewish people. They said to him: For what reason do you say this? He said to them: He did such and such to me. They said to him: Nevertheless, forgive him, as he is a great Torah scholar. He said to them: For your sakes I forgive him, provided that he will not be accustomed to behave like this.

Immediately, Rabbi Elazar ben Rabbi Shimon entered the study hall and taught: A person should always be pliable like a reed, and not inflexible like a cedar. It is for this reason that the reed merited to have a quill taken from it, with which to write Torah scrolls, phylacteries, and *mezuzot*.

(*Ta'anit* 20a–b)

> Further reading: Even today, Torah scrolls, phylacteries, and *mezuzot* are written with a quill; see *A Concise Guide to Halakha*, pp. 541, 590.

Stories from the Sages

Stories from the Sages

A Woman, a Young Boy, and a Young Girl

Rabbi Yehoshua ben Hananya recounts three occasions when he lost an argument. Some involved explicit or tacit criticism of his qualities.

Rabbi Yehoshua ben Hananya said: No person has ever prevailed over me in a dispute except for a woman, a small boy, and a small girl. What is the incident involving a woman? Once I was being hosted at a certain inn and the hostess prepared beans for me. On the first day I ate them and left nothing over. On the second day I also left nothing over. On the third day she oversalted them, rendering them inedible. As soon as I tasted them, I withdrew my hand from them and did not eat.

She said to me: Rabbi, why aren't you eating? I said to her: I already ate earlier in the day. She said to me: You should have withdrawn your hand from the bread [as then you would have had an appetite to eat the beans]. She said to me: Rabbi, perhaps you did not leave over food on the corner of your plate on the first days.[45] Isn't this what the Sages said: One does not leave over food in the corner of the pot, but one leaves over food in the corner of the plate?

What is the incident involving a young girl? Once I was walking along the way, and the way passed through a field, and I was walking along it. A certain young girl said to me: Rabbi, isn't this a field?[46] I said to her: Isn't it a well-trodden path [on which it is permitted to walk through a field]? She said to me: Robbers like you have trodden it.

What is the incident involving a young boy? Once I was walking along the way, and I saw a young boy sitting at the crossroads. I said to him: On which path shall we walk to the city? He said to me: This path is short and long, and that one is long and short. Rabbi Yehoshua continued: I walked on the path that was short and long. When I approached the city I found that it was surrounded by gardens and orchards and there was no access to the city.

I retraced my steps and said to the young boy: My son, didn't you tell me that this way is short? He said to me: But didn't I tell you that it is long too? I kissed him on his head and said to him: Happy are you, Israel, as you are all exceedingly wise, from your old to your young.

(*Eiruvin* 53b)

---

45. Etiquette demands leaving something over on the plate. The hostess said that perhaps Rabbi Yehoshua did not eat in order to compensate for his lapse in etiquette on the first two days.

46. It is prohibited to walk through a field due to the damage caused to the seeds and crops.

Hillel Would Not Get Angry

Hillel the Elder was renowned for his patience. Even at times that were exceedingly stressful for him, people were unsuccessful in causing him to lose his temper.

There was an incident involving two people who wagered with each other, saying: Whoever will go and aggravate Hillel will receive four hundred dinars from the other. One of them said: I will aggravate him. That day was the day before Shabbat, and Hillel was washing his hair. The man went and passed the entrance to Hillel's house and impertinently said: Who here is Hillel; who here is Hillel? Hillel wrapped himself in a garment and went out to greet him. He said to him: My son, what do you seek? The man said to him: I have a question to ask. Hillel said to him: Ask, my son, ask. The man asked: Why are the heads of Babylonians oval? He said to him: My son, you asked an outstanding question. It is because they do not have capable midwives.[47]

The man went and waited a short while, and he returned and said: Who here is Hillel; who here is Hillel? Hillel wrapped himself in a garment, went out to greet him. He said to him: My son, what do you seek? He said to him: I have a question to ask. Hillel said to him: Ask, my son, ask. He asked: Why are the eyes of the residents of Tadmor bleary? Hillel said to him: My son, you asked an outstanding question. It is because they live among the sands.[48]

He went and waited a short while, and he returned, and said: Who here is Hillel; who here is Hillel? Hillel wrapped himself in a garment and went out to greet him. He said to him: My son, what do you seek? He said to him: I have a question to ask. He said to him: Ask, my son, ask. He asked: Why do Africans have wide feet? Hillel said to him: You asked an outstanding question. It is because they live in marshlands.[49]

The man said to him: I have many questions to ask, but I am afraid to ask them lest you get angry. Hillel wrapped himself and sat before him. He said to him: Ask all of the questions that you have to ask. The man said to him: Are you Hillel whom they call the *Nasi* of Israel? Hillel said to him: Yes. He said to him: If you are he, then may there not be many like you in Israel. Hillel said to him: My son, for what reason do you say this? The man said to him: It is because I lost four hundred dinars on your account. Hillel said to him: Be vigilant of your spirit [avoid wagers of this sort]; Hillel is worthy of

---

47. Capable midwives know how to shape the baby's head properly.
48. Their eyes are bleary because the sand that enters irritates the eyes.
49. Having wide feet enables them to walk on the swampy land.

having you lose four hundred dinars and four hundred dinars more on his account, as long as Hillel will not get angry.[50]

(*Shabbat* 30b–31a)

Martyrs: Rabbi Akiva

Ten prominent Jewish martyrs were executed by the Roman government in the years preceding and following the destruction of the Second Temple. The most famous of them was Rabbi Akiva, who continued to teach Torah publicly even when doing so endangered his life. He was apprehended and executed while being horrifically tortured. Yet, at the moment of his death, he sanctified the name of God by reciting *Shema*.

Once, the evil Roman Empire decreed that Israel may not engage in the study and practice of Torah. Pappos ben Yehuda came and found Rabbi Akiva convening public assemblies and engaging in Torah study. Pappos asked him: Akiva, don't you fear the authorities?

Rabbi Akiva said to him: I will relate a parable. To what can this matter be compared? It can be compared to a fox walking along a riverbank who saw fish gathering and swimming from place to place. The fox said to them: What are you fleeing from? They said to it: We are fleeing from the nets that people cast upon us. The fox said to them: Do you wish to come up onto dry land, and we will reside together, just as my ancestors resided with your ancestors? The fish said to him: Are you the one of whom they say that he is the cleverest of animals? You are not clever; you are a fool. If we are afraid in the water, which is our natural habitat and keeps us alive, then in a habitat that causes our death, all the more so do we have what to fear.

Rabbi Akiva continued: So too, we Jews, if we fear for our lives now, when we are sitting and engaging in Torah study, about which it is written: "For it is your life and the length of your days" (Deuteronomy 30:20), then if we proceed to remain idle from its study, all the more so should we fear for our lives.

The Sages said: Only a few days passed before they seized Rabbi Akiva and incarcerated him in prison, and they also seized Pappos ben Yehuda and incarcerated him alongside him. Rabbi Akiva said to him: Pappos, who brought you here? Pappos said to him: Happy are you, Rabbi Akiva, that you were arrested for engaging in Torah study. Woe unto Pappos, who was arrested for engaging in idle matters.

---

50. It is better that you lose money than Hillel lose his temper.

When they took Rabbi Akiva out to be executed, it was the time for the recitation of *Shema*. While they were raking his flesh with iron combs, he was reciting *Shema*, thereby accepting upon himself the yoke of Heaven. His students said to him: Our teacher, even now, when you are suffering so greatly, can you recite *Shema*? He said to them: All my days I have been troubled by the verse from *Shema*: "With all your soul" (Deuteronomy 6:5), which the Sages interpret to mean: Even if God takes your soul. I said to myself: When will the opportunity be afforded me to fulfill this? Now that I have the opportunity, shall I not fulfill it? He prolonged the word: One [*ehad*], until his soul left his body as he uttered: One. A divine voice descended and said: Happy are you, Rabbi Akiva, that your soul left as you uttered: One.

The ministering angels said before the Holy One, blessed be He: This is Torah and this is its reward? This is as the verse states: "From death, by Your hand, Lord, from death from the world" (Psalms 17:14).[51] God told them the end of the verse: "Whose portion is life."[52] A divine voice subsequently emerged and announced: Happy are you, Rabbi Akiva, as you are destined for life in the World to Come.

(*Berakhot* 61b)

📖 Further reading: For more on martyrdom, see *A Concise Guide to Mahshava*, p. 198.

Martyrs: Rabbi Hanina Ben Teradyon

Rabbi Hanina ben Teradyon, in contrast to Rabbi Yosei ben Kisma, maintained that one should not seek the favor of the Roman government. He taught Torah despite the severe prohibition against doing so, and he too was executed while being tortured.

When Rabbi Yosei ben Kisma fell ill, Rabbi Hanina ben Teradyon went to visit him. Rabbi Yosei ben Kisma said to him: Hanina my brother, don't you know that this nation [Rome] has been crowned by a decree from Heaven [and therefore, it is preferable not to provoke them]? The proof is that Rome has destroyed God's Temple, burned His Sanctuary, killed His pious ones, and destroyed His elites, and the empire still exists.[53] Yet I heard about you that you sit and engage in Torah study and convene assemblies in public, with a Torah scroll placed in your lap.

---

51. The hand of God kills and does not rescue.
52. Even those who die, if they are righteous they are destined for eternal life for their souls.
53. Apparently, their actions were sanctioned by God.

Rabbi Hanina ben Teradyon said to him: From the heavens they will have mercy and protect me. Rabbi Yosei ben Kisma said to him: I am stating reasonable claims to you, and you tell me: From the heavens they will have mercy? I wonder whether the Romans will not burn you and the Torah scroll in fire …

The Sages said: Not even a few days passed and Rabbi Yosei ben Kisma died of his illness. And all of the Roman notables went to bury him, and they eulogized him with a great eulogy. Upon their return, they found Rabbi Hanina ben Teradyon sitting and engaging in Torah study and convening assemblies in public, with a Torah scroll placed in his lap.

They brought him and wrapped him in the Torah scroll, encircled him with bundles of thin branches, and set fire to it. They brought tufts of wool and soaked them in water, and placed them on his heart, so that his soul would not depart his body quickly. His daughter said to him: Father, how can I see you like this? Rabbi Hanina ben Teradyon said to her: Were I being burned alone, it would be difficult for me. Now that I am burning along with a Torah scroll, He who seeks retribution for the affront to the Torah scroll will seek retribution for the affront to me, as well.[54]

His students said to him: Our teacher, what do you see? Rabbi Hanina said to them: I see the scroll's parchment burning, and its letters flying to the heavens. They said: You, too, open your mouth so the fire will enter you and hasten your death. Rabbi Hanina said to them: It is preferable that He who gave my soul will take it, and he [referring to himself] will not do harm to himself.

The executioner said to him: Rabbi, if I increase the flame and take the tufts of wool from upon your heart [thereby hastening your death and minimizing your suffering], will you bring me to the life of the World to Come? Rabbi Hanina said to him: Yes. The executioner requested: Take an oath to me that you will do so. Rabbi Hanina took an oath to him. The executioner immediately increased the flame and took the tufts of wool from upon his heart, and his soul left his body quickly. The executioner too, leaped and fell into the fire and died.

A divine voice emerged and said: Rabbi Hanina ben Teradyon and the executioner are destined for the life of the World to Come. Rabbi Yehuda HaNasi wept, and said: There is one who acquires his place in the World to

54. God will administer to them an appropriate punishment.

Come in one moment, like the executioner, and there is one who acquires his place in the World to Come only after many years.

(*Avoda Zara* 18a)

The Passing of Rabbi Yohanan Ben Zakkai

Just before they died, Sages of Israel would convey their last will and testament as well as words of encouragement. These incorporated central principles of their personal philosophy.

When Rabbi Yohanan ben Zakkai fell ill, his students entered to visit him. Upon seeing them, he began to cry. His students said to him: Lamp of Israel, the right pillar, the mighty hammer,[55] why are you crying?

He said to them: If they were leading me before a king of flesh and blood, who is here today and in the grave tomorrow; who, if he were angry with me, his anger would not be eternal; if he imprisoned me, his imprisonment would not be eternal imprisonment; and if he killed me, his killing would not be for eternity,[56] and I would be able to appease him with words or bribe him with money, nevertheless, I would cry. Now that they are leading me before the supreme King of kings, the Holy One, blessed be He, who lives and endures forever and all time: If He is angry with me, His anger is eternal; if He imprisons me, his imprisonment is eternal imprisonment; if He kills me, His killing is for eternity; and I am unable to appease Him with words or bribe him with money; and moreover, I have two paths before me, one to the Garden of Eden and one to Gehenna, and I do not know on which they are leading me, how can I not cry?

His students said to him: Our teacher, bless us. He said to them: May it be God's will that the fear of Heaven shall be upon you like the fear of flesh and blood. His students said to him: Is that all?[57] He said to them: If only one could achieve that level of fear. Know that when one commits a transgression, he says to himself: I hope that no man will see me.[58]

At the time of his death, Rabban Yohanan ben Zakkai said to them: Remove the vessels due to the ritual impurity,[59] and prepare a chair for Hizkiyahu king of Judea, who is coming to accompany me to the World to Come.

(*Berakhot* 28b)

---

55. These are expressions of great praise.
56. Even if he executes me in this world, there is life in the World to Come.
57. The students' question is: Shouldn't one fear God more than he fears people?
58. One who commits a transgression is more concerned that a person might see him than he is about God seeing him.
59. Any vessels that are under the same roof as a corpse become ritually impure.

Stories from the Sages

The Passing of Rabbi Yehuda HaNasi

Rabbi Yehuda HaNasi, known simply as Rabbi, was the redactor of the Mishna and *Nasi* of the Sanhedrin. One of the most prominent Sages, he merited Torah, greatness, and honor in the course of his lifetime. His passing was a dramatic, formative event, and the Sages described in detail his final hours and how the news of his death was received.

The Sages taught: At the time of the passing of Rabbi Yehuda HaNasi, he said: I need my sons. His sons entered his room, and he said to them: Be careful with the honor of your mother. My lamp should be kindled in its place, my table should be set in its place, and my bed should be made in its place. As for Yosef Hofni and Shimon Efrati, they attended to me during my lifetime and they will attend to me in my death....

Rabbi Yehuda HaNasi said to his attendants: I need the Sages of Israel. The Sages of Israel entered his room, and he said to them: Do not eulogize me in the towns,[60] and resume Torah study at the academy after thirty days. My son Shimon is a Sage; my son Gamliel is the *Nasi*;[61] Hanina bar Hama will sit at the head of the academy....

He said to them: I need my younger son. Rabbi Shimon entered his room and he transmitted to him the order of wisdom.[62] He said to them: I need my older son. Rabban Gamliel entered his room, and he transmitted to him the protocols of the office of the *Nasi*. Rabbi Yehuda HaNasi instructed Rabban Gamliel: My son, conduct your term as *Nasi* boldly and cast fear upon the students....

On that day when Rabbi Yehuda HaNasi died, the Sages decreed a fast, and prayed for divine mercy that he would not die. They said: Anyone who says that Rabbi Yehuda HaNasi has died will be stabbed with a sword.

Rabbi Yehuda HaNasi's maidservant ascended to the roof and said: The upper worlds are requesting the presence of Rabbi Yehuda HaNasi, and the lower worlds, the Jews, are also requesting Rabbi Yehuda HaNasi. May it be the will of God that the lower worlds impose their will upon the upper worlds. But when she saw how many times he would enter the bathroom and first have to remove his phylacteries, and then come out and put them back on, and how he was suffering from his intestinal disease, she said: May it be the will of God that the upper worlds impose their will upon the lower worlds. [It would be preferable that he die.]

---

60. Have eulogies only in the cities, where large crowds will gather.
61. Although my son Shimon is wise, my son Gamliel will succeed me as *Nasi*.
62. He conveyed to him the leadership protocols and the fundamental principles of Torah.

But the Sages would not be silent and continued praying for mercy [preventing Rabbi Yehuda HaNasi's death]. She took a jug and threw it from the roof to the ground. Due to the sudden noise, the Sages were momentarily silent from praying for mercy, and Rabbi Yehuda HaNasi passed away.

The Sages said to bar Kappara: Go and ascertain the condition of Rabbi Yehuda HaNasi. He went and found that Rabbi Yehuda HaNasi had died. He rent his garments but reversed the tear behind him [so that it would not be noticed. When he returned to the other Sages] he opened his remarks by saying: The angels and the righteous mortals both clutched the holy ark [a reference to Rabbi Yehuda HaNasi], but the angels triumphed over the righteous, and the holy ark was taken captive. They said to him: Has he died? He said to them: You said it; I did not say it.

At the time of Rabbi Yehuda HaNasi's death, he straightened his ten fingers heavenward and declared: Master of the Universe, it is revealed and known before You that I toiled with my ten fingers in the Torah, and I have not derived pleasure from this world even equivalent to my smallest finger. May it be Your will that there will be peace in my repose. A divine voice emerged and announced: "May he depart in peace; rest on their resting places" (Isaiah 57:2).

(*Ketubot* 103a–104a)

Sages on Life

Love of Israel

The Sages teach that love and camaraderie are central values on which the entire Torah is based. This chapter cites statements of the Sages on the centrality of love of one's neighbor, the importance of avoiding disputes, and the virtue of peace.

Love of Other People

Loving other people is one of the foremost, fundamental principles in the Torah. By contrast, the opposite trait, baseless hatred, is an extremely grave sin, to the extent that the Sages maintain that, in terms of its gravity, it is the equivalent of the three cardinal transgressions of idolatry, bloodshed, and immorality.

So said the Holy One, blessed be He, to Israel: My sons, have I withheld anything from you? What do I ask of you? I ask only that you love one another and respect one another, and be fearful of each other, and that there should be no sins, or robbery, or any ugliness between you ... so that you will never behave in an unseemly manner, as it is stated: "He told you, man, what is good, and what the Lord demands from you: Only to execute justice, to love kindness, and to walk humbly with your God" (Micah 6:8). Do not read: "Walk humbly with your God" (*im Elohekha*), but rather interpret the verse: Walk humbly, and your God will be with you (*ve'imkha Elohekha*). As long as you are with Him [by following His ways] discreetly and humbly, He will be with you discreetly. Therefore, it is stated: "Walk humbly with your God."

"Love your neighbor as yourself" (Leviticus 19:18). Rabbi Akiva says: This is an essential principle of the Torah.

Why was the First Temple destroyed? Because of three matters that were prevalent during the First Temple period: idol worship, forbidden sexual relations, and bloodshed .... But considering that the people during the Second Temple period were engaged in Torah study, observance of mitzvot, and acts of kindness, and they did not perform the sinful acts that were performed during the First Temple period, why was the Second Temple destroyed? Because there was baseless hatred during that period. This serves to teach you that baseless hatred is the equivalent of the three cardinal transgressions: idol worship, forbidden sexual relations, and bloodshed.

(*Eliyahu Rabba* 26; *Sifra, Kedoshim* 2; *Yoma* 9b)

📖 **Further reading:** For more on the love of Israel and its centrality in Judaism, see *A Concise Guide to Mahshava*, p. 113.

Making Peace

It is a great mitzva to bring peace to the world, to reconcile enemies to each other, and to avoid dispute and vengeance.

We learned [in Mishna *Avot* 1:18] that Rabban Shimon ben Gamliel says: The world stands on three things: on judgment, on truth, and on peace.

Rabbi Mona says: The three of them are one matter; if judgment is achieved, truth is achieved and peace is achieved.[1] All three of them are mentioned in the same verse, as it is stated: "Administer truth, justice, and peace in your gates" (Zechariah 8:16). Wherever there is justice there is peace, and wherever there is peace there is justice.

Who is the mightiest of the mighty? … Some say: One who turns his enemy into his friend.

It is written: "You shall not take vengeance, you shall not bear any grudge against members of your people" (Leviticus 19:18). To what can this be compared? It can be compared to one who was cutting meat, and the knife struck his hand. Would he retaliate by striking his other hand?[2]

(Derekh Eretz Zuta, Perek Shalom; Avot deRabbi Natan, version A, chap. 23; Jerusalem Talmud, Nedarim 9:4)

Great Is Peace

The Sages are effusive in extolling the virtue of peace, to the extent that they even stated that *Shalom*, Peace, is one of God's names.

Hizkiyya said: Great is peace, as regarding all the mitzvot of the Torah it is written "if," [e.g.]: "If you see" (Exodus 23:5);[3] "if you encounter" (Exodus 23:4);[4] "if a bird's nest will happen before you" (Deuteronomy 22:6);[5] "if you build" (Deuteronomy 22:8);[6] which indicate that if the opportunity to fulfill the mitzva comes before you, you are required to perform it. But peace, what

---

1. Judgment leads to truth, and truth leads to peace.
2. It is equally absurd for one Jew to retaliate against another Jew, as they are both parts of one unit.
3. If you find a lost item, return it to its owner.
4. If you encounter a person who is having difficulty leading his animal, assist him.
5. If you come upon a bird's nest with fledglings or eggs, send away the mother bird before taking the offspring.
6. If you build a house, build a parapet for the roof.

is written in its regard? "Seek peace and pursue it" (Psalms 34:15): Seek it in your place, and actively pursue it elsewhere.[7]

Rabbi Yehoshua says: Great is peace, as [one of the] names of God is Peace.

Rabbi Shimon ben Halafta says: The Holy One, blessed be He, found no receptacle more suitable to contain His blessing for Israel than peace, as it is stated: "The Lord gives strength to His people; the Lord will bless His people with peace" (Psalms 29:11).

(*Derekh Eretz Zuta, Perek Shalom* 4:13; Mishna *Okatzin* 3:12)

---

7.   It is not sufficient to wait until you happen to encounter peace.

Husband and Wife

The stability of the Jewish home is based on the relationship between husband and wife. The Sages deal extensively with this topic, from the early stages of finding the right partner, through marriage and marital life, to the loss of one's spouse. The chapter that follows presents statements of the Sages regarding the importance of marriage; a suitable match; the joy of marriage; the mutual respect and love between husband and wife, which are the foundation of the home; and the deep bond between spouses.

Everything Is Thanks to the Wife

Married life is vital for a man, and he is not considered whole until he finds his partner. A man's blessing, happiness, and joy are attained thanks to his wife.

"It is not good that the man shall be alone; I will make for him a helper alongside him" (Genesis 2:18).[8] Rabbi Yaakov taught: Anyone who does not have a wife is without goodness, without a helper…without joy…without atonement…without blessing….

Rabbi Shimon says in the name of Rabbi Yehoshua ben Levi: He is even without peace…Rabbi Yehoshua of Sakhnin says in the name of Rabbi Levi: Even without life….

Rabbi Hiyya bar Gamda: He is not even a whole man, as it is stated: "He blessed them, and He called their name Man" (Genesis 5:2), indicating that the two of them together are called Man. Some say: It even diminishes the image,[9] as it is stated: "As He made man in the image of God" (Genesis 9:6); what is written immediately after it? "And you, be fruitful, and multiply" (Genesis 9:7).

The Sages taught: Who is wealthy…Rabbi Akiva says: Anyone who has a wife who is pleasant in her deeds.

"Therefore, everyone who is devoted to You should pray at the time of searching" (Psalms 32:6). Rabbi Hanina said: "The time of searching" – this

---

8. This was stated by God prior to creation of Woman.
9. It diminishes, as it were, the image of God.

is referring to a prayer to find a wife, as it is stated: "He who has found a wife has found goodness and elicits favor from the Lord" (Proverbs 18:22).

In the West [the Land of Israel], when a man married a woman, customarily they would ask him: *Matza* or *motzeh*?[10] *Matza*, as it is written: "He who has found [*matza*] a wife has found goodness and elicits favor from the Lord," or *motzeh*, as it is written: "I find [*motzeh*] more bitter than death the woman" (Ecclesiastes 7:26).

(Bereshit Rabba 17; Shabbat 25b; Berakhot 8a)

Matches

It is so difficult to make matches between a man and a woman that the Sages say this has been God's primary pursuit since creating the world. Some matches are determined by people's deeds, while other matches are predetermined.

God pairs a woman with a man only according to the man's actions … Rabba bar bar Hana says that Rabbi Yohanan says: It is as difficult to pair them as the splitting of the Red Sea, as it is stated regarding the exodus: "God settles the lonely in a home; He joyously leads forth prisoners" (Psalms 68:7).[11]

Is that so? But didn't Rav Yehuda say that Rav says: Forty days before an embryo is formed, a divine voice [*bat kol*] emerges and says: The daughter of so-and-so is destined to marry so-and-so…the field of so-and-so is destined to belong to so-and-so. It is not difficult: The predetermined pairing is with regard to a first match, while that pairing that is according to one's actions is with regard to a second match.

A certain Roman noblewoman asked Rabbi Yosei bar Halafta a question, saying to him: In how many days did the Holy One, blessed be He, create His world? He replied: In six days…. She said to him: What has He been doing from that moment until now? He said to her: The Holy One, blessed be He, sits and makes matches: The daughter of so-and-so is for so-and-so; the widow of so-and-so is for so-and-so; the property of so-and-so is for so-and-so.

She said to him: Is that His vocation? I too can do the same! I have many slaves and many maidservants; I can pair them in a short while. He said to her: Although it is easy in your eyes, it is as difficult before the Holy One, blessed be He, as the splitting of the Red Sea. Rabbi Yosei bar Halafta went on his way.

---

10. Implicit in this is a question regarding the nature of the woman he is marrying.
11. Creating a home for the lonely is comparable to the exodus.

What did the Roman noblewoman do? She took one thousand slaves and one thousand maidservants, and positioned them in rows facing each other; she said: Slave so-and-so will marry maidservant so-and-so, and maidservant so-and-so will marry slave so-and-so, and she paired them all in a single night. The next day they came to her; this one's skull was cracked, this one's eye was dislocated, and this one's leg was broken. She said to them: What happened to you? This maidservant said: I don't want this man, and that slave said: I don't want this woman. She immediately sent for and brought Rabbi Yosei bar Halafta before her, and said to him: There is no god like your God; your Torah is true, pleasant, and praiseworthy; you spoke well.

The students of Rabbi Dostai son of Rabbi Yannai asked him: Why does a man typically court a woman, but a woman does not court a man? Rabbi Dostai answered: This can be compared to a person who lost an item. Who searches for what? Certainly, it is the owner of the lost item who searches for his item.[12]

More than a man wants to marry, a woman wants to get married.

Reish Lakish said: It is preferable to sit together as two bodies than to sit alone like a widow.[13]

(*Sota* 2a; *Bereshit Rabba* 68; *Nidda* 31b; *Yevamot* 103a; *Kiddushin* 7a)

The Wedding

The rejoicing at a wedding is of great significance. It is a mitzva to bring joy to a bride and groom, who on their wedding day are likened to a king and queen.

The Sages taught: One should interrupt Torah study to attend the removal of a corpse, to attend a funeral, and to attend the entry of a bride to the wedding feast.

Anyone who partakes in the wedding feast of a groom but does not cause him to rejoice contravenes the five voices [*kolot*] written in the context of a wedding celebration, as it is stated: "The sound of gladness and the sound of joy, the sound of a groom and the sound of a bride, the sound of those who say: Give thanks to the Lord of hosts" (Jeremiah 33:11).

What is his reward if he causes the groom to rejoice? Rabbi Yehoshua ben Levi says: He is privileged to acquire the Torah, which was given with

---

12. The man, who, as it were, lost one of his sides, from which the woman was created, seeks the woman.
13. Any partner is preferable to loneliness.

five sounds [*kolot*][14]…Rabbi Abbahu said: Causing a groom to rejoice is as though one offered a thanks offering in the Temple…Rav Nahman bar Yitzhak said: It is as though he rebuilt one of Jerusalem's ruins.

A groom is like a king: Just as a king does not venture out into the marketplace alone, so too a groom does not venture out into the marketplace alone. Just as a king wears splendid vestments, so too does a groom wear splendid vestments all seven days of rejoicing following the wedding. Just as everyone praises a king, so too do they praise a groom. Just as the face of a king shines like the light of the sun, so too does the face of a groom shine like the light of the sun.

(*Ketubot* 17a; *Berakhot* 6b; *Pirkei deRabbi Eliezer* 16)

Further reading: For more about the wedding ceremony, its laws and customs, and its meanings, see *A Concise Guide to Mahshava*, p. 16; *A Concise Guide to Halakha*, p. 47.

Love and Honor

A man is commanded by the Sages to be vigilant regarding his wife's honor, and to be attentive and sensitive to her needs.

The Sages taught: One who loves his wife as himself, and who honors her more than himself, and who instructs his sons and daughters in an upright path, and who marries them near the time when they reach maturity [marriageable age], the verse says about him: "You will know that your tent[15] is at peace" (Job 5:24).

Rav says: A person must always be careful not to mistreat his wife.[16] Since her tears are easily generated, punishment for her mistreatment is immediate…. And Rabbi Helbo says: A person must always be vigilant in honoring his wife, for blessing is found in a person's house only thanks to his wife, as it is stated: "And he benefited Abram for her sake, he acquired sheep, oxen" (Genesis 12:16). That is what Rava said to the residents of Mehoza: Honor your wives, so that you will become wealthy.

A person should always eat and drink less than the means at his disposal, and he should dress and cover himself in accordance with the means at his disposal, and he should honor his wife and children with more than the means at his disposal – as they are dependent on him, and he is dependent on the One who spoke and the world came into being.

(*Yevamot* 62b; *Bava Metzia* 89a; *Hullin* 84b)

---

14. The word *kol* is stated five times in the account of the revelation at Sinai.
15. This is a reference to the home.
16. He should ensure that she suffers no distress.

The Loss of a Spouse

The death of a beloved spouse is a very jarring blow.

Rabbi Yohanan says: For any man whose first wife dies, it is as though the Temple was destroyed in his days…Rabbi Alexandri says: Any man whose wife dies in his days, the world is dark for him…Rabbi Yosei bar Hanina says: His steps get shorter…Rabbi Abbahu says: His wisdom fails.

Rabbi Shmuel bar Nahman says: Everything has a replacement, except for the wife of one's youth…. A man dies only to his wife, and a woman dies only to her husband.[17]

(*Sanhedrin* 22a–b)

Further reading: For more on couples, see *A Concise Guide to Mahshava*, p. 179.

---

17. The spouse is the one who experiences suffering and mourning most acutely.

Faith and Trust in God

Faith in God is the foundation of all the mitzvot of the Torah, and of the bond between people and their Creator. Reliance on God – absolute trust in the One who created the world – is the most complete manifestation of faith. The chapter that follows presents statements of the Sages regarding the virtue of faith, the great reward that awaits true believers, the essence of faith, and the source for trust in God.

Great Is Faith

Thanks to their faith, the Jewish people merited divine revelation, and thanks to their enduring faith, they will merit redemption in the future. In fact, the essence of Torah and mitzvot can be condensed into faith, on which everything is built.

Great is the faith that the Israelites placed in the One who spoke and the world came into being. In reward for the Israelites' belief in God, divine inspiration rested on them and they recited the song [at the Red Sea], as it is stated: "And they believed in the Lord and in Moses, His servant" (Exodus 14:31), and it is stated [immediately afterward]: "Then Moses and the children of Israel sang this song to the Lord" (Exodus 15:1).

Rabbi Simlai taught: Six hundred and thirteen mitzvot were stated to Moses in the Torah, 365 prohibitions corresponding to the number of days in the solar year, and 248 positive mitzvot corresponding to the number of a person's limbs…. King David came and consolidated the 613 mitzvot to eleven mitzvot,[18] as it is written: "A psalm by David. Lord, who may sojourn in Your tent? Who may dwell on Your holy mountain? He who walks with integrity and does righteous works, and speaks the truth in his heart. He who does not gossip with his tongue, nor does evil to his neighbor, nor tolerates disgrace for his friend. In his own eyes he is despised and repugnant, but he honors those who fear the Lord. He abides by his oaths, even if they cause him harm. He does not lend with usury, nor does he take bribes

Sages on Life

---

18. David condensed them into eleven fundamental mitzvot, as recorded in these verses from the Psalms.

against the innocent. Whoever behaves in this manner will never stumble" (Psalms 15:1–5).

Isaiah came and consolidated the 613 mitzvot to six, as it is written: "One who walks righteously and speaks fairly, spurns the profit of exploitations, shakes off his hands from being supported by bribery, stops his ears from conspiring bloodshed, and shuts his eyes from conceiving evil" (Isaiah 33:15).

Micah came and consolidated them to three, as it is written: "He told you, man, what is good, and what the Lord demands from you: Only to perform justice, and to love kindness, and to walk humbly with your God" (Micah 6:8).

Isaiah then consolidated [his original six mitzvot] to two, as it is stated: "So said the Lord: Maintain justice and act with righteousness, for it is nigh that My salvation is to come and My righteousness is to be revealed" (Isaiah 56:1).

Habakkuk came and consolidated them to one, as it is stated: "But the righteous will live by his faith" (Habakkuk 2:4).[19]

(*Mekhilta deRabbi Yishmael, Beshalah, Mesekhta deVayhi* 6;
Makkot 23b–24a)

Trust in God

It is futile to pin one's hopes on other people, whose days are numbered and whose existence in this world is transient. It is preferable to rely on the eternal God.

Rabbi Yehuda Nesia asked Rabbi Ami: What is the meaning of that which is written: "Trust in the Lord forever, for God the Lord is an everlasting [*olamim*][20] Rock" (Isaiah 26:4)? Rabbi Ami said to him: For anyone who places his trust in the Holy One, Blessed be He, He will be his refuge in this world [*olam hazeh*] and in the World to Come [*olam haba*].

This is the meaning of that which the verse stated: "Do not trust in princes, in man in whom there is no salvation" (Psalms 146:3): Rabbi Shimon said in the name of Rabbi Yehoshua ben Levi: Anyone who trusts in the Holy One, blessed be He, will merit to be similar to Him [as it were]. From where is this derived? It is derived from a verse, as it is stated: "Blessed is the man who trusts in the Lord; the Lord is his haven" (Jeremiah 17:7). But anyone who trusts in idolatry is liable to be like a worthless idol. From

---

19. Isaiah, Micah, and Habakkuk, along with those mentioned in the unabridged version of this midrash, were all prophets.
20. *Olamim* is the plural form of *olam*.

where is this derived? It is derived from a verse, as it is stated: "May their makers become like them; so too, all who put their faith in them" (Psalms 115:8). The Sages say: Anyone who trusts in transient flesh and blood, his protection afforded by that person is likewise transient, as it is stated: "In man in whom there is no salvation" (Psalms 146:3). What is written immediately afterward? "His spirit departs, he returns to the earth" (Psalms 146:4).

The Holy One, blessed be He, said to [the people of Israel who seek rescue from their difficulties]: Trust in My name and it will stand firm for you, as it is stated: "Let him trust in the name of the Lord" (Isaiah 50:10). And why? For I rescue anyone who trusts in My name; and likewise, David says: "In You, Lord, I have taken refuge; I shall never be ashamed" (Psalms 71:1).

(*Menaḥot* 29b; *Devarim Rabba* 5; *Yalkut Shimoni* 2:473)

Further reading: For more about hope in all situations, see *A Concise Guide to Mahshava*, p. 311.

Truth

The Torah commands people to distance themselves from falsehood, and the Sages likewise stress the virtue of adherence to truth and distance from falsehood. The chapter that follows presents statements of the Sages regarding truth as the firm basis for the existence of society and the world, "white lies," and the repugnance of hypocrisy.

The Foundations of the World

Truth is one of the three foundations on which the entire world rests.

Rabban Shimon ben Gamliel says: The world stands on three things: on judgment, on truth, and on peace.

(Mishna Avot 1:18)

The Seal of God

Truth is a name of God and His seal. It endures forever, while falsehood will ultimately collapse and fall.

Rabbi Hanina says: The seal of the Holy One, blessed be He, is truth.

Rabbi Akiva says [regarding the Hebrew letter] *alef*: What is the meaning of *alef*? It teaches that the Torah says: Truth teach your mouth,[21] so that you will merit life in this world; your mouth teach truth,[22] so that you will merit life in the World to Come. Why is this so? Because the Holy One, blessed be He, is called truth. He sits on His Throne in truth forever, His countenance will be preceded by kindness and truth, all His statements are words of truth, all His judgments are judgments of truth, and all His ways are kindness and truth.

For what reason are the letters of the word "truth" [*emet*] scattered,[23] whereas the letters of the word "falsehood" [*sheker*] are juxtaposed to each

---

21. The letters of the word *alef* are an acronym for *emet* – truth, *lamed* – teach, *pikha* – your mouth.
22. The letters of the word *alef* reversed are an acronym for *pikha lamed emet*.
23. Its first letter, *alef*, is the first letter of the Hebrew alphabet, its middle letter, *mem*, is in the middle of the alphabet, and its last letter, *tav*, is the final letter of the alphabet.

other?[24] It is because truth is hard to accomplish,[25] while falsehood stands readily accessible next to one's ear…. For what reason do each of the letters of *emet* stand on two legs, while the letters of *sheker* stand on one leg?[26] It is because when anyone performs truth, the result endures forever, and he inherits a share in the World to Come, and he will not stumble in this world … but falsehood does not endure forever.

(*Shabbat* 55a; *Otiyot deRabbi Akiva*, version A, chap. 1)

Falsehood

One must be resolute in refraining from falsehood in his speech, whether the lie is large or small, explicit or implicit.

Rabbi Elazar said: Anyone who alters the truth in his speech, it is as though he worships idols.

Shmuel said: It is prohibited to deceive people, even to deceive a gentile.

Rabbi Zeira said: A person should not say to a child: I will give you something, and not give it to him, because he thereby teaches the child to lie.

This is the punishment of the liar: Even if he speaks the truth, people do not listen to him.

(*Sanhedrin* 92a; *Ḥullin* 94b; *Sukka* 46b; *Sanhedrin* 89b)

Flatterers and Hypocrites

The Sages are extremely critical of certain forms of lying, flattery and hypocrisy.

King Yannai said to his wife: Do not fear the Pharisees,[27] and those who are not Pharisees.[28] Rather, beware of the hypocrites who appear to be Pharisees,[29] whose actions are like the act of Zimri[30] and yet they request a reward like Pinhas.[31]

Rava said: Any Torah scholar whose interior does not correspond to his exterior[32] is not a true Torah scholar.

---

24. The three letters preceding the final letter in the Hebrew alphabet are *kof, resh,* and *shin,* which, in a different order, spell *sheker.*
25. Like harvesting scattered items, which is much more difficult than harvesting gathered items.
26. This refers to the form of these letters as they are written in a Torah scroll.
27. The sect that accepted the oral rabbinic tradition in interpreting the Torah and the mitzvot.
28. The reference is to the Saduccees, the sect that did not accept the oral rabbinic tradition.
29. People who put on a façade of righteousness while sinning in private.
30. Zimri publicly engaged in sexual relations with a Midyanite princess.
31. Pinhas was zealous on behalf of the Lord and executed Zimri.
32. The reference is to a Torah scholar who is a hypocrite.

Sages on Life

Rabbi Elazar says: As for any person who has the trait of flattery, even fetuses in their mothers' wombs curse him…. Rabbi Elazar says: Any person who has the trait of flattery falls into Gehenna…. Rabbi Elazar says: Anyone who flatters another ultimately falls into his hands; if he does not fall into his hands, he falls into his children's hands. And if he does not fall into his children's hands, he falls into his grandchild's hands…. Rabbi Elazar says: Any congregation in which there is flattery will ultimately be exiled…. Rabbi Yirmeya bar Abba says: Four factions will not greet the Divine Presence: the faction of scorners, the faction of flatterers, the faction of liars, and the faction of slanderers.

(*Sota* 22b; *Yoma* 72b; *Sota* 41b–42a)

📖 **Further reading:** For the *halakhot* related to telling the truth, see *A Concise Guide to Halakha*, p. 603.

The Land of Israel

The Land of Israel, the eternal inheritance of the Jewish people, was given to us by God. It is not merely a land belonging to a people, but rather the center and the source of blessing and plenty for the entire world. The chapter that follows presents statements of the Sages regarding the elevated status of the Land of Israel, the special merit of those who live there, and what will transpire there at the end of days.

The Right to the Land

The Land of Israel belongs to the Jewish people, not by force of conquest but as a gift from the Creator of the world, who allocated it to His children.

"He tells the power of His deeds to His people, to give them the portion of nations" (Psalms 111:6). For what reason did the Holy One, blessed be He, reveal to Israel what was created on the first day and what was created on the second day? It is due to the nations of the world, so that they would not upset Israel and say to them: Aren't you a nation of plunderers? Israel can respond to them and say to them: The Land of Israel was first plundered by you,[33] as "Kaftorim, who emerged from Kaftor, destroyed them, and settled in their place" (Deuteronomy 2:23).[34] The world and all that it holds[35] belong to the Holy One, blessed be He;[36] when He wished, He gave the Land of Israel to you, and when He wished, He took it from you and gave it to us. This is the meaning of what is written: "He tells the power of His deeds to His people, to give them the portion of nations": He told them of all the generations.[37]

(*Bereshit Rabba* 1)

---

33. You, too, conquered the Land of Israel from the nations who resided there before you.
34. In the western Negev. Initially the Avim resided there, then the residents of the island of Kaftor conquered it from them and resided there until the Israelites reached that region.
35. See Psalms 24:1.
36. That is why the Torah describes God's creation of the world in such great detail.
37. The sequence of the creation of the world, the descent of the generations, and the peoples who resided in the Land of Israel before the Israelites.

A Cherished Land

The Land of Israel is the spiritual center of the world, and the Sages describe its virtues at length.

The Land of Israel is the might of the world.

Those standing outside the Land of Israel direct their hearts[38] toward the Land of Israel and pray, as it is stated: "And they will pray via their land" (II Chronicles 6:38). Those standing in the Land of Israel direct their hearts toward Jerusalem and pray, as it is stated: "And they pray to You via this city that You have chosen" (II Chronicles 6:34). Those standing in Jerusalem direct their hearts toward the Temple, as it is stated: "And pray toward this House" (II Chronicles 6:32). Those standing in the Temple direct their hearts toward the Holy of Holies[39] and pray, as it is stated: "They will pray toward this place" (I Kings 8:30). Consequently, all Israel pray toward one place.

The Sages taught: The Land of Israel was created first and the rest of the world was created thereafter…the Holy One, blessed be He, waters the Land of Israel Himself, and He waters the rest of the world through an intermediary…. The Land of Israel absorbs rainwater and the rest of the world absorbs from the residue of rainwater left in the clouds…. The Land of Israel absorbs first, and the rest of the world thereafter.

Ten measures of wisdom descended to the world; the Land of Israel took nine and the rest of the world took one. Ten measures of beauty descended to the world; Jerusalem took nine and the rest of the world took one.

The air of the Land of Israel makes one wise.

This can be explained by means of a parable of a king who had concubines and many sons from them. He also had a son from a certain noblewoman, and he was inordinately fond of that son. The king gave fields and vineyards to all the sons of the concubines, and then he gave his favorite son a specific orchard from which the king's entire stock was produced. The son sent a message and said to his father: You gave the sons of the concubines fields and vineyards, but you gave me only one orchard. His father said to him: I take an oath by your life! My entire stock is produced from this orchard, and because I am fonder of you than of all your brothers, that is why I gave it to you. Likewise…the Holy One, blessed be He, distributed fields and vineyards to the other nations of the world…and to Israel He gave the

---

38. They should direct their faces and their hearts toward the Land of Israel.
39. The inner sanctum at the western edge of the Sanctuary.

Land of Israel, which is the source of God's stock: Offerings are from it, the showbread is from it, the first fruits are from it;[40] all the goodness in the world is from it.

There is no Torah like the Torah of the Land of Israel, and no wisdom like the wisdom of the Land of Israel.

The Holy One, blessed be He, said: The elders of the exile are beloved to Me, but a small faction of Torah scholars in the Land of Israel is more beloved to Me than the Great Sanhedrin when it is outside the Land of Israel.

(*Sifrei Devarim, Va'ethanan* 4; *Tosefta Berakhot* 3:15–16; *Ta'anit* 10a; *Kiddushin* 49b; *Bava Batra* 158b; *Tanḥuma, Kedoshim*; *Bereshit Rabba* 16; Jerusalem Talmud, *Nedarim* 6:8)

The Merit of Those Who Live in the Land

It is a great merit to live in the Land of Israel, and likewise it is praiseworthy to traverse the land and build it.

Rabbi Meir would say: Concerning anyone who dwells in the Land of Israel, the Land of Israel atones for him, as it is stated: "The people who live in it are forgiven iniquity" (Isaiah 33:24) … and likewise, Rabbi Meir would say: Concerning anyone who resides in the Land of Israel and recites *Shema* in the morning and evening, and speaks in the holy tongue of Hebrew, he is destined for the World to Come.

Anyone who resides in the Land of Israel dwells without transgression, as it is stated: "The people who live in it are forgiven iniquity" (Isaiah 33:24).

"I am the Lord your God, who brought you out from the land of Egypt, to give you the land of Canaan, to be your God" (Leviticus 25:38). From here[41] the Sages said: Any Jew who resides in the Land of Israel thereby accepts upon himself the kingdom of Heaven, and concerning whoever leaves for a country outside the Land of Israel, it is as though he worships idols.

Rabbi Yohanan says: Why did Omri king of Israel merit to assume the monarchy? He added one city[42] in the Land of Israel.

---

40. All offerings brought from produce, the showbread, and the first fruits must be from produce grown in the Land of Israel.
41. Based on the juxtaposition in the verse between the Lord bringing us to the land and His being our God.
42. He built the city of Samaria.

Rabbi Hiyya bar Abba says: One who walks four cubits[43] in the Land of Israel is assured of a place in the World to Come.

(Sifrei Devarim, Ha'azinu 28; Ketubot 111a; Sifra, Behar 5; Sanhedrin 102b; Yalkut Shimoni 2:366)

The Land of Israel in the Messianic Era

In the days of the messiah, the Land of Israel will become the permanent residence for the people of Israel. Indeed, it will expand and become a center that will attract the entire world.

Rabbi Elazar HaKappar says: The synagogues and the study halls in Babylonia are destined to be transported and reestablished in the Land of Israel.

The Holy One, blessed be He, said: In this world, everyone longed for the Land of Israel, but due to your sins you were exiled from it. But in the messianic era, when you will have no sins or transgressions, I will plant you within it in a tranquil manner. From where is this derived? As it is stated: "I will plant them on their land, and they will not be uprooted from their land that I gave them" (Amos 9:15).

It is written: "It shall be that on each and every New Moon and on each and every Sabbath all flesh will come to prostrate themselves before Me, said the Lord" (Isaiah 66:23). But how is it possible that all flesh would come to Jerusalem on every Sabbath and on the first of every month?[44] Rabbi Levi says: Jerusalem is destined to be like the Land of Israel,[45] and the Land of Israel like the entire world. But still, how can people come on the first of the month and on the Sabbath from the ends of the earth? Rather, clouds will come and carry them and bring them to Jerusalem, and they will pray there in the morning. And this is why the prophet praises them in these terms: "Who are these who fly like a cloud?" (Isaiah 60:8).

(Megilla 29a; Devarim Rabba 3; Yalkut Shimoni 2:503)

Further reading: For more about the spiritual centrality of the Land of Israel, see *A Concise Guide to Mahshava*, p. 132.

---

43. A distance roughly equivalent to 2 m.
44. How will there be space in Jerusalem for all mankind?
45. Jerusalem will expand to the size of the present-day Land of Israel.

The Coming of the Messiah

The belief in the ultimate coming of the messiah is one of the fundamental principles of Jewish faith. His arrival will usher in the redemption of the world and achieve the purpose of its creation. The Sages describe this period and its significance as an era of material and spiritual prosperity. In this section they address the importance of belief in and anticipation of the coming of the redeemer, the events that will precede the redemption, the process of redemption, the identity of the messiah, and the end of days.

Belief in the Coming of the Messiah

Awaiting redemption is one of the most basic tenets of Judaism, and it is thanks to this very anticipation that the people of Israel will merit redemption.

When they bring a person in to heavenly judgment after his death, they say to him: Did you conduct business faithfully and equitably? Did you designate fixed times for Torah study? Did you engage in procreation? Did you await salvation?[46]

Even if Israel has in its favor only the anticipation for redemption, they are worthy of redemption in reward for that anticipation.

(*Shabbat* 31a; *Yalkut Shimoni* 2:736)

The Approach of the Messiah

The Sages describe the time just preceding the arrival of the messiah as a tumultuous period, as the redemption will sprout from the spiritual low point that will characterize that era.

In the times of the approach of the messiah, impudence will increase and the cost of living will increase. The vine will produce its fruit, but wine will be expensive.[47] The monarchy will turn to heresy, and there will be no one wor-

Sages on Life

---

46. The reference is to the coming of the messiah.
47. Despite the increase in supply, the demand will increase even more due to excessive drinking of wine.

thy of giving reproof. The meeting place of the Sages will become a place of promiscuity, the Galilee shall be destroyed, the Golan will become desolate, and the men of the border[48] will go around from city to city to seek charity but they will find no mercy. The wisdom of scribes will putrefy, people who fear sin will be held in disgust, and the truth will be absent. Youth will shame elders; elders will stand before minors. "The daughter rises[49] against her mother, the daughter-in-law against her mother-in-law; the members of his household are a man's enemies" (Micah 7:6).[50] The face of the generation will be like the face of a dog;[51] a son will not be ashamed before his father. And on what is there for us to rely? On our Father in Heaven.

The messiah son of David will not come until informers proliferate; alternatively, until the students [Torah scholars] decrease; alternatively, until the *peruta*[52] will cease from the purse; alternatively, until the Jewish people despair of the redemption[53] … as though there were no supporter or helper for the Jewish people….

Rabbi Hama bar Hanina says: The son of David will not come until the arrogant cease from among the Jewish people…. Rabbi Simlai says in the name of Rabbi Elazar son of Rabbi Shimon: The son of David will not come until all the worthy judges and officers cease from among the Jewish people…. Rabbi Yohanan says: If you see a generation whose troubles inundate it like the flow of a mighty river, await the coming of the messiah…

If you see kingdoms clashing with one another, anticipate the approaching steps of the messiah.

(Sota 49b; Sanhedrin 97a; Sanhedrin 98a; Bereshit Rabba 42)

Further reading: For more on the coming of the messiah, see *A Concise Guide to Mahshava*, p. 145.

Hastening the Redemption

The Sages note that there are certain factors that can hasten the redemption and the coming of the messiah.

Great is repentance, as it hastens the redemption.

---

48. The reference is to residents of border towns.
49. The daughter rebels.
50. All family relationships will be dysfunctional.
51. They will feel no shame before one another.
52. A *peruta* is a small coin. Even the smallest coin will be absent from the purse, i.e., no one will have any money.
53. They give up hope that the redeemer will come.

Great is charity, as it hastens the redemption.

The Holy One, blessed be He, said: If Israel performs justice and righteousness, they are immediately redeemed.

The generations will be redeemed only in the merit of the righteous women in that generation.

(*Yoma* 86b; *Bava Batra* 10a; *Shoḥar Tov*, Psalms 119;
Yalkut Shimoni 2:606)

📖 **Further reading:** For more about repentance, see *A Concise Guide to the Torah*, p. 502, *A Concise Guide to Mahshava*, p. 316. For more about charity, see pp. 240, 245, 426, 458; *A Concise Guide to Halakha*, p. 615.

Calculating the End of Days

We do not know the time appointed for the redemption, the end of days. Is it appropriate to attempt to calculate it?

There are three matters that come only by means of diversion of attention[54] from those matters, and they are: The messiah,[55] a lost item, and a scorpion….

May those who calculate the end of days be cursed, as they might say that since the end [of days according to their calculations has] arrived and the messiah did not come, he will no longer come at all….

Rav says: All the ends [of days that were calculated have] passed, and the matter is dependent only on repentance and good deeds.

If a person will tell you when the end of the redemption will come, do not believe him, as it is stated: "For it was a day of vengeance[56] in My heart" (Isaiah 63:4). If the heart does not reveal the time of the redemption to the mouth, to whom can the mouth reveal it?[57]

(*Sanhedrin* 97b; *Yalkut Shimoni* 2:507)

The Time of the Redemption

Although the Sages did not seek to calculate the precise date of the future redemption, they did consider certain times auspicious for the coming of the messiah.

---

54. The person is taken by surprise.
55. People will be unaware of the onset of the end of days.
56. The end of redemption is a day of vengeance against the wicked.
57. The information remains, as it were, in the heart of the Creator, and He does not reveal it to anyone.

It is written [concerning the messiah's arrival, that it will occur]: "In its time" (Isaiah 63:4), and it is also written [in the same verse]: "I will hasten it."[58] If they merit,[59] God will hasten it; if they do not merit, the messiah will come at the designated time.

Six thousand years is the duration of the world. The first two thousand are characterized by emptiness,[60] the next two thousand are characterized by Torah,[61] and the last two thousand are the period appropriate for the coming of the messiah.

Rabbi Eliezer says…the Israelites were redeemed from Egypt in the Hebrew month of Nisan and they are destined to be redeemed with the coming of the messiah in the month of Tishrei. Rabbi Yehoshua says: They were redeemed in Nisan and they are destined to be redeemed in Nisan.

(*Sanhedrin* 97a–b; *Rosh HaShana* 10b)

The Process of Redemption

The Sages discuss the process of the redemption. How will the messiah arrive? Will the redemption be completed in a single moment?

It is written: "I was seeing in night visions, and behold, with the clouds of the heavens, like a person was coming" (Daniel 7:13), and it is written: "Humbly, and riding on a donkey" (Zechariah 9:9).[62] The resolution is: If the Jewish people are worthy, the messiah will come miraculously, "with the clouds of the heavens." If they are not worthy, the messiah will come "humbly, and riding on a donkey."

Rabbi Hiyya the Great and Rabbi Shimon ben Halafta were walking in the Arbel valley at dawn, and they saw the early morning light emerging. Rabbi Hiyya the Great said to Rabbi Shimon ben Halafta: Honorable rabbi! So is the redemption of Israel: At first little by little, but as it continues, it keeps increasing.

(*Sanhedrin* 98a; Jerusalem Talmud, *Berakhot* 1:1)

Further reading: For more about destruction as a part of the redemption process, see p. 327.

---

58. There is an apparent contradiction between the two parts of the verse.
59. i.e., if they conduct themselves properly.
60. This was the state of the world before the Torah was given.
61. The Torah was given at the start of the third millennium.
62. There is an apparent contradiction between these two descriptions of the coming of the messiah.

The Messiah

The Sages address the identity of the messiah. From where will he arrive? What will be his name? Likewise, they portray his exalted status.

Rabbi Yehoshua ben Levi found Elijah the prophet standing at the entrance to the burial cave of Rabbi Shimon ben Yohai.... Rabbi Yehoshua ben Levi asked Elijah: When will the messiah come? Elijah said to him: Go and ask him. Rabbi Yehoshua ben Levi asked: Where is he sitting? Elijah answered: At the entrance to the city of Rome. Rabbi Yehoshua ben Levi asked: And what is his identifying sign? Elijah answered: He is sitting among the poor who are suffering from illnesses. All of them untie all their bandages at once and then retie them, but the messiah unties one bandage and reties it, and only then another one. The reason is that the messiah says [to himself]: Perhaps I will be needed [to bring the redemption. Therefore, I will never untie more than one bandage, so] that I will not be delayed.

Rabbi Yehoshua ben Levi went to the messiah and said to him: *Shalom* to you, my rabbi and my teacher. The messiah replied: *Shalom* to you, ben Levi. Rabbi Yehoshua ben Levi asked him: When will the master come? The messiah answered: Today.

Rabbi Yehoshua ben Levi later came to Elijah, who said to him: What did the messiah say to you? He told Elijah that the messiah had said: *Shalom* to you, ben Levi. Elijah said to him: He thereby guaranteed that you and your father will enter the World to Come.[63] Rabbi Yehoshua ben Levi said to Elijah: The messiah lied to me, as he told me that he will come "today," but he did not come. Elijah said to him: This is what he told you: "Even today, would you only heed His voice" (Psalms 95:7).[64]

What is the messiah's name? The school of Rabbi Sheila says: Shilo[65] is his name, as it is stated: "Until Shilo arrives [and to him, nations shall assemble]" (Genesis 49:10). The school of Rabbi Yannai says: Yinon is his name, as it is stated: "May his name endure forever. May his name be praised [*yinon*] as long as the sun shines" (Psalms 72:17). The school of Rabbi Hanina says: Hanina is his name, as it is stated: "As I will not grant you clemency [*hanina*]" (Jeremiah 16:13). And some say that Menahem ben Hizkiyya is

---

63. By virtue of the fact that the messiah mentioned Rabbi Yehoshua's father's name and greeted Rabbi Yehoshua with *shalom*.

64. The messiah did not say he would come today; he alluded to the verse. If you heed God's voice, he will come immediately.

65. Each school ascribed to the messiah a name similar, or identical, to the name of the head of that school.

his name, as it is stated: "For a comforter [*menahem*], restorer of my soul, has grown distant from me" (Lamentations 1:16). And the Rabbis say that the leper of the house of Rabbi Yehuda HaNasi is his name, as it is stated: "Indeed, he bore our illnesses and carried our pains, and we regarded him as plagued, struck by God and afflicted" (Isaiah 53:4).

Rav Nahman says: If the messiah is one who is among the living in this generation, he is a person such as me…. Rav says: If the messiah is among the living in this generation, he is a person such as our saintly Rabbi Yehuda HaNasi. If he is among the dead,[66] he is a person such as Daniel, the beloved man.[67]

"Behold, My servant will succeed; he will be elevated and raised and will become very lofty" (Isaiah 52:13).[68] This is the anointed king [the messiah]…who will be more "elevated" than Abraham…and "raised" higher than Moses, and loftier than the ministering angels.

In the case of a king of flesh and blood, no one else wears his crown, and yet the Holy One, blessed be He, will in the future place His crown on the anointed king.

The Torah that a person studies in this world[69] is relatively insignificant in comparison to the Torah that the messiah will teach.

(*Sanhedrin* 98a–b; *Yalkut Shimoni* 2:476; *Shemot Rabba* 8; *Kohelet Rabba* 11)

Further reading: For more about the identity of the messiah, see *A Concise Guide to Mahshava*, p. 149.

The Messianic Period

The messianic period is described by the prophets. The Sages richly embellish and elaborate on that description on the basis of traditions they received. They portray, at times using metaphor, the messianic era as a period of miraculous abundance and prosperity in all areas of life: health, fertility, agriculture, and more, accompanied by a spiritual renaissance and eternal life.

The Holy One, blessed be He, is destined to transform the fast of *Tisha Be'Av* into gladness and joy, and a happy festival, and He Himself will rebuild Jeru-

66. People who lived in the past.
67. The reference is to the subject of the biblical book of Daniel.
68. The verse enumerates the virtues of the messiah.
69. The Torah studied in the time of the exile.

salem and gather the exiles, as it is stated: "The Lord is the builder of Jerusalem; He gathers in the dispersed of Israel" (Psalms 147:2).

Avimi son of Rabbi Abbahu taught: The messianic era will last seven thousand years for the Jewish people….

Rav Yehuda says that Shmuel says: The duration of the messianic era is like the duration of the period from the day the world was created until now….

Rav Nahman bar Yitzhak says: Its duration is like from the days of Noah until now.

A woman is destined to give birth every day….[70]

Trees are destined to produce fruits every day….

The Land of Israel is destined to produce baked goods and silk garments that grow from the ground.

Wheat is destined to grow as tall as a palm tree and ascend to the mountaintops. Lest you say that if so there will be great exertion for its reaper… the Holy One, blessed be He, will bring wind from His storehouse and cause it to blow on the wheat, and this will detach the wheat kernels for the flour from the stalks, and a person will go out to the field and bring back a palmful of kernels, from which his sustenance and the sustenance of the members of his household will be provided….

Each wheat kernel is destined to be as large as the two kidneys of a large ox….

The World to Come is not like this world. In this world, harvesting and pressing grapes involves great exertion. But in the World to Come, a person will bring one grape in a wagon or on a boat[71] and place it in a corner of his house, and supply from it enough wine to fill a large barrel; and with the wood of its vine he will kindle a fire under a cooked dish. You will not have even one grape that does not contain enough liquid to fill thirty *gerev*[72] of wine.

The synagogues and the study halls in the Diaspora are destined to be transported and reestablished in the Land of Israel.

The Holy One, blessed be He, said: In this world, few people prophesied, but in the World to Come, all of Israel will become prophets.

In the messianic era, all the sick people will be healed.

_____

70. She will give birth on the day she conceives.

71. Due to the large size of each grape.

72. A liquid measure; each *gerev* measures approximately 8 L.

Sages on Life

In this world, one's lifespan is shortened due to the evil inclination, but in the messianic era: "He will eliminate death forever" (Isaiah 25:8).[73]

Rabbi Hanina says: In the messianic era, death will exist only among the gentiles. Rabbi Yehoshua ben Levi says: Death will not exist among Jews nor among gentiles, as it is stated: "He will eliminate death forever and the Lord God will wipe tears from all faces" (Isaiah 25:8).[74]

Just as new moons are sanctified and renewed[75] in this world, so will Israel be sanctified and renewed in the future.

Jerusalem is destined to be a metropolis[76] for all lands.

(*Yalkut Shimoni* 2:1043; *Sanhedrin* 99a; *Shabbat* 30b; *Ketubot* 111b; *Megilla* 29a; *Tanḥuma, Behaalotekha*; *Bereshit Rabba* 30; *Tanḥuma, Yitro*; *Bereshit Rabba* 26; *Pirkei DeRabbi Eliezer* 51; *Shemot Rabba* 23)

📖 **Further reading:** For more on miracles and wonders, see *A Concise Guide to Mahshava*, p. 213. For more about the new moon as a symbol of renewal, see *A Concise Guide to Mahshava*, p. 41.

---

73. People will live eternal life.
74. "All faces," including the gentiles, will live forever.
75. With the renewal of the moon, the first day of the new month is sanctified.
76. It will be a significant capital city.

Health and Illness

Maintaining health is a mitzva, and accordingly the Sages address health, illness, and medicine from various perspectives, ranging from recommendations for a healthy way of life and advice on remedies, to a discussion on whether gravely ill patients are obligated to observe certain mitzvot. The chapter that follows presents statements of the Sages regarding the treatment of patients, the causes of disease and the remedy provided by Torah study, illness as means to forgiveness for sins, doctors, and the significant mitzva incumbent on the healthy: Visiting the sick.

Healing the Ill

Typically, prohibitions are suspended in order to heal the ill. Only in rare circumstances does one leave a sick person in danger due to a prohibition that would be violated by his treatment. Even the fast of Yom Kippur is overridden if it would endanger a patient.

Abaye and Rava both said: Anything that contains an element of healing is not prohibited due to the ways of the Emorite.[77]

When Ravin came from the Land of Israel to Babylonia, he said that Rabbi Yohanan said: One may heal himself with any item[78] except for those prohibited due to idolatry, forbidden sexual relations, and bloodshed.

[On Yom Kippur], a sick person is fed in accordance with the advice of medical experts.[79] If there are no experts there, one feeds him according to his own assessment, until he says that he has eaten enough.

Rabbi Yannai said: If a sick person says he needs to eat and a doctor says he does not need to eat, one heeds the sick person. What is the reason? "The heart knows its own bitterness" (Proverbs 14:10).[80] If a doctor says that the sick person needs to eat but the sick person says he does not need to

---

77. Since there are measurable medical benefits to such a practice, it is not included in the prohibition against adopting the superstitious practices of gentiles.
78. Even with items from which it is prohibited to derive benefit.
79. On Yom Kippur, one feeds the sick person based on a medical expert who determines that fasting will endanger him.
80. The patient himself knows the severity of his pain, and the doctor cannot dismiss his suffering.

eat, one heeds the doctor. What is the reason? It is because confusion may have overcome the sick person [impairing his judgment].

In the case of one who is afflicted with overwhelming, ravenous hunger,[81] one may feed him even forbidden foods until his eyes recover.[82]

(*Shabbat* 67a; *Pesaḥim* 25a–b; *Yoma* 82a, 83a; Mishna *Yoma* 8:6)

📖 **Further reading:** For more regarding the laws of relating to the ill on Yom Kippur, see *A Concise Guide to Halakha*, p. 165.

Causes of Disease

Sometimes a person's death is caused by disease, but generally it is cold, heat, or negligence that causes death. On occasion, the causes of an illness may be spiritual.

Rabbi Ḥanina, because he lived in Tzipori,[83] where it is cold, would say: Ninety-nine people out of a hundred die from excessive cold, and only one dies at the hands of heaven. Rabbi Shmuel bar Naḥman said in the name of Rabbi Yonatan: Ninety-nine die from excessive heat, and one dies at the hands of heaven. And the Rabbis say: Ninety-nine die from their own negligence, and one dies at the hands of heaven.

Rabbi Hunya Yaakov from Ofratim said in the name of Rabbi Yehuda HaNasi: When the verse states: "The Lord will remove from you all illness" (Deuteronomy 7:15), this is referring to fever. Rabbi Huna said, and some teach this in the name of Rabbi Elazar ben Yaakov: When the verse states: "The Lord will remove from you all illness," this is referring to troubling thoughts … Rabbi Avun says: When the verse states: "The Lord will remove from you all illness," this is referring to the evil inclination, whose beginning is sweet but its end is bitter.[84]

(Jerusalem Talmud, *Shabbat* 14:3)

Torah Study

Engaging in Torah study is a remedy. It is both a preventive remedy and a treatment and cure for maladies.

Rabbi Shimon ben Lakish said: Concerning one who engages in Torah study, afflictions distance themselves from him.

---

81. A condition that could lead to loss of consciousness and blindness.
82. Until he regains his consciousness and vision.
83. Tzipori is a city in northern Israel.
84. Initially one experiences pleasure, but ultimately he bears the consequences.

One who feels pain in his head should engage in Torah study, as it is stated concerning the Torah: "For they will be a graceful adornment for your head" (Proverbs 1:9). One who feels pain in his throat should engage in Torah study, as it is stated: "And necklaces for your neck" (Proverbs 1:9). One who feels pain in his intestines should engage in Torah study, as it is stated: "It will be healing for your navel" (Proverbs 3:8). One who feels pain in his bones should engage in Torah study, as it is stated: "And an elixir for your bones" (Proverbs 3:8). One who feels pain in his entire body should engage in Torah study, as it is stated: "And healing for all his flesh" (Proverbs 4:22).

Rav Yehuda son of Rabbi Hiyya said: Come and see that the ways of flesh and blood are not like the ways of the Holy One, blessed be He. The way of flesh and blood is that when a person gives a potion to another, it is good for this ailment but it is harmful for that other ailment. But the way of the Holy One, Blessed be He, is not so. He gave the Torah to the Jewish people, and it is a potion of life for one's entire body, as it is stated: "And healing for all his flesh."

(Berakhot 5a; Eiruvin 54a)

Merits and Forgiveness for Sins

Sometimes a person is afflicted with illness to inspire him to repent. The merit he has accrued during his life protects him during his illness. If a sick person recovers from his illness and is cured, it is a clear sign that his sins have been forgiven.

Rav Yitzhak son of Rav Yehuda said: A person should always pray that he will not become ill, for if he becomes ill they say to him in Heaven: First bring proof of your merit,[85] then be rid of your illness.

Rabbi Alexandri said that Rabbi Hiyya bar Abba said: A sick person recovers from his illness only when God forgives him for all his sins, as it is stated: "It is He who forgives all your sins, who heals all your diseases" (Psalms 103:3).

"You change his bedding during his illness" (Psalms 41:4).[86] Rav Yosef said: This is to say that illness causes his studies to be forgotten.

---

85. Bring proof of the good deeds that you have to your credit.
86. The verse literally means that being bedridden causes all his knowledge to be overturned and confused.

Rabbi Levi said: As the parable says: A gate that is not open for mitzvot will ultimately be open for the doctor.[87]

"For I am lovesick" (Song of Songs 2:5). The congregation of Israel said before the Holy One, blessed be He: Master of the Universe, all the illnesses that You bring upon me are in order to cause me to love You.[88]

(*Shabbat* 31b; *Nedarim* 41a; *Shir HaShirim Rabba* 6; *Shir HaShirim Rabba* 2)

The Doctor

A sick person is obligated to try to be cured. Therefore, one must not live in a place where there is no doctor, and likewise one must hire a skilled doctor, regardless of the cost.

"And he shall provide healing" (Exodus 21:19). It is derived from here that permission is granted to a doctor to heal.[89]

A Torah scholar is not permitted to reside in any city that does not have these ten features: …a doctor.

A doctor who heals for nothing is worth nothing…a distant doctor will cause the eye to go blind.[90]

Rabbi Elazar ben Pedat said: As the parable says: Honor your doctor before you need him.[91]

The best of doctors is destined for Gehenna.[92]

(*Bava Kamma* 85a; *Sanhedrin* 17b; *Shemot Rabba* 21; Mishna *Kiddushin* 4:14)

Visiting the Sick

Visiting the sick is a great mitzva, and there is no limit to or measure for this obligation. Even God Himself treats the sick and visits them.

The Sages taught: The mitzva of visiting the sick has no measure. What is the meaning of "has no measure"? Rav Yosef thought to say: There is no fixed

---

87. Failure to observe mitzvot undermines one's immunity from illness.
88. They will cause me to repent and to deepen my love of God.
89. We do not say that healing a sick person is countering the will of God.
90. Once he receives payment, he will no longer care about his patient. A local doctor will provide treatment until he is sure that his patient has recovered.
91. Honor him so that if the need arises, he will provide you with the proper treatment.
92. The punishment of a doctor who believes that he is superior to others and does not conduct a thorough examination is severe.

measure for the granting of its reward. Abaye said to him: And do all other mitzvot have a fixed measure for the granting of their reward? Didn't we learn: Be as meticulous in observance of a minor mitzva as in a major one, as you do not know the granting of reward for mitzvot? Abaye said a different explanation: Even a prominent person should pay a visit to a lowly person.[93] Rava said: Even one hundred times a day is appropriate.[94]

Rav Aha bar Hanina said: Anyone who visits a sick person removes from him one-sixtieth of his suffering. The Sages said to him: If so, let sixty people enter to visit him, and thereby restore him to full health. Rav Aha bar Hanina said to them: It is like the tenths of the school of Rabbi Yehuda Ha-Nasi.[95] [Furthermore, visiting is effective in easing the suffering only when the visitor is] the same age [as the sick person].

Ravin said that Rav said: From where is it derived that the Holy One, blessed be He, feeds a sick person? As it is stated: "The Lord will support him on his sickbed" (Psalms 41:4). And Ravin said that Rav said: From where is it derived that the Divine Presence is resting above the bed of a sick person? As it is stated: "The Lord will support him on his sickbed."

This is also taught [in a *baraita*]: One who enters to visit a sick person may sit neither on the bed nor on a bench nor on a chair. Rather, he [deferentially] wraps himself in his prayer shawl and sits on the ground, because the Divine Presence rests above the bed of a sick person, as it is stated: "The Lord will support him on his sickbed."[96]

What is the difference between one who is dangerously ill and one who is merely ill? One who is ill suffers from a standard illness [which follows a slow pattern of development], whereas for one who is dangerously ill, the acute illness comes upon him suddenly. In the case of one suffering from a standard illness, those close to him enter to visit him immediately and those who are distant come after three days, whereas if the illness comes upon him suddenly, both these and those enter to visit him immediately.[97]

(Nedarim 39b, 40a; Jerusalem Talmud, Gittin 6:5)

Further reading: For more about the mitzva of visiting the sick, see *A Concise Guide to Halakha*, p. 606.

---

93. The statement "there is no measure" relates to a difference in social standing.
94. There is no measure to the number of times one should visit a sick person.
95. In other words, each visitor removes one-sixtieth of what remains after the previous visitor has left. Therefore, some of the illness will always remain (see *Ketubot* 68a).
96. This is interpreted literally; God is on his sickbed.
97. This is due to the concern that his end is near.

Parenthood

People, by their very nature, desire to have children, and when they are born, children are more important to their parents than anything else. A parent's love for his children is immense, as is the responsibility for their safety, well-being, and education. The chapter that follows presents statements of the Sages regarding parents' love for their children, the mitzva of education, obligations incumbent on the parents, and what they must refrain from doing.

Parents' Love for Their Children

There is no love greater than the love of parents for their children.

There was an incident involving a man who made a will and said: My son will not inherit from me until he becomes a fool. Rabbi Yosei son of Rabbi Yehuda went to Rabbi Yehoshua ben Kor a to inquire about this incident.[98] They peered from the outside and they saw Rabbi Yehoshua ben Korha stamping on his hands and feet, with a rope of reed grass in his mouth, and he was following his son and playing with him. When they saw him, they hid themselves. When they entered his house and asked him about that incident, he began laughing and said to them: I take an oath by your lives, this incident about which you asked me just happened to me [as I just now acted like a fool]. They said to him: From here one can learn that when a person sees his children and interacts with them, it is as though he becomes a fool.[99]

(*Yalkut Shimoni* 2:846)

Educating One's Children

Parents must train their children to fulfill the mitzvot and to study Torah from a young age. If they fail to develop good habits in their youth, it will be very hard to teach them later.

The Sages taught: A minor who knows how to wave the *lulav* on *Sukkot* is obligated in the mitzva of *lulav*; a young boy who knows how to wrap himself in a garment is obligated in the mitzva of ritual fringes; if he knows to

---

98. What is the meaning of that stipulation, and is there any way to execute that will?
99. The man meant that his son will inherit from him only when his son fathers a child, as then, he too will act like a fool with his small child.

preserve the sanctity of *tefillin* [in a state of bodily cleanliness],[100] his father buys him *tefillin*; when he knows how to speak, his father teaches him Torah and *Shema*. What is the Torah that his father teaches him first? Rav Hamnuna said: "Moses commanded us the Torah, a heritage of the assembly of Jacob" (Deuteronomy 33:4). And what is the *Shema* that his father teaches him? The first verse of *Shema*.[101]

"Educate the lad in accordance with his way" (Proverbs 22:6). Rabbi Eliezer and Rabbi Yehoshua each interpreted this verse. Rabbi Eliezer said: If you educate your son in matters of Torah while he is a lad, he will mature with them as his guide, as it is stated: "Even when he grows old, he will not turn from it" (Proverbs 22:6). And Rabbi Yehoshua said: It is like an ox that did not learn to plow, and therefore it ultimately finds plowing difficult; or like a vine branch, which if you do not bend it when it is moist, you will not succeed in bending it when it is rigid.

(Sukka 42a; *Midrash Mishlei* [Buber] 22)

Raising Children and Ensuring Their Well-Being

Parents must raise their children and see to all their needs, a task that is at times far from easy.

It is written: "To the woman He said: I will increase your suffering and your pregnancy; in pain you shall give birth to children" (Genesis 3:16)[102] ... "your suffering"; this is a reference to the pain of raising children.

A father is obligated with regard to his son to circumcise him, to redeem him,[103] to teach him Torah, to marry him to a woman, and to teach him a trade. Some say: To teach him to swim, as well. Rabbi Yehuda says: Any father who does not teach his son a trade effectively teaches him banditry.[104]

(Eiruvin 100b; *Kiddushin* 29a)

Preferential Treatment Is Prohibited

Showing preference to one child over the others is deplorable and is apt to lead to negative consequences.

---

100. So he will not defile the *tefillin*.
101. "Hear, Israel: The Lord is our God, the Lord is one" (Deuteronomy 6:4).
102. This is Eve's punishment for eating from the Tree of Knowledge.
103. If he is a firstborn, his father redeems him when he is thirty days old.
104. If he does not have a profession, he will be forced to support himself in this manner.

A person should never distinguish one of his children from among the other children [with preferential treatment], as due to the extra two-*sela* weight[105] of the tunic of fine wool that Jacob gave to Joseph above that which he gave to the rest of his sons, Joseph's brothers became jealous of him, and the episode unfolded and our forefathers descended to Egypt.[106]

With regard to one who wrote a document bequeathing his property to others and left his sons with nothing, what he did is done and the transaction is valid, but the Sages are not pleased with him.

(*Shabbat* 10b; *Bava Batra* 133b)

📖 Further reading: For more on parenting and education, see *A Concise Guide to Mahshava*, p. 186.

---

105. This is a relatively small weight.
106. This led to Jacob and all his sons moving to Egypt, which ultimately led to the enslavement of the children of Israel there.

Pregnancy and Childbirth

Pregnancy and childbirth are among the wonders of creation. It is a period accompanied by great joy and anticipation on the one hand, but physical difficulties on the other. The Sages addressed this topic from several perspectives. The chapter that follows presents statements of the Sages regarding the divine partnership in creating the fetus, what the fetus experiences in the womb, and the difficulties of pregnancy and childbirth.

Partnership

A child is the product of a partnership between God and his parents.

There are three partners in the creation of a person: the Holy One, blessed be He; his father; and his mother.

(*Nidda* 31a)

The Fetus in the Womb

While a fetus is in its mother's womb, all its needs are cared for, and it even learns the entire Torah. Its stay there is so pleasant that it is forced to leave against its will, but not before the fetus is made to take an oath that it will follow the upright path in the world.

Rabbi Hanina bar Pappa taught: The angel appointed over conception is called: Night. And this angel takes a drop of semen and presents it before the Holy One, blessed be He, and says before Him: Master of the Universe, what will become of this drop? [Will it produce one who is] mighty or weak, clever or stupid, wealthy or poor? But the angel does not say: Will the person be wicked or righteous?[107]

Rabbi Simlai taught: To what can a fetus in its mother's womb be compared? It can be compared to a ledger that is folded and arranged: Its hands on its two temples, its two elbows on its two shanks, its two heels on its two buttocks. Its head is placed between its knees, its mouth is closed, and

---

107. Because that is dependent on the person himself.

its umbilicus is open. It eats from what its mother eats, and it drinks from what its mother drinks, and it does not expel excrement lest it kill its mother. Once it emerges into the atmosphere of the world, the closed [its anus] opens, and the open [its umbilicus] closes, as otherwise it could not live for even one hour.

A lamp is kindled for it above the fetus's head [in the womb], and it gazes from one end of the world to the other. The angels teach the fetus the entire Torah…but when it emerges into the atmosphere of the world, an angel comes and slaps it on the mouth, and causes it to forget the entire Torah….

The fetus does not emerge from the womb until angels administer an oath to it…and what is the oath that they administer to the fetus? Be righteous and do not be wicked; and even if the entire world says to you: You are righteous, consider yourself wicked.[108] Know that the Holy One, blessed be He, is pure, and His ministers are pure, and the soul that He placed within you is pure. If you preserve it in purity, good; but if not, I will take it from you….

The Sages taught: During the first three months of pregnancy, the fetus resides in the lower compartment[109] of the womb; in the middle three months, the fetus resides in the middle compartment; and during the last three months, the fetus resides in the upper compartment. Once its time to emerge arrives, it overturns and emerges.

The Holy One, blessed be He, says to the spirit of man: Enter into this drop of semen…the spirit begins to speak and says before God: I am satisfied with the world where I have resided from the day You created me. Why do You wish to insert me into this putrid drop, as I am holy and pure, and I am cut from the cloth of Your glory?

Immediately, the Holy One, blessed be He, says to the spirit: The world into which I am introducing you is better for you than that in which you reside. From the moment I created you, I created you only for this drop. Immediately, the Holy One, blessed be He, places the spirit there against its will, and then the angel returns and places the spirit into its mother's womb.

They prepare two angels for the spirit, and they guard it so that it will not emerge from there and it will not be miscarried…and one angel takes it and leads it to the Garden of Eden and shows it the righteous sitting in glory with their crowns on their heads. The angel says to that spirit: Do you know

_____

108. Consider yourself as one who still has much to improve.
109. The part of the womb farthest from the cervix.

who these are? The spirit says to the angel: No, my lord. The angel again says to it: These who you can see were originally created like you within their mother's womb, and they emerged to the world and observed the Torah and mitzvot, which is why they merited and they encountered this goodness that you see....

In the evening, the angel leads the spirit to Gehenna and shows it the wicked there...and that angel further says to that spirit: Do you know who these are? The spirit says: No, my lord. The angel says to it: These who are burning in the fires of Gehenna were created like you, and they emerged to the world but they did not observe the Torah and the statutes of the Holy One, blessed be He, which is why they received the ignominy that you see....

The angel walks with the spirit from morning to evening, and he shows it the place where it is destined to die and the place where it is destined to be buried. He then leads it and walks with it across the entire world and shows it the righteous and the wicked, and shows it everything. In the evening the spirit returns into its mother's womb, and the Holy One, blessed be He, fashions for it there a lock and doors.

Eventually, its time comes to emerge into the world. Immediately, that same angel comes and says to the spirit: At this designated hour, your time to emerge into the world will arrive. The spirit says to the angel: Why do you wish to take me out into the world?... The spirit does not wish to emerge from the womb until the angel strikes it and extinguishes the lamp that is lit above its head, and takes it out into the world against its will. Immediately, upon its emergence from the womb, the baby forgets everything it saw and everything it knows. Why does a baby cry upon its emergence into the world? It is because it has lost a place of respite and well-being; and [it cries in longing for the world] from which it emerged.

(*Nidda* 16b, 30b; *Tanḥuma, Pekudei*)

Further reading: For more about the experiences of the fetus in the course of the pregnancy, see *A Concise Guide to Mahshava*, p. 4.

Labor Pains

Childbirth involves pain. This is an element of the decree issued against Eve after the sin of eating from the Tree of Knowledge. The Sages speak about the emotional process that this experiences entails, and women who merit a painless birth.

The students of Rabbi Shimon ben Yoḥai asked him: For what reason does the Torah say that a woman after childbirth shall bring an offering? He said

to them: At the time that she crouches to give birth, her pain is so great that she impulsively takes an oath that she will not engage in relations with her husband.[110] Therefore, the Torah says: She shall bring an offering.[111]

[The verse states with regard to the mother of Moses]: "The woman conceived and bore a son" (Exodus 2:2).... The verse serves to juxtapose her birthing him to her conceiving him: Just as her conceiving him was painless, so too, her birthing him was painless. From here it is derived that righteous women are not included in the verdict of Eve.[112]

(*Nidda* 31b; *Sota* 12a)

📖 **Further reading:** For more about laws and customs tied to childbirth, see *A Concise Guide to Halakha*, p. 3.

Against Your Will You Are Born

A birth is certainly a happy event, but the joy is mitigated by great responsibility and concern: How will this child act, and what experiences does his future hold?

Against your will you are formed, against your will you are born, against your will you live, against your will you die, and against your will you are destined to give an account and a reckoning before the King, King of all kings, the Holy One, blessed be He.

"A good name is better than fragrant oil; and the day of death than the day of one's birth" (Ecclesiastes 7:1).... When a person is born, they await [in the heavens, to see what will become of] him, until his death,[113] and once he has died, they await [to see what became of] him, until he is granted life.[114] When a person is born, everyone is happy; when he dies, everyone weeps. But it should not be so; rather, when a person is born, one should not be happy for him, as it is unknown what will be his fate and what deeds he will perform: Whether he will be righteous or wicked, good or evil. It is when he dies that they should be happy, as he passed away with a good name.

This can be compared to two ships that set sail on the Mediterranean Sea; one was leaving the port and one was entering the port. For the one leaving the port, everyone was happy, but for the one entering the port, they were not happy. There was a certain perceptive individual there who said

---

110. The pain is so intense that she does not want to become pregnant again.
111. The offering is to atone for the fact that she has no intention of fulfilling her oath.
112. "In pain you shall give birth" (Genesis 3:16).
113. They wait to see how he will live his life and how he will leave this world.
114. i.e., in the World to Come.

to them: I see matters to the contrary: As for the one leaving the port, they should not be happy for it, as no one knows what its fate will be: How many days it will remain at sea and how many storms it will encounter. When it enters the port, everyone should be happy, as it entered in peace.

So, too, when a person dies, everyone should be happy and praise God, as he passed away in peace from the world with a good name. This is the meaning of what Solomon said: "And the day of death than the day of one's birth." You find that when the righteous are born, no person senses [his greatness], but when they die, everyone senses [his greatness].

(Mishna *Avot* 4:22; *Kohelet Rabba* 7)

Further reading: For more about pregnancy and birth with regard to a person's spiritual development, see *A Concise Guide to Mahshava*, p. 4.

Friendship

According to the Sages, the value of a good friend who can provide one with guidance cannot be overestimated. One must make an effort to acquire a good friend. The chapter that follows presents statements of the Sages regarding the ways to acquire a friend, the value of friends, proper and worthy friendship, and the honor that is due a friend.

Acquire a Friend for Yourself

Two are better than one. In mundane matters, in the study of Torah, and in the performance of mitzvot, it is advantageous to have a good friend who can provide assistance when needed.

Rabbi Yohanan said to his outstanding disciples: Go out and see which is the right path to which a person should adhere...Rabbi Yehoshua says: A good friend.[115]

Yehoshua ben Perahya would say: Get yourself a teacher, and acquire a friend for yourself.

And acquire a friend for yourself; how so? This teaches that a person should acquire a friend for himself, and he can eat with him, drink with him, study the written Torah with him, study the Oral Law with him, reside with him, and reveal all his secrets to him – both Torah esoterica and his secret thoughts on worldly matters. For when they sit and engage in Torah together, and one of them errs in understanding a *halakha* or subject matter, or if he says about ritual impurity that it is pure, or about ritual purity that it is impure, his friend can correct him. From where is it derived that when his friend corrects him and studies the written Torah with him they receive a better reward for their efforts? As it is stated: "Two are better than one, because they have a better reward for their toil" (Ecclesiastes 4:9).

If you have friends, some who reprove you and some who praise you, love those who reprove you and hate those who praise you, because those

---

115. This refers either to the acquisition of a good friend or to acting as a good friend to others.

who reprove you will bring you to life in the World to Come,[116] and those who praise you remove you from that world.[117]

"Worry in the heart of a man, he should suppress it [yash'hena]" (Proverbs 12:25). Rabbi Ami and Rabbi Asi disagree. One said: He should remove worry [yesihena] from his mind. And one said: He should tell [yesihena] others his worries.[118]

Either friendship or death.

If you want a beloved friend to cleave to you, you should advocate for him.

(Mishna *Avot* 2:9, 1:6; *Avot deRabbi Natan*, version A, chaps. 8, 29;
Yoma 75a; *Ta'anit* 23a; *Avot deRabbi Natan*, version B, chap. 26)

Further reading: Read the story of Honi HaMe'agel, who, toward the end of his life, suffered from a lack of friendship, p. 354.

True Love

True love is one that is free of any personal interests.

Concerning any love that is dependent on another matter, when the matter ceases to exist, the love ceases. But a love that is not dependent on another matter never ceases. Which is the love that is dependent on another matter? This is the love of Amnon[119] for Tamar. Which is the love that is not dependent on another matter? This is the love between David and Jonathan.

(Mishna *Avot* 5:16)

Honor of One's Friend

A person should honor his friends just as he would like others to honor him, and he should greatly value the good deeds that a friend does on his behalf.

Rabbi Eliezer says: The honor of your friend should be as precious to you as your own, and [as for you,] do not be easy to anger.

The honor of your friend should be as precious to you as your own; how so? This teaches that just as one is concerned with his honor, so too, he should be concerned with the honor of his friend. And just as a person does

---

116. His rebuke will lead you to improve your actions and thereby gain you entry into the World to Come.

117. His praise will cause you to be complacent and refrain from self-examination and repentance, causing you to lose your share in the World to Come.

118. The Hebrew root *yod-sin-het* has more than one meaning.

119. Amnon loved his half-sister Tamar and desired her, until he raped her, and his love for her ceased.

not want a bad reputation compromising his honor, so too, a person should not want a bad reputation compromising the honor of his friend.

If you did slight harm to your friend, it should be considered significant in your eyes. If you did significant good for your friend, it should be considered slight in your eyes. By contrast, if your friend did you a minor favor, it should be considered significant in your eyes. If he did significant harm to you, it should be considered slight in your eyes… and be forgiving of affronts to you.

Renounce your desire in favor of the desire of your friend…but renounce your desire and the desire of your friend in favor of the desire of Heaven.

(Mishna *Avot* 2:10; *Avot deRabbi Natan,* version A, chaps. 15, 41;
Derekh Eretz Zuta 1)

Dreams

Dreams and their meanings have occupied people since the dawn of time. There are various approaches in the statements of the Sages regarding how seriously one should relate to a dream. The chapter that follows presents approaches of the Sages to dreams, suggestions of the meaning of certain dreams, and what to do to avoid the effects of bad and worrisome dreams.

Do Dreams Have Meaning?

There are several opinions found among the Sages when it comes to dreams. Do dreams have meaning? Are they a portent of future events? Or do they have no meaning at all?

A dream is one-sixtieth prophecy.[120]

Rav Hisda said: Let a person have a dream any time, but not during a fast.[121]

And Rav Hisda said: A dream that was not interpreted is like a message that was not read.[122] And Rav Hisda said: Neither is a good dream entirely fulfilled, nor is a bad dream entirely fulfilled. And Rav Hisda said: A bad dream is preferable to a good dream.[123]

And Rav Hisda said: A bad dream, its sadness is enough for him; a good dream, its joy is enough for him….[124]

And Rav Hisda said: A bad dream is worse than lashes….

Rabbi Yohanan said in the name of Rabbi Shimon bar Yohai: Just as it is impossible for grain to grow without straw, so too, it is impossible to dream without some element of insignificant matters. Rabbi Berekhya said: Even if part of a dream is fulfilled, its entirety is not fulfilled….

Shmuel, when he would have a bad dream, would say: "And the dreams speak falsehood" (Zechariah 10:2). When he would have a good dream, he

---

120. This means that it contains an element of prophecy.
121. A dream on a fast is a bad omen.
122. It is the interpretation that determines the effect of a dream.
123. The bad dream causes him pain and leads him to repent.
124. The sadness and the joy are considered fulfillment of the bad and good dreams, respectively.

would say: Do dreams speak falsehood? Isn't it written: "In a dream, I will speak to him" (Numbers 12:6)?[125]

Rabbi Yohanan said that three dreams are fulfilled: a dream in the morning, a dream that another person dreamed about him, and a dream that is interpreted within a dream. And some say a recurring dream as well....

Rabbi Shmuel bar Nahmani said that Rabbi Yonatan said: A person is shown in a dream only from the thoughts of his heart [when he was awake]... Know that this is so, as one is shown in a dream neither a golden palm tree nor an elephant passing through the eye of a needle....

There were twenty-four interpreters of dreams in Jerusalem. One time, I dreamed[126] a dream and went to each of them for an interpretation. What one interpreted for me the other did not interpret for me, yet all of their interpretations were realized in me, to fulfill what is stated: All dreams follow the word of the interpreter.

Matters appearing in dreams have no effect.

Dreams during twilight on the eve of Shabbat have no substantive meaning.

(*Berakhot* 57b, 55a; *Gittin* 52a; *Yoma* 83b)

Improving a Bad Dream

The Sages formulated a prayer to be recited before sleep, in which one requests that he not experience any disturbing or frightening dreams. They also composed a prayer for one who already experienced a troubling dream.

Rav Yehuda said that Rav said: Three matters require God's mercy[127] [to facilitate them]: a good king, a good year, and a good dream....

Ameimar and Mar Zutra and Rav Ashi were sitting together. They said: Let each and every one of us say something that the other has not heard. One of them began, saying: Someone who saw a dream and does not understand what he saw[128] should stand before the priests at the time that they raise their hands for the Priestly Blessing and recite this:

Master of the Universe, I am Yours and my dreams are Yours, I dreamed a dream and I do not understand what it is. Whether I have dreamed about

---

125. God states that He speaks to all prophets except Moses in dreams, indicating that some dreams are prophetic.
126. This is cited in the name of Rabbi Bena'a.
127. One should pray that God provide those three matters.
128. But he is concerned that it might have been a bad dream.

myself, whether my friends have dreamed about me, or whether I have dreamed about others: If they are good, strengthen them and reinforce them like the dreams of Joseph,[129] and if the dreams require healing, heal them like the sweetening of the bitter waters of Mara by Moses our teacher, and like Miriam from her leprosy, and like [King] Hizkiya from his illness,[130] and like the bitter waters of Jericho by [the prophet] Elisha. Just as You transformed the curse of Bilam the wicked into a blessing, so too, transform for me all my dreams for the best.

He concludes his prayer together with the priests, so that the congregation responds amen [both to the blessing of the priests and to his individual request]. If he is not able to recite that entire formula, he should recite this: Majestic One on High, who dwells in might, You are peace and Your name is Peace. May it be Your will that You bestow peace on us.

If a person sees in his dream as though a sword is cutting his thigh, what should he do? He should rise early to go to the synagogue and stand before the priests and listen to the Priestly Blessing, and no evil matter will harm him.

One who goes to sleep on his bed recites from *Shema Yisrael* to *Vehaya im shamoa*.[131] Then he recites [the following formula]: Blessed are You, Lord our God, King of the Universe, who makes the bands of sleep fall on my eyes and slumber on my eyelids, and illuminates the pupil of the eye. May it be Your will, Lord my God, that You have me lie down in peace and give me my portion in Your Torah, and accustom me to mitzvot and do not accustom me to transgression, and do not lead me into error, or into iniquity, or into temptation, or into disgrace. May the good inclination have dominion over me, and may the evil inclination not have dominion over me. Save me from an evil mishap and evil diseases. Let neither bad dreams nor troubling thoughts disturb me. May my bed be flawless before You,[132] and enlighten my eyes lest I sleep to death. Blessed are You, Lord, who gives light to the whole world in His glory.

(*Berakhot* 55a; *Bemidbar Rabba* 11; *Berakhot* 60b)

---

129. Joseph's dreams were realized.
130. Both Miriam and Hizkiya were cured.
131. He recites the verse, "Hear, Israel: The Lord is our God, the Lord is one" (Deuteronomy 6:4), and then the first paragraph of *Shema*.
132. May all my offspring be righteous.

The Meaning of Dreams

Although some Sages are of the opinion that dreams have no substantive meaning, other Sages detailed a long list of examples of dreams and their meaning.

Rabbi Hanina said: One who sees a well in a dream sees peace ... Rabbi Natan said: He has found Torah[133] ... Rava said: The well in the dream symbolizes actual life ....

The Sages taught: One who sees a reed in a dream should expect wisdom ... if he sees many reeds, he should expect understanding ... Rabbi Zeira said: Pumpkin, heart of palm, wax, and reed are all a good omen for [a person when they appear in his] dream ....

The Sages taught: Five matters are stated about dreams involving an ox. One who dreams that he ate from its flesh will become wealthy. One who dreams that it gored him will have sons who are Torah scholars, as they [will metaphorically] gore each other in an attempt to better understand Torah. If he dreamed that the ox bit him, suffering is coming to him. If he dreamed that it kicked him, he will have occasion to travel a great distance. If he dreamed that he was riding it, he will rise to prominence .... One who sees a donkey in a dream should anticipate salvation ....

Concerning one who sees grapes in a dream, if they were white, whether it was in their season or not in their season, it is a good omen. If he sees black grapes, [if it was] in their season, it is a good omen; if it was not in their season, it is a bad omen. Concerning one who sees a white horse in a dream, whether walking or running, it is a good omen for him. If he saw a red horse walking, it is a good omen; if it was running, it is a bad omen.

Concerning one who sees Ishmael in a dream, his prayer will be heard. But this refers specifically to Ishmael son of Abraham, not a random Arab.[134] Concerning one who sees a camel in a dream, it is an omen that death was decreed on him from Heaven but he was spared from it .... Concerning one who sees Pinhas in a dream, a miracle will be performed on his behalf. Concerning one who sees an elephant [pil] in a dream, miracles [pela'ot] will be performed for him. If he sees multiple elephants in a dream, miracles upon miracles will be performed for him ....

Rabbi Hiyya bar Abba said: One who sees wheat in a dream has seen peace ... One who sees barley in a dream has received a sign that his iniquities have been taken away .... Concerning one who sees a vine laden with grapes

---

133. Torah is likened to water.
134. Arabs are called Ishmaelites.

in a dream, his wife will not miscarry…If he sees a planted vine branch, he should anticipate the messiah….

Concerning one who sees a fig tree in a dream, it is an omen that his Torah is preserved within him…. Concerning one who sees pomegranates in a dream, if they were small, his business will flourish like the [numerous] seeds of a pomegranate; if they were large, his business will increase like a pomegranate. In a case where he saw slices of pomegranates, if he is a Torah scholar he should anticipate Torah…and if he is an ignoramus, he should anticipate mitzvot….

Concerning one who sees olives in a dream, if they were small, it is an omen that his business will flourish, increase, and be sustainable like olives. These matters are stated only regarding the fruit of an olive tree, but if he sees olive trees, he will have many children…. Some say that one who sees an olive tree in a dream, a good reputation will spread for him…. One who sees olive oil in a dream should anticipate the light of Torah…. Concerning one who sees palm trees [temarim] in a dream, it is a sign that his transgressions have ceased [tamu]….

Rav Yosef says: Concerning one who sees a goat in a dream, his year will be blessed; if he sees many goats, his years will be blessed…. Concerning one who sees myrtle in a dream, his property will be successful. If he does not own property, it is an omen that he will receive an inheritance from elsewhere. Ulla said, and some say that it was taught in a baraita: This is the case only where he saw the myrtle growing in the ground. Concerning one who sees an etrog in a dream, it is a sign that he is honored [hadur][135] before his Creator…. Concerning one who sees a lulav in a dream, he has but one heart for his Father in Heaven[136]…. One who sees a goose in a dream should anticipate wisdom….

Concerning one who dreams that he entered a large city, his desires will be fulfilled…. Concerning one who shaves his head in a dream, it is a good omen for him; if he shaved his head and his beard, it is a good omen for him and his entire family…. Concerning one who sits in a boat in a dream, if it is a small boat, it is an omen that a good reputation will spread for him; if it is in a large boat, a good reputation will spread for him and his entire family. This applies only if the boat was floating high on the waves….

One who ascends to the roof in a dream will ascend to greatness. If he descended, it is an omen that he will descend from the greatness he

_____

135. The verse refers to an etrog as a peri etz hadar.
136. The word lulav is expounded as a portmanteau of the words lo lev – he has a heart.

Sages on Life

achieved. Abaye and Rava both said: Once one has ascended to the roof in his dream, he has ascended[137] .... Concerning one who lets blood in a dream, it is an omen that his transgressions have been forgiven ....

Concerning one who sees a snake in a dream, it is an omen that his livelihood will be accessible to him. If the snake bit him in his dream, it is an omen that his livelihood will double. If he killed the snake, it is a sign that he will lose his livelihood.

(*Berakhot* 56b)

📖 **Further reading:** For more on dreams and their interpretations, see *A Concise Guide to the Torah*, pp. 92, 101.

_____

137. Once he has ascended, the good portent will remain in effect, even if he descends.

Anger

The Sages consider anger so abhorrent that they liken one who becomes angry to an idol worshipper. When a person is angry he loses his wisdom, and if he is a prophet, his spirit of prophecy abandons him. A person must control his temper and suppress his anger.

A Person's Anger Conveys His Character

One must make an effort not to submit to his anger but to overcome it. To a great extent, this is a test of a person's character.

There are four types of temperaments: Concerning one who is easy to anger and easy to appease, his virtue is overshadowed by his flaw.[138] Concerning one who is difficult to anger and difficult to appease, his flaw is overshadowed by his virtue.[139] One who is difficult to anger and easy to appease is a pious person. One who is easy to anger and difficult to appease is a wicked person.

Rabbi Elai said: In three matters the true character of a person is exemplified: Through his cup [*koso*],[140] his pocket [*kiso*],[141] and his anger [*ka'aso*]. Some say through his laughter as well.

Rabbi Shimon ben Elazar says in the name of Hilfa bar Agra, who said it in the name of Rabbi Yohanan ben Nuri: Concerning one who rends his garments in his anger, or who breaks his vessels in his anger, or who scatters his money in his anger, he should be like an idol worshipper in your eyes, as that is the craft of the evil inclination: Today it tells him do this,[142] and tomorrow it tells him do that, until ultimately it tells him: Worship idols, and he goes and worships idols.

(Mishna *Avot* 5:11; *Eiruvin* 65b; *Shabbat* 105b)

---

138. His admirable quality of being easily appeased is overshadowed by his quick temper.
139. His shortcoming of being difficult to appease is overshadowed by the fact that he is not easily angered.
140. How he acts after drinking.
141. How he acts when he needs to spend money.
142. Violate a minor prohibition.

A Man of Fury Abounds in Transgression

Anger is useless, and one who repeatedly succumbs to his anger brings on himself lack of focus, confusion, and dread.

At the moment one grows angry, even the Divine Presence is not important to him....

Rabbi Yirmeya of Difti said: He forgets his learning and adds foolishness....

Rav Naḥman bar Yitzḥak said: It is clear that his sins are more numerous than his merits, as it is stated: "And a man of fury abounds in transgression" (Proverbs 29:22).

Reish Lakish said: In the case of any person who grows angry, if he is a wise man, his wisdom departs from him; if he is a prophet, his prophecy departs from him.

Elijah the prophet said to Rav Yehuda brother of Rav Sala Ḥasida: Do not get angry and you will not sin.

Bar Kappara taught: An irritable person has succeeded only in acquiring the irritability.[143]

(*Nedarim* 22b; *Pesaḥim* 66b; *Berakhot* 29b; *Kiddushin* 40b–41a)

Further reading: For the story of Hillel, who refused to allow a man to anger him, see p. 363. For the story of Rav Michel of Zelochov, who refrained from anger, see *A Concise Guide to Mahshava*, p. 77.

_____

143. Anger is unproductive, so he is left with nothing but the anger.

Constellations

Do the heavenly bodies and the stars have import for one's life and fate? The Sages discuss the extent of the influence, if any, of the constellations on the people of Israel. They also explain the significance of the time a person is born and its effect on his personality.

When Were You Born?

The Sages offer various suggestions regarding the effect that the time of a person's birth, both the day of the week and the hour, has on his character.

It was written in Rabbi Yehoshua ben Levi's ledger: One who was born on the first day of the week will be a person who will not have one in him. What is the meaning of: Who will not have one in him? If you say that there is not one good quality in him, that is difficult: But didn't Rav Ashi say: I was born on the first day of the week [and he certainly had good qualities]. Rather, it means that there is not one bad quality in him. But didn't Rav Ashi say: Dimi bar Kakuzta and I were born on the first day of the week; I am a king [head of a yeshiva], and he became head of a gang of thieves. Rather, one born on the first day of the week is either completely good or completely bad. What is the reason? It is because light and darkness were created on the first day of Creation.[144]

One who was born on the second day of the week will be an irritable person. What is the reason? It is because on that second day of Creation, the upper and lower waters were divided.[145]

One who was born on the third day of the week will be a rich man and an adulterer. What is the reason? It is because on that third day of Creation, vegetation was created.[146]

One who was born on the fourth day of the week will be a wise and enlightened person. What is the reason? It is because the lights were suspended in the heavens on that fourth day.[147]

---

144. Therefore, one is either completely light, good; or completely dark, bad.
145. Therefore, it is a day of dispute and petulance.
146. Different species of grasses, flowers, and trees grow intermingled, an allusion to promiscuity and adultery.
147. The sun, moon, and stars were fixed in their places in the heavens, and wisdom is likened to light.

One who was born on the fifth day of the week will be a person who performs acts of kindness. What is the reason? It is because on that day fish and birds were created.[148]

One who was born on the day before Shabbat will be a seeker. Rav Nahman bar Yitzhak said: This means he will be a seeker of mitzvot.[149]

One who was born on Shabbat will die on Shabbat, because the great day of Shabbat was already desecrated once on his behalf.[150] Rava bar Rav Sheila said: He will be called a person of great sanctity.[151]

Rabbi Hanina said to his students: Go tell Rabbi Yehoshua ben Levi: It is not the astrology of the day of the week that determines a person's nature; rather, it is the astrology of the star of the hour that determines his nature.

One who was born under the influence of the sun will be a radiant person. He will eat from his own resources and drink from his own resources, and his secrets will be exposed.[152] If he steals, he will not succeed.

One who was born under the influence of Venus will be a rich and adulterous person. What is the reason? It is because fire was created in it.[153]

One who was born under the influence of Mercury will be an enlightened man, because Mercury is the sun's scribe.[154]

One who was born under the influence of the moon will be a person who suffers pains, who builds and dismantles, and dismantles and builds. He eats not from his own resources and drinks not from his own resources, and his secrets are hidden.[155] If he steals, he will succeed.

One who was born under the influence of Saturn [Shabbetai] will be a man whose plans are constantly nullified.[156] And some say that everything that others think [or plot against him] will be nullified.

One who was born under the influence of Jupiter [Tzedek] will be a just person [tzadkan]. Rav Nahman bar Yitzhak said: He will be just in the performance of mitzvot.

---

148. Fish and birds receive their food without exertion by the grace of God.
149. Just as one makes an effort to prepare for Shabbat on Friday, one born on that day makes an effort to fulfill mitzvot.
150. They did what needed to be done to assist the baby and the mother.
151. He is so called because he was born on the great and sacred day of Shabbat.
152. Just as the sun is beautiful and self-sustaining, and its light is visible to all, so too is the person born under its influence.
153. Fire symbolizes the fire of the evil inclination that is constantly burning within him.
154. Mercury is the closest planet to the sun, which provides light, and wisdom is likened to light.
155. He is likened to the moon, which constantly changes, whose light is not consistent and is not its own, and which at times is obscured.
156. The term Shabbetai is from the root shin-bet-tav, meaning to put to rest, or abrogate.

One who was born under the influence of Mars will be one who spills blood. Rav Ashi said: He will be either a bloodletter, a thief, a ritual slaughterer, a butcher, or a circumciser. Rabba said: I was born under the influence of Mars and I do not perform any of those activities. Abaye said: My master also punishes and kills [in his capacity as a judge].

(*Shabbat* 156a)

Is There Astrology for Israel?

The Sages disagreed with regard to whether or not there is astrology for Israel. In other words, does the movement of the heavenly bodies influence the lives of Jews, their actions, and their fates, or is it only one's deeds and merits that determine his fate?

It is stated that Rabbi Ḥanina says: Astrology makes one wise[157] and astrology makes one wealthy, and astrology does have influence on the Jewish people. Rabbi Yoḥanan said: There is no astrology for the Jewish people. And Rabbi Yoḥanan followed his own reasoning,[158] as Rabbi Yoḥanan said: From where is it derived that there is no astrology for the Jewish people? As it is stated: "So said the Lord: Do not learn the way of the nations, and from the signs of the heavens do not be dismayed, for the nations are dismayed by them" (Jeremiah 10:2). The verse indicates that the other nations are dismayed by the signs of the heavens, but not the Jewish people.

Rav, too, maintains that there is no astrology for the Jewish people, as Rav Yehuda said that Rav said: From where is it derived that there is no astrology for the Jewish people? As it is stated with regard to God and Abraham: "He took him outside, and said: Look now toward the heavens, and count the stars, if you can count them; and He said to him: So shall be your descendants" (Genesis 15:5). Abraham said before the Holy One, blessed be He: Master of the Universe, "Behold, to me You have not given descendants, and a member of my household[159] is my heir" (Genesis 15:3). God said to him: No. "Rather, one who shall emerge from your loins, he shall be your heir" (Genesis 15:4).

Abraham said before God: Master of the Universe, I have looked into my astrological map, and according to it I am not fit to have a son. God re-

Sages on Life

---

157. A person's wisdom is dependent on astrology.
158. This refers to a statement that Rabbi Yoḥanan said previously.
159. The reference is to Abraham's servant.

sponded: Set aside your astrology,[160] as there is no astrology for Israel. What do you think? Is it because Jupiter [*Tzedek*] is situated in the west that you cannot have children? I will restore it and situate it in the east. That is the meaning of what is written with regard to Abraham: "Who awakens from the east, righteousness [*tzedek*] ... attends his footstep [*leraglo*]" (Isaiah 41:2).[161]

From what happened to Shmuel, one also concludes that there is no astrology for the Jewish people. As Shmuel and the gentile astrologer Ablet were sitting together, and they saw several people going to a lake, Ablet said to Shmuel [pointing to one of them]: That person will go and he will not return, because a snake will bite him and he will die. Shmuel said to him: If he is a Jew, he will go and return. As they were sitting there, that person went and returned.

Ablet stood, took the person's knapsack off of him, and found inside of it a snake cut in half. Shmuel said to the man: What did you do [to merit being saved from death]? The person said to him: Every day we give of our bread and eat together.[162] Today, there was one of us who didn't have bread to share and he was embarrassed because of this. I told the others: I will go and collect the bread. When I came to the man with no bread, I feigned as though I took from him so that he would not be embarrassed. Shmuel said to the man: You performed a mitzva. Shmuel later went out and taught: "Righteousness delivers from death" (Proverbs 10:2), meaning not only from an unusual death but even from death itself.

From what happened to Rabbi Akiva, too, one can conclude that there is no astrology for the Jewish people. As Rabbi Akiva had a daughter, and Chaldean astrologers told him that on the very day that she enters the wedding canopy, a snake will bite her and she will die. She was very concerned about this matter. On that day, she took an ornamental pin from her hair and stuck it into the wall for safekeeping, and it happened that it penetrated the eye of a snake. In the morning, when she removed the pin, the snake was pulled and came with it.

Her father said to her: What did you do to merit being saved from the snake? She said to him: In the evening a poor person came and knocked on the door, while everyone was preoccupied with the wedding feast and there was no one to hear him knocking at the door. I got up, took the portion of food that you had given me at the feast, and gave it to him. Rabbi Akiva said

---

160. "God took him outside" means outside his astrology.
161. God established Jupiter [*Tzedek*] in the east on behalf of [*leraglo*] Abraham.
162. We share our food.

to her: You performed a mitzva. Rabbi Akiva went out and taught: "Righteousness delivers from death" (Proverbs 10:2), meaning not only from an unusual death but even from death itself.

"For these nations from whom you are taking possession heed soothsayers and sorcerers; but you, not so did the Lord your God give to you" (Deuteronomy 18:14).

There was an incident involving Rabbi Yannai and Rabbi Yohanan, who were sitting at the Tiberias city gate. There were two astrologers there, who saw two Jews going out to work. Those two astrologers said: Those two men are going out to work, but they will not reach their destination; a snake will bite them. Rabbi Yannai and Rabbi Yohanan heard this. What did they do? They sat at the city gate to find out if those two people entered their destination city to perform their labor. They did enter, and Rabbi Yannai and Rabbi Yohanan saw them.

Rabbi Yannai and Rabbi Yohanan said to the astrologers: Didn't you say that these two people will go out but will not reach their destination, as a snake will bite them? The astrologers said to them: Yes. Rabbi Yannai and Rabbi Yohanan said to them: They went out in peace and reached their destination in peace. The astrologers looked at those two men. The astrologers said to them: Tell us, what did you do today? The men told them: We did not do anything special; we did what we are accustomed to doing: We recited *Shema* and we prayed. The astrologers said to them: You are Jews; the pronouncements of astrologers do not affect you, because you are Jews. The midrash concludes: That is the meaning of what is written: "But you, not so did the Lord your God give to you" [i.e., the Jewish people are not affected by the constellations].[163]

(*Shabbat* 156a–b; *Tanḥuma, Shofetim*)

Life, Children, and Sustenance

Comparing the very different lives of two righteous individuals teaches us that there are certain matters that are not dependent on a person's deeds, but on his astrology.

Rava said: Concerning length of life and health, children, and sustenance, the matter is not dependent on merit but on astrology. For Rabba and Rav Hisda were both righteous Sages, as this Sage [Rabba] would pray during a

---

163. Divination by means of heavenly bodies and sorcery are not the path that God has provided for Israel.

drought and rain would fall, and that Sage [Rav Hisda] would pray during a drought and rain would fall.[164]

Nevertheless, Rav Hisda lived ninety-two years, and Rabba lived forty years.[165] In the household of Rav Hisda there were sixty weddings; in the household of Rabba there were sixty bereavements.[166] In the household of Rav Hisda they baked bread from the finest flour even for the dogs, and it was not lacking [as there was so much food]. In the household of Rabba, they had coarse barley bread even for the people, and even that was hard to find.[167]

(*Shabbat* 156a; *Moed Katan* 28a)

📖 **Further reading:** For more about the influence of the constellations on the Jewish people, see *A Concise Guide to Mahshava*, p. 46.

---

164. They were both righteous men.
165. This indicates that life expectancy is not dependent on deeds but on astrology.
166. Deaths of children, indicating that fertility and the lives of children are dependent on astrology.
167. This indicates that sustenance, too, is not dependent on righteousness.

Prophecy

Prophecy is one of the foundations of faith. It is the medium through which the Creator transmits His messages. The Sages address many aspects of prophecy, among them the characteristics common to prophets and the hierarchy of the prophets. They also provide explanations of different prophetic revelations. The chapter that follows presents statements of the Sages about the resting of the Divine Presence on an individual, the prophets who arose for the people of Israel over the generations, the levels of prophecy, and prophecy in our times.

The Resting of the Divine Presence

The Divine Presence rests upon a person only in the wake of appropriate preparation. The nature of the preparation determines the nature of the prophecy.

The Divine Presence does not rest on an individual in an atmosphere of sadness, or laziness, or laughter, or frivolity, or idle conversation, but rather in an atmosphere of the joy of a mitzva.

Rabbi Yona says: Jonah son of Amitai[168] was among the festival pilgrims, and only after he participated in the Celebration of the Place of the Water Drawing[169] [*Simhat Beit HaSho'eva*] did divine inspiration rest on him. This serves to teach you that the Holy Spirit rests only on one with a happy heart.

I call on the heavens and earth to testify: Whether Jew or gentile, man or woman, slave or maidservant: In accordance with the deed he performs, so the Holy Spirit rests on him.

(*Pesaḥim* 117a; Jerusalem Talmud, *Sukka* 5:1;
Tanna deVei Eliyahu Rabba 9)

Prophecy for Posterity

Many prophets arose over the generations, but the prophecies of only a few of them were included in the Bible.

---

168. The eponymous prophet of the book of Jonah.
169. A celebration in the Temple on each night of the festival of *Sukkot*.

Many prophets arose for the Jewish people, double the number of Israelites who left Egypt.[170] Nevertheless, only a prophecy that was necessary for future generations was written in the Bible, but one that was not necessary for future generations was not written in the Bible.[171]

(Megilla 14a)

Levels of Prophecy

There are many different levels of prophecy. The level attained by Moses is unlike that of any other prophet.

What is the difference between Moses and all the other prophets? Rabbi Yehuda son of Rabbi Elai and the Rabbis disagreed on the matter. Rabbi Yehuda son of Rabbi Elai said: The other prophets would see a divine vision through nine crystals... and Moses would see through only one crystal, as it is stated: "And a vision that is not in riddles" (Numbers 12:8). And the Rabbis say: All other prophets would see through a murky crystal, as it is written: "[I spoke to the prophets, I proliferated visions] and granted imagery[172] to the prophets" (Hosea 12:11)... whereas Moses would see through a polished crystal, as it is written: "And a picture of the Lord he will behold" (Numbers 12:8).

Rava said: Everything that the prophet Ezekiel saw, Isaiah saw as well.[173] To what can Ezekiel be compared? To a villager[174] who saw the king; and to what can Isaiah be compared? To a city dweller[175] who saw the king.

(Vayikra Rabba 1; Ḥagiga 13b)

Prophecy Today and in the Messianic Era

Prophecy, as it existed in biblical times, no longer exists. Nevertheless, the Sages note several situations and contexts that contain characteristics of prophecy. In the messianic era, the spirit of God will imbue everything, and all the Jews will be worthy of prophecy.

---

170. i.e., double the 600,000 men between the ages of twenty and sixty who left Egypt and were counted in the census – 1.2 million prophets.

171. This is the reason that so few of them appear in the Bible.

172. They sensed images, but did not see directly.

173. The same vision was revealed to both prophets. Both described the revelation of God and His hosts: Ezekiel expansively and Isaiah tersely.

174. Unaccustomed as he is to seeing the king, the villager excitedly describes every detail at great length.

175. Accustomed as he is to the royal pageantry, he provides a concise description.

Rabbi Yoḥanan said: If one awoke early in the morning and a verse happened into his mouth,[176] this is a minor prophecy.[177]

Rabbi Avdimi from Haifa says: From the day that the Temple was destroyed, prophecy was taken from the prophets and given to the Sages.... Rabbi Yoḥanan said: From the day that the Temple was destroyed, prophecy was taken from the prophets and given to imbeciles and small children.

The Holy One, blessed be He, said: In this world, individuals prophesied, but in the World to Come[178] all Israel will become prophets, as it is stated: "Thereafter, it shall be that I will pour My spirit upon all flesh and your sons and your daughters will prophesy; your elders will dream dreams; your young men will see visions" (Joel 3:1).

(*Berakhot* 55b; *Bava Batra* 12a; *Bemidbar Rabba* 15)

📖 **Further reading:** For more about prophets and prophecy, see *A Concise Guide to Mahshava*, p. 203.

---

176. A certain verse comes to mind.
177. It is an allusion that the content of the verse will be fulfilled.
178. In this context, the World to Come is a reference to the messianic era.

Humility and Pride

A humble individual is especially beloved by God. By contrast, pride is an unacceptable trait that one must uproot from his heart. The chapter that follows presents statements of the Sages on the great virtue of humility, how God draws unassuming people near to Him, the reward of the humble, and the condemnation of pride.

God Is Exalted but He Sees the Lowly

God lowers Himself, as it were, to the lowly and self-effacing. Through them He is praised and glorified, and He is particularly close to them.

Rav Yosef says: A person should always learn conduct from the wisdom of his Creator, as the Holy One, blessed be He, rejected all the mountains and hills and rested His Divine Presence at the giving of the Torah on [the relatively small] Mount Sinai. [Similarly, when appearing to Moses,] He forsook all the beautiful trees and rested His Divine Presence in the bush[179]....

Rav Avira expounded, and some say it was Rabbi Elazar: Come and see that the manner of the Holy One, blessed be He, is not like the manner of flesh and blood. The manner of flesh and blood is that the exalted sees the exalted,[180] but the exalted does not see the lowly. But the manner of the Holy One, blessed be He, is not like that: He is exalted but He sees the lowly, as it is stated: "Though the Lord is exalted, He sees the lowly" (Psalms 138:6).

Rav Hisda says, and some say it is Mar Ukva: Concerning any person who has arrogance within him, the Holy One, blessed be He, says: He and I cannot dwell together in the world, as it is stated: "I will not tolerate [oto lo ukhal] anyone with a proud demeanor or a lustful heart. [My eyes are on the faithful of the land;] they will dwell with me" (Psalms 101:5–6). Do not read: "Oto [lo ukhal]," but rather: "Itto [lo ukhal]."[181]

---

179. A low, thorny bush in which God appeared to Moses (see Exodus 3:2).
180. People tend to ascribe importance to their peers but not to those who belong to a lower social stratum.
181. Not: I will not tolerate him, but: I cannot tolerate being with him.

Rabbi Alexandri says: If an ordinary person uses broken utensils, it is disgraceful for him. But the utensils of the Holy One, blessed be He, are broken, as it is stated: "The Lord is near to the brokenhearted" (Psalms 34:19); "He heals the brokenhearted" (Psalms 147:3); "For so said the Exalted and Most High...and I will be with the downtrodden and humble" (Isaiah 57:15).

(Sota 5a; Vayikra Rabba 7)

Further reading: For more on humility and pride, see pp. 74, 148, 457.

One Who Humbles Himself and One Who Exalts Himself

It is the humble individual, who does not seek greatness for himself, who ultimately merits honor and distinction.

For three years Beit Shammai and Beit Hillel disagreed.[182] These said: The *halakha* is in accordance with our opinion, and those said: The *halakha* is in accordance with our opinion. Ultimately, a divine voice emerged and said: Both these and those are the words of the living God, but the *halakha* is in accordance with the opinion of Beit Hillel. Now, since both these and those are the words of the living God, why were Beit Hillel privileged to have the *halakha* established in accordance with their opinion? It is because they were agreeable and forbearing, and would teach both their statements and the statements of Beit Shammai. Moreover, they would cite the statements of Beit Shammai before their own statements...This teaches you that concerning anyone who humbles himself, the Holy One, blessed be He, exalts him, and anyone who exalts himself, the Holy One, blessed be He, humbles him. Likewise, concerning anyone who seeks greatness, greatness flees from him, and anyone who flees from greatness, greatness seeks him.

Rav Yehuda said that Rav said: Concerning anyone who acts haughtily, if he is a Torah scholar, his wisdom departs from him; if he is a prophet, his prophecy departs from him.

Rabbi Eliezer HaKappar says: Do not be like a lintel that people cannot reach, or like an elevated threshold that obscures faces,[183] or like a slightly elevated threshold that strikes the feet.[184] Rather, be like a low threshold on

---

182. They had halakhic disputes regarding a long series of issues.
183. It is so elevated that people are forced to bend their heads in order to avoid bumping them on the lintel.
184. People trip and fall over it.

which everyone treads, as eventually even if the entire structure is demolished, the threshold remains in its place.

(*Eiruvin* 13b; *Pesaḥim* 66b; *Avot deRabbi Natan*, version A, chap. 26)

Humility Is Greater than All

The quality of humility is more praiseworthy than any other good quality.

Rabbi Yehoshua ben Levi says: Humility is greater than all the other positive qualities.

Who is destined for the World to Come? One who is modest and humble, who hunches forward when he enters and hunches forward as he exits,[185] and who studies Torah regularly, and who does not take credit for himself.

Rabbi Meir says: … And be humble before every person.

This is the adage that people say: A coin in an empty barrel calls: *Kish, kish.*[186]

(*Avoda Zara* 20b; *Sanhedrin* 88b; Mishna *Avot* 10:4; *Bava Metzia* 85b)

---

185. He does not draw attention to himself.
186. Like empty barrels, empty people make the most noise and seek to make the greatest impression.

Kindness to Animals

It is permitted to use animals for one's own purposes, but one must avoid causing them unnecessary pain. The chapter that follows presents statements of the Sages regarding the severity of the prohibition against causing the suffering of animals, the proper treatment of animals, and the leaders of Israel who were found suitable for their positions due to their considerate treatment of animals.

Grass in Your Field for Your Animals

It is an absolute prohibition to cause pain to animals. Furthermore, it is incumbent upon a person to tend to the needs of the animals in his care before taking care of himself.

It is prohibited by Torah law to cause animals to suffer.

Rav Yehuda said that Rav said: It is prohibited for a person to taste anything before he gives food to his animals, as it is stated: "I will provide grass in your field for your animals"; and only then does it say: "And you will eat and you will be satisfied" (Deuteronomy 11:15).

It is permitted for a person to purchase animals, beasts, or birds for himself only if he prepares food for them.

(*Shabbat* 128b; *Berakhot* 40a; *Tanḥuma, Mishpatim*)

And His Mercy Extends to All His Creations

God has compassion on all His creatures, people and animals alike. We too must adopt that same approach.

If a person boards a ship with an animal, and a storm arose at sea, what do people do? They cast the animal into the sea and spare the person, because one does not have mercy on an animal as one has mercy on a person. But the way of the Holy One, blessed be He, is not so; rather, just as He has mercy on people, so He has mercy on animals. Know that this is so, as at the moment that the Holy One, blessed be He, sought to destroy His world in the generation of the flood, at the moment that they sinned, He drew a parallel

between people and animals, as it is stated: "The Lord said: I will obliterate man whom I have created from the face of the earth; from man to animal, to crawling creatures, to birds of the heavens" (Genesis 6:7).[187] And when He came to reconcile Himself[188] with the world, just as He reconciled Himself with humankind and had mercy on them, so, too, He had mercy on the animals. This can be derived from what we read regarding that matter: "God remembered Noah and all the beasts and all the animals that were with him in the ark" (Genesis 8:1).

The suffering of Rabbi Yehuda HaNasi[189]...came due to an incident and ceased due to an incident. It came due to an incident; what is the incident? A certain calf was being led to the slaughter, and it went and hung its head on the corner of Rabbi Yehuda HaNasi's garment and wept. Rabbi Yehuda HaNasi said to it: Go, as you were created for this purpose. The angels said: Since he was not compassionate to the calf, let suffering come on him. His suffering ceased due to an incident, as one day the maidservant of Rabbi Yehuda HaNasi was sweeping his house. There were young weasels lying there, and she swept them away. Rabbi Yehuda HaNasi said to her: Leave them, as it is written: "The Lord is good to all; and His mercy extends to all His creations" (Psalms 145:9). The angels said: Since he was compassionate to the weasels, we will have compassion on him; and he was cured.

(*Tanḥuma* [Buber], *Noah*; *Bava Metzia* 85a)

A Test of Leadership

In order to ascertain whether a potential leader of Israel is blessed with the qualities suited for leadership of His people, God assesses them on the basis of their approach to animals.

"The Lord tests the righteous" (Psalms 11:5). On what basis does He test them? It is on the basis of herding sheep. He assessed David on the basis of his treatment of the flock, and found him to be a fine shepherd...he would prevent older sheep from eating before the younger ones; and he would take out the younger ones so they could graze from the soft grass;[190] and then take out the older ones so they could graze from the intermediate quality-grass;

---

187. The destruction of man and animal are mentioned in the same verse, indicating that they are equal in the eyes of the Lord.
188. The reconciliation with humankind that led Him to end the flood.
189. Rabbi Yehuda HaNasi suffered from a chronic intestinal ailment over the course of many years.
190. He did so to ensure that the young, frail sheep would not go hungry.

and only afterward would he take out the youthful, vigorous sheep so they would eat the rough grass. The Holy One, blessed be He, said: One who knows how to herd the flock in this manner, each animal in accordance with its attributes, is worthy to shepherd My people.

Concerning Moses, too, the Holy One, blessed be He, assessed him only on the basis of his treatment of the flock. Our Sages said: When Moses our teacher, may he rest in peace, was herding Yitro's flock in the wilderness, a goat fled from him, and Moses chased after it until he came to a shelter. When he arrived at the shelter, he happened upon a pool of water, and the goat stood there to drink. When Moses reached it, he said: I did not know that you were running due to your thirst. You must be tired. He carried the goat on his shoulders and walked back like that. The Holy One, blessed be He, said: You have the mercy to lead a flock belonging to flesh and blood in this manner; I take an oath by your life that you will shepherd My flock, Israel.

(*Shemot Rabba* 2)

📖 Further reading: To learn about the laws relating to the suffering of animals, see *A Concise Guide to Halakha*, p. 613. With regard to the eating of meat from a living animal, see *A Concise Guide to Mahshava*, p. 122.

Judging Others

The manner in which people typically assess the actions of others is discussed at length in rabbinic literature. The Sages condemn the haste with which we assess what transpires around us and with which we condemn others. The chapter that follows presents statements of the Sages regarding the need to judge others favorably and to refrain from suspecting the innocent.

Judging People Favorably

One should view the actions of others in the most favorable light and not be too hasty in judging them. If we treat others in this manner, God will treat us in the same way.

One should judge every person favorably.

Do not judge another until you have arrived in his place.[191]

The Sages taught: One who judges another favorably is himself judged favorably. There was an incident involving a certain person who came down from the Upper Galilee and was hired by a landlord in the south to work for three years. On the eve of the Day of Atonement, he said to his employer: Give me my wages, and I will go and feed my wife and children. His employer told him: I have no money. The worker said to him: In that case, give me my wages in the form of produce. His employer told him: I have none. The worker said to him: Give me land. His employer told him: I have none. The worker said to him: Give me animals. His employer told him: I have none. The worker said to him: Give me cushions and blankets. His employer told him: I have none. The worker slung his tools over his shoulder behind him and went home in anguish.

After the festival of *Sukkot*, the employer took the worker's wages in his hand, along with three donkeys, one laden with food, one with drink, and one with all types of sweets, and he went to the worker's home. After they ate and drank, the employer gave him his wages and said to him: When you said to me: Give me my wages, and I said: I have no money, of what did you suspect me? The worker answered: I said: Perhaps the opportunity to purchase merchandise at a cheap price presented itself, and you purchased it with the money that you owed me. The employer asked: And when you

---

191. The reference is to the physical, social, or emotional place that causes a person's negative behavior.

said to me: Give me animals, and I said: I have no animals, of what did you suspect me? The worker answered: I said: Perhaps the animals are rented to others. The employer asked: When you said to me: Give me land, and I said: I have no land, of what did you suspect me? The worker answered: I said: Perhaps the land is leased to others.[192] The employer asked: And when I said: I have no produce, of what did you suspect me? The worker replied: I said: Perhaps they are not tithed.[193] Finally, the employer asked: And when I said: I have no cushions or blankets, of what did you suspect me? The worker answered: I said: Perhaps he consecrated all his property to Heaven.[194]

The employer said to him: I take an oath by the Temple service that you were correct. I had vowed and consecrated all my property on account of Hyrcanus, my son, as he would not engage in Torah study.[195] And when I came to the Sages in the South, they annulled all my vows for me. And you, just as you judged me favorably, so may God judge you favorably.

(Mishna *Avot* 1:6, 1:2; *Shabbat* 127b)

📖 Further reading: For stories of parents who sought to disinherit their children for studying Torah, see p. 332.

One Who Suspects the Innocent

It is inappropriate to suspect a person based merely on the superficial impression created by his actions. Nevertheless, the one suspected of wrongdoing must make an effort to refrain from actions apt to arouse suspicion.

"Hannah answered Eli the High Priest and said:[196] No, my master. I am an embittered woman; I did not drink wine or intoxicating drink but poured out my soul before the Lord" (I Samuel 1:15). Ulla said, and some say it was Rabbi Yosei son of Rabbi Hanina, that she said to him: With regard to this matter, you are not a master,[197] and divine inspiration does not rest on you, as you incorrectly suspect me of this.

Some say that this is what she said to him: Aren't you a master?[198] The Divine Presence and divine inspiration are not with you, as you judged me

Sages on Life

---

192. The employer did not have access to his rented animals and leased land.
193. It is prohibited to eat untithed produce or to give it to others.
194. The consecrated property belongs to the Temple and it is prohibited for the employer to utilize it for his own purposes.
195. He was angry at his son and sought to disinherit him.
196. Eli saw her praying silently and thought that she was intoxicated.
197. The allusion to this is from the fact that Hannah called him "my master."
198. i.e., it was not a statement but rather a rhetorical question.

unfavorably, and you did not judge me favorably. Didn't you know that I am an embittered woman and I did not drink wine or intoxicating drink? Rabbi Elazar said: From here it is derived that one who is suspected of something of which he is not guilty must inform the other of his error.[199]

"Eli answered and said: Go in peace" (I Samuel 1:17). Rabbi Elazar said: From here it is derived that in the case of one who suspects another of something of which he is not guilty, the one who suspected him must appease him. Moreover, he must even bless him, as it is stated that Eli blessed her: "And may the God of Israel grant your request" (I Samuel 1:17).

Reish Lakish said: One who suspects the innocent will be afflicted in his body.

Rabbi Yosei said: May my portion be with one who is suspected of some wrongdoing but is innocent.[200]

(*Berakhot* 31b; *Shabbat* 97a; *Moed Katan* 18b)

---

199. He must inform his accuser of his innocence.
200. His sins are atoned for via the suffering he experiences due to the false suspicion.

Joy

"Serve the Lord with joy; come before Him with song" (Psalms 100:2). Joy is an inseparable component of the fulfillment of the mitzvot, and the "joy of a mitzva" is especially praiseworthy. The chapter that follows presents statements of the Sages regarding the virtue of joy, the merit of providing joy to others, and the great joy that will be experienced in the messianic era.

The Joy of a Mitzva

The proper form of rejoicing is delighting in God and His mitzvot. The more the Jewish people rejoice in observance of the mitzvot, the more God will afford them joyous occasions.

"So I praised joy" (Ecclesiastes 8:15);[201] this is a reference to the joy of a mitzva. "And of joy: What does it achieve?" (Ecclesiastes 2:2);[202] this is a reference to joy that is not joy of a mitzva. This serves to teach you that the Divine Presence does not rest on an individual in an atmosphere of sadness, or of laziness, or of laughter, or of frivolity, or of idle conversation, or of idle chatter, but rather from an atmosphere imbued with the joy of a mitzva. As it is stated: "Now, bring me a musician. It was as the musician played, and the hand of the Lord was upon him" (II Kings 3:15). Rav Yehuda said: Likewise, one should be joyful over a matter of *halakha*.[203]

Come and see how much the people of Israel cherish the mitzvot, as they incur expenses in order to observe the mitzvot and rejoice in them. The Holy One, blessed be He, declares: If you observe the mitzvot and rejoice in them, I will add joy to you, as it is stated: "The humble will increase their joy in the Lord" (Isaiah 29:19).

(*Shabbat* 30b; *Tanḥuma, Tazria*)

Those Who Are Destined for the World to Come

The joy one brings to others provides an especially significant merit.

Sages on Life

---

201. This and the following verse were stated by King Solomon.
202. What is the use of joy?
203. In order to reach a halakhic conclusion, one should approach the matter with joy.

Rabbi Beroka of Hoza'a was often found in the marketplace of Bei Lefet, and Elijah the prophet would frequently appear to him there. Once Rabbi Beroka said to Elijah: Of all the people who come here, is there anyone in this marketplace worthy of the World to Come? Elijah said to him: No....

Meanwhile, two others came to the marketplace. Elijah said to Rabbi Beroka: These two...are destined for the World to Come. Rabbi Beroka went over to the men and said to them: What is your occupation? They told him: We are jesters, and we cheer up the depressed. Also, when we see two people who have a quarrel, we strive to make peace between them.

(*Ta'anit* 22a)

Then Will Our Mouths Fill with Laughter

At present, joy is incomplete, but in the future our joy will be absolute, not mitigated by suffering or worry.

Rabbi Yohanan said in the name of Rabbi Shimon ben Yohai: It is prohibited for a person to fill his mouth with mirth in this world, as it is stated: "Then our mouths will be filled with laughter, and our tongues with song" (Psalms 126:2). When will that be? At a time when "the nations will say: The Lord has done great things for them" (Psalms 126:2). The Sages said about Reish Lakish that after he heard this statement from his teacher, Rabbi Yohanan, he never again filled his mouth with laughter in this world.

"And you shall be completely joyous" (Deuteronomy 16:15). What is the meaning of "completely joyous"? You find that although a person can be happy in this world, his joy is never complete. How so? In this world, when children are born to a person, he worries over them whether or not they will survive,[204] and therefore, he is always somewhat concerned. By contrast, in the messianic era, the Holy One, blessed be He, will eliminate death, as it is stated: "He will eliminate death forever" (Isaiah 25:8), and then the joy will be complete, as it is stated: "Then our mouths will be filled with laughter" (Psalms 126:2).

Alternatively: "And you shall be completely joyous." A person is joyous in this world. A festival arrives and he acquires meat for himself, which he cooks in his home to rejoice on the festival. When he comes to eat it, he gives a portion to each of his children, and one of them inevitably complains: My brother's portion is bigger than mine, and consequently, he is up-

---

204. He does not know whether they will reach adulthood and old age, or die in infancy or childhood.

SAGES _____ Sages on Life > Joy

set even in the midst of his joy. By contrast, in the messianic era, the pots will themselves cook[205] [whatever one needs], and one will watch and rejoice over them. This is the meaning of what is written: "Lord, You will establish [*tishpot*][206] peace for us" (Isaiah 26:12). At that moment, one's joy will be complete.

"And I will transform their mourning into gladness" (Jeremiah 31:12). For in this world, joy is ultimately transformed into mourning. How so? The seven days of mourning for the dead correspond to the seven days of a wedding feast.[207] By contrast, in the World to Come, God says, I will restore the mourning into joy, as it is stated: "And I will transform their mourning into gladness, and I will console them and cheer them from their sorrow" (Jeremiah 31:12).

(*Berakhot* 31a; *Pesikta deRav Kahana, Parasha Aḥeret*;
Yalkut Shimoni 2:314)

---

205. The pots will cook on their own.
206. The term *tishpot* is interpreted homiletically as an expression of placing [*shefita*] a pot on the fire.
207. The joy of marriage will be replaced by sorrow when one's spouse dies.

Silence and Speech

Speech is an ability unique to human beings, who can use it for good or for evil. The Sages underscore the power of speech and the significance of carefully monitoring it. The chapter that follows presents statements of the Sages regarding the virtue of silence, the unique power of the tongue, and the value of scrupulous insistence on clean speech.

Silence Is Good

Silence is praiseworthy and preferable to speech. If this applies to Torah study, it all the more so applies regarding nonsensical matters.

Shimon the son of [Rabban Gamliel] would say: All my life I grew up among the Sages, and I have found nothing better for the body than silence. It is not the study that is essential, but rather the deed. And anyone who speaks excessively engenders sin.

A safeguard for wisdom is silence.[208]

Rabbi Yehuda of Kefar Geboraya, and some say of Kefar Gibor-Hayil, expounded: What is the meaning of what is written: "For You … silence is praise" (Psalms 65:2)? The best remedy for everything is silence. When Rav Dimi came from the Land of Israel to Babylonia, he said: In the West [the Land of Israel], they say the following adage: A word for a *sela*, silence for two.[209]

Bar Kappara taught: Silence is good for the wise; all the more so[210] for the foolish. Likewise, King Solomon says: "Even a fool, being silent, is considered wise" (Proverbs 17:28), and it goes without saying that the same is true of a wise person who remains silent.

(Mishna *Avot* 1:17, 3:13; *Megilla* 18a; Jerusalem Talmud, *Pesaḥim* 9:9)

Further reading: For more about appropriate speech, see p. 147.

---

208. Caution in this regard leads to wisdom.
209. Silence is worth twice the value of a word, which is worth a *sela* coin.
210. This is a logical inference: If silence is advisable for the wise, who have the capacity to speak words of wisdom, all the more so it is advisable for the foolish, who lack that capacity.

Sages on Life

Death and Life Are Controlled by the Tongue

The tongue has the ability to facilitate good and evil. A person can achieve through his speech what he cannot achieve with any other limb.

Rabban Shimon ben Gamliel said to his servant Tavi: Go and buy a good cut of meat for me from the marketplace. Tavi went and bought him tongue. Rabban Shimon ben Gamliel said to him: Go and buy a bad cut of meat for me from the marketplace. He again went and bought him tongue. Rabban Shimon ben Gamliel asked him: What is this, that when I say to you a good cut of meat, you buy tongue for me, and when I say to you a bad cut of meat, you also buy tongue for me?

Tavi explained to him: Good is from the tongue and bad is from the tongue. When the tongue is good, there is nothing better than it,[211] and when it is bad, there is nothing worse than it.

Rabbi Yehuda HaNasi prepared a meal for his students. He brought before them soft tongues and hard tongues. They selected portions among the soft ones and left the hard ones. He said to them: Consider what you are doing. Just as you select the soft ones and leave the hard ones, your tongues should be the same.[212]

Rava said: For one who seeks life, it is in his tongue; for one who seeks death, it is in his tongue.

There was an incident involving the king of Persia, who became ill. The doctors said to him: There is no cure for you unless they bring you the milk of a lioness, and we will prepare a remedy for you. One man spoke up and said: I will bring you the milk of a lioness if you wish, but give me ten goats. The king told his servants to give the goats to that man, and they gave them to him.

The man went to a lions' den and a lioness was there, suckling her cubs. On the first day, he stood from afar and cast one goat to the lioness, and she ate it. On the second day, he drew slightly nearer and cast another goat to her. He did so, drawing closer each day, until he was able to play with the lioness, at which point he took some of her milk and returned to the king.

When he was halfway to the king, he saw in a dream that his limbs were arguing with one another. The legs said: None of the other limbs can compare to us. Had we not walked to the lions' den, the man would not have been able to take the milk. The hands said: There is none like us; had

---

211. There is nothing with more potential for good than the tongue.
212. You should be soft-spoken and you should not speak with a harsh tongue.

we not acted, there would have been nothing.[213] The heart said: Had I not provided the counsel,[214] what use would any of you have been? The tongue responded: Had I not stated the matter to the king, what would the rest of the man have done?

All the other limbs responded to the tongue: How dare you compare yourself to us! You are situated in a place of darkness,[215] and you do not have discernment like the other limbs. The tongue said to them: Today, you will say that I control you.

The man heard this exchange and then went to the king and said to him: My lord, the king, here is the milk of a female dog. The king was enraged, and commanded the man be hanged. As he walked to his death, the other limbs began to weep. The tongue said to them: Didn't I tell you that you lack substance? If I save you, will you acknowledge that I am superior to you? They answered: Yes. The man said to those about to hang him: Return me to the king; perhaps I will be spared. They returned him to the king, and the man asked him: Why did you command to hang me? The king said to him: You brought to me the milk of a female dog [*kalba*]! The man said to him: What do you care, provided that you are cured? Furthermore, a lioness is also called *kalba*.[216] The king's servants took some of the milk and sampled it, and found it to be the milk of a lioness. The other limbs said to the tongue: We concede to you that you were right.

This is the meaning of: "Death and life are in the power of the tongue" (Proverbs 18:21).

(*Vayikra Rabba* 33; *Arakhin* 15b; *Yalkut Shimoni* 2:721)

Euphemism

Vulgarity is despicable, and one should make every effort to refrain from mentioning negative matters, even incidentally. Not only do the Sages condemn speech of that kind, they even condem listening to it.

Rabbi Yehoshua ben Levi said: A person should never express a crude matter. Indeed, a verse was distorted by the addition of eight superfluous letters in order that it would not be expressed in a crude matter, as it is stated:

---

213. We cast the goats and took the milk.
214. Without the plan, the hands and the legs would not have been successful.
215. You are in the mouth.
216. In fact, I brought you the milk of a lioness.

"From the pure animal, and from the animal that is not pure" (Genesis 7:8).[217] Rav Pappa said: A different verse added nine letters, as it is stated: "If there will be among you a man, who will not be pure[218] due to a nocturnal incident" (Deuteronomy 23:11). Ravina said: Actually, it is ten letters because of the *vav* in the word *tahor* [pure].[219] Rav Aha bar Yaakov said: Yet another verse adds sixteen letters, as it is stated: "As he said: It is incidental; he is impure, as he is not purified" (I Samuel 20:26).[220]

A person should always converse euphemistically....

There were two students who were sitting before Hillel the Elder, and one of them was Rabban Yohanan ben Zakkai. And some say it was before Rabbi Yehuda HaNasi, and one of them was Rabbi Yohanan. One said: Why must one be careful to harvest grapes in a state of ritual purity, but one need not harvest olives in a state of ritual purity? And one said [the same idea, only he worded it differently]: Why must one harvest grapes in ritual purity, but one may harvest olives in a state of ritual impurity? Their teacher said: I am certain that this [first student, who spoke euphemistically, will] issue halakhic rulings in Israel. It was not even a short while later that he issued halakhic rulings in Israel.

Due to the sin of vulgar speech, troubles abound, and harsh decrees are renewed, and the youth of the enemies of Israel[221] die, and orphans and widows cry for help and are not answered....

Rabbi Hanan bar Rava said: Everyone knows why a bride enters the wedding canopy.[222] Nevertheless, anyone who speaks in a vulgar manner about it, even if the angels on High sealed for him a decree of seventy years of good fortune, they will reverse it to bad fortune because of this sin.

Rabba bar Sheila said that Rav Hisda said: Concerning anyone who speaks in a vulgar manner, Gehenna is deepened for him...Rav Nahman bar Yitzhak said: The same applies even to one who hears vulgar speech and remains silent.[223]

Sages on Life

---

217. Instead of "from an impure animal." In Hebrew, this would have taken eight fewer letters to express.
218. Instead of "who will be impure," which would have taken nine fewer letters to express in the Hebrew phrase.
219. The word *tahor* in the verse from the Torah is written with an "extra" letter, the letter *vav*.
220. Instead of using the three-letter Hebrew word *tameh*, impure, the prophet says, "he is impure, as he is not purified," which in Hebrew has sixteen extra letters.
221. This is a euphemism for Israel.
222. Everyone knows that the marriage will be consummated, but it is improper to speak of it.
223. Anyone who does not protest the vulgar speech and reprimand the one who spoke it.

Bar Kappara expounded: What is the meaning of what is written: "And a spade shall be for you with your weapons [*azenekha*]" (Deuteronomy 23:14)? Do not read it as "your weapons [*azenekha*]." Rather, read it as: On your ear [*oznekha*], meaning that if a person hears an inappropriate matter, he should place his finger [which is shaped like a spade] into his ears. And that is what Rabbi Elazar said: Why are the fingers of a person similar to spades? So that if a person hears an inappropriate matter, he will place his fingers in his ears.

A Sage of the school of Rabbi Yishmael taught: Why is the entire ear hard and the earlobe soft? So that if a person hears an inappropriate matter, he will bend his earlobe into his ear to seal it.

Rabbi Eliezer ben Yaakov says: If a person is fine and laudable and yet he utters a foul expression from his mouth, to what can this be compared? It can be compared to a large hall that has the opening of a tanner's sewer[224] fixed inside it. Every passerby says: How fine would this hall be were it not for the tanner's sewer fixed inside it. The same applies to a fine and laudable person who utters a foul expression from his mouth.

(*Pesaḥim* 3a–b; *Shabbat* 31a, 33a; *Ketubot* 5a;
Derekh Eretz Rabba, Ben Azzai 1)

Further reading: For more on inappropriate speech, see *A Concise Guide to Halakha*, p. 598.

---

224. Tanneries have an especially foul stench.

Torah

The Torah and its study are at the heart of the Sages' worldview. They extensively praise the Torah and its virtue, and consider its study a most important value. The chapter that follows presents statements of the Sages regarding the significance of the Torah; the fact that everything is included in it; the Torah's ability to elevate man, but also to degrade him; and the completeness and unity of all parts of the Torah, its interpretations, and its laws.

Equal to All of Them

Engaging in Torah study is one of the pillars on which the world stands and is equal in value to many important mitzvot.

These are the matters that have no fixed measure: … performing acts of kindness and Torah study. These are the matters whose profits a person enjoys in this world, while the principal remains for him for the World to Come: honoring one's father and mother, performing acts of kindness, and bringing peace between one person and another. And Torah study is equal to all of them.

Shimon the Righteous was among the last surviving members of the Great Assembly.[225] He would say that the world stands on three matters: on the Torah, on the Temple service, and on performing acts of kindness.

(Mishna *Pe'a* 1:1; Mishna *Avot* 1:2)

Everything Is in It

The Torah encompasses everything, and a person can always find in the Torah what he is seeking.

Ben Bag Bag says: Delve into it, delve into it,[226] for everything is in it; and in it you will see and understand. Grow old and worn with it.[227] Do not budge from it, as there is nothing better than it.

Rabbi Hiyya bar Abba said that Rabbi Yohanan said: What is the meaning of what is written: "The guardian of a fig tree will eat its fruit" (Proverbs

---

225. The 120-member tribunal that served as a legislative body during the return to Zion and the early Second Temple period.

226. Search it well, and engage in its study constantly from different perspectives.

227. Engage in Torah study until the infirmity of old age prevents you from doing so.

27:18)? Why are matters of Torah likened to a fig tree? Just as with regard to a fig tree, whenever a person searches it, he finds figs in it that he did not find previously,[228] so too, with matters of Torah: Whenever a person contemplates them, he finds in them meaning that he did not find previously.

Why is the Torah likened to a fig tree? Because in all the other fruits there is waste: In dates there are pits, in grapes there are pits, and in pomegranates there are rinds; but the fig is entirely edible. Likewise, in matters of Torah there is no waste, as it is stated: "For it is not an empty thing for you" (Deuteronomy 32:47).

"And may they proliferate like fish in the midst of the earth" (Genesis 48:16).[229] Just as fish grow in water, and yet when a single drop falls on them from above, they receive it thirstily as one who never tasted water in his life, the same is true of Israel: They grow in the water of Torah, and yet when they hear a new matter from the Torah, they receive it thirstily as though they have never heard a matter of Torah in their lives.

(Mishna *Avot* 5:22; *Eiruvin* 44a–b; *Yalkut Shimoni* 2:2; *Bereshit Rabba* 97)

A Potion of Life and a Potion of Death

Torah study can elevate a person to great heights, but if he is unworthy and studies the Torah improperly, it can bring him down to the lowest depths.

Rabbi Yehoshua ben Levi said: What is the meaning of what is written: "And this is the Torah that Moses placed [*sam*] before the children of Israel" (Deuteronomy 4:44)? If one is worthy,[230] the Torah becomes a potion [*sam*] of life for him;[231] if one is not worthy, the Torah becomes a potion of death for him.[232] This is what Rava said: For one who studies Torah for its own sake,[233] it is a potion of life; but for one who studies Torah not for its own sake, it is a potion of death.[234]

---

228. Not all figs on a tree ripen at the same time; therefore, whenever he goes to the tree he can find a fig that was not there previously.
229. This was Jacob's blessing to his grandsons, Ephraim and Manasseh.
230. If he studies properly, with sanctity and fear of God.
231. The Torah is a remedial cure for him; the word "placed" [*sam*, spelled *sin, mem* in Hebrew] is expounded as "potion" [*sam*, spelled *samekh, mem* in Hebrew].
232. It is poison for him.
233. He studies only for the sake of fulfilling the mitzva of studying Torah.
234. See the next chapter, which explores the issue of Torah study not for its own sake in more detail.

Rabbi Shmuel bar Nahmani said that Rabbi Yonatan raised a contradiction: It is written: "The precepts of the Lord are upright, gladdening the heart" (Psalms 9:19), and it is written: "The word of the Lord is refining" (Psalms 18:31).[235] He resolves the contradiction: For one who is worthy, the Torah gladdens him; for one who is not worthy, it refines him.

The Sages taught: There are three types of people over whom the Holy One, blessed be He, cries every day: one who is able to engage in Torah study and does not engage in it; one who is unable to engage in Torah study but engages in it;[236] and a leader who is domineering over the community.

(*Yoma* 72b; Ḥagiga 5b)

📖 **Further reading:** For more about the study of Torah for its own sake, see *A Concise Guide to Mahshava*, p. 276.

Better than Any Merchandise

The Torah is more precious and valuable than any money or merchandise, and it accompanies a person in this world and in the World to Come. Even if one loses all his property, his Torah remains with him.

Rabbi Yosei ben Kisma said: Once I was traveling and a man encountered me. He greeted me and I returned his greeting. He said to me: Rabbi, from what place are you? I said to him: I am from a great city of Sages and scholars. He said to me: Rabbi, would you like to live with us in our place? I will give you thousands upon thousands of gold coins, precious stones, and pearls.

I said to him: Even were you to give me all the silver, gold, precious stones, and pearls in the world, I would live only in a place of Torah. Likewise, it is written in the book of Psalms by David king of Israel: "The teaching of Your mouth is better for me than thousands of gold and silver pieces" (Psalms 119:72).

Furthermore, when a person passes away from this world, neither silver, nor gold, nor precious stones, nor pearls accompany him, but rather Torah and good deeds alone, as it is stated: "It will guide you when you walk; when you lie down, it will protect you, and when you awaken, it will be your conversation" (Proverbs 6:22). "It will guide you when you walk," in this world; "when you lie down, it will protect you," in the grave; "and when you awaken, it will be your conversation," in the World to Come. And the verse

_____

235. The Torah purifies by passing the person through a crucible of fire.
236. He continues to study despite not understanding what he learns.

states: "Mine is the silver, and Mine is the gold, the utterance of the Lord of hosts" (Haggai 2:8).

There was an incident involving a certain Torah scholar who was on a ship with many merchants. They said to that scholar: Where is your merchandise? He responded: My merchandise is greater than yours. They searched the entire ship but found nothing that was his, and they began laughing at him.

Later, pirates attacked them, looted their merchandise, and took everything that was in the boat. The people on the boat disembarked onto dry land and entered the city. They had no food to eat or garments to wear.

What did that scholar do? He entered the study hall and sat and taught Torah. Upon seeing that he was very learned in Torah, the residents of that city stood and treated him with great deference, and they determined to provide him with a commensurate income, appropriate to live respectably and in dignity. The leaders of the congregation began to walk on his right and left and accompany him.

When the merchants saw this, they came to him and sought to placate him for their earlier insult, and they said to him: We request of you, do us a favor and speak on our behalf to the residents of the city,[237] as you know what we were and what we lost on the ship. We request of you, perform a kindness on our behalf and speak to them so that even a slice of bread might be placed in our mouths, and we will live and not die of starvation.

The scholar said to them: Didn't I tell you that my merchandise is greater than yours? Yours is lost and mine is intact. This is the meaning of: "For a good lesson [lekah] I have given you" (Proverbs 4:2).[238]

(Mishna *Avot* 6:9; *Tanḥuma, Teruma*)

The Unity of Torah

Along with the Written Torah that was given to Moses at Mount Sinai, the Oral Torah, which includes the interpretations of the laws and inferences from the verses of the Written Torah, was also given.

"These are the statutes and ordinances and laws which the Lord gave between Him and the children of Israel at Mount Sinai by the hand of Moses" (Leviticus 26:46). "The statutes," this is the Midrash;[239] "ordinances," these

---

237. Speak to them so they will provide us with sustenance and garments.
238. The verse is referring to the Torah, and the Sages expound that *lekah* means acquisition [*lekiha*].
239. The *halakhot* derived from a careful reading of the precise language of the text.

are the laws; "and laws,"[240] this teaches that two Torahs were given to Israel, one written and one oral....

"At Mount Sinai by the hand of Moses." This teaches that the entire Torah: its *halakhot*, inferences, and interpretation, were all given through Moses at Sinai.

"The Lord said to Moses: Ascend to Me, to the mountaintop, and be there; and I will give you the stone tablets and the law and the commandment that I have written, to teach them" (Exodus 24:12). Rabbi Levi bar Hama said that Rabbi Shimon ben Lakish said: What is the meaning of what is written: "And I will give you the stone tablets and the law and the commandment that I have written, to teach them"? "Tablets," these are the Ten Commandments; "law," these are the Five Books of Moses; "and the commandment," this is the Mishna; "that I have written," these are the Prophets and Writings; "to teach them," this is the Talmud. This teaches that they were all given to Moses at Sinai.

"Because he scorned the word of the Lord" (Numbers 15:31); this is referring to one who says that the Torah did not originate from Heaven.[241] And even if one said: The entire Torah is from Heaven except for this verse,[242] and even if one said: The entire Torah originated from Heaven except for this inference[243] by the Sages, or except for this *a fortiori* inference, or except for this verbal analogy,[244] this is included in: "Because he scorned the word of the Lord."

(Sifra, Behukotai 26; Berakhot 5a; Sanhedrin 99a)

📖 Further reading: For more about the concepts of Torah from Heaven and the sanctity of all components of the Torah, see *A Concise Guide to Mahshava*, p. 269.

---

240. Written in the plural.
241. i.e., he claims that the Torah was written by man.
242. i.e., he claims that one verse was written by man.
243. i.e., he denies the validity of one inference from the wording of the verse.
244. A law derived based on the incidence of an identical term in two different places in the Torah.

Torah Study

The Sages also address the approaches to studying Torah and the ways to attain Torah knowledge. The chapter that follows presents statements of the Sages regarding the requisite humility for those who toil in Torah study; who is worthy of studying Torah, the proper intention for Torah study; and the nature of teaching Torah to others, with all the associated difficulties.

Humility

The quality of humility is vital for one who seeks to study the Torah properly.

Rabbi Hanina bar Idi said: Why are matters of Torah likened to water, as it is written: "Ho, everyone thirsty, go to water" (Isaiah 55:1)? This verse serves to tell you: Just as water leaves a high place and flows to a low place, so too, matters of Torah are retained only by one whose spirit is humble.

Rabbi Oshaya said: Why are matters of Torah likened to these three liquids: to water, wine, and milk?... This serves to tell you: Just as these three liquids are maintained only in the lowliest of vessels,[245] so too, matters of Torah are retained only by one whose spirit is humble.

(Ta'anit 7a)

Who Is Worthy of Studying Torah?

Although ideally one should study Torah only for the sake of the mitzva, this does not mitigate his obligation to study Torah even if his motives are not pure. The Sages disagree concerning who is worthy of studying Torah: Is it only those who are wise and of distinguished lineage, or should it be available even to people of more modest lineage?

Rav Yehuda said that Rav said: A person should always engage in Torah study and mitzvot even not for their own sake,[246] as through their performance not for their own sake, one comes to perform them for their own sake.[247]

Beit Shammai say: One should teach only a person who is wise, humble, of distinguished lineage, and wealthy. Beit Hillel say: One should teach

---

245. Wine keeps best in the simplest earthenware vessel. It spoils in gold and silver vessels.
246. If he did so not in order to fulfill the mitzva and to fulfill the will of God, but rather to attain honor or for some other unrelated reason.
247. He will ultimately study Torah and fulfill mitzvot for the right reason.

any person, as there were many transgressors in Israel who were drawn to Torah study and they became righteous, pious, and decent individuals.

(*Nazir* 23b; *Avot deRabbi Natan*, version A, chap. 2)

From My Students More than All of Them

It is not always easy to engage in the study of Torah and completely understand its content. It is incumbent on the rabbi teaching his student to explain matters again and again, as often as necessary. Despite the difficulties inherent to studying and teaching, the cross-pollination that results from the exchanges between great Sages and their young students is one of the ways in which they glorify the Torah.

Matters of Torah are likened to silk garments: Just as you do not purchase silk garments quickly but you can tear them quickly,[248] so too, matters of Torah are difficult to acquire but easy to lose.[249] By contrast, inconsequential matters can be compared to sackcloth garments: Just as with regard to sackcloth garments, you purchase them quickly but you do not tear them quickly, so too, inconsequential matters are easy to acquire and difficult to lose.

Rabbi Perida had a certain student whom he would teach four hundred times, and ultimately he would learn the material. One day, some people sought Rabbi Perida's presence for a matter of a mitzva after the lesson. Rabbi Perida taught his student four hundred times as usual, but the student did not learn the material successfully. Rabbi Perida said to him: What is different today that you are unable to grasp the lesson? The student said to him: From the moment they said to the master that there is a matter of a mitzva for which he is needed, my mind was distracted from the lesson. Each moment I said: Now the master will stand; now the master will stand.[250]

Rabbi Perida said to him: Pay attention this time and I will teach you again, as you now know that I will not leave until you have mastered the lesson. He again taught him another four hundred times. A divine voice emerged and said to Rabbi Perida: Would you prefer that they add four hundred years to your life, or that you and your generation will merit the World to Come? He said: I prefer that I and my generation merit the World to Come. The Holy One, blessed be He, said to the angels: Give him this reward and that one.

---

248. One does not purchase silk quickly because it is expensive, but one can tear it quickly because it is delicate.

249. Torah is easily forgotten.

250. I was unable to concentrate because each moment I expected you to leave.

Sages on Life

Rav Nahman bar Yitzhak said: Why are Torah matters likened to a tree, as it is stated: "It is a tree of life for those who hold on to it" (Proverbs 3:18)? It serves to tell you that just as a small piece of wood kindles a large piece,[251] so too, young Torah scholars sharpen the great Torah scholars. This is what Rabbi Hanina said: I have learned much from my teachers and even more from my friends, but from my students I have learned more than from all of them.

(*Avot deRabbi Natan*, version B, chap. 31; *Eiruvin* 54b; *Ta'anit* 7a)

📖 **Further reading:** For more about the proper way to study Torah, see *A Concise Guide to Mahshava*, p. 276; *A Concise Guide to Halakha*, p. 509.

---

251. One uses twigs and kindling to start the fire, with the larger logs sustaining the fire.

Prayer

Standing before God in prayer is one of the central features of Jewish life. The Sages address the topic of prayer extensively, from the institution of the basic prayers and their laws to the meaning of prayer and its place in our lives.

The chapter that follows presents statements of the Sages regarding the service of prayer; preparation for and intent during prayer; prayer for the future and prayer for the past; and God, who hears prayer.

The Service of Prayer

The Sages define prayer as a service of the heart, and they consider it a substitute for the bringing of offerings after the Temple's destruction.

"To love the Lord your God, and to serve Him with all your heart and with all your soul" (Deuteronomy 11:13). Which is the service of God that is performed in the heart?[252] You must say that this is prayer.

"I am sleeping, but my heart is awake" (Song of Songs 5:2). "I am sleeping," from bringing the offerings;[253] "but my heart is awake," for the reciting of *Shema* and prayer. "I am sleeping," from the Temple; "but my heart is awake," for synagogues and study halls.

(*Ta'anit* 2a; *Shir HaShirim Rabba* 5)

Preparation and Intent of the Heart

Prayer requires both preparation and intent of the heart: One must approach prayer unhurriedly and with consideration, with a joyous state of mind, and after having performed an act of kindness for the poor.

The Sages taught: One may not stand to pray in an atmosphere of sadness or out of laziness, or while laughing, or while engaging in mundane conversation, or while engaging in frivolity, or while engaging in idle activity. Rather, one must stand to pray in an atmosphere imbued with the joy of performing a mitzva.

---

252. Which is the service that requires the intent of the heart?
253. When a person is unable to bring an offering he is likened to a sleeping person.

Rabbi Elazar would first give a *peruta*[254] to a poor person, and only then would he pray. He said that is as it is written: "Truly [*betzedek*], I shall see Your face" (Psalms 17:15).[255]

Rav Hana bar Bizna says that Rabbi Shimon Hasida says: One who prays must see himself as though the Divine Presence itself were opposite him, as it is stated: "I set the Lord before me always" (Psalms 16:8).

One stands and begins to pray only from a state of seriousness. The early pious men would wait one hour and pray,[256] so that they would direct their hearts to their Father in Heaven. Even if a king greets a person, he should not respond to him; and even if a snake is wound around his heel, he should not interrupt his prayer.

The Sages taught: There was an incident involving a particular pious man who was praying while on the road when a high-ranking gentile officer came and greeted him, but the pious man did not respond with a greeting. The officer waited for him until he completed his prayer.

After he completed his prayer, the officer said to him: Empty one![257] Isn't it written in your Torah: "Only beware, and protect your lives" (Deuteronomy 4:9)? And it is also written: "You shall greatly beware for your lives" (Deuteronomy 4:15). When I greeted you, why didn't you respond with a greeting? Were I to behead you with a sword, who would hold me accountable for your blood?[258]

The pious man said to him: Wait for me to appease you with my words. The man said to him: Had you been standing before a flesh-and-blood king and someone else came and greeted you, would you return his greeting? The officer said to him: No. The pious man continued: And had you returned his greeting, what would the king's officers have done to you? The officer said to him: They would have beheaded me with a sword.

The pious man said to him: Isn't this matter an *a fortiori* inference? You, who were [hypothetically] standing before a flesh-and-blood king who is here today and in the grave tomorrow, you would have done so and not responded. I, who was standing before the Supreme King of kings, the Holy One, blessed be He, who lives and endures for all eternity, all the more so

---

254. A *peruta* is a small coin.
255. *Betzedek* is an allusion to charity [*tzedaka*]. After dispensing *tzedaka*, one can approach and see God's face, in prayer.
256. During that hour they would prepare themselves for prayer.
257. You are a flighty and irresponsible person.
258. Could anyone hold me responsible? You failed to respond to me; therefore, it was you who endangered your life.

that I could not respond. The officer was immediately appeased, and that pious man returned home in peace.

(*Berakhot* 2a; *Bava Batra* 10a; *Sanhedrin* 2a; Mishna *Berakhot* 5:1; *Berakhot* 32b–33a)

A Prayer in Vain

Prayer is relevant when making requests regarding the future. Requests for changing past occurrences are prayers in vain.

Concerning one who cries out over the past, this is a prayer in vain. How so? If one's wife was pregnant and he says: May it be God's will that my wife will give birth to a male child, this is a prayer in vain. Or if one was coming on the path home and he heard the sound of a scream in the city, and he says: May it be God's will that this scream will not be from the members of my household, this is a prayer in vain.

(Mishna *Berakhot* 9:3)

He Who Hears Prayer

God is called "He who hears prayer." The Sages explain several ways in which this characterization is manifest.

"The one who hears prayer, all flesh comes to You" (Psalms 65:3). What is the meaning of: "The one who hears prayer"? Rabbi Pinhas said in the name of Rabbi Meir, and Rabbi Yirmeya said in the name of Rabbi Hiyya bar Abba: When Israel prays, you do not find that they all pray as one. Rather, each and every assembly prays by itself; first this assembly, and afterward that assembly....

After all the assemblies have completed all the prayers, the angel appointed over the prayers takes all the prayers that were prayed in all the assemblies and fashions them into crowns, which he places on the head of the Holy One, blessed be He, as it is stated: "All flesh comes to You [*adekha*]," and *adekha* means nothing other than a crown, as it is stated: "As you will don all of them like jewelry [*ka'adi*]" (Isaiah 49:18). And it likewise says: "Israel, in whom I glory" (Isaiah 49:3), which teaches that the Holy One, blessed be He, adorns Himself with the prayers of Israel....

Alternatively: "The one who hears prayer":...you find that flesh and blood cannot hear the conversation of two people simultaneously, but regarding the Holy One, blessed be He, it is not so. Rather, everyone prays before Him simultaneously, and He hears and accepts all their prayers.

Sages on Life

Alternatively: "The one who hears prayer": Rabbi Yehuda bar Shalom said in the name of Rabbi Elazar: With regard to flesh and blood, if a pauper comes to say something to him, he does not listen to him, but with regard to the Holy One, blessed be He, it is not so. Rather, everyone is equal before Him: women, slaves, the poor, and the wealthy.

(*Shemot Rabba* 25)

📖 Further reading: For more about prayer, see *A Concise Guide to Mahshava*, p. 300.

The Prayer of God

Not only do we pray, but God, too, as it were, prays. His prayer is that He should have mercy on Israel and treat them with kindness, beyond the letter of the law.

Rabbi Yohanan said in the name of Rabbi Yosei: From where is it derived that the Holy One, blessed be He, prays? As it is stated: "I will bring them to My holy mountain and I will bring them joy in My house of prayer" (Isaiah 56:7). It does not state "their [house of] prayer," but "My [house of] prayer." From here it is derived that the Holy One, blessed be He, prays.

What does God pray? Rav Zutra bar Toveya said that Rav said: God's prayer is: May it be My will that My mercy will overcome My anger, and may My mercy prevail over My other attributes,[259] and may I act toward My children with the attribute of mercy, and may I enter before them beyond the letter of the law.[260]

The Sages taught that Rabbi Yishmael ben Elisha the High Priest said: Once on Yom Kippur I entered the innermost sanctum, the Holy of Holies, to offer incense, and in a vision I saw Akatriel Ya,[261] the Lord of hosts, seated on a high and exalted throne. He said to me: Yishmael My son, bless Me. I recited before Him [the prayer that God prays]: May it be Your will that Your mercy will overcome Your anger, and may Your mercy prevail over Your other attributes, and may You act toward Your children with the attribute of mercy, and may You enter before them beyond the letter of the law. And God nodded His head in agreement.

(*Berakhot* 7a)

📖 Further reading: For the *halakhot* of various prayers, see *A Concise Guide to Halakha*, p. 483.

---

259. For example, it should overcome the attribute of justice.
260. May I treat them with benevolence even when they do not deserve it.
261. This is one of God's names.

Repentance

The opportunity available to an individual to rectify his actions, to regret having performed them, and to improve his ways; in other words, to repent, is a central concept that the Sages discuss at length. The chapter that follows presents statements of the Sages regarding how God teaches people to repent and anticipates their repentance; the demand that the individual engage in perpetual repentance; the great virtue of penitents; and how one moment of repentance is capable of repairing an entire lifetime of sin.

God Teaches the Path of Repentance

The existence of repentance as an option for the sinner is not self-evident. Ostensibly, the sinner should be held responsible for his actions and bear the consequences. It is God alone who offers people this opportunity.

Rabbi Pinhas said: "Good and upright is the Lord" (Psalms 25:8). Why is He good? Because He is upright. And why is He upright? Because He is good. "Therefore He instructs sinners in the way" (Psalms 25:8), as He instructs them in the way of repentance.

They asked wisdom: What is the fitting punishment of a sinner? Wisdom said to them: "Evil pursues sinners" (Proverbs 13:21). They asked prophecy: What is the punishment of a sinner? Prophecy said to them: "The soul that sins, it will die" (Ezekiel 18:4). They asked the Holy One, blessed is He: What is the punishment of a sinner? He said to them: Let him repent and the sin will be atoned for him.

This is the meaning of what is written: "Therefore He instructs sinners in the way"; He instructs sinners in the path of repentance.

(Jerusalem Talmud, *Makkot* 2:6)

Great Is Repentance

The Sages are expansive in praising the virtue of repentance, which reaches the heavenly Throne and is capable of transforming even a person's most severe sins into merits.

Rabbi Levi said: Great is repentance, as it reaches the heavenly Throne....

Rabbi Yonatan said: Great is repentance, as it facilitates the redemption, as it is stated: "A redeemer will come to Zion and to those who repent from transgression in Jacob" (Isaiah 59:20).

Reish Lakish said: Great is repentance, as intentional sins are transformed for him into unwitting transgressions.... Is that so? Didn't Reish Lakish himself say: Great is repentance, as intentional sins are transformed for him into merits?... This is not difficult: Here, one repents out of love [and his sins transform into merits]; there, one repents out of fear [and his sins transform into unwitting transgressions].

Rabbi Shmuel bar Nahmani said that Rabbi Yonatan said: Great is repentance, as it lengthens a person's years....

The Sages taught that Rabbi Meir would say: Great is repentance, as due to one individual who repents, the heavenly court forgives the entire world.

(*Yoma* 86a–b)

May Sin Be Removed, Not Sinners

Berurya, Rabbi Meir's wife, spurred him to understand that it is not the sinners who should be eliminated from the world, but rather sin itself.

There were hooligans in Rabbi Meir's neighborhood who were causing him a great deal of anguish. Rabbi Meir would pray for God to have mercy on them, that they should die. Rabbi Meir's wife, Berurya, said to him: What is your thinking? Is it because it is written: "May sinners [*hata'im*][262] be removed [from the earth]" (Psalms 104:35)? But is it written, "May sinners [*hotim*] be removed"? Rather, *hata'im* is written. Furthermore, go to the end of the verse: "And may the wicked be no more." This is apparently superfluous, as once the sinners are removed, then of course the wicked will be no more. Rather, the beginning of the verse is referring to sins, not sinners, and therefore pray for God to have mercy on them, that they should repent, and then "the wicked will be no more." Rabbi Meir agreed, and prayed for God to have mercy on them, and they repented.

(*Berakhot* 10a)

---

262. The term *hata'im* literally means sins, but in this verse it is understood to mean sinners.

At All Times, May Your Garments Be White

A person does not know when his time will come and he will be called before his Creator. It is therefore advisable for one to rectify his ways each and every day, rather than procrastinate and miss his opportunity.

We learned there: Rabbi Eliezer says: Repent one day before your death.

Rabbi Eliezer's students asked him: But does a person know the day on which he will die? He said to them: All the more so; one should repent today lest he die tomorrow, and one will thereby spend his entire life engaged in repentance. King Solomon also said in his wisdom: "At all times, may your garments be white and may the oil on your head not be lacking" (Ecclesiastes 9:8). Rabban Yohanan ben Zakkai said: This can be explained by means of a parable of a king who invited his servants to a feast and did not set a precise time for them to come. The wise among them adorned themselves and sat at the entrance to the king's house,[263] saying: Is the king's house lacking anything?[264] The fools among them went to their work, saying: Is there a feast without the toil of preparation?[265]

Suddenly, the king requested that his servants come to the feast. The wise among them entered before him adorned in their finery, and the fools entered before him dirty. The king was happy at the approach of the wise ones and angry at the approach of the fools. He said: These wise servants who adorned themselves for the feast will sit and eat and drink, whereas these fools who did not adorn themselves for the feast will stand and watch.

(Mishna *Avot* 2:10; *Shabbat* 153a)

Open for Me an Entrance

God anticipates and waits for His children to repent. When they indeed repent, it is as though they are created anew and merit a status that even the righteous do not attain.

As long as a person is alive, the Holy One, blessed be He, awaits his repentance. Once he dies, his hope is lost, as it is stated: "With the death of a wicked man, hope is lost" (Proverbs 11:7).

Rabbi Yoshiya said: It is due to three matters that the Holy One, blessed be He, is patient[266] with the wicked in this world: Perhaps they will repent;

---

263. They were waiting expectantly for the king to summon them.
264. It will not take them long to prepare the feast.
265. We have time, as it takes a while to prepare a feast.
266. He is patient and does not punish them immediately.

or perhaps they will perform mitzvot for which the Holy One, blessed be He, will want to reward them in this world; or perhaps righteous children will emerge from them. As we found in the Bible that God was patient with the wicked Ahaz, and Hizkiyahu emerged from him, with Amon,[267] and Yoshiyahu[268] emerged from him, and with Shimi,[269] and Mordekhai emerged from him.

Prayer is likened to a ritual bath, and repentance is likened to a sea. Just as a ritual bath is sometimes open and sometimes locked, so too, the gates of prayer are sometimes locked and sometimes open. By contrast, the sea is always open; so too, the gates of repentance are always open.

"Open for me" (Song of Songs 5:2). Rabbi Yisa said that the Holy One, blessed be He, said to Israel: My children, open for Me one entrance of repentance even the size of the eye of a needle, and I will open for you entrances through which carriages and wagons can enter.

"Let this be recorded for the last generation" (Psalms 102:19):[270] It can be derived from here that the Holy One, blessed be He, accepts penitents. "So that those yet to be born may praise the Lord" (Psalms 102:19): This teaches that the Holy One, blessed be He, will fashion penitents into new creations.[271]

In the place[272] where penitents stand, completely righteous individuals cannot stand.

(*Kohelet Rabba* 7; *Eikha Rabba* 3; *Shir HaShirim Rabba* 5;
Vayikra Rabba 30; *Berakhot* 34b)

One Who Acquires His Share in the World to Come in a Single Moment

In a single moment of sincere repentance, a person can rectify the sins of an entire lifetime.

They said about Rabbi Elazar ben Durdaya that he did not leave a single prostitute in the world with whom he did not engage in intimate relations. Once he heard that there was a prostitute in one of the cities overseas who

---

267. Ahaz was a wicked king of Judah, as was his great-grandson, Amon.
268. Hizkiyahu was a righteous king of Judah, as was his great-grandson, Yoshiyahu.
269. Shimi son of Gera cursed King David when he fled from Avshalom (II Samuel 16:7).
270. The word "last" is not used in this context in a chronological sense, but rather is a reference to those whose actions are last qualitatively.
271. It will be as if they were created anew.
272. The reference is to their place in the World to Come.

would take a purse full of dinars as her payment. He took a purse of dinars and went and crossed seven rivers to reach her.

When they were engaged in the customary matters [a euphemism for intercourse], she passed wind and said: Just as this passed wind will not return to its place, so too, Elazar ben Durdaya, they will not accept him in repentance.

Elazar ben Durdaya went and sat between two mountains and hills, he said: Mountains and hills, pray for mercy on my behalf. They said to him: Before we pray for mercy on your behalf, we must pray for mercy on our behalf… He said: Sun and moon, pray for mercy on my behalf. They said to him: Before we pray for mercy on your behalf, we must pray for mercy on our behalf… He said: Stars and constellations, pray for mercy on my behalf. They said to him: Before we pray for mercy on your behalf, we must pray for mercy on our behalf….

Elazar ben Durdaya said: Clearly the matter of repentance is dependent only on me. He placed his head between his knees and wept bitterly until his soul departed his body. A divine voice emerged and said: Rabbi Elazar ben Durdaya is destined for life in the World to Come.

When Rabbi Yehuda HaNasi heard this, he wept, and said: There is a person who acquires his share in the World to Come only after many years of toil, and there is one who acquires his share in the World to Come in a single moment. And Rabbi Yehuda HaNasi said: It is not sufficient that they accept the penitents, but they even call them: Rabbi.[273]

A single moment of repentance and good deeds in this world is preferable to all the life in the World to Come.

(*Avoda Zara* 17a; Mishna *Avot* 4:17)

📖 Further reading: For more on repentance, see *A Concise Guide to Mahshava*, p. 316.

Sages on Life

---

273. The divine voice referred to the newly penitent lifelong sinner with the honorific Rabbi.

Passages from the Talmud

How the Prayers Were Instituted

This passage, which appears in the Babylonian Talmud, tractate *Berakhot* 26b, seeks to ascertain precisely what the source for prayer is and who first instituted it. The question that arises is: Were prayers established parallel to offerings, as a replacement for offerings after the destruction of the Second Temple; or do they have an independent source unrelated to the Temple service? One opinion identifies the historical source of the institution of prayer to the founding fathers of the Jewish nation, Abraham, Isaac, and Jacob, who themselves prayed. The other opinion is that the prayer is structured to correspond to the times of the daily offering in the Temple. Although these opinions are not necessarily contradictory, the Talmud contrasts them and draws a conclusion based on a synthesis of the two: Prayer is an obligation whose source is an ancient ordinance dating back to the patriarchs, while at the same time the specific details of the protocols of prayer and their times were instituted at a later stage, based on the sacrificial service in the Temple.

The Source of the Obligation to Pray

The Torah commands a person to pray. This mitzva appears in the verse: "To love the Lord your God, and to serve Him with all your heart and with all your soul" (Deuteronomy 11:13). The Sages said: Which is the service of God that is performed in the heart?... It is prayer (*Ta'anit* 2a). This obligation is stated in general terms. In practice, it was instituted that one must pray three times on each day of the week: morning, afternoon, and evening; and pray an additional prayer on Shabbat and festivals, the *Musaf* prayer.

A Discussion between *Amora'im*

The passage begins with the presentation of the opinions of two *amora'im*[1] regarding the source of the institution of prayer.

---

1. *Amora'im*: The Sages of the Talmud (Babylonia and the Land of Israel, circa 200–550 CE).

It was stated that **Rabbi Yosei son of Rabbi Hanina**[2] **said: The prayers were instituted by the patriarchs,** Abraham, Isaac, and Jacob. **Rabbi Yehoshua ben Levi**[3] **said: The prayers were instituted**[4] **based on the daily** burnt **offerings** sacrificed every morning and evening in the Temple.

Introduction of a Proof from a *Baraita*

The Talmud suggests that a proof can be brought from a *baraita* in support of the opinions of each of the *amora'im*.

It was taught in a *baraita*[5] **in accordance with** the opinion **of Rabbi Yosei son of Rabbi Hanina and it was taught** in a *baraita* **in accordance with** the opinion **of Rabbi Yehoshua ben Levi.**

Presentation of the Proof from a *Baraita*

The Talmud cites proof from a *baraita* in support of the opinion of Rabbi Yosei son of Rabbi Hanina that the patriarchs instituted the prayers.

It was taught in a *baraita* **in accordance with** the opinion **of Rabbi Yosei son of Rabbi Hanina: Abraham instituted the morning prayer, as it is stated: "Abraham arose early in the morning to the place where he stood** before the Lord" (Genesis 19:27), **and** the verb **standing** in this verse means **nothing other than**[6] **prayer.** The proof for this is **that it is stated: "Pinhas stood up to carry out judgment,** and the plague was stopped" (Psalms 106:30). Just as the verb "stood" is used in the context of Pinhas's prayer to halt the plague, here too, when Abraham stood early in the morning it was for the purpose of prayer.

---

2. Rabbi Yosei son of Rabbi Hanina: A third-generation *amora* of the Land of Israel, and a student of Rabbi Yohanan.
3. Rabbi Yehoshua ben Levi: A first-generation *amora* of the Land of Israel, who headed the talmudic academy in Lod and Tiberias.
4. The prayers were instituted by the patriarchs: In principle, "one does not learn anything from what preceded the revelation at Sinai" (see Jerusalem Talmud, *Moed Katan* 3:5). Accordingly, no *halakha* can be derived from the conduct of the patriarchs, as they lived before the nation of Israel received the Torah. Here, by contrast, the Talmud is seeking the source for the custom and the obligation to pray, not the halakhic authority of the obligation.
5. *Baraita*: Literally, "external," a *baraita* is a passage from tannaitic literature that was not included in the Mishna.
6. Means nothing other than: In halakhic midrash of this kind, a specific meaning is ascribed to an ambiguous word. The interpretation is based on another verse in the Bible where that term is employed in a clear, unambiguous context.

Isaac instituted the afternoon prayer, as it is stated: "Isaac went out to walk [*lasuah*] **in the field toward evening"** (Genesis 24:63), **and** the term *siha* in this verse means **nothing other than prayer.** And the proof is **that it is stated: "The prayer of a poor man, when he feels overwhelmed and pours out his woes** [*siho*] **before the Lord"** (Psalms 102:1). This indicates that Isaac was the first to pray as evening approached, at the time of the afternoon prayer.

Jacob instituted the evening prayer, as it is stated: "He came upon ⌊*vayifga*⌋ **the place, and stayed the night there** because the sun had set" (Genesis 28:11), **and** the term *pegia* in this verse means **nothing other than prayer.** And the proof is **that it is stated,** when God spoke to the prophet Jeremiah: **"And you, do not pray on behalf of this people, and do not lift up a cry or a prayer on their behalf, and do not plead** [*tifga*] **with Me,** for I am not listening to you" (Jeremiah 7:16).

Proof from a *Baraita*

The Talmud cites proof from a *baraita* in support of the opinion of Rabbi Yehoshua ben Levi.

And it was taught in a *baraita* **in accordance with** the opinion **of Rabbi Yehoshua ben Levi,** as the *baraita* explicitly links the times of prayer to the times of the daily offerings: **Why did** the Rabbis **say** that **the morning prayer** may be recited **until noon? Because** the **daily morning** burnt **offering** may be **sacrificed until noon. And Rabbi Yehuda says: Until four hours,**[7] **because the daily morning offering** may be **sacrificed until four hours.**

And why did the Rabbis **say** that **the afternoon prayer** may be recited **until the evening? Because the daily afternoon offering**[8] **is sacrificed until the evening. Rabbi Yehuda says:** The afternoon prayer may be re-

7. Hours: Although, typically, an hour refers to a fixed period of sixty minutes, in certain halakhic contexts the period of daylight is divided into twelve, and each twelfth of that period is one temporal hour. Consequently, the duration of the temporal hour will vary depending on the length of the period of daylight during the different seasons of the year.

8. The daily morning offering…the daily afternoon offering: A burnt offering brought twice daily, once in the morning and once toward evening (see Numbers 28:3–6). The afternoon offering is called by this name because it is typically sacrificed nine and a half hours into the day. The earliest time that the afternoon offering was sacrificed was when the day before Passover coincided with Friday, in which case it was brought six and a half hours into the day. "Afternoon" [*bein ha'arbayim*] is a general term for the period of time from when the sun tends westward, shortly after midday, until sunset.

cited only **until the midpoint of the afternoon,**[9] **as the daily afternoon offering is sacrificed until the midpoint of the afternoon.**

And why did they say that **the evening prayer is not fixed,** it does not have a set time during the night? **Because** the internal **limbs and fats**[10] of the animal offerings that were **not consumed** by the fire on the altar **until the evening** remained on the altar and were **offered continuously** throughout **the entire night.**

And why did the Rabbis **say** that **the additional prayer** may be recited **all day? Because the additional offering is brought** throughout **the entire day. Rabbi Yehuda says:** The additional prayer may be recited **until the seventh hour, because the additional offering may be sacrificed until the seventh hour...**

A Difficulty

The Talmud raises a difficulty to the opinion of Rabbi Yosei son of Rabbi Hanina from the *baraita* that supports the opinion of Rabbi Yehoshua ben Levi.

...Let us say that **this should be a conclusive refutation**[11] of the opinion **of Rabbi Yosei son of Rabbi Hanina,** who maintains that the patriarchs instituted the prayers, whereas the *baraita* expressly states that the prayers correspond to the offerings.

The Resolution

The Talmud resolves the difficulty by suggesting a more nuanced analysis of the opinion of Rabbi Yosei son of Rabbi Hanina.

Rabbi Yosei son of Rabbi Hanina could have **said to you: Actually, I will say to you** that **the patriarchs instituted the prayers, and the Sages based** the times and characteristics of prayer **on the Temple offerings.**[12]

---

9. The midpoint of the afternoon: Halfway between the time of bringing the afternoon offering, at nine and a half hours of the day, and sunset.

10. Because the limbs and fats: The Jerusalem Talmud (*Berakhot* 4:1) cites an alternative explanation: The evening prayer is not fixed because they did not find any offering corresponding to it, and the Sages instituted it independently.

11. Let us say that this should be a conclusive refutation: This expression indicates a difficulty raised from a tannaitic source with regard to the opinion of an *amora*. Literally, it means: Let us say that it is a response, meaning that this is a response to and a refutation of the statement of the *amora*, or that the *amora* himself must respond to this difficulty because it is an especially strong challenge.

12. And the Sages based them on the Temple offerings: The enactments of the Sages are often modeled on earlier precedents in the Torah, or on more explicit *halakhot*: "Everything that the Sages instituted, they instituted parallel to Torah law" (see *Yevamot* 11a).

Reinforcing the Resolution

The Talmud proves that there is no alternative to the proposed resolution.

As, if you do not say so,[13] that the laws of offerings and the laws of prayers are related, it is unclear: **According to Rabbi Yosei son of Rabbi Hanina, who instituted the additional prayer?** It is not one of the prayers instituted by the patriarchs. **Rather,** there is no alternative to the aforementioned resolution: According to Rabbi Yosei son of Rabbi Hanina, **the prayers were instituted by the patriarchs and the Sages based** the times and characteristics of prayer on the laws of the **offerings.**

Summary

This passage comprises three stages: 1) The presentation of the opinions of the *amora'im*: Were the prayers instituted by the patriarchs, or did the Sages institute them parallel to the daily offerings? 2) *Baraitot* that support the statements of the *amora'im*: A *baraita* in the style of a halakhic midrash that supports the opinion of Rabbi Yosei son of Rabbi Hanina that the patriarchs instituted the prayers, and a *baraita* in accordance with the opinion of Rabbi Yehoshua ben Levi that establishes that the daily prayers are modeled after the times of the daily offerings in the Temple. 3) The difficulty and its resolution: The Talmud raises a difficulty to the opinion of Rabbi Yosei son of Rabbi Hanina from a *baraita*, and suggests that the opinion of Rabbi Yosei son of Rabbi Hanina does not in fact diverge from the opinion in that *baraita*. Rather, he is proposing a more complex understanding: Although the patriarchs instituted the prayers, the Sages structured them on the basis of the daily offerings. In that way, the Sages were able to institute the additional prayer; despite the fact that there is no corresponding patriarch, it was modeled after the additional offering brought in the Temple.

Ramifications

The halakhic ruling: Were the prayers instituted by the patriarchs or based on the daily offerings? Since the Talmud does not present this as a clear-cut dispute, some halakhic authorities are inclined toward the opinion that the prayers were instituted to correspond to the daily offerings. Therefore,

---

13. As, if you do not say so: This expression introduces a proof by process of elimination. A certain assumption is posited, and it is then shown that it leads to an illogical conclusion, which must be rejected.

matters relevant to the laws of the offerings apply to prayer as well, e.g., the obligation to pray in a fixed place, just as offerings were brought in the Temple; and the fact that an improper thought can invalidate a prayer, just as it can invalidate an offering (see *Tur, Oraḥ Ḥayim* 98). The Rambam, too, presents the times of the prayers as corresponding to the offerings (*Mishneh Torah*[14] *Sefer Ahava, Hilkhot Tefilla* 1:4), although elsewhere he states that the prayers were instituted by the patriarchs (*Mishneh Torah, Sefer Shofetim, Hilkhot Melakhim* 9:7). Some explain that the Rambam rules in accordance with the opinion that the structure of the prayers was fixed parallel to the offerings (*Kesef Mishneh*[15]), while others explain that he holds there is no dispute between the Sages with regard to this point (*Leḥem Mishneh*[16]). The authorities also discuss possible practical differences between these opinions. For example, may one recite a voluntary prayer at his own initiative however he wishes, or whether even a voluntary prayer, too, must be recited in accordance with the principles governing a gift offering in the Temple.

The Ordinance of Prayer

The Mitzva of Prayer

The obligation to pray is derived from the verse: "To love the Lord your God, and to serve Him with all your heart and with all your soul" (Deuteronomy 11:13). Which is the service of God that is performed in the heart? ... This is prayer (*Ta'anit* 2a). The Rambam[17] maintains that the mitzva is to pray every day (*Mishneh Torah, Sefer HaMitzvot*, positive commandment 5), whereas the Ramban contends that the mitzva is to pray whenever a person finds himself in times of trouble and feels a need to turn to God (Ramban's comments on Rambam, *Mishneh Torah, Sefer HaMitzvot*, positive commandment 5).

---

14. *Mishneh Torah*: The great halakhic work by Rabbi Moshe ben Maimon, the Rambam, twelfth century, Spain and Egypt.
15. *Kesef Mishneh*: Written by Rav Yosef Karo, sixteenth century, Safed, it identifies and explains the sources of the rulings of the Rambam in his *Mishneh Torah*.
16. *Leḥem Mishneh*: The name of a commentary on the *Mishneh Torah* by Rav Avraham de Boton, sixteenth century, Salonica.
17. Ramban: An acronym for Rabbi Moshe ben Naḥman, who wrote a commentary on the Torah and the Talmud. He was also a halakhic authority, kabbalist, doctor, and philosopher, thirteenth century, Spain.

The Formula of Prayer

The formula of the prayers evolved over time, from the prayers of biblical figures until their consolidation into the Sephardic and Ashkenazic prayer books in use today. The general structure and formula began to take shape in the early Second Temple period, when the members of the Great Assembly composed the *Amida* prayer (*Megilla* 17b). The Mishna and Gemara already mention several sections of the prayers, among them the morning blessings, the verses of song from the book of Psalms, the Daily Psalm, *Hallel*, and the blessings of *Shema*, but these are not presented in a systematic or precise order, and it is difficult to ascertain the order in which these sections are to be recited.

The complete prayer formula, from beginning to end, dates back to the geonic period, and it first appears in the prayer books of Rav Amram Gaon[18] and Rav Se'adya Gaon[19] (including Kaddish inserted between the various sections, and the blessings before and after the verses of song) and in the order of prayers at the end of *Mishneh Torah, Sefer Ahava,* of the Rambam. In later generations, the *hasidim* of Ashkenaz,[20] the Ari[21] and his disciples, and the leaders of the Hasidic movement all continued editing, formulating, and revising on the basis of earlier versions of the prayer book, primarily on the basis of mysticism. They even added certain sections to the prayer book. In that way, the formula of the different prayer books was consolidated.

Prayer Times

The obligation to pray three times a day is based on a verse in the book of Daniel: "Three times a day he knelt on his knees" (Daniel 6:11). The time for each of these prayers corresponds to the time of the sacrifice of the fixed offerings brought in the Temple in Jerusalem. The calculations of the correct times of day and night are affected by the position of the earth relative to the sun during the various seasons of the year, as well as the geographic location of the one praying. Consequently, the time for prayer varies from place to place. The appropriate time to pray is influenced by the situation of the specific individual in question as well: His employment, his involve-

---

18. Rav Amram Gaon: Head of the talmudic academy of Sura in the geonic period, ninth century, Babylonia.
19. Rav Se'adya Gaon: Head of the talmudic academy of Sura in the geonic period, tenth century, Egypt and Iraq.
20. The *hasidim* of Ashkenaz: This specific reference is primarily to one of the leaders of this movement, Rabbi Elazar of Worms, author of *Sefer HaRokeah*, thirteenth century, Germany.
21. The Ari: An acronym for the great kabbalist, Rav Yitzhak Ashkenazi Luria, sixteenth century, Safed.

ment in public affairs, the place where he is located, his ability to pray with proper intent, and his proximity to a place of prayer. In accordance with the above variables, one is often obligated to pray slightly earlier or later than the prescribed times of the fixed prayers.

How Is the Composition of a Court Determined?

This passage, from the Babylonian Talmud, tractate *Sanhedrin* 23a, addresses the question of how to maintain the objectivity of judges, while at the same time providing the litigants with a feeling of trust in them and their ability to understand and consider the position of each of the parties. Should each side be permitted to select its judges, or should the members of the court be determined irrespective of their interests?

The mishna presents a complex model, in which each party can select a judge acceptable to him, with the third judge chosen by the selected judges. The Talmud first seeks to ascertain whether the mishna means that each party chooses an entire tribunal of judges, and the two tribunals determine the final composition, or whether each party selects only one judge, and those two judges select the third judge.

In the course of its analysis of the mishna, the Gemara takes several factors relevant to the matter into consideration: the level of expertise of the court ("laymen's courts in Syria" or "a court of experts"), the nature of the claim (a loan as opposed to other disputes regarding monetary law), and the extent to which the claimant can impose on the respondent to try the case before another court ("they compel him and it is adjudicated in his city").

Monetary law is a system of statutes tied to the resolution of interpersonal financial disputes. These monetary cases are adjudicated before a court of three judges, and in certain cases, even before three laymen; and sometimes even before a single expert, as explained at the beginning of tractate *Sanhedrin*. The mishna that follows opens the chapter that addresses the protocols of judgment in cases involving monetary law.

Mishna

How do the litigants select a court?

The mishna addresses the process of selecting a court, in accordance with the preferences of the parties to the dispute. **Mishna:** Cases of **monetary law** are adjudicated by **three** judges. **This** litigant **chooses one for himself and that** litigant **chooses one for himself, and the two of them choose one more for themselves;** this is **the statement of Rabbi Meir. And the Rabbis say:** The **two judges** who were chosen, not the litigants, **choose one more** judge **for themselves.**

Clarification

The Talmud clarifies the meaning of the statement that opens the mishna.

Gemara: At the beginning of the discussion, the Gemara assumes that "one" means an entire tribunal, composed of three judges. It therefore asks: **What** is the meaning of: **This** litigant **chooses**[22] **one for himself and that** litigant **chooses one for himself?** Isn't it **sufficient** to adjudicate the case **with three** judges? There is no need to select two entire courts, a total of six judges, to choose three other judges.

Response

The Talmud suggests an alternative explanation of the mishna's ruling.

This is what the mishna **is saying:** In a situation **where this** litigant **chooses one court for himself,** in accordance with his preference, **and that** litigant **chooses one court for himself** that he prefers, **both of them** must reach a compromise and **choose one additional** court **for themselves.** They must agree on the composition of the court that will judge them.

---

22. This litigant chooses: This passage in the Gemara has been explained in several different ways. Some explain that the problem is not that there are too many judges participating in the selection process, but rather the opposite; the problem is that the number of judges diminishes. This interpretation assumes that the word *one* in the mishna in fact refers to one judge, and understands that each party selects a judge and disqualifies the judge of the other party, until they ultimately agree upon one judge. Judges who were disqualified do not sit in judgment, leaving only one judge to try the case. This is problematic, as the mishna explicitly states: Cases of monetary law are adjudicated by three (Ran). Others explain that the difficulty is merely with the formulation of the mishna, which creates the impression that each party is obligated to choose a judge or a court, even if he does not want to do so (*Tosafot*).

A Difficulty

The Talmud raises a difficulty to the ruling of the mishna from a statement of Rabbi Elazar.

In light of the fact that the mishna spoke in general terms about a claimant and respondent who may determine the members of the court, the Gemara asks: And **can even a debtor prevent** selection of the court, and refuse to be judged before a court that he rejects? **But doesn't Rabbi Elazar**[23] **say:** The Sages **taught** that **only a creditor**[24] can refuse to be judged by a court chosen by the debtor, due to his desire to be judged by a prominent court, **but a debtor** cannot refuse in a like manner, as **they compel him** to **be judged** in the court that convenes **in** the creditor's **city.**

The Resolution

The Talmud resolves the apparent contradiction between the ruling of the mishna and the statement of Rabbi Elazar by explaining the situation to which the mishna refers.

The Gemara answers: It is **as Rabbi Yohanan**[25] **said** elsewhere: The Sages **taught with regard to** the laymen's **courts**[26] **in Syria.**[27] **Here, too,** the mishna is addressing a similar situation: **They taught** the *halakha* in the mishna[28] **with regard to** the laymen's **courts in Syria,** where even a debtor can refuse

---

23. Rabbi Elazar: Rabbi Elazar ben Pedat, a third-generation *amora* in the Land of Israel, and a student of Rabbi Yohanan. Rabbi Elazar immigrated to the Land of Israel from Babylonia.

24. The Sages taught that only a creditor: Rabbi Elazar restricts the right of a debtor to choose a more prominent court instead of his local court. The reason is that the cost of traveling to that place and remaining there could amount to more than the sum of the loan, and the lender is accorded an advantageous position vis-à-vis the debtor, in accordance with the verse: "A borrower is a servant to a man who lends" (Proverbs 22:7). See also *Sanhedrin* 31b.

25. Rabbi Yohanan: A second-generation *amora* in the Land of Israel, head of the talmudic academy in Tiberias.

26. Laymen's courts [*arkaot*]: From the Greek ἀρχή, *arkhē*, meaning magistracy, administration, and the like. The use of the letter *ayin* in the Hebrew spelling may be a result of the similarity in meaning to the Hebrew word *erekh*, value, or *arikha*, arrangement.

27. Syria: Syria is the name used in the Mishna and Gemara to refer to the lands to the north and northeast between the Land of Israel and the Euphrates River. Most of Syria (Aram) was conquered by King David, but this conquest rendered Syria halakhically equivalent to the Land of Israel only concerning specific matters, e.g., the obligation of first fruits, whereas concerning other *halakhot*, e.g., *orla* and *halla*, it was accorded an intermediate halakhic status between that of the Land of Israel and the countries outside Israel.

28. They taught the *halakha* in the mishna: During the period of the Mishna and Gemara, the scholars would review the *mishnayot* orally, and at times they would interject an explanation or clarification to the text of the mishna when reciting it.

to be judged before the court chosen by the creditor, and claim that they are not worthy judges. **But,** by inference, if the creditor chooses a court of **experts,** the debtor does **not** have the right to refuse to be judged before them.

An Alternative Resolution

The Talmud suggests a different resolution of the apparent contradiction between the ruling of the mishna and the statement of Rabbi Elazar.

In the previous answer of Rabbi Yohanan, it was stated that the mishna is addressing the situation regarding laymen's courts. Rav Pappa[29] offers a different resolution: **Rav Pappa said:** One can understand the mishna **even if you say** that the mishna is referring to courts of **experts, like the courts of Rav Huna[30] and of Rav Hisda,[31]** who were both experts and resided in the same city.

The Talmud explains why in that situation the debtor can refuse judgment before a court of experts: **As,** in that case, the debtor **can say to** the creditor: **Am I imposing on you** by requesting that you go for judgment elsewhere? According to Rav Pappa's response, the debtor may refuse judgment before a court of experts in that city. Although he may not compel the creditor to go to another city, in accordance with the opinion of Rabbi Elazar that the creditor may force the debtor to appear in the court that convenes in his own city, the debtor may insist on judgment before a different court of experts in that city.

An Additional Difficulty to the Explanation of the Mishna

The Talmud proceeds to clarify the ruling in the mishna according to the opinion of the Rabbis, who disagree with Rabbi Meir.

The Gemara cites an excerpt from the mishna. **We learned** in the mishna: **And the Rabbis say:** The **two judges** who were chosen **choose one more for themselves.** The Gemara asks: **If it enters your mind** to interpret the mishna **as we said** before, that "one" refers to one court, is it possible that **after** each **court was disqualified** by one of the litigants, as each party is able to disqualify the court chosen by the other side, that the members of both

---

29. Rav Pappa: A fifth-generation Babylonian *amora*, and a student of the *amora'im* Abaye and Rava.
30. Rav Huna: A second-generation Babylonian *amora*, and a student of the *amora* Rav and his replacement as the head of the talmudic academy in Sura.
31. Rav Hisda: A third-generation Babylonian *amora*, and a student of Rav Huna and his replacement as the head of the talmudic academy in Sura.

courts can **go and choose another court for themselves?** It is illogical that judges who have been disqualified from judgment, for whatever reason, will be the ones who select the court that will ultimately try the case.

Yet Another Difficulty

And furthermore, there is another difficulty: **What** is the meaning of: **This** litigant **chooses one for himself and that** litigant **chooses one for himself,** which is formulated as a command? After all, choosing a court is the prerogative of each of the parties, not an obligation they must fulfill.

A New Proposed Explanation of the Mishna

The Talmud presents a different explanation of the mishna, in light of the difficulties it raised against the previous interpretation.

Rather, the term "one" is not referring to the court, and instead it means one judge, and **this** is what the mishna **is saying;** this is how the entire sentence in the mishna should be explained: **When this** litigant **chooses one judge for himself,** before whom he requests to be judged, **and that** litigant **chooses one** other **judge for himself,** to be a member of that tribunal, **the two** judges then **choose one** additional judge **for themselves** as the third judge on the court. According to this interpretation, the selection of the court is achieved in two stages: First, each side chooses the judge he prefers, and then the two judges jointly select the third member of the tribunal.

The Logic behind the New Explanation

Having drawn a conclusion regarding the meaning of the text of the mishna, the Gemara seeks to ascertain the reason for the *halakha*: **What is different** about this procedure, i.e., **that** the selection of the judges is **performed** specifically **in this** manner, with each side choosing a judge?

The Gemara answers by citing a halakhic tradition from the Land of Israel. The Sages **in the West,** the Land of Israel, **say in the name of Rabbi Zeira** that the reason for the mishna's ruling is: **As a result of** the fact **that this** litigant **chooses one judge for himself, and that** litigant **chooses one judge for himself, and the two** judges **choose one more** judge **for themselves, the true judgment will emerge.** Since each party chooses his own judge, and together the two judges select the additional judge, this will lead to a verdict that is just and true.

Passages from the Talmud

The true judgment will emerge: How will this procedure facilitate emergence of a true verdict? The Jerusalem Talmud (*Sanhedrin* 3:1) cites a statement of Rav Zeira in this regard: "Because he selected [his judge], [that judge] will plead in his favor."

Some explain that the Gemara characterizes this ruling a true judgment due to its enforceability. The two parties will obey the court's decision because they know that had the judge they selected been able to proffer a claim in their favor, he would have done so (Rashi). Even one who is found liable to pay will acknowledge that the ruling did not result from bias, but rather because the court realized they had no alternative but to rule against him (Rivan). Some add that a court selected in this way will feel freer to explore the merits of each claim, because its members were selected by both parties (Rashi).

Summary

This passage comprises three interwoven sections: 1) Interpreting the term "one" in the mishna: Does it mean one judge or one court? 2) A clarification of the *halakha* stated in the mishna: The Talmud seeks to reconcile the blanket statement of the mishna, which appears to apply in all cases, with the opinion of the *amora* Rabbi Elazar, who restricts the rights of a debtor to choose a court. In this regard, the passage presents two amoraic opinions. According to Rabbi Yohanan, the general ruling of the mishna applies to so-called "laymen's courts in Syria," but in the case of an expert court the debtor does not have the right to choose. Rav Pappa maintained that the *halakha* in the mishna refers to a case where two courts are located in the city where both the creditor and the debtor live, but the debtor cannot compel the creditor to come to judgment before a court that is situated elsewhere. 3) An explanation of the reasoning for the law stated in the mishna: After analyzing the formulation of the mishna and basic logic, the Gemara sought a more profound understanding of the mishna. It cited a tradition from the Land of Israel in the name of Rabbi Zeira that the procedure is designed to create a balance between the parties and their positions, so that ultimately "the true judgment will emerge."

Ramifications

The halakhic ruling: The *halakha* is in accordance with the opinion of the Rabbis; each of the litigants selects one judge, and the two judges in turn

select the third member of the tribunal, even if he is not acceptable to the litigants (*Shulḥan Arukh*,[32] *Ḥoshen Mishpat* 13:1). The Rema adds that in a place where there is a publicly appointed permanent court, where all the residents of the city go for judgment, the respondent is not entitled to select a judge in accordance with the procedure described in the mishna, and the claimant may compel him to come before that court for judgment (Rema,[33] *Shulḥan Arukh, Ḥoshen Mishpat* 13:1). Contemporary halakhic authorities disagree with regard to whether a permanent court exists today.

If the parties prefer mediation rather than judgment, they must agree to the third judge selected by the other two judges, as the entire concept of mediation is based on the judges coming to a consensus about the decision and the litigants acceding to it (*Tur, Ḥoshen Mishpat* 13 and *Baḥ*[34] there; *Shakh*[35] on *Shulḥan Arukh, Ḥoshen Mishpat* 13:1).

Objectivity

The *halakha* prohibits a judge from distorting judgment in favor of one of the litigants, based on the verse: "You shall not distort judgment, you shall not give preference" (Deuteronomy 16:19). The halakhic authorities discuss how the *halakha* of this mishna, which allows litigants to select their own judges, can be implemented without compromising their objectivity. The Rosh[36] explains that the judge does not do all he can in order to enable the litigant who selected him to win the case. He is certainly prohibited from acting as a lawyer does for a client, advancing a claim that he knows to be incorrect, even if the other judges would accept it. Rather, he must carefully weigh the legitimate claims of the party who selected him, and present those claims in a clear manner to the third judge. When each of the selected judges presents their considerations before the third judge, the ruling will be clarified better than if a judge had not made any effort to present the claim of the litigant who selected him.

---

32. *Shulḥan Arukh*: The classic halakhic work by Rav Yosef Karo, sixteenth century, Safed.
33. Rema: An acronym for Rabbi Moshe Isserles, sixteenth century, Poland.
34. *Baḥ*: An acronym for *Bayit Ḥadash*, a commentary on the halakhic code *Tur*. It was written by Rabbi Yoel Sirkis, sixteenth century, Poland.
35. *Shakh*: An acronym for *Siftei Kohen*, a commentary on the halakhic code *Shulḥan Arukh*. It was written by Rabbi Shabbetai HaKohen, seventeenth century, Lithuania.
36. Rosh: An acronym for Rabbeinu Asher, thirteenth century, Germany and Spain.

Family Mitzvot

This passage, from the Babylonian Talmud, tractate *Kiddushin* 29a–30a, addresses mitzvot incumbent upon parents, particularly the mitzva of teaching Torah. The Torah is knowledge that is transmitted from generation to generation, and the father teaching his son plays a special role in fulfillment of the mitzva of Torah study, as depicted in the relevant verses.

This selection discusses unique expressions that appear in the mishna: Mitzvot of the son with regard to the father and mitzvot of the father with regard to the son. One of the reasons why these expressions require clarification is that although "father" and "son" in the Mishna often refer exclusively to father and son in the literal sense, they can also refer to parent and child in the broader sense, including mother and daughter. Furthermore, the phrase "with regard to the father" does not make it clear whether it is referring to an obligation that the father must perform on behalf of his son, or a duty of the son vis-à-vis his father. The same dilemma applies to the phrase "with regard to the son." The Talmud proceeds to clarify the halakhic ramifications of these different meanings: Does the mitzva of honoring one's parents apply only to sons, or to daughters as well? Is the mitzva of teaching Torah an obligation incumbent upon the father alone, or upon the mother as well?

The mitzva of Torah study is mentioned in several verses in the Torah, e.g.: "You shall teach them to your sons to speak of them" (Deuteronomy 11:19); "And you shall learn them, and you shall take care to perform them" (Deuteronomy 5:1); "And you shall impart them to your children and to your children's children" (Deuteronomy 4:9). The mitzva to honor one's parents is one of the Ten Commandments: "Honor your father and your mother" (Exodus 20:11), and elsewhere the Torah commands one to fear his parents: "Each of you shall fear his mother and his father" (Leviticus 19:3). In this passage, the Talmud explains how the mitzvot to honor and fear one's parents are complementary aspects of the same command.

The mitzva to marry is not mentioned explicitly in the Torah, but the Sages explain that it is an integral part of the mitzva to be fruitful and multiply, which appears in *Parashat Bereshit*: "Be fruitful, and multiply, and fill the earth" (Genesis 1:28), and in *Parashat Noah*: "And you, be fruitful, and multiply" (Genesis 9:7).

Mishna

The following passage presents the Mishna's explication of the obligations of parents to their children and children to their parents.

Mishna: The mishna establishes principles governing obligations in mitzvot performed concerning parents and concerning children. With regard to **all mitzvot of a son with regard to** his **father, men are obligated** to perform them **and women are exempt. And** with regard to **all mitzvot of a father with regard to his son, both men and women are obligated** to perform them.

Clarification

The talmudic discussion begins with clarification of the meaning of the mishna text.

What is the meaning of: **All mitzvot of a son with regard to** his **father? If you say** that it means **all mitzvot that the son is obligated to perform for** his **father,** i.e., the obligations incumbent upon a son toward his father…

Contradiction

This explanation contradicts a halakhic midrash cited in a *baraita*.

If we maintain that "all mitzvot of a son with regard to his father" refers to those mitzvot that a son is obligated to perform for his father, and the mishna rules that "women are exempt," are **women exempt** from these mitzvot? This is contradicted by a *baraita*: **But isn't it taught** in a *baraita* concerning a verse that addresses the mitzva of honoring one's father and mother: **"Each of you** [*ish*, literally man] shall fear his mother and his father" (Leviticus 19:3). **I have** derived **only** that **a man** is obligated in this mitzva. **From where** do I derive that **a woman** is also obligated to honor her parents? The source is from the same verse. **When it says: "Each of you shall fear** [*tira'u*] **his mother and his father"** (Leviticus 19:3), *tira'u* is a plural verb, indicating that **there are two** obligated **here,** son and daughter.

The halakhic midrash cited in the *baraita* teaches that a daughter is also commanded to fear her mother and father. Consequently, "all mitzvot of a son with regard to his father," with regard to which the mishna states that women are exempt, cannot be explained as referring to obligations of a son toward his father.

The Resolution

The Talmud proposes an alternative interpretation of the mishna.

Rav Yehuda[37] **said** that **this is what** the mishna **is saying** in the expression "all mitzvot of a son with regard to his father": With regard to **all mitzvot of a son that are incumbent upon** his **father to perform for his son, men,** i.e., fathers, **are obligated** in them **and women,** mothers, **are exempt.** In other words, the obligations that the Torah imposes on a father to perform on behalf of his son are not incumbent upon his mother.

Proof

The Talmud bolsters the above explanation based on a different *baraita.*

The Gemara notes that the obligations of a father toward his son are also taught in a different *baraita*: **We learned** this *halakha*, **as the Sages taught** in a *baraita*: **A father is obligated with regard to his son to circumcise him; and to redeem him,** a firstborn son, with payment of five shekels to a priest; **and to teach him Torah; and to marry him to a woman; and to teach him a trade. And some say:**[38] A father is **also** obligated **to teach** his son **to swim. Rabbi Yehuda**[39] **says:**[40] **Any** father **who does not teach his son a trade teaches him banditry,** to be a robber and a crook.

Difficulty and Resolution

The Talmud questions the formulation of the *baraita*, and then explains its intent.

Does it **enter your mind** that any father who does not teach his son a trade actually teaches him **banditry?** Does a father who does not teach his son a profession, teach him to rob? **Rather,** one should adjust the formulation slightly: With regard to a father who does not teach his son a trade, it is **as though he teaches him banditry.** Since the son has no profession, he is likely to seek his livelihood dishonestly.

---

37. Rav Yehuda: A second-generation Babylonian *amora*, founder of the talmudic academy in Pumbedita.
38. Some say: This term indicates the introduction of another opinion in a mishna or *baraita*. Sometimes this opinion does not disagree with the previous ruling but merely adds to it, while the name of its author is omitted by the editor of the text for some reason.
39. Rabbi Yehuda: Rabbi Yehuda bar Ilai, a fourth-generation *tanna* in the Land of Israel, who was a resident of Usha.
40. Rabbi Yehuda says: Later in the passage (30b), the Gemara explains that Rabbi Yehuda wants a father to teach his son a constructive profession, and not merely how to be a merchant or a businessman. He reasons that one who deals in commerce, when he cannot find a good deal, is frequently tempted to swindle people.

Search for the Halakhic Source

The Talmud seeks the biblical source for the father's obligation to teach his son Torah.

Concerning the father's obligation **to teach** his son **Torah** that is mentioned in the *baraita*, the Gemara asks: **From where** in the Torah **do we** derive it? **As it is written: "You shall teach them to your sons** to speak of them" (Deuteronomy 11:19). This is the source for the requirement of a father to teach his son Torah.

On the basis of that source, one might conclude that this obligation is incumbent exclusively on the father, and therefore, if the father neglected to do so, the son is exempt from the obligation to study Torah himself. The Gemara explains that this is not the *halakha*: **And** in a situation **where his father did not teach him, he is obligated to teach himself, as it is written**: **"And you shall learn them,** and you shall take care to perform them" (Deuteronomy 5:1). Consequently, if one's father did not teach him Torah, he must study Torah on his own.

Search for the Halakhic Source

The Talmud inquires into the biblical source for the ruling in the Mishna that a mother is exempt from the obligation to teach her son Torah.

She, the mother, **from where do we** derive **that she is not obligated** to teach her son Torah? The Gemara explains: **As it is written: "You shall teach them** to your sons to speak of them" (Deuteronomy 11:19), and it is also stated: **"And you shall learn them,** and you shall take care to perform them" (Deuteronomy 5:1). It is derived from the similar expressions that there is a link between the obligation to teach others and the obligation to study oneself: **Anyone who is commanded to study** Torah **is commanded to teach** it to others, **and anyone who is not commanded to study is not commanded to teach** it to others. Since a woman is not obligated to study Torah, she is likewise not obligated to teach it to others.

Search for the Halakhic Source

The Talmud seeks the biblical source for the fact that women themselves are not obligated to study Torah.

The above explanation established a principle according to which the obligation to teach is derived from the obligation to study: "Anyone who is commanded to study is commanded to teach," based upon which it exempted women. But how it is known that women are not obligated to study Torah?

And she, women, **from where do we** derive **that she is not obligated to teach herself** Torah? The Gemara answers: **As it is written: "You shall teach them** to your sons" (Deuteronomy 11:19), and it is written: **"And you shall learn them,** and you shall take care to perform them" (Deuteronomy 5:1). This indicates a logical connection that can be formulated: **Anyone whom others are commanded to teach is commanded to teach himself, and anyone whom others are not commanded to teach is not commanded to teach himself.**

Search for the Halakhic Source

The Talmud seeks the biblical source for the fact that others are not obligated to teach women Torah.

The Gemara established a causal link between those whom others are obligated to teach and those who are themselves obligated to study Torah: Anyone whom others are commanded to teach is commanded to teach himself. This *halakha* itself requires a source. **And from where** is it derived **that others are not commanded to teach** a woman? The Gemara explains the source: **As the verse states: "You shall teach them to your sons"** (Deuteronomy 11:19), from which it is inferred that the obligation is to teach **your sons, but not your daughters.** Accordingly, there is no obligation for others to teach women.

A Baraita

The Talmud cites a *baraita* that addresses the question: Which takes priority, studying Torah or getting married?

The Sages taught in a *baraita*: If one is obligated **to study Torah and** has reached the appropriate age **to marry a woman,** which takes priority? **He should study Torah** first **and afterward marry a woman. And if it is impossible for him** to be **without a wife,** for whatever reason, **he should marry a woman and then study Torah.**

The Halakhic Ruling

The Talmud presents a halakhic ruling that was stated with regard to this matter.

Rav Yehuda says that **Shmuel**[41] **says:**[42] The *halakha* is that one should **marry a woman and afterward study Torah.**

Criticism and an Alternative Position

The Talmud presents a contrary opinion, that of Rabbi Yohanan, which criticizes Shmuel's ruling.

Is it possible to marry before fulfilling the obligation to study Torah? **Rabbi Yohanan**[43] **says:** How can one do so? With **a millstone** hanging **from his neck,** with the yoke of providing for his wife and children weighing on him, can he find the time to **engage in Torah** study?

Resolving the Halakhic Rulings

The Talmud suggests that in fact there is no dispute between the halakhic rulings.

The Gemara explains that there is in fact no dispute between Shmuel and Rabbi Yohanan, and suggests reformulating the *halakha* based on where one lives. **And** the *amora'im* **do not disagree,** as each spoke of a different set of circumstances: **This,** Shmuel's ruling, **is for us,** the residents of Babylonia, **and that,** the statement of Rabbi Yohanan, **is for them,**[44] who reside in the Land of Israel. The inhabitants of Babylonia can marry and then study Torah

---

41. Shmuel: A first-generation Babylonian *amora*, one of the Sages of Neharde'a and the founder of the talmudic academy in Sura.

42. Rav Yehuda says that Shmuel says: In other words, Rav Yehuda stated this matter in the name of Shmuel.

43. Rabbi Yohanan: A second-generation *amora* in the Land of Israel, head of the talmudic academy in Tiberias.

44. This is for us and that is for them: The Talmud does not specify who is "us" and who is "them," nor does it explain why in one place they would study before marriage, while in the other place they would get married first and then study Torah. The majority of the commentaries maintain that as the Babylonian Talmud was written in Babylonia, it is logical to assume that the term "us" refers to the residents of Babylonia and "them" refers to the inhabitants of the Land of Israel. Concerning the different customs in the two countries, there are various opinions among the commentaries. Some assert that the key factor is the nature of Torah study: Young men from Babylonia would typically travel to the Land of Israel to study. Since they were far from home they would not be burdened with the yoke of providing for their households, while the residents of the Land of Israel, who studied locally, had to assume responsibility for support of their families (Rashi).

Others contend that the difference is due to the economic conditions in each place: In Babylonia the women would work after marriage, and therefore their husbands could concentrate on their studies, while in the Land of Israel the men were responsible for being the breadwinners (Meiri). Yet others suggest a different explanation. The strong passion of the people of Babylonia would prevent them from studying if they did not marry first, while it was specifically the Torah study in the Land of Israel that suppressed their desires (*Tosefot Rabbeinu Yitzḥak HaZaken*).

without concern about the needs of their household, while the residents of the Land of Israel should study Torah first, as once they are married they will be unable to study Torah properly.

A Discussion

The Talmud discusses the obligation to study Torah.

To what extent, with regard to the generational range and the scope of the material, **is a person obligated to teach his son Torah? Rav Yehuda says** that **Shmuel says:** One should emulate the education of, **for example, Zevulun ben Dan, whose father's father taught him Bible, Mishna, Talmud,**[45] *halakhot,* **and** *aggadot.*

Summary

This passage comprises three sections: 1) An inquiry into the textual meaning of the mishna: The Gemara discussed the formula "all mitzvot of a son with regard to a father." Is this referring to the obligations of a son toward his father, or those of a father to his son? The Gemara decided that the second interpretation is preferable, as it is consistent with the *halakha* as it appears in other sources. 2) An inquiry into the source of the *halakha* of the mishna. In addition, the Talmud sought the biblical source for the exemption of a mother from teaching her son Torah. In doing so, it touched upon the fundamental principles of the obligation to teach and study Torah. 3) A discussion concerning the *halakha:* The Talmud cited an apparent dispute about whether one should marry or study Torah first, after which it stated that there is no dispute between the two opinions. Rather, they represent different customs that stem from different circumstances in different geographic places. Other halakhic matters raised address the question whether a grandfather is also obligated to teach Torah to his grandsons, and what material is one obligated to teach his son and his grandson.

---

45. Talmud: For the Sages of the Babylonian Talmud, the word Talmud does not refer to a particular work, but rather is a general term for the analysis of the Mishna and its rulings. The Mishna was written in a terse style, and the inquiries into the reasons for its rulings, and clarification of *halakhot* that were not incorporated into the Mishna, were called Talmud.

Ramifications

The halakhic ruling: Both a son and a daughter are obligated to honor their father and mother (Rambam, *Mishneh Torah, Sefer Shofetim, Hilkhot Mamrim* 6:8).

Who Is Obligated to Study and Teach Torah

A father is obligated to teach his son Torah. One who was not taught by his father must teach himself (*Shulḥan Arukh, Yoreh Deʾa* 1). A mother is not obligated to teach her son Torah, as only those who are commanded to study are commanded to teach others. Nevertheless, a woman who studies Torah receives a reward, like those who fulfill a mitzva that they are not obligated to perform (Rema on *Shulḥan Arukh, Yoreh Deʾa* 246:6).

To Study Torah or Marry a Woman

A man should first study Torah and then marry, because if he marries first he will not be free to focus on his studies. If his desires prevent him from concentrating on his studies, he should marry first and then study Torah (Rambam *Mishneh Torah, Sefer HaMadda, Hilkhot Talmud Torah* 1:5). Some claim that as a man is obligated to know the entire Torah and to not forget any of it, he could theoretically spend his entire life studying Torah and never marry. This approach is not suitable for everyone, and as the mitzva of procreation has been described as "greater than all the mitzvot" and it is impossible to have another fulfill this mitzva on one's behalf, it is proper to marry after studying all the *halakhot* of the Torah and their reasons in brief (*Shulḥan Arukh HaRav*[46] 3:1; *Kuntres Aḥaron* on *Shulḥan Arukh HaRav* 3:1).

The basic mitzva is for one to teach his son the entire Written Torah, or to hire a teacher to do so (Rambam *Mishneh Torah, Sefer HaMadda, Hilkhot Talmud Torah* 1:7). This minimal requirement is in effect even if the father is occupied with earning a livelihood, but if he has the ability, he must teach his son Mishna, Talmud, *halakhot*, and *aggadot* (*Tur*[47]).

---

46. *Shulḥan Arukh HaRav*: A halakhic work by Rabbi Shneur Zalman of Liadi, eighteenth century, Russia.
47. *Tur*: A halakhic work by Rabbi Yaʾakov *Baʾal HaTurim*, thirteenth century, Spain.

Glossary

Glossary

Adar – Month of the Jewish calendar, occurring during February/March.

afikoman – Part of the middle matza at the Passover Seder, which is set aside during *Yahatz* and eaten at *Tzafun*, after the meal.

aggada (pl. aggadot) – Rabbinic story meant to impart an educational lesson.

Al HaNisim – Lit. "for the miracles"; a paragraph added to the *Amida* and the Grace after Meals on Purim and Hanukkah, thanking God for the miracles He wrought on behalf of the Jewish people.

aliya – Subdivision of the weekly Torah portion; the honor of being called up to the Torah for the reading of such a subdivision.

Amen – A response to a blessing indicating agreement with it and belief in its content..

Amida – A prayer comprising nineteen blessings that forms the central part of the prayer service. Also known as *Shemoneh Esreh* (lit. eighteen), because its original formulation had eighteen blessings.

arava (pl. aravot) – Willow branch, one of the four species taken on *Sukkot*.

ark – Repository in the prayer hall for Torah scrolls.

Ashkenazim (adj. Ashkenazic) – Segment of the Jewish population; broadly, Jews of European descent.

aufruf – Yiddish for "calling up." In Ashkenazic custom, a groom is called up to the Torah on the Shabbat before his wedding. This is observed as a celebratory event.

Av – Month of the Jewish calendar, occurring during July/August.

bar mitzva, bat mitzva – When a Jewish child reaches maturity and becomes formally obligated in mitzva observance. For a boy this occurs at the age of thirteen, for a girl at twelve.

baraita – A tannaitic statement that does not appear in the Mishna.

Barekhu – An invitation by the prayer leader to the congregation to recite a blessing. This marks the beginning of the blessings before *Shema* and of the blessings recited when one is called up to the Torah.

bima – The table in the synagogue upon which the Torah scroll is placed for Torah reading.

Birkot HaShahar – Morning Blessings.

Blessings over the Torah – Blessings said as part of the Morning Blessings, thanking God for the Torah and requesting His assistance to cleave to it.

brit – Circumcision ritual in which the baby is given his name.

dreidel – A four-sided spinning top played with on Hanukkah.

Edot HaMizrah – A general term for Sephardic congregations or the version of liturgy they use in their prayer services.

eiruv – A solution instituted by the Sages with regard to Shabbat prohibitions against carrying between domains and against walking far out of one's town; commonly used to refer to one type of *eiruv, eiruv hatzerot.*

eiruv hatzerot – The symbolic joining of private domains belonging to different people, thereby allowing them to carry from one place to another on Shabbat. This is accomplished when food belonging to the different residents is placed in one location.

eiruv tavshilin – When Shabbat falls on the day after a festival day, one must set aside bread and a cooked dish for a Shabbat meal before the festival begins. This allows him to cook or to carry out other preparations for Shabbat on the festival.

eiruv tehumin – The placement of food in a particular location, which establishes that location as a person's Shabbat residence. This allows him to travel two thousand cubits, the maximum distance one may travel on Shabbat (see *tehum Shabbat*), from that new location, rather than from his home.

Elul – Month of the Jewish calendar, occurring during August/September.

etrog – Citron, one of the four species taken on *Sukkot.*

farbrengen – Gathering of Chabad hasidim that may include the teaching of hasidic ideas, the telling of stories, and the singing of songs, as well as refreshments.

Full Kaddish – An Aramaic prayer of praise of God that is recited in the synagogue service, often by mourners.

gabbai – The synagogue sexton, who oversees the services.

gebrokts – Yiddish term for matza that has come into contact with liquid. Many Jews of hasidic descent have a custom not to eat *gebrokts* on Passover.

gematriya – A system in which each Hebrew letter is given a numerical value. It often highlights connections, sometimes mystical ones, between words.

geniza – Storeroom or repository in a synagogue used for discarded, damaged, or defective sacred books, papers, and objects.

Grace after Meals – Blessings recited after eating bread. Known in Hebrew as *Birkat HaMazon* and in Yiddish as *Bentching*.

hadas – Myrtle branch, one of the four species taken on *Sukkot*.

haftara – A portion from the Prophets read after the Torah reading on Shabbat, festivals, and public fasts.

haggada (pl. haggadot) – The text that presents the order of the Passover Seder. It contains instructions for the different parts of the Seder, and includes the text traditionally recited as fulfillment of the mitzva to retell the story of the redemption from Egypt.

HaGomel – Blessing said by one who is saved from a dangerous situation.

hakafot sheniyot – The seven rotations taken with the Torah, accompanied by music and dancing, on the night following *Simhat Torah*. This is customary in some communities.

halaka – Ceremonial first haircut, given to boys at age three; means haircut in Arabic. The Yiddish term is *upsherin*.

halakha (pl. halakhot) – Jewish law.

halakhic hour – One-twelfth of the period of daylight, may be longer or shorter than ordinary hours.

Half Kaddish – A shortened version of the Kaddish prayer (see Full Kaddish) that is recited by the prayer leader at certain points in the synagogue prayer service.

halla (pl. hallot) – Braided bread eaten on Shabbat and festivals. The name derives from the mitzva of *halla*, which is to separate a piece of dough and give it to a priest. Nowadays, however, the dough is destroyed.

Hallel – A series of psalms of praise recited on festivals.

hametz – Leavened grain products, which are prohibited for consumption on Passover.

HaMotzi – The blessing before eating bread.

Hanukkah – Eight-day holiday in the winter commemorating the victory of the Hasmoneans over the Seleucid Empire and the rededication of the Temple. On each day candles are lit.

hanukkiya – Hanukkah menora, the eight- or nine-branched candelabrum on which Hanukkah candles are lit.

hasid – Literally, a pious person. A member of the hasidic movement founded by the Baal Shem Tov in the eighteenth century.

hasidic – Having to do with Hasidism.

Hasidism – Pietist, anti-elitist movement founded by Rabbi Yisrael Baal Shem Tov in the eighteenth century. Hasidism emphasizes the service of God in all of one's actions, especially through ecstatic prayer and celebration, and the connection to God through the intervention of a *tzaddik*, a saintly person. Within a generation, Hasidism also became an intellectual movement, applying kabbalistic thought to an individual's religious life.

hatan me'ona – The name given in Sephardic communities to the penultimate *aliya* to the Torah before concluding the Torah on *Simhat Torah*.

hatan Torah – Literally, bridegroom of the Torah. The person who receives the *aliya* for the reading of the last section of the Torah on *Simhat Torah*.

Havdala – The ceremony for concluding the Sabbath. The blessing is said over a cup of wine, and with a candle and sweet-smelling spices.

hazan – Prayer leader in the synagogue, cantor.

hevra kadisha – Burial society, responsible for both preparing the deceased for burial and the actual interment.

hitbodedut – Seclusion practiced by Breslov hasidim for personal communication with God.

hitbonenut – Deep contemplation or meditation on one matter until the person has a spiritual experience regarding that matter. *Hitbonenut* combines intellectual study and spiritual passion.

Hol HaMoed – Intermediate days of *Sukkot* and Passover. On these days certain activities are prohibited, but there is no general prohibition of performing labor.

Hoshana Rabba – The seventh day of *Sukkot*, called *Hoshana Rabba* due to the custom of circling the *bima* seven times in a procession while reciting prayers that begin with the word *hoshana*.

huppa – Literally wedding canopy; *huppa* also refers to the wedding ceremony as a whole.

Isru Hag – The day after Passover, *Shavuot*, and *Sukkot*.

Iyar – Month of the Jewish calendar, occurring during April/May.

Kabbala – The Jewish tradition of mystical theory and practice.

Kabbalat Shabbat – The prayer service said at the onset of Shabbat on Friday night, as instituted by the Sages of Safed in the sixteenth century.

kabbalists – Thinkers who make use of the traditions of Kabbala

Kaddish – Prayer praising God that is said at particular intervals during the prayer service. See Mourner's Kaddish, Half Kaddish, and Rabbis' Kaddish.

kasher – To render a pot or a utensil kosher, usually by immersing it in boiling water or by heating it directly.

kashrut – The theory and practice of ritually kosher food.

Kedusha – Literally, sanctification. In this prayer, said during the repetition of the *Amida*, Israel joins forces with the angels in sanctifying God.

keli rishon – Primary vessel (lit. "first vessel"). The vessel in which something is cooked, even after it has been removed from a heat source.

kelipa (pl. kelipot) – Literally, husk. The kabbalistic term for those elements of existence that are forces of evil that need to be removed.

ketuba – A marriage contract that guarantees the wife a certain sum of money in the event of divorce or her husband's death.

kezayit – Olive-bulk, a halakhic measure of volume that generally corre-

sponds to the amount of food one needs to consume in order to fulfill a mitzva or be liable to punishment for a transgression. According to the most prevalent halakhic opinion, an olive-bulk is about 27 ml.

Kiddush – The blessing made over wine at the beginning of Shabbat and festival meals. The *Kiddush* said on Friday night includes a blessing consecrating Shabbat.

kiddush – Light meal at which *Kiddush* is said on Shabbat morning.

Kiddush Levana – The blessing said once a month at the appearance of the new moon. Usually said on Saturday night at the close of Shabbat.

kiddushin – The part of the wedding ceremony involving the groom giving the ring to the bride. Once *kiddushin* has been performed they are formally married.

kimha depis'ha – Aramaic for "Passover flour," also known as *ma'ot hittin* (lit. "money for wheat"). Charity given before Passover to enable the poor to buy food for the holiday.

kinnot – The liturgical poems that lament the destruction of the Temple and other tragedies, recited on *Tisha BeAv*.

Kislev – Month of the Jewish calendar, occurring during November/December.

kitniyot – Foods derived from edible seeds such as rice, beans, and lentils. These are not *hametz*, but are prohibited on Passover in the Ashkenazic tradition.

kittel – A white robe worn by many married men on Yom Kippur, Seder night and other occasions.

kohen (pl. kohanim) – A person of priestly lineage, a descendant of Aaron.

kol hane'arim – The *aliya* on *Simhat Torah* in which all the children of the community are called to the Torah. An adult recites the blessing.

Kol Nidrei – The prayer said at the onset of Yom Kippur in which the prayer leader asks to nullify all the vows made in the community that year.

Lag BaOmer – The thirty-third day of the *omer*, the eighteenth of the month of Iyar. *Lag BaOmer* is the day of the passing of Rabbi Shimon bar Yohai and also, in many customs, the end of the mourning period of the *omer*.

Various customs of *Lag BaOmer* include lighting bonfires and visiting Rabbi Shimon's grave at Meron.

lehem mishneh – Two whole loaves of bread that are used for the blessing at the beginning of a Shabbat meal.

Lekha Dodi – Liturgical poem composed by Rabbi Shlomo Alkabetz that is traditionally sung on Friday evening during *Kabbalat Shabbat.*

lulav – Palm branch, one of the four species that are taken together on *Sukkot.* Often, *lulav* is used to refer to all four species.

Ma'ariv – The evening prayer.

maftir – The additional reading at the conclusion of the Torah reading on Shabbat, festivals, and fast days. The person who receives the *maftir aliya* also reads the *haftara.*

maggid – In Eastern Europe before the Holocaust, a *maggid* was a person who gave sermons and admonished the community, e.g., the Maggid of Koznitz.

mahzor – Prayer book for festivals, Rosh HaShana, or Yom Kippur.

Marheshvan – Month of the Jewish calendar, occurring during October/November.

mashgiah – (1) *Kashrut* supervisor; (2) In many yeshivot, the person in charge of the spiritual development of the students.

matanot la'evyonim – Literally, gifts to the poor. Giving a gift to at least two poor people is one of the obligations of Purim.

matza (pl. matzot) – Unleavened bread that is eaten on Passover.

matza sheruya – See *gebrokts.*

megilla – Literally, scroll; often refers to the book of Esther.

melakha – Productive, creative activity (lit. "labor"), which is prohibited on Shabbat.

melaveh malka – Literally, "accompanying the queen." The meal customarily served on Saturday night to acknowledge the end of Shabbat.

messiah – Literally, "the anointed one." The anointed king from the house of David who will appear at the end of days and rule Israel righteously.

mezuza (pl. mezuzot) – The scroll affixed to the doorposts of a Jewish home

containing the verses beginning *Shema Yisrael.*

mikva – Ritual bath. Food utensils acquired from gentiles must be immersed in a *mikva* before being used. A woman immerses herself in a *mikva* a week after her menstrual period before she resumes relations with her husband. Some men have the practice of immersing themselves in a *mikva* either every morning or every week.

Minha – The afternoon prayer service.

minyan – The quorum of ten men required for public prayer and Torah reading.

mishlo'ah manot – Gifts of food given on Purim.

mishnayot – Plural of mishna.

mishteh – Feast, one of the mitzvot on Purim.

mitnagged (pl. mitnaggedim) – Opponents of Hasidism. The original *mitnaggedim* fiercely opposed the innovations of the Baal Shem Tov and his followers. Once Hasidism became established, the *mitnaggedim* became a competing ideological movement that was centered in the great yeshivot of Eastern Europe.

mitzva (pl. mitzvot) – Literally, commandment. Traditionally there are 613 commandments in the Torah. Mitzva is often also used more loosely to refer to any religious obligation.

mohel – One who performs a ritual circumcision.

molad – The moment when the new moon becomes visible. See *Kiddush Levana.*

Morning Blessings – Blessings said upon rising in the morning celebrating the beginning of a new day.

Mourner's Kaddish – Kaddish said by mourners, usually by children for a parent, commemorating and elevating the soul of the deceased. See Kaddish.

muktze – An item that may not be handled on Shabbat or festivals. An item is *muktze* either because it serves no purpose (e.g., sticks and stones) or because its purpose involves a prohibited action on Shabbat or a festival (e.g., a pen).

Musaf – The additional prayer service said after the morning service on Shabbat and holidays.

Musar – (1) A type of Jewish literature devoted to moral development and spiritual and psychological growth; (2) A movement begun in the second half of the nineteenth century by Rabbi Yisrael Salanter that emphasized moral reflection and self-improvement, often through the study of Musar literature.

Ne'ila – The closing prayer service on Yom Kippur.

Nisan – Month of the Jewish calendar, occurring during March/April.

nisu'in – The second part of the Jewish marriage ceremony, in which blessings are recited under the wedding canopy.

nolad – An item that has just come into being. This concept is used in various *halakhot*, including those of festivals.

nusah – Version of a prayer used by a particular community.

Nusah Sefarad – Version of the prayer service used by those of hasidic heritage.

Old Yishuv – Ultra-Orthodox communities that were present in the Land of Israel prior to the various waves of Zionist immigration in the nineteenth and early twentieth centuries.

omer – An offering brought from the new crop of barley on the sixteenth of Nisan; the period from the sixteenth of Nisan until *Shavuot.*

onen – An acute mourner, one whose close relative has died but has not yet been buried. An *onen* does not perform any positive mitzvot.

panim hadashot – Literally, a new face. In order to recite the seven blessings celebrating the bride and groom during the week following the wedding, there must be *panim hadashot,* a person who was not present at the wedding.

parasha – The weekly Torah portion.

pareve – Food containing neither dairy nor meat ingredients.

pe'ot – Sideburns. Jewish men are forbidden to remove their sideburns above about half the ear. Some hasidic groups have the custom of growing their *pe'ot* long.

pesik reisha – Performing an action that will unintentionally bring about the performance of labor on Shabbat or a holiday is permitted. However, if such an unintentional result will necessarily occur, the action is called a *pesik reisha* and is prohibited. For example, it is prohibited to open a refrigerator on Shabbat if that action will necessarily cause an incandescent light bulb to be lit in the refrigerator, even if one opened the refrigerator with no intention of turning on the light.

Pesukei DeZimra – The psalms said at the beginning of the morning service.

pidyon haben – Redemption of the firstborn, performed on firstborn sons of Israelite lineage on the thirtieth day of life.

pikuah nefesh – Saving a life. Saving a life overrides all mitzvot in the Torah except for the prohibitions against murder, illicit sexual relations, and idolatry.

prozbol – Legal transfer of the responsibility for the collection of one's debts to the court. *Prozbol* is performed during the Sabbatical Year in order to avoid the cancellation of those debts.

Rabbis' Kaddish – The Kaddish prayer that is said after studying Torah. It includes a passage praying for the welfare of Torah scholars and their students.

Retzeh – (1) The third-to-last blessing of the *Amida*, in which we pray for the renewal of the Temple service; (2) The addition to Grace after Meals for Shabbat.

Rosh Hodesh – The first of the month, which is a minor holiday. Jewish months have either 29 or 30 days. When the preceding month had 30 days, *Rosh Hodesh* is celebrated on the 30th day of the preceding month and the first of the new month. When the preceding month had 29 days, *Rosh Hodesh* is celebrated only on the first of the new month.

sandak – The person at a circumcision ceremony who holds the baby during the actual circumcision. To be *sandak* is regarded as an honor, often given to one of the newborn's grandfathers.

Sanhedrin – The High Court of the Jewish people, composed of 71 members. The Sanhedrin continued to exist after the destruction of the Second Temple for about 350 years.

seder – Literally, order; one of the six sections of the Mishna.

Seder – Ceremonial Passover meal in which four cups of wine are drunk, matza and bitter herbs are eaten, and those present read the haggada.

sefer Torah – Torah scroll, in which the entire Pentateuch is written by hand, using special calligraphy.

Sefira (pl. Sefirot) – The ten different manifestations of the Divine according to Kabbala. The *Sefirot* bear structured relationships with one another, and the relationships between them serve to explain every aspect of Being.

Sefirat HaOmer – The counting of the *omer,* the mitzva to count the days and weeks beginning on the second day of Passover and concluding on the day before *Shavuot.*

segula – An object or practice that serves as a favorable omen or a talisman for receiving some benefit.

sekhakh – *Sukka roofing. Sekhakh must be made from a plant that is no longer attached to the earth and is not edible or any sort of utensil (and therefore is not subject to ritual impurity).*

Selihot – Prayers, mostly composed as liturgical poems, that petition God for mercy and forgiveness. *Selihot* are said on fast days, during the days before and between Rosh HaShana and Yom Kippur, and on Yom Kippur itself.

Sephardim (adj. Sephardic) – Jews who trace their traditions and liturgy back to medieval Spain and Portugal. Today, most Sephardic families trace their more recent origins to Middle Eastern countries, from Morocco in the west to Iran in the east.

seuda shelishit – The third Shabbat meal.

seudat havra'a – The meal prepared for mourners upon their return from the funeral, by their friends and neighbors.

seudat mitzva – A celebratory meal held in honor of the performance of a mitzva, including a wedding, bar mitzva, circumcision, and *siyum.*

Shabbat (pl. Shabbatot) – Saturday. Shabbat is the day of rest and the *halakha* proscribes thirty-nine specific labors on that day.

Glossary

Shabbat Hatan – Literally, groom's Shabbat. On the Shabbat either immediately before or after a wedding the groom's family and friends gather to celebrate. The groom usually receives an *aliya* to the Torah.

Shaharit – The morning prayer service.

Shalom Zakhar – Traditional Ashkenazic ceremony in which family and friends gather on the Friday evening after the birth of a baby boy to sing, share words of Torah, and celebrate the birth.

Sheheheyanu – The blessing recited on the occasion of a new experience: when one makes a significant purchase, upon eating a fruit or vegetable that was previously out of season, the first time one performs a mitzva, and at the beginning of holidays.

Shekhina – The Divine Presence, the manifestation of God in the world. In Kabbalistic thought, the *Shekhina* is identified with the *Sefira* of *Malkhut*.

sheloshim – The thirty-day period of mourning after the death of a close relative.

Shema – The verse "Hear, Israel: the Lord is our God, the Lord is one" (Deut. 6:4). It is a mitzva to recite the *Shema* (along with other verses) every morning and evening. The *Shema* is a declaration of one's acceptance of the yoke of Heaven and is the ultimate expression of a Jew's loyalty to and faith in God. As such it has often been recited by martyrs at their deaths.

Shemini Atzeret – The eighth day of the festival of *Sukkot*, which is in many ways a separate holiday, as the mitzvot of *Sukkot* such as *lulav* and *sukka* do not apply to it.

sheva berakhot – The seven blessings recited at a wedding and at subsequent meals made for the couple in celebration of their wedding in the following week.

Shevat – Month of the Jewish calendar, occurring during January/February.

shevut – Actions on Shabbat that the Sages prohibited beyond those prohibited by Torah law.

shiva – The seven-day mourning period observed after the death of a close relative.

Glossary

shofar – A hollowed-out ram's horn that is sounded on Rosh HaShana.

siddur – Jewish prayer book.

Simhat Beit HaSho'eva – The celebration of the drawing of the water, a celebration that took place in the Temple on *Sukkot* in honor of the water libation that was brought on that festival. *Simhat Beit HaSho'eva* has become a general term for a celebration held on the festival of *Sukkot*.

Simhat Torah – The last day of the festival of *Sukkot*. In Israel, *Simhat Torah* is celebrated on *Shemini Atzeret*, while in the diaspora it is celebrated on the following day. On this day the yearly cycle of Torah reading is completed and begun again.

sitra ahra – Literally, the other side. In kabbalistic thought, the *sitra ahra* is the metaphysical locus of the forces of evil.

Sivan – Month of the Jewish calendar, occurring during May/June.

siyum – A celebration marking the completion of the study of a talmudic tractate or some other significant work of Torah literature.

sukka – A covered booth (see *sekhakh*). On *Sukkot*, it is a mitzva to dwell in a *sukka* rather than in one's house.

Sukkot – The festival beginning on the fifteenth of Tishrei, in which we are commanded to dwell in *Sukkot* and to take up the four species. *Sukkot* lasts seven days, concluding on the eighth day with *Shemini Atzeret* and in the diaspora extending a ninth day with *Simhat Torah*.

Tahanun – A petitionary prayer recited on weekdays following the *Amida* in both the morning and afternoon services. It is the custom in Ashkenazic (and some Sephardic) synagogues to lean over and cover one's face with one's arm during this prayer.

tallit – A prayer shawl, a four-cornered garment with *tzitzit* that is worn by men during the morning service.

Tamuz – Month of the Jewish calendar, occurring during June/July.

tanna – A Sage of the period of the Mishna.

tefillin – Phylacteries, leather boxes containing scrolls upon which are written passages from the Torah. The boxes are attached to one's forehead and one's upper arm with leather straps. *Tefillin* are worn by Jewish men during weekday morning prayers.

Glossary

tehum Shabbat – The Shabbat limit, the maximum distance one may travel on Shabbat: two thousand cubits beyond one's place of dwelling, or in a city, from the city limit.

tena'im – Literally, conditions. The contract explicating the monetary commitments of both sides in a marriage and the consequences for each side if they do not go through with the marriage. In many communites today, this is not done at all or if it is, it is merely a ritualized formality.

tereifa – An animal that has a certain type of physical defect that renders it non-kosher. The most common type of defect is a hole in the lung.

Tevet – Month of the Jewish calendar, occurring during December/January.

Three Weeks – The three-week period between the Seventeenth of Tammuz and Tisha BeAv, a period of mourning for the destruction of the two Temples.

tikkun – A set text of prayers and readings from the Bible and from rabbinic and kabbalistic works, read on evenings when it is customary to study Torah at night. These occasions include *Shavuot, Hoshana Rabba*, and the eve of the seventh day of Passover. Each day has its own *tikkun*.

tisch – Literally, table. A gathering of hasidim around their rebbe, with singing and Torah discourses.

Tisha BeAv – The ninth day of the month of Av, which is the anniversary of the destruction of both the first and second Temples. as well as of other disasters that befell the Jewish people. *Tisha BeAv* is a day of mourning and a fast day.

Tishrei – Month of the Jewish calendar, occurring during September/October.

Tu BeAv – The fifteenth of the month of Av. It is a minor holiday in commemoration of an ancient practice recorded in the Mishna (*Ta'anit* 4:8) whereby young women would dance in the vineyards in search of a bridegroom.

Tu BeShvat – The fifteenth of the month of Shevat, known as the New Year for the trees. This date has halakhic significance in terms of the calculation of the year for the purpose of tithes. Many have the custom to hold special celebrations on this day.

Glossary

tza'ar ba'alei hayim – Causing unnecessary pain to animals. Not only is this forbidden, but one is also obligated to alleviate the pain of animals in one's possession.

tzadik (pl. tzadikim) – In general, a *tzadik* is a righteous person. In Hasidism, a *tzadik* is an extraordinary individual who has a special connection to God. Ordinary people can connect to God through a *tzadik*, either by becoming his hasidim, his followers, or by his acting as an intermediary for them.

tzedaka – Charity, or more generally, righteousness. *Tzedaka* is used specifically to denote monetary gifts to the poor.

tzedaka box – A small box into which people put small amounts of money for charity.

tzimtzum – Literally, contraction. The kabbalistic/theological principle that God "contracted" Himself in order to create a "space" for the universe to exist.

tzitzit – Ritual fringes that one is commanded to place at the corners of a four-cornered garment.

Wayfarer's Prayer – A prayer one recites when he travels between cities, to request divine protection.

Ya'aleh VeYavo – The prayer inserted into the *Amida* and Grace after Meals on Rosh Hodesh and festivals.

yad soledet bo – The temperature at which one's hand spontaneously recoils from an item's heat. Used for *halakhot* of Shabbat and *kashrut*.

yahrzeit – The anniversary of someone's death. On that day Kaddish is recited by his or her children.

Yedid Nefesh – A liturgical hymn composed by Rabbi Elazar Azikri in the sixteenth century. In many communities it is sung at the beginning of Friday night prayers. It is also often sung at the third meal on Shabbat.

yeshiva – A traditional institution for Torah study. The focus of the curriculum is usually the Talmud.

yetzer hara – The evil inclination, the aspect of the human personality that desires to sin. In some contexts the *yetzer hara* is conceived of as a metaphysical force.

yihud room – The room in which the bride and groom briefly seclude themselves following their wedding ceremony.

Yizkor – A prayer said in memory of the deceased. Usually said by his or her children on the last day of each festival and on Yom Kippur.

Zeved HaBat – Celebration for the birth of a girl.

zimmun – The invitation to recite Grace after Meals, added when three men (or three women) eat together.

A Concise Guide to the Sages

Rabbi Adin Even-Israel Steinsaltz

nsaltz Center

English Edition

Executive Director, Steinsaltz Center
Rabbi Meni Even-Israel

Editor in Chief
Rabbi Jason Rappoport

Executive Editor
Rabbi Joshua Schreier

Translator
Avi Steinhart

Editor
Rabbi Yehoshua Duker

Technical Staff
Adena Frazer
Adina Mann

Designer
Eliyahu Misgav

Typesetters
Rina Ben-Gal
Estie Dishon

Copy Editors

Caryn Meltz, Manager
Rachelle Emanuel
Deena Nataf
Dvora Rhein
Ilana Sobel

Hebrew Edition

Senior Editors
Menachem Brod
Amechaye Even-Israel

Editors
Elad Shlezinger
Uriel Segal
Passages from the Talmud